IF YOU THINK YOU'VE HEARD IT ALL, YOU PROBABLY HAVEN'T HEARD . . .

In 2011 came a revelation that challenges one of the backbones of scientific theory. An experiment that fired tiny particles called neutrinos through Earth toward a detector seemed to show these subatomic particles traveled slightly faster than the speed of light, affecting everything we've known to be true up to this point, including the basis of heat, gravity, and radio waves.

Apa Sherpa of Nepal, climbing leader of the Eco Everest Expedition 2011, reached the summit of Mount Everest for a record breaking 21st time on May 11, 2011.

The most expensive painting made by an elephant, entitled *Cold Wind, Swirling Mist, Charming Lanna I*, was created at the Maesa Elephant Camp in Chiang Mai, Thailand, and sold for $32,970.

Accreditation

Guinness World Records Limited has a very thorough accreditation system for records verification. However, while every effort is made to ensure accuracy, Guinness World Records Limited cannot be held responsible for any errors contained in this work. Feedback from our readers on any point of accuracy is always welcomed.

Abbreviations & Measurements

Guinness World Records Limited uses both metric and imperial measurements. The sole exceptions are for some scientific data where metric measurements only are universally accepted, and for some sports data. Where a specific date is given, the exchange rate is calculated according to the currency values that were in operation at the time. Where only a year date is given, the exchange rate is calculated from December of that year. "One billion" is taken to mean one thousand million. "GDR" (the German Democratic Republic) refers to the East German state, which was unified with West Germany in 1990. The abbreviation is used for sports records broken before 1990. The USSR (Union of Soviet Socialist Republics) split into a number of parts in 1991, the largest of these being Russia. The CIS (Commonwealth of Independent States) replaced it and the abbreviation is used mainly for sporting records broken at the 1992 Olympic Games. Guinness World Records Limited does not claim to own any right, title or interest in the trademarks of others reproduced in this book.

General Warning

Attempting to break records or set new records can be dangerous. Appropriate advice should be taken first and all record attempts are undertaken at the participant's risk. In no circumstances will Guinness World Records Limited have any liability for death or injury suffered in any record attempt. Guinness World Records Limited has complete discretion over whether or not to include any particular records in the book. Being a Guinness World Records record holder does not guarantee you a place in the book.

GUINNESS WORLD RECORDS 2013

BANTAM BOOKS
NEW YORK

2013 Bantam Books Mass Market Edition

GUINNESS WORLD RECORDS™ 2013
Copyright © 2012 Guinness World Records Limited.
Published under license.

GUINNESS WORLD RECORDS™ is a trademark of Guinness World Records Limited and is reproduced under license by Bantam Books, an imprint of The Random Hosue Publishing Group, a division of Random House, Inc., New York.

Revised American editions copyright © 2013, 2012, 2011, 2010, 2009, 2008, 2007, 2006, 2005, 2004, 2003, 2002, 2001, 2000, 1999, 1998, 1997, 1996, 1995, 1994, 1993, 1992, 1991, 1990, 1989, 1988, 1987, 1986, 1985, 1984, 1983, 1982, 1981, 1980, 1979, 1978, 1977, 1976, 1975, 1974, 1973, 1972, 1971, 1970, 1969, 1968, 1966, 1965, 1964, 1963, 1962, 1960 by Guinness World Records Ltd.

For more information address: Guinness World Records Ltd.

BANTAM BOOKS and the rooster colophon are registered trademarks of Random House, Inc.

ISBN: 978-0-345-54711-8

Printed in the United States of America

www.bantamdell.com

9 8 7 6 5 4 3 2 1

Bantam Books mass market edition: May 2013

GUINNESS WORLD RECORDS
2013

EDITOR-IN-CHIEF
Craig Glenday

CONTENTS

Look out for cross-references to related record.

INTRODUCTION

TO THE LIMITS

EXPLORING THE EXTREMES OF BREAKING RECORDS

It took 50,000 years of evolution for a human to run a mile in less than four minutes; within two months, the record had been beaten . . . twice!

Do world records have their limits? Is there a point beyond which a record cannot be broken? This is a key question here at Guinness World Records, because one of the fundamental criteria for us is that a record is breakable (apart from significant "firsts," of course). Yet, surely, there is an upper limit to every record . . .

For this year's book, we have asked our consultants, advisers, and records managers to explore the outer limits of some popular categories. The question, each time, is how far can a record be pushed? So, what's the greatest age to which a human can live? Or the heaviest weight an athlete can lift in competition? Or the tallest tower we can build?

You'll find these features at the beginning of each chapter. What you may not find is a definitive answer to each question—some extremes are impossible to predict, of course, but we can at least explore the fascinating factors that define their limits.

THE BIG QUESTIONS . . .

- How Much Climate Change Can We Survive? (pp. 33–36)
- How Big Can Animals Get? (pp. 57–61)
- How Long Can We Live? (pp. 99–104)
- How Heavy Can We Lift? (pp. 139–142)
- How Deep Can We Go? (pp. 203–206)
- How Rich Can You Get? (pp. 255–259)
- How Tall Can We Build? (pp. 311–316)
- What's the Speed Limit? (pp. 365–368)
- How Famous Can You Get? (pp. 405–408)
- How Fast Can We Run? (pp. 451–454)

FACT: The speed of light is considered the absolute speed limit in the universe; in theory, nothing is faster . . .

CAN YOU LIVE TO 130 YEARS? Gerontology is the study of aging (the word comes from the Greek for "old man" and "study"). To help us assess claims from the world's oldest people, we enlist the help of gerontologist Robert Young. His task is to ensure that claimants provide all the required documentation to support their stories.

In "How Long Can We Live?" on pp. 99–104, Robert looks at the limits to old age. Will a man ever live longer than Christian Mortensen (left), the oldest man ever at 115 years 252 days? Will *anyone* ever exceed the 122 years 164 days of Jeanne Calment (below), the oldest person ever. And crucially, will they be able to prove it?!

1895 (20 YEARS) 1915 (40 YEARS) 1935 (60 YEARS)

1988 (113 YEARS) 1997 (122 YEARS)

TALLEST TOWERS At 2,716 ft. 6 in. (828 m) to the top of its spire, the Burj Khalifa is currently the **tallest building** on Earth. Is the 3,280-ft.-tall (1-km) tower planned for Saudi Arabia even possible?

FACT: The last 11 years are among the top 12 warmest years on record. Can we survive global warming?

HOW LOW CAN YOU GO? In March 2012, moviemaker James Cameron (Canada, above right) made the deepest solo dive, reaching the bottom of the Marianas Trench in the Pacific Ocean. Now, Richard Branson (UK, above left) hopes to visit the deepest points in each ocean. But what is the absolute limit to our deepest desires? GWR's adventure adviser Mike Flynn takes us in search of the Earth's final frontiers on pp. 203–206.

EDITOR'S LETTER

A big thank-you to everyone who's helped to make Guinness World Records a superlative success over the past year . . .

In the last 12 months, we've received an incredible 16,611 record applications from the United States. Of these, just 581 made it through our rigorous ratification process, ranging from the **highest jump on a pogo stick** (9 ft. 6 in.; 2.9 m) in Utah and **fastest 100-m dash in clogs** (17.78 seconds) in Connecticut to the **longest dog tail** (26 in.; 66.04 cm) in Colorado and the **most marathons completed in one year** (113), from Texas.

Globally, GWR records managers processed around 50,000 applications over the past year, and the U.S.A.'s contribution to record-breaking was second to none, placing it above the UK at the top of the list of claimants.

One of the most exciting and gratifying aspects of working with this superlative organization is that there is no let-up in the enthusiasm for record-breaking. This year marks my 10th year at Guinness World Records, and I can say with authority that inspiring accomplishments continue to flood in, pushing the boundaries of what's possible.

A newspaper journalist once asked me why we bother to continue monitoring record-breaking, given that every record worth breaking has been broken. Well, you ask that question to the likes of filmmaker and explorer James Cameron, who, at the time of writing, has just made the **first solo dive to the deepest point in the ocean** (see p. 203), or the crew of the *Turanor*, the **first ship to circumnavigate the globe on solar power** (p. 207), or 12-year-old Tom Schaar, who has just pulled off the **first 1080 on a skateboard**—a trick that has defied even the most experienced skaters (p. 604).

It's been 100 years since Roald Amundsen made the **first visit to the South Pole** (p. 213), but the desire for exploration and discovery is as healthy as it has always been, as our Adventure chapter (pp. 201–232) proves. There, you'll find a timeline of pioneering, plus an awe-inspiring collection of the recent records from explorers, trailblazers, and globetrotters, all of whom continue to widen our horizons.

LONGEST CHAIN OF BRACELETS A total of 600 students at Owingsville Elementary School in Kentucky—winners of the Carson Dellosa Classroom Challenge—stood as one on May 20, 2011, when they linked 3,799 friendship bracelets together: a total length of 810 ft. (246.89 m).

MOST TWINKIES EATEN IN ONE MINUTE Takeru Kobayashi of Japan appeared on *The Wendy Williams Show* on January 23, 2012, as part of Wendy's "Save the Twinkie" campaign. There, the multiple record-holder added one more certificate to his collection by devouring 14 Twinkies in one minute!

MOST PEOPLE DOING JUMPING JACKS IN 24 HOURS As part of her "Let's Move" campaign to fight childhood obesity, First Lady and fitness fan Michelle Obama led 464 children doing jumping jacks for one minute on the White House lawn on October 11, 2011. The event, organized by *National Geographic Kids* (U.S.A.), was part of a worldwide workout which involved 300,265 kids at 1,050 locations on October 11–12, 2011. GWR's Stuart Claxton (above) was on hand to witness the White House event, along with *Today Show* personality Al Roker and Olympic figure skater Michelle Kwan.

Inspired by this question of the limits of record-breaking, we've included a feature at the start of each chapter that explores the absolutes of human accomplishment. The questions are simple—how fast can an athlete run? how tall can we build? how long can we live?—but, as you'll discover, the answers are far from straightforward. You'll find a list of what's in these "To the Limits" features on pp. xii–xiv. And talking of the limits of human abilities, we've all been gripped by Olympic fever here at GWR. At www.guinnessworldrecords.com/bonuschapter, we've issued a digital update to our sports chapter that collates every new world record set at the Olympics.

If you're a sports fan who enjoys the quirkier side of life, and you've not yet downloaded our *Wacky Sporting Champions* ebook, then visit www.guinnessworldrecords.com/sport and take a look at our sideways glance at sporting superlatives. Breaking the 100-m sprint record is one thing, but how fast would Usain Bolt be in a pair of high heels? Or wearing a pair of swim fins?

As well as the hundreds of claims we deal with each day, we receive thousands of new and updated records from a team of consultants. We are particularly indebted to our science consultant David Hawksett for his contribution to our Green Earth chapter (pp. 31–54). This looks at the good, the bad, and the ugly aspects of our treatment of the planet and takes as balanced a view as possible, based on our current understanding of this topic.

Thanks, too, to Dan Barrett, GWR's online Community Manager, for his invaluable help with the new social media feature (pp. 304–308). We're living through an incredible digital revolution, in which records are being broken every second. Fortunately, Dan gets to spend all day in conversation with our vast online community, helping us stay up to date on all the latest traffic figures.

LONGEST FINGERNAILS ON A PAIR OF HANDS It took the small matter of 18 years to achieve, but Chris "The Dutchess" Walton (U.S.A.) eventually grew the five fingernails on her left hand to a length of 10 ft. 2 in. (309.8 cm) and the five nails on her right to 9 ft. 7 in. (292.1 cm), for a grand total of 19 ft. 9 in. (601.9 cm), as measured in Las Vegas on February 21, 2011.

MOST BEHIND-THE BACKBOARD-SHOTS (ONE MINUTE) Most of us would have difficulty making 18 shots in one minute from in front of the hoop. The NBA's Ricky Rubio (Spain) achieved this feat from *behind the backboard* at the NBA All-Star Jam Session 2012 in Orlando, Florida, on February 24!

MEDICAL RECORDS Kaiser Permanente, the Oakland-based healthcare consortium, broke 12 health-related records to help raise awareness of medical issues. The records include the **largest skin cancer screening**, which involved 780 participants in San Diego, California, on August 4, 2011.

LARGEST FUZZY DICE The Las Vegas Convention and Visitors Authority chose the supposedly lucky date of November 11, 2011—or 11/11/11—to unveil the world's largest fuzzy dice. The sides of each die measured 4 ft (1.22 m), as confirmed by GWR's Danny Girton, Jr. in front of the iconic "Welcome to Las Vegas" signpost.

MOST COSMETIC MAKEOVERS IN 24 HOURS It was girly heaven on the New York set of *Good Morning America* on May 9, 2012. A team of five makeup artists from Ulta Beauty and *Lucky* magazine (both U.S.A.) completed 387 cosmetic makeovers in 24 hours.

FACT: GWR's Mike Janela helped adjudicate the record, while Lara Spencer (above in middle) presented the show.

FACT: The makeup artists tailored the cosmetic colors to suit the skin tone of each individual—all 387 of them!

LONGEST CAREER AS A SPORTS BROADCASTER Sports fans have been listening to Bob Wolff (U.S.A.) for 73 years. He began broadcasting in 1939 while a student at Duke University, Durham, North Carolina, and, at the age of 91, he continues to appear on-air for Cablevision News 12.

LONGEST ROCK TOUR Rock band Thirty Seconds to Mars (U.S.A.) took considerably longer than 30 seconds to tour the world. Promoting the album *This Is War*, they started their 309-concert tour on November 11, 2009, and finally ended it over two years later at Hammerstein Ballroom, New York, on December 7, 2011—when GWR's Stuart Claxton rocked up.

This year's book is bursting with the usual array of spectacular original photos that you'll not find anywhere else. Picture Editor Michael Whitty has been touring the globe with his team to bring you the best in new photography. Among his favorite record-holders this year are Abbie Girl (**longest wave surfed by a dog**, p. 94), the giant Westech truck (**largest mining truck**, p. 311) and Darlene Flynn (**largest collection of shoes**, p. 176). Look out for Michael's behind-the-scenes accounts in the SNAPSHOT features included with the photos.

LARGEST BIKINI PARADE Panama City Beach, Florida, turned into a giant runway on March 6, 2012, when 450 participants took part in a bikini parade organized by Panama City. As well as their bikinis, the participants sported hats and wristbands to show they were part of the record attempt. GWR's Philip Robertson was the lucky man who got to adjudicate this record.

LARGEST AFRO A GWR first this year was our "mummy blogger" event, in which we invited parent bloggers and their children to our New York office to meet record holders including Aevin Dugas, whose Afro stands 7.3 in. (18.5 cm) high and is 4 ft. 4 in. (132.1 cm) in circumference.

MOST VIEWED PROGRAM IN U.S. TELEVISION HISTORY America came to a standstill as the New York Giants clinched a last-gasp 21–17 victory over the New England Patriots in Super Bowl XLVI on February 5, 2012. The game attracted an average of 111.3 million viewers, peaking at 114 million for Madonna's (U.S.A.) half-time show.

LARGEST BOTTLE MOSAIC Some say the Jack Daniel's bottle, with its distinctive square corners and black label, is a work of art in itself. However, Herb Williams (U.S.A.) used 2,120 of the bottles to create another work of art—a portrait of Jack Daniel himself, the creator of the Tennessee whiskey. The mosaic, made on September 1, 2011, at South Street Seaport in New York, was in celebration of Jack's 161st birthday.

MOST SIGNATURES ON AN ITEM OF SPORTS MEMORABILIA A total of 515 signatures were squeezed onto a replica basketball at the NBA All-Star Jam Session 2012 at the Orange County Convention Center in Orlando, Florida, on February 24–26, 2012. Among the signatures were those of retired NBA stars Chris Webber and Robert Horry, comedian and actor J. B. Smoove, and GWR's very own Mike Janela (left).

MOST CONSECUTIVE SOCCER PENALTY KICKS Some of soccer's big shots—including David Beckham (England), Thierry Henry (France), and former American international Alexi Lalas (left)—helped achieve 742 consecutive penalty kicks in Major League Soccer's "PK Challenge" at Herald Square in New York on July 25, 2011. The event was organized to help celebrate the MLS All-Star Game being hosted by the New York Red Bulls.

As ever, there's so much more: our *Star Wars* feature to celebrate the 30th anniversary of *Return of the Jedi* (U.S.A., 1983) on pp. 440–444; a snapshot of the global economy to mark a year of recession and austerity on p. 275; and, to take your mind off the gloom, a fun exploration of the weirder side of record-breaking with consultant Dr. Karl Shuker's "mysterious world" on pp. 279–284, which manages to encompass Scotland's Loch Ness Monster, spontaneous human combustion, and even a collection of "haunted" dolls!

I hope you'll agree that the records in this year's book are more exciting, more inspiring, and more spectacular than ever. Of course, if you think you can do better, then please do get in touch. There are plenty of ways to get your name in the pages of the world's biggest-selling copyright book (see pp. xxvi–xxix) and, with your help, the next 10 years of record-breaking will be as fruitful as the last.

Craig Glenday
Editor-in-Chief
Follow me at twitter.com/@craigglenday

GWR DAY

Every year in mid-November, thousands of people around the world try to set or break records for Guinness World Records Day. It's a celebration of determination, ingenuity, craziness . . . and it's a lot of fun! You, too, can help raise money and awareness for your favorite charity. If you've got a special record you'd like to achieve, visit www.guinnessworldrecords.com to find out how to start. Who knows—you could be on these pages next year!

HIGHLIGHTS FROM OUR GWR DAY 2011 . . .

Country	Record/event	Description
1. Ireland	Largest gathering of leprechauns	262, on *The Mooney Show* (RTE1)
2. Japan	Tallest tower	2,080 ft. (634 m), for the Tokyo Sky Tree
3. Germany	Longest radio show broadcast by a team	73 hours, by Nora Neise and Tolga Aka for KISS FM Radio
4. UK	Most people in one pair of underpants	57, by Pants to Poverty
5. UK	Tallest basketball player	7-ft. 7.25-in. (231.8-cm) Paul "Tiny" Sturgess

HIGHLIGHTS FROM OUR GWR DAY 2011 . . .

6. Netherlands	Most water rockets launched simultaneously	443, by students at Teylingen College in Noordwijkerhout
7. Japan	Largest rice cracker	5-ft. 2-in. (1.6-m) diameter, by Inzai City Tourism Association
8. UK	Fastest motorized shopping cart	42.8 mph (69 km/h), by Tesco plc and The Big Kick
9. Germany	Most bottle caps removed with head (1 minute)	24, by Ahmed Tafzi
10. Germany	Longest full-body burn run (without oxygen)	393 ft. 8.4 in. (120 m), by Denni Düsterhöft
11. UK	Fastest time to wrap a person in newspaper	3 min. 7 sec., by Francesca Librae for the *Daily Star Sunday*
12. UK	Fastest time to wrap a person in newspaper (by a team of eight)	1 min. 31 sec., by *First News*
13. U.S.A.	Oldest yoga teacher	91-year-old Bernice Mary Bates (b. June 30, 1920)
14. UK	Largest cream tea party	334, by The English Cream Tea Company
15. Romania	Largest chocolate coin	584 lb. 3.5 oz. (265 kg), by the Sun Plaza shopping mall
16. China	Longest kissing chain	351, by Jiayuan.com
17. U.S.A.	Largest hula-hoop workout	221, by students from Longleaf Elementary School
18. UK	Most chin-ups (one hour)	993, by Stephen Hyland
19. Lebanon	Largest collection of model automobiles	27,777, by Nabil Karam
20. Germany	Most pine boards broken by a weight attached to the hair in one minute	10, by Janna Vernunft at the Joe Alexander Entertainment Group gym in Hamburg

BE A RECORD BREAKER

HAVE YOU GOT A RECORD-BREAKING TALENT?

You don't need to be a superathlete, a world-famous explorer, or a multibillionaire to have a Guinness World Record. We believe there's a world record in everyone—so why not attempt one yourself?

If you've got a world-beating skill, however offbeat you may think it is, get in touch with us! You could set or break a new world record online, at one of our live events, or even on television. To find out how, simply read on . . .

HOW TO BE A RECORD BREAKER *Follow Jonny on his mission to break the Guinness World Record for the most T-shirts worn at once. Everyone who wants to register a claim must follow this application process. Be sure to give us plenty of warning—at least a month.*

START:
I want to be a record breaker.
Do you have a record in mind?

NO:
Read the book, watch the TV shows, or visit www.guinnessworld records.com to see the kind of records we usually accept.

YES:
Tell us as much as you can about your record idea at www.guinness worldrecords.com. If it's an existing record, we'll send you the official guidelines that the previous claimant followed. If it's a new idea, and we like it, we'll write new guidelines for you.

FACT: Our most frequently broken record is that of **oldest living woman**.

Have we sent guidelines for your claim?

NO:
If we don't think your idea is suitable for a record, we can help you adapt it so that it is worthy of a record.

YES:
The guidelines explain how to attempt the record and how to collate the evidence. At the same time, we'll send you details of the current record—this is the figure you'll have to beat!

You're now ready to attempt the record. Be sure to follow every rule in the guidelines. If you're not sure about anything, let us know before you start.

Have you collated the evidence we've asked for?

NO:
Gather the evidence we ask for, such as photographs, video footage, press clippings, and eyewitness signatures.
YES:
If you think you've broken the record, send all your evidence to our adjudicators. The investigation can take a few weeks.

FINISH:
If you've followed the rules and beaten the existing record (or set a new one), you will receive a letter of confirmation. You will also be sent your official Guinness World Records certificate welcoming you into the record-breaking family. Congratulations!

FACT: The **most T-shirts worn at once** is 257, achieved by Sanath Bandara (Sri Lanka) in 2011.

EVIDENCE

Here's the kind of proof we need to show that you've followed our guidelines:

- 📷 Photographs
- 📹 Full (unedited) video
- 📄 Witness statements
- 📋 Logbook
- ✂ Newspaper clippings
- 📒 Professional qualifications
- 🧭 GPS readings
- = Birth certificates

Each record is different, so please read your guidelines carefully.

RECORDS SERVICES Aspiring record holders can take advantage of various premium records services:
- Fast-track your claim
- Invite a GWR adjudicator to your event
- Launch a record-breaking product
- Promote your attempt using the official GWR logo

See **www.guinnessworldrecords.com** for more information.

BREAK YOUR RECORD AT A LIVE EVENT SHOW Guinness World Records hosts live events in supermarkets, shopping malls, vacation resorts—wherever there's space for us! We stage record attempts every hour, on the hour. There are practice stations, and GWR adjudicators are on hand to officiate. To find out when we'll be in your area, visit **www.guinnessworldrecords.com/live-event**. Above right, GWR's Talal Omar (far right) is in attendance as Chris Wones and Stuart Aitken (both U.S.A.) receive their certificate for the **most football passes in one minute by a pair (101)**. On the left, GWR's Science Show visits Butlins in Bognor, UK.

BREAK YOUR RECORD ON TV When you make your record application through our website, let us know if you think your attempt would work well on television. We're always on the lookout for visually amazing records for our international TV shows. On the left, GWR adjudicator Kristian Teufel is pictured with Bollywood star Preity Zinta, host of *Guinness World Records—Ab India Todega*. Above right, GWR's Marco Frigatti and Lorenzo Veltri line up with two diminutive record holders on Italy's *Lo Show dei Record*. And on January 10, 2010, Brendan Mon Tanner (Australia, above right, closely watched by GWR's Chris Sheedy), set a record for the **most fire torches extinguished with the mouth in one minute (88)** on the set of *Australia Smashes Guinness World Records*.

BREAK YOUR RECORD ONLINE If you want to start attempting world records *right now*, then be a GWR Challenger! Simply visit us at **www .guinnessworldrecords.com/ challengers** and pick a world record you'd like to try—or suggest a new record you think you can set. Once we've given you the go-ahead, you're free to carry out your record attempt, but be sure to film yourself doing it. Next, upload your video and wait to hear from us—we adjudicate the best new videos every week. Who knows, you could be joining Silvio Sabba (Italy, left)—**most Ferrero Rocher chocolates stacked (12)**—and Stephen Kish (UK, above right)—**most coins stacked into a tower in 30 seconds (44)**—as Guinness World Record holders on Challengers!

Be a Record Breaker

PEACE ONE DAY

SEPTEMBER 21 . . .

"When you build a house, you start with one brick. If we want to build peace, we start with one day. That day has arrived." *Jeremy Gilley, founder, Peace One Day*

Guinness World Records is proud to support Peace One Day—a global initiative to encourage an annual day of nonviolence on Peace Day (September 21) and provide an opportunity for aid organizations to carry out essential life-saving work in war-torn communities. Already, the campaign has resulted in the vaccination of millions of children in Afghanistan. But there is much more to do . . . and you can be part of it.

By the time you read this, and if all goes according to plan, the world will have experienced the largest reduction of violence ever recorded on a single day. The day in question—September 21, 2012—is the focus of Peace One Day's Global Truce 2012 campaign, and is part of the ongoing initiative to establish an annual day of cease-fire and non-violence.

How it all began Peace One Day was the brainchild of British actor-turned-moviemaker Jeremy Gilley, who, in the late 1990s, "became preoccupied with questions about the fundamental nature of humanity and the issue of peace." His idea was a seemingly simple one: to achieve just one day of cease-fire around the world—an effort that would manifest in a documentary movie following his attempts to secure

---

OTHER RECORD-BREAKING PEACE INITIATIVES

Jeremy Gilley's Peace One Day campaign joins a host of other record-worthy initiatives to reduce poverty, encourage cease-fire, and redress the imbalance of power on our planet.

Indeed, the **largest Guinness World Records attempt ever staged** was a worldwide United Nations program—"Stand Up Against Poverty" in October 2008. In support of the program, a total of 116,993,629 participants in 7,777 events around the globe got to their feet to raise awareness of the "Global Call to Action Against Poverty" campaign.

FACT: A copy of the Hittite version of the treaty (see page xxxi) remains in the Karnak Temple in Luxor, Egypt.

---

this day of peace. From this audacious start, Gilley has spearheaded a successful global crusade to have an annual day of global ceasefire and nonviolence with a fixed date adopted by all United Nations member states. The resulting film, *The Day After Peace*, has inspired countless individuals, corporations, organizations and governments to recognize September 21 as an annual day of global unity.

Seeing results Peace Days have already been a fantastic success. In Afghanistan, an initiative led by Peace One Day has achieved incredible results: on Peace Day 2008, the UN recorded a 70% reduction in violent incidents in that country. And on Peace Day 2010, more than 50,000 children and women of child-bearing age across 23 high-risk locations in greater Kabul were vaccinated against deadly diseases including polio, meningitis, diphtheria, and tetanus. In addition, a nationwide polio immunization campaign to target 8 million children was launched. Already 4.5 million children have benefited from life-saving polio vaccinations as a result of Peace Day agreements since 2007.

Across the world It's not just in Afghanistan that Peace Day activities have made an impact. In 2010, Peace One Day instigated a total of 88 life-saving and humanitarian activities by 28 organizations in 31 countries. And the campaign's aim is not simply to stop violence in war-torn countries. Backed by Peace One Day ambassadors Jude Law and Thandie Newton (pictured on page xxxiii), and Baroness Scotland of Asthal (bottom left), Peace One Day partnered the Eliminate Domestic Violence Global Foundation (EDV) for Peace Day 2012. Domestic violence affects people in all countries, and can have major consequences for children who see and hear it or even suffer from it at home.

FIRST PEACE TREATY The earliest known surviving peace treaty was drawn up ca. 1271 B.C. and signed by the Egyptian pharaoh Ramses II and Hattusilis III, King of the Hittites and ruler of Hatti (in present-day Turkey). Two copies of the treaty were made, one in hieroglyphics, the other in the Mesopotamian language of Akkadian (or Babylonian-Assyrian). Both parties agreed to end years of warring and form an alliance in the event of foreign aggression.

JEREMY GILLEY IN HIS OWN WORDS

We all want answers to the big questions in the world: why is there so much starvation, destruction, and killing of innocent people? But like most of us, I didn't think I could do anything about it. I had no qualifications (except a "D" in pottery!) and worked in acting. I began filmmaking, and wanted to make a film about peace, but there needed to be more than a series of sound bites and images. There had to be a mountain to climb. That's when I had the idea, a starting point for peace—could I create an annual day of global unity, a day when humanity comes together and realizes that we're all in this together?

I wanted the day to be September 21 because 21 was my grandfather's favorite number. He fought in World War II and died when I was 11. In one expedition, 700 men in his regiment left to fight, 23 came back and two died on the boat, leaving only 21 survivors.

The launch

So I launched Peace One Day in 1999, inviting hundreds of press organizations, but none turned up! A total of 114 people were there—but they were mostly my friends and family. It didn't matter—it was a start; it made a statement.

Gradually, after lots of letter-writing and telephoning, people started coming on board. Mary Robinson, United Nations Commissioner for Human Rights, said it was an idea whose time has come. UN Secretary General Kofi Annan told me the day would help his UN peacekeeping troops on the ground.

So on September 7, 2001, the UK and Costa Rican governments sponsored a resolution, with 54 cosponsors, at the General Assembly of the United Nations, seeking to establish this annual day of non-violence on the UN International Day of Peace, fixed in the calendar as September 21. It was unanimously adopted by the member states of the United Nations—every single nation in the world! I was there at the top of the General Assembly, looking down, and I saw it happen. It really was a magnificent moment.

I was going to be present at a press conference with Kofi Annan on the morning of September 11, 2001, to announce the creation of the day. But obviously, after the planes crashed into the World Trade Center, Kofi Annan never arrived and the conference was canceled. For me, though, the events of 9/11 simply confirmed exactly why we had to work harder. I left New York anxious but empowered—and inspired to stop events like 9/11 from ever happening again.

Be a part of Peace Day So how can you get involved? Every year on September 21, Peace One Day invites you to celebrate peace in your community. It may be a soccer match—on Peace Day 2010, in a campaign entitled One Day One Goal, over 3,000 soccer matches took place in all 192 UN member states. You could also organize an event in any other sport, or put on a dance, theatrical, or musical performance. According to the UN, 100 million people were active on Peace Day by 2007, and you can join them by simply contacting the organization through its website (www.peaceoneday.org).

You can also encourage teachers to download free education resources at the website. School teacher Betsy Sawyer from Groton, Massachusetts, U.S.A., uses these resources in her after-school peace book club, called the Bookmakers and Dreamers. The teenagers in the club have Skyped fellow teenagers in rural Afghanistan and they found out exactly how important a sense of peace was in a country that has endured war for 30 years. For Afghani children, peace is not a grandiose ideal—like all children, they have the right to grow up without fearing for their safety.

LARGEST BOOK OF SIGNATURES Amnesty International gathered 10 million signatures from 125 countries in its one-year-long "Get Up, Sign Up" campaign, pledging support for the Universal Declaration of Human Rights. The signatures were compiled into a book and presented to Kofi Annan, the UN Secretary General, in Paris, France, on the 50th anniversary of the Universal Declaration of Human Rights on December 10, 1998. Pictured is the Dalai Lama adding his autograph to the book.

FACT: Your own Peace Day event could qualify as a new world record. Find out how to apply on p. xxvi.

NOBEL PEACE PRIZES

The Nobel Peace Prize is one of the five categories of award bequeathed by Alfred Nobel (Sweden), the inventor of dynamite. It is awarded annually "to the person who shall have done the most or the best work for fraternity between nations, for the abolition or reduction of standing armies, and for the holding and promotion of peace congresses." Notable laureates include:

Laureate	Year	Why?
A. Henry Dunant (Switzerland) & Frédéric Passy (France)	1901	**First Peace Laureates** (awarded jointly)— Dunant, for being a principal founder of the Red Cross and Passy for organizing the first Universal Peace Congress
Bertha von Suttner (Austria)	1905	**First female Peace Laureate**, for her novel *Lay Down Your Arms* (1889) and for assisting Alfred Nobel in founding the Peace Prize
Aung San Suu Kyi (Burma)	1991	For her nonviolent struggle for democracy; endured the **longest house arrest** of the 20th century (lasting 5 years 355 days)
B. Rigoberta Menchú Tun (Guatemala)	1992	**Youngest Peace Laureate** (at the age of 33), for her work in asserting the rights of indigenous peoples
C. Barack Obama (U.S.A.)	2009	For his efforts to strengthen international diplomacy and cooperation; the United States has the **most Peace Prizes by nationality**, with 272 recipients

LARGEST ANTIWAR RALLY On February 15, 2003, antiwar rallies took place across the globe—the largest occurring in Rome, Italy, where a crowd of 3 million gathered to protest the U.S.A.'s threat to invade Iraq (pictured). Police figures report that millions more demonstrated in nearly 600 cities worldwide. On the same day, 1.3 million rallied in Barcelona, Spain, and 1 million people participated in a peace march through the streets of London, UK.

SPACE

CONTENTS

HOW FAR WILL WE EXPLORE?

WHAT ARE THE LIMITS TO SPACE TRAVEL?

The distances between the stars are vast and are measured using a unit called "light-years." One light-year is the distance traveled by light in one year. The speed of light is 671 million mph (299,792,458 m/s), so one light-year is the same as 5,878,625,373,183.608 miles (9,460,730,472,580.8 km)!

Our Sun is 8.3 "light-minutes" away (i.e., it takes 8.3 minutes for sunlight to reach Earth), and the Moon—the farthest place humans have ever visited—just 1.3 "light-seconds" away. So when we consider that our next nearest star is 4.2 light-years away, what chances have we got of ever reaching it? Even if we consider light as our theoretical speed limit, how far *can* we expect to travel from Earth? Our journey starts at bottom left of the page . . .

So rapid was humanity's progress in the development of flight that, for 18 years, Orville Wright (coinventor of the **first powered airplane**) and Neil Armstrong (**first man on the Moon**) were alive at the same time!

LARGEST CONCENTRATION OF OBSERVATORIES The 13 telescopes on Hawaii's Mauna Kea include the world's largest infrared and submillimeter telescopes, along with some of the largest optical telescopes. Operated by 11 countries, the observatories are near the 13,796-ft.-high (4,205-m) summit of the Mauna Kea volcano. Because the atmosphere above the summit is dry, free of pollutants, and rarely cloudy, astronomers can see the faintest galaxies at the edge of the observable universe. This photograph was taken at the summit with a long exposure so that, as Earth rotates, the stars appear to leave trails.

KEY

The history of exploring objects in space points to a trend of key stages:

 1. Study from Earth using telescopes

 2. Study briefly at close range using a flyby probe

 3. More in-depth, close-range study using an orbiting probe

 4. Land on the surface using a robotic probe

 5. Bring back samples using a robotic probe

 6. Send humans to explore

The distance stated at each stage is the average distance from Earth in astronomical units (AU), in which 1 AU is the distance between Earth and the Sun (roughly 92,955,807 miles/149,597,870.7 km).

OGLE-2005-BLG-390L *(stage 1)* Near the center of the Milky Way, orbiting this red dwarf star, is OGLE-2005-BLG-390Lb, the most **distant extrasolar planet** discovered to date. Even if we could travel at 157,077 mph (252,792 km/h), it would take us 92 million years to get there!

1.3×10^9 AU (21,500 LIGHT-YEARS)

GLIESE 581 *(stage 1)* This red dwarf star system is home to the planet Gliese 581 d, which lies in the "habitable zone" of its solar system and is, therefore, a contender for life (see panel, p. 6). A radio signal sent there in 2008 is due to arrive in 2029.

1.28 MILLION AU (20.3 LIGHT-YEARS)

PROXIMA CENTAURI *(stage 1)* At 4.24 light-years away, this red dwarf is the **nearest star to the Sun**. Even traveling at the **fastest spacecraft speed yet achieved** (*Helios 2* at 157,077 mph/252,792 km/h), it would take some 18,000 years to reach. To put this into perspective, 18,000 years ago our ancestors were creating cave art and using stone tools.

268,136 AU (4.24 LIGHT-YEARS)

PLUTO *(stage 2)* Despite its demotion from planet to dwarf planet, Pluto is the most distant Solar System object currently targeted by a robotic mission. NASA's *New Horizons* spacecraft is en route and will perform a flyby of Pluto and its four moons in July 2015.

39.5 AU (3.67 BILLION MILES)

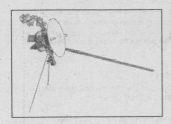

VOYAGER 1 Currently nearly 11.2 billion miles (120 AU) from Earth

EUROPA *(stage 3)* The *Galileo* orbiter (1995–2003) suggested that, with its icy surface and the potential of liquid water oceans, this Jovian moon offers one of the best chances yet of finding extraterrestrial life. A robotic lander mission to Europa is under discussion as a concept but will launch no earlier than around 2030.

5.2 AU (483.4 MILLION MILES)

MARS *(stage 4)* The USSR *Mars 2* and *Mars 3* missions were the **first spacecraft to reach the surface of Mars**, in 1971. We have yet to see a successful sample return mission, but the first visit by humans should happen within the next few decades.

1.5 AU (139.4 MILLION MILES)

ITOKAWA ASTEROID *(stage 5)* On June 13, 2010, the unmanned spacecraft *Hayabusa* (Japan) landed on Earth with its cargo of tiny grains of material collected from the surface of the asteroid Itokawa. It was the **first spacecraft to lift off from an asteroid** and the farthest land-and-return sample mission launched.

0.706 AU (65.6 MILLION MILES)

APOLLO 13 Reached 248,655 miles (400,171 km) from Earth

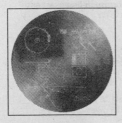

MOST REMOTE MAN-MADE OBJECT As of February 12, 2012, NASA's *Voyager 1*, launched in 1977 to help us study the outer Solar System, was 11,160,000,000 miles (120 AU) from the Sun. Should it ever be found by aliens, it contains a gold-plated disk carrying data on the human race, including photographs and music.

MOON *(stage 6) Apollo 11*, which landed on the Moon on July 20, 1969, was the first mission to reach stage 6; also counted as the first sample return mission (stage 5).

0.0027 AU (250,980 MILES)

VOSTOK 1 Reached apogee (farthest point from Earth) of 203 miles (327 km)

HIGHEST ALTITUDE ACHIEVED The farthest distance ever traveled from Earth by humans is 248,655 miles (400,171 km), by the crew of *Apollo 13* (Jack Swigert, Jim Lovell, and Fred Haise, all U.S.A.) on April 15, 1970.

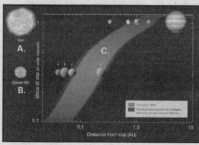

A. *SUN*   B. *GLIESE 581*   C. *HABITABLE ZONE*

FIRST CONFIRMED EXOPLANET THAT COULD SUPPORT EARTHLIKE LIFE The "habitable zone" is the region around a star in which planets can sustain liquid surface water. Within this region of the star Gliese 581 is at least one planet ("d"); Gliese 581 is smaller than our Sun, but "d" is correspondingly closer to its star.

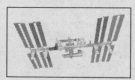

INTERNATIONAL SPACE STATION Orbits at an altitude of 205–255 miles (330–410 km)

> **FACT:** To make the trip to Proxima Centauri—our nearest star neighbor—would take 100 times more energy than our civilization currently generates.

FIRST MANNED SPACEFLIGHT Cosmonaut Flight Major (later Col.) Yuri Alekseyevich Gagarin (USSR) became the first human to travel into space, orbiting Earth in *Vostok 1* on April 12, 1961.

LONGEST HIGH-FIDELITY SPACEFLIGHT SIMULATION Mars-500 was a collaboration between the European Space Agency, Russia, and China to simulate a 500-day manned mission to Mars. The crew of six men entered their sealed facility in Moscow, Russia, in June 2010 and emerged in November 2011. The project included a 20-minute time delay in communications between the crew and the outside world, just like a real Mars mission would.

With current conventional rocket technology, a trip to the nearest star is out of the question. Even if we could develop an interstellar spacecraft (artist's impression, top right), Albert Einstein has taught us that as this theoretical spacecraft approached the speed of light, it would appear to gain mass, making it increasingly difficult to accelerate.

More advanced rocket technology, such as nuclear thermal or nuclear pulse, could theoretically send a manned mission to the nearest stars at a significant fraction of the speed of light—albeit at a great cost—within a century. If anyone manages to invent sci-fi technology, such as a warp drive, it could happen much sooner!

How Far Will We Explore?

VENUS

Largest planet without a moon Of the eight major planets of the solar system, only Mercury and Venus have no natural satellite. It is possible that Venus once had a moon, which crashed into the surface. With a 7,520.8-mile (12,103.6-km) diameter, Venus is similar in size to Earth.

Largest impact crater on Venus Mead crater, north of a highland area called Aphrodite Terra, has a diameter of around 174 miles (280 km). Mead is shallow, suggesting it may have been filled by lava or impact melt after its formation.

Planet with the longest day Venus has the longest rotation period (day) of all the major planets in the solar system. While Earth takes 23 hr. 56 min. 4 sec. to complete one rotation, Venus takes 243.16 "Earth days" to spin once through 360 degrees. Because it is closer to the Sun, the length of Venus's year is shorter than Earth's, lasting 224.7 days, so a day on Venus is actually longer than its year!

HOTTEST PLANET Venus has an average surface temperature of 896°F (480°C). This scorching heat is hot enough to melt lead and, coupled with the atrocious atmosphere, makes exploration of the surface by landers very difficult. The circular forms and radiating concentric cracks seen in the main photograph above are known as arachnoids, because they resemble spiderwebs. They may have been caused by volcanic processes. The smaller picture is a colorized version of one of the images taken by the Soviet *Venera 13* and *14* landers, which touched down on Venus in 1982.

FACT: Mercury is closer to the Sun, but it has no atmosphere to trap heat. Venus does, and so it is hotter.

Brightest planet seen from Earth Seen from Earth, the brightest of the five planets usually visible to the naked eye (Jupiter, Mars, Mercury, Saturn, and Venus) is Venus, with a maximum magnitude of -4.4. Venus appears so bright because around 80% of the sunlight that reaches the planet is bounced back by its reflective cloud cover (see below). At maximum elongation, it is visible for some time before and after sunrise and sunset.

Thickest planetary atmosphere Often referred to as the closest place to hell in the solar system, Venus's atmosphere is the thickest of any planet, with a pressure nearly 100 times that of Earth's atmospheric pressure at sea level. The gases in the thick atmosphere cause a greenhouse effect, which means the temperature on the surface reaches 896°F (480°C). Europe's *Venus Express* spacecraft is currently performing the most intensive study of Venus's atmosphere ever made (see p. 11).

Most acidic rain in the solar system The highly reflective white clouds of Venus, which prevent direct viewing of the surface from space, are due to a layer of sulfuric acid 30–36 miles (48–58 km) above the surface. Rain of almost pure sulfuric acid falls from these clouds but never reaches the surface. At an altitude of around 18.5 miles (30 km), the rain evaporates; it is recycled into the Venusian clouds.

First successful interplanetary mission *Mariner 2* (U.S.A.) performed a flyby of Venus on December 14, 1962, within 35,000 km (21,750 miles) of the planet's surface. Results from the flyby revealed the extremely hot nature of the planet's surface. *Mariner 2*, now without power, is still in orbit around the Sun.

LARGEST PLANET WITH NO MAGNETIC FIELD Unlike Earth, Venus does not have a magnetic field. This allows particles from the solar wind to interact with the atmosphere, stripping away around 2×10^{24} hydrogen atoms into space every second. This image was pieced together from data from NASA's *Magellan* spacecraft, which used radar to map the surface.

Largest highland region on Venus Close to Venus's equator lies Aphrodite Terra, one of two major highland "continents" on the planet. First mapped in detail by the Soviet *Venera 15* and *16* orbiters in 1984, it covers an area of around 30 million km² (11.6 million miles²), which is approximately the same size as Africa. The fractured appearance of Aphrodite suggests it has been subject to huge forces of compression in its geological history.

Tallest mountain on Venus Maxwell Montes, on the Ishtar Terra plateau, is the highest point on Venus, up to 6.8 miles (11 km) above the average surface level of the planet.

VENUS AT A GLANCE

The vital statistics of this cloud-enshrouded planet

- **Mass:** 5.29×10^{21} tons (4.8×10^{21} tonnes)

- **Volume:** 22.2×10^{10} miles³ (9.38×10^{11} km³)

- **Equatorial (and polar) radius:** 3,760.4 miles (6,051.8 km)

- **Diameter:** 7,520.8 miles (12,103.6 km)

- **Surface gravity:** 0.9 *g* (8.9 m/s²)

- **Major atmospheric gases:** 96.5% carbon dioxide; 3.5% nitrogen

- **Mean surface temperature:** 896°F (480°C)

- **Closest distance to Earth:** 23.7 million miles (38.3 million km)

- **Rotation:** Retrograde. Venus and Uranus rotate in the opposite direction to all other planets in the solar system. On both planets, the Sun rises in the west and sets in the east.

First detection of lightning on Venus On October 26, 1975, the spectrometer onboard the Soviet *Venera 9* spacecraft detected optical flashes—consistent with lightning—in the Venusian atmosphere on the dark side of the planet. This represents the only time lightning has been witnessed optically by a spacecraft in the atmosphere of Venus.

On December 25, 1978, in its descent to Venus's surface, the USSR's *Venera 11* lander picked up a sound that scientists believe to be the first thunder heard on another planet.

Longest channel in the solar system Baltis Vallis on Venus is around 4,300 miles (7,000 km) in length and has an average width of around 1 mile (1.6 km). It was discovered by the *Magellan* radar mapper, which orbited Venus from August 1990 to October 1994. Experts believe that the channel was originally formed by molten lava.

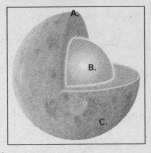

VENUSIAN GEOLOGY

A. CRUST The crust of Venus was analyzed by Soviet landers and is basaltic in nature, with a thickness of around 30 miles (50 km). Underneath is the mantle, which is around 1,900 miles (3,000 km) thick.

B. CORE Probably a semimolten, metallic mass, like the Earth's core.

C. ATMOSPHERE Mainly carbon dioxide (96.5%) and a small amount of nitrogen (3.5%). Smaller traces of sulfur dioxide, argon, water, carbon monoxide, helium, and neon.

NB: The heavy cloud cover and extremely hostile conditions on Venus have made it very difficult for scientists to gather useful data about the internal composition of the planet. The mantle and core of the planet are still mysteries and require fuller investigation.

FIRST EUROPEAN VENUS ORBITER *Venus Express*, the European Space Agency's (ESA) first mission to Venus, is designed for long-term study of the Venusian atmosphere. The spacecraft is an orbiter with a complex array of instruments. It successfully entered orbit around Venus on April 11, 2006, after a main engine burn of just over 50 minutes, allowing the spacecraft to be captured by the planet's gravity. It has been operational ever since and is the only spacecraft currently studying the planet. Its discoveries to date include the first clear images of the planet's south pole and the discovery of an ozone layer in the upper atmosphere.

EARTH'S EVIL TWIN

If Venus is considered to be a twin planet to Earth, it's certainly an *evil* twin! Here are some of the hazards that make Venus the closest place to hell in the solar system:

 You'd be suffocated by the thick carbon dioxide (CO_2) atmosphere . . .

 . . . fried by the surface temperature of 896°F (480°C) . . .

 . . . and crushed by the pressure, which is 92 times greater than on Earth.

 The beautiful white clouds of Venus are actually made of caustic sulfuric acid.

 And if the atmosphere's not already nasty enough, there are trace elements of sulfur dioxide, carbon monoxide, and hydrogen chloride.

 Superfast winds blow at speeds up to 186 mph (300 km/h) in the upper atmosphere.

 There's a total absence of liquid water, all of which evaporated a long time ago . . . and to make matters worse, if you weren't instantaneously crushed, suffocated, and fried, just a single day on this hellish planet would last the equivalent of 243 days on Earth!

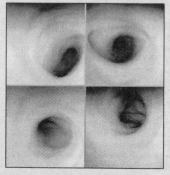

LARGEST VENUSIAN ATMOSPHERIC VORTICES Huge double-eye vortices (whirlpool-like spirals in the atmosphere) up to 1,240 miles (2,000 km) across swirl around the north and south poles of Venus. The northern vortex was discovered by *Mariner 10* (U.S.A.) in 1974 and the southern vortex in 2006 by the ESA orbiter *Venus Express*. These swirling clouds are highly dynamic, shifting regularly between "S" shapes, "8" shapes, and more chaotic patterns.

THE SUN

Fastest wind in the Solar System The solar wind is a steady stream of (mostly) electrons and protons that is emitted from the Sun in all directions. The fastest component of the solar wind travels outward at around 470 miles/sec (750 km/sec) and is thought to originate from areas of open magnetic field lines around the Sun's poles.

Largest object in the Solar System The Sun dominates the Solar System. With a mass of 1.98×10^{30} kg, or 332,900 times that of Earth, and a diameter of 865,000 miles (1,392,000 km), it accounts for some 99.86% of the mass of the Solar System.

Largest explosions in the Solar System Coronal mass ejections are often, although not always, associated with solar flares. They are huge bubbles of plasma threaded with magnetic field lines, which erupt from the Sun over a period of several hours. They can contain up to 220.5 billion lb. (100 billion kg) of matter moving at 620 miles/sec (1,000 km/sec), with the equivalent energy of a billion hydrogen bombs. The next solar maximum, in 2013, could see several of these erupt from the Sun every day.

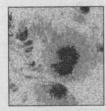

COOLEST PART OF THE SUN Sunspots form on the Sun's photosphere as a result of magnetic activity and have a temperature of ca. 3,700 K, compared with ca. 5,700 K for the surrounding photosphere. (The photosphere is the point at which the Sun becomes opaque and is regarded as its "surface.") These large spots would glow brightly if they could be seen against the background of space.

LONGEST TOTAL SOLAR ECLIPSE A total solar eclipse occurs when the Moon completely obscures the Sun. The longest total solar eclipse since the year 1001 occurred on June 20, 1955, west of the Philippines, and lasted for 7 min. 8 sec.; the gridded area shows the areas that fell into full or partial darkness. The longest possible solar eclipse is 7 min. 31 sec.; an eclipse of 7 min. 29 sec. will occur in the mid-Atlantic Ocean on July 16, 2186.

FACT: The strength of the Sun's magnetic field varies. When it peaks, dark "sunspots" appear.

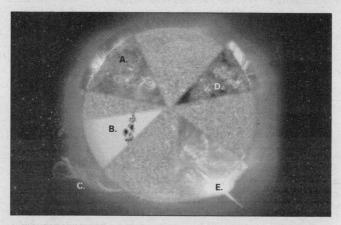

A. HIGHEST NUMBER OF SUNSPOTS IN THE CURRENT SOLAR CYCLE On October 21, 2011, observations of the Sun showed a total of 207 sunspots, the highest seen to date in the current solar cycle—number 24. Despite the sunspot number, flare activity was fairly light with only one X-class eruption event to date since then.

B. LARGEST SUNSPOT GROUP The most extensive group of sunspots ever recorded was in the Sun's southern hemisphere on April 8, 1947. Its area was about 7 billion sq. miles (18 billion km²), with an extreme longitude of 187,000 miles (300,000 km) and an extreme latitude of 90,000 miles (145,000 km).

C. LARGEST SOLAR PROMINENCE "Prominences" are large, eruptive features of relatively cool plasma, or ionized gas, at around 144,000ºF (80,000ºC). Trapped within the Sun's magnetic field lines, they often form loops and can appear to twist and evolve above the Sun's photosphere for longer than a month. The largest to date have been around 310,000–435,000 miles (500,000–700,000 km) long.

D. LARGEST SOLAR FLARE IN THE CURRENT SOLAR CYCLE On January 8, 2008, the Sun began its most recent solar cycle since records began in 1755. On August 9, 2011, a solar flare with an X-ray magnitude of X6.9 erupted from sunspot 1263, near the western limb of the Sun. The associated coronal mass ejection caused some minor short-wave radio disruptions on Earth.

E. LARGEST RECORDED SOLAR FLARE Solar flares—huge bursts of energy on the Sun—are graded at three levels: C class (minor), M class (medium), and X class. M- and X-class events can have repercussions here on Earth, such as radio blackouts. On November 4, 2003, a flare erupted from the Sun's surface that was rated an X28 event by the Space Environment Center of the National Oceanic and Atmospheric Administration (NOAA) in Boulder, Colorado, U.S.A.

Largest magnetic structure in the Solar System The magnetic field of the Sun is contorted into a vast spiral shape by the Sun's rotation and motion of the solar wind. Resembling the shape of a spinning ballerina's skirt, and known as the "Parker spiral," it extends all the way to the edge of the Solar System, into a region known as the "heliosheath." The magnetic structure of the Parker spiral is approximately 160–200 AU across, or 15–18 billion miles (24–30 billion km).

Strongest magnetic fields on the Sun's surface Sunspots can have magnetic field strengths of up to 0.4 tesla, around 1,000 times that of their surrounding areas and around 13,000 times the strength of Earth's magnetic field at the Equator.

Longest continuous observational science data Astronomers have access to a continuous set of observational data of the number of sunspots on the Sun, dating back to 1750.

Longest solar minimum The "solar minimum" is a period during the Sun's solar cycle when few sunspots are visible and solar activity is low. The Maunder minimum lasted from 1647 to 1715, during which it appeared as if the solar cycle had broken down altogether. This period corresponded with a period of savage winters in Earth's northern hemisphere that became known as the "Little Ice Age."

Largest solar granules Convection currents within the Sun cause a phenomenon known as "granulation" on the photosphere. Each granule is formed as hot hydrogen rises in its center and then falls again around its edge. A typical granule is around 620 miles (1,000 km) across and can last for less than 20 minutes. Discovered in the 1950s, supergranules measure

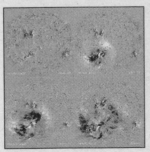

LARGEST SOLAR "TSUNAMIS" First captured using time-lapse imagery, left, in 1959, and subsequently confirmed by observations from spacecraft, Morton waves are the Sun's equivalent of tsunamis. Generated by eruptive solar flares, they travel across the solar surface like ripples from a stone dropped into water. They can reach speeds of 930 miles/sec (1,500 km/sec) in a radiating wave of hot plasma and magnetism that grows up to 62,130 miles (100,000 km) tall.

FACT: The term "solar cycle" refers to a period of flux in the Sun's magnetic field. It lasts for around 11 years.

around 18,640 miles (30,000 km) across and represent larger-scale currents in the Sun, which has several thousand of these features at any time.

Hottest place in the Solar System Scientists estimate that the temperature at the Sun's core is around 28,000,000°F (15,600,000°C). The pressure there is around 250 billion times that of sea level on Earth.

SIZING UP THE SUN

The Sun dwarfs the planets in the Solar System. But when it comes to some of the other stars in the Milky Way, our Sun is pretty small-fry (even if these stars weigh relatively little compared with their colossal size). Let GWR take you on an interstellar voyage:

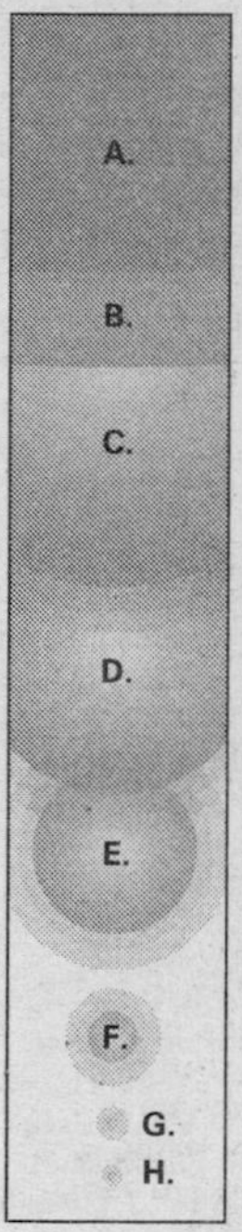

A. Betelgeuse
Diameter: 807.8 million miles
(ca. 15–20 x solar mass, the mass of our own Sun)

B. Antares
Diameter: 602.7 million miles
(15–18 x solar mass)

C. Rigel A
Diameter: 60.3 million miles
(ca. 17 x solar mass)

D. Aldebaran
Diameter: 37.14 million miles
(ca. 2 x solar mass)

E. Arcturus
Diameter: 22.37 million miles
(ca. 1.5 x solar mass)

F. Pollux
Diameter: 6.9 million miles
(ca. 2 x solar mass)

G. Sirius A
Diameter: 1.45 million miles
(ca. 2 x solar mass)

H. Sun
Diameter: 865 thousand miles
Mass: 1.98×10^{30} kg.

FACT: Sunspots can be huge. The largest may reach 50,000 miles (80,000 km) in diameter.

LIVING IN SPACE

FIRST . . .

Manned spaceflight Soviet cosmonaut Yuri Gagarin was the first man in space when he orbited Earth in *Vostok 1* on April 12, 1961. Gagarin ejected 108 minutes into the flight as planned and landed back on Earth 10 minutes later by parachute. The maximum altitude on the 25,394.8-mile (40,868.6-km) flight was 203 miles (327 km), with a top speed of 17,560 mph (28,260 km/h). Gagarin, invested a Hero of the Soviet Union and awarded the Order of Lenin and the Gold Star Medal, was killed in a jet plane crash in March 1968.

Flight between space stations Mir EO-1 was the first expedition to the new Soviet *Mir* space station. Its crew, Leonid Kizim and Vladimir Solovyov, launched from Earth on March 13, 1986, docking with *Mir* two days later. They remained on *Mir* for six weeks, changing the station's orbit to match that of the *Salyut 7* space station. On May 5, 1986, the crew undocked their *Soyuz* spacecraft from *Mir* and flew to *Salyut 7*, the first flight between space stations. It took 29 hours. On June 25, the crew undocked from *Salyut 7* and returned to *Mir*, bringing equipment from the old station to the new.

Live music concert broadcast to space Paul McCartney (UK) became the first artist to broadcast live to space when he sent a "wake-up call" to the *International Space Station* from his concert in Anaheim, California, U.S.A., on November 12, 2005. In 2008, "Across the Universe," by McCartney's old band, The Beatles, became the **first song to be beamed**

FIRST PERSON TO SHOWER IN SPACE The U.S. space station *Skylab* orbited Earth from its launch on May 14, 1973, to its reentry on July 11, 1979. During its life, it was home to three crews of three astronauts, who all enjoyed the use of a shower. Users stood inside a ring on the floor and then lifted a circular curtain, which attached to the ceiling. A hose would spray 3 quarts (2.8 liters) of water, which was collected afterward using a special vacuum cleaner.

FACT: *Apollo* 10 was intended as a "dry run" for *Apollo* 11, which saw the first Moon landing.

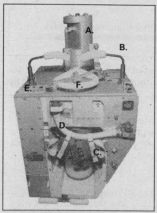

MOST EXPENSIVE TOILET SYSTEM
When the space shuttle *Endeavour* launched on January 13, 1993, it carried a U.S. $23.4-million unisex toilet. The facility, described by NASA as a "complete sewage collection and treatment plant," works by suction instead of gravity. It contains 4,000 parts, including footholds and thigh bars to keep the user in place. In case of failure, the space shuttle carried fecal and urine collection bags.

A. Waste compactor
B. Thigh bars
C. Footholds
D. Urine hose
E. Control panel
F. Seat

into deep space. NASA sent the song, at a speed of 186,000 miles per second (300,000 km per second), to celebrate the 50th anniversary of NASA's founding and the 40th anniversary of the song being recorded.

Untethered space walk NASA astronaut Bruce McCandless II performed an untethered space walk from the space shuttle *Challenger* on February 7, 1984. His space walk was the first test of the Manned Maneuvering Unit backpack, which cost U.S. $15 million to develop.

Food smuggled into space *Gemini III* was an orbital mission with a duration of 4 hr. 52 min. on March 23, 1965, crewed by U.S. astronauts Gus Grissom and John Young. During the mission, Young was authorized to eat preapproved space food, while Grissom was not scheduled to eat at all during the flight. However, Young, aware of Grissom's love of corned beef sandwiches, smuggled one onboard for his fellow astronaut. Young and Grissom were disciplined by NASA for this act.

Person to make an orbit of Earth on a bicycle *Skylab 3* was the second manned mission to the U.S. *Skylab* space station, from July 28 to September 25, 1973. During the flight, Alan Bean, who walked on the Moon during *Apollo 12*'s mission, spent just over 90 minutes on a stationary bicycle, pedaling throughout a whole orbit of the Earth.

Person to vomit in space Space sickness is similar to motion sickness and is caused by the changes in gravity. The first to have it was Soviet

FACT: *Skylab*'s three crews spent 171 days 13 hr. 14 min. in orbit and made 2,476 revolutions of Earth.

cosmonaut Gherman Titov, who experienced nausea and vomiting on his *Vostok 2* flight on August 6, 1961. Some form of space sickness is felt by around half of all people who fly in space.

Fire on a space station On February 23, 1997, a fire broke out onboard the Russian space station *Mir*, caused by lithium perchlorate "candles," which supplied oxygen to the station. Although the fire was extinguished, the six-man crew came close to abandoning the station in their *Soyuz* "lifeboat," which was docked with *Mir*.

Commercial filmed in space An advertising campaign for Tnuva Milk, showing cosmonaut Vasily Tsibliyev drinking milk onboard the Russian *Mir* space station, was broadcast on August 22, 1997.

Dog in space "Laika" became the first dog in space in November 1957 on board *Sputnik 2*, more than three years before the first human. She died early in the mission—her vehicle was not designed to return to Earth.

LONGEST . . .

Continuous human presence in space *Expedition 1*'s *Soyuz TM-31* was launched to the *International Space Station* on October 31, 2000, and its crew of three remained onboard for 136 days. This marked the longest uninterrupted human presence in space to date, with over 10 years of continuous occupation of the space station.

Mission by a spacesuit On February 3, 2006, Russian cosmonaut Valery Tokarev and U.S. astronaut Bill McArthur jettisoned an old Russian Orlan M spacesuit from the *International Space Station*. Equipped with a transmitter, "SuitSat-1" broadcast nearly 3,500 radio messages and data on the temperature inside the suit, which were picked up by amateur radio operators on Earth. The last transmission from SuitSat-1 was received on February 18, 2006, shortly before its battery died.

FIRST CREW TO SHAVE IN SPACE Thomas Stafford, John Young, and Gene Cernan, the crew of NASA's *Apollo 10* mission, May 18–26, 1969, were the first men to shave in space. They found the mechanical shaver developed by NASA inadequate, and resorted to razors and shaving cream.

MOST PEOPLE TOGETHER IN SPACE When the space shuttle *Endeavour* docked on the *International Space Station* on July 17, 2009, it brought the number of people on the station to 13. The Russian space station commander, Gennady Padalka, rang a ceremonial bell to welcome the seven new *Endeavour* astronauts as they floated onboard.

FIRST PERSON TO SLEEP IN SPACE Gherman Titov (USSR) slept onboard his 25-hour flight on *Vostok 2* in August 1961. He awoke to find his arms were floating in front of him, causing a hazard to the switches.

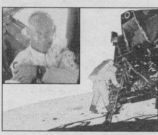

FIRST PERSON TO RELIEVE HIMSELF ON THE MOON After landing on the Moon on July 20, 1969, *Apollo 11* crew Neil Armstrong and Buzz Aldrin descended the ladder to the lunar surface. While still on the ladder, Aldrin urinated into a special collection bag within his spacesuit.

Running space grocery delivery program Russia's *Progress* vehicles are unmanned spacecraft designed to resupply cosmonauts in orbit with water, food, and oxygen, as well as equipment for experiments and repairs. They have been in use since the first one was launched on January 20, 1978. Today's *Progress* vehicles can carry 3,748 lb. (1,700 kg) of supplies in a 212-cu.-ft. (6-m³) space. Upon docking to the *International Space Station*, it remains in place for months, during which time it is filled with trash from the station before undocking and burning up in a controlled deorbit.

LARGEST MENU IN SPACE The Russian crew of the *International Space Station* have access to more than 300 dishes, including borscht (beet soup), goulash (spicy stew), rice with meat, and dried beef.

USING A TOILET IN SPACE

Here, quoting directly from the NASA Missions Operations handbook, are the instructions on using the Space Shuttle's Waste Collection System (WCS):

Foot/Toe Restraints – down, locked
Strap your feet into the WCS to ensure accurate positioning; body and thigh straps can also be used once seated.

VAC VLV – OP
Unstow urinal hose from Velcro strap, install hose in cradle
Open the vacuum pump; remove the urinal hose from its housing and mount it in its cradle.

✓CRADLE – AUTO
✓MODE – AUTO
FAN SEP SEL sw – "1"
Unstow hose from cradle (✓Airflow)
Check that the urinal hose is functioning (you can feel the suction using your hand); set the WCS to automatic and turn the "fan separator selector" switch to position "1" (this turns on an airflow that separates waste liquid off to a waste-water tank).

✓WCS ON IT – on
Check that the WCS light is on.

Unstow, install WCS Container, Bag & Hose, Mirror, Elbow Bag Dispenser
Ventline mated in aux
✓Wet Trash
Solid waste goes down the commode; liquids down the urinal tube; nonhuman waste (paper, wet wipes) is collected in a bag, so remove from container and attach to WCS; use mirror to check that you are aligned correctly; check that ventline is connected to Wet Trash hose; connect self to urinal hose; use.

SPACE WARFARE

First gun in space Soviet cosmonaut Yuri Gagarin, the first man in space, allegedly carried a Makarov pistol on his historic *Vostok 1* flight on April 12, 1961. The weapon was to be used in self-defense in case he landed back on Earth in hostile territory or amid dangerous wildlife.

First space-based submarine surveillance satellite SEASAT was a U.S. satellite designed to use synthetic aperture radar to monitor the oceans. Launched on June 27, 1978, it operated for only 105 days before malfunctioning. An unexpected feature of the radar system onboard SEASAT was its ability to detect the movement of submerged submarines by seeing their "wake" on the ocean surface. This has led some people to conjecture that the satellite's malfunction is a cover story—they believe it was taken over by the U.S. military upon discovery of its submarine-detecting ability.

First military space shuttle mission STS-4, the fourth U.S. space shuttle mission, was the first to handle a military payload. It launched on June 27, 1982, and landed back on Earth on July 4, 1982. Its payload, known as P82-1, consisted of two sensors designed to detect missile launches from space. Both sensors reportedly failed. Mission commander Ken Mattingly referred to the payload as "a rinky-dink collection of minor stuff they wanted to fly."

SMALLEST ROBOTIC SPACE PLANE The U.S. Boeing *X-37B* is an unmanned space plane that launches on an Atlas V rocket and returns to Earth as a glider, like the retired space shuttles, before touching down on wheels. Measuring 29 ft. 2 in. (8.9 m) long with a wingspan of 14 ft. 9 in. (4.5 m) and a loaded mass of around 11,000 lb. (4,990 kg), it is only the second type of space vehicle to land unmanned on wheels, after the Soviet *Buran* shuttle. Two *X-37B*s exist to date; the first was launched into orbit on April 22, 2010, and landed on December 5, 2010. The mission for a second vehicle began on March 5, 2011. The precise mission and payload of both flights are secret. The X-37 project was started by NASA in 2004 and taken over by the U.S. Air Force in 2006—its potential military applications include reconnaissance of enemy armed forces and the jamming of enemy satellites.

FIRST MILITARY SPACE STATION *Salyut 2* was the first of the Soviet Union's Almaz military space stations. Measuring 47 ft. 9 in. (14.55 m) long with a diameter of 13 ft. 7 in. (4.15 m), it was launched on April 3, 1973. It was intended to be manned and conduct military activities, including espionage from orbit. However, shortly after entering orbit, it was struck by debris from the Proton rocket that had launched it. It remained in orbit for 55 days before reentering the atmosphere and burning up and crashing into the Pacific Ocean, without having been visited by a crew.

First stealth satellite When the space shuttle *Atlantis* launched on February 28, 1990, it carried into orbit a classified payload for the U.S. Department of Defense. Two days later, *Atlantis* deployed what is believed to be the first of the U.S.A.'s MISTY satellites. These spy satellites allegedly use an inflatable outer shell to reduce their visibility to radar.

Largest combat satellite The Soviet *Polyus* satellite was an orbital weapons platform measuring 121 ft. 4 in. (37 m) long and 13 ft. 5 in. (4.1 m) in diameter, with a mass of 176,370 lb. (80 tonnes). It could be equipped with an antisatellite recoilless cannon, a sensor-blinding laser to confuse hostile satellites, and a nuclear space-mine launcher. Only one was ever launched, on May 15, 1987. It failed to reach orbit and crashed into the Pacific. It is unclear which weapon systems it had.

Largest military satellite constellation Initiated in 1973, the U.S.A.'s Global Positioning System (GPS) is a coordinated constellation of at least 24 satellites in orbit around the Earth. They provide, via radio signals, precise 3D navigation data across the world, enabling users to quickly pinpoint their location using a receiver. The GPS constellation is operated by the U.S. Air Force 50th Space Wing and was only available for military use until 1996.

LARGEST SPY SATELLITE On November 21, 2010, the U.S.A. launched the highly classified *NROL-32* satellite from Cape Canaveral, Florida, U.S.A. Believed to be the latest in the series of Mentor-class satellites, *NROL-32* was claimed to be the largest ever put into space by the Director of the National Reconnaissance Office, the U.S. body responsible for spy satellites. Although details of both the satellite and its mission are secret, some experts believe *NROL-32* has a main antenna larger than 328 ft. (100 m) across.

LARGEST HANDHELD FIREARM IN SPACE From 1986 to 2007, the Soviet Union began equipping their cosmonauts with a TP-82 firearm, a triple-barrel combination pistol/carbine/shotgun and flare gun with a detachable stock that conceals a machete. Cosmonauts would use the weapon, which weighed 5.3 lb. (2.4 kg), to protect themselves from wild animals if they landed in the Siberian wilderness.

Highest-altitude satellite destroyed from Earth On January 11, 2007, the Chinese government launched a missile from the ground at its *Fegyun-1C* satellite, orbiting at an altitude of 537 miles (865 km). The missile, a type referred to as "kinetic kill," struck the satellite and destroyed it using its own kinetic energy, rather than with an explosive warhead. According to NASA, some 2,841 pieces of space debris were created in the collision. NASA is worried that the debris will endanger spacecraft in low orbit around Earth.

Longest unexplained explosion detected from space The *Vela* satellites were launched by the U.S.A. to monitor Earth and detect illegal nuclear weapons tests that contravened the 1963 Partial Test Ban Treaty. On September 22, 1979, a double flash was detected by the *Vela 6911* satellite over the Indian Ocean between Crozet Islands and Prince Edward Islands. It was estimated that a 2–3-kiloton nuclear explosion would have been needed to create a double flash of such magnitude. However, no radioactive debris was ever unambiguously detected.

FIRST ALLEGED SHOT AT A MANNED SPACECRAFT According to some sources, the Soviet Union aimed a laser at the space shuttle *Challenger*, above, during the STS-41-G mission in 1984. As *Challenger* was orbiting over the Soviet Union, the crew allegedly felt unwell, as well as losing communications and experiencing other technical difficulties. The theory that the Terra-3 laser complex in Kazakhstan was used to fire at the shuttle is firmly denied by NASA.

FACT: The first V2 attack hit Paris on September 2, 1944; the last was aimed at Antwerp on March 28, 1945.

MOST HEAVILY ARMED SPACE STATION Of all the space stations to orbit Earth, only the Soviet *Salyut 3*, launched in 1974, was armed. For defense, it was fitted with a 1-in (23-mm) Nudelman aircraft cannon.

FIRST WEAPON IN SPACE During World War II, Germany developed military rocket technology, culminating in the V2, which was used to attack its enemies, mainly in London, UK, and Antwerp, Belgium. The rocket was 45 ft. 11 in. (14 m) long and weighed 27,558 lb. (12,500 kg), with an operational range of 200 miles (320 km). The first successful firing of the V2—on October 3, 1942, from Peenemünde on Germany's Baltic coast—was the first time any man-made object had entered space. The V2's speed—about 3,580 mph (5,760 km/h)—and trajectory—it reached altitudes of about 62 miles (100 km)—made it invulnerable to antiaircraft guns and fighters.

ARMING ORBITAL SPACE

The Cold War saw countless pieces of military hardware sent into space, from space stations in low orbit to top-secret satellites thousands of miles above us.

VELA SATELLITES
62,760 to 69,600 miles (101,000 to 112,000 km)

MILSTAR COMMUNICATIONS SATELLITES
22,236 miles (35,786 km)

GPS SATELLITES
12,551 miles (20,200 km)

GLONASS
11,868 miles (19,100 km)

LACROSSE 5
444 miles (715 km)

STS-4
227 miles (365 km)

X37B
197 miles (318 km)

KEYHOLE SPY SATELLITES
174–624 miles (281–1,005 km)

***ALMAZ 2* STATION**
160–173 miles (257–278 km)

Highest-altitude nuclear explosion A 1.7-kiloton nuclear weapon was detonated 466 miles (749 km) above Earth on September 6, 1958, as part of the U.S.A.'s secret Operation Argus test series. The 218-lb. (98.9-kg) W-25 warhead was launched by a modified three-stage Lockheed X-17A missile from the warship USS *Norton Sound*, located in the South Atlantic. There were two other Operation Argus nuclear explosions at lower altitudes. The aim was to create belts of trapped radiation that would destroy and disrupt enemy satellites and communication systems.

COSMIC CURIOSITIES

Fastest matter in the universe Blobs of superheated plasma are ejected from black holes in the cores of highly active galaxies known as blazars. These blobs, with as much mass as the planet Jupiter, move at 99.99% of the speed of light.

Fastest approaching galaxy Despite the overall expansion of the universe, a small number of galaxies are approaching our own. M86, a lenticular galaxy about 52 million light-years away, in the Virgo Cluster, is moving toward our Milky Way at 260 miles per sec. (419 km/sec).

Fastest star in the galaxy On February 8, 2005, a team of astronomers from the Harvard-Smithsonian Center for Astrophysics in Cambridge, Massachusetts, U.S.A., announced their discovery of a star traveling at more than 1.5 million mph (2.4 million km/h). Named SDSS J090745.0+24507, the star was probably accelerated by an encounter with the supermassive black hole at the center of our Milky Way galaxy nearly 80 million years ago.

DARKEST EXTRA-SOLAR PLANET On August 10, 2011, U.S. astronomers announced their discovery of the planet TrES-2b, around 750 light-years away in the constellation of Draco. Compared with Earth, which reflects about 37% of the light it receives, TrES-2b reflects less than 1%, making it darker than coal. The Jupiter-sized planet has an estimated temperature of 2,192°F (1,200°C), giving it a reddish glow.

FACT: The darkness of TrES-2b may be due to materials such as gaseous sodium in its atmosphere.

Fastest spinning star VFTS 102 is a star approximately 25 times more massive than the Sun and 100,000 times more luminous. It lies within the Tarantula Nebula in the Large Magellanic Cloud, around 160,000 light-years away. Announced on December 5, 2011, VFTS 102 rotates at an estimated 300 times faster than our Sun, at around 1.2 million mph (2 million km/h). If it rotated any faster, it would be in danger of tearing itself apart with centrifugal forces.

Flattest star The least spherical star studied to date in our galaxy is the southern star Achenar (Alpha Eridani). Observations made using the VLT Interferometer at the European Southern Observatory's Paranal Observatory in Atacama, Chile, have revealed that Achenar is spinning so rapidly that its equatorial diameter is more than 50% greater than its polar diameter. The observations were made between September 11 and November 12, 2002, and the results were released on June 11, 2003.

Most luminous star in the galaxy The latest observations of LBV 1806-20, which is 45,000 light-years from Earth, indicate that it is between 5 and 40 million times more luminous than the Sun. It has a mass of at least 150 times the mass of the Sun and is at least 200 times the Sun's diameter.

Shortest-lived stars Less than 0.1% of the stars in our galaxy are blue supergiants. With masses of around 100 times that of the Sun, they burn through their fuel very quickly and can last as little as 10 million years. Their blue color is a result of their high surface temperatures, around 36,000–90,000°F (20,000–50,000°C). One of the best known is Rigel in the constellation of Orion. It is the sixth brightest star in the sky, despite being around 900 light-years away.

Smallest stars Neutron stars may have a mass around 1.5 times that of the Sun, but only have diameters of 6–19 miles (10–30 km).

LARGEST DISTANT GALAXY CLUSTER "El Gordo" is the nickname of a massive galaxy cluster some 7 billion light-years away. It is actually two galaxy clusters that are colliding at a rate of several million miles per hour. Its combined mass is around 2×10^{15} times the mass of our Sun. Its discovery was announced on January 10, 2012.

NEAREST SUPERMASSIVE BLACK HOLE
Sagittarius A* is the supermassive black hole that resides in the center of our Milky Way galaxy, some 27,000 light-years away. With a mass around 4 million times greater than our Sun, this black hole is orbited by several massive stars.

Heaviest black hole On December 5, 2011, astronomers using the Gemini North, Keck II, and Hubble Space Telescope observatories reported their discovery of a supermassive black hole in the center of the elliptical galaxy NGC 4889, some 336 million light-years away. Its mass is estimated at around 21 billion times that of the Sun.

Largest structure in the universe In October 2003, a team of astronomers from Princeton University in New Jersey, U.S.A., announced that they had discovered a huge wall of galaxies an estimated 1.37 billion light-years long. The breakthrough had been made using data from the Sloan Digital Sky Survey, which mapped the locations of one million galaxies in the universe.

Largest circumstellar disk M17-SO1 is a protostar (early stage of star formation) in the Omega Nebula, some 5,000–6,000 light-years away. In 2005, it was discovered to have a disk of material orbiting it with a diameter of some 20,000 astronomical units, or around 18.6 trillion miles (30 trillion km). This is around 100 times greater than our heliosphere (the distance from our sun to the point at which its gravitational force fades).

Most distant dwarf galaxy On January 18, 2012, astronomers using the Keck II telescope on Mauna Kea, Hawaii, U.S.A., announced that they had discovered a dwarf galaxy orbiting a large elliptical galaxy 10 billion light-years away. It was found using a method called gravitational lens-

DENSEST OBJECTS IN THE UNIVERSE Black holes are the remnants of stars that ended their lives as supernovae. They are characterized by a region of space in which gravity is so strong that not even light can escape. The boundary of this region is known as the event horizon, and at the center of the black hole is the "singularity," where the mass of the dead star is compressed to a single point of zero size and infinite density. It is this singularity that generates the powerful gravitational field of a black hole.

FIRST PROVEN COLLISION OF WHITE DWARF STARS
SNR 0509-67.5 was a type 1a supernova in the Large Magellanic Cloud, a satellite galaxy of our own, which occurred around 400 years ago. The remnant of the explosion is a bubble of gas some 23 light-years across, and expanding at more than 11.2 million mph (18 million km/h). In January 2012, astronomers studying the remnant proved that the supernova was caused by two white dwarf stars colliding. The remnant is around 160,000 light-years away.

FARTHEST OBJECT EVER VISIBLE TO THE EYE
Gamma-ray bursts—the birth cries of black holes—are the largest explosions in the universe. At 2:12 EDT on March 19, 2008, a gamma-ray burst in a galaxy 7.5 billion light-years away was visible for around 30 seconds and captured by a robotic telescope.

ing, in which the mass of a foreground galaxy distorts and magnifies light from a much more distant galaxy behind it.

Most distant object in the universe In January 2011, scientists announced that the Hubble Space Telescope had successfully imaged a galaxy so old that its light has taken 13.2 billion years to reach us. This means the galaxy as we see it today was formed less than 480 million years after the Big Bang, making it the earliest object to form in the universe.

STARSTRUCK

How well do you know those twinkling lights in the night sky?

• Stars mostly consist of plasma (superhot matter) and gas.

• They form in dust-and-gas clouds called "nebulae."

• Scientists estimate there may be as many as 400 billion stars in our galaxy, the Milky Way. But there are more than 100 billion galaxies in our universe. And there may be more than 100 billion stars in each . . .

• Blue and white stars are hotter than orange or red stars. The temperature of a blue star may reach 45,000–75,000°F (25,000–40,000°C).

• Neutron stars are the core remnants of huge stars that have exploded. Although only around 12.5 miles (20 km) in diameter, their mass is approximately 1.5 times that of the Sun.

FACT: Later named GRB 080319B, the burst (artist's impression above) reached a brightness of magnitude 5.8.

Visit the cutting edge of science on p. 369..

SUN AND STARS

Our galaxy, the Milky Way, is around 100,000 light-years in diameter and has a spiral shape. The Sun is around 30,000 light-years from its center, located on one of the "arms" of the spiral:

KEY

1. Disk   2. Nucleus
3. Bulge   4. Sun

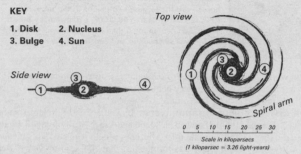

Top view

Side view

Spiral arm

```
0   5   10   15   20   25   30
Scale in kiloparsecs
(1 kiloparsec = 3.26 light-years)
```

STAR SIZES

Stars range greatly in size, from the most massive supergiants (at 559 million miles/900 million km in diameter) down to the stellar remnants known as neutron stars (12.5–25 miles/20–40 km wide).

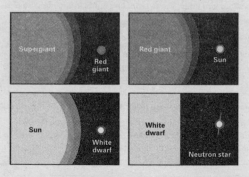

GREEN EARTH

CONTENTS

HOW MUCH CLIMATE CHANGE CAN WE SURVIVE?

FIGURE 2

FIGURE 1

LARGEST CAVE Hang Son Doong ("Mountain River Cave") is around 655 ft. (200 m) high, 490 ft. (150 m) wide, and at least 4 miles (6.5 km) long. Located in Phong Nha-Ke Bang National Park, Bo Trach District, Quang Binh Province, Vietnam, this gigantic cave might be even larger than first thought, because it had not been completely surveyed as of February 2012. Hidden by forest, it was found in 1991 by a local farmer named Ho Khanh. In April 2009, he led a team of British cavers to the cave, and they made an initial survey of it.

FACT: The figure nearest to us in this photograph is more than half a mile away from the figure in the background.

DO WE HAVE A FUTURE ON THE EARTH?

The Earth's changing climate is one of the most complex systems ever studied. It is difficult to refute the data gathered by scientists, especially when very different methods show the same overall trend. The biggest questions are why is it changing, how much is human activity responsible, and can we survive as a race?

The Earth's climate has changed before. The planet has undergone periods of severe glaciation (ice ages), which have occurred with no influence from humans. Around 14,600 years ago, as the ice sheets of the last ice age were retreating, a catastrophe happened. The partial collapse of the Antarctic ice sheet saw global sea levels rise by 66 ft. (20 m) in less than 500 years.

Back then, however, there were no massive cities on the coastlines. In 2005, the U.S. city of New Orleans was devastated by Hurricane Katrina, leaving more than 1,500 people dead. A sea-level rise of just 3 ft. (1 m) could flood 17% of Bangladesh, creating tens of millions of refugees. Some island nations, such as the Maldives, would be completely submerged. Sea-level rise will destroy some of the world's largest cities, and contaminate fresh water for many of the others.

Illustrated here are three key influences on the climate, with a prognosis of how they might affect our future survival on the Earth.

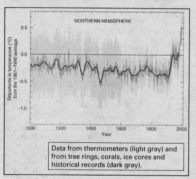

Data from thermometers (light gray) and from tree rings, corals, ice cores and historical records (dark gray).

HOCKEY STICK GRAPH
Published by the UN's Intergovernmental Panel on Climate Change in 2001, this graph is one of the most controversial in science. It is based on the one first published by U.S. scientists Michael Mann, Raymond Bradley, and Malcolm Hughes in 1998. It uses scientific data, including tree-ring studies, ice cores, historical records, and coral and instrument data to show an overall rise in the Earth's atmospheric temperature after 1900. The graph's name comes from the shape of the line.

Meet pioneering polar explorers on p. 211.

FACT: Pine Island glacier in Antarctica is shrinking by at least 52 ft. (16 m) per year—and may be gone in 100 years.

ICE CAPS CAUSE: The Earth's average temperature has increased by around 0.9°F (0.5°C) in the last 100 years. This has an effect on the size of the planet's ice caps. Ice is white, so it reflects more solar radiation back into space. As the ice caps shrink, they reflect less and allow more solar radiation to be absorbed, meaning it can contribute to further warming. This is known as "positive feedback."

EFFECT: Antarctica is a land mass covered by a vast ice cap, but the Arctic is an ocean on which the ice floats. The ice grows and shrinks with the seasons. In summer 2007, the Arctic experienced the greatest shrinkage in the ice cap, reducing in size to an area of 1.58 million sq. miles (4.11 million km^2). In summer 2011, it shrank to 1.67 million sq. miles (4.33 million km^2), the second smallest Arctic ice cap recorded.

FUTURE: If the Arctic ice cap disappeared, it would not affect global sea levels. Why not? Because the ice is already floating on the ocean. However, massive changes to Antarctica could change sea levels considerably. There is enough ice in Antarctica to raise the level of the oceans by around 200 ft. (61 m), and the Greenland ice cap contains enough water to cause a 23-ft. (7-m) rise. A recent report predicts a rise of 4 ft. 7 in. (1.4 m) by the end of the century. This could have devastating results for coastal cities.
A. London today . . .
B. . . . and under 23 ft. of water

ACID OCEANS CAUSE: The oceans are a natural "sink" for atmospheric carbon dioxide (CO_2)—they absorb about 24.5 million tons (22 million metric tonnes) of CO_2 every day. CO_2 in the atmosphere comes from various natural sources, including volcanic activity and the respiration of animals, as well as human activity. The concentration of CO_2 in the atmosphere has increased since the beginning of the Industrial Revolution (ca. 1750 onward).

EFFECT: The absorption of CO_2 into the oceans is gradually changing their pH value, which is a measure of their acidity/alkalinity. (A pH value of 7 is neutral.) Between 1751 and 1994, the average pH of the oceans' surface water decreased from around 8.25 to around 8.14. The current rate of change of ocean acidity is around 100 times greater than at any time in the last 20 million years.

FUTURE: If the overall acidity of the oceans continues to rise, there will be various effects. Some species—for example, sea grasses—flourish in water with elevated CO_2 in it. Other species, including some invertebrates, will find it tougher to form their shells, and some studies suggest up to 70% of corals (pictured) could be under threat by the end of the century.

How Much Climate Change Can We Survive?

CO_2 **CAUSE:** CO_2 is a natural component of the atmosphere. It only accounts for a small part of it but it has a significant effect on the Earth's ability to trap in heat from the Sun. Most sources of CO_2 are natural, but the study of air bubbles trapped in Antarctic ice cores shows a steady increase since 1832, corresponding to the increase in man-made emissions since the start of the Industrial Revolution. Exactly how much human activity has contributed to this remains unknown.

EFFECT: From the 1950s to 2011, the atmospheric concentration of CO_2 increased in volume from around 315 to 391.1 parts per million—the highest it has been in the last 800,000 years, and possibly a lot longer. After water vapor, CO_2 is the most abundant "greenhouse gas" in our atmosphere.

FUTURE: If CO_2 levels in the atmosphere keep on rising, it will lead to an increase in the Earth's natural greenhouse effect, which, in turn, will make the planet warmer. A hotter atmosphere is expected to lead to not only sea-level rise but also a more energetic climate in general, with more tropical cyclones, droughts, flooding, and heatwaves.

POLLUTION

Worst air pollution (country) According to a 2011 World Health Organization report, Mongolia has the worst air pollution, with an annual average of 279 micrograms of "PM10" particles per cubic meter (about 35.3 cu. ft.). In Mongolia, many factories burn coal and a lot of people live in *gers*, felt-lined tents with stoves in which coal or wood is burned. Ulan Bator, the Mongolian capital, which means "Red Hero," has been rechristened by the locals as Utan Bator, or "Smog Hero." It is the second most polluted city after Ahvaz (see main image and record on p. 38).

Highest levels of CO_2 According to the National Oceanic and Atmospheric Administration (U.S.A.), the atmospheric carbon dioxide level for

January 2011 was 391.19 parts per million (ppm). This is up on the average for 2010, which was 387.35 ppm.

Largest national producer of CO$_2$ emissions According to the United Nations, as of 2008 China was responsible for 7,751 million tons (7,031.9 million metric tonnes) of carbon dioxide emissions. This represented 23.33% of the global total. The rest of the top five:

2. U.S.A.: 18.11%
3. India: 5.78%
4. Russia: 5.67%
5. Japan: 4.01%

Worst SO$_2$ fire A fire at a sulfur plant near Mosul, Iraq, which began on June 24, 2003, released an average of 23,100 tons (21,000 metric tonnes) of sulfur dioxide per day for nearly a month. In all, 661,386 tons (600,000 metric tonnes) escaped—representing the greatest man-made release of sulfur dioxide and exceeding the sulfur dioxide output from most volcanic eruptions.

LARGEST LANDFILL RECLAMATION PROJECT The Fresh Kills Landfill at Staten Island, New York, U.S.A., was opened in 1947. It was officially closed in early 2001—although it temporarily reopened to receive debris from the 9/11 attack on the World Trade Center. At 2,200 acres (890 ha), it is three times bigger than Central Park—and, in places, it is 223 ft. (68 m) high, taller than the Statue of Liberty. In October 2009, work began on a 30-year project to turn it into a public park.

LARGEST DDT PRODUCER The insecticide DDT has been banned for agricultural use, but it is still used to control malaria and the bubonic plague. India is the largest national producer—it made 6,967 tons (6,344 metric tonnes) in 2007.

LARGEST RED MUD SPILL On October 4, 2010, the collapse of a dam at the Ajkai Timföldgyár alumina plant in Ajka, Hungary, resulted in the release of about 35 million cu. ft. (1 million m^3) of toxic red mud waste. The mud flooded nearby villages in a wave up to 6.6 ft. (2 m) high. At least four people were killed and more than 100 injured as the mud covered around 15.4 sq. miles (40 km^2). The flood also killed all life in the nearby Marcal River.

FIRST GLOBAL LIGHT POLLUTION MAP Light pollution in urban areas drowns out much of the natural night sky. In addition to representing energy waste, it can lead to confusion in nocturnal species. In 2001, Italian and American astronomers released the first global map highlighting the problem. According to the data, around 20% of the world's population can no longer see the Milky Way in the night sky from their homes. The Falkland Islands at the foot of South America have a surprising amount of light pollution because of light from fishing fleets and the gas flares on offshore oil and gas rigs.

CITY WITH THE WORST AIR POLLUTION According to a 2011 report by the World Health Organization (WHO), which measured air quality in 1,100 urban areas, Ahvaz, Iran, has the world's worst air pollution. (The main photo shows the oil fields of Ahvaz.) Air pollution is measured by the amount of particles less than 10 micrometers across per cubic meter (about 35.3 cu. ft.). Ahvaz has an annual average of 372 micrograms of these "PM10" particles per cubic meter, nearly 20 times the WHO's recommended safe level. The city with the least air pollution is Whitehorse in Yukon, Canada, with an annual average of three micrograms of PM10 particles per cubic meter.

BIGGEST CONTRIBUTOR TO THE ATMOSPHERIC BROWN CLOUD First observed in 1999 over parts of Asia, the Atmospheric Brown Cloud is a complicated mixture of air pollutants that can be 1.86 miles (3 km) thick. This type of pollution is caused by industrial activity, vehicle emissions, and wood burning. The biggest single component of the cloud is black carbon "soot," the result of incomplete burning, which makes up around 55% of the cloud.

LARGEST E-WASTE SITE Guiyu, a group of villages in Guangdong province, China, is the world capital of electronic waste. Around 1.65 tons (1.5 million metric tonnes) of discarded computers, phones, and other electronics are processed here each year, within an area of 20.1 sq. miles (52 km²). As a result, the area has high levels of heavy metal and acid pollution.

Most lethal smog About 3,500 to 4,000 people, mainly the elderly and children, died in London, UK, from acute bronchitis caused by thick smog between December 4 and 9, 1952. It was caused by the burning of fossil fuels combined with a weather inversion that trapped smoke particles near the ground. Visibility in the streets was only 12 in. (30 cm) and movie theaters had to close because it was impossible to see the screens.

Most acidic acid rain A pH reading of 2.83 was recorded over the Great Lakes, U.S.A./Canada, in 1982 and a reading of 1.87 was recorded at Inverpolly Forest, Highland, Scotland, in 1983. These are the lowest pH levels ever recorded in acid precipitation, making it the most acidic acid rain.

Largest single oil spill On March 14, 1910, an uncontrolled gusher began at the Midway-Sunset Oil Field in California, U.S.A. The eruption of pressurized crude oil destroyed the mining derrick and produced a crater that prevented engineers from controlling the oil geyser. The leak, known as the Lakeview Gusher, lasted for 18 months and released around 9 million barrels (50.5 million cu. ft.; 1.43 billion liters) of oil before the well sealed itself naturally.

Largest ocean landfill site The North Pacific Central Gyre is a vast vortex of slow, clockwise-revolving, high-pressure ocean water that naturally concentrates floating garbage in its center. In 2002, environmental studies revealed that the center of the Gyre contains about 13 lb. (6 kg) of waste plastic for every 2.2 lb. (1 kg) of natural plankton.

Largest marine oil spill During Iraq's retreat in the 1991 Gulf War, Saddam Hussein ordered troops to release oil from refineries and tankers in Kuwait. Some 2–4 million barrels (11.2–22.4 million cu. ft.; 318–635 million liters) of oil was released into the sea.

Worst nuclear waste accident In December 1957, an explosion at the nuclear plant at Kyshtym, Russia, released radiation that dispersed over 8,900 sq. miles (23,000 km^2). More than 30 villages in a 460-sq.-mile (1,200-km^2) area were eliminated from maps of the USSR in the three years following the accident, and about 17,000 people were evacuated. A 1992 report indicated that 8,015 people died as a direct result of discharges.

Longest-lasting pollution Nuclear waste, formed as a by-product of nuclear fission, gradually loses its radioactivity over time, until it can be considered "safe." "Half-life" is the time it takes for half of a quantity of radioactive material to lose its radioactivity. Iodine-129, an unstable isotope of iodine, produced by the fission of uranium and plutonium in reactors, has a half-life of 15.7 million years.

TOP 10 TOXIC POLLUTION PROBLEMS

The Blacksmith Institute's 2011 report on *The World's Worst Toxic Pollution Problems* reveals the most polluting industries, the key pollutants, and the numbers of people directly at risk:

1. Artisanal gold mining
Key issue: Mercury pollution
At risk: 3,506,600

2. Industrial estates
Key issue: Lead pollution
At risk: 2,981,200

3. Agricultural production
Key issue: Pesticide pollution (considering only local impact)
At risk: 2,245,000

4. Lead smelting
Key issue: Lead pollution
At risk: 1,988,800

5. Tannery operations
Key issue: Chromium pollution
At risk: 1,848,100

6. Mining/ore processing
Key issue: Mercury pollution
At risk: 1,591,700

7. Mining/ore processing
Key issue: Lead pollution
At risk: 1,239,500

8. Lead-acid battery recycling
Key issue: Lead pollution
At risk: 967,800

9. Naturally occurring arsenic in ground water
Key issue: Arsenic pollution
At risk: 750,700

10. Pesticide manufacturing and storage
Key issue: Pesticide pollution
At risk: 735,400

Source: Blacksmith Institute/Green Cross (Switzerland)

NUCLEAR ENERGY

First commercial nuclear power station Calder Hall, in Cumbria, UK, was the first nuclear power station to provide electricity commercially. It was officially opened on October 17, 1956, by Queen Elizabeth II. Its four Magnox reactors were each capable of producing 60 MWe (megawatts). Its initial purpose was to produce weapons-grade plutonium; electricity generation was a by-product. It was decommissioned in 2003.

Country with the highest percentage of nuclear power use France currently generates more than 75% of its electricity needs from nuclear power. There are 58 reactors in the country, with a total generating power of 63 GWe (gigawatts).

First nuclear reactor in space On April 3, 1965, the U.S.A. launched the System for Nuclear Power (SNAP) 10A into a polar orbit around the earth. Designed to test remotely operated nuclear reactors, SNAP 10A began producing electricity at more than 600 W some 12 hours after launch. After 43 days of operation, the reactor shut down due to an electrical component failure. The spacecraft is still in orbit, about 746 miles (1,200 km) above the earth, and is not expected to reenter the atmosphere for around 4,000 years.

FIRST NUCLEAR-POWERED PACEMAKER
In the late 1960s, two companies, Alcatel (France) and Medtronic (U.S.A.), created a nuclear pacemaker. It was first implanted into a patient in 1970. Before, patients would need surgery every few years to replace battery-powered pacemakers. Powered by a tiny piece of plutonium-238, the nuclear pacemaker resembled a hockey puck. In the 1980s, pacemakers powered by lithium batteries, which last around 10 years, superseded it.

LARGEST MAIL IRRADIATION PROGRAM In October 2001, deadly anthrax spores were discovered in mail sent to congressional leaders and journalists in the U.S.A., resulting in five deaths. In response, the U.S. government initiated the irradiation of mail sent to key addresses. Between November 2001 and April 2008, around 1.2 million containers of federal mail were irradiated. All mail addressed to the White House is still reportedly irradiated.

SMALLEST NUCLEAR-POWERED ATTACK SUBMARINE France currently operates six Rubis-class submarines, each of which has a length of 241 ft. (73.6 m) and a displacement of 2,860 tons (2,600 metric tonnes) when submerged. Powered by a pressurized-water nuclear reactor, they have unlimited range and were designed to have an operational lifetime of around 25 years.

On December 22, 2006, the French government placed an order for six Barracuda submarines, which are expected to start replacing the Rubis subs by 2016. The Barracudas will be 326 ft. (99.4 m) long.

First floating nuclear power station MH-1A, a pressurized-water reactor, was built inside a converted cargo ship for the U.S. Army, and began operation in 1967. The ship, whose engines had been removed to make way for the reactor, was towed to the Panama Canal, where it provided electrical power to the Panama Canal Zone between 1968 and 1975. It was capable of providing 10 MWe of power.

LONGEST SUSTAINED FUSION REACTION In 2002, scientists at the experimental Tore Supra reactor in Cadarache, France, sustained a nuclear fusion reaction of 3 MW for 210 seconds. The picture shows a technician checking the heating system inside the reactor. Cadarache will be the site of the International Thermonuclear Experimental Reactor (ITER). When operational (planned for 2018), ITER is hoped to be the first large-scale fusion reactor to produce more energy than is used to initiate its fusion reactions.

FACT: Nuclear fusion occurs all the time in stars—nuclei fuse together, releasing energy in the form of light and heat.

Longest-operating nuclear power station The nuclear reactor in Obninsk, Russia, ran from June 27, 1954, until it was decommissioned on April 30, 2002. It was the world's first operating civilian nuclear reactor. Obninsk is known as Russia's first science city, or *naukograd*.

Largest nuclear-powered lighthouse program During the Cold War, the USSR required navigational aids for shipping along its vast northern coast. Its solution was a chain of lighthouses powered by radio-isotope thermal generators, which are more like "nuclear batteries" than reactors. These generators allowed isolated lighthouses to operate without supervision. After the fall of the USSR, the network of around 132 nuclear lighthouses began to fail, and some have been plundered by thieves for their metals.

LARGEST NUCLEAR POWER STATION Until going offline in March 2012, Kashiwazaki-Kariwa nuclear power station in Japan had a total output of 8,212 MWe. It supplied electricity to 16 million households and was the fourth largest electric-generating station in the world behind the hydroelectric plants at Itaipu on the Brazil-Paraguay border, Three Gorges Dam in China, and Guri Dam in Venezuela.

HIGHEST FOOD IRRADIATION DOSE The irradiation of food is aimed at preventing the spread of disease. It can also increase the storage life of food. In 2003, the Codex Alimentarius, established in 1963 by the World Health Organization and the UN to maintain food standards, removed any upper limit on recommended radiation doses for food. Today, the highest dose in general use is around 70 kGy (kilograys), to which some hospital food is subjected. About 0.0056–0.0075 kilograys would be a lethal dose to humans.

LARGEST RADIOACTIVE EXCLUSION ZONE The accident at the Chernobyl nuclear power plant in Ukraine on April 26, 1986, resulted in a permanent exclusion zone about 19 miles (30 km) around the power plant. No one is officially allowed to live inside this zone, although some people are believed to have returned illegally.

Largest particle detector The ATLAS Detector, part of the Large Hadron Collider (LHC) at the European Organization for Nuclear Research (CERN), measures 151 ft. (46 m) long, 82 ft. (25 m) wide, and 82 ft. (25 m) high. It weighs 7,700 tons (7,000 metric tonnes) and contains 100 million sensors to measure particles produced in proton-proton collisions in the LHC. ATLAS is being used to investigate the forces that have shaped the universe since the start of time, including the way particles gain mass, the differences between matter and antimatter, and the possibility of extra dimensions in space.

First commercial food irradiation In 1957, a facility in Stuttgart, then West Germany, began irradiating spices with an electron beam to increase their storage life.

Highest nuclear fusion energy output The highest energy output achieved using nuclear fusion is 16 MW, by the Joint European Torus (JET) tokamak nuclear fusion reactor, Culham, Oxfordshire, UK, in 1997.

Largest nuclear reactor building program China is currently building 27 new nuclear power stations, around 40% of the total under construction worldwide. The country's 13 operational nuclear power stations provide only around 2% of its electricity. The Chinese government suspended approval for additional facilities after an earthquake and tsunami wrecked the nuclear plant at Fukushima, Japan, in March 2011.

Longest operation for a pressurized-water reactor On October 6, 2009, the TMI-1 reactor at Three Mile Island, Pennsylvania, U.S.A., was shut down for refueling after 705 days of continuous operation. There are more than 200 pressurized-water reactors worldwide. Three Mile Island is famous for the partial meltdown of TMI-2 in March 1979.

Most powerful nuclear-powered cargo ship Designed for Russia's northern sea route, the USSR-built *Sevmorput*, an icebreaking container-cargo vessel, began active service in 1988. With a KLT-40 pressurized-water reactor, rated at 135 MWt, she is the most powerful of only four nuclear cargo ships ever built and the last in operation.

Strongest force The four fundamental forces in the universe which account for all interactions between matter and energy are: the strong nuclear (which holds nuclei together), the weak nuclear (responsible for radioactive decay), electromagnetic, and gravity. The strongest of these is the strong nuclear force, which is 100 times stronger than the electromagnetic force—the next strongest. Gravity, the weakest, is 10^{40} times weaker than the electromagnetic force.

For science stats and facts, turn to p. 368.

NUCLEAR
FISSION & FUSION

The nucleus of an atom is held together by strong forces, which means that the atom contains a huge amount of energy. Harnessing this energy means tapping into a source of power more than a million times more efficient than burning coal. There are two fundamental ways of releasing this energy: fission and fusion.

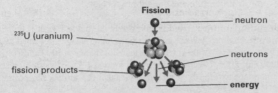

Fission

neutron
^{235}U (uranium)
neutrons
fission products
energy

Basics: Splitting of atomic nuclei into smaller fragments.
Occurrence: Very rare in nature.
Waste products: Many types of unwanted by-products requiring massive disposal efforts with short-, medium-, and long-term environmental risks.
Energy released: Around a million times the energy released by chemical reactions.
Requirements: Critical mass of the fissile material plus high-speed neutrons.
Use history: Chicago Pile 1 was first tested in 1942. Commercial power supply from fission began in 1956.

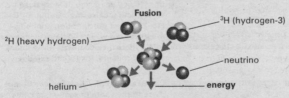

Fusion

^{3}H (hydrogen-3)
^{2}H (heavy hydrogen)
neutrino
helium
energy

Basics: The fusing together of two atoms to make a larger one.
Occurrence: Stars are powered by natural fusion reactions in their cores, where hydrogen is fused into helium and, later in a star's life, to heavier elements.
Waste products: None, apart from when a "fission trigger" is used.
Energy released: Between three and four times the energy released in fission.
Requirements: Very high temperatures and densities.
Use history: First lab demonstration in 1932. Longest sustained man-made fusion reaction stands at 210 seconds. No commercial use yet.

BIOMES

Geographical area with greatest biodiversity The tropical Andes region covers 485,716 sq. miles (1,258,000 km²) and runs through Venezuela, Colombia, Ecuador, Peru, Bolivia, Chile, and a small area in north Argentina. So far, 45,000 species of vascular plants have been recorded (15–17% of the world's species) as well as 1,666 bird species, 414 mammal species, and 1,309 reptile and amphibian species.

Fastest-declining biome Tropical rainforests are being lost at a higher rate than any other biome. A 2002 study, using satellite images, revealed that around 22,394 sq. miles (58,000 km²) a year were lost between 1990 and 1997. Between 2000 and 2005, Central America lost around 1.3% of its rainforests each year and about two-thirds of its rainforest has been turned into pasture since 1950.

Smallest ecosystem In October 2008, scientists discovered the first ecosystem on the Earth with only one species. The bacteria *Desulforudis audaxviator* was found 1.7 miles (2.8 km) underground in the Mponeng gold mine, in South Africa. It exists in total isolation and total darkness in temperatures of around 140°F (60°C).

YOUNGEST BIOME Arctic tundra, which encircles the North Pole along the northern coastlines of Russia and Canada, as well as parts of Greenland, was formed only 10,000 years ago. It is treeless, windy, and receives only about 6–10 in. (15–25 cm) of precipitation annually—mostly as snow. The 48 animal species found there include bears, polar bears, wolves, rodents, foxes, and reindeer.

LARGEST BIOME The open ocean, not close to the shore or seabed, is known as the pelagic zone. Globally, its volume is around 319 million cu. miles (1,330 million km³). This biome contains many of the largest animals on the Earth, including *the* largest, the blue whale (left), as well as bluefin tuna and giant squid.

FACT: About 90% of marine life lives in the top 636 ft. (200 m) of the ocean where the sunlight can reach.

> **FACT:** Rainforest trees are so dense that rain falling on the canopy can take 10 minutes to land on the floor.

BIOME WITH THE GREATEST BIODIVERSITY The total number of animal and plant species in the world's tropical rainforests is unknown. However, current estimates of rainforest biodiversity suggest that perhaps 50–75% of all the earth's living species are concentrated in rainforests, although they cover only 6–7% of the Earth's surface. The Wooroonooran National Park in Queensland, Australia, left, contains some of the oldest rainforests.

OLDEST TERRESTRIAL BIOME Tropical rainforests, such as the Amazon rainforest (left), have been established for at least a million years. The last ice age, which ended about 10,000 years ago, covered much of the world's forests in ice, but left the equatorial forests uncovered.

Highest concentration of heathers The *fynbos* (Afrikaans for "fine bush") plant ecosystem, exclusive to South Africa's Cape floristic region, has more than 600 species of heather (*Erica*). Only 26 species of heather occur in the rest of the world.

LARGEST . . .

Temperate deciduous forest biome Temperate deciduous forests are those with trees that lose their leaves each year and receive an average of 30–60 in. (75–150 cm) of rainfall annually. They exist across eastern U.S.A., New Zealand, and eastern China, but the largest example covers 3.5 million sq. miles (9.06 million km²) across Russia and Scandinavia.

Tropical rainforest The Amazon rainforest covers an area of 2.12 million sq. miles (5.5 million km²) across nine different South American countries: Brazil, Colombia, Peru, Venezuela, Ecuador, Bolivia, Guyana, Suriname, and French Guiana. The second largest contiguous rainforest is in the Congo Basin, Africa.

Alpine biome There are alpine biomes occurring in mountain regions across the world—the largest being the Tibetan alpine steppe in China, which covers about 309,000 sq. miles (800,000 km²). They begin around 10,000 ft. (3,000 m) and continue up to the snow line. The harsh conditions mean there are no cold-blooded animals, and plants tend to grow close to the ground because of the wind and cold. Alpine animals cope with the cold by hibernating, migrating, or growing layers of insulating fat.

FACT: The scaly-foot gastropod (or snail, bottom, lives near the vents and has a foot armored with iron sulphides.

DEEPEST HYDROTHERMAL VENT Hydrothermal vents, discovered in 1977, spew hot water laden with minerals from the ocean floor. The deepest ones found to date are in the Beebe Vent Field, south of the Cayman Islands, at a depth of 16,272 ft. (4,960 m). Bacteria are able to convert minerals found in the vents' fluids into energy through chemosynthesis. They form the basis of the food chain, because, at these depths, there is no light for plants to photosynthesize.

Marine reserve The Papahānaumokuākea Marine National Monument covers 137,791 sq. miles (356,879 km^2) of the Pacific Ocean surrounding the northwestern Hawaiian islands and atolls. The coral reefs here are home to more than 7,000 species, one-quarter of which are unique to the region. It was designated a marine reserve on June 15, 2006, and was made a UNESCO World Heritage Site in 2010.

Tropical forest reserve The largest tropical forest reserve is the Tumucumaque National Park in the northern Amazonian state of Amapá, Brazil. Measuring some 15,010 sq. miles (38,875 km^2) in area, the reserve contains sloths, jaguars, freshwater turtles, eagles, and agouti (a species of rodent). The creation of the park was announced on August 22, 2002, by Brazilian president Fernando Henrique Cardoso.

FOREST BIOMES

Broadly speaking, there are three types of forest biome:

• **Boreal or taiga forest**, in the far north, is dominated by evergreen conifers, especially spruces and firs. In the long winters, many mammals hibernate and many birds migrate south.

• **Temperate deciduous forest** dominates in Europe and North America and has trees that shed their leaves in fall. Even in summer, a lot of sun penetrates the canopy, so forest-floor plants can photosynthesize and cold-blooded animals, such as snakes and frogs, can survive.

• **Tropical rainforest** near the equator has hundreds of species of trees, and the same species rarely grow next to each other. Vegetation is dense, so little light reaches the forest floor. Many vines and epiphytes (plants that perch on other plants) cling to the branches.

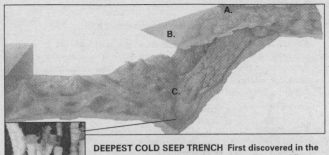

DEEPEST COLD SEEP TRENCH First discovered in the Gulf of Mexico in 1983, cold seeps are an ocean floor biome sustained by methane and sulfide-rich fluids seeping from the seabed. The deepest yet discovered lies 24,035 ft. (7,326 m) below sea level in the Japan Trench off the coast of Japan in the Pacific Ocean.
Cold-seep ecosystems rely on the bacteria feeding on the escaping fluids, which, in turn, attract animals, including mussels, clams, and the *Lamellibrachia* tube worm, inset. *Lamellibrachia* tube worms are believed to live for up to 250 years.
A. Japan
B. Pacific Ocean
C. Japan Trench

Coastal mangrove forest The Sundarbans (from the Bengali word for "beautiful forest") is a forested region stretching almost 6,000 sq. miles (15,540 km²) across India and Bangladesh. This acts as a natural barrier against tsunamis and cyclones that blow in from the Bay of Bengal. With saltwater-tolerant roots, this forest's mangrove trees sometimes exceed 70 ft. (21 m) in height above islands of layered sand and gray clay, which have been deposited by rivers that flow 1,000 miles (1,609 km) from the Himalayas to the Bay of Bengal.

Marine animal structure The Great Barrier Reef, off Queensland, Australia, covers an area of 80,000 sq. miles (207,000 km²) and consists of billions of living and dead stony corals (order Madreporaria or Scleractinia). Over 350 species of coral are currently found there, and it is estimated to have formed over 600 million years. It was made a UNESCO World Heritage Site in 1981.

Unbroken intertidal mudflats Stretching along some 311 miles (500 km) off the northern European coastline from the Netherlands to Denmark lies the Wadden Sea. Its total area of around 3,861 sq. miles (10,000 km²) contains many habitats, including tidal channels, sea-grass meadows, sandbars, mussel beds, and salt marshes. About 10–12 million migratory birds pass through each year, with up to 6.1 million present at any one time.

TREES

First tree The earliest surviving species of tree is the maidenhair (*Ginkgo biloba*) of Zhejiang, which first appeared in China about 160 million years ago, during the Jurassic era. It was rediscovered by Engelbert Kaempfer (Germany) in 1690. It has been grown in Japan since ca. 1100, where it is now known as *ichou*.

Don't be stumped, turn to p. 479.

LARGEST DEFORESTATION Between 2005 and 2010, some 31,199,525 acres (12,626,000 ha) of forest were cleared in Brazil—an average rate of 6,239,410 acres (2,525,000 ha) per year. Data from the UN Food and Agriculture Organization shows that between 2000 and 2010, deforestation across 121 tropical countries averaged a total of 23,079,642 acres (9,340,000 ha) per year. At current rates, more than half of it will be lost by 2030.

Longest-living forests The forests of Patagonian cypresses (*Fitzroya cupressoides*) in the Andean mountains of southern Chile and Argentina have an average age of 2,500 years.

Highest ring count The greatest number of rings counted on a tree is 4,867. They belonged to a bristlecone pine (*Pinus longaeva*) known as "Prometheus," which was cut down in 1963 on Mount Wheeler, Nevada, U.S.A.

Largest tree transplanted An oak tree (*Quercus lobata*) named "Old Glory," at the age of 180–220 years and weighing about 916,000 lb. (415.5 tonnes), was moved 0.25 miles (0.4 km) by the Senna Tree Company (U.S.A.) to a new park in Los Angeles, California, U.S.A., on January 20, 2004. The tree was 58 ft. (17.67 m) tall and had a branch span of 104 ft. (31.6 m).

Longest pinecone Steve Schwarz (U.S.A.) of Cuyahoga Falls, Ohio, U.S.A., collected a pinecone measuring 22.9 in. (58.2 cm) on October 15, 2002.

Fastest-growing tree The princess tree (*Paulownia tomentosa*), also known as the empress or foxglove tree, can grow 20 ft. (6 m) in its first year and up to 1 ft. (30 cm) in three weeks. Native to central and western China, but naturalized in the U.S.A., this large tree has purple foxglove-like flowers and produces 3–4 times more oxygen during photosynthesis than any other species of tree.

Highest tree The highest altitude at which trees have been discovered is 15,000 ft. (4,600 m). A silver fir (*Abies squamata*) was found in southwestern China at this height. Himalayan birch trees (*Betula utilis*) have also been discovered near this altitude.

LARGEST LIVING TREE BY VOLUME "General Sherman," the giant sequoia (*Sequoiadendron giganteum*) in Sequoia National Park, California, U.S.A., has a volume of 52,508 cu. ft. (1,487 m³).

LARGEST CORK TREE The "Whistler Tree" is named for the songbirds that sing in its branches in the Alentejo region of Portugal. The tree is harvested every nine years by cutting the bark away with axes. The last harvest in 2009 produced 1,818 lb. (825 kg) of raw cork—enough for 100,000 bottles of wine. The average tree produces enough cork for 40,000 bottles.

OLDEST LIVING TREE "Old Tjikko," a spruce tree at an altitude of 2,985 ft. (910 m) in Dalarna Province, Sweden, has a root system that has been growing for 9,550 years, according to radiocarbon dating completed in April 2008. The roots are able to spawn new trees after each one dies. The oldest continuously standing tree is "Methuselah," a bristlecone pine (*Pinus longaeva*) in California's White Mountains, U.S.A., dated in 1957 as being 4,600 years old.

Most dangerous tree The trunk of the manchineel (*Hippomane mancinella*), native to the Florida Everglades, U.S.A., and Caribbean coast, exudes a sap so acidic that the merest contact with human skin causes a breakout of blisters, and blindness can occur if it touches a person's eyes. In addition, a single bite of its small, green, applelike fruit causes blistering and severe pain, and it can be fatal. And if the tree catches fire, its smoke can cause blindness.

Most parasitic tree Unlike normal plants, the albino coastal redwoods (*Sequoia sempervirens*) lack chlorophyll and, therefore, are unable to feed themselves via photosynthesis. Instead, they permanently attach themselves to the roots of "parent" trees, from which they draw all of their sustenance. The trees are white with thin, limp, waxy needles, hence their nicknames "vampire redwoods" and "everwhites." Only between 25 and 60 exist, all in California, U.S.A.

Fastest-growing tree by volume per year "General Grant," a giant sequoia (*Sequoiadendron giganteum*) in Grant Grove, Kings Canyon National Park, California, U.S.A., increased its trunk volume by a yearly average of 79 cu. ft. (2.23 m³), from 43,038 cu. ft. (1,218 m³) in 1931 to 46,608 cu. ft. (1,319 m³) in 1976.

GREATEST GIRTH OF A LIVING TREE: "El Arbol del Tule" (the Tree of Tule), a Montezuma cypress (*Taxodium mucronatum*) in Oaxaca state, Mexico, when measured in 1998, had a girth (circumference) of about 119 ft. (36 m).

> **FACT:** Redwoods use fog for more than 30% of their water needs—absorbing it directly into their leaves.

TALLEST TREES Redwoods, a type of softwood tree, and eucalyptuses, often called gum trees, are the world's tallest tree species. This redwood from Prairie Creek Redwoods State Park in California, U.S.A., was photographed with a camera suspended from the upper branches of the forest canopy, so it could shoot the trunk all the way up from about 50 ft. (15.24 m) away. A total of 84 photos were montaged together to create this image. This redwood is 300 ft. (91.44 m) tall—but even this is dwarfed by the tallest living tree, "Hyperion," a coast redwood (*Sequoia sempervirens*) in the Redwood National Park, California, U.S.A., which measured 379 ft. (115.54 m) in September 2006.

A. 300 ft. (91.44 m)
B. 275 ft. (83.83 m)
C. 250 ft. (76.2 m)
D. 225 ft. (68.58 m)
E. 200 ft. (60.96 m)
F. 175 ft. (53.34 m)
G. 150 ft. (45.72 m)
H. 125 ft. (38.1 m)
I. 100 ft. (30.48 m)
J. 75 ft. (22.86 m)
K. 50 ft. (15.24 m)
L. 25 ft. (7.62 m)
M. 0

Most cold-tolerant trees The trees most "tolerant" of cold weather are the larches (genus Larix). These include the tamarack larch (*L. laricina*), native to northern North America, mostly Canada, which can survive winter temperatures of at least -85°F (-65°C) and commonly occur at the Arctic tree line at the edge of the tundra.

Most expensive tree A single Starkspur Golden Delicious apple tree (*Malus domestica*) from near Yakima, Washington, U.S.A., was sold to a garden nursery in 1959 for U.S. $51,000—which is equivalent to U.S. $525,000 at today's prices.

Most trees destroyed by storms Approximately 270 million trees were felled or split by storms that hit France on December 26 and 27, 1999.

HIGHEST TREE NEST: Nests of the marbled murrelet (*Brachyramphus marmoratus*), a small north Pacific member of the auk family of seabirds, have been discovered as high as 147 ft. (45 m), usually on moss-covered branches of old conifer trees.

TALLEST HARDWOOD TREE: "Centurion," a specimen of Australian swamp gum tree (*Eucalyptus regnans*) located in Tasmania, Australia, stands 331.36 ft. (101 m) tall.

Remotest tree The world's loneliest tree is believed to be a solitary Norwegian spruce (*Picea abies*)—which is more than 100 years old—located on Campbell Island in Antarctica. Its nearest companion is more than 119.8 nautical miles (137.9 miles; 222 km) away on the Auckland Islands.

Slowest-growing tree The white cedar (*Thuja occidentalis*) is the slowest-growing tree—one on a cliff in the Canadian Great Lakes area grew to less than 4 in. (10.2 cm) tall after 155 years. It averaged a growth rate of 0.003 oz. (0.11 g) of wood each year.

FOREST FACTS

The Forestry Department of the Food and Agriculture Organization (FAO) collects data from around the world in order to help nations manage their forests in a sustainable way.

 AREA: In 2010, forests covered about 31% of the world's total land area—about 9.966 billion acres. This is an area just over four times the size of the U.S.A.

 NATURAL vs. PLANTED: About 93% of the world's forest cover is natural forest and 7% is planted.

 DEFORESTATION: Between 2000 and 2010, an estimated 32 million acres of forest was affected by deforestation per year—an area more than twice the size of France over 10 years.

 NET LOSS: Afforestation projects and natural expansion help to replace lost trees at a rate of over 17.3 million acres a year (an area the size of Ireland). However, the net loss is still 12.8 million acres of forest. The good news, at least, is that this figure is down from 20.5 million acres lost per year in the 1990s.

ANIMALS

CONTENTS

HOW BIG CAN ANIMALS GET?

LONGEST LIVING SNAKE Meet Medusa, a reticulated python (*Python reticulatus*) owned by Full Moon Productions Inc. of Kansas City, Missouri, U.S.A. When measured on October 12, 2011, this outsize serpent was 25 ft. 2 in. (7.67 m) long—which also makes her the **longest captive snake ever.** She eats live animals, from rats right up to deer. And although she doesn't bite, she can "butt" people and bring them down. Medusa is the star attraction at Kansas City's The Edge of Hell Haunted House—some of whose grisly denizens are lending a helping hand here.

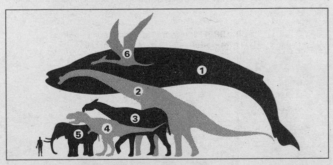

SIZE COMPARISON Here, we see the relative sizes of the mightiest creatures on the Earth. Nothing on land has ever exceeded ca. 110 tons (100 metric tonnes); in the oceans, the upper limit is a 176-ton (160-metric-tonne) whale.

KEY

1: Blue whale
2: *Argentinosaur*
3: *Paraceratherium*
4: Giganotosaur
5: African elephant
6: *Quetzalcoatlus*

FACT: The blue whale has the largest heart of any animal—about the same size as a Volkswagen Bug car!

IS THERE A SIZE LIMIT TO ANIMAL LIFE?

Despite their epic size, dinosaurs were not the largest creatures to have ever lived. We don't need to look into prehistory to find this absolute record holder. We currently share our planet with the **largest animal that ever lived**—the blue whale (see p. 59). But does the blue whale represent the absolute in animal size? What about terrestrial creatures or birds? Here, GWR zoologist Dr. Karl Shuker sizes up the planet's largest inhabitants.

A 176-ton (160-metric-tonne) blue whale can exist because of the support it receives from the water. But on land, the upper weight limit—based on fossil evidence—is around 77–110 tons (70–100 metric tonnes) in the case of the herbivorous *Argentinosaurus*, which existed 95 million years ago.

A figure of about 110 tons is also the limit reached theoretically when examining the stress limits of bones—and the corresponding increase in muscle size—in terrestrial animals. Such a creature is feasible but would be limited by gravity, the availability of resources, the turnaround of offspring (larger animals produce fewer babies), and a lack of adaptability in times of crisis (such as a food shortage).

So, if we were going to find an animal bigger than the blue whale, it would have to be in the oceans. Could the mysterious "Bloop" (see p. 398) be a contender?

Guinness World Records is indebted to Schleich for supplying the models used in this feature.

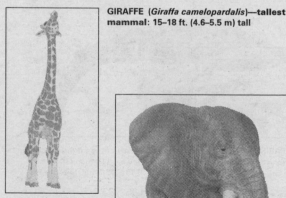

GIRAFFE (*Giraffa camelopardalis*)—tallest mammal: 15–18 ft. (4.6–5.5 m) tall

AFRICAN ELEPHANT (*Loxodonta africana*)—largest ungulate and largest land mammal: 9 ft. 10 in.–12 ft. 1 in. (3–3.7 m) to shoulder; 8,800–15,400 lb. (4–7 metric tonnes)

ALASKAN MOOSE (*Alces alces gigas*)—**largest deer**: 7 ft. 8 in. (2.34 m) to shoulder

EASTERN LOWLAND GORILLA (*Gorilla beringei graueri*)—**largest primate**: 5 ft. 9 in. (1.75 m) tall; 360 lb. (163 kg)

ALDABRA GIANT TORTOISE (*Aldabrachelys gigantea*)—**largest tortoise**: 48 in. (1.22 m) wide

HUMAN (*Homo sapiens*): 5 ft. 5 in. (1.65 m) tall; 130 lb. (60 kg)

POLAR BEAR (*Ursus maritimus*)—**largest land carnivore**: 7 ft. 10 in.–8 ft. 6 in. (2.4–2.6 m) nose to tail; 880–1,320 lb. (400–600 kg)

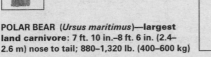

BLUE WHALE (*Balaenoptera musculus*)—**largest mammal**: 80 ft. (24 m) long; 176 tons (160 metric tonnes)

EMPEROR PENGUIN (*Aptenodytes forsteri*)—**largest penguin**: 3 ft. 3 in. (1 m) tall; 95 lb. (43 kg)

QUETZALCOATLUS (*Quetzalcoatlus northropi*)—**largest flying creature**: 39 ft. (12 m) wingspan; 250 lb. (113 kg)

AMERICAN BISON (*Bison bison*)—**largest migrant on land**: 6 ft. 5 in. (2 m) to shoulder; ca. 2,200 lb. (1 metric tonne)

How Big Can Animals Get?

THEROPODS ("beast-footed" dinosaurs)—largest ever land carnivores: up to 43 ft. (13 m) long; 13,230 lb. (6 metric tonnes)

RED KANGAROO (*Macropus rufus*)—largest kangaroo: 5 ft. 11 in. (1.8 m) tall; 198 lb. (90 kg)

HIPPOPOTAMUS (*Hippopotamus amphibius*)—heaviest artiodactyl: up to 8,000 lb. (3,630 kg); 4 ft. 7 in. (1.4 m) to shoulder

SOUTHERN WHITE RHINOCEROS (*Ceratotherium simum simum*)—largest rhino: 11 ft. 6 in.–15 ft. (3.5– 4.6 m) long; 7,700 lb. (3,500 kg)

NORTH AFRICAN OSTRICH (*Struthio camelus camelus*)— largest bird: 9 ft. (2.75 m) tall; 345 lb. (156.5 kg)

SALTWATER CROCODILE (*Crocodylus porosus*)—largest crocodilian: 23 ft. (7 m) long; 1,150 lb. (520 kg)

WOLF (*Canis lupus*)—largest canid: 39.5–63 in. (1–1.6 m) body length; 35.25–176.5 lb. (16–80 kg)

SIBERIAN TIGER (*Panthera tigris altaica*)— largest felid: 10 ft. 4 in. (3.15 m) nose to extended tail; 580 lb. (265 kg)

GREAT WHITE SHARK (*Carcharodon carcharias*)—largest predatory fish: 14–15 ft. (4.3–4.6 m) average length; 1,150–1,700 lb. (520–770 kg)

WHALE SHARK (*Rhincodon typus*)—**largest fish: 41 ft. 6 in. (12.65 m) long; 16.5–23.1 tons (15–21 metric tonnes)**

SHARKS

First use of the term "shark" Sailors originally described sharks as "sea dogs." The first use of the term "shark" occurred when sailors from the second expedition of 16th-century English seaman Sir John Hawkins exhibited a specimen in London in 1569 and referred to it as a "sharke." This soon became the accepted name for the creature.

Shark with the most gill slits Most modern-day shark species have five pairs of gill slits. However, a few have six pairs, and two—the sharpnose sevengill shark (*Heptranchias perlo*) and the broadnose sevengill shark (*Notorhynchus cepedianus*)—have seven pairs. These sevengill species are related to some of the most ancient sharks; fossil sharks from the Jurassic period, 200 to 145 million years ago, also had seven pairs.

LARGEST FISH The rare, plankton-feeding whale shark (*Rhincodon typus*) is found in the warmer areas of the Atlantic, Pacific, and Indian oceans. The largest scientifically recorded example was 41 ft. 6 in. (12.65 m) long, and weighed an estimated 33,000–46,200 lb. (15–21 tonnes). It was captured on November 11, 1949, off Baba Island, near Karachi, Pakistan. A whale shark has also produced the **largest egg** by any living creature. It was found on June 29, 1953, in the Gulf of Mexico and measured 12 x 5.5 x 3.5 in. (30.5 x 14 x 8.9 cm).

FACT: Hammerheads swim so close to the surface, they can get sunburn.

FASTEST SHARK The shortfin mako (*Isurus oxyrinchus*), with recorded swimming speeds exceeding 34.8 mph (56 km/h), is the fastest shark. By comparison, the fastest human swims at only 4.7 mph (7.5 km/h). The shortfin mako is also the **highest leaping shark**. It can jump 19 ft. 8 in. (6 m) out of the water—that's longer than the average school bus. It has even leaped directly into fishermen's boats.

SHARK WITH THE LARGEST TEETH (RELATIVE TO BODY) The largetooth cookiecutter (*Isistius plutodus*) measures only 1 ft. 4 in. (40 cm) in length—however, its lower jaw's 19 triangular teeth with rectangular bases are huge in proportion. They are twice as large, relative to its total body length, as the great white shark's (*Carcharodon carcharias*) teeth are in relation to its own total body length. The shark uses the teeth to gouge flesh from larger fish.

Largest shark pups The basking shark (*Cetorhinus maximus*) is the world's second largest shark species and it gives birth to the largest pups. A sexually mature female will give birth to one or two live pups at a time, each of which is about 5 ft. 7 in. (1.7 m) long.

Most poisonous shark The Greenland shark (*Somniosus microcephalus*) is the most poisonous species. Although its flesh is popularly eaten in Greenland and Iceland, it must be boiled in several changes of water first. This removes its poison—a neurotoxin known as trimethylamine oxide—which causes effects resembling extreme drunkenness.

Fish with greatest sense of smell Sharks have a better sense of smell than any other fish. They can detect one part of mammalian blood in 100 million parts of water.

Most recently discovered shark family The newest zoological family of sharks is Megachasmidae, which was created in 1981 for a large and dramatically different species of shark discovered as recently as November 1976.

LARGEST HAMMERHEAD Of the nine currently recognized species of hammerhead shark, by far the largest is the great hammerhead (*Sphyrna mokarran*). It attains a maximum length of 20 ft. (6.1 m)—at least one-third longer than any other hammerhead species. The great hammerhead inhabits tropical waters around the world's continents and, despite its size, can sometimes be encountered in reefs as shallow as 3 ft. 3 in. (1 m).

LARGEST PREDATORY FISH Adult great white sharks (*Carcharodon carcharias*) average 14–15 ft. (4.3–4.6 m) long, and generally weigh 1,150–1,700 lb. (520–770 kg). There are many claims of huge specimens up to 33 ft. (10 m) long, but few have been properly authenticated. However, there is plenty of circumstantial evidence to suggest that some great whites grow to more than 20 ft. (6 m) long.

In that year, an adult male specimen, measuring 14 ft. 9 in. (4.5 m) long, attempted to swallow the anchor of a U.S. Navy research vessel near Oahu, Hawaii. It was hauled out of the water to the astonishment of the scientific world. On account of its huge mouth, the species became known as the megamouth shark (*Megachasma pelagios*). Up to August 2011, only 51 megamouth sharks had been found.

Shark with the least varied diet The crested bullhead shark (*Heterodontus galeatus*) is the fussiest eater of all the sharks. Despite measuring about 4 ft. 11 in. (1.5 m) in length, this species feeds almost exclusively on red sea urchins.

Shark with the most varied diet Nicknamed the "garbage-can shark," the tiger shark (*Galeocerdo cuvier*) eats almost anything that moves. Confirmed prey of this 16-ft. 5-in.-long (5-m) predator includes seals; dolphins; seabirds, such as cormorants and pelicans; reptiles, including marine turtles and sea snakes; bony fishes; other sharks; invertebrates, such as lobsters, octopuses, and crabs; and any land mammals that end up in the sea, including dogs, rats, and even cattle.

Longest gestation The common frilled shark (*Chlamydoselachus anguineus*), native to all oceans, has a gestation period (pregnancy) of 3.5 years, the longest known of any animal species.

Most bioluminescent shark The cookiecutter shark (*Isistius brasiliensis*) from the central regions of the Atlantic and Pacific is the brightest shark. It is named after Isis, an Egyptian goddess associated with light. Up to 5 ft. (1.5 m) long, it has a dull brown upper surface, but underneath it is often covered entirely with photophores, light-producing organs that emit a very bright, ghostly green glow. The purpose of this bioluminescence is unclear—it may serve to attract sharks of its own species or to attract prey, or it may even act as camouflage if viewed from below.

> **FACT:** The hammerhead shark's "hammer" is known as a "cephalofoil."

SHARK ATT🕱X
Galeophobia

Galeophobia is the fear of sharks, but you have little to worry about. Movies such as *Jaws* (U.S.A., 1975)—the **first blockbuster movie**—have unfairly portrayed sharks as ferocious man-eaters, but statistics show you're more likely to be killed by lightning or a falling coconut than by a shark. However, sharks *are* apex predators and will attack you if they mistake you for prey.

A. ALL SHARKS
B. SHARKS THAT ATTACK HUMANS

There are **>360** species of shark but only **35** have been reported to attack humans; of these, only a few are responsible for major incidents.

Top 5 attacking species

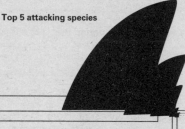

Great white: 10.6%
Tiger: 5.8%
Bull: 3.0%
Hammerhead: 0.9%
Lemon: 0.5%

 26 average age in years of a shark-attack victim

Global shark attacks

Year	Total	Fatalities
2000	80	11
2001	73	5
2002	65	3
2003	53	4
2004	65	7
2005	59	4
2006	56	4
2007	69	1
2008	53	4
2009	63	6
2010	79	6

ANIMAL LIFE

MATING

Highest-pitch mating call The male Colombian *Arachnoscelis* katydid (a type of cricket) rubs its forewings together to create an intense burst of chirps, peaking at a frequency of 130 kHz. This mating call is beyond the hearing threshold of humans.

Largest bowers The bowerbirds of Australia and New Guinea construct and decorate elaborate "bowers" to attract females for mating purposes. The largest bowers are those of the Vogelkop gardener bowerbird (*Amblyornis inornata*) from New Guinea. These hutlike structures are some 5 ft. 3 in. (160 cm) across and 3 ft. 3 in. (100 cm) high, often with a front lawnlike area several square yards in size. To attract mates to the bower, the male clears this "lawn" of forest debris and then decorates it with bright, shiny objects, such as pieces of fruit, flowers, shells, and even shiny beetle wing cases.

Most frequent mating Native to the deserts of North Africa, a small gerbil-related rodent species known as Shaw's jird (*Meriones shawi*) has been scientifically observed mating 224 times in just two hours.

SMALLEST PLACENTAL MAMMAL BABY RELATIVE TO ADULT The giant panda (*Ailuropoda melanoleuca*) produces the smallest baby of any placental mammal (that is, a mammal other than marsupials or those who lay eggs). A newborn panda is pink, hairless, blind, about 5 in. (12 cm) long, and weighs about 3.5 oz (100 g). It is about 1/900th the size of its mother.

Smallest semelparous mammal The male brown antechinus (*Antechinus stuartii*), a marsupial mouse from east Australia, is the world's smallest "semelparous" mammal, meaning that it has just one reproductive period during its life. Every year, the entire adult male population spends two weeks mating with as many females as possible before dying. Their deaths are believed to result from the stress of chasing females and fighting off rival males, causing their immune system to shut down and leaving them vulnerable to ulcers, infection, or, because they neglect to eat, starvation.

Longest baculum In many mammals, the penis has a bone called the baculum (although not in humans, whales, marsupials, rabbits, hyenas, and some hooved species). The walrus (*Odobenus rosmarus*) has the longest mammalian baculum; it can measure 29.5 in. (75 cm)—the length of a human thigh bone.

PREGNANCY

Longest gestation "Gestation" is the period of development of an embryo or fetus inside the mother (pregnancy). The longest gestation is that of the common frilled shark at 3.5 years (see p. 63).

Amphibian: The longest gestation period not just for an amphibian but for any terrestrial vertebrate is 1,156 days (39 months), as exhibited by the alpine salamander (*Salamandra atra*), native to the Swiss Alps.

Mammal: The Asian elephant (*Elephas maximus*) has an average gestation of 650 days and a maximum of 760 days—more than twice as long as a human pregnancy.

The **shortest mammal gestation** is ca. 12 days 8 hours for the short-nosed bandicoot (*Isoodon macrourus*) of Oceania.

MOST MACAWS BORN IN A YEAR From January 26 to October 30, 2009, 105 macaws were born at the Xcaret Eco-Park on the Riviera Maya in Cancun, Mexico—a world record for one facility. Xcaret also holds the record for the **most dolphins born in a single facility in one year**, with 11 in 2008.

See p. ■■■ for other creatures that are long in the tooth.

LARGEST NEWBORN MARSUPIAL Newborn marsupials are born at a very early stage and continue to develop in their mothers' pouches. The red kangaroo (*Megaleia rufa*) produces the largest newborn marsupial, but even this weighs only 0.02 oz. (0.75 g)—less than a paper clip. It would take at least 36,000 newborn babies to equal its mother's weight.

Largest newborn At the time of its birth, an Australian stump-tailed skink, or bobtail (*Tiliqua rugosa*), can weigh more than a third of its mother's weight—equivalent to a woman giving birth to a baby the size of a six-year-old child!

EGGS, ETC.

Most prolific chicken The highest authenticated rate of egg-laying is 371 in 364 days, by a white leghorn in an official test that ended on August 29, 1979, at the University of Missouri in Columbia, Missouri, U.S.A.

LARGEST BIRD EGG RELATIVE TO BODY SIZE The brown kiwi (*Apteryx australis*) of New Zealand lays the largest eggs relative to its body size. One female kiwi weighing 3 lb. 12 oz. (1.7 kg) laid an egg weighing 14 oz. (406 g), which is almost one-quarter of her total body mass. Weights of 1 lb. (510 g) have been reliably reported for other kiwi eggs.

LARGEST INSECT EGG The largest egg laid by an insect belongs to the 6-in.-long (15-cm) Malaysian stick insect (*Heteropteryx dilitata*). At 0.5 in. (1.3 cm) in length, each egg is larger than a shelled peanut. Some insects, notably mantids and cockroaches, lay egg *cases* that are much larger, but these contain as many as 200 eggs.

Most eggs laid by a dinosaur The largest clutch of eggs laid by a single dinosaur is 34, as discovered by paleontologists alongside a fossilized skeleton of *Psittacosaurus*. This beaked dinosaur was around 3 ft. 3 in. (1 m) tall, walked on two feet, and lived in Mongolia 105–115 million years ago, during the Cretaceous period.

Biggest dinosaur nest The biggest dinosaur nest on record measured 9 ft. 10 in. (3 m) in diameter and contained 28 long, cylindrical eggs, each roughly 12 in. (30 cm) in length. The nest and eggs were from a *Macroelongatoolithus*, a dinosaur that lived in China about 70–90 million years ago.

Fewest eggs produced by a fish in one spawning The mouth-brooding fish *Tropheus moorii* of Lake Tanganyika in east Africa produces seven eggs or fewer during normal reproduction. As each egg is released, the female takes it into her mouth, where it is fertilized by the male.

Smallest bird egg The smallest egg laid by any bird is that of the vervain hummingbird (*Mellisuga minima*) of Jamaica and two nearby islets. Two specimens, measuring less than 0.39 in. (10 mm) in length, weighed 0.0128 oz. (0.365 g) and 0.0132 oz. (0.375 g)—you would need at least 136 of these to equal the weight of a medium-size hen's egg.

Most protective female tortoise The female Burmese brown tortoise (*Manouria emys*) remains close to her nesting site, guarding it from potential egg-snatchers, for several days after laying her eggs. Other tortoises, conversely, either show no maternal interest in their eggs at all after laying them, or spend no more than an hour or so concealing their eggs and the nesting site.

Most fertile stick insect The world's most fertile stick insect is *Acrophylla titan*, a species from north Australia that can grow to 12 in. (30 cm). A single female can lay more than 2,000 eggs at a time.

ANIMAL LONGEVITY

LONG-LIVED SPECIES

Alligator The greatest authenticated age for a crocodilian is 66 years, for a female American alligator (*Alligator mississippiensis*) that arrived at Adelaide Zoo, South Australia, on June 5, 1914, when she was two years old. She died on September 26, 1978.

LONGEST-LIVED VENOMOUS LIZARD The Mexican beaded lizard (*Heloderma horridum*) is a black-and-yellow, forest-dwelling species that measures up to 2 ft. 11.4 in. (90 cm) long. One specimen lived in captivity for 33 years 11 months.

Amphibian The Artis Zoo in Amsterdam, Netherlands, owned two giant Japanese salamanders (*Andrias japonicus*), both of whom reached 52 years—the oldest confirmed age for an amphibian. The first giant Japanese salamander was given to the zoo in 1839, where it lived until 1881; the second arrived in 1903 and died in 1955.

Chelonian The greatest authentic age recorded for a chelonian (tortoise, turtle, or terrapin) is at least 188 years, for a Madagascar radiated tortoise (*Astrochelys radiata*) that was presented to the Tonga royal family by Captain Cook in either 1773 or 1777. The animal was called Tui Malila and remained in their care until its death in 1965.

Insect On May 27, 1983, a golden buprestid (*Buprestis aurulenta*) appeared from the staircase woodwork in the home of Mr. W. Euston of Prittlewell, Southend-on-Sea, Essex, UK. The beetle had spent at least 47 years as a larva. How do we know? The staircase had been in Mr. Euston's house for the whole of this period, and because the beetle was a tropical species, not native to the UK, it must have already been present in the lumber before the staircase was installed.

Lungfish The longest-lived species of lungfish is the Australian lungfish (*Neoceratodus forsteri*). Popularly deemed to be more primitive in form than its South American and African relatives, it has lived to 19 years 8 months 12 days in captivity.

Marsupial The oldest marsupial whose age has been reliably recorded was a common wombat (*Vombatus ursinus*) that was 26 years 22 days old when it died on April 20, 1906, at London Zoo. Although not verified, it is possible that the larger species of kangaroo can live to 28 years in the wild.

Mollusk A quahog clam (*Arctica islandica*) that had been living on the seabed off the north coast of Iceland was dredged by researchers from Bangor University's School of Ocean Sciences, UK, in 2006. On October 28, 2007, sclerochronologists (experts who examine growth patterns in algae and invertebrates) from Bangor University announced that they had studied the annual growth rings in the clam's shell and determined that it was 405–410 years old. It was nicknamed "Ming," after the Chinese dynasty that had been in power when the clam was born.

FACT: Armadillos curl up if threatened. Their hard, leathery shell gives them 360-degree protection.

LONGEST-LIVED ARMADILLO The La Plata three-banded armadillo (*Tolypeutes matacus*) is native to northern Argentina, southwestern Brazil, Paraguay, and Bolivia. A female specimen of this species was acquired by Lincoln Park Zoo in Chicago, Illinois, U.S.A., in 1971, and died there in 2005 at the age of 36 years 9 months 18 days old.

OLDEST CARNIVOROUS MARSUPIAL One captive Tasmanian devil (*Sarcophilus harrisii*) was at least 13 years old when it died at Rotterdam Zoo, Netherlands, in 2005.

The **longest-lived species of freshwater bivalve mollusk** is the freshwater pearl mussel (*Margaritifera margaritifera*). Russian malacologist Dr. Valeriy Zyuganov determined, in 2000, the maximum lifespan of this endangered Holarctic species to be 210–250 years, a discovery verified independently in 2008 by a team of malacological researchers in Finland.

Sponge The longest-lived species of sponge is *Scolymastra joubini*, the Antarctic hexactinellid or glass sponge. It grows extremely slowly in this region's exceedingly cold waters, and an estimate of age for one 6-ft. 6-in.-tall (2-m) specimen in the Ross Sea gave a result of 23,000 years. Admittedly, this sea's fluctuating levels suggests that it could not survive there for more than around 15,000 years. Yet even if that latter, lower figure is itself an overestimate, this sponge is still one of the oldest—if not *the* oldest—specimens on the planet.

LONGEST-LIVED AUK The common murre or European guillemot (*Uria aalge*) is a puffin-related species of auk. Based on records obtained from ringed specimens, it can live to 38 years in the wild. The murre returns to land to breed, but otherwise passes most of its life at sea.

FACT: Female murres lay eggs one at a time—on a ledge! The egg's conical shape helps stop it from rolling off.

LONGEST-LIVED LYNX The bobcat or red lynx (*Lynx rufus*) ranges from southern Canada through much of continental U.S.A. into northern Mexico. It is smaller than the Canada lynx (*L. canadensis*), with which it shares part of its range, but lives longer, with a maximum recorded longevity of 32 years 3 months 18 days, as opposed to 26 years 9 months 18 days for the Canada lynx.

LONGEST-LIVED WOODPECKER The longest-lived species of woodpecker is the red-bellied woodpecker (*Melanerpes carolinus*). Native to deciduous forests and with a breeding range spanning southern Canada and northeastern U.S.A., this species has been known to live more than 20 years 8 months in its wild state.

Wild bird The oldest recorded age for a bird in the wild is 50 years for a Manx shearwater (*Puffinus puffinus*), a small seabird. It was first ringed in 1957 (when it was five years old) and then again in 1961, 1977, and finally in 2002. It was captured on Bardsey, an island off the Lleyn Peninsula, Wales, UK, on April 3, 2002.

Wild buffalo The longest-lived species of wild buffalo is the anoa or dwarf buffalo (*Bubalus depressicornis*) of Celebes, Indonesia. The world's second smallest buffalo species, it has been recorded as living to 36 years 1 month 6 days in captivity.

BECOME A LIZARD WIZ!

• Lizards smell with their tongues, as do snakes.

• Some lizards can squirt blood 4 ft. (1.2 m) from their eyes as a defense tactic.

• Common lizards (*Zootoca vivipara*) can give birth to both live offspring and eggs.

• The tails of some lizards detach if grabbed.

SHORT-LIVED SPECIES

Fish The shortest-lived fishes are various species of toothcarp, including several South American *Nothobranchius* species, which live for only about eight months in the wild. These small fishes thrive in temporary water sources, such as drainage ditches and even water-filled animal footprints. As soon as these sources dry up, however, the fishes die, but the eggs that they have laid in the meantime survive in the mud. When the rain returns and fills the pool, the eggs hatch and the fishes rapidly grow to their full size, then spawn, before their temporary homes dry out again.

Jackal Based upon maximum recorded longevity, the shortest-lived species of jackal is the African side-striped jackal (*Canis adustus*). Its maximum recorded longevity is 13 years 8 months 12 days, in comparison with 18 years 9 months 18 days for the golden jackal (*C. aureus*) and 16 years 8 months 12 days for the African black-backed jackal (*C. mesomelas*).

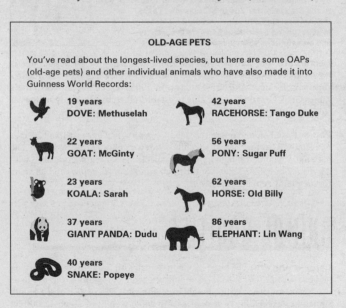

OLD-AGE PETS

You've read about the longest-lived species, but here are some OAPs (old-age pets) and other individual animals who have also made it into Guinness World Records:

19 years
DOVE: Methuselah

22 years
GOAT: McGinty

23 years
KOALA: Sarah

37 years
GIANT PANDA: Dudu

40 years
SNAKE: Popeye

42 years
RACEHORSE: Tango Duke

56 years
PONY: Sugar Puff

62 years
HORSE: Old Billy

86 years
ELEPHANT: Lin Wang

FACT: The blue iguana is rated as Critically Endangered on the IUCN Red List of Threatened Species.

SHORTEST-LIVED TAPIR Also the smallest tapir, the mountain tapir *Tapirus pinchaque* (which lives in Colombia, Ecuador, and Peru) has a maximum known longevity of 28 years 6 months.

LONGEST-LIVED LIZARD In 1950, an adult male Grand Cayman blue iguana (*Cyclura lewisi*) nicknamed "Godzilla" (right) was captured alive on Grand Cayman by naturalist Ira Thompson, who estimated Godzilla's age to be 15 years at that time. In 1985, the iguana was purchased from Thompson and imported into the U.S.A. by an animal dealer, who donated him in 1990 to the Gladys Porter Zoo in Brownsville, Texas, U.S.A. Here, Godzilla remained until his death in 2004, giving a period of 54 years in captivity and an estimated total lifespan of 69 years.

Vertebrate The animal with the shortest lifespan of all vertebrates is the coral-reef pygmy goby (*Eviota sigillata*), which has been recorded as surviving for an average of 59 days. In 2005, researchers at Australia's James Cook University were able to establish their age by studying the ear stones of 300 pygmy gobies, which collect daily growth rings.

Zebra Based on maximum recorded longevity, the shortest-lived species of zebra is also the largest species—Grévy's zebra (*Equus grevyi*). The maximum recorded longevity for this species is 31 years, compared with 33 years 2 months 12 days for the mountain zebra (*E. zebra*) and 38 years for the plains zebra (*E. burchelli*).

ANIMAL ODDITIES

Largest unicorn The largest ever mammal with a single central horn on its head was *Elasmotherium*, a prehistoric rhinoceros often referred to as the "giant unicorn." With a height exceeding 8 ft. 2.5 in. (2.5 m), a length sometimes exceeding 16 ft. 5 in. (5 m), and a weight of about 11,000 lb. (5 metric tonnes), this rhino survived until at least as recently as 50,000 years ago, during the Late Pleistocene epoch in the Black Sea region of Russia, extending north as far as Siberia. The horn, believed to be at least 6 ft. 7 in. (2 m) long, is thought to have been used for defense, attracting mates, and digging for roots and water.

Fish with most eyes The six-eyed spookfish (*Bathylychnops exilis*), which inhabits depths of 300–3,000 ft. (91–910 m) in the northeastern Pacific, was only discovered by biologists in 1958. A slender 17-in.-long (45-cm) pikelike species, it has a second, small pair of eyes—known as secondary globes—positioned, pointing downward, within the lower half of its principal eyes. Each secondary globe possesses its own lens and retina, and may help to increase the spookfish's sensitivity to light in its shadowy surroundings. Moreover, located behind the secondary globes is a third pair of eyes, which lack retinas but divert incoming light into the fish's large principal eyes.

Most cannibalistic amphibian Several amphibian species eat others of their own species, but the world's most cannibalistic amphibian is the alpine salamander (*Salamandra atra*), native to Europe's alpine regions. The female of this species carries up to 60 fertilized eggs in her body, but most of them are eaten by the first few salamander embryos that hatch inside her, so that only between one and four young are actually born.

Most colorful cattle It was announced on January 17, 2012 that a male calf, lilac and white in color, was born in Jezdina village near the city of Čačak in Serbia. Its owner is considering naming it Milkan, after the purple cow emblem of Milka chocolate. Only one previous purple cow is known—she was discovered in Florida in 1948.

Largest item of clothing woven from spider silk In 2011, after eight years' work, 80 workers completed weaving a wide, full-length lady's cape with matching 13-ft. 1-in.-long (4-m) brocade scarf. Both cape and scarf were made from the golden-colored silk of more than one million female Madagascan golden orb spiders (*Nephila madagascariensis*). Each day, the workers collected thousands of spiders from their webs in the wild and then used hand-powered machines to extract the silk from their spinnerets, after which the spiders were released unharmed. The cape alone contains 3.3 lb. (1.5 kg) of silk. The project was masterminded by fashion designer Nicholas Godley (U.S.A.) and textiles expert Simon Peers (UK).

LARGEST AMPHIPOD CRUSTACEAN
Amphipods are a large zoological order of superficially shrimplike crustaceans with thin bodies. Most amphipods are very small, no more than around an inch or so long. However, the world's largest species of amphipod is *Alicella gigantea*—one specimen has been measured at 1 ft. 1 in. (34 cm) long.

FACT: Pictured is an 11-in.-long (28-cm) "supershrimp" amphipod caught off New Zealand in February 2012.

FACT: Amphipods live at the bottom of oceans, where the pressure is 1,000 times greater than at sea level.

LARGEST COLLECTION OF TWO-HEADED ANIMALS Former Grammy award-winning producer Todd Ray (U.S.A.) has 22 different specimens of two-headed animals, including an albino hog-nosed snake, a goat, a terrapin, a king snake, and a bearded dragon (a species of lizard) named Pancho and Lefty. He also has the world's only living three-headed creature: a turtle named Myrtle, Squirtle, and Thirdle (above right). The smallest head is the middle one and consists of only eyes and a beak poking out from the carapace.

Pictured here is Rosi, a Goliath bird-eating spider owned by Walter Baumgartner (Austria). This species has a record leg span of 11 in. (28 cm).

LARGEST SPIDER In July 2011, with the help of the Natural History Museum (NHM) in London, UK, GWR finally put to rest the notion that the Hercules baboon spider (*Hysterocrates hercules*) might be the world's largest spider species. According to GWR, the record holder is—and always has been—the Goliath bird-eating spider (*Theraphosa blondi*, above), a fact now confirmed by Dr. George Beccaloni, Curator of Orthopteroid Insects. Using the NHM's own specimens, Dr. Beccaloni used Archimedes' Principle to perform a volume test. This revealed that the Goliath is, in fact, more than twice the size of the Hercules. Case closed!

SMALLEST CHAMELEON The tiny leaf chameleons (*Brookesia minima*) of Madagascar are between 0.87 in. (22 mm) and 1.89 in. (48 mm) long, from head to tail.

MOST BLOODTHIRSTY BIRD The vampire finch (*Geospiza difficilis septentrionalis*)—which only inhabits Wolf Island and Darwin Island in the Galápagos Islands, Ecuador—lands on the tails of large seabirds (mainly the Nazca booby and blue-footed booby), pecks at the base of the wing feathers, and then drinks the blood that seeps from the wound. It also eats seeds, eggs, and invertebrates.

Most clothing used in a bird's nest In 1909, a 1,323-lb. (600-kg) nest of a white stork (*Ciconia ciconia*) was removed from Colmar Cathedral, in Alsace in eastern France, to prevent the tower from toppling over. The nest's walls included 17 ladies' black stockings, five fur caps, three shoes, a sleeve from a white silk blouse, a large piece of leather, and four buttons from the uniform of a railroad porter!

Strongest bird gizzard The gizzard is the portion of a bird's stomach that grinds food into small pieces. The world's strongest recorded gizzard is that of the turkey *Meleagris gallopavo*. One specimen had crushed 24 walnuts in their shells within four hours, and it had also ground surgical lancet blades into grit within 16 hours.

Most legs Despite their names, centipedes do not have 100 legs and millipedes do not have 1,000. Normally, millipedes have only about 300 pairs of legs, although a millipede called *Illacme plenipes*, first discovered in California, U.S.A., in 1926, had 375 pairs (750 legs).

Longest surviving Janus cat A Janus cat is a domestic cat possessing two near-separate faces as a result of a very rare congenital condition known as diprosopia. In 2011, it was established that the world's longest-lived Janus cat was Frank and Louie, from Minnesota, U.S.A., whose last-reported age, in June 2006, was six years old.

> **FACT:** Dr. Beccaloni used his wife's former pet female Goliath spider—called Tracy—in the test!

SMALLEST FROG *Paedophryne amauensis* **of Papua New Guinea is, on average, between 0.27 in. (7 mm) and 0.3 in. (7.7 mm) in length from snout to vent when fully grown.**

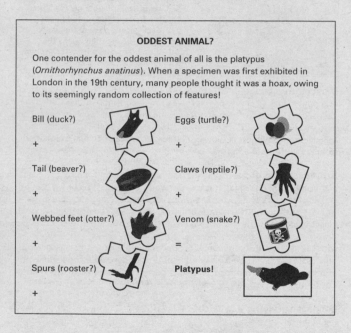

ODDEST ANIMAL?

One contender for the oddest animal of all is the platypus (*Ornithorhynchus anatinus*). When a specimen was first exhibited in London in the 19th century, many people thought it was a hoax, owing to its seemingly random collection of features!

Bill (duck?)

+

Tail (beaver?)

+

Webbed feet (otter?)

+

Spurs (rooster?)

+

Eggs (turtle?)

+

Claws (reptile?)

+

Venom (snake?)

=

Platypus!

In fall 2011, GWR was contacted by Marty Stevens—Frank and Louie's owner, now living in Massachusetts—who revealed that his now-famous two-faced cat was still alive and in good health, and in September 2011 celebrated his 12th birthday! Normally, Janus cats rarely survive more than a day or so following their birth. Since his first appearance in GWR last year, Frank and Louie has become an unlikely media star, appearing in countless newspaper reports and online news videos throughout the world.

TEETH, TUSKS & HORNS

Dinosaur with the most teeth *Edmontosaurus*, a hadrosaur (duck-billed dinosaur) that lived in the late Cretaceous period, 65–61 million years ago, had more than a thousand teeth. They were diamond-shaped and set in columns known as "tooth batteries."

The **land mammal with the most teeth** is the giant armadillo (*Priodontes maximus*) of South America, which typically has up to 100 teeth.

The numbat or marsupial anteater (*Myrmecobius fasciatus*) of Western Australia is the **marsupial with the most teeth**, up to 52, including a unique cheek tooth sited between the premolars and the molars.

LARGEST CAT FANGS The 6-in.-long (15-cm) daggerlike canine teeth of *Eusmilus*, a false saber-toothed cat, were the largest feline fangs relative to body size—almost as long as its skull. It lived around 37–29 million years ago.

LARGEST HORNED TOAD The horned lizards of North America, popularly dubbed "horned toads," are named after the horns on their head—which are true horns, having a bony core. The largest species is the giant or long-spined horned lizard (*Phrynosoma asio*), which has a total length of up to 7.9 in. (20 cm). It lives in desert regions along southern Mexico's Pacific coast.

LONGEST WHALE TOOTH The spiraled ivory tusk of the male narwhal (*Monodon monoceros*) was once thought to be the horn of the fabled unicorn when it was found washed up with dead male narwhals. Narwhal tusks reach an average length of 6 ft. 6 in. (2 m), but occasionally exceed 9 ft. 10 in. (3 m) and weigh up to 22 lb. (10 kg), with a maximum girth of approximately 9 in. (23 cm). Narwhals live in the waters of the Arctic.

FACT: Horned lizards squirt jets of blood from the corners of their eyes if they feel threatened.

LARGEST HORN SPREAD FOR DOMESTIC CATTLE (LIVING) "JR," a Texas Longhorn owned by Michael and Lynda Bethel (Australia), has a horn spread of 9 ft. 1 in. (277 cm). He was measured in Queensland, Australia, on October 2, 2011.

Largest teeth used for eating

The largest teeth employed for eating (as opposed to tusks used for defense purposes) belonged to *Livyatan melvillei*—a prehistoric species of sperm whale that lived around 12 million years ago during the Miocene epoch. Its teeth were up to 1 ft. 2 in. (36 cm) long.

Longest elephant tusks (relative to body)

Anancus was a prehistoric gomphothere (an extinct family of elephantine mammals) that lived from the late Miocene epoch to the early Pleistocene epoch, 3–1.5 million years ago. Each of its two long, straight tusks measured up to 13 ft. (4 m)—almost as long as its body!

LARGEST ANTLERS An antler spread or "rack" of 6 ft. 6.5 in. (1.99 m) was recorded for a moose (*Alces alces*) killed near the Stewart River, Canada, in October 1897. It is now housed in the Field Museum in Chicago, Illinois, U.S.A.

LONGEST BEETLE WITH ENLARGED JAWS Almost a third of the length of the male giant sawyer beetle (*Macrodontia cervicornis*) is accounted for by its huge jaws. The longest specimen on record was 10 in. (17.7 cm), and was collected in Peru in 2007.

FACT: An Asian water buffalo (*Bubalus arnee*) shot in 1955 had horns measuring 13 ft. 10 in. (4.24 m) from tip to tip.

HEAVIEST HORN FOR A HORNBILL
The hornbills, native to tropical Africa and Asia, are named after the hornlike structure, or "casque," on top of their bill's upper mandible. Usually, the casque is very light, being hollow, but, uniquely, in the helmeted hornbill (*Rhinoplax vigil*) of Malaysia and Indonesia it is solid. The skull of this species (including its casque) can account for up to 10% of the bird's weight of about 6 lb. 10 oz. (3 kg).

Longest prehistoric tusks The straight-tusked elephant (*Hesperoloxodon antiques germanicus*), which lived about 2 million years ago, had an average tusk length in adults of 16 ft. 4.8 in. (5 m).

The **longest tusks (nonprehistoric)** belong to an African elephant (*Loxodonta africana*) from the Democratic Republic of the Congo, now housed at the New York Zoological Society in New York City, U.S.A. The right tusk measures 11 ft. 5 in. (3.49 m) along the outside curve; the left is 10 ft. 11 in. (3.35 m).

Heaviest mammoth tusks A pair of mammoth tusks found near Campbell, Nebraska, U.S.A., in April 1915 weighs 498 lb. (226 kg). One is 13 ft. 9 in. (4.21 m) long, the other 13 ft. 7 in. (4.14 m). They are in the University of Nebraska Museum, U.S.A.

The **heaviest tusks (nonprehistoric)**, are a pair of African elephant tusks in the Natural History Museum, London, UK, from a bull shot in Kenya in 1897. They weigh 240 lb. (109 kg) and 225 lb. (102 kg)—giving a total weight of 465 lb. (211 kg).

Longest horns on a sheep The longest sheep horn measured 6 ft. 3 in. (191 cm) and belonged to a Marco Polo sheep (*Ovis ammon polii*). The species is indigenous to only the Pamir Mountains bordering Tajikistan, Afghanistan, Pakistan, and China.

Most horns on a sheep Ewes and rams of the Jacob sheep breed—a rare "polycerate" (multihorned) sheep—typically grow two or four horns, but six is not uncommon. Of sheep that have four horns, one pair usually grows vertically, often to more than 2 ft. (60 cm), while the other pair curls around the side of the head.

LONG IN THE TOOTH

When it comes to animal dentition, some creatures are way out ahead of the rest. GWR brushes up on the longest teeth in the animal world, from the prehistoric past to the present:

WOOLLY MAMMOTH: 16.5 ft.

AFRICAN ELEPHANT: 10 ft.

NARWHAL: 6.5 ft.

WALRUS: 40 in.

HIPPOPOTAMUS: 20 in.

TYRANNOSAURUS REX: 12 in.

WARTHOG: 9 in.

SPERM WHALE: 7 in.

LION: 3.5 in.

ALLIGATOR: 1.5 in.

Most horns on a giraffe A giraffe usually has three "ossicones" (horn-like projections under the skin): a pair on top of its head and a single one at the center of its brow. A Rothschild's giraffe (*Giraffa camelopardalis rothschildi*) discovered in 1901 in Uganda, however, boasted five ossicones. It had an extra pair at the back of its head, behind its ears.

BIG CATS

Largest cat not classed as a "true" big cat There are five species of "true" big cats (all from the *Panthera* genus)—the lion, tiger, leopard, jaguar, and snow leopard. However, four other large species—the clouded leopards, puma, and cheetah—are often classified with them. The puma (*Puma concolor*)—also known as the cougar, mountain lion, catamount, and painter—is the largest cat species apart from the true cats (only the lion, tiger, and jaguar are bigger). It is up to 9 ft. (2.75 m) long, stands 1 ft. 11 in.–2 ft. 11 in. (0.6–0.9 m) at the shoulder, and weighs 116 lb. 13 oz.–220 lb. 7 oz. (53–100 kg). The puma also has the **greatest north–south range for a big cat**. It lives in the New World from Alaska, U.S.A., and Yukon, Canada, in the north down to Tierra del Fuego, an island group at the southern tip of South America—a distance of 8,950 miles (14,400 km).

First big cat in Europe The earliest species of "true" big cat in Europe was the European jaguar (*P. gombaszoegensis*). Larger than present-day New World jaguars, this apex predator existed about 1.5 million years ago, during the early–mid Pleistocene epoch.

LARGEST JAGUAR The jaguar (*Panthera onca*) is the third largest species of cat (after the lion and tiger), and is, therefore, the largest cat in the New World. The largest subspecies of jaguar is the Pantanal jaguar (*P. o. palustris*), native to the Pantanal tropical wetlands in Brazil and Paraguay, as well as northeast Argentina. An adult of this subspecies weighs more than 300 lb. (135 kg).

FACT: "Black panthers," such as Boogie from Tbilisi Zoo in Georgia (in Europe), are jaguars with an excess of dark melanin pigment.

SMALLEST BIG CAT The world's smallest species of "true" big cat (*Panthera* genus) is the snow leopard (*Panthera uncia*). Native to the mountain ranges of central and south Asia, this rare and highly elusive species has a head and body length of 2 ft. 5 in.–4 ft. 3 in. (0.75–1.3 m), a tail length of 2 ft. 7 in.–3 ft. 3 in. (0.8–1 m), and a shoulder height of 1 ft. 11 in. (0.6 m). It generally weighs around 59–121 lb. (27–55 kg), although an extra-large male can weigh 165 lb. (75 kg).

Highest-altitude big cat specimen The famous frozen carcass of a leopard (*Panthera pardus*) discovered in 1926 at the rim of Mount Kilimanjaro's Kibo Crater in Tanzania, at a height of 18,700 ft. (5,700 m), is the highest-found true big cat specimen. The highest-recorded cat of any species was a puma observed during the early 1990s at an altitude of 19,028 ft. (5,800 m) in the South American Andes mountain range.

Largest population of white tigers Nandankanan Zoo, in the state of Orissa, India, is home to the world's largest population of white tigers, with at least 34 specimens. The zoo has bred many white tigers, and has sent them to zoos all over the world.

Largest litter of tigers born in captivity Eight tiger cubs were born to a Bengal tiger (*Panthera tigris tigris*) named Baghdad on April 15, 1979, at Marine World/Africa U.S.A., Redwood City, California, U.S.A. (now called Six Flags Marine World and located at Vallejo, California).

Least genetically diverse big cat The big cat with the least genetic diversity is the cheetah (*Acinonyx jubatus*). Studies conducted in the 1980s, using two different populations of South African cheetah, revealed that the cheetah not only exhibits less genetic diversity than any other species of cat but also less than almost any other species of large mammal.

Newest big cat The newest species of big cat is the Bornean clouded leopard (*Neofelis diardi*). Traditionally classed merely as a subspecies of the mainland clouded leopard (*Neofelis nebulosa*), it was reclassified in December 2006 after studies showed that its DNA and outward appearance were sufficiently distinct.

First record of a lion/tiger hybrid Lion/tiger hybrids have frequently been bred in captivity, and are known as ligers if sired by a lion and tiglons or tigons if sired by a tiger. The earliest confirmed record of a lion/tiger hybrid is a color plate of one that was prepared in 1798 by French naturalist Étienne Geoffroy Saint-Hilaire. The liger is the **largest hybrid of the cat family**, typically growing larger than both parents and reaching lengths of 10–12 ft. (3–3.6 m).

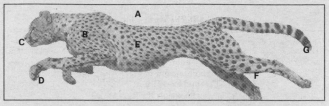

FASTEST MAMMAL ON LAND Over a short distance, the cheetah can maintain a steady maximum speed of approximately 62 mph (100 km/h) on level ground. In a timed run, Sarah, an eight-year-old cheetah, ran 100 m. (328 ft.) in 6.13 seconds on a specially designed course at Cincinnati Zoo, Ohio, U.S.A., on September 10, 2009. If Usain Bolt had run against her, he would be just past halfway when she crossed the finish line. Here's why . . .

A. Flexible spine allows limbs to swing freely
B. Large heart and lungs take in extra oxygen
C. Large nostrils and sinuses increase air intake
D. Ridged foot pads and blunt claws maximize grip on ground
E. Slender body with flat rib cage reduces air resistance
F. Long, loose, muscular limbs enhance speed
G. Large, flat tail aids balance and steering

MOST WIDELY DISTRIBUTED BIG CAT Even today, after having become extinct in many parts of the world during the past century, the leopard (*Panthera pardus*) remains the world's most widely distributed true big cat. Inhabiting a range of habitats, it still exists throughout much of sub-Saharan Africa, northwest Africa, parts of the Middle East and west Asia, most of tropical Asia, and in isolated zones in eastern Russia, northern China, the Korean peninsula, Sri Lanka, and Java.

LONGEST GESTATION PERIOD FOR A CAT SPECIES The gestation period of a lion (*Panthera leo*) varies between 100 and 114 days, with an average of 110 days. Close behind is the tiger (*P. tigris*), with a gestation period ranging from 93 to 112 days. The Asian elephant (*Elephas maximus*) has the **longest gestation period for a mammal,** taking an average of 650 days to give birth.

FACT: At top speed, the cheetah takes strides of about 23 ft. (7 m)—the same stride length as a horse!

"FRANKENSTEIN" CATS

Several big cat species have been crossbred—almost always in zoos instead of in the wild. Hercules, right, is a liger from South Carolina, U.S.A., while the four tiglon cubs were born in Haikou city, China.

Breed	Hybrid name	Characteristics
Lion/tiger	Liger (from male lion)	Huge, sociable
	Tiglon/tigon (from male tiger)	Smaller than parents
Lion/leopard	Lipard (from male lion)	Large lionlike head
	Leopon (from male leopard)	Larger than leopards
Lion/jaguar	Liguar (from male lion)	Anecdotal evidence
	Jaglion (from male jaguar)	Build of jaguar
Tiger/leopard	Tigard/tipard (from male tiger)	Anecdotal evidence
	Leoger (from male leopard)	One recorded example
Tiger/jaguar	Tiguar (from male tiger)	One recorded example
	Jagger (from male jaguar)	No evidence
Leopard/jaguar	Leguar/lepjag (from male leopard)	Bigger than leopards
	Jagupard (from male jaguar)	Small, size of jaguar

Rarest tiger hybrids In 1977, at Southam Zoo in Warwickshire, UK, a cub was born to a tigress that had mated with a black, or melanistic, leopard (commonly known as a black panther). The media dubbed the cub a "pantig," although strictly it is a "leoger." The only offspring ever to survive as a result of a tiger/leopard mating, it was sold to an American zoo as an adult. Despite his father's all-black coat, the pantig closely resembled a normal leopard in coat color, but its face was distinctly tiger-like. There has also been only one tiger/jaguar hybrid. Born at Altoplano Zoo in San Pablo Apetatlan, Mexico, in 2009, this "tiguar" was born to a Siberian, or Amur, tiger (*P. tigris altaica*) father and a jaguar mother from the Chiapas jungle, Mexico. It was named Mickey.

Smallest leopard The smallest subspecies of leopard is the recently recognized, and critically endangered, Arabian leopard (*Panthera pardus nimr*). Males weigh about 66 lb. (30 kg), and females 44 lb. (20 kg)—notably smaller than any of the leopard's other eight subspecies. In the past, the Somali leopard was deemed the smallest leopard, but it is no longer recognized as a separate subspecies. The clouded leopard (*Neofelis nebulosa*)—native to Asia—is a different species from the leopard. An adult weighs about 33–51 lb. (15–23 kg).

Largest captive lion The largest lion was a black-maned male named Simba, who had a shoulder height of 44 in. (1.11 m) in July 1970. He lived in the UK until he died on January 16, 1973, at 14 years old.

MAMMAL WITH MOST NAMES The puma (*Puma concolor*) has 40 common names—including deer tiger, ghost cat, and mountain screamer—in the English language alone.

COMPARING CATS

A selection from the feline family in descending order of average weight:

 Tiger (*Panthera tigris*)
9 ft. 10 in. (3 m); 441 lb. (200 kg)

 Lion (*Panthera leo*)
9 ft. 10 in. (3 m); 400 lb. (180 kg)

 Jaguar (*Panthera onca*)
6 ft. 10 in. (2.1 m); 220 lb. (100 kg)

 Puma (*Puma concolor*)
7 ft. 5 in. (2.27 m); 190 lb. (86 kg)

 Leopard (*Panthera pardus*)
6 ft. 6 in. (2 m); 140 lb. (63 kg)

 Cheetah (*Acinonyx jubatus*)
6 ft. 6 in. (2 m); 100 lb. (46 kg)

 Eurasian lynx (*Lynx lynx*)
3 ft. 11 in. (1.2 m); 66 lb. (30 kg)

 Ocelot (*Leopardus pardalis*)
3 ft. 7 in. (1.1 m); 30 lb. (13.5 kg)

 Serval (*Leptailurus serval*)
2 ft. 7 in. (0.8 m); 30 lb. (13.5 kg)

 Domestic cat (*Felis catus*)
2 ft. 5 in. (0.75 m);10 lb. (4.5 kg)

FACT: The Asiatic lion (*Panthera leo persica*) is now found only in the wild in the Gir forest in Gujarat, India.

ON THE FARM

Most abundant farm mammal The domestic cattle *Bos taurus* is the most abundant farm mammal. There are an estimated 1.3 billion individuals alive today around the world, which means that among large mammals of any kind, only our own species, *Homo sapiens*, is more abundant.

Largest dairy goat population The greatest population of dairy goats in the world is found in China's Fuping County, which contains approximately 320,000 individuals. By comparison, there are around 310,000 dairy goats in the whole of the U.S.A. Almost all of Fuping's dairy goats are Saanen goats, a large, all-white breed named after Switzerland's Saanen Valley.

Greatest milk-yielding goat breed The breed of domestic goat (*Capra hircus*) that yields the greatest amount of milk is the Saanen goat, the largest of the dairy goat breeds. A Saanen nanny produces an average daily milk yield of 1 gallon (3.8 liters).

Goat breed with the shortest ears First bred in Oregon, U.S.A., the breed of goat with the shortest ears is the LaMancha, of which there are two types in terms of ear size. The earlobes of those with so-called "gopher" ears are either nonexistent or measure no more than 1 in. (2.54 cm) and contain little or no cartilage, whereas those with "elf" ears measure 2 in. (5.08 cm) at most. Neither has normal outer earlobes; on first sight LaMancha goats often appear earless.

Least dense goat coat The breed of domestic goat with the least dense coat is the angora goat, from which mohair is derived. Other breeds of goat produce a double coat, consisting of coarse outer hair and softer underdown, but the angora goat's coat normally lacks any coarse outer hair, consisting only of a very fine, fleecy underdown.

SHORTEST HORSE Charly, a male five-year-old sorrel pony born in 2007, measures just 25 in. (63.5 cm) to the withers (between the shoulders). He can be a little bad-tempered, but is affectionate toward his owner, Bartolomeo Messina (Italy), who has trained Charly to take part in equine exhibition shows.

If you have a penchant for pets, see p. 260.

Animals

Largest donkey sanctuary The world's largest donkey sanctuary is the Sidmouth Donkey Sanctuary in Devon, UK. Founded in 1969 by the late Elisabeth Svendsen (UK), MBE, it currently owns eight farms in the UK, and has cared for more than 13,500 donkeys since it opened. It also oversees sanctuaries, foster homes, and holding bays for donkeys in seven other European countries, as well as conducting international operations in Africa, Asia, and Mexico.

Most widely used animal fiber Wool from the domestic sheep (*Ovis aries*) is the most widely used natural fiber derived from animals. It is utilized throughout the inhabited world wherever sheep are farmed. There are just over a billion domestic sheep individuals currently in existence worldwide.

TALLEST LIVING HORSE Big Jake is a nine-year-old gelding Belgian draft horse who measured 20 hands 2.75 in. (6 ft. 10 in.; 210.19 cm), without horseshoes, at Smokey Hollow Farms in Poynette, Wisconsin, U.S.A., on January 19, 2010. Jerry Gilbert is the manager of Smokey Hollow Farms, and his daughter Caley is holding the reins here.

The **tallest horse ever** was the shire gelding Sampson (renamed Mammoth), bred by Thomas Cleaver (UK). This horse, foaled in 1846, measured 21.2 1/2 hands (7 ft. 2.5 in.; 2.19 m) in 1850.

FACT: Big Jake is 2.75 in. (7 cm) taller than the previous tallest horse, a Clydesdale named Remington.

SHORTEST BULL Archie—a Dexter bull named and fully registered in the Northern Ireland livestock inventory in County Antrim, UK—measured 30 in. (76.2 cm) from the hoof to the withers on November 22, 2011, when he was 16 months old.

The smallest breed of cattle is the Vechur breed of Kerala, India. Its average height from the ground to a hump near its shoulders (a feature of certain cattle breeds) for the cow is 31–35 in. (81–91 cm) and 32–41 in. (83–105 cm) for the bull.

Hairiest domestic pig The domestic pig (*Sus scrofa*) with the most hair is the Mangalitza. Uniquely among living breeds of pigs, the Mangalitza grows a remarkably long coat that resembles the fleece of sheep. The Mangalitza is divided into three breeds—the blonde Mangalitza (which is white), the swallow-bellied Mangalitza (which has a black body with white feet and belly), and the red Mangalitza (which is orange). Mangalitzas originated in Hungary.

Largest sheep population The country with the world's greatest domestic sheep population is China, which has more than 136 million sheep. Most of these belong to the fat-tailed breed, which is raised mainly for meat and dairy products because the quality of its wool is usually low. Australia is in second place, with around 79 million sheep.

Smallest breed of goat According to the American Goat Society and Dairy Goat Association, adult males (bucks) of the Nigerian Dwarf breed should measure less than 23.6 in. (60 cm) at the withers, and adult females (does) less than 22.4 in. (57 cm).

TALLEST LIVING DONKEY Oklahoma Sam, a four-year-old American Mammoth Jackstock, measured 15.3 hands (5 ft. 3 in.; 160.02 cm) tall on December 10, 2011. Jake's owner is Linda Davis of Watsonville, California, U.S.A. Mammoth Jackstocks were bred by U.S. president George Washington, who strongly advocated the use of large mules for farmwork instead of horses.

FACT: Archie's parents are both Dexter cows, too, but their other calves are far larger than him.

DONKEY LOWDOWN

• Donkeys (*Equus asinus*) can live for more than 40 years in captivity. They became domesticated around 4,000 years ago.

• They are descendants of Africa's wild ass (*E. africanus*).

• Donkeys have to shelter in rain—unlike horses, their coats are not waterproof.

• Males are dubbed "jacks"; females are called "jennies."

• Mules are the offspring of a male donkey and a female horse. Female donkeys and male horses produce ninnies. Both these cross-breeds are usually sterile.

THE PRODUCE WE PRODUCE . . .

We rely on farms for our basic food staples. In 2010 alone, the world's farmers produced the following jaw-dropping amounts of food and drink. It all adds up to more than 13 quadrillion calories!

 MILK More than 200.7 million gallons (or 304 Olympic-size swimming pools—enough to fill a milk bottle more than twice the height of Nelson's Column, London, UK)

 EGGS 75.9 million tons (enough to make an omelet the size of Northern Ireland)

 POULTRY 107.9 million tons (around 16.4 times heavier than the Great Pyramid at Giza, Egypt)

 PIG MEAT 120.3 million tons (some 4,430 times heavier than the **heaviest statue,** New York's Statue of Liberty)

 BEEF AND BUFFALO MEAT 72.4 million tons (enough to create a burger with an area nearly 2.5 times greater than that of Mauritius)

 SHEEP AND GOAT MEAT 15 million tons (more than 40 times heavier than the Empire State Building)

 FISH (farmed, not wild fish) 61.7 million tons (around 560 times heavier than the world's **largest cruise ship,** the MS *Allure of the Seas*)

Source: Food and Agriculture Organization of the United Nations Statistical Yearbook 2012

Smallest breed of domestic pig The Kunekune pig comes from New Zealand with a name that means "fat and round" in Maori. They grow up to 30 in. (76 cm) and weigh up to 240 lb. (108.9 kg).

Shortest donkey KneeHi, a brown miniature Mediterranean jack who lives at Best Friends Farm in Gainesville, Florida, U.S.A., measured 25.29 in. (64.2 cm) to the top of the withers on July 26, 2011. KneeHi is owned by Jim and Frankie Lee (U.S.A.).

ANIMALYMPICS

FASTEST . . .

Guinea pig A guinea pig appropriately named Flash took 8.81 seconds to run 32 ft. 9 in. (10 m) on July 27, 2009 in London, UK.

Skateboarding dog Tillman, an English bulldog, covered a 328-ft. (100-m) stretch of parking lot on a skateboard in 19.678 seconds at X Games XV in Los Angeles, California, U.S.A., on July 30, 2009.

Canine rat catcher During the 1820s, a 26-lb. (11.8-kg) "bull and terrier" dog named Billy dispatched 4,000 rats in 17 hours, a remarkable feat considering that he was blind in one eye. His most notable feat was killing 100 rats in 5 min. 30 sec. at the Cockpit in Tufton Street, Westminster, London, UK, on April 23, 1825.

Time for a dog to weave through 12 poles Champion Mach Blazer, owned by Elaine Havens (U.S.A.), wove between 12 poles in a remarkable 1.87 seconds on the set of Animal Planet's *Guinness World Records: Amazing Animals* in Los Angeles, California, U.S.A., on September 24, 2005.

Mad for sport? Then race on to p. 449!

FISH WITH THE LARGEST REPERTOIRE OF TRICKS Albert Einstein, a calico fantail goldfish, can perform a range of tricks, including eating from his owner's hand, swimming through a hoop, passing through a tunnel, fetching a ball from the bottom of his tank, and swimming under a limbo bar. He even plays soccer by pushing a tiny ball along the floor of his tank and into a goal. He was trained by his owner, Dean Pomerleau (U.S.A.), at the Fish School in Gibsonia, Pennsylvania, U.S.A.

HIGHEST JUMP BY A DOG Greyhound Cinderella May a Holly Grey, owned by Kate Long and Kathleen Conroy of Miami, Florida, U.S.A., cleared 5 ft. 8 in. (1.72 m) at the Purina Incredible Dog Challenge National Finals at Gray Summit, Missouri, U.S.A., on October 7, 2006. Her name derives partly from the rescue home that she came from, Hollydogs; "Grey" refers to her breed.

The **fastest time for a dog to weave between 24 poles** is 5.88 seconds, by Alma, owned by Emilio Pedrazuela Cólliga (Spain), on the set of *Guinness World Records* in Madrid, Spain, on January 16, 2009.

Tortoise A tortoise named Charlie covered an 18-ft. (5.48-m) course in 43.7 seconds—a speed of 0.28 mph (0.45 km/h)—during the National Tortoise Championship at Tickhill, UK, on July 2, 1977. The course had a gradient of 1:12.

HIGHEST JUMP BY A . . .

Dolphin Some bottlenose dolphins (*Tursiops truncatus*) have been trained to jump as high as 26 ft. (8 m) above the surface of the water.

Dog (leap and scramble) The canine high-jump record for a leap and scramble over a smooth wooden wall (without ribs or other aids) is 12 ft. 2.5 in. (3.72 m), achieved by an 18-month-old lurcher dog named Stag at the annual Cotswold Country Fair in Cirencester, Gloucester, UK, on September 27, 1993. The dog was owned by Mr. and Mrs. P. R. Matthews of Redruth, Cornwall.

> **FACT:** Abbie Girl set her record at the Surf City Surf Dog event, beating more than 20 other paw-ticipants!

LONGEST WAVE SURFED BY A DOG (OPEN WATER) A kelpie named Abbie Girl surfed a 351-ft. 8-in.-long (107.2-m) wave at Ocean Beach Dog Beach in San Diego, California, U.S.A., on October 18, 2011. Kelpies are an Australian dog breed. They herd sheep, occasionally jumping on the backs of stubborn individuals to steer them while balancing on top—exactly the same balancing skills needed for surfing! Abbie has also happily gone skydiving with her owner, Michael Uy (U.S.A.).

MOST RACES WON BY A SHEEP When it comes to racing, a sheep named Lamborghini is way ahead of the pack. Born in January 2011, this woolly whirlwind has won 165 out of 179 races at Odds Farm Park in High Wycombe, UK. The track is approximately 820 ft. (250 m) long and features hurdles and hairpin bends. Each competitor carries a jockey—although in the case of sheep racing, the jockeys are soft toys. Lamborghini—a Friesland/Dorset Down breed—races once a day from May to the end of October, when he has a well-earned rest.

MOST SLAM DUNKS BY A PARROT IN ONE MINUTE Who's a pretty smart boy, then? Zac the parrot, from the Happy Birds Performing Parrot Show in San Francisco, California, U.S.A., pulled off an impressive 22 slam dunks in 60 seconds on November 11, 2011, using his specially designed basketball net.

Guinea pig When it comes to high jumps, one guinea pig soars above the rest. Patch, owned by Philippa Sale (UK) and her family, cleared 8.7 in. (22 cm) on October 11, 2011.

Horse Unbroken now for more than 60 years, the Fédération Equestre Internationale record for a high jump by a horse outdoors is 8 ft. 1.25 in. (2.47 m), by Huaso ex-Faithful, ridden by Captain Alberto Larraguibel Morales (Chile). The record was set at Viña del Mar in Santiago, Chile, on February 5, 1949.

The **highest indoor jump by a horse** measured 7 ft. 10.5 in. (2.4 m) and was set by Optibeurs Leonardo, ridden by Franke Sloothaak (Germany), at Chaudefontaine, Switzerland, on June 9, 1991.

FACT: A greyhound named Bang set the doggy long-jump record with a leap of 29 ft. 11 in. (9.14 m).

Miniature pygmy horse A pygmy horse called Lovebug, owned by Krystal Cole (U.S.A.), performed a 24-in. (61-cm) high jump on the set of Animal Planet's *Guinness World Records: Amazing Animals*. The jump took place on September 24, 2005, in Los Angeles, California, U.S.A.

Pig An 18-month-old pot-bellied pig named Kotetsu performed a 27.5-in. (70-cm) high jump on August 22, 2004, at the Mokumoku Tedsukuri Farm in Mie, Japan. He was trained by Makoto Ieki (Japan).

Rabbit The highest rabbit jump is 39.2 in. (99.5 cm) and was achieved by Mimrelunds Tösen, owned by Tine Hygom (Denmark), in Herning, Denmark, on June 28, 1997.

LONGEST JUMP BY A . . .

Frog The greatest confirmed distance ever leaped by a frog is 33 ft. 9 in. (10.3 m)—about half the length of a basketball court! The jump was made by a South African sharp-nosed frog (*Ptychadena oxyrhynchus*) named Santjie at a frog derby held at Lurula Natal Spa, Petersburg, KwaZulu-Natal, in eastern South Africa, on May 21, 1977.

Guinea pig Truffles the guinea pig cleared an 18-in. (48-cm) gap in Rosyth, Fife, UK, on April 6, 2012.

Kangaroo The greatest confirmed long-jump by a kangaroo occurred during a chase in New South Wales, Australia, in January 1951, when a female red kangaroo made a series of bounds, including one measuring 42 ft. (12.8 m).

FACT: Lamborghini may be speedy, but he'd need to run 14 times faster to beat the automobile of that name!

ANIMAL SPEED

The list below charts the speeds recorded by a selection of creatures. As you'll see, humans just can't compete when racing against the animal kingdom . . .

Bird (dive): 167 mph Peregrine falcon, 30° dive

Bird (level): 78.9 mph Albatross, timed over 8 hours

Fish: 68 mph Sailfish, over 300 ft.

Cat: 65 mph Cheetah, over 220 yards

Bird (flightless): 45 mph Ostrich, burst speed

Horse: 43.97 mph Winning Brew, over 2 furlongs

Greyhound: 41.83 mph Star Title, over 400 yards

Insect: 36 mph Dragonfly, short bursts

Ungulate: 35 mph Pronghorn, over 4 miles

Shark: 34.8 mph Shortfin mako, burst speed

Human: 23.35 mph Usain Bolt, over 100 meters

Reptile: 21.7 mph Iguana, burst speed

Snake (on land): 12 mph Black mamba, burst speed

WEIGHTLIFTING WONDER

What about humans versus animals in the strength stakes? Again, puny *Homo sapiens* just can't compare . . .

 x 850

The **strongest animals**, relative to body size, are the Scarabaeidae beetles. Larger members of this family support up to 850 times their own body weight—the human equivalent of the average man lifting 10 fully grown African elephants!

Animals

HUMANS

CONTENTS

HOW LONG CAN WE LIVE?

WHAT'S THE OLDEST AGE WE CAN REACH?

Guinness World Records' founding editor, Norris McWhirter, once stated: "No single subject is more obscured by vanity, deceit, falsehood, and deliberate fraud than the extremes of human longevity." Extraordinary claims of old age continue to surface in the media, but what, realistically, is the upper age limit for the human race? No authenticated account can be found of someone living beyond 122 years—and only one person ever reached this extreme age. However, is this the absolute limit to life? Here, GWR gerontologist Robert Young explains the limiting factors of longevity and makes his prediction for the oldest possible age . . .

SHORTEST LIVING MAN The shortest man alive—and, indeed, the shortest living person on the Earth—is Chandra Bahadur Dangi (Nepal), who measured 21.5 in. (54.6 cm) tall at the CIWEC Clinic Travel Medicine Center in Lainchaur, Kathmandu, Nepal, on February 26, 2012. This measurement means that Chandra is also the shortest man in history whose height has been verified beyond doubt.

According to his identity card, Chandra is 72 years old, which would also make him the oldest person to have achieved the shortest man record. He hails from the remote mountain village of Reemkholi, in the Dang district of Nepal, and made his first ever visit to the Nepali capital to have his height confirmed by Guinness World Records.

FACT: Telomeres give an indication of life expectancy. Can we lengthen our lives by using gene therapy to lengthen our telomeres?

HOW LONG WILL YOU LIVE?

The table below reveals the odds of life. On the left, we look at the likelihood of *you*, the reader, reaching a given age. On the right is the likelihood that *anyone in history* ever lived to a given age.

Age	Odds of you surviving to this age	Likelihood of one person ever reaching this age
120	1 in 10 billion	48%
121	1 in 20 billion	24%
122	1 in 40 billion	12%
123	1 in 80 billion	6%
124	1 in 160 billion	3%
125	1 in 320 billion	1.50%
126	1 in 640 billion	0.75%
127	1 in 1.28 trillion	0.38%
128	1 in 2.56 trillion	0.19%
129	1 in 5.12 trillion	0.09%
130	1 in 10.24 trillion	0.05%

Calculations are based on current world life expectancy and assuming that annual mortality above 110 is .5.

OLDEST MAN EVER Men fare relatively poorly in the survival stakes (there is only one man in the list of top ten oldest living people; see p. 109). The greatest ever authenticated age for a male is 115 years 252 days by Denmark's Christian Mortensen (1882–1998).

OLDEST PERSON EVER The greatest fully authenticated age to which any human has ever lived is 122 years 164 days by Jeanne Louise Calment (France, 1875–1997). She led an extremely active life, taking up fencing at 85 years old and still riding a bicycle at 100. Her keys to long life were olive oil, chocolate, and port; she gave up smoking at 120 years old.

FACT: After the age of about 20 years, you lose around .035 oz. of brain mass every year.

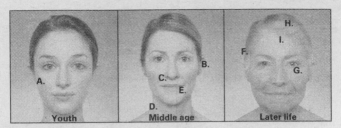

Youth   Middle age   Later life

SURVIVING OLD AGE As we age, we all undergo inevitable physiological changes, some of which we can counteract or at least slow down. Those who live longer tend to "look young" as the effects of aging unfold at a slower rate than normal.

A. SKIN: In our youth, the skin is full of moisture and very elastic; retain that youthful look by using moisturizers and avoiding the sun.

B. HEARING: With every passing year, the range of frequencies we can hear reduces, especially higher pitches.

C. SMELL: We tend to lose our sense of smell as we age, and our taste buds become increasingly dulled.

D. BONES: Aging skeletons lose their density and become brittle as calcium levels drop. A diet rich in Vitamin D and calcium will slow this process.

E. RESPIRATORY SYSTEM: The lungs can lose their elasticity as you age, leading to shortness of breath, fatigue, and increased risk of infection. Avoid smoking, and get regular exercise.

F. HAIR: Graying occurs as pigment cells in the hair follicles die off. When the follicles themselves atrophy (waste away), the hair falls out. Hormonal differences between men and women result in differing patterns of baldness between the sexes.

G. SIGHT: The lenses in our eyes slowly lose their ability to "accommodate"— that is, focus. As the focal length shortens, glasses are needed for reading. The pupils also shrink and it becomes difficult to see in lower light.

H. NERVOUS SYSTEM: Reaction times slow as signals take longer to pass from the nerves to the muscles.

I. MEMORY: Brain cells start to die from your early 20s, so by the time you reach your senior years, short-term memory will usually be affected.

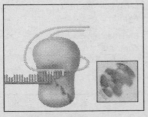

GENETIC LIMITS Human cells tend to divide only 50 times, and the average human cell lives two years, so that's a limit of 100 years. Even for those who age 15% slower than normal, that's age 115. So, living beyond 115 is difficult at present, due to the inevitable aging process. Some of the research into extending life is being directed on "telomeres"—the molecular strands attached to our chromosomes (pictured) that get shorter as we age.

How Long Can We Live?

25 Dina Manfredini
Born: Apr. 4, 1897
Birthplace: **Italy**
Aged: **115**

24 Marie Brémont
Born: Apr. 25, 1886
Birthplace: **France**
Died: Jun. 6, 2001
Age: **115**

23 Maud Farris-Luse
Born: Jan. 21, 1887
Birthplace: **U.S.A.**
Died: Mar. 18, 2002
Age: **115**

22 Hendrikje van Andel-Schipper
Born: June 29, 1890
Birthplace: **Netherlands**
Died: Aug. 30, 2005
Age: **115**

21 Augusta Holtz
Died: Aug. 3, 1871
Birthplace: **Germany**
Died: Oct. 24, 1986
Age: **115**

20 Susie Gibson
Born: Oct. 31, 1890
Birthplace: **U.S.A.**
Died: Feb. 16, 2006
Age: **115**

19 Maria de Jesus
Born: Sep. 10, 1893
Birthplace: **Portugal**
Died: Jan. 2, 2009
Age: **115**

18 Julie Winnefred Bertrand
Born: Sep. 16, 1891
Birthplace: **Canada**
Died: Jan. 18, 2007
Age: **115**

17 Bettie Wilson
Born: Sep. 13, 1890
Birthplace: **U.S.A.**
Died: Feb. 13, 2006
Age: **115**

16 Emiliano Mercado del Toro
Born: Aug. 21, 1891
Birthplace: **Puerto Rico**
Died: Jan. 24, 2007
Age: **115**

15 Gertrude Baines
Born: Apr. 6, 1894
Birthplace: **U.S.A.**
Died: Sep. 11, 2009
Age: **115**

14 Margaret Skeete
Born: Oct. 27, 1878
Birthplace: **U.S.A.**
Died: May 7, 1994
Age: **115**

13 Mary Ann Rhodes
Born: Aug. 12, 1882
Birthplace: **Canada**
Died: Mar. 3, 1998
Age: **115**

12 Edna Parker
Born: Apr. 20, 1893
Birthplace: **U.S.A.**
Died: Nov. 26, 2008
Age: **115**

11 Charlotte Hughes
Born: Aug. 1, 1877
Birthplace: **UK**
Died: Mar. 17, 1993
Age: **115**

10 Christian Mortensen
Born: Aug. 16, 1882
Birthplace: **Denmark**
Died: Apr. 25, 1998
Age: **115**

9 **Besse Cooper**
Born: Aug. 26, 1896
Birthplace: **U.S.A.**
Age: **115**

8 **Maggie Barnes**
Born: Mar. 6, 1882
Birthplace: **U.S.A.**
Died: Jan. 19, 1998
Age: **115**

7 **Elizabeth Bolden**
Born: Aug. 15, 1890
Birthplace: **U.S.A.**
Died: Dec. 11, 2006
Age: **116**

6 **Tane Ikai**
Born: Jan. 18, 1879
Birthplace: **Japan**
Died: Jul. 12, 1995
Age: **116**

5 **Maria Esther de Capovilla**
Born: Sep. 14, 1889
Birthplace: **Ecuador**
Died: Aug. 27, 2006
Age: **116**

4 **Marie-Louise Meilleur**
Born: Aug. 29, 1880
Birthplace: **Canada**
Died: Apr. 16, 1998
Age: **117**

3 **Lucy Hannah**
Born: Jul. 16, 1875
Birthplace: **U.S.A.**
Died: Mar. 21, 1993
Age: **117**

2 **Sarah Knauss**
Born: Sep. 24, 1880
Birthplace: **U.S.A.**
Died: Dec. 30, 1999
Age: **119**

1 **Jeanne Calment**
Born: Feb. 21, 1875
Birthplace: **France**
Died: Aug. 4, 1997
Age: **122**

PROOF OF AGE Living to a grand old age is one thing, but proving it is another. To qualify for a GWR certificate, claimants must provide sufficient proof of birth (preferably with an original certificate, issued at the time of birth; later-life certification does not count). Supporting documentation is then required to place a claimant at given key points in their life—so, national service papers, census reports, marriage certificates, medical reports, and so on. Note: Passports only really provide confirmation of nationality, not proof of age.

Will you be joining the 110+ club? The chart below details the chances of survival of supercentenarians (those over 110 years). It reveals that the longevity of Jeanne Calment, the **oldest person ever** (see p. 107) is an anomaly, with the next oldest at 119 (only one person), two at 117, and three at 116.

SUPERCENTENARIAN SURVIVAL RATES

Age	Surviving	Deaths	Survival rate		Mortality rate	
			Yearly	Cumulative	Yearly	Cumulative
123	0		0.00%			
122	1	−1	50.00%	0.00%	100.00%	100.00%
121	1	0	100.00%	0.07%	0.00%	99.92%
120	1	0	100.00%	0.07%	0.00%	99.92%
119	2	−1	50.00%	0.07%	50.00%	99.92%
118	2	0	100.00%	0.15%	0.00%	99.84%
117	4	−2	50.00%	0.15%	50.00%	99.84%
116	7	−3	57.14%	0.30%	42.86%	99.70%
115	23	−16	30.43%	0.52%	69.57%	99.48%
114	78	−55	29.49%	1.70%	70.51%	98.30%
113	167	−89	46.71%	5.77%	53.29%	94.23%
112	354	−187	47.18%	12.36%	52.82%	87.64%
111	683	−329	51.83%	26.20%	48.17%	73.80%
110	1,351	−668	50.56%	50.56%	49.44%	49.44%

To reach a record-breaking age, you will need to be a "longevity hybrid"—someone optimized for endurance, just as runners are optimized for strength. A diet low in fat and calories, and high in fresh fruit and vegetables, will help, as will regular, moderate exercise, a stimulated mind, and a positive attitude to life. However, you must also be capable of avoiding or managing disease and disability (and avoiding debilitating falls).

An increasing number of humans and the effects of better health care across a lifetime mean that we can and should expect humans to live longer in the future—and that a 130-year life span is possible.

OLDEST . . .

Living mixed twins Pauline Shipp Love and Paul Gerald Shipp (both U.S.A.) were born on April 22, 1911. As of March 23, 2012 they were 100 years 11 months 1 day old.

As of April 16, 2012, the **highest aggregate age for two siblings** was 213 years 3 months 27 days for sisters Marjorie Phyllis Ruddle (b. April 21, 1907) and Dorothy Richards (b. December 15, 1903; both UK). Dorothy lives in Stamford, Lincolnshire, while Marjorie resides in Peterborough in Cambridgeshire (both UK).

Abseiler Intrepid pensioner Doris Cicely Long, MBE (UK, b. May 18, 1914) completed a descent of 197 ft. (60 m) from the top of Millgate House in Portsmouth, UK, on May 21, 2011, at the age of 97 years 3 days.

Acrobatic salsa dancer (female) The UK's Sarah Paddy Jones (b. July 1, 1934) won first prize on Spain's TV talent show *Tú Sí Que Vales* (*You Are Worth It*) on December 2, 2009, at the age of 75 years 5 months 1 day.

Act to release a new album Australian artist Smoky Dawson (1913–2008) released a new album of original songs, *Homestead of My Dreams*, at the age of 92 years 4 months 14 days. The album went on sale on August 22, 2005.

On September 17, 2011, at the age of 87 years 5 months 14 days, 1950s screen favorite Doris Day (U.S.A., née Doris Kappelhoff, b. April 3, 1924) became the **oldest act to achieve a UK Top 10 album with a new recording** when *My Heart* peaked at No. 9.

The star's 29th studio release featured eight new recordings, along with four songs that had appeared on earlier albums.

Author to have a first book published Bertha Wood's (UK, b. June 20, 1905) *Fresh Air and Fun: The Story of a Blackpool Holiday Camp* was published on her 100th birthday.

OLDEST LIVING MAN Jiroemon Kimura (Japan) was born on April 19, 1897, and celebrated his 115th birthday in 2012. Seen here with GWR's Frank Foley, he is the only man verifiably born in the 19th century who is still alive today.

OLDEST LIVING PERSON Besse Cooper (U.S.A., b. August 26, 1896)—seen here with GWR consultant Robert Young—became the world's oldest person on June 21, 2011, at the age of 114 years 10 months. As of May 11, 2012, she was 115 years 250 days old. Like Jiroemon Kimura, the **oldest living man** (see above), she puts her exceptional longevity down to a good diet and no junk food.

FACT: The year that Besse was born saw the staging of the first Olympic Games held in modern times.

OLDEST LIVING DWARF Lowell DeForest Mason (U.S.A.) was born on August 14, 1937 and currently resides in Missouri, U.S.A. He was at the age of 74 years 6 months 2 days as of February 16, 2012.

BASE jumper James Talbot Guyer (U.S.A., b. June 16, 1928) parachuted off the 486-ft.-high (148-m) Perrine Bridge near Twin Falls, Idaho, U.S.A., on August 2, 2002, at 74 years 1 month 17 days old.

Bodybuilder (male) Competitive bodybuilder Raymond "Ray" Moon (Australia, b. 1929) performed at the NABBA International Bodybuilding Figure and Fitness Championships in Melbourne, Australia, on May 23, 2010, at the age of 81.

Ballroom dancer Frederick Salter (UK, b. February 13, 1911) passed his IDTA Gold Bar Level 3 exams in Latin and Ballroom with Honours, aged 100 years 8 months 2 days, in London, UK, on October 15, 2011.

Darts player As of February 24, 2012, Candy Miller (UK, b. October 21, 1920) was still competing in darts matches in the Bournemouth and District Ladies Darts League, in Parkstone, Bournemouth, UK, at the age of 91 years 123 days.

Movie director Manoel de Oliveira (Portugal, b. December 11, 1908) began directing in 1931. His most recent movie was *O Estranho Caso de Angélica* (*The Strange Case of Angelica*, Portugal/Spain/France/Brazil, 2010).

Indoor bowls player As of March 1, 2012, Jean Ella Cowles (UK, b. August 31, 1917) was a member of Spalding and District Indoor Bowls Club in Spalding, Lincolnshire, UK, at the age of 94 years 183 days.

Lifeguard (active) Louis Demers (U.S.A., b. September 3, 1923) of Quincy, Illinois, U.S.A., was 88 years 6 months 4 days old as of March 7, 2012. He has been a lifeguard since 1954.

MOBO winner In 1998, B. B. King (U.S.A., b. Riley B. King, September 16, 1925) picked up the Music of Black Origin (MOBO) Award

OLDEST LIVING FEMALE TWINS Evelyn Middleton (above far left) and Edith Ritchie (left; both UK) were born on November 15, 1909. They are pictured celebrating their 102nd birthdays and (below) in their youth.

for Lifetime Achievement at the age of 73. Over a recording career stretching back to 1949, King has won an impressive 16 Grammy Awards, including a Lifetime Achievement Award in 1987. His 1969 track "The Thrill is Gone" has also received a Grammy Hall of Fame Award.

Nobel laureate Professor Francis Peyton Rous (U.S.A., 1879–1970) shared the Physiology or Medicine prize in 1966 at the age of 87.

Patient Jeanne Calment (France, 1875–1997)—the **oldest person ever**—was at the age of 114 years 11 months when she had a hip operation in January 1990.

Storekeeper Jack Yaffe (UK) ran his hardware store in Prestwich, Greater Manchester, UK, for 78 years. He retired in January 2012, on his 103rd birthday.

Person to complete a marathon Dimitrion Yordanidis (Greece) completed a 26-mile (42-km) marathon in Athens, Greece, on October 10, 1976, at the age of 98. He finished the race in 7 hr. 33 min.

On December 12, 2010, at the age of 92 years 19 days, Gladys Burrill (U.S.A.) completed the Honolulu Marathon in Hawaii, U.S.A., making her the **oldest woman to complete a marathon**. Burrill completed the race in 9 hr. 53 min. 16 sec.

Person to swim the English Channel Roger Allsopp (UK, b. April 6, 1941) swam the Channel from Shakespeare Beach, Dover, UK, to Calais, France, in 17 hr. 51 min. 19 sec., at 70 years 4 months 24 days old, on August 30, 2011.

The **oldest woman to swim the English Channel** is the UK's Linda Ashmore (b. October 21, 1946), who crossed from England to France in 15 hr. 11 min., at 60 years 9 months 29 days old, on August 19, 2007.

OLDEST NEWSPAPER DELIVERY PERSON
Ted Ingram (UK, b. February 14, 1920) was still delivering the *Dorset Echo* in Weymouth, Dorset, UK, at the age of 92 years 8 days, as of February 22, 2012.

The oldest female newspaper delivery person, Joyce Pugh (UK, b. September 10, 1931), delivers the *Shropshire Star* in Shrewsbury, Shropshire, UK. She was 80 years 6 months 3 days old as of March 13, 2012.

FACT: During his long career, Ted has delivered around 500,000 newspapers!

OLDEST ACTIVE FLIGHT ATTENDANT As of May 21, 2012, at the age of 88 years 14 days, Robert Reardon (U.S.A., b. May 7, 1924, near left) was still working as a flight attendant with Delta Air Lines. He took up his first post as a flight attendant in 1951.

Ronald "Ron" Byrd Akana (U.S.A., b. September 8, 1928, far left) has enjoyed the **longest career as a flight attendant**. He joined United Airlines on December 16, 1949, and, as of March 22, 2012, had worked for 62 years 3 months 6 days.

OLDEST GYMNAST Johanna Quaas (Germany, b. November 20, 1925) is a regular competitor in the amateur competition Landesseniorenspiele, staged in Saxony, Germany.

She performed a floor-and-beam routine on the set of *Lo Show dei Record* in Rome, Italy, in April 2012 and can still perform cartwheels at the age of 86!

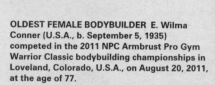

OLDEST FEMALE BODYBUILDER E. Wilma Conner (U.S.A., b. September 5, 1935) competed in the 2011 NPC Armbrust Pro Gym Warrior Classic bodybuilding championships in Loveland, Colorado, U.S.A., on August 20, 2011, at the age of 77.

Solo parachute jumper Milburn Hart (U.S.A.) made a solo parachute jump near Bremerton National Airport, Washington, U.S.A., on February 18, 2005, at the age of 96 years 2 months 1 day.

Sylvia Brett (UK) was 80 years 5 months 13 days old when she parachuted over Cranfield in Bedfordshire, UK, on August 23, 1986, making her the **oldest woman to make a solo parachute jump**.

Wing walker At the age of 91 years 16 days, Thomas Lackey (UK, b. May 22, 1920) completed a wing walk across the English Channel from Lydd Airport, Kent, UK, to Calais Airport, France, on June 7, 2011.

FACT: Johanna was a relatively late starter—she didn't take up gymnastics until she was in her 30s.

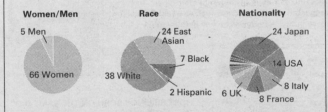
BIRTHS

HEAVIEST . . .

Birth In February 2012, the birth of baby Chun Chun to mother Wang Yujuan in Henan Province, China, made headlines because of his impressive weight of 15.5 lb (7.03 kg)—twice the average birth weight. As remarkable as this delivery was, it pales when compared with the heaviest birth of all time. On January 19, 1879, Anna Bates (Canada, pictured on page 111), who measured 7 ft. 5.5 in. (2.27 m) tall, gave birth to a boy weighing 23 lb. 12 oz. (10.8 kg)!

Twins The world's heaviest twins, with a combined weight of 27 lb. 12 oz. (12.58 kg), were born to Mary Ann Haskin of Fort Smith, Arkansas, U.S.A., on February 20, 1924.

Triplets The heaviest triplets ever weighed 24 lb. (10.9 kg) and were born to Mary McDermott (UK) on November 18, 1914.

Quadruplets Two girls and two boys, with a total weight of 22 lb. 15.75 oz. (10.42 kg), were born to Tina Saunders (UK) at St. Peters Hospital in Chertsey, UK, on February 7, 1989.

Quintuplets There have been two recorded cases of quintuplets with a combined birth weight of 25 lb. (11.35 kg): on June 7, 1953, to Liu Saulian (China) and on December 30, 1956, to a Mrs. Kamalammal (India).

MOST SETS OF MIXED TWINS Lightning struck twice for mixed-race parents Dean Durrant and Alison Spooner (both UK) when, in March 2009, Alison gave birth to a second set of twins with entirely different skin colorations: Leah and Miya. In 2001, she gave birth to the dark-skinned Hayleigh and fair-skinned Layren. Dr. Sarah Jarvis, from the UK's Royal College of General Practitioners, has suggested that the odds of such an event happening twice in this way "must be one in millions."

MOST SIBLINGS BORN ON THE SAME DAY There are only five verified examples of a mother producing two sets of twins with the same birthdays in different years. The most recent case is that of Tracey Bageban (UK), who gave birth to Armani Jafar and Diego Mohamed on February 27, 2008, and Elisia Christina and Dolcie Falimeh three years later on February 27, 2011.

FACT: The odds of a mixed-race couple having just *one* set of twins of differing color are around 500 to 1.

HEAVIEST & LONGEST BIRTH Giantess Anna Bates (Canada), who was 7 ft. 5.5 in. (2.27 m) tall, gave birth to a 23-lb. 12-oz. (10.8-kg), 30-in.-long (76-cm) boy on January 19, 1879.

LIGHTEST . . .

Birth The lowest confirmed birth weight for a surviving infant is 9.17 oz. (260 g), in the case of Rumaisa Rahman (U.S.A.), who was born at Loyola University Medical Center, Maywood, Illinois, U.S.A., on September 19, 2004, after a gestation period of 25 weeks 6 days.

Twins The lowest combined birth weight recorded for a surviving set of twins is 1 lb. 13.57 oz. (847 g) in the case of Hiba (1 lb. 4.4 oz.; 580 g) and Rumaisa (9.17 oz.; 260 g) Rahman, who were born to Mahajabeen Shaik (India). The twins were born by Cacsarean section (or C-section).

Triplets With a combined weight of 3 lb. 0.8 oz. (1,385 g), Peyton (1 lb. 4.6 oz.; 585 g), Jackson (14.8 oz.; 420g), and Blake (13.4 oz.; 380g) Coffey (all U.S.A.) became the lightest triplets to survive when they were born by Caesarean section at the University of Virginia Hospital (U.S.A.) on November 30, 1998.

HEAVIEST WOMAN TO GIVE BIRTH Donna Simpson of New Jersey, U.S.A., weighed 532 lb. (241 kg) when she gave birth to her daughter Jacqueline on February 13, 2007, at Akron City Hospital in Akron, Ohio, U.S.A. Jacqueline was born after a gestation period of 37 weeks 4 days, and weighed 8 lb. 14 oz. (4 kg) at birth. Donna, who wears size XXXXXXXL clothing and was reportedly consuming around 15,000 calories a day at one point, has embarked on a diet since giving birth to Jacqueline. She had shed around 85 lb. (38.5 kg) by December 2011.

MOST . . .

Prolific mother The wife of Russian peasant Feodor Vassilyev bore a total of 69 children. In 27 pregnancies from 1725 to 1765, she had 16 pairs of twins (the **most sets of twins born**), seven sets of triplets, and four sets of quadruplets (the **most sets of quadruplets born**). See page 113 for more information.

The **most sets of triplets born** to one mother is 15, by Maddalena Granata (Italy, b. 1839).

Children delivered at a single birth Nine children (nonuplets) were born to Geraldine Brodrick in Sydney, Australia, on June 13, 1971. Unfortunately, none of the children lived for longer than six days.

Children delivered at a single birth to survive Nadya Suleman (U.S.A.) gave birth to six boys and two girls at the Kaiser Permanente Medical Center, Bellflower, California, U.S.A., on January 26, 2009. The babies were conceived with the aid of *in vitro* fertilization (IVF) treatment and were nine weeks premature when they were delivered by Caesarean section.

HEAVIEST TRIPLETS AT BIRTH (CURRENT) Shown from left to right are Gabriel James, Lilliana Mary, and Nathan Andrew Kupresak (all Canada), who had a combined weight of 17 lb. 2.7 oz. (7.7 kg) when they were born on November 6, 2008, at Mount Sinai Hospital in Toronto, Canada. The triplets were born after a gestation period of 37 weeks, four weeks longer than the average period for triplets. Two years after their birth, there was still a significant size difference between the three children, with Gabriel and Lilliana weighing approximately 24 lb. (10.8 kg) each and Nathan weighing around 36 lb. (15.4 kg).

TRIPLET FACTS AND FIGURES

• More than 90% of triplets are born prematurely.

• Women who have children after the age of 30, especially those who use fertility treatment, have an increased chance of having triplets. Taller or heavier women are also more likely to give birth to triplets.

• Identical triplets have 100% of their DNA in common. They are of the same sex and the color of their hair and eyes is the same, as is their blood type, although their fingerprints will be different.

Check out more young achievers on p. 187.

Caesarean sections Kristina House of California, U.S.A., gave birth to 11 children (six girls and five boys), all by Caesarean section, between May 15, 1979, and November 20, 1998.

Premature James Elgin Gill was born to Brenda and James Gill (both Canada) on May 20, 1987. He was 128 days premature and weighed 1 lb. 6 oz. (624 g).

OLDEST . . .

Father Les Colley (Australia, 1898–1998) had his ninth child to his third wife at the age of 92 years 10 months. Colley met Oswald's Fijian mother in 1991 through a dating agency.

MOST CHILDREN BORN TO ONE MOTHER

The peasant Feodor Vassilyev of Shuya, Russia, lived between ca. 1707 and ca. 1782 and fathered 69 children with his first wife (whose name is not recorded). The births came in 27 confinements and consisted of four quadruplets, seven triplets, and 16 twins!*

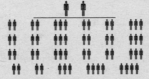

The case was reported to the government in Moscow on February 27, 1782, by the Monastery of Nikolsk, where the births were recorded. The report revealed that Vassilyev married a second time and fathered another 18 children in eight confinements of two triplets and six twins:

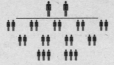

By the time of the 1782 report, Vassilyev was in "perfect health" at the age of 75 and boasted a total of 87 surviving children!

The sexes of the children were not reported

You're never too old! Turn to p. 113.

Mother to give birth Following IVF treatment, Maria del Carmen Bousada Lara (Spain, 1940–2009) gave birth by Caesarean section to twin boys, Christian and Pau, at the age of 66 years 358 days in Barcelona, Spain, on December 29, 2006. This achievement also gave Maria the record for the **oldest mother to give birth to twins**.

On August 20, 1997, a baby was born to Dawn Brooke (UK) who, at the age of 59 years, became the **oldest mother to conceive naturally** (i.e., without the aid of fertility treatments). She conceived him accidentally, having ovulated past her last period.

Woman to give birth to her grandchildren At the age of 56 years, Jacilyn Dalenberg of Wooster, Ohio, U.S.A., acted as surrogate mother for her daughter, Kim Coseno (U.S.A.), and carried and delivered her own grandchildren: three girls. The triplets were delivered—two months premature—by Caesarean section.

WEDDINGS

BRIDAL WEAR

Most expensive wedding dress Jeweler Martin Katz and bridal couturier Renee Strauss (both U.S.A.) created a U.S. $12-million gown bedecked with 150 carats' worth of diamonds for the Luxury Brands Lifestyle Bridal Show held on February 26, 2006, at the Ritz-Carlton in Marina del Rey, California, U.S.A.

MOST EXPENSIVE WEDDING The wedding of Vanisha Mittal, daughter of billionaire Lakshmi Mittal, to investment banker Amit Bhatia (all India) was a wallet-busting affair. The six-day event, held in Versailles, France, in 2004, included a reenactment of the couple's courtship and an engagement ceremony at the Palace of Versailles—the only private function ever to have been held there. The entertainers at the reception included Shah Rukh Khan and Kylie Minogue. The bride's father picked up a bill for U.S. $55 million.

Most crystals on a wedding dress Özden Gelinlik Moda Tasarım Ltd. (Turkey) created a wedding dress adorned with 45,024 crystals that was presented at the Forum Istanbul Shopping Mall, in Istanbul, Turkey, on January 29, 2011.

Longest wedding dress train Measuring 1.54 miles (2.48 km), the longest wedding train—created by Lichel van den Ende (Netherlands)—was presented and measured in Zoetermeer, Netherlands, on December 22, 2009.

Longest wedding veil At the wedding of Sandra Mechleb to Chady Abi Younis (both Lebanon) in Arnaoon, Lebanon, on October 18, 2009, Sandra wore a veil 2 miles (3.35 km) long.

LARGEST UNDERWATER WEDDING The marriage ceremony between Francesca Colombi and Giampiero Giannoccaro (both Italy) was attended by 261 divers at an event organized by the company Mares SpA (Italy) at the Morcone beach, Capoliveri, Elba, Italy, on June 12, 2010. The bride and groom were able to communicate by watches provided by Mares with a special "yes" and "no" function on their screens. The mayor of Capoliveri, who conducted the ceremony, was able to communicate with the couple using waterproof plastic boards on which prewritten text had been inscribed.

CAKES

Most expensive wedding cake slice A piece of the Duke and Duchess of Windsor's 1937 wedding cake sold at Sotheby's, New York, U.S.A., on February 27, 1998 for U.S. $29,900 to Benjamin and Amanda Yin of San Francisco, U.S.A.

Oldest wedding cake Two pieces of the wedding cake of Queen Victoria and Prince Albert, preserved since their wedding day on February 10, 1840, went on display at the Drawings Gallery, Windsor Castle, Windsor, UK, for the first time on April 27, 2007. On the opening day of the exhibition, which celebrated royal marriages, the cake was 167 years 2 months 17 days old.

OLDEST . . .

Bride At the age of 102, Minnie Munro (Australia) married 83-year-old Dudley Reid (both Australia) at Point Clare, New South Wales, Australia, on May 31, 1991.

Bridegroom Harry Stevens became the oldest bridegroom at the age of 103 when he married Thelma Lucas (both U.S.A.), then 84 years old, at the Caravilla Retirement Home in Wisconsin, U.S.A., on December 3, 1984.

Bridesmaid On March 31, 2007, Edith Gulliford (UK, b. October 12, 1901; d. April 29, 2008) was bridesmaid at the wedding of Kyra Harwood and James Lucas (both UK) at Commissioner's House, Chatham, UK, at the age of 105 years 171 days.

Best man Gerald W Pike (U.S.A., b. October 12, 1910) served as best man at the marriage of Nancy Lee Joustra and Clifford Claire Hill (both U.S.A.) at the age of 93 years 166 days on March 26, 2004, at Kent County in Michigan, U.S.A.

7.5 tons

HEAVIEST WEDDING CAKE Weighing a belt-busting 7.5 tons, or 15,032 lb. (6.818 tonnes), the largest wedding cake was displayed during the New England bridal showcase at the Mohegan Sun Hotel and Casino, Uncasville, Connecticut, U.S.A., on February 8, 2004. The seven-tiered cake could have fed 59,000 people and weighed more than a bull elephant. It was created by the Mohegan Sun's chef Lynn Mansel and a team of 57 chefs and "pastry artisans." Two fork-lift trucks were used to help raise each tier.

Humans

Couple to marry (combined age) On February 1, 2002, François Fernandez (France, b. April 17, 1906) and Berthe Andrée "Madeleine" Francineau (France, b. July 15, 1907) exchanged marriage vows at the rest home Le Foyer du Romarin, Clapiers, France, at the age of 96 years 290 days and 94 years 201 days, respectively. Their aggregate age at the time of the ceremony totaled 191 years 126 days.

UNUSUAL WEDDINGS

Most wedding guests On September 7, 1995, more than 150,000 people witnessed the wedding of V. N. Sudhakaran to N. Sathyalakshmi (both India). The ceremony—shown on screens at the 50-acre (20-ha) grounds in Madras, India—was followed by the **largest wedding reception!**

First zero-gravity wedding Erin Finnegan and Noah Fulmor (both U.S.A.) were sky high when they got married on June 23, 2009—their weightless wedding took place aboard *G-Force One*, a modified Boeing 727-200.

Most weddings in a TV soap opera A total of 79 wedding ceremonies have been celebrated on the British TV soap opera *Coronation Street*. The first took place on March 8, 1961.

LARGEST DOG WEDDING Some people even want their pets to get hitched! A group of 178 pooch pairs wed at the "Bow Wow Vows" event set up by the Aspen Grove Lifestyle Center (U.S.A.) on May 19, 2007.

LARGEST MASS WEDDING CEREMONY IN A PRISON On June 14, 2000, a group of 120 inmates of Carandiru prison, São Paulo, Brazil, married their fiancées in a mass ceremony organized by prison officers and volunteers from 19 local churches.

Although the brides wore traditional white dresses, the grooms were required to wear their prison trousers along with formal jackets and ties.

HIGHEST MARRIAGE RATES

Some nations are more in love with the idea of marriage than others. Below is a list of the countries with the highest marriage rates. (Number of marriages per 1,000 population; figures for 2009 or last available year.)

Rank	Country	Rate
10	Barbados	0.1
9	Jordan	10.4
8	Bermuda	11.2
7	Iran	11.3
6	Mongolia	12.4
5	Guam	13.3
4	Tajikistan	13.7
3	British Virgin Islands	19.6
2	Antigua & Barbuda	21.7
1	Virgin Islands (U.S.)	35.8

LOWEST MARRIAGE RATES

Marriage isn't for everyone, of course. Here's a list of those nations who don't care so much for the sound of wedding bells ...

Rank	Country	Rate
1	Colombia	.7
2	Qatar	.2
3	Botswana	2.5
4	Venezuela	2.5
5	Peru	2.7
6	St. Lucia	2.8
7	Argentina	3.0
8	Andorra	3.1
9	Chile	3.2
10	Slovenia	3.3

Source: The Economist

Most couples married underwater simultaneously On Valentine's Day 2001 (February 14), 34 couples from 22 countries exchanged wedding vows at the same time, 32 ft. 9 in. (10 m) underwater near Kradan Island, Southern Thailand. The submarine service was organized by Trang Chamber of Commerce and Thai Airways International.

First robot wedding A robot named I-Fairy conducted the wedding ceremony between robotics enthusiasts Tomohiro Shibata and Satoko Inoue (both Japan) in Tokyo, Japan, on May 16, 2010.

BODY PARTS

Longest tongue Stephen Taylor (UK) holds the record for the longest tongue, which stretches 3.86 in. (9.8 cm) from the tip to the middle of his closed top lip. It was measured at Westwood Medical Centre in Coventry, UK, on February 11, 2009.

The **woman with the longest tongue** is Chanel Tapper (U.S.A.). Her lengthy licker was found to be 3.8 in. (9.75 cm) from the tip to the middle of the lip when measured in California, U.S.A., on September 29, 2010.

Most teeth As of October 17, 2008, both Kanchan Rajawat (India) and Luca Meriano (Italy) could boast a more-than-full set of 35 adult teeth.

Oldest person to grow a new tooth Spare a thought for Brian Titford (Australia, b. January 14, 1933): in March 2009, two of his upper wisdom teeth erupted when he was 76 years old. His dentist subsequently removed the teeth to restore the stability of Brian's denture.

Youngest person to have a wisdom tooth extracted Matthew Adams (U.S.A., b. November 19, 1992) had his lower two wisdom teeth

removed at Midland Oral and Maxillofacial Surgery in Michigan, U.S.A., on October 24, 2002. He was at the age of just 9 years 339 days.

GREATEST EXTERNAL FOOT ROTATION
Moses Lanham (U.S.A.) turns heads when he turns his feet around. He rotated them outward, through an angle of 120 degrees, on the set of *Lo Show dei Record* in Milan, Italy, on March 10, 2011. On the same day, Moses also achieved the record for the **fastest time to walk 20 m (65.6 ft.) with the feet facing backward**. He achieved the act of rapid reverse pedestrianism in a time of 19.59 seconds.

FACT: Moses is constantly being asked to show off his foot rotation at parties.

SNAPSHOT

• At 14 years old, Moses fell off some gym bars at school and landed awkwardly, with his feet bent and apparently broken. Surprisingly, he didn't find it too painful . . .

• After a lot of X-rays and tests, the doctors confirmed that Moses had a unique muscle and ligament makeup that he had probably endured since birth. It means he has the ability to turn his feet back to front.

• Moses' son can also bend his feet to an unusual degree.

44.6 in. high

TALLEST MOHICAN When it comes to Mohican hairstyles, one man's achievements tower above the rest. Kazuhiro Watanabe (Japan) had a mammoth 44.6-in. (113.5-cm) Mohican as of October 28, 2011. Kazuhiro's lofty achievement easily broke his own world record: on January 10, 2011, his Mohican had been measured at "just" 41.3 in. (105 cm) in Sapporo, Hokkaido, Japan—a hair-raising 9.8 in. (25 cm) taller than the previous record holder.

Most fingers and toes on a living person

The greatest number of fingers and toes on a living person is 25, comprising 12 fingers and 13 toes. Two Indian citizens hold this record: Pranamya Menaria (b. August 10, 2005) and Devendra Harne (b. January 9, 1995). This digital abundance is the result of the congenital conditions polydactyly (a multiplicity of finger or toe) and syndactyly (in which fingers or toes have become fused together).

Fewest toes Some members of the Wadomo tribe of the Zambezi Valley, Zimbabwe, and the Kalanga tribe of the eastern Kalahari Desert, Botswana, are born with only two toes. The three central toes are missing and the two outer toes are turned inward. The condition is passed down via a single mutated gene.

Largest feet ever Robert Wadlow (U.S.A., 1918–40), the **tallest man ever**, wore U.S. size 37AA shoes (UK size 36 or approximately a European size 75), equivalent to 18.5 in. (47 cm) in length.

Excluding cases of elephantiasis, the **largest feet on a living person** are those of Brahim Takioullah (Morocco), whose left foot measures 1 ft. 3 in. (38.1 cm) and right foot measures 1 ft. 2.76 in. (37.5 cm). He was measured in Paris, France, on May 24, 2011.

Longest fingernails ever (male) The fingernails of Melvin Boothe (U.S.A., 1948–2009) totaled 32 ft. 3.8 in. (9.85 m) when measured in Troy, Michigan, U.S.A., in May 2009.

When last measured in 2004, the fingernails on the left hand of Shridhar Chillal (India) totaled 23 ft. 1.5 in. (7.05 m) in length, the **longest fingernails on one hand**.

Longest fingernails ever (female) Lee Redmond (U.S.A.) began growing her fingernails in 1979 and nurtured them to a length of 28 ft. 4.5 in. (8.65 m), as verified in Madrid, Spain, on February 23, 2008. Sadly, in early 2009, Lee lost her nails in an automobile accident.

The current owner of the **longest fingernails (female)** is singer Chris "The Dutchess" Walton (U.S.A.). Her left fingernails total 10 ft. 2 in. (309.8 cm) and her right nails total 9 ft. 7 in. (292.1 cm)—an overall length of 19 ft. 9 in. (601.9 cm)—as measured in Las Vegas, Nevada, U.S.A., on February 21, 2011.

Longest eyeball pop Keith Smith (U.S.A.) kept his eyes popped out of their sockets for 53.01 seconds. The eye-watering record attempt took place in Madrid, Spain, on January 28, 2009.

Hairiest family Victor "Larry" Gomez, Gabriel "Danny" Ramos Gomez, Luisa Lilia De Lira Aceves, and Jesus Manuel Fajardo Aceves (all Mexico) are four members of a family of 19, spanning five generations, all of whom have a condition called congenital generalized hypertrichosis, characterized by excessive facial and torso hair. The women have a light-to-medium coat of hair, while the men have thick hair on around 98% of their bodies.

Longest hair (female) Xie Qiuping's (China) hair measured 18 ft. 5.54 in. (5.62 m) on May 8, 2004.

Longest beard ever The beard of Hans N. Langseth (Norway) measured 17 ft. 6 in. (5.33 m) at the time of his burial at Kensett, Iowa, in 1927, after 15 years' residence in the U.S.A. His record-breaking beard was presented to the Smithsonian Institution, Washington, D.C., U.S.A., in 1967.

The **longest beard on a living man** can be combed out to 8 ft. 2.5 in. (2.49 m). It belongs to Sarwan Singh (Canada), head priest of the Guru Nanak Sikh temple in Surrey, British Columbia, Canada.

Longest nose ever There are historical accounts that Thomas Wedders, who lived in England during the 1770s and was a member of a traveling circus, had a nose measuring 7.5 in. (19 cm).

The **longest nose on a living person** measures 3.46 in. (8.8 cm) and belongs to Mehmet Ozyurek (Turkey).

LONGEST HUMAN HAIRS

Hairs are threadlike, fine strands of protein (largely keratin, which is also a part of the finger- and toenails) that grow on every part of the body apart from a few areas, such as the soles, the palms, and the lips.

Eyelash	2.75 in. (6.99 cm)	Ear hair	7.1 in. (18.1 cm)
Arm hair	5.75 in. (14.61 cm)	Eyebrow	7.1 in. (18.1 cm)
Nipple hair	6 in. (15.16 cm)	Chest hair	9 in. (22.8 cm)
Leg hair	6.5 in. (16.51 cm)		

> **FACT:** In 2003, a peat farmer in Ireland discovered a 2,300-year-old corpse sporting a Mohican.

Stretchiest skin Garry Turner (UK) has a rare medical condition called Ehlers-Danlos Syndrome, a disorder of the connective tissues affecting the skin, ligaments, and internal organs. He is able to stretch the skin of his stomach to a distended length of 6.25 in. (15.8 cm). The condition makes the collagen that strengthens the skin, and determines its elasticity, defective. Its effects include a loosening of the skin and "hypermobility" of the joints.

BIZARRE BEAUTY

Most extensive scarification Women of the Tiv and Nuba peoples of Nigeria in west Africa endure extreme scarification rituals as part of a rite of passage (as in the case of the Nuba) or to accentuate their beauty. The scars are made using a knife or, more traditionally, stone or shards of glass or coconut shell. The deep wounds are rubbed with toxic plant juices to create swollen welts or "keloids."

Largest lip plates For the Surma people of Ethiopia, lip plates serve a financial purpose. The process of inserting these plates (made by the women themselves from local clay) begins around a year before marriage and the final size indicates the number of cattle required by the girl's family from her future husband for her hand. The plates can reach 6 in. (15 cm) in diameter, which would require a payment of 50 cattle.

Longest neck The maximum known extension of a human neck is 15.75 in. (40 cm). It was created by the successive fitting of copper coils—practiced by the women of the Padaung or Kareni tribe of Myanmar as a sign of beauty.

TATTOOS

Most tattooed person The acme of multilayered tattooing is represented by the chainsaw-juggling, unicycling, sword-swallowing Lucky Diamond Rich (Australia, b. New Zealand), who has spent more than 1,000 hours having his body modified. He began with a collection of colorful designs from around the world tattooed over his entire body. Lucky next opted for a 100% covering of black ink, including eyelids, the delicate skin between the toes, down into the ears, and even his gums. He is now being tattooed with white designs on top of the black, and colored designs on top of the white.

Most tattooed senior citizen Tom Leppard (UK, b. ca. 1934) has 99.9% of his body covered in tattoos. Tom opted for a leopard-skin design, with all the skin between the dark spots tattooed saffron yellow. Having lived alone in a cabin on the Isle of Skye, UK, for 20 years, he moved to one of the island's villages, Broadford, in 2008.

The **most tattooed female senior citizen** is Isobel Varley (UK, b. 1938), who had covered 93% of her body with tattoos, as revealed on the set of *Lo Show dei Record*, in Milan, Italy, on April 25, 2009.

Longest tattoo session (multiple people) Michael Cann (U.S.A.) tattooed multiple people in a marathon session lasting 35 hr. 8 min. at Skipass 2010 in Suffolk, Virginia, U.S.A., from November 18 to 19, 2011.

The **longest tattoo session by a team of two** lasted for 50 hours and was achieved by tattooist Tyson Turk and tattooee Chris Elliott (both U.S.A.) at the Tyson Turk Body Mod Studio, Texas, U.S.A., on September 9–11, 2011.

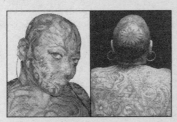

MOST TATTOOED WOMAN
Licensed medical practitioners determined on March 31, 2011, that Cynthia J. Martell (U.S.A.) had tattoos covering slightly more than 96% of her body. Cynthia—from Parker, Arizona, U.S.A.—was regularly tattooed for five years to attain her record-breaking skin coverage.

FACT: Cynthia's palms and the soles of her feet are the only areas of her body that have no tattoos.

INK-REDIBLE TATTOOS

• **Most bone tattoos:** As of April 27, 2011, Rick "Rico" Genest (Canada) had 139 bones tattooed on his body. By the same date, he also had the **most insect tattoos**: 176.

• **Most flag tattoos:** Guinness Rishi (India) was tattooed with 366 tattoos of flags between July 2009 and July 2011.

• **Most jigsaw-puzzle piece tattoos:** Artist The Enigma (U.S.A., aka Paul Lawrence) had 2,123 tattoos in the shape of jigsaw-puzzle pieces as of April 13, 2011.

Most tattoos in 24 hours by a single artist Hollis Cantrell (U.S.A.) performed 801 tattoos in 24 hours at Artistic Tattoo in Phoenix, Arizona, U.S.A., on November 16, 2008.

The **most tattoos by a single artist in eight hours** is 331 and was achieved by John McManus (U.S.A.) at Joker's Tattoo Studio in Louisiana, U.S.A., on October 31, 2008.

PIERCINGS

Most piercings in a lifetime (female) Since first receiving a skin piercing in January 1997, Elaine Davidson (Brazil/UK) had been pierced a total of 4,225 times as of June 8, 2006. The former restaurant owner is constantly adding and replacing jewelry, mostly in her face; this number reflects her repiercings.

Elaine also holds the record for the **most piercings in a single count**. On examination on May 4, 2000, she was found to have a total of 462 piercings: 192 piercings on her facial area, including ears, forehead, eyebrows, chin, nose, and tongue (30); and 56 piercings on her body, including the stomach and hands.

The **most pierced man** is Rolf Buchholz (Germany). Rolf had 453 piercings, including 158 around his lips, as of February 22, 2012.

MOST PIERCED TONGUE As of February 17, 2012, Francesco Vacca (U.S.A.) of Belleville, New Jersey, U.S.A., had 16 piercings in his tongue. Francesco actually wants to take all of his piercings out . . . but only so that he can space them out more efficiently. Then he's aiming to fit in double the amount!

SNAPSHOT

• Francesco's piercer, who also came along to the photo shoot, knows another GWR body mod legend—Lucky Diamond Rich.

• Francesco is a licensed bounty hunter in his home state of New Jersey, U.S.A.

Most 18-gauge surgical needle piercings Jeremy Stroud (U.S.A.) had 1,197 18-gauge surgical needle body piercings inserted into his body at the Tyson Turk Tattoo Studio in Arlington, Texas, U.S.A., on May 2, 2009. Jeremy broke the previous record with his back alone, which received 901 needles.

Most people pierced in one hour by one person Rhonda Polley (Australia) pierced 64 people at Body Pleasure Piercing Studio in Melbourne, Australia, on September 18, 2010.

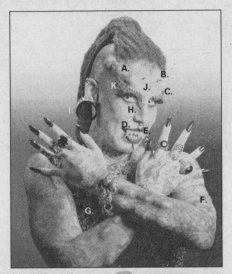

MOST BODY MODIFICATIONS María José Cristerna (Mexico) has undergone a total of 49 body modifications, including significant tattoo coverage, a range of transdermal implants on her forehead, chest, and arms, and multiple piercings in her eyebrows, lips, nose, tongue, earlobes, belly button, and nipples.

A. Subdermal (under the skin) forehead implants (and on the chest and forearms)
B. Exposed titanium horn implants
C. Ten piercings in left eyebrow
D. Dental implants (fangs)
E. Three lip piercings
F. Tattoos cover around 95% of her body
G. Five chest implants
H. One inner nose ring
I. Both earlobes expanded with a "septum"
J. Four upper-nose bars
K. Nine piercings in right eyebrow

FACT: María is sometimes referred to as "The Mexican Vampire Lady."

MOST FACIAL PIERCINGS
Axel Rosales, from Villa Maria, Argentina, had a total of 280 piercings on his face as of February 17, 2012. On the day of the GWR adjudication itself, the count came in at 271 piercings. Axel wanted a round number for his record, however, and so invited his piercer friend to add nine more to reach a final total of 280.

COSMETIC SURGERY

Tattoos, piercings, and body modifications aren't for everyone, of course. The quest for idealized beauty is seeing more and more people turn to cosmetic surgery. GWR takes a look at the world of nips and tucks.

Top five cosmetic surgical procedures

In 2011, there were more than 13 million cosmetic surgery operations in the U.S.A.:

 1. **Breast augmentation:** 307,180 (up 4% from 2010)

 2. **Nose reshaping:** 243,772 (down 3% from 2010)

 3. **Liposuction:** 204,702 (up 1% from 2010)

 4. **Eyelid surgery:** 196,286 (down 6% from 2010)

 5. **Face-lift:** 119,026 (up 5% from 2010)

 Kristina Ray (Russia) has had more than 100 silicone injections to boost the size of her lips.

Top five cosmetic "minimally invasive" procedures

When it comes to less dramatic surgery, botox implants are way out in front:

 1. **Botox:** 5,670,788 (up 5% from 2010)

 2. **"Soft-tissue" implants (such as collagen):** 1,891,158 (up 7% from 2010)

3. **Chemical peel:** 1,110,464 (down 3% from 2010)

 4. **Laser hair removal:** 1,078,612 (up 15% from 2010)

5. **Microdermabrasion:** 900,439 (up 9% from 2010)

(Source: American Society of Plastic Surgeons. Figures for 2011)

LARGEST . . .

HEAVIEST . . .

Man The heaviest person in medical history was Jon Brower Minnoch (U.S.A., 1941–83), who had lived with obesity since childhood. He was 6 ft. 1 in. (185 cm) tall and weighed 392 lb. (178 kg) in 1963, 700 lb. (317 kg) in 1966, and 975 lb. (442 kg) in September 1976.

In March 1978, Minnoch was admitted to University Hospital in Seattle, Washington, U.S.A., where consultant endocrinologist Dr. Robert Schwartz calculated that he must have weighed more than 1,400 lb. (635 kg), a great deal of which was water accumulation due to his congestive heart failure.

Woman Rosalie Bradford (U.S.A., 1943–2006) was claimed to have registered a peak weight of 1,200 lb. (544 kg) in January 1987.

The **heaviest woman living** is Pauline Potter (U.S.A.) of Sacramento, California, U.S.A., who weighed 643 lb. (291.6 kg) on May 13, 2010.

Twins Billy Leon (1946–79) and Benny Loyd (1946–2001) McCrary, alias McGuire (both U.S.A.), were average in size until the age of six. In November 1978, Billy and Benny weighed 743 lb. (337 kg) and 723 lb. (328 kg) respectively. Each brother had waists measuring 84 in. (213 cm) in circumference.

FACT: To date, Sharran has won four gold medals in sumo competitions around the world.

HEAVIEST SPORTSWOMAN The heaviest competing sportswoman is Sharran Alexander of London, UK, who weighed 448 lb. (203.21 kg) on December 15, 2011. Sharran actively competes around the world as an amateur sumo wrestler and is recognized by the British Sumo Federation in the UK. The 6-ft. (180-cm) sumo star is looking to retire from competition level in 2013, when she will turn 48 years old.

FACT: Sharran dines on pasta, meat pies, cornflakes, chicken, and rice—5,000 calories a day!

TALLEST . . .

Actor Matthew McGrory (U.S.A., 1973–2005) stood 7 ft. 6 in. (229 cm) tall. His movie career began in 1999 with *The Dead Hate the Living!* (U.S.A., 2000). He also featured in Tim Burton's *Big Fish* (U.S.A., 2003), playing the role of Karl the Giant alongside Ewan McGregor.

Two actors hold the title for the **tallest actor in a leading role**, with a height of 6 ft. 5 in. (194 cm). Christopher Lee (UK) has played most of the major horror characters in movies since 1958. Vince Vaughn (U.S.A.) had his first leading role in *Return to Paradise* (U.S.A., 1998).

Four women share the record for the **tallest actress in a leading role**. Margaux Hemingway (U.S.A., 1955–96), Sigourney Weaver (U.S.A.), Geena Davis (U.S.A.), and Brigitte Nielsen (Denmark) all stand 6 ft. (182 cm) tall.

Basketball player Suleiman Ali Nashnush (1943–91) was 8 ft. 0.25 in. (245 cm) tall when he played for the Libyan national team in 1962.

HEAVIEST PERSON TO FINISH A MARATHON Kelly Gneiting (U.S.A.) completed the 2011 Los Angeles Marathon weighing 400 lb. (181.44 kg) in California, U.S.A., on March 20, 2011. He finished in 9 hr. 48 min. 52 sec.

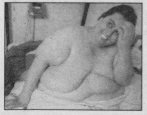

HEAVIEST MAN LIVING The heaviest living man is Manuel Uribe (Mexico), who weighed 980 lb. (444.6 kg) as of March 2012. At his absolute heaviest, in January 2006, Manuel peaked at 1,235 lb. (560 kg). Since then—and with some medical assistance—he has gradually been able to lose weight. Although he has been bed-bound since 2002, Manuel married his second wife, Claudia Solis, in 2008.

TALLEST TEENAGER EVER At the age of 17, Robert Wadlow (U.S.A., 1918–40) was 8 ft. 0.38 in. (245 cm) tall. And he became the tallest man ever—at 8 ft. 11.1 in. (272 cm) when measured on June 27, 1940. He's pictured far left, at the age of 18, with his family, and near left, at 10 years old, with an 11-year-old boy.

TALLEST LIVING TWINS Michael and James Lanier (U.S.A.) stand 7 ft. 3 in. (223 cm) tall. Ann and Claire Recht (U.S.A.) are the tallest female twins, at 6 ft. 7 in. (201 cm). Both sets of twins are identical.

Boxer The tallest professional boxer was Gogea Mitu (Romania, 1914–36). In 1935, he was 7 ft. 4 in. (223 cm) tall and weighed 327 lb. (148 kg). John Rankin, who won a fight in New Orleans, Louisiana, U.S.A., in November 1967, measured 7 ft. 4 in. tall, too. Jim Cully (Ireland), "The Tipperary Giant" who fought as a boxer and wrestled in the 1940s, was reputedly also this height.

Crown prince The current heir apparent to the Spanish throne, Príncipe de Asturias, Don Felipe de Borbón y Grecia (Spain), stands at 6 ft. 5.5 in. (197 cm).

Ice hockey player (NHL) At 6 ft. 9 in. (205 cm) tall, Zdeno Chára (Slovakia), of the Boston Bruins (U.S.A.), is the tallest player in National Hockey League history.

TALLEST LIVING WOMAN Yao Defen (China, left) was 7 ft. 7 in. (231 cm) tall when last documented. Zeng Jinlian (China) (1964–82) measured 8 ft. 1.6 in. (248 cm) when she died, making her the tallest woman ever.

TALLEST FEMALE TEENAGER Anna Haining Bates, born Anna Haining Swan (Canada, 1846–88), had grown to 7 ft. 11 in. (241 cm) by the time she was 15 years old. And as an adult, she set another world record—see p. 109.

Shoot to p. 493 for basketball world beaters.

Professional model Amazon Eve (U.S.A.) topped out at 6 ft. 7.4 in. (201 cm) when measured on February 25, 2011.

Grand Slam tennis player Ivo Karlović (Croatia) stands at 6 ft. 10 in. (208 cm), taller than any other Grand Slam player in history.

Juan Martín Del Potro (Argentina) measured 6 ft. 6 in. (198 cm) when he triumphed in the 2009 U.S. Open in New York, U.S.A., on September 14, 2009, making him the **tallest tennis player ever to win a Grand Slam**.

NATIONS BY HEIGHT

According to Statistics Netherlands, the Dutch are, on average, the world's **tallest citizens**, at 5 ft. 11.2 in. (181 cm); the **shortest citizens** are the Cambodians at 5 ft. 3.1 in. (160.3 cm). The average is 5 ft. 6.2 in. (168.1 cm).

Cambodians: 5 ft. 3.1 in.
Average: 5 ft. 6.2 in.
Dutch: 5 ft. 11.2 in.

NATIONS BY WEIGHT

Body Mass Index (BMI) is a calculation made by dividing your body weight by the square of your height. It was devised by Adolphe Quetelet (Belgium) in the 19th century to track the problem of obesity in the population. According to the Global Burden of Metabolic Risk Factors of Chronic Diseases Collaborating Group, Nauru in the South Pacific has the heaviest citizens, with an average BMI of 34.4; Bangladesh has the lightest citizens, averaging 20.4.

Bangladeshis: 20.4
Average: 25.5
Nauruans: 34.4

Sources: Interbasket; Global Burden of Metabolic Risk Factors of Chronic Diseases Collaborating Group

TALLEST MAN Sultan Kösen (Turkey) is the tallest person alive today. He was last measured in Ankara, Turkey, on February 8, 2011, at the age of 26 years, when he stood at an incredible 8 ft. 3 in. (251 cm).

This photo shoot took place on a basketball court in Manhattan, New York, U.S.A. Sultan is a big basketball fan—as a teenager, he was signed to the Galatasaray team but proved *too* big to play!

SHORTEST . . .

Shortest siblings Bridgette and Brad Jordan (both U.S.A.) are 2 ft. 3 in. (69 cm) and 3 ft. 2.5 in. (98 cm) tall respectively, a combined height of 5 ft. 5.5 in. (167 cm). Their reduced height is caused by the condition Majewski osteodysplastic primordial dwarfism type II. They both enjoy full and active lives; Bridgette wants to become a model.

SHORTEST MAN In February 2012, Guinness World Records traveled to the Nepalese capital of Kathmandu to investigate the case of a 72-year-old man supposedly standing 2 in. (5 cm) shorter than the current shortest living man, Junrey Balawing (Philippines) at 1 ft. 11.5 in., or 23.5 in. (59.9 cm). Following a series of measurements (see below) at the CIWEC Clinic Travel Medicine Center in the Lainchaur district, Chandra Bahadur Dangi from Reemkholi, Nepal, did indeed prove to be shorter, averaging 1 ft. 9.5 in., or 21.5 in. (54.6 cm). This also makes him the **shortest man ever measured.**

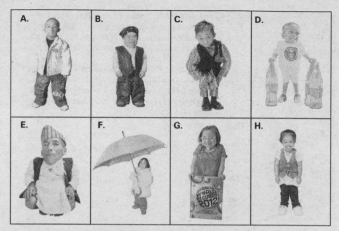

RECENT "SHORTEST" RECORD HOLDERS

A. He Pingping
2 ft. 5.3 in. (74.6 cm)

B. Edward "Niño" Hernández
2 ft. 3.6 in. (70.2 cm)

C. Khagendra Thapa Magar
2 ft. 2.4 in. (67 cm)

D. Junrey Balawing
1 ft. 11.5 in. (59.9 cm)

E. Chandra Bahadur Dangi
1 ft. 9.5 in. (54.6 cm)

F. Elif Kocaman
2 ft. 4.5 in. (72.6 cm)

G. Bridgette Jordan
2 ft. 3.0 in. (69 cm)

H. Jyoti Amge
2 ft. 0.7 in. (62.8 cm)

SHORTEST FACTS

Pictured here are the eight shortest record holders from the past five years.

• Over this period, the male record has fallen an incredible 7.8 in. (20 cm).

• In the female category, height has dropped nearly 4 in. (10 cm).

• At the (unconfirmed) age of 72, Chandra Bahadur Dangi, the current **shortest living man**, is by far the oldest person to attain this record.

• Extreme short stature is usually the result of a medical condition. Each person in our lineup has a form of dwarfism.

SHORTEST EVER...
Woman: Pauline Musters (Netherlands, left) measured exactly 24 in. (61 cm) in March 1895.
  Man: Prior to Dangi taking the title, Gul Mohammed (India, below left) held the record at 22.5 in. (57 cm).

Shortest twins Matyus and Béla Matina (1903–ca. 1935) of Budapest, Hungary, who later became naturalized American citizens, both measured 30 in. (76 cm). Primordial dwarfs, they appeared in *The Wizard of Oz* (U.S.A., 1939), billed as Mike and Ike Rogers.

The **shortest identical twin sisters** are 4-ft. 1-in. (124.4-cm) Dorene Williams and Darlene McGregor (both U.S.A., b. 1949).

Shortest married couple Brazilian couple Douglas Maistre Breger da Silva and Claudia Pereira Rocha measured 2 ft. 11 in. (90 cm) and 3 ft. 0.6 in. (93 cm) respectively when married on October 27, 1998, in Curitiba, Brazil.

Shortest newborn baby Nisa Juarez (U.S.A.) was born on July 20, 2002, measuring just 9.4 in. long (24 cm), at the Children's Hospital and Clinic in Minneapolis, Minnesota, U.S.A. (The average newborn length in the U.S.A. is 17 in., or 43 cm.) Born 108 days premature, Nisa weighed 11.3 oz. (320 g)—over 10 times smaller than the average weight of 7 lb. (3.5 kg). She was discharged from hospital on December 6, 2002.

MEASURING STATURE

When assessing absolute "shortest" and "tallest" claims, Guinness World Records insists on making a series of measurements over the duration of a day. The principal assessment is standing height, or stature, which is the length of the claimant standing as straight as possible, measured using a stadiometer (a ruler with a vertical sliding headpiece). Three measurements are taken, then averaged.

Lightest person Lucia Zarate (Mexico, 1863–89) of San Carlos, Mexico, an emaciated ateleiotic dwarf who stood 2 ft. 2 in. (67 cm) tall, weighed 2 lb. 6 oz. (1.1 kg) at birth and only 4 lb. 11 oz. (2.1 kg) at the age of 17. She had fattened up to 13 lb. (5.9 kg) by the time of her 20th birthday.

Most variable stature Adam Rainer (Austria, 1899–1950) measured 3 ft. 10.5 in. (118 cm) at the age of 21. He then suddenly started growing at a rapid rate and, by 1931, he had reached the height of 7 ft. 1.8 in. (218 cm). Unfortunately, he became so weak as a result of his growth spurt that he was bedridden for the rest of his life.

JUNREY BALAWING In June 2011, shortly after we went to press with *Guinness World Records 2012*, our adjudicators visited the home of Junrey Balawing in the Philippines to confirm him as the **shortest living man**. Measured three times on the advent of his 18th birthday, Balawing reached 1 ft. 11.5 in. (59.9 cm) and claimed the title from Khagendra Thapa Magar from Nepal. Yet he held the record for less than a year before ceding it to another Nepali, Chandra Bahadur Dangi, as this year's book went to print.

DWARFISM

• An adult is regarded as a dwarf if he or she is less than 4 ft. 10 in. (147 cm) in height.

• Body growth is stimulated by the activation of different hormones. If this process is disrupted, the individual can experience delayed or extremely slow body growth, resulting in dwarfism.

• There are around 200 forms of the condition.

• Pygmies—native to various regions worldwide, including central Africa, the Philippines, and Brazil—also have a reduced height, but not because of dwarfism. Their smaller size is hereditary.

SHORT AND SHORTER

The difference in height between He Pingping and Chandra Bahadur Dangi is illustrated here in actual size, with their fellow record-breakers included for comparison.

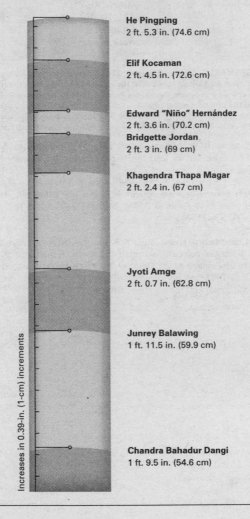

He Pingping
2 ft. 5.3 in. (74.6 cm)

Elif Kocaman
2 ft. 4.5 in. (72.6 cm)

Edward "Niño" Hernández
2 ft. 3.6 in. (70.2 cm)
Bridgette Jordan
2 ft. 3 in. (69 cm)

Khagendra Thapa Magar
2 ft. 2.4 in. (67 cm)

Jyoti Amge
2 ft. 0.7 in. (62.8 cm)

Junrey Balawing
1 ft. 11.5 in. (59.9 cm)

Chandra Bahadur Dangi
1 ft. 9.5 in. (54.6 cm)

Increases in 0.39-in. (1-cm) increments

SHORTEST WOMAN On December 16, 2011, former **shortest living teenager** Jyoti Amge (India) reached the age of 18 and so took the title of **shortest living woman.** Dr. Manoj Pahukar, an orthopedic consultant, performed the official measurements at the Wockhardt Hospital in Nagpur, India, in the presence of GWR's Rob Molloy. Jyoti's average height was 2 ft. 0.7 in. (62.8 cm)—2.3 in. (6.2 cm) shorter than the previous record holder.

Shortest actor in a leading adult role The Indian actor Ajay Kumar, who performed in the lead role of his debut feature movie, *Albhutha Dweep* (India, 2005), measures 2 ft. 6 in. (76 cm) in height.

Tamara de Treaux (U.S.A., 1959–90) was, at 2 ft. 6.3 in. (77 cm) tall, the **shortest actress ever to appear in a leading adult role**. Her most celebrated (shared) role was as E.T. in Steven Spielberg's *E.T. The Extra-Terrestrial* (U.S.A., 1982).

Shortest stuntman Kiran Shah (UK, b. Kenya) is the shortest professional stuntman currently working in movies, standing 4 ft. 1.7 in. (126 cm) when measured on October 20, 2003. He has appeared in 52 movies since 1976 and performed stunts in 31 of them. He doubled as Elijah Wood in the *Lord of the Rings* trilogy.

HUMAN
ACHIEVEMENT

CONTENTS

FASTEST TIME TO FIT INTO A BOX
Contortionist extraordinaire Skye Broberg (New Zealand) crammed herself into a 20.4 x 17.7 x 17.7-in. (52 x 45 x 45-cm) box in just 4.78 seconds at the Melia Whitehouse Hotel in London, UK, on September 15, 2011. Once Skye's body was entirely inside the box, the lid was closed from the outside and the clock was stopped.

Along with fellow New Zealanders Nele Siezen and Jola Siezen, Skye also set the record for the **longest time spent in a box by three contortionists**. The elastic trio remained inside a 26 x 27 x 22-in. (66 x 68.5 x 55.8-cm) box for 6 min. 13.52 sec. on the set of *NZ Smashes Guinness World Records* at the Sylvia Park shopping mall in Auckland, New Zealand, on September 20, 2009.

HOW HEAVY CAN WE LIFT?

WHAT IS THE HEAVIEST WEIGHT A HUMAN CAN LIFT?

The superheavyweight category of Olympic weightlifting can, arguably, be considered the ultimate test of a human's lifting ability. Powerlifters may well disagree, but whoever holds the total record in the over-105-kg category at the Olympics—the combined weight of a snatch lift plus the clean and jerk—can rightly consider themselves the strongest in the world. However, it's not just about brute strength—technique is equally as important. So what's the lifting limit in competition?

HOSSEIN REZAZADEH Double Olympic champion and the athlete dubbed the "strongest man in the world" by his peers, Iran's Hossein Rezazadeh holds the total lifting record in the over-105-kg category (athletes compete in different classes, depending on their body mass). He achieved this twice in the Olympics (2000 and 2004) with snatches of 212.5 and 210 kg, and clean and jerks of 260 and 263.5 kg.

472.5 kg

SUPPORT BELTS Weightlifting rules allow competitors to wear a belt—no wider than 4.72 in. (12 cm)—outside their clothing, to provide support and protection. The belt stiffens the torso and increases intra-abdominal pressure, allowing the muscles to work more efficiently; it also gives the torso more of an elastic "bounce" during lifts.

A. HEIGHT: The average height of recent record-breaking lifters (see p. 141) is 6 ft. (1.84 m). The taller the lifter, the more difficult it is to stand up from the squat position (see steps 3 and 4, pp. 141–142).

B. HEART: Weightlifting is anaerobic, meaning that it does not need oxygen. This means the cardiopulmonary aspect of the training is less important than the musculoskeletal.

C. BODYWEIGHT: In the over-105-kg category, there is no upper weight limit for the athlete, so any increase in body weight is justified as long as it results in even a small increase in performance—it could make the difference between gold and silver. Ideally, of course, it will be as muscle, not fat.

D. BODY SHAPE: Thick and solid barrel shape; muscle needs to be developed only in those areas that need it.

E. BACK MUSCLES: Strong development of fast-twitch (Type II) muscle is needed for the split-second anaerobic bursts of power needed to raise the bar.

F. LIMBS: Short arms and legs make better levers (but too short and the corresponding reduction in bodyweight means the risk of dropping down a category in competition).

G. LEG MUSCLES: The quadriceps and hamstrings work with the back muscles (spinal erectors) and the glutes to provide most of the lifting power.

H. STANCE: Bad positioning and technique can effectively add weight to a lift: moving the bar just 0.4 in. (1 cm) away from the vertical (as opposed to lifting straight up) adds a load of up to 4.8 kg to the total.

I. MOBILITY: Getting the body *under* the bar during the "clean" is just as important as getting the bar *over* the head. Lifters must be flexible and nimble enough to react quickly.

J. FEET: Flexibility is needed to move the feet through a range of movements. Approved "lifting shoes" provide stability, keep the foot at the optimal angle, and help balance the lifter during holds.

NEW WORLD RECORD HOLDERS OF
SUPER HEAVYWEIGHT CATEGORY

472.5 kg
HOSSEIN REZAZADEH
(Iran)
Sydney, Australia (2000)

465 kg
RONNY WELLER
(Germany)
Reisa, Germany (1998)

462.5 kg
ANDREI CHEMERKIN
(Russia)
Chiang Mai, Thailand (1996)

457.5 kg
ALEXANDER KURLOVICH
(Belarus)
Istanbul, Turkey (1994)

450 kg
ANDREI CHEMERKIN
Sokolov, Czech Rep. (1994)

442.5 kg
RONNY WELLER
Melbourne, Australia (1993)

*In 1993 and 1998, the weight
categories were reclassified—
therefore Leonid Taranenko's
1988 record of 475 kg is no
longer recognized.*

475 kg
LEONID TARANENKO
(USSR)
Canberra, Australia (1988)

472.5 kg
ALEXANDER KURLOVICH
Ostrava, Czech Rep. (1987)

467.5 kg
ANTONIO KRASTEV
(Bulgaria)
Reims, France (1987)

465 kg
ALEXANDER GUNYASHEV
(USSR)
Reims, France (1984)

1. The clean and jerk is the heaviest lift over the head. Grab the bar, palms down, with a shoulder-wide grip.

2. The clean—pulling the barbell to shoulder height —must be done in one continuous movement. So, without stopping . . .

3. . . . extend the body, pulling the bar upward. At the same time, bend at the knees to descend under the bar, flip the wrists, and bring the bar to the clavicle.

For more sporting greats, see pp. 449–562.

4. From the squat position, stand up straight with the bar, completing the "clean" part of the two-part lift.

5. Bend at the knee to begin the "jerk." (There are various jerk options—pictured is a "split jerk" with the feet apart.)

6. Finish the lift by standing upright, raising the bar and holding it above the head with locked arms.

Rezazadeh's total record of 472.5 kg has stood for more than a decade (although his eight-year reign as snatch world record holder ended in November 2011, when fellow Iranian, Behdad Salimikordasiabi, lifted 214 kg).

Combining the heaviest-ever biathlon results—a 216-kg snatch by Antonio Krastev (Bulgaria) in 1987 and a 266-kg clean and jerk by Leonid Taranenko (USSR) in 1988, both of which are now considered unofficial following the recategorizing of classes—gives a theoretical upper limit of 482 kg. As simplistic as this calculation is, it certainly gives current contenders something to aspire to.

STRENGTH

HEAVIEST . . .

Vehicle lifted with the breath On July 23, 2011, at the Arrowhead Mall in Muskogee, Oklahoma, U.S.A., Brian Jackson (U.S.A.) lifted a 2011 Ford Fiesta weighing 2,520 lb. (1,143 kg) by blowing into a bag that, when inflated, raised the vehicle off the ground.

Weight lifted by both eye sockets Yang Guang He (China) lifted two buckets of water weighing 51 lb. 12.96 oz. (23.5 kg) with both eye sockets on the set of *Lo Show dei Record* in Milan, Italy, on April 28, 2011. Yang rested hooks on the bones under his eyes and connected them to the buckets.

328 kg

ZHOU LULU Lifting is not just for the boys—women have been competing at Olympic level since 2000. Pictured is Zhou Lulu (China), the current world record holder for the "total" in the over-75-kg category—the heaviest female class. She achieved a snatch of 146 kg and a clean and jerk of 182 kg to give a world-beating total of 328 kg at the World Weightlifting Championships in Paris, France, on November 13, 2011.

Combined weight of aircraft pulled simultaneously
More than 200 Hong Kong citizens pulled four aircraft weighing 1,046,578 lb. (474.72 metric tonnes) for 164 ft. (50 m) at Hong Kong International Airport in Hong Kong, China, on March 17, 2011. The aircraft were a Boeing 747-400, an Airbus 330-343, an Airbus 300-200, and a Zlin Z-242 L, and the feat took 2 min. 53 sec.

Weight lifted by a fingernail
Chikka Bhanu Prakash (India) deadlifted a weight of 19.11 lb. (8.67 kg) with just one fingernail in Hyderabad, Andhra Pradesh, India on November 20, 2011.

Vehicle pulled by a woman with her hair
Rani Raikwar (India) pulled a 19,479-lb. (8,835.5-kg) truck on the set of *Guinness World Records—Ab India Todega* in Lalitpur, Bhopal, India, on March 3, 2011. Ajit Kumar Singh (India) holds the record for **heaviest vehicle pulled by a man with his hair**. He pulled a 20,690-lb. (9,385-kg) truck in Nawada, Bihar, India, on September 21, 2010.

Weight lifted by tongue
Thomas Blackthorne (UK) lifted a 27-lb. 8.96-oz. (12.5-kg) weight hooked through his tongue on the set of *El Show Olímpico*, in Mexico City, Mexico, on August 1, 2008.

MOST WORLD'S STRONGEST MAN WINS Nicknamed "The Dominator," "Super Mariusz," and "Pudzian," Mariusz Pudzianowski (Poland) has won the World's Strongest Man competition five times: in 2002, 2003, 2005, 2007, and 2008. Magnús Ver Magnússon and Jón Páll Sigmarsson (both Iceland) have each won the title four times.

> **FACT:** Events in the World's Strongest Man include the farmer's walk, shown above.

FASTEST 100-M LIGHT AIRCRAFT PULL Montystar Agarawal (India) pulled a light aircraft 100 m (328 ft.) in 29.84 seconds on the set of *Guinness World Records—Ab India Todega* in Baramati, Maharashtra, India, on February 23, 2011.

FASTEST TIME TO PUSH A CAR ONE MILE On February 28, 2011, Konda Sahadev (India) pushed a Tata Winger van one mile (1.61 km) down Shamshabad Airport Road in Hyderabad, India, in 11 min. 39 sec. The van weighed 5,952 lb. (2,700 kg).

Dead lift in one hour (male) Nick Molloy (UK) dead lifted 100,755 lb. (45,702 kg) in an hour at the White Swan pub in London, UK, on May 25, 2011. For his total, Molloy completed 164 repetitions of a 166-lb. (75.5-kg) barbell and 490 repetitions of a 150-lb. (68-kg) barbell to reach his total.

Dead lift in one minute (male) Markus Rücker (Germany) dead lifted 10,317 lb. (4,680 kg) at the Marktplatz in Eilenburg, Germany, on June 13, 2011. Rücker lifted a bar and weighted plates, with a combined weight of 264 lb. (120 kg), for 39 repetitions.

Vehicles to run over the stomach Tom Owen (U.S.A.) had nine pick-up trucks, each weighing between 6,614 lb. (3,000 kg) and 8,818 lb. (4,000 kg), run over his stomach on the set of *Lo Show dei Record*, in Milan, Italy, on April 26, 2009.

HEAVIEST BARBELL LIFTED BY A PAIR
Matthias Steiner and Almir Velagić (both Germany) lifted a barbell weighing 734.8 lb. (333.3 kg) in Wiesbaden, Germany, on February 5, 2011.

Consecutive bench presses underwater Marcello Paredi (Italy) achieved 20 bench presses while holding his breath underwater on the set of *Lo Show dei Record* in Rome, Italy, on February 25, 2010. His barbell weighed 110 lb. (50 kg).

Weight lifted by arm curls in one hour In Castlebar, County Mayo, Ireland, on November 12, 2011, Keith Cresham (Ireland) used arm curls to lift 65,191.8 lb. (29,570.5 kg) in one hour. Keith completed 1,253 repetitions of 52.02 lb. (23.6 kg) during the record attempt.

Chin-ups in 24 hours Lucas Garel (Canada) completed 5,045 chin-ups in 24 hours at Fitness Force gym in Keswick, Ontario, Canada, on July 17–18, 2011.

HEAVIEST AIRCRAFT PULLED MORE THAN 100 M BY A WHEELCHAIR TEAM
A team of Belgian wheelchair users from Blijf Actief (Stay Active) pulled an aircraft weighing 148,128.59 lb. (67.19 metric tonnes) at Melsbroek Air Base in Brussels, Belgium, on May 29, 2011. The team consisted of 84 connected individuals who pulled a C-130 Hercules, without stopping, for nearly four minutes.

For weighty humans, turn to p. 127.

Stacked benches held between the teeth For 10 seconds, Huang Changzhun (China) held 17 benches between his teeth on the set of *CCTV Guinness World Records Special* in Beijing, China, on August 19, 2011.

Consecutive 90-degree push-ups Starting from a headstand, Jesus Villa (U.S.A.) completed 13 consecutive push-ups, attaining a 90-degree angle at the elbow on each, in Las Vegas, Nevada, U.S.A., on September 18, 2011.

World's Strongest Woman wins Aneta Florczyk (Poland) has won the World's Strongest Woman competition on four occasions, in 2003, 2005, 2006, and 2008. The annual event is staged by the International Federation of Strength Athletes.

FASTEST . . .

Farmer's walk more than 20 m On the set of *CCTV Guinness World Records* in Beijing, China, on December 5, 2011, Laurence Shahlaei (UK) completed a 20-m (66-ft.) farmer's walk (see p. 143) in 6.73 seconds, carrying a 330-lb. (150-kg) weight in each hand. Laurence won England's Strongest Man competition in 2009.

20 m carrying 300 kg on shoulders Derek Boyer (Australia) carried a 300-kg (661-lb.) weight between his shoulders for 20 m (66 ft.) in 6.88 seconds on the Gold Coast in Queensland, Australia, on September 2, 2011.

20 m carrying an automobile on the shoulders Žydrunas Savickas (Lithuania) carried an automobile 20 m (66 ft.) strapped to his shoulders in 14.44 seconds on the set of *Lo Show dei Record*, in Milan, Italy, on March 10, 2011.

Bus-pull more than 50 m by an individual Jarno Hams (Netherlands) pulled a bus weighing 37,920 lb. (17.2 tonnes) more than 50 m (164 ft) in 1 min. 13.12 sec. on the set of *CCTV Guinness World Records Special* in Beijing, China, on August 16, 2011. Jarno has won Holland's Strongest Man competition on six occasions, most recently in 2010.

LONGEST . . .

Time holding a 500-kg weight with shoulders Kevin Fast (Canada) held a 500-kg (1,102.31-lb.) weight on his shoulders for 1 min. 1.4 sec. on the set of *CCTV Guinness World Records Special* in Beijing, China, on August 19, 2011.

HEAVIEST DEAD LIFT

TWO-ARM

1,003 lb. (455 kg)
Andy Bolton (UK)
November 4, 2006

ONE-FINGER

354.72 lb. (116.90 kg)
Benik Israelyan (Armenia)
June 11, 2011

ONE-ARM

663 lb. 8 oz. (301 kg)
Hermann Goerner (Germany)
October 29, 1920

LITTLE-FINGER

230 lb. 3 oz. (104.43 kg)
Kristian Holm (Norway)
November 3, 2008

MOST PUSH-UPS IN ONE MINUTE CARRYING . . .

40 lb. (18 kg) pack
Paddy Doyle (UK) — 61

160 lb. (27 kg) pack
Neil Bryant (Australia) — 50

80 lb. (36 kg) pack
Paddy Doyle (UK) — 38

100 lb. (45 kg) pack
Paddy Doyle (UK) — 34

MOST WEIGHT LIFTED IN ONE HOUR . . .

BENCH PRESS: 305,296 lb. (138,480 kg)

BARBELL ROWS: 80,213 lb. (36,384 kg)

DUMBBELL ROWS: 72,157 lb. (32,730 kg)

LATERAL RAISES: 43,210 lb. (19,600 kg)

All held by multiple record holder Eamonn Keane (Ireland).

MOST PULL-UPS

 = **993** Nov 16, 2011

 = **3,288** Jul 23, 2011

= **4,020** Jul 23, 2011

All set by Stephen Hyland (UK) in Stoneleigh, Surrey, UK.

Time restraining two aircraft Using ropes, Chad Netherland (U.S.A.) prevented two Cessna planes from taking off by pulling in opposite directions for 1 min. 0.6 sec. at Richard I. Bong Airport in Wisconsin, U.S.A., on July 7, 2007.

TEAMWORK

LARGEST ENSEMBLES

• **Air guitar:** On September 22, 2011, a group of 2,377 air-guitar aficionados performed at an event organized by San Manuel Indian Bingo & Casino (U.S.A.) in Highland, California, U.S.A.

• **Carol singers:** 15,111 singers performed eight Christmas carols at the Hong Myung-bo Charity Soccer Game in Seoul, South Korea, on December 25, 2010, in an event organized by the Hong Myung-bo Foundation (South Korea).

• **Choir:** The Art of Living (India) assembled a 121,440-strong choir that sang in unison in Perungalathur, Chennai, India, on January 30, 2011.

• **Gospel choir:** 1,138 gospel singers performed 17 songs in an event organized by Mano Ezoh (Germany) at the Olympiahalle, Munich, Germany, on October 15, 2011.

• **Human beat boxers:** A group of 2,081 human beat boxers—including Shlomo and Testament (both UK), and staff at Google (Ireland)—performed at The Convention Centre, Dublin, Ireland, on November 14, 2011.

MOST PEOPLE ON ONE MOTORCYCLE
The greatest number of people mounted on one moving motorcycle is 54 and was achieved by the Army Service Corps Motorcycle Display Team "Tornadoes" (all India) at Air Force Station Yelahanka in Bangalore, India, on November 28, 2010. The men rode a single 500 cc Royal Enfield motorcycle a distance of 3,609 ft. (1,100 m) and were supervised by Major M. K. Jha. The overladen motorcycle was driven by Havi Idar Ram Pal Yadav and was modified, as permitted in the GWR guidelines, with a platform around the edge to carry all the riders. None of the participants touched the ground during the attempt.

- **Ukulele players:** On August 20, 2011, a group of 1,547 ukulele players strummed "Leende Guldbruna Ögon," by Vikingarna, in Helsingborg, Sweden, in an event organized by ABF, Folkuniversitetet, and Studieförbundet Vuxenskolan (all Sweden).

- **Violinists:** 4,645 violinists played at Changhua Stadium in Chinese Taipei, China, on September 17, 2011, in a performance set up by the Changhua County Government.

- **Whistlers (one venue):** 672 members of the Make-A-Wish Club at the Nazareth Area Middle School whistled "God Bless America" and "America the Beautiful" in the Andrew S. Leh Stadium at the Nazareth Area High School in Nazareth, Pennsylvania, U.S.A., on May 27, 2011.

MOST PEOPLE . . .

On a theme-park ride (costumed) A total of 330 riders took to the Steel Force ride in costume at Dorney Park & Wildwater Kingdom in Pennsylvania, U.S.A., on August 18, 2011.

21 People

MOST PEOPLE CRAMMED INTO A MINI COOPER The maximum number of people to have squeezed into a Mini Cooper (old model) is 21 and was last achieved by female members of the Caless Dance School (Japan) on the set of *100 Beautiful Women Who Have Guinness World Records*, at the Shiodome Nihon TV Studios in Tokyo, Japan, on May 5, 2011. How do you fit 21 dancers into a Mini Cooper? Twelve in the back of the car, eight in the front, and one person in the trunk! This superlative feat of tight-fitting equaled an existing record, achieved by 21 students from INTI College Subang Jaya at INTI College Subang Jaya Campus in Selangor, Malaysia, on June 17, 2006.

> **FACT:** You can fit even more people in the new-style Mini—the record is 27, achieved in Eastbourne, UK, on November 18, 2011.

MOST PEOPLE DRESSED AS . . .

Category	People	Organizer/event	Location	Event date
Pirates	8,734	Angie Butler and the town of Penzance (both UK)	Penzance, Cornwall, UK	Jun. 26, 2011
Zombies	4,093	New Jersey Zombie Walk (U.S.A.)	Asbury Park, New Jersey, U.S.A.	Oct. 30, 2010
Wally/Waldo (A)	3,872	Street Performance World Championship (Ireland)	Dublin, Ireland	Jun. 19, 2011
Bees	2,176	Yateley and Westfield schools campus (UK)	Hampshire, UK	Apr. 6, 2011
Skeletons (B)	2,018	Jokers' Masquerade (UK)	Swansea, UK	Oct. 8, 2011
Comic-book characters	1,530	Opening ceremony of International Animation CCJOY LAND (China)	Changzhou City, Jiangsu Province, China	Apr. 29, 2011
Star Trek characters	1,040	Official *Star Trek* Convention	Las Vegas, Nevada, U.S.A.	Aug. 13, 2011
Vampires	1,039	Kings Dominion (U.S.A.)	Doswell, Virginia, U.S.A.	Sep. 30, 2011
Turkeys	661	44th Annual Capital One Bank Dallas YMCA Turkey Trot (U.S.A.)	Dallas, Texas, U.S.A.	Nov. 24, 2011
Superman (C)	437	Nexen Inc. (Canada)	Calgary, Alberta, Canada	Sep. 28, 2011

MOST PEOPLE DRESSED AS . . .

Category	People	Organizer/event	Location	Event date
Video game characters	425	BUYSEASONS, Inc. (U.S.A.)	New Berlin, Wisconsin, U.S.A.	Oct 5, 2011
Garden gnomes	331	Bayview Glen Day Camp (Canada)	Don Mills, Ontario, Canada	Jul. 19, 2011
Cows (D)	250	Bel Nederland BV, Maud Peters, and John Smit (all Netherlands)	Wassenaar, Netherlands	Sep. 10, 2011
Sunflowers (E)	229	Thorndown Community Infant School and Junior School (both UK)	St. Ives, Cornwall, UK	May 27, 2011

Head shaving at once On September 19, 2010, in Port Colborne, Ontario, Canada, 57 people shaved their heads at once in an event set up by Nancy Salvage (Canada).

Inside a soap bubble Fan Yang, Deni Yang, and Melody Yang (all Canada) popped 118 people into a soap bubble at the Discovery Science Center in Santa Ana, California, U.S.A., on April 4, 2011.

MOST PEOPLE DRESSED AS GANDHI On January 29, 2012, a group of 485 children dressed up as Mohandas "Mahatma" Gandhi in Kolkata, India, in an event organized by the charity Training Resource and Care for Kids (TRACKS). The children, all of whom were from disadvantaged backgrounds, were aged 10 to 16 and had been taught about Gandhi's philosophy prior to the attempt. TRACKS has been rehabilitating underprivileged young women and their children since 1991.

FACT: GWR's Andrea and Lucia checked that all the children remained garbed as Gandhi for a full 10 minutes.

Wearing underwear Clad only in their underwear, 2,270 people (all U.S.A.) met up at the Utah Undie Run in Salt Lake City, U.S.A., on September 24, 2011.

CIRCUS ARTS

FIRE-BREATHERS

Most flames blown in one breath The most consecutive flames blown without refueling was 129, by Ambika Niraula (Nepal) in Kathmandu, Nepal, on February 27, 2012.

Most torches put out in 30 seconds On February 21, 2011, Hubertus Wawra (Germany) extinguished 39 torches in 30 seconds using only his mouth in Mumbai, India.

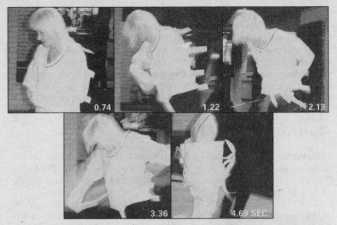

0.74 1.22 2.13

3.36 4.69 SEC

FASTEST ESCAPE FROM A STRAITJACKET Sofia Romero (UK) escaped from a regulated Posey straitjacket in 4.69 seconds at the Aylestone Leisure Centre in Leicester, UK, on June 9, 2011.

Greatest flame distance blown by a fire-breather Reg Morris (UK) blew a flame from his mouth to a distance of 31 ft. (9.4 m) at The Miner's Rest, Chasetown, Staffordshire, UK, on October 29, 1986.

ACROBATS

Longest neck hang Rebecca Peache (UK) and Donovan Jones (U.S.A.) carried out a neck hang lasting 1 min. 12.29 sec. for *CCTV—Guinness World Records Special* in Beijing, China, on August 14, 2011.

Farthest indoor aerial trapeze flight The leader of Russian aerial flying team "The Tur," Sergei Tur, flew 62 ft. 4 in. (19 m) through the air between two swinging cradles, to be caught by a fellow acrobat. The feat was performed at the Anaheim Pond in Anaheim, California, U.S.A., on July 29, 1998.

First . . .
• **flying return trapeze act** Jules Léotard (France) demonstrated the first flying return trapeze act at Cirque Napoleon in Paris, France, on November 12, 1859.

> **FACT:** Antonio used liquid paraffin as fuel for his fire-breathing. *Definitely* don't try this at home!

Circus Arts

• **triple somersault on the trapeze** This feat was first performed in public at the Chicago Coliseum in Illinois, U.S.A., in 1920.

• **double-back somersault on the flying return trapeze** Eddie Silbon (UK) performed this feat for the first time at the Paris Hippodrome in Paris, France, in 1879.

• **triple-back somersault on the flying return trapeze** The debut performance of a triple-back somersault on the flying trapeze was by Lena Jordan (Latvia) to Lewis Jordan (U.S.A.) in Sydney, Australia, in April 1897.

TIGHTROPE WALKERS

Longest tightrope crossing (supported) The longest walk by any funambulist was 11,368 ft. (3,465 m), achieved by Henri Rochetain (France) along a wire slung across a gorge at Clermont-Ferrand in France on July 13, 1969.

Longest tightrope crossing by bicycle Nik Wallenda (U.S.A.) cycled across a 235-ft. (71.63-m) tightrope in Newark, New Jersey, U.S.A., on October 15, 2008.

HIGHEST FLAME BY A FIRE-BREATHER Antonio Restivo (U.S.A.) blew himself into the record books with a 26-ft. 5-in.-high (8.05-m) flame at a warehouse in Las Vegas, Nevada, U.S.A., on January 11, 2011. In fact, Antonio succeeded in hitting the warehouse ceiling with the fire!

FARTHEST TIGHTROPE WALK (UNSUPPORTED) The greatest distance for an unsupported tightrope walk is 429 ft. (130 m) and was achieved by funambulist Bello Nock (U.S.A.) across a wire attached to poles on board Royal Caribbean International's *Majesty of the Seas* cruise ship, in Coco Bay, The Bahamas, on November 10, 2010.

FACT: The walk lasted 15 minutes—not an easy feat when the sea is moving the ship all the time!

2 hours plus!

LONGEST DURATION JUGGLING FOUR OBJECTS Zdeněk Bradáč (Czech Republic) juggled four objects, without dropping any of them, for 2 hr. 46 min. 48 sec. in Jablonec nad Nisou, Czech Republic, on November 30, 2010. The prolific Zdeněk also holds another 15 GWR records!

Steepest tightrope Aisikaier Wubulikasimu (China) and Maurizio Zavatta (Australia) walked a tightrope set at a 36-degree angle in Changzhou City, China, on November 28, 2011.

Fastest motorcycle wheelie on a tightrope On August 13, 2005, Johann Traber (Germany) performed a 33-mph (53-km/h) motorcycle wheelie on a tightrope in Flensburg, Germany.

Oldest tightrope walker In 1948, William Ivy Baldwin (U.S.A.) crossed the Eldorado Canyon in Colorado, U.S.A., on a tightrope on his 82nd birthday.

JUGGLERS AND JOGGLERS

Fastest 100 m joggling three objects (women) In July 1990, Sandy Brown (U.S.A.) ran 100 m while joggling three objects in 17.2 seconds at the International Juggling Association's Joggling Championships in Los Angeles, California, U.S.A.

Longest duration juggling three objects blindfolded On August 11, 2011, Niels Duinker (Netherlands) juggled three objects for 6 min. 29 sec. while blindfolded in Rotterdam, Netherlands.

Farthest distance on a unicycle juggling three objects On April 25, 2011, Chayne Hultgren (Australia) unicycled 3,297 ft. (1,005 m) while juggling three objects at the Royal Easter Show in Sydney, Australia.

Most juggling catches in one minute (three firestaffs) Johan Eklund (Sweden) caught three lit firestaffs 48 times in one minute in Skyttorp, Sweden, on January 5, 2011.

Hungry for more risky thrills? Try p. 196.

FACT: Dr. Adamovich (aka "The Great Throwdini") practiced for five years before aiming his knives at a human.

ESCAPOLOGY

Fastest escape from a straitjacket (suspended) Peng Deming (China) escaped from a suspended straitjacket in 25.37 seconds on the set of *CCTV—Guinness World Records Special* in Beijing, China, on August 17, 2011.

The **fastest straitjacket escape while suspended and chained** is 19.2 seconds, by Lucas Wilson (Canada) in Simcoe, Ontario, Canada, on October 8, 2011.

HISTORY OF THE SHALLOW DIVE

Inch by inch, the record for the highest shallow dive edges ever more skyward. As per GWR rules, daredevil divers are allowed just 12 in. (30 cm) of water in which to land, cushioned by a mattress a mere 10 in. (25 cm) thick . . .

Current GWR—36.7 ft. Darren Taylor, U.S.A. (2011) Changzhou City, Jiangsu, China

36 ft. Darren Taylor (2010) Louisville, Kentucky, U.S.A.

35.76 ft. Darren Taylor (2009) Atlanta, Georgia, U.S.A.

35.5 ft. Darren Taylor (2008) Tokyo, Japan

35.27 ft. Darren Taylor (2007) Cologne, Germany

35 ft. Darren Taylor (2006) Madrid, Spain

33.8 ft. Darren Taylor (2005) Denver, Colorado, U.S.A.

Largest-ever increase in record (4.4 ft.)

29.4 ft. Danny Higginbottom, U.S.A. (2004) Twickenham, Middlesex, UK

29 ft. Danny Higginbottom (2000) Therme Erding Spa, Germany

29 ft. Danny Higginbottom (1999) Metairie, Louisiana, U.S.A.

The current Guinness World Record holder, Darren Taylor, aka Professor Splash, hits the water at an estimated speed of 33 mph (53 km/h)!

Regulation-size paddling pool: 12 in. (30 cm) deep, 6 ft. (1.82 m) wide, 12 ft. (3.65 m) long.

MOST KNIVES THROWN AROUND A HUMAN TARGET IN ONE MINUTE Dr. David R. Adamovich (U.S.A.) hurled 102 throwing knives around his partner, "Target Girl" Tina Nagy (U.S.A.), in one minute in Freeport, New York, U.S.A., on December 26, 2007.

Fastest handcuff escape blindfolded Zdeněk Bradáč (Czech Republic) escaped from handcuffs—while blindfolded—in just 4.06 seconds on November 29, 2010.

FUN WITH FOOD

AGAINST THE CLOCK

Lasagna (30 sec.): Rafael Bujotzek (Germany) ate 12.6 oz. (358 g) of lasagna in 30 seconds at the Theatre Cinedom in Cologne, Germany, on August 3, 2006.

Mashed potatoes (30 sec.): On November 23, 2011, Hasib Zafar (UK) consumed 9.38 oz. (266 g) of mashed potatoes at the British Potato Conference in Harrogate, North Yorkshire, UK.

Brussels sprouts (1 min.): Linus Urbanec (Sweden) downed a record 31 Brussels sprouts in one minute in Rottne, Sweden, on November 26, 2008.

Jaffa Cakes (1 min.): Gustav Schulz (Germany) scoffed eight Jaffa Cakes in a minute in Essex, UK, on October 9, 2009. His feat was matched by Connor Whiteford (UK) in Hull, UK, on October 6, 2011.

Marshmallows (1 min.): Prolific record setter Ashrita Furman (U.S.A.) consumed

MOST MASHED POTATOES EATEN IN ONE MINUTE Amy Varney (U.S.A.) ate 12.875 oz. (365 g) of mashed potatoes in one minute at Sierra Studios, in East Dundee, Illinois, U.S.A., on January 14, 2012.

12 marshmallows in a minute at the Panorama Café in New York City, U.S.A., on January 13, 2011.

Mincemeat pies (1 min.): Luke Chilton, Catherine Jones, and Michael Xuereb (all UK) each ate two mincemeat pies in one minute at the offices of *Real People* magazine in London, UK, on November 22, 2010.

AN APPETITE FOR BREAKING RECORDS Patrick Bertoletti (U.S.A.) has stacked up a mouthwatering array of food-related records. They include the **most chicken nuggets eaten in one minute** (12)—at Sierra Studios in East Dundee, Illinois, U.S.A., on January 14, 2012. And on the set of ABC's *Live with Regis & Kelly* in New York City, U.S.A., he set the record for the **most ice cream eaten in 30 seconds** (13.5 oz. [382 g]). But that's just an appetizer: See his other records—all set in one minute!

A. JELLY DOUGHNUTS: 3
B. GRAPES: 40
C. YOGURT: 2 lb. 12.875 oz. (1.272 kg)
D. OLIVES: 30
E. BANANAS PEELED AND EATEN: 8
F. CREAM-FILLED COOKIES: 7
G. CHOCOLATE BARS: 3. Record shared with Joey Chestnut (U.S.A.)

H. MINI GHERKINS: 16
I. GARLIC CLOVES: 36
J. PEANUT-BUTTER-AND-JELLY SANDWICHES: 6
K. SHRIMP: 5.89 oz. (167 g)
L. FERRERO ROCHER CHOCOLATES: nine. Record shared with Peter Czerwinski (Canada)

Oranges peeled and eaten (3 min.): Ashrita Furman (U.S.A.) ate six oranges, which he had also peeled, at the Panorama Café in New York City, U.S.A., on July 14, 2010.

Sausages (1 min.): On July 22, 2001, Stefan Paladin (New Zealand) chomped his way through eight whole sausages at the Ericsson Stadium in Auckland, New Zealand.

Dumplings (2 min.): Seth Grudberg (U.S.A.) ate a stomach-bulging 18 dumplings in just two minutes at the Third Annual Tang's Natural NYC Dumpling Festival in New York City, U.S.A., on September 17, 2011.

Baked beans (3 min.): Nick Thompson (UK) consumed 136 baked beans from a plate with a toothpick in three minutes at an event organized by the advertising agency Claydon Heeley Jones Mason (UK) at Harrow School, Harrow-on-the-Hill, Middlesex, UK, on August 18, 2005.

Grapes (3 min.): Ashrita Furman (U.S.A.) downed 186 grapes in three minutes at the Sri Chinmoy Center in New York City, U.S.A., on May 31, 2011.

Jam doughnuts (3 min.): Lup Fun Yau downed six sugared jam doughnuts, without licking his lips, in three minutes at the offices of *The Sun* in London, UK, on May 2, 2007. This equaled the 2002 record set by Steve McHugh (UK).

Oysters (3 min.): Colin Shirlow (UK) ate a belt-busting 233 oysters in three minutes at the annual World Oyster Eating Championship held in Hillsborough, County Down, UK, on September 3, 2005.

MOST GELATIN EATEN WITH CHOPSTICKS IN ONE MINUTE Ashrita Furman (U.S.A.) tucked away 1 lb. 5 oz. (610 g) of gelatin (jello) in one minute—using a pair of chopsticks—at the Panorama Café in New York City, U.S.A., on December 7, 2010.

MOST HOT DOGS EATEN IN THREE MINUTES Takeru Kobayashi (Japan) worked his way through six hot dogs in three minutes for *Bikkuri Chojin 100 Special #2* (Fuji TV) at Kashiwanohakoen Sogokyogijo, Kashiwa, Japan, on August 25, 2009. Takeru's healthy appetite has earned him a few GWR records and seen him become a big cheese in the world of competitive eating . . .

Takeru won Nathan's Annual Hot Dog Eating Contest a record six times in a row! Other feasting feats include:

Most hamburgers eaten in three minutes: 10

Most meatballs eaten in one minute: 29

Most Twinkies (cake snacks) eaten in one minute: 14

Fastest time to eat 3.5 oz. (100 g) of pasta: 45 sec.

Fastest time to eat a 12-in. (30.5-cm) pizza: 1 min. 9.36 sec.

THE FIZZ-ICS OF CANDY-SODA FOUNTAINS

Physicists at Appalachian State University in Boone, North Carolina, U.S.A., have applied their scientific minds to explaining—and perfecting—the ever-popular candy-soda fountain:

1. For optimum results, use Mentos mint candies. They're not as smooth as they seem: they're covered in layers of liquid sugar, creating a surface of microscopically tiny pits.

2. Sodas are fizzy because carbon dioxide (CO_2) is dissolved in the liquid. Bubbles of CO_2 get released when the molecules come into contact with tiny bumps—such as minute scratches on a drinking glass or flecks of dust—known as "nucleation points."

3. Bubbles of CO_2 quickly form on all the millions of nucleation points on the Mentos, creating a raging foam as the mints sink to the bottom. This release of pressure forces the foaming liquid upward and outward!

4. The best soda to use is Diet Coke—it contains the sweetener aspartame, which lowers the surface tension of the liquid, allowing the CO_2 to escape more easily. (Caffeine-free Diet Coke works just as well!)

Human Achievement

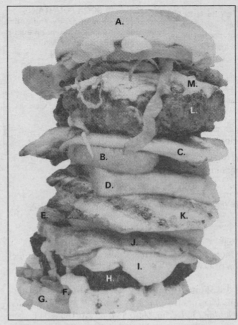

MOST CALORIFIC BURGER As of February 2012, Oscar's Diner in Telford, Shropshire, UK, is serving a 2-lb. 8-oz. (1.1-kg) hamburger packing 4,200 calories for £15 (U.S. $24). Finish it off, along with complementary milk shake, fries, and coleslaw, within 45 minutes and you'll win a free meal, T-shirt, and photo to mark the event. One customer did it in seven minutes!

A. Bun (50 calories); mayonnaise (150 calories); tomato slice (20 calories); lettuce (0 calories)
B. Onion rings (100 calories)
C. Chicken breast (200 calories)
D. Potato waffle (100 calories)
E. Onion rings (100 calories)
F. Sliced pickle (20 calories); chopped onions (10 calories)

G. Bun (50 calories); lettuce (0 calories)
H. Beef patty (1,150 calories)
I. Mozzarella cheese (100 calories); bacon slices (300 calories)
J. Bacon slices (300 calories)
K. Chicken breast (200 calories)
L. Beef patty (1,150 calories)
M. Mozzarella cheese (100 calories)

Shrimp (3 min.): On February 26, 2003, William E. Silver (U.S.A.) worked his way through 9.6 oz. (272.1 g) of shrimp in three minutes at the Calabash West Restaurant in Asheville, North Carolina, U.S.A.

Baked beans (5 min.): Gary Eccles (UK) consumed a total of 258 baked beans with a toothpick in five minutes on March 18, 2011.

You'll find more tasty records on p. 163.

MENTOS AND SODA FOUNTAINS
A total of 2,865 mint-candy-and-soda fountains were unleashed in an event organized by Perfetti Van Melle (Philippines) at the SM Mall of Asia Complex in Manila, Philippines, on October 17, 2010 (pictured left).

FASTEST TIME TO EAT . . .

A raw onion Peter Czerwinski (Canada) consumed a raw onion in 43.53 seconds in Mississauga, Ontario, Canada, on November 2, 2011.

A lemon Ashrita Furman (U.S.A.) peeled then ate a lemon in 8.25 seconds at the Songs of the Soul offices in New York City, U.S.A., on May 3, 2010.

Three eclairs Jonathan Coull (UK) scoffed three pastry eclairs in 1 min. 11 sec. at the offices of *Zoo* magazine, London, UK, on November 17, 2011, in celebration of GWR Day.

Three chiles (Bhut Jolokias) Birgit Tack (Germany) ate three Bhut Jolokia chiles in 1 min. 11 sec. on *Guinness World Records: Wir holen den Rekord nach Deutschland* in Berlin, Germany, on April 2, 2011.

MOST . . .

Competitors in a hot-dog eating contest A total of 3,189 participants took part in a hot-dog eating contest at an event organized by Oscar Mayer (Spain) in Puente de las Flores, Valencia, Spain, on March 12, 2011.

Watermelons crushed with the head (1 min.) Tafzi Ahmed (Germany) smashed 43 watermelons with his head in a minute at the Rose Festival, Saxony-Anhalt, Germany, on May 27, 2011.

Apples snapped (1 min.) The greatest number of apples snapped in one minute is 40, a feat achieved by Ashrita Furman (U.S.A.) in New York City, U.S.A., on December 31, 2011.

Ashrita, who has recently turned to food in order to satisfy his hunger for breaking records, also holds records for the **most bananas snapped with both hands (1 min.)**—he broke 99 of them at the Sri Chinmoy Center in New York City, U.S.A., on May 4, 2010—and the **most cucumbers snapped (1 min.)**—118 at the Smile of the Beyond Luncheonette in New York City, U.S.A., on March 24, 2011.

BIG FOOD

LARGEST . . .

- **Cheese slice:** Long Clawson Dairy (UK) created a 243-lb. 9.7-oz. (110.5-kg) piece of Stilton cheese. It was presented and weighed in Long Clawson, Leicestershire, UK, on September 20, 2011.

- **Chocolate Easter egg:** Tosca (Italy) made an Easter egg that measured 34 ft. 1.05 in. (10.39 m) tall on April 16, 2011.

- **Doner:** On August 26, 2011, Doner Restaurant (UAE) created a 1,031-lb. 12-oz. (468-kg) doner on Jumeirah Beach Road, in Dubai, UAE.

- **Falafel:** The Santa Clarita Valley Jewish Food and Cultural Festival (U.S.A.) prepared a 52-lb. 12-oz. (23.9-kg) falafel ball at the College of the Canyons in Valencia, California, U.S.A., on May 15, 2010.

- **Lasagna:** Weighing a titanic 8,179 lb. 2 oz. (3.71 tonnes), and measuring 70 x 7 ft. (21.33 x 2.13 m), the largest lasagna was created by the Food Bank for Monterey County at Salinas, California, U.S.A., on October 14, 1993.

HEAVIEST PINEAPPLE Tipping the scales at 18 lb. 4 oz. (8.28 kg), and measuring 12.5 in. (32 cm) long, is the pineapple (left) picked in November 2011 by amateur gardener Christine McCallum (Australia). The prodigious pineapple has a girth of 25.9 in. (66 cm) and took two and a half years to grow in Christine's yard in Bakewell, Northern Territory, Australia.

LONG LUNCH

- Peckish? Try the longest cooked salami, at 52 ft. 9.46 in. (16.09 m), made by Fratelli Daturi snc (Italy).

- Some greens, perhaps? The longest cucumber is 42.1 in. (107 cm) and was grown by Ian Neale (UK).

- To finish, how about the longest ice-cream dessert, a 150-ft. (45.72-m) sundae made by the parents of the Parent and School Association of St. Anne School, Bethlehem, Pennsylvania (U.S.A.)?

• **Pasty:** On August 19, 2010, the Proper Cornish Food Company made a "pasty" (a meat-filled pastry) that weighed 1,604 lb. (728 kg) in Fowey, Cornwall, UK.

• **Ploughman's lunch:** Sylwia Ciszewski, from Seriously Strong Cheddar (UK), made a "ploughman's lunch" weighing 4,086 lb. (1,853.9 kg). It was shown in London, UK, on July 29, 2011.

LARGEST SERVING OF . . .

• **Baked potatoes:** Shopping center El Mirador (Spain) baked 2,460 lb. 5.7 oz. (1,116 kg) of potatoes at Las Palmas de Gran Canaria, Spain, on May 28, 2011. The dish—*papas arrugadas* ("wrinkly potatoes")—is popular in the Canary Islands.

• **Chili con carne:** On July 19, 2003, the Keystone Aquatic Club (U.S.A.) cooked up a pot of chili con carne that weighed 1,438 lb. 5.1 oz. (652.4 kg) at the Broad Street Market, Harrisburg, Pennsylvania, U.S.A.

LARGEST HOT DOG COMMERCIALLY AVAILABLE Made by Gorilla Tango Novelty Meats (U.S.A.), the Big Hot Dog weighs 7 lb. (3.18 kg) and is available for U.S. $89.95 as of December 2011. Pictured here is the CEO of Gorilla Tango Novelty Meats, Dan Abbate (U.S.A.), with his hands full of one of the record-breaking snacks. The hot dog—which is made from veal, beef, and pork—is 16 in. (40.64 cm) long and has a diameter of 4 in. (10.16 cm). Just one of these humongous hunger-quashers can provide 40 regular servings!

SNAPSHOT

• Dan's original plan was to create a rectangular frankfurter that wouldn't spin out of the bun when pressed. That idea didn't take off, so he decided to go really big and aim for a Guinness World Record.

• During the photo shoot, a small dog named Dorian went by, licking his lips. He ended up eating a lot of one end of the supersize snack. Dorian is a dachshund—also called a "sausage dog" . . .

FACT: U.S. baseball fans gobble up around 26 million hot dogs every season.

HEAVIEST FRUIT & VEG

The largest produce grown in our vegetable gardens is the pumpkin, the mightiest of which is the 1,810-lb. 8-oz. (821.23-kg) monster grown by Chris Stevens (U.S.A.) of Wisconsin, U.S.A. The pumpkin is 10 times heavier than its nearest rival, the cabbage, as this list of garden produce reveals . . .

Cabbage. . . . . . . 127 lb. (57.61 kg)
Sweet potato. . . . 81 lb. 9 oz. (37 kg)
Radish . . . . 68 lb. 9 oz. (31.1 kg)
Cantaloupe . . . . . 64 lb. 13 oz. (29.4 kg)
Zucchini . . . . 64 lb. 8 oz. (29.25 kg)
Celery. . . . . 63 lb. 4.8 oz. (28.7 kg)
Cauliflower . . . . . 54 lb. 3 oz. (24.6 kg)
Beet . . . . 51 lb. 9.4 oz. (23.4 kg)
Turnip. . . . . 39 lb. 3 oz. (17.7 kg)
Broccoli . . . . 35 lb. (15.87 kg)
Cucumber . . . . . . 27 lb. 5 oz. (12.4 kg)
Leek . . . . 20 lb. 5 oz. (9.2 kg)
Carrot. . . . . 18 lb. 13 oz. (8.61 kg)
Brussels sprout . . 18 lb. 4 oz. (8.3 kg)
Pineapple. . . . . . . 18 lb. 4 oz. (8.3 kg)
Onion . . . . 17 lb. 15 oz. (8.15 kg)
Parsnip. . . . . 17 lb. 4 oz. (7.8 kg)
Lemon . . . . 11 lb. 9 oz. (5.26 kg)
Potato . . . . 10 lb. 14 oz. (4.98 kg)
Tomato. . . . . 7 lb. 12 oz. (3.51 kg)
Mango . . . . 7 lb. 8 oz. (3.43 kg)
Grapefruit . . . . . . 7 lb. 1.2 oz. (3.21 kg)
Pear . . . . 6 lb. 8 oz. (2.94 kg)
Avocado. . . . . 4 lb. 13 oz. (2.19 kg)
Apple . . . . 4 lb. 1 oz. (1.84 kg)
Garlic . . . . 2 lb. 10 oz. (1.19 kg)
Peach . . . . 1 lb. 9 oz. (725 g)
Pepper . . . . 10.08 oz. (290 g)
Strawberry. . . . . . 8.14 oz. (231 g)
Cherry . . . . 0.76 oz. (21.69 g)
Blueberry . . . . 0.4 oz. (11.28 g)

Pictured is record vegetable grower Peter Glazebrook (UK) with his prize-winning onion, weighed at the Harrogate Flower Show in Yorkshire, UK, on September 16, 2011.

• **Fish and "chips":** Weighing in at 101 lb. 7 oz. (45.83 kg), the heftiest helping of fish with fries was created by the Wensleydale Heifer hotel (UK) in West Witton, Yorkshire, UK, on July 2, 2011.

LARGEST MEATBALL This mountain of meat weighs 1,110 lb. 7.84 oz. (503.71 kg)—making it about 5,926 times larger than a more conventional 3-oz. (85-g) meatball—and has a diameter of 4 ft. 6.5 in. (1.38 m). It was prepared by the Columbus Italian Club (U.S.A.) at the St. John's Italian Festival, in Columbus, Ohio, U.S.A., between October 5 and 8, 2011. The meat and spices were mixed in batches of 50 lb. (22.5 kg), then refrigerated, moved to another location, packed into a podlike vessel, and cooked in a specially made oven.

• **Fried chicken:** Weighing 2,372 lb. 2.7 oz. (1,076 kg), the largest serving of fried chicken was produced by NOAS FM (Japan) at the Fourth Karaage Festival at AEON Mall Sanko in Nakatsu City, Oita, Japan, on September 23, 2011.

• **Potato salad:** Spilva Ltd. (Latvia) exhibited a 7,209-lb.1-oz. (3.27-tonne) potato salad at the International Exhibition Centre of the Riga Technical University in Latvia, on September 1, 2002.

• **Risotto:** On November 26, 2004, the Ricegrowers' Association of Australia served a 16,556-lb. 11-oz. (7.51-tonne) helping of risotto at First Fleet Park, Sydney, Australia.

LARGEST BOX OF POPCORN Cineplexx International (Austria/Serbia/Croatia) made a 1,857-cu.-ft. (52.59-m³) popcorn box. It was filled in 1 hr. 57 min. at an event near Avenue Mall in Osijek, Croatia, on April 16, 2011, to mark the opening of two new malls, along with two new Cineplexx movie theaters, in Croatia.

FACT: Native Americans were popping corn in North America 5,000 years ago!

- **Salsa:** A team led by Bob Blumer (Canada) created a supersize salsa weighing 2,672 lb. (1,212 kg) at the 26th Annual Tomato Festival in Jacksonville, Texas, U.S.A., on June 12, 2010.

- **Snails:** The Câmara Municipal de Loures (Portugal) created a 2,449-lb. (1,111-kg) serving of snails in Loures, Portugal, on July 11, 2009.

- **Stir-fry:** On September 5, 2011, the University of Massachusetts Dining Services (U.S.A.) created a 4,010-lb. (1,818.91-kg) stir-fry in Amherst, Massachusetts, U.S.A.

- **Vegetable stew:** The city council of Tudela (Spain) created a 4,497-lb. 6.8-oz. (2,040-kg) vegetable stew in Tudela, northern Spain, on April 30, 2011. The recipe included locally grown artichokes, peas, fava beans, green beans, asparagus, onions, and garlic.

SWEET TREATS

FASTEST TIME TO SORT 30 JELLY BABIES
Alfie Binnie (UK) sorted 30 jelly babies by color using chopsticks in a record time of 40 seconds in London, UK, on February 17, 2012.

FACT: The Chinese have used licorice plants as a medicine for thousands of years.

FACT: You could circle the earth more than five times with all the jelly beans eaten last year!

FACT: The earliest samples of chocolate (found in Honduras, Central America) date back to 1150 B.C.

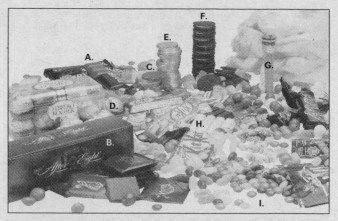

A. **CADBURY'S DAIRY MILK** The **best-selling chocolate bar** is Cadbury's Dairy Milk, which generates annual sales worth U.S. $852 million globally. It is especially popular in the UK—the British go through an average of 19 lb. (8.6 kg) of chocolate per person every year.

B. **AFTER EIGHTS** Anthony Falzon (Malta) downed a record-breaking 10 After Eight thin mints in one minute, without using his hands, in Sliema, Malta, on December 14, 2011.

C. **COCONUT ICE** A 459-ft. 9-in.-long (140.14-m) coconut candy was made to celebrate the Coconut Festival at Tecolutla, Mexico, on February 28, 1998.

D. **FERRERO ROCHER** Silvio Sabba (Italy) stacked a record 12 Ferrero Rocher chocolates on top of each other in Pioltello, Milan, Italy, on January 30, 2012.

E. **CHOCOLATE COINS** The world's **largest chocolate coin** was unveiled at the Sun Plaza shopping center in Bucharest, Romania, on November 17, 2011. The enormous 1,325,000-calorie coin measured 5.5 in (14 cm) thick with a diameter of 4 ft. 5 in. (1.35 m) and weighed in at 584 lb. 3.5 oz. (265 kg). If it had been made from gold, it would have cost $15 million (£9.5 million)!

F. **OREO COOKIES** The world's **best-selling cookie** is the Oreo, with total sales in excess of 500 billion since its introduction in the U.S.A. in 1912. If every Oreo ever made were to be stacked on top of each other, the pile would reach to the Moon and back more than six times.

G. **PEZ DISPENSERS** In May 1998, David Welch (U.S.A.) sold three Pez dispensers for U.S. $6,000 each—a total of U.S. $18,000—making them the **most expensive candy dispensers**. About 50 years old at the time, they had three separate designs: a one-piece shiny gold elephant, a Mickey Mouse softhead, and a headless dispenser embossed with the words "PEZ-HAAS." All three were bought by an anonymous dealer.

H. **KITKAT** The KitKat is the **chocolate bar with the greatest number of flavor variants**. To date, the standard four-finger KitKat has been available in more than 120 flavors, including cucumber, wasabi, watermelon, and salt—and, of course, milk chocolate.

I. **M&M'S** With annual sales worth U.S. $1.8 billion in the U.S.A. alone as of 2007, the world's **most popular candy** is the M&M. These candy-coated chocolate drops were introduced in 1941 by Americans Forrest Mars, Sr. and R. Bruce Murrie, who named the product after themselves.

J. COTTON CANDY The longest cotton candy (candy floss) measures 4,593 ft. 2 in. (1,400 m) and was spun by Kocaeli Fuar Müdürlüğü (Turkey) in Izmit, Kocaeli, Turkey, on July 10, 2009.

K. HERSHEY'S KISS The largest individual chocolate was a Hershey's Kiss weighing 30,540 lb. (13,852.71 kg). It was made to celebrate the iconic chocolate's 100th anniversary and was displayed at Chocolate World, Hershey, Pennsylvania, U.S.A., on July 7, 2007.

L. SMARTIES Using chopsticks, Kathryn Ratcliffe (UK) ate a record 170 Smarties in three minutes at the Guinness World Records 2005 Roadshow at the Trafford Centre, Manchester, UK, on November 27, 2004.

M. PICK 'N' MIX A 1-lb. 12-oz. (800-g) bag of "pick 'n' mix" candies, including cola bottles, white mice, and jelly worms, sold for £14,500 (U.S. $23,653) at a charity auction for Retail Trust (UK) on February 21, 2009. It was the last pick 'n' mix to be sold by the now-defunct Woolworth's chain. Proceeds went toward a helpline for retail workers and their families affected by the closure.

N. MALTESERS The farthest distance to blow a Malteser with a straw is 46 ft. 1 in. (14.07 m), achieved by Ashrita Furman (U.S.A.) in the gymnasium of the Jamaica YMCA, New York City, U.S.A., on November 29, 2010.

O. HIGHEST CHOCOLATE CONSUMPTION Switzerland has the highest per capita chocolate consumption. On average, its citizens manage to consume 23 lb. 4 oz. (10.55 kg) of chocolate each per year—hardly surprising, given the legendary quality of Swiss chocolate.

P. FUDGE The largest slab of fudge weighed 5,754 lb. (2.61 metric tonnes) and was made by Northwest Fudge Factory (Canada) in Levack, Ontario, Canada, on October 23, 2010.

Q. BUBBLEGUM The largest bubblegum bubble blown through the nose had a diameter of 11 in. (27.94 cm). It was created by Joyce Samuels (U.S.A.) on the set of *Guinness World Records: Primetime* in Los Angeles, U.S.A., on November 10, 2000.

> **FACT:** It took a week to make this bumper block of vanilla-, chocolate-, and maple-flavored fudge.

TITANIC TREATS

Jar of jelly beans
9 ft. 9 in. tall

Chocolate Easter egg
33 ft. 9 in. tall

Piece of toffee
8 ft. 2 in.

Chocolate bar
13 ft. 1 in. tall
13 ft. 1 in. wide

String of licorice
800 ft. long

Gummy bear candy
2 ft. 8 in. tall

LARGEST CHOCOLATE BAR Made by Thorntons plc (UK) in Alfreton, Derbyshire, UK, on October 7, 2011, the largest chocolate bar weighed 12,770 lb. 4.48 oz. (5,792.50 kg) and measured 13 ft. 1.48 in. x 13 ft. 1.48 in. x 1 ft. 1.78 in. (4 x 4 x 0.35 m). The bumper-size bar was made as part of the celebrations for Thorntons' centenary.

HE COLLECTS . . .

Airline boarding passes Miguel Fernández Díaz (Spain) had a collection of 1,020 airline boarding passes from 54 airlines as of May 2009.

Armored vehicles As of February 3, 2007, Jacques Littlefield (U.S.A.) had 229 deactivated armored fighting vehicles, including a German Panzer IV tank, displayed at his ranch in California, U.S.A.

Autographed baseballs Dennis M. Schrader (U.S.A.) had collected 4,020 baseballs, all autographed by different professional baseball players, as of August 2011.

Autographed books As of March 11, 2011, Richard Warren of Lake Forest, California, U.S.A., had collected 2,381 books, all signed by their original authors.

Back scratchers Manfred Rothstein (U.S.A.) has amassed 675 back scratchers from 71 countries, housed in his dermatology clinic in Fayetteville, North Carolina, U.S.A.

Beatles memorabilia Rodolfo Renato Vazquez (Argentina) had 7,700 different Beatles-related items, as of August 2011.

Candles Lam Chung Foon (Hong Kong) owned 6,360 different candles, as of December 23, 2011. He keeps them in four temperature-regulated showrooms.

HARRY POTTER MEMORABILIA The largest collection of Harry Potter memorabilia belongs to Steve Petrick of Pittsburgh, U.S.A., and consisted of 608 individual items as of October 30, 2011. Steve's huge hoard includes life-size cardboard cutouts of all the main characters, adult and children's versions of the books, Quidditch trophies, goggles and snitches, and a large assortment of toy owls and wands. He also has numerous soft toys, including one of Hagrid's three-headed dog, Fluffy.

SUPERMAN MEMORABILIA As of February 22, 2012, Herbert Chavez (Philippines) had a collection of 1,253 Superman-related items. They include life-size statues, figurines, clothing, cushion and duvet covers, and comics and posters. Herbert has taken his obsession with the Man of Steel to even greater extremes—he has admitted to having a nose job, chin augmentation, silicone lip injections, and thigh implants to make himself look like his (super)hero.

***Charlie's Angels* memorabilia** Jack Condon (U.S.A.) has 5,569 items of *Charlie's Angels* memorabilia, which he has been collecting since 1976.

Dioramas Nabil Karam (Lebanon) has 333 unique dioramas (three-dimensional models of a scene). Nabil also has the **largest collection of model automobiles**, with 27,777 items (see pp. xxiv–xxv). Both collections were counted on November 17, 2011.

"Do Not Disturb" signs Jean-François Vernetti (Switzerland) has collected 11,111 different "Do Not Disturb" signs from hotels in 189 countries since 1985.

Firefighter's patches Bob Brooks (U.S.A.) has 8,158 firefighter's patches, all of which he displayed at the Albany Fire Department in Albany, Oregon, U.S.A., on June 22, 2011. Bob was a firefighter for 35 years.

Hats Roger Buckey Legried (U.S.A.) has collected hats since 1970 and, as of March 2, 2010, he had 100,336 of them.

Horse-related items Edgar Rugeles (Colombia) had 2,149 horse-related items, as of August 26, 2011.

License plates Brothers Péter and Tamás Kenyeres (both Hungary) had 11,345 different license plates from 133 countries, as of April 2011. They have been collecting since 1990.

Miniature champagne bottles Christoph Bermpohl (Germany) had 1,030 different miniature champagne bottles, as of July 2011.

VOMIT BAGS Niek Vermeulen (Netherlands) had 6,290 airline air-sickness bags from 1,191 different airlines from more than 160 countries, as of February 28, 2012, which he has accumulated since the 1970s. All the vomit bags have an airline company name or company logo printed on them. His favorite bag, however, is not from an airline—it's from the NASA space shuttle *Columbia*.

MINIATURE BOOKS Jozsef Tari (Hungary) owns 4,500 miniature books, including one that measures only 0.10 in. (2.75 mm) high and 0.07 in. (1.75 mm) wide. Jozsef, a printer by trade, has been collecting miniature books since 1972 and has made some of his own miniature books. He has a special bookcase for his collection—each shelf is about half the height of a matchbox.

Moutai bottles Zhang Jinzhong (China) had 432 different bottles of Moutai liquor, as of May 2011. He's been collecting since 2003.

Movie cameras Richard LaRiviere (U.S.A.) owns 894 different movie cameras that he has collected since 1960.

Movie projectors Christos Psathas (Greece) had 1,919 movie projectors, as of July 29, 2011.

Pizza-related items Brian Dwyer (U.S.A.) had 561 different pizza-related items, as of July 31, 2011. He has been collecting only since 2010. His collection includes games, puzzles, and matchboxes.

YOUR COLLECTIONS

Do you have a record-breaking collection? If you see a record here that you think you can break, or have a collection that's not already featured in the book, let us know—you might even get your name in the next edition!

1. A record-breaking collection is based on the number of items of a particular kind that are distinguishable in some way (no two items should be the same).

2. All items should have been accumulated personally (rather than by an organization).

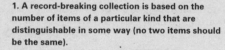

3. An inventory of all the items should be compiled in the presence of two independent witnesses. The witnesses should not be family members, friends, or teachers and, preferably, one of them should be an expert in collections (such as a museum curator or librarian). The final total should be included in statements submitted by your two (unrelated) independent witnesses.

4. Owing to the huge number of items it is possible to collect, priority will be given to those that reflect proven widespread interest.

5. We will ask you for photographs or video of your entire collection.

For full details on how to register your claim, visit www.guinnessworldrecords.com.

SHE COLLECTS . . .

Angels Since 1976, Joyce and Lowell Berg (both U.S.A.) have collected 13,165 angelic objects, including angel and cherub figurines, music boxes, and even an angel smoke alarm.

Bells Myrtle B. Eldridge (U.S.A.) has built up a collection of 9,638 bells since the 1980s.

Butterflies As of September 2011, Nina Merinova (Russia) owned a total of 735 different butterfly ornaments. She started her collection in 1996 and makes many of the ornaments herself.

Cats Carmen de Aldana (Guatemala) had 21,321 different cat-related items as of March 14, 2011. She began her collection in 1954 with three ceramic kittens, one of which she still owns.

HELLO KITTY MEMORABILIA Asako Kanda (Japan) had amassed 4,519 different Hello Kitty items as of August 14, 2011. Her house is filled with a huge range of products relating to the white bobtail cat whose full name is Kitty White, including a skillet, an electric fan, and even a Hello Kitty toilet seat!

FACT: According to Mattel, there are in excess of 100,000 collectors of Barbie dolls worldwide.

SHOES Darlene Flynn (U.S.A.) had 15,665 unique shoe-related items as of March 20, 2012, in a collection that dates back to 2000. It's still growing, too—Darlene receives shoes from well-wishers around the world. Her favorite movies are *Cinderella* and *The Wizard of Oz* and, as you might expect, she owns replicas of both Cinderella's glass slippers and Dorothy's red shoes. Darlene lives close to Denise Tubangui—the owner of the largest collection of cows (2,429, as of March 2011)—and they speak to each other regularly about their joint passion for collecting.

BARBIE DOLLS Bettina Dorfmann shares her home in Düsseldorf, Germany, with 15,000 unique Barbie dolls. She received her first doll back in 1966, but has only been collecting seriously since 1993. Barbie was first released by U.S. toy giants Mattel in 1959. Her full name is Barbara Millicent Roberts, the name of the daughter of Mattel founders Elliot and Ruth Handler (U.S.A.).

SNAPSHOT

• Bettina posed for this photo in October 2011, when her collection surpassed 15,000 dolls.

• She received her first doll when she was five years old, but it wasn't Barbie—it was Midge, Barbie's best friend.

• She's now the proud owner of an original (and rare) 1959 Barbie.

• Got a broken Barbie? Bettina runs a doll hospital, where she fixes broken legs, untangles matted hair, and replaces missing limbs!

Coca-Cola memorabilia Rebecca Flores (U.S.A.) began collecting Coca-Cola items in 2005. As of December 15, 2008, she had 945 unique objects.

Donald Duck memorabilia As of March 2011, Mary Brooks (U.S.A.) had 1,411 objects related to Donald Duck. Her collection began more than 35 years ago and it now occupies a spare room in her house.

Flamingos Sherry Knight (U.S.A.) owned 619 flamingo-related items as of February 19, 2011. Her collection is displayed at the Path Shelter Store in Lecanto, Florida, U.S.A.

Refrigerator magnets Louise J. Greenfarb (U.S.A.) has amassed a total of 35,000 nonduplicated refrigerator magnets. Her collection dates back to the 1970s.

Gnomes and pixies As of March 2011, Ann Atkin (UK) had 2,042 unique garden gnomes and pixies.

Handmade dolls Isabel Romero Jorques (Spain) has made 500 felt dolls by hand, each 3.9 in. (10 cm) high. She made dolls as a child, but it was only at the age of 69, prompted by her grandchilden, that she began creating her record-breaking collection.

Mickey Mouse memorabilia Janet Esteves (U.S.A.) owned 2,760 different Mickey Mouse items as of December 11, 2008.

Pandas Miranda Kessler (U.S.A.) had put together a collection of 1,225 unique panda items by March 2011.

Pigs Anne Langton (UK) has a collection of 16,779 pig items, which she has been collecting for more than 40 years.

Pokémon memorabilia Lisa Courtney (UK) was the proud owner of 14,410 different items of Pokémon memorabilia as of October 14, 2010, after more than 14 years of collecting.

Rubber ducks Charlotte Lee (U.S.A.) owned 5,631 unique rubber ducks by April 10, 2011.

Spice Girls memorabilia As of April 2011, Elizabeth West (UK) owned 2,066 different Spice Girls items.

FACT: The **oldest known leather shoe** dates back 5,500 years. It was found in Armenia in 2008.

COLLECTORMANIA
13,788,795

total number of unique items collected by Guinness World Records collectors*

only current holders; not including public collections amassed by libraries or universities

Top 10 largest collections

🔳	Matchbook covers	3,159,119
🦷	Human teeth	2,000,744
📕	Books (privately owned)	1,500,000
🔳	Matchbox labels	1,054,221
🖼	Cigarette cards	1,000,000
⚫	Buttons	439,900
🍺	Beer labels	424,868
▨	Scratchcards	319,011
✒	Ballpoint pens	285,150
🖊	Cigar bands	211,104

10

items in the ***smallest*** record-breaking collection: playable musical instruments made of matchsticks. A total of 106,000 matches were used to make, among other instruments, a violin, a mandolin, a recorder, and a ukulele! The collection is owned by Tony Hall (UK).

Top 10 collecting nations

U.S.A.: 34.0%	**ITALY: 3.9%**
UK: 13.9%	**CANADA: 3.1%**
GERMANY: 9.3%	**THE NETHERLANDS: 3.1%**
INDIA: 4.6%	**SPAIN: 3.1%**
CHINA: 3.9%	**SWEDEN: 2.3%**

Male vs. female collectors

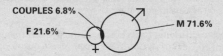

COUPLES 6.8%

F 21.6%

M 71.6%

Most hotly contested collections

Certain items are more appealing to collectors. Here are the most popular objects to collect—each record has been broken five times in the last 10 years:

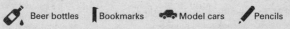

Beer bottles   Bookmarks   Model cars   Pencils

BIGGEST...

Artificial climbing wall Scared of heights? The tallest artificial climbing wall measured 137.42 ft. (41.89 m) and was constructed at Historic Banning Mills in Whitesburg, Georgia, U.S.A. It was scaled in 12 minutes by experienced climber Kalib Robertson on December 9, 2011.

Bar chimes Consisting of 1,221 parts, the largest playable bar chimes reach 64 ft. 2 in. (19.58 m) in length. They were built by Universal Percussion Inc., TreeWorks Chimes, Tom Shelley, and Mitch McMichen (all U.S.A.) and presented and played at the Drum Festival in Columbiana, Ohio, U.S.A., on August 28, 2011.

Bed On May 28, 2011, the biggest bed was created by Commissie Zomerfeesten St. Gregorius Hertme (Netherlands) in Hertme, Netherlands. It is 86 ft. 11 in. (26.5 m) long and 53 ft. 11 in. (16.44 m) wide.

Cup of coffee At 3,394 U.S. gal. (12,847.69 liters), the largest cup of coffee contained around 54,304 regular servings. It was made by Puerto RicolsCoffee.com and served at the Puerto Rico Coffee Expo 2011 held in San Juan, Puerto Rico, on October 9, 2011.

Drum A drum measuring 18 ft. 2 in. (5.54 m) in diameter and 19 ft. 6 in. (5.96 m) tall, weighing 15,432 lb. 5.76 oz. (7 metric tonnes), was built by the Yeong Dong-Gun local government and Seuk Je Lee (all South Korea) in Simcheon-Meon, South Korea, on July 6, 2011.

Flag (flown) The city of Piedras Negras in Coahuila, Mexico, raised a flag measuring 112 ft. 6.39 in. x 196 ft. 10.2 in. (34.3 m x 60 m) on December 2, 2011.

The **largest draped flag**, unveiled in Rayak, Lebanon, on October 10, 2010, in honor of the Lebanese Army, was 1,066 ft. x 666 ft. (325 m x 203 m).

Garden gnome A giant garden gnome built by Ron Hale (Canada) in 1998 reached a record height of 25 ft. 11 in. (7.91 m). It was measured officially on August 19, 2009.

LARGEST SPADE At 12 ft. 9 in. (3.90 m) tall, with a blade 1 ft. 11 in. (64 cm) wide, the biggest spade was produced by Yeoman Quality Garden Products (UK) on October 4, 2011, in Droitwich, UK.

BIGGEST DRUM KIT The largest drum kit comprises 340 pieces, is owned by Dr. Mark Temperato (U.S.A.), and was counted in Lakeville, New York, U.S.A., on October 31, 2011. A huge converted truck is used to transport the drum kit around the U.S.A. when Dr. Temperato is on tour.

Jacket A jacket measuring 42 ft. 6 in. (12.95 m) from collar to bottom and 50 ft. 3 in. (15.32 m) across from sleeve to sleeve was made at St. George's Church (UK) in Stockport, UK, on June 29, 2011.

Jigsaw puzzle When measured by number of pieces, the largest jigsaw is a 551,232-piece puzzle completed on September 24, 2011, by 1,600 students of the University of Economics of Ho Chi Minh City (Vietnam), at a local stadium. It had an overall size of 48 ft. 8.64 in. x 76 ft. 1.38 in. (14.85 x 23.20 m).

The **largest jigsaw by area** comprised 21,600 pieces and measured 58,435 sq. ft. (5,428.8 m²). It was devised by Great East Asia Surveyors & Consultants Co. Ltd. and assembled on November 3, 2002, by 777 people at the former Kai Tak Airport in Hong Kong.

Magazine An edition of *Veronica Magazine* (Netherlands) was the largest magazine ever, at 6 ft. 2 in. x 8 ft. 10 in. (190 cm x 270 cm). It was measured in Hilversum, Netherlands, on October 31, 2011.

BIGGEST GLOVE Taking a whopping 128 hours to manufacture, the biggest glove measures 9 ft. 3 in. (2.82 m) tall and 3 ft. (93 cm) wide and was created by Held GmbH (Germany). It was presented in Burgberg im Allgäu, Germany, on April 20, 2011.

BIGGEST SKATEBOARD At 36 ft. 7 in. (11.14 m) long, 8 ft. 8 in. (2.63 m) wide, and 3 ft. 7.5 in. (1.10 m) high, the largest skateboard was created by MTV presenter Rob Dyrdek with Joe Ciaglia and team from California Skateparks (all U.S.A.) in Los Angeles, U.S.A. It made its grand entrance on February 25, 2009, on *Rob Dyrdek's Fantasy Factory*.

Pocket knife When opened, the world's largest pocket knife measures 17 ft. 33 in. (6.02 m) and has a steel blade 8 ft. 1 in. (2.46 m) long. It was designed and manufactured by Garima Foundation and Pankaj Ojha (all India) and was presented at the Pink Square Mall, Jaipur, India, on December 21, 2010.

BIGGEST TELEPHONE The largest operational telephone was exhibited on September 16, 1988, to celebrate the 80th birthday of Centraal Beheer, an insurance company in Apeldoorn, Netherlands. It was 8 ft. 1 in. (2.47 m) high and 19 ft. 11 in. (6.06 m) long, and weighed 3.8 tons (3.5 tonnes). The handset, at 23 ft. 5 in. (7.14 m) long, had to be lifted by crane for a call to be made.

For big things with whiskers, turn to p. 83.

Screwdriver A giant screwdriver was created by Biswaroop Roy Chowdhury (India) and was unveiled in New Delhi, India, on April 20, 2011. It is 89.2 in. (2.27 m) long and has an acrylic handle, measuring 9.5 in. (24.13 cm) at its widest point and 28 in. (71.12 cm) long. The steel shaft is 3.5 in. (8.89 cm) thick and can be extended another 61.2 in. (1.55 m).

Sock A massive sock measuring 32 ft. 7 in. x 22 ft. 6 in. x 8 ft. 2 in. (9.93 m x 6.86 m x 2.49 m) was displayed on December 2, 2011 at the Rhode Island Convention Center in Providence, Rhode Island, U.S.A. Made by Project Undercover, Inc. (U.S.A.), it was designed to resemble a "sock monkey" puppet.

Tea bag Capable of producing over 50,000 cups of tea, the biggest tea bag weighs 264 lb. 8.8 oz. (120 kg) and was achieved by All About Tea (UK) onboard HMS *Warrior* in Portsmouth, Hampshire, UK, on November 16, 2011. The tea bag is 8 ft. 1.64 in. (2.48 m) in length and width.

White cane On August 27, 2011, the largest white cane measured 77 ft. 3.16 in. (23.55 m) and was achieved by the Swiss Federation of the Blind and Visually Impaired Fribourg Section (Switzerland) in Fribourg, Switzerland.

Wineglass At 11 ft. (3.37 m) tall and 5 ft. 8 in. (1.73 m) at its widest, the biggest wineglass was completed by the Limassol Municipality in Cyprus on September 8, 2011. It was revealed at the Limassol wine festival, where it was filled with five bottles of wine.

FANTASTIC FASHION

For the gentleman or lady with the fuller figure, we present the Guinness World Records wardrobe of outsize outfits.

PANTS
26 ft. (7.92 m) wide
42 ft. 3 in. (12.9 m) tall

KNITTED HAT
22 ft. 7 in. (6.9 m)

UNDERPANTS
65 ft. 7 in. (20 m) wide
39 ft. 3 in. (12 m) tall

SHOE
18 ft. (5.5 m)

PAIR OF SOCKS
45 ft. (13.72 m)

BUT IS IT ART?

LARGEST . . .

Drawing (one artist) A pencil drawing by Ashok Nagpure (India) measuring 324 x 8 ft. (98.75 x 2.43 m), depicting the life of Indian moviemaker Dadasaheb Phalke, was shown in Nashik, Maharashtra, India, on May 24, 2010.

Finger painting On November 26, 2009, a total of 3,242 students created a finger painting measuring 22,619.51 sq. ft. (2,101.43 m²). The event was organized by the Organizing Committee of the Anti Youth Drug Abuse Campaign at Victoria Park in Hong Kong, China.

Handprint painting A handprint painting covering 63,431 sq. ft. (5,893 m²)—larger than an American football field—was created by 5,000 children in an event organized by the UN Relief and Works Agency. It was made at the Khan Younis Stadium in Southern Gaza, Palestinian Entity (West Bank-Gaza) on July 21, 2011 and depicted the United Nations logo as the Sun rising over the Gaza Strip.

Painting by numbers In celebration of GWR Day 2010, a painting-by-numbers artwork measuring 33,696.95 sq. ft. (3,130.55 m²) was unveiled by the Ecole de Dessin in Lagos State, Nigeria.

LARGEST MODEL OF A HUMAN ORGAN Pfizer Japan Inc. created a 16-ft. 5-in. x 18-ft. 11-in. (5.02 x 5.78-m) model of a human lung at Ario Sapporo, Sapporo, Hokkaido, Japan, on October 2, 2010. One side displayed a healthy lung; the other showed a smoker's lung.

FACT: Only around 10% of the human lung is solid tissue. The remaining 90% is filled with air.

LARGEST ART CONTEST A total of 4,850,271 children from 6,601 schools across India entered the All India Camel Colour Contest, which was judged on December 8, 2011.

 **LARGEST SAND PAINTING** More than 2,500 participants created a sand painting measuring 97,176.19 sq. ft. (9,028 m²), based on the theme of "peace," on November 26, 2010. The event was organized by the Brahma Kumaris (India) at Firodia School in Ahmednagar, Maharashtra, India.

Footprint painting On May 29, 2011, in an event organized by Creative Campus in Ealing, London, UK, 200 participants created a 16,000-sq.-ft. (1,489.45-m²) painting using their feet.

Painting by mouth R. Rajendran (India) painted a 30 x 20-ft. (9.14 x 6.10-m) artwork, as a tribute to Mother Teresa, with his mouth. It was measured on October 30, 2007.

Spray-painted picture Made for Coca-Cola İçecek by 580 Turkish students, the largest spray-painted image measured 8,183.58 sq. ft. (760.28 m²). It was completed at Hezarfen Airport, Istanbul, Turkey, on August 16, 2004.

Underwater painting Alexander Belozor (Ukraine) created an 8.61-sq.-ft. (0.8-m²) submarine painting at diving site El Mina in the Red Sea, off the coast of Hurghada, Egypt, on December 18, 2010.

LONGEST . . .

Cartoon strip (team) The longest cartoon strip made by a team measured 3,320 ft. (1,012 m). It was created by students of Ecole Emile Cohl, ECAM, and Centrale Lyon (all France) in an event staged by Lyon BD Organisation in Lyon, France, on May 28, 2011.

Graffiti scroll Almeersegraffiti (Netherlands) organized 300 participants in the creation of a gigantic graffiti scroll measuring 5,171 ft. 6 in. (1,576.3 m)—longer than 22 747 jumbo jets—in Almere, Netherlands, on July 2, 2011.

FACT: The skull-pture was designed to highlight the huge levels of waste that humanity produces.

Painting A 19,690-ft.-long (6-km) artwork on the theme of government transparency was painted by 3,000 students from local schools (all Mexico) at an event held at Parque Tangamanga in San Luis Potosí, Mexico, on May 28, 2010.

The **longest painting by an individual** measured 6,587 ft. (2,008 m) and was created by Thommes Nentwig (Germany). It was completed, presented, and measured in Vechta, Germany, on July 10, 2008.

The **longest anamorphic painting**—that is, a distorted artwork that when viewed from the correct angle looks three-dimensional—measures 422 ft. 3 in. (128.7 m) and was created by Qi Xinghua (China). Entitled *Macao's One Impression*, it was unveiled at the One Central Macao shopping mall in China on December 6, 2011. (See p. 187 for an example of anamorphic sidewalk art.)

MOST PLASTIC BAGS USED IN AN ARTWORK Miha Artnak (Slovenia) created *Plastic Bag Monster* in November 2010, using 40,000 plastic bags (and 7,500 plastic cups).

LARGEST MODELING BALLOON SCULPTURE Adam Lee (U.S.A., lower left) created a balloon sculpture in the shape of a gigantic spider measuring 22 ft. 2 in. (6.76 m) long and 45 ft. 2 in. (13.77 m) wide. Consisting of 2,975 balloons, it was measured at the Grand Mound Great Wolf Lodge in Washington, DC, U.S.A., on October 6, 2011.

2,975 balloons

LARGEST PANORAMIC PAINTING A 32,424.82-sq.-ft. (3,012.36-m²) panoramic painting entitled *Splendid Central Plains* was unveiled by the Henan Administration of Radio Film and Television (China) at the Tower of Fortune in Zhengzhou City, Henan Province, China, on April 26, 2011.

MOST EXPENSIVE ART

Art is big business. And business is getting bigger all the time . . .

 The **most expensive book illustration sold at auction** is a Beatrix Potter (UK) watercolor titled *The Rabbits' Christmas Party*. Created in the 1890s, it was bought on July 17, 2008, by a British collector for £289,250 (U.S. $579,232).

 The **most expensive photograph** is an image of the Rhine taken by the German artist Andreas Gursky (b. 1955). It sold for U.S. $4,338,500, including buyer's premium, at Christie's in New York City, U.S.A., on November 8, 2011. (See p. 268.)

 Danseuse au repos (ca. 1879), a pastel of a ballet dancer by French artist Edgar Degas, sold for £17,601,500 (U.S. $27,854,400) at Sotheby's, London, UK, on June 28, 1999, making it the **most expensive work of art on paper**.

 The **most expensive drawing by an Old Master** is the *Head of a Muse* by Raphael (Italy), which sold for £29,200,000 (U.S. $47,788,400) on December 9, 2009, at Christie's, London, UK.

 The **most valuable sculpture** sold at auction is Alberto Giacometti's (Switzerland) bronze sculpture entitled *L'Homme qui marche I* (*The Walking Man I*, 1960), which sold to an anonymous bidder at Sotheby's, London, UK, for a record £65,000,000 (U.S. $103,676,000) on February 3, 2010.

 Damien Hirst (UK) made U.S. $200.8 million during an auction on September 15 and 16, 2008, the **most money made at auction by an artist**. Of the 167 works that went on sale at Sotheby's in London, UK, only three were not sold.

 The **most expensive painting in private sale** is French artist Paul Cézanne's *The Card Players*. One of a series of five, it was sold to the royal family of Qatar for more than U.S. $250 million in 2011. *Vanity Fair* magazine broke news of the sale in February 2012.

All currency conversions have been calculated as of the date of sale when known.

LARGEST ANAMORPHIC SIDEWALK ART
Joe Hill of 3D Joe and Max (both UK) created an anamorphic sidewalk artwork measuring 12,490.93 sq. ft. (1,160.45 m²). The sensational street art was unveiled at West India Quay, London, UK, to celebrate Guinness World Records Day, on November 17, 2011.

Painting by numbers Entitled *Birds and Wetlands*, the longest painting by numbers measures 3,147 ft. 5 in.(959.35 m). It was created by 2,041 participants in an event organized by the Hong Kong Wetland Park at their premises in Hong Kong, China, on October 17, 2009.

Woodblock print A group of 80 students from De Eindhovense School (Netherlands) made a woodblock print 497 ft. (151.5 m) long. It was exhibited at their school in Eindhoven, Netherlands, on January 30, 2009. Entitled *Holland and Nicaragua*, it was created to raise awareness of Chinandega—Eindhoven's twin city in Nicaragua.

YOUNGEST . . .

You might be surprised at just how young some GWR record holders are! Here's a selection of remarkably young achievers, listed by ascending age.

No. 1 box-office star Movie star Shirley Temple (U.S.A., b. April 23, 1928) was seven years old when she became No. 1 at the box office in 1935, retaining the title until 1938.

Temple's great popularity saw her become the **youngest millionairess (noninherited)**. She had earned more than U.S. $1 million before she reached the age of 10.

The **youngest millionaire (noninherited)** was the American child film actor Jackie Coogan (1914–84), who was born in Los Angeles, California, U.S.A. In 1923–24, he was earning U.S. $22,000 per week and retained approximately 60% of his movies' profits. By the age of 13, Coogan had become a millionaire in his own right.

DRUMMER The youngest professional drummer is Julian Pavone (U.S.A., b. May 14, 2004). As of January 24, 2012, he was 7 years 8 months 10 days old. Julian started off by playing while seated on his father's lap, at the age of just three months, and released his first CD, *Go Baby!*, at the age of just 23 months. He plays a 22-piece kit, including 17 cymbals.

Club DJ Jack Hill (UK, b. May 20, 2000) played at CK's Bar and Club in Weston-super-Mare, Somerset, UK, on August 26, 2007, at the age of 7 years 98 days.

Movie director The youngest director of a professionally made feature-length movie is Kishan Shrikanth (India, b. January 6, 1996), who directed *C/o Footpath* (India, 2006)—about an orphaned boy who wants to go to school—when he was nine years old.

Graduate Michael Kearney (U.S.A.) obtained his BA in anthropology from the University of South Alabama, U.S.A., in June 1994, at the age of 10 years 4 months. He went on to gain his Master of Science degree in biochemistry on August 9, 1998, at the age of just 14 years 8 months.

AUTHOR OF A BEST-SELLING BOOK SERIES Born on November 17, 1983, Christopher Paolini (U.S.A.) is the author of the *Inheritance Cycle* series. It had sold in excess of 20 million copies as of May 2011 and remains a firm favorite of fantasy fans the world over.

PROFESSIONAL POKER PLAYER Joe Cada (U.S.A., b. November 18, 1987) became the youngest winner of the World Series of Poker main event at the age of 21 years 357 days on November 10, 2009. Joe earned $8,547,044 (£5,250,449).

Chess grandmaster Child prodigy Sergey Karjakin (Ukraine, b. January 12, 1990) qualified as an international chess grandmaster on August 12, 2002, at the age of 12 years 212 days. The title has been in existence since 1950.

Doctorate On April 13, 1814, Carl Witte of Lochau, Austria, was made a Doctor of Philosophy (PhD) at the University of Giessen, Germany, at the age of 12.

Olympic gold medalist The youngest female Olympic champion was Kim Yun-mi (South Korea, b. December 1, 1980), at the age of 13 years 85 days, in the 1994 women's 3,000 m (9,843 ft.) short-track speed-skating relay event.

Composer of a musical Adám Lörincz (Hungary, b. June 1, 1988) was 14 years 76 days old when his 92-minute musical *Star of the King* was performed on August 16, 2002, in Székesfehérvár, Hungary.

FIFA World Cup finals goal-scorer Pelé (b. Edson Arantes do Nascimento) was 17 years 239 days old when he scored for Brazil against Wales at Gothenburg, Sweden, on June 19, 1958.

NBA player Jermaine O'Neal (U.S.A., b. October 13, 1978) made his debut for the Portland Trail Blazers against the Denver Nuggets on December 5, 1996, at the age of 18 years 53 days.

Hollywood producer Steven Paul (U.S.A.) was 20 when he produced and directed *Falling in Love Again* (U.S.A., 1980), starring Elliott Gould and Susannah York, which saw the movie debut of actress Michelle Pfeiffer. He has produced another 28 movies and directed the 1993 *NYPD Blue* TV series.

X GAMES GOLD MEDALIST Lyn-z Adams Hawkins (U.S.A., b. September 21, 1989) became the youngest female to win a gold medal at the X Games in any discipline when she won the Skateboard Vert competition at 14 years 321 days old at X Games 10, Los Angeles, California, U.S.A., on August 7, 2004.

Super Bowl player At 21 years 155 days, Jamal Lewis (U.S.A., b. August 26, 1979) of the Baltimore Ravens is the youngest player to ever appear in the Super Bowl. Lewis ran for 102 yards (93 m) and a touchdown in a 34–7 romp over the New York Giants at Super Bowl XXXV on January 28, 2001.

Oscar winner (Best Actress) On March 30, 1987, at the age of 21 years 218 days, Marlee Matlin (U.S.A., b. August 24, 1965) won the Best Actress award for playing Sarah Norman in *Children of a Lesser God* (U.S.A., 1986).

The **youngest winner of an Oscar for Best Actor** is Adrien Brody (U.S.A., b. April 14, 1974). He picked up the award on March 23, 2003, for his performance as Wladyslaw Szpilman in *The Pianist* (France/Germany/UK/Poland, 2002), at 29 years 343 days old.

Formula One World Champion Sebastian Vettel (Germany, b. July 3, 1987) won his first Formula One World Championship at the age of 23 years 134 days. He took the title on November 14, 2010, at the Abu Dhabi Grand Prix in the United Arab Emirates.

Vettel is also the **youngest driver to win a Formula One World Championship race**. He was 21 years 72 days old when he won the Italian Grand Prix on September 14, 2008, driving for Toro Rosso.

Prime minister William Pitt (1759–1806) was 24 years 205 days old when he assumed office on December 19, 1783. He had previously declined the premiership at the age of 23 years 275 days. (In fact, the term "prime minister" wasn't officially used to describe the role until 1905.)

Astronaut Major (later Lieutenant-General) Gherman Stepanovich Titov (USSR, b. September 11, 1935) was at the age of 25 years 329 days when he launched in *Vostok 2* on August 6, 1961.

FACT: As of 2010, an estimated 52% of the world's population was under the age of 30.

The **youngest female astronaut** was Valentina Tereshkova (USSR, b. March 6, 1937), who was 26 years 102 days old when she became the **first woman in space** on June 16, 1963, in *Vostok 6*.

Antarctic solo trekker On December 20, 1998, 26-year-old Swede Ola Skinnarmo arrived on his own, unaided, at the Scott Base in Antarctica after a 47-day, 750-mile (1,200-km) trek on skis across the frozen continent. Ola was pulling a sled that weighed approximately 260 lb. (120 kg) when fully laden, yet still managed to finish 10 days earlier than he had expected.

Chief Scout The youngest Chief Scout is Edward "Bear" Grylls (UK). He was 34 years old when he received the appointment from The Council of the Scout Movement in London, in 2009.

BIRTH RATES

Average number of children per woman (estimated, 2010–15)

Highest			Lowest	
1 Niger	7.2		1 Hong Kong	1.0
2 Afghanistan	6.6		Macau	1.0
3 Mali	6.5		3 Bosnia	1.2
Timor-Leste	6.5		4 Hungary	1.3
5 Somalia	6.4		Japan	1.3
Uganda	6.4		Malta	1.3
7 Chad	6.2		Poland	1.3
Zambia	6.2		Romania	1.3
9 Congo-Kinshasa	6.1		Singapore	1.3
10 Malawi	6.0		Slovakia	1.3
			South Korea	1.3

YOUNG PLANET

Figures from the U.S. Census Bureau for 2010 revealed that there were more than 2.4 billion people under 19 years old on the Earth:

	0–4	5–9	10–14	15–19
Male	320,032,992	306,710,315	306,644,307	309,742,265
Female	299,175,551	288,524,929	285,899,964	288,768,476

CURIOUS CONTESTS

MOST WINS

World Conker Championships (men) The most World Conker Championships won in the men's category is three, by P. Midlane (UK), who took the title in 1969, 1973, and 1985, and J. Marsh (UK), who won in 1974, 1975, and 1994. The annual contest was started in Ashton, Northamptonshire, UK, in 1965.

Gurning World Championships (women) Between 1977 and 2010, Anne Woods (UK) won 27 Women's Gurning World Championships at the Egremont Crab Fair in Cumbria, UK.

Tommy Mattinson (UK) has recorded the **most wins of the Men's Gurning World Championships**, with 12. His flexible face took top prize at the annual Gurning World Championships at the Egremont Crab Fair in 1986–87 and 10 times between 1999 and 2010.

Horseshoe Pitching World Championships (women) Vicki Chappelle Winston (U.S.A.) won 10 Women's Horseshoe Pitching World Championships. She took the first of her titles in 1956, and the last in 1981.

Log Rolling World Championships (men) Between 1956 and 1969, Jubiel Wickheim (Canada) triumphed in 10 Log Rolling World Championships.

World Pea Shooting Championships (men) Mike Fordham (UK) won an unprecedented seven Championships, in 1977–78, 1981, 1983–85, and 1992.

Sandra Ashley (UK) has picked up the **most Women's World Pea Shooting Championships**, producing three wins consecutively in 2005–07.

MOST UNDERWATER CHECKERS PLAYERS The most people playing checkers (draughts) underwater is 88, at an event organized by Normunds Pakulis (Latvia) in Riga, Latvia, on May 21, 2011.

FACT: Usually, around 60 divers enter these championships in Latvia. The games last up to six minutes.

Find more conventional sports on p. 450.

MOST TIDDLYWINKS WORLD CHAMPIONSHIPS "Winker" extraordinaire Larry Kahn (U.S.A.) won 21 World Championships singles titles from 1983 to 2011. He discovered the game in 1971 as a student at Massachusetts Institute of Technology (MIT), U.S.A.

Sauna World Championships Timo Kaukonen (Finland) has won the Sauna World Championships in Heinola five times, in 2003, 2005–07, and 2009.

Tiddlywinks World Championships (pairs) Larry Kahn (U.S.A.) has won the greatest number of pairs titles at the Tiddlywinks World Championships. He secured 16 victories between 1978 and 2011.

Toe Wrestling World Championships (men) Alan Nash (UK) has won six World Championships, in 1994, 1996–97, 2000, 2002, and 2009. Nash, nicknamed "Nasty," has also had the honor of being knighted by His Majesty King Leo 1st of Redonda in the West Indies.

The contest is held annually at Ye Olde Royal Oak, Wetton in Staffordshire, UK. Contestants must push an opponent's foot to the other side of a ring called a "toerack," using only their toes.

Karen Davies (UK) won four times consecutively in the women's category, between 1999 and 2002—the **most Women's Toe Wrestling World Championships**.

MOST WORLD GRAVY WRESTLING CHAMPIONSHIPS The most prolific winner of the World Gravy Wrestling Championships, held annually at the Rose 'n' Bowl pub in Stacksteads, Lancashire, UK, is Joel Hicks (UK). Out of the four competitive tournaments held to date, he has won the title twice, in 2009 and 2011.

MOST WOMEN'S LOG ROLLING CHAMPIONSHIPS Tina Bosworth (U.S.A., née Salzman) has taken 10 International Championships for log rolling. She won the contest—part of the Lumberjack World Championships—in 1990, 1992, and 1996–2003.

MOST MEN'S HORSESHOE PITCHING WORLD CHAMPIONSHIPS Alan Francis (U.S.A.) won the men's championships a record 15 times between 1989 and 2009.

Most Wife Carrying World Championships (male) Margo Uusorg (Estonia) won the World Championships five times, in 2000–01, 2003, and 2005–06.

The **most Wife Carrying World Championships won by a female** is two. The record is shared by four Estonians: Annela Ojaste (1998–99), Birgit Ullrich (2000–01), Egle Soll (2003 and 2005), and Inga Klauso (2004 and 2007).

Wok Racing World Championships (team) Two teams have won the Wok Racing World Championships twice each: ProSieben (Germany) in 2004–05 and TV Total (Germany) in 2009–10.

World Conker Championships (women) Two women have won the World Conker Championships twice: Sheila Doubleday (UK) won the inaugural women's event in 1988 and took the title again in 1993, in a competition organized by Ashton Conker Club, UK. Tina Stone (UK) won the event in 1994 and 2007.

THE ART OF LOG ROLLING

- Both competitors ("birlers") step off a dock and onto a floating log. Assistants offer them poles so that they can steady themselves.

- The two birlers push away from the dock. When both are balanced, they dispense with the poles and set the log spinning quickly.

- Each opponent tries to slow or stop the log to dislodge their rival and send them into the water ("wetting"). If neither falls within a set time limit, they continue on a smaller log.

MOST WOK RACING WORLD CHAMPIONSHIPS In wok racing, competitors make timed runs down Olympic bobsled tracks on modified Chinese woks. Georg Hackl (Germany) won six Wok Racing World Championships, in 2004–05 and 2007–10. Georg is pretty good at more conventional sports, too. He has picked up five medals at consecutive Olympic Games in the luge contest, **the most consecutive individual event Olympic medals won.**

World Unicycle Hockey titles UNICON, the world championships of unicycling, has been held every two years since 1984. Unicycle hockey was added to the program of events in 1994, since then nine tournaments have been contested. The Swiss Power Team (Switzerland) has won the title a record three times, in 2004, 2006, and 2010.

FASTEST TIME IN THE . . .

Men's World Bog Snorkeling Championships Andrew Holmes (UK) completed the course in 1 min. 24.22 sec. at Llanwrtyd Wells, Powys, UK, on August 28, 2011.

Men's World Mountain Bike Bog Snorkeling Championships Graham Robinson (UK) won the men's World Mountain Bike Bog Snorkeling Championships in 51 min. 37 sec. at the 2010 games in Llanwrtyd Wells, Powys, UK.

World Roof Bolting Championships This vocational "sport" tests competitors' accuracy and skill with a roof-bolting drill machine. Brian McArdle and Les Bentlin (both Australia) secured the 1998 World Championships by finishing the required tasks in 1 min. 50.85 sec. at Fingal Valley, Tasmania.

Wife Carrying Championships On July 1, 2006, Margo Uusorg and Sandra Kullas (both Estonia) completed the 831-ft. 8-in. (253.5-m) obstacle course at the World Wife Carrying Championships in 56.9 seconds. This is the fastest time since a minimum "wife weight" was introduced in 2002.

Woolsack race (male) Pete Roberts (UK) achieved the fastest men's individual time of 45.94 seconds in the 2007 World Woolsack Championships. The event is held annually at Tetbury in Gloucestershire, UK, and involves competitors racing up and down the 1-in-4 Gumstool Hill while carrying a 60-lb. (27.21-kg) bag of wool on their shoulders.

The **fastest woolsack race by a woman** in the event is 1 min. 6.3 sec. in 2009, by Zoe Dixon (UK). Women competitors carry a 30-lb. (13.6-kg) bag of wool on their shoulders.

THE COTSWOLD OLIMPICKS

The modern Olympic Games was the brainchild of France's Baron de Coubertin at the end of the 19th century. However, 284 years prior to the Games' revival, the Cotswold Olimpicks in Gloucestershire, UK, were first staged. Once described as a "unique blend of history, eccentricity, amateurism, and enthusiasm bordering on the obsessive," this competition involves a range of curious disciplines:

DANCING
The medieval Morris-dancing equivalent of *Dancing with the Stars*

CHESS
It's not all physical—this is a mental match of minds

COCKFIGHTING
Pitting one angry, aggressive rooster against another to the death

JUMPING IN SACKS
Jumping. In sacks.

PIKE DRILL
Wielding a long spear with grace and aplomb

SHIN KICKING
Kicking your opponent to the ground by stamping on their shins

SPURNING THE BARRE
Middle England's version of Scotland's Highland Games caber toss

HAY BALE RACING
Moving a bundle of hay using a wheelbarrow at high speed

RISKY BUSINESS

FASTEST TIME TO . . .

Change a wheel on a spinning car Terry Grant (UK) changed a wheel on a spinning car in 3 min. 10 sec. on the set of *Lo Show dei Record* in Rome, Italy, on March 4, 2010.

Drink a pint of stout upside down Peter Dowdeswell (UK) imbibed a pint of stout while being held upside down in 5.24 seconds on the set of *Lo Show dei Record* in Milan, Italy, on April 21, 2011.

Eat a drinking glass The fastest time to eat a drinking glass is 1 min. 27 sec. and was achieved by Patesh Talukdar (India) on the set of *Guinness World Records—Ab India Todega* in Mumbai, India, on March 10, 2011.

Pierce four coconuts with one finger Ho Eng Hui, aka "Master Ho" (Malaysia), took just 12.15 seconds to pierce four coconuts with a finger on the set of *Lo Show dei Record* in Milan, Italy, on April 21, 2011.

Climb the Burj Khalifa The fastest time to climb the world's **tallest building** (see p. 311) is 6 hr. 13 min. 55 sec. by Alain Robert (France). "Spiderman," as he is known, climbed it barehanded (and with the aid of only rubber-sole shoes) between 6:03 p.m. and 12:17 a.m. on March 29–30, 2011.

HEAVIEST WEIGHT LIFTED BY . . .

Eye socket Manjit Singh (UK) lifted a 30-lb. 13.7-oz. (14-kg) weight with his eye socket in Punjab, India, on July 7, 2011.

Beard On December 18, 2010, Antanas Kontrimas (Lithuania) raised a female model weighing 139 lb. 12 oz. (63.4 kg) a distance of 3.9 in. (10 cm) off the ground using only his beard on the set of *Zheng Da Zong Yi—Guinness World Records Special* in Beijing, China.

Little fingers The heaviest dead lift using the pinkie fingers is 148 lb. 12 oz. (67.5 kg), achieved by Kristian Holm (Norway) in Herefoss, Norway, on November 13, 2008.

Neck Frank Ciavattone (U.S.A.) lifted a weight of 808 lb. (366.5 kg) supported by the neck at the New England Weightlifting Club in Walpole, Massachusetts, U.S.A., on November 15, 2005.

FASTEST TIME TO JUMP OVER THREE MOVING AUTOMOBILES The fastest time to leap over three moving automobiles head-on is 1 min. 11.79 sec. and was achieved by Aaron Evans (U.S.A.) on the set of *Guinness World Records Gone Wild* at the Staples Center in Los Angeles, U.S.A., on September 28, 2011. Each of the automobiles was driven head-on toward Aaron at a speed of 25 mph (40 km/h). He took a run-up toward each vehicle before jumping off the ground and performing a front flip over it, clearing its length completely without touching any part of the vehicle itself.

FACT: Aaron's feat was inspired by a video in which NBA star Kobe Bryant seems to jump a moving Aston Martin.

MOST KICKS TO THE HEAD IN ONE MINUTE (SELF) The greatest number of self-administered kicks to the head in one minute is 115, by Joshua William Reed (U.S.A.) on the set of *Guinness World Records Gone Wild* at the Staples Center in Los Angeles, California, U.S.A., on September 28, 2011.

MOST...

Champagne bottles sabered simultaneously A group of 196 participants sabered champagne bottles at once in an event organized by Centro Empresarial e Cultural de Garibaldi (Brazil) at the Fenachamp 2011 champagne festival in Garibaldi, Rio Grande, Brazil, on October 8, 2011.

Concrete blocks broken in a stack with the head Wasantha De Zoysa (Sri Lanka) broke a stack of 12 concrete blocks using only his head in Anuradhapura, Sri Lanka, on August 23, 2009.

Most concrete blocks broken on the head with a bowling ball John Ferraro (U.S.A.) stacked 45 concrete blocks on his head and had his assistant smash them by dropping a 16-lb. (7.3-kg) bowling ball onto them on the set of *Lo Show dei Record* in Milan, Italy, on April 14, 2011.

Cups kicked off a head (one minute) David Synave (France) kicked 89 plastic cups off the head of an assistant in one minute in Nord-Pas-de-Calais, France, on September 17, 2011.

MOST ARROWS CAUGHT BLINDFOLDED (TWO MINUTES) Joe Alexander (Germany) caught four arrows blindfolded in two minutes at the gym of Joe Alexander Entertainment Group in Hamburg, Germany, on November 16, 2011. He was 26 ft. 3 in. (8 m) from the archer, Peter Dubberstein (Germany). Joe also holds the record for the **most arrows caught (two minutes)**—43 in all—set on November 17, 2010.

BORN TO BURN

When it comes to fiery daredevils, Jayson has some company . . .

• The **greatest number of simultaneous full-body burns** is 17 and was achieved during an event set up by Ted Batchelor and the "Ohio Burn Unit" (all U.S.A.) in South Russell, Ohio, U.S.A., on September 19, 2009.

• Ted also holds the record for the **longest distance run while on fire**—492 ft. 10 in. (150.23 m)—set at King's Home in Chelsea, Alabama, U.S.A., on December 4, 2011.

• The **longest distance pulled by a horse while on full-body burn** was 1,551 ft. 2 in. (472.8 m) by Halapi Roland (Hungary) in Kisoroszi, Hungary, on November 12, 2008.

MOST CHAINSAW-JUGGLING CATCHES Ian Stewart (Canada) showed he was a cut above the rest by making 94 chainsaw-juggling catches at the Hants County Exhibition in Windsor, Nova Scotia, Canada, on September 25, 2011.

LONGEST DURATION FULL-BODY BURN (WITHOUT OXYGEN) Jayson Dumenigo (U.S.A.) endured a full-body burn without oxygen for 5 min. 25 sec. in Santa Clarita, California, U.S.A., on March 27, 2011. Having set a new world record, Jayson stopped the attempt earlier than planned to allow assistants to free him from his protective layers and let him breathe freely again. He has worked on a number of big-budget blockbusters, including *Fantastic Four, Ocean's Eleven, Ocean's Twelve,* and the first three installments of *Pirates of the Caribbean*.

Jayson beat the previous record by 40 seconds.

UNDER RISK UNDERWATER

If a record doesn't feel quite demanding enough, why not try it underwater? These people did . . .

Greatest depth cycled underwater

- 218 ft. 2 in. (66.5 m)
- Vittorio Innocente (Italy)
- Santa Margherita Ligure, Liguria, Italy
- July 21, 2008

Farthest distance cycled underwater

- 1.87 miles (3.04 km)
- Ashrita Furman (U.S.A.)
- Complexo Olímpico de Piscinasde Coimbra, Coimbra, Portugal
- September 22, 2011

Farthest distance on a pogo stick underwater

- 1,680 ft. (512.06 m)
- Ashrita Furman (U.S.A.)
- Nassau County Aquatic Center, East Meadow, New York, U.S.A.
- August 1, 2007

Fastest escape from a straitjacket underwater

- 15.41 seconds
- Matthew Cassiere, aka "Matt the Knife" (U.S.A.)
- *Zheng Da Zong Yi—Guinness World Records Special*, CCTV Studios, Beijing, China
- September 13, 2007

Fastest escape from handcuffs underwater

- 4 seconds
- Zdeněk Bradáč (Czech Republic)
- Jablonec nad Nisou swimming pool, Jablonec nad Nisou, Czech Republic
- February 15, 2011

Longest submergence underwater in a controlled environment

- 4 days 4 hours (100 hours total)
- Ronny Frimann (Norway)
- Central Station, Oslo, Norway
- June 14–18, 2007

Longest time breath held underwater voluntarily

- 21 min. 33 sec.
- Peter Colat (Switzerland)
- Ebikon, Switzerland
- September 17, 2011

Deepest underwater escape using equipment

- 601 ft. (183 m)
- Norman Cooke and Hamish Jones (both UK)
- From submarine HMS *Otus* in Bjørnefjorden, off Bergen, Norway
- July 22, 1987

ADVENTURE

CONTENTS

LONGEST JOURNEY BY QUAD BIKE Quad Squad Expedition team members Valerio De Simoni, Kristopher Davant, and James Kenyon (all Australia) started out from Istanbul, Turkey, on August 10, 2010, and went on to set a new record for the longest journey on a quad bike (ATV) by covering 34,945 miles (56,239 km). The trip ended in Sydney, Australia, with a 500-strong motorcycle escort, on October 22, 2011, after 437 days 19 hr. 9 min. The team had traversed 37 countries.

HOW DEEP CAN WE GO?

WHAT'S THE GREATEST DEPTH WE CAN REACH?

With his Virgin Oceanic project, Richard Branson (UK) hopes to achieve a solo trip to the deepest points in every ocean. However, just how far will he be able to descend in his *Deep Flight Challenger* submersible? What's the absolute limit when it comes to plumbing the depths of our planet?

695 FT. (212 M) DEEPEST HALF MARATHON: A competition between 11 racers in the Bochnia salt mine in Poland on March 4, 2004.

1,044 FT. (318.2 M) DEEPEST SCUBA DIVE: Nuno Gomes (South Africa) descended a fifth of a mile in the Red Sea off Dahab, Egypt, on June 10, 2005.

3,345 FT. (1 KM) DEEPEST OPERATIONAL COMBAT SUBMARINE: No
military sub has gone deeper than the Russian K-278.

4,166 FT. (1.3 KM) DEEPEST CONCERT: Agonizer (Finland) played in the
Pyhäsalmi Mine Oy at Pyhäjärvi, Finland, on August 4, 2007.

1.2 MILES (2 KM) DEEPEST DIVE BY A MAMMAL: A bull sperm whale
(*Physeter macrocephalus*) was studied off the coast of Dominica
in the Caribbean in 1991.

1.3 MILES (2.191 KM) DEEPEST CAVE: In September
2007, Ukrainian cavers (speleologists) reached a
new record depth at the Krubera Cave in the Arabika
Massif of Georgia.

1.5 MILES (2.4 KM) DEEPEST LIVE TV BROADCAST BY A PRESENTER:
Alastair Fothergill (UK) relayed *Abyss Live* for the BBC on September 29,
2002, from inside a Mir submersible, along the Mid-Atlantic Ridge off the
eastern coast of the U.S.A.

**0.8–2.2 MILES (1.3–3.6 KM) DEEPEST LAND-DWELLING
CREATURE:** The 0.02-in.-long (0.5-mm) nematode
worm *Halicephalobus mephisto*—aka the "worm from
hell"—was found in a South African gold mine in 2011.

2.4 MILES (3.9 KM) DEEPEST MINE: The TauTona gold mine near
Carletonville, South Africa, began operation in 1962. By 2008, it had reached
2.4 miles (3.9 km) deep. The elevator journey can take one hour.

DEEPEST POINTS IN EACH OCEAN
Arctic: 3.5 miles (5.60 km)
Southern: 4.5 miles (7.23 km)
Indian: 5 miles (8.04 km)
Atlantic: 5.2 miles (8.38 km)
Pacific: 6.8 miles (11.03 km)

> **FACT:** At these depths, the oceans rarely get above 39°F (4°C)—even in the warmest tropical regions.

2.5 MILES (4 KM) WRECK OF RMS *TITANIC*: The pride of the White Star Line (UK) was sunk on April 15, 1912, off Newfoundland, Canada, with the loss of 1,517 lives. The youngest person to dive to the *Titanic* is Sebastian Harris (UK), who was 13 years old when he visited the site in the *Mir 2* submersible on August 2, 2005.

3.6 MILES (5.8 KM) DEEPEST SHIPWRECK: World War II German blockade runner SS *Rio Grande*, discovered in 1996 at the bottom of the South Atlantic Ocean on November 30, 1996.

4 MILES (6.5 KM) DEEPEST SUBMERSIBLE IN SERVICE: Built in 1990, the Shinkai 6500 is a Japanese three-man research submarine with a 2.9-in.-thick (7.35-cm) hull. It made its 1,000th dive in 2007.

5.2 MILES (8.4 KM) DEEPEST FISH: An 8-in.-long (20-cm) species of cusk eel (*Abyssobrotula galatheae*) found in the Puerto Rico Trench of the Atlantic Ocean.

ON LAND

Even at 7.6 miles (12.2 km), the deepest borehole (see next page) is barely a scratch on the Earth's surface. The planet's outer crust comprises 21.5 miles (35 km) of solid rock. Assuming we could stop water seeping into our hole—a constant problem in mines—we'd also have to contend with temperatures that rise the deeper we go; at the bottom of the 2.4-mile (3,900-m) TauTona mine shaft (see previous page), our current depth limit on land, the heat rises to 131°F (55°C).

On breaking through the crust, we'd then face the challenge of the mantle: 1,864 miles (3,000 km) of superheated rock at 752–1,652°F (400–900°C), depending on depth. Temperatures here are far beyond the operational limits of any known heatproof suit. Still want to keep digging?

How Deep Can We Go?

6.2 MILES (10.1 KM) DEEPEST OIL WELL: The *Deepwater Horizon* semisubmersible drilling rig operated to this depth in the Tiber oil field in the Gulf of Mexico.

6.7 MILES (10.9 KM) DEEPEST DESCENT BY A MANNED VESSEL: Jacques Piccard (Switzerland) and Donald Walsh (U.S.A.) piloted the bathyscaphe *Trieste* to the "Challenger Deep" section of the Mariana Trench (see below) on January 23, 1960. On March 25, 2012, James Cameron (U.S.A.) made the same journey alone—the deepest solo descent—in the *DEEPSEA CHALLENGER* (pictured), a "vertical torpedo" that allowed him to make the first ever exploration of the trench.

6.8 MILES (11 KM) DEEPEST PART OF THE OCEAN: The Mariana Trench in the Pacific Ocean is the deepest natural point on the surface of the Earth.

7.6 MILES (12.3 KM) DEEPEST PENETRATION INTO THE EARTH'S CRUST: A geological exploratory borehole near Zapolyarny on the Kola peninsula of Arctic Russia. It was begun on May 24, 1970, and had reached this record depth by 1983, when work stopped because of a lack of funds.

IN THE OCEAN

Human beings evolved to live on land. Under the water, we soon discover the limits this places on us. We can't breathe, our senses become dulled, and the pressure exerted by the water as we travel deeper becomes increasingly dangerous. Here, we are little more than well-equipped cavemen, using technology to plunge our Stone Age bodies into the abyss.

However, by shielding our fragile bodies from the effects of pressure, nitrogen narcosis, and oxygen toxicity, we can voyage to the deepest, darkest crevices of our oceans. Because humans have already traveled to the deepest known point in the ocean, this is one record that has already reached its absolute limit. The Virgin team now faces the added challenge of making the first solo dives to the deepest points in the oceans. Good luck!

CIRCUMNAVIGATION

FIRST . . .

Ever circumnavigation History's first circumnavigation of the world was accomplished on September 8, 1522, when the Spanish vessel *Vittoria*, under the command of the Spanish navigator Juan Sebastián de Elcano, reached Seville in Spain. The ship had set out from Sanlúcar de Barrameda, Andalucía, Spain, on September 20, 1519, along with four others as part of an expedition led by the Portuguese explorer Ferdinand Magellan. They rounded Cape Horn, crossed the Pacific via the Philippines, and returned to Europe after sailing around the Cape of Good Hope. *Vittoria* was the only ship to survive the voyage.

By walking The first person reputed to have walked around the world is George Matthew Schilling (U.S.A.), from 1897 to 1904. The first verified achievement was by David Kunst (U.S.A.), who walked 14,450 miles (23,250 km) through four continents from June 20, 1970, to October 5, 1974.

By aircraft without refueling Richard G. "Dick" Rutan and Jeana Yeager (both U.S.A.) circumnavigated the world westward from Edwards Air Force Base, California, U.S.A., in nine days from December 14 to 23, 1986, without refueling.

Via both poles by aircraft Captain Elgen M. Long (U.S.A.) achieved the first circum-polar flight in a twin-engined Piper PA-31 Navajo from November 5 to December 3, 1971. He covered 38,896 miles (62,597 km) during the course of 215 flying hours.

Via both poles by helicopter Jennifer Murray and Colin Bodill (both UK) flew around the world, taking in both poles, from December 5, 2006, to May 23, 2007, in a Bell 407 helicopter. The journey started and finished in Fort Worth, Texas, U.S.A.

FASTEST CIRCUMNAVIGATION BY BICYCLE The speediest circumnavigation by bicycle took 106 days 10 hr. 33 min. and was achieved by Alan Bate (UK), who cycled a distance of 18,310.47 miles (29,467.91 km) and traveled 26,475.8 miles (42,608.76 km), including transfers. The journey lasted from March 31 to August 4, 2010, starting and finishing at the Grand Palace in Bangkok, Thailand.

> **FACT:** *Banque Populaire* V sailed 21,600 nautical miles (24,870 miles; 40,030 km).

FASTEST CIRCUMNAVIGATION BY YACHT On their arrival at Ushant, France, on January 6, 2012, Loïck Peyron (France) and the 13-man crew of *Banque Populaire V* became record holders. They had sailed their yacht around the world in a time of 45 days 13 hr. 42 min. 53 sec.—more than two days faster than the previous record set by Franck Cammas (France). The feat saw the team take the Jules Verne Trophy—a competition for the fastest circumnavigation by yacht—which Peyron's brother Bruno has won three times.

FASTEST . . .

Sailing solo Francis Joyon (France) sailed the world nonstop in 57 days 13 hr. 34 min. 6 sec., from November 23, 2007, to January 20, 2008, in the 97-ft. (29.5-m) maxitrimaran *IDEC II*. The 21,600-nautical-mile (24,170-mile; 38,900-km) trip began and ended in Brest, France.

The **fastest solo sailed circumnavigation by a woman** was achieved by Ellen MacArthur (UK). She sailed nonstop around the world in 71 days 14 hr. 18 min. 33 sec., from November 28, 2004, to February 7, 2005, in the trimaran *B&Q*.

By passenger aircraft The fastest flown circumnavigation under the Fédération Aéronautique Internationale (FAI) rules, which permit flights that exceed the length of the Tropic of Cancer or Capricorn (22,858.8 miles; 36,787.6 km), was one of 31 hr. 27 min. 49 sec. The aircraft was an Air France Concorde, piloted by captains Michel Dupont and Claude Hetru (both France). The flight lasted from August 15 to 16, 1995; a total of 80 passengers and 18 crew were also on board.

By balloon solo Steve Fossett (U.S.A.) flew around the world alone in 13 days 8 hr. 33 min. in *Bud Light Spirit of Freedom* from June 19 to July 2, 2002. He took off from Northam, Western Australia, and landed at Eromanga in Queensland, Australia.

By helicopter Edward Kasprowicz (U.S.A.) and crewman Stephen Sheik flew around the world in an easterly direction in an AgustaWestland Grand helicopter in 11 days 7 hr. 5 min., completing their epic trip on August 18, 2008. The journey started and finished in New York, U.S.A., traveling via Greenland, UK, Italy, Russia, U.S.A., and Canada.

> **FACT:** At 101 ft. (31 m) long and with a displacement of 85 metric tonnes, TÛRANOR *PlanetSolar* is the **largest solar-powered boat**.

FIRST CIRCUMNAVIGATION BY SOLAR-POWERED BOAT MS *TÛRANOR PlanetSolar* (Switzerland) circumnavigated the world in a westward direction from Monaco in 1 year 7 months 7 days from September 27, 2010 to May 4, 2012. The catamaran's upper surface is covered in 5,780 sq. ft. (537 m²) of solar panels, allowing it to be powered by solar energy alone.

FIRST CIRCUMNAVIGATION IN A HYDROGEN-POWERED VEHICLE Mercedes-Benz (Germany) was the first manufacturer to circumnavigate the world with a hydrogen-powered "fuel cell" vehicle. Three identical automobiles (based on the company's B-Class hatchback) carried out the 125-day journey to mark the automaker's 125th anniversary. The trip started and finished in Stuttgart, Germany.

GOING GLOBAL

These are the current rules for a "true" circumnavigation, as defined in the official GWR guidelines:

• A circumnavigation must pass through two antipodes (opposite points of the Earth's surface).

• The traveler must start and finish at the same point—and travel in only one direction.

• All lines of longitude must be crossed.

• A minimum distance of 24,855 miles (40,000 km), or 21,600 nautical miles (24,870 miles; 40,030 km), should be covered.

• Claimants must be 16 or older.

By car The record for the first and fastest man and woman to have circumnavigated the Earth by car covering six continents under the rules applicable in 1989 and 1991, embracing more than an equator's length of driving (24,901 road miles; 40,075 km), is held by Saloo Choudhury and his wife Neena Choudhury (both India). The journey took 69 days 19 hr. 5 min. from September 9 to November 17, 1989. The couple drove a 1989 Hindustan "Contessa Classic" starting and finishing in Delhi, India.

A CENTURY OF ADVENTURE (1912–2012)

 Circumnavigation   Mountaineering   Sea

 Polar   Land & Air

 January 17, 1912: Captain Robert Scott (UK, left) and four comrades reach the South Pole, 34 days too late to claim the record as **first expedition to reach the South Pole**. This accolade goes to Roald Amundsen (Norway) and his team, who reached the Pole on December 14 the previous year.

March 7, 1912: Roald Amundsen arrives at Hobart in Tasmania, Australia, with confirmation of his successful polar trip.

March 29, 1912: Scott and his crew perish on their return journey from the South Pole.

 1914–15: Ernest Shackleton (UK) attempts to cross Antarctica via the South Pole but his ship, *Endurance*, freezes in pack ice and eventually sinks.

 **June 14, 1919:** John Alcock and Arthur Brown (UK) fly from Newfoundland in Canada to Connemara in Ireland, the **first nonstop transatlantic flight**. They touch down the following day and win themselves a £10,000 prize (equivalent today of U.S. $570,000).

1924: First Olympic medal for alpinism (mountain climbing) is awarded at the Chamonix Winter Games to the team led by Brigadier Charles Bruce (UK) for the (failed) 1922 Mount Everest expedition.

June 4, 1924: A British duo set off on an attempt to be the first climbers to summit Mount Everest—but disappear. George Mallory (pictured) and Andrew Irvine are last seen a few hundred yards from the summit, but we will never know if they reached the peak. Mallory's body is eventually found in 1999.

September 28, 1924: Two U.S. Army Douglas DWC seaplanes complete the **first circumnavigation by aircraft**; they do so in a series of 57 "hops," starting and finishing in Seattle, Washington, USA.

May 20, 1927: Charles Lindbergh (USA) sets off on the **first solo flight across the Atlantic Ocean** in his monoplane *Spirit of St. Louis*.

May 31, 1928: Charles Kingford Smith (Australia) captains the **first transpacific flight**, from the USA to Australia.

November 29, 1929: Richard Byrd (USA) captains the **first flight over the South Pole** in the *Floyd Bennett* Ford trimotor.

July 26, 1930: Charles Creighton and James Hargis (both USA) set off from New York on the **fastest drive across the USA in reverse**; they arrive at Los Angeles, California, without once stopping the engine.

POLAR JOURNEYS

FASTEST . . .

Solo journey to the South Pole (unsupported and unassisted)
On January 13, 2011, Christian Eide (Norway) completed a solo and un-supported trek to the South Pole in 24 days 1 hr. 13 min. He set off on the 715-mile (1,150-km) adventure on December 20, 2010, and covered an average of 29 miles (47 km) per day. Eide smashed the previous record—Todd Carmichael's (U.S.A.) 39 days 7 hr. 49 min.—and has set a benchmark that many polar explorers consider nearly impossible to beat.

Ray Zahab, Kevin Vallely, and Richard Weber (all Canada) reached the South Pole from the Hercules Inlet, Antarctica, on January 7, 2009 after 33 days 23 hr. 30 min., the **fastest journey to the South Pole by a team (unsupported and unassisted)**.

FIRST FEMALE TO SKI SOLO ACROSS ANTARCTICA Felicity Aston (UK) became the first woman to ski solo across Antarctica when she arrived at the Hercules Inlet on the Ronne Ice Shelf on January 23, 2012, after a 1,084-mile (1,744.5-km) journey lasting 59 days. She made the trip while pulling two sleds and without the assistance of kites or any other propulsion aids.

YOUNGEST PERSON TO SKI TO THE SOUTH POLE Amelia Hempleman-Adams (UK, b. June 1, 1995) was at the age of just 16 years 190 days when she reached the South Pole on December 9, 2011, after skiing 97 miles (156 km). She and her father David spent 17 nights in Antarctica, enduring whiteouts and temperatures as low as −58°F (−50°C).

Trek to the North Pole David J. P. Pierce Jones (UK), Richard Weber, Tessum Weber (both Canada), and Howard Fairbanks (South Africa) trekked to the North Pole in 41 days 18 hr. 52 min., from March 3 to April 14, 2010. The team set out on March 3 from 82°58'02"N, 77°23'3"W and were picked up after reaching the North Pole, 90°N, on April 14, 2010.

Trek to the North Pole by a female (unsupported) Cecilie Skog (Norway) made an unsupported trek to the North Pole in 48 days 22 hr. She left Ward-Hunt Island with teammates Rolf Bae and Per Henry Borch (both Norway) on March 6, 2006 and reached the North Pole on April 24, 2006.

Owing to this trek, Skog is also the **fastest female to complete the Three-Poles Challenge** (conquering both poles and Mount Everest), taking just 1 year 336 days.

FIRST . . .

Person to reach the North Pole The question of who first reached the North Pole has long been a matter of debate. Robert Peary, traveling with Matt Henson (both U.S.A.), indicated he had reached the North Pole on April 6, 1909. Frederick Cook (U.S.A.) claimed he had done so a year earlier, on April 21, 1908. Neither claim has been convincingly proven.

Person to reach the South Pole A Norwegian party of five men, led by Captain Roald Amundsen, reached the South Pole at 11 a.m. on December 14, 1911, after a 53-day march with dog sleds from the Bay of Whales, Antarctica.

Surface crossing of Antarctica A party of 12, led by Sir Vivian Ernest Fuchs (UK), completed a crossing of Antarctica on March 2, 1958 after a trek of 2,158 miles (3,473 km), lasting 99 days from November 24,1957. They crossed from Shackleton Base to Scott Base via the Pole.

Person to visit both poles Dr. Albert Paddock Crary (U.S.A.) reached the North Pole in a Dakota aircraft on May 3, 1952. On February 12, 1961, he arrived at the South Pole by Sno-Cat on a scientific traverse party from the McMurdo Station.

FASTEST OVERLAND JOURNEY TO THE SOUTH POLE To mark the 100th anniversary of Amundsen's epic polar trip (see p. 213), Jason De Carteret and Kieron Bradley (both UK) traveled to the South Pole in a record time of 1 day 15 hr. 54 min. They set off on December 18, 2011 in the Thomson Reuters Polar Vehicle, driving from Patriot Hills at an average speed of 17.34 mph (27.9 km/h)—also beating the record for the fastest average speed for a South Pole journey.

MOST SOUTH POLE TREKS IN A YEAR There were 19 Antarctic expeditions in 2011, mostly to mark the centenary of the race to the South Pole between Roald Amundsen and Captain R. Scott.

Person to walk to both poles Robert Swan (UK) led the three-man "In the Footsteps of Scott" expedition, which arrived at the South Pole on January 11, 1986. Three years later, he headed the eight-man "Icewalk" expedition, reaching the North Pole on May 14, 1989.

Person to walk to both poles solo and unsupported Marek Kamiński (Poland) reached the North Pole from Ward Hunt Island on May 23, 1995, a 546-mile (880-km) trip, in 72 days. He trekked 870 miles (1,400 km) to the South Pole from Berkner Island, Antarctica, in 53 days, arriving on December 27, 1995.

Aircraft flight over the North Pole The first verified flight over the North Pole was achieved on May 12, 1926, by the crew of a 348-ft. (106-m) airship led by Norwegian explorer Roald Amundsen and Umberto Nobile (Italy), the airship's designer and pilot.

Ivan André Trifonov (Austria) flew a one-man Thunder and Colt Cloudhopper balloon 0.6 miles (1 km) over the geographic North Pole at 4:30 p.m. GMT on April 20, 1996, the **first hot-air balloon flight over the North Pole**.

Hot-air balloon flight over the South Pole Ivan André Trifonov floated over the geographic South Pole at an altitude of 15,000 ft. (4,570 m) with two Spanish crew members on January 8, 2000.

Winter expedition to the North Pole Matvey Shparo and Boris Smolin (both Russia) began the earliest winter expedition to the North Pole on December 22, 2007, the day of winter solstice, from the Arktichesky Cape, the northern point of the Zevernaya Zemlya Archipelago. They reached the North Pole on March 14, 2008, eight days before the vernal equinox, the official beginning of the polar "day."

Unsupported journey to the North Pole Along with husband Thomas, Tina Sjögren (both Sweden) made the journey in 68 days, from

---

POLAR OPPOSITES

• As well as the geographic poles (the most northerly and southerly points of the Earth) there are magnetic North and South Poles. These are the most northerly and southerly points of the Earth's magnetic field.

• Antarctica is far colder than the Arctic. In 1983, it saw the **lowest-ever temperature**: −128.6°F (−89.2°C).

• Unlike the geographic South Pole, the North Pole is covered by a floating ice cap. There is no land beneath it.

March 22 to May 29, 2002. The couple received no external support on their trek.

Tina is also the **first woman to complete an unsupported journey to the South Pole**. With her husband, she made the journey from the Hercules Inlet in 63 days, from November 30, 2001, to February 1, 2002.

Prior to her polar treks, Tina had summited Mount Everest on May 26, 1999; the mountain is often regarded as a "pole" because of its inaccessibility. Tina's success at reaching all three landmarks constitutes the **first completion by a female of the Three Poles Challenge**.

Married couple to reach both poles Mike and Fiona Thornewill (UK) skied to the South Pole on January 4, 2000, and the North Pole on May 6, 2001. Both trips were air-supported and on both the duo were accompanied by teammate Catharine Hartley (UK). She and Fiona became the first British women to walk to the North and South Poles.

Person to complete the Three Poles Challenge Erling Kagge (Norway) became the first person to complete the trio of the North Pole (reached on May 8, 1990), the South Pole (on January 7, 1993), and the peak of Mount Everest (on May 8, 1994).

Person to complete the Explorers' Grand Slam Park Young-Seok (South Korea) reached the North Pole on foot on April 30, 2005, becoming the first person to achieve the Explorers' Grand Slam. This involves climbing the highest peaks on all seven continents (the "Seven Summits") and the 14 peaks over 26,246 ft. (8,000 m), and reaching the North and South Poles on foot.

FARTHEST UNSUPPORTED SOLO SKI JOURNEY Aleksander Gamme (Norway) skied 1,410 miles (2,270 km) across Antarctica, from Hercules Inlet to the South Pole and returning to a point 0.6 miles (1 km) from his start. There, he waited almost five days to cross the finish line, on January 24, 2012, with skiers James Castrission and Justin Jones (both Australia), who had traveled a similar route.

FACT: Aleksander traveled without the aid of food drops, snowmobiles, kites, or any form of assistance.

A CENTURY OF ADVENTURE (1912–2012)

 Circumnavigation

 Mountaineering

 Sea

 Polar

Land & Air

May 21, 1932: Female aviator Amelia Earhart (U.S.A.) becomes the **first woman to fly solo across the Atlantic.**

July 22, 1933: Wiley Post (U.S.A.) is the **first person to fly around the world solo** in the Lockheed Vega *Winnie Mae*, starting and finishing in New York, U.S.A.

August 15, 1934: William Beebe and Otis Barton (both U.S.A.) descend to a then-record 3,028 ft. (923 m) in a tethered bathysphere, the **first deep-ocean dive.**

February 20, 1935: Caroline Mikkelsen (Denmark), the wife of a Norwegian whaling captain, makes history by becoming the **first woman to set foot on Antarctica.**

July 2, 1937: Amelia Earhart vanishes over the Pacific Ocean during an attempt at flying around the world.

July 24, 1938: A German-Austrian team solve the "last great problem of the Alps" by completing the first ascent of the north face of the Eiger in Switzerland.

1943: Jacques Cousteau (pictured) and Émile Gagnan (both France) develop the Aqua-Lung, giving divers an unprecedented degree of freedom to explore.

1946: Alpinism is dropped as an Olympic sport.

1946–47: Operation Highjump sees the **largest expedition to Antarctica** as a 4,700-strong U.S. Navy force establishes a presence on the continent.

October 14, 1947: U.S. test pilot Chuck Yeager takes his Bell X-1 through the sound barrier, the **first supersonic flight.**

1949: Otis Barton (U.S.A.) breaks his own record for deepest ocean dive with a 4,500-ft. (1,372-m) dive in his benthoscope submersible. This remains the deepest solo descent by a cable-suspended submersible.

July 19, 1950: Ben and Elinore Carlin (both Australia) begin the first—and to date only—successful circumnavigation by amphibious auto. Wife Elinore abandons their jeep *Half-Safe*—and their marriage—when taking a rest break during the trip.

MOUNTAINEERS

Deadliest mountain According to the Himalayan Database, between 1950 and 2009 the death toll at Annapurna I was 62 from 1,524 attempts (in 169 expeditions), giving the peak a 4.07% mortality rate. (The mean death rate in the Himalayas is 1.55%.) The latest fatalities came in October 2011, when Young-Seok Park, Dong-Min Shin, and Gi-Seok Gin (all South Korea) perished during their descent.

First person to climb all 8,000-m peaks Reinhold Messner (Italy) became the first person to climb the world's 14 peaks over 8,000 m, or 26,246 ft., when he summited Lhotse (27,890 ft.; 8,501 m), between Nepal and Tibet, on October 16, 1986. His quest started in June 1970, and the difficulty of his feat is illustrated by the fact that by the first half of 2012, only 27 people had achieved it.

Messner, who was the first person to summit the world's three highest mountains, is considered the greatest climber of all time. He achieved all of the 14 ascents without supplementary bottled oxygen, making him the

first person to climb all 8,000-m peaks without oxygen—a feat that, to date, has been achieved by only 12 climbers.

FIRST WOMAN TO CLIMB ALL 8,000-M PEAKS On May 17, 2010, Edurne Pasaban Lizarribar (Spain) became the first woman to climb all 14 of the peaks over 8,000 m (26,246 ft.). She began her conquest of the "8,000-ers" by reaching the top of Mount Everest on May 23, 2001, and completed it by summiting Shishapangma in Tibet, the lowest of the 14 peaks.

FACT: Mount Everest is known to locals as Qomolangma, meaning "holy mother."

FASTEST TIME TO CLIMB THE SEVEN SUMMITS BY A MARRIED COUPLE Rob and Joanne Gambi (UK) achieved the fastest (and **first**) Seven Summits ascent by a married couple, climbing the highest peak on each continent in 404 days for the Kosciuszko list (which takes Mount Kosciuszko as the highest point in Australasia). The couple later climbed the Carstensz Pyramid, or Puncak Jaya (Australasia's highest point, if Indonesia is included), in 799 days.

MOST CONQUESTS OF MOUNT EVEREST Apa Sherpa (Nepal), Climbing Leader of the Eco Everest Expedition 2011, reached the summit of Mount Everest for a record-breaking 21st time on May 11, 2011. Apa made his first ascent of Everest back in May 1990 (see above right). He is pictured here receiving his official GWR certificate in Gyalthum, Sindhupalchowk, Nepal, in February 2012, while trekking on the 1,056-mile-long (1,700-km) Great Himalayan Trail.

Fastest time to climb all 8,000-m peaks Jerzy Kukuczka (Poland) conquered all of the 14 main peaks over 8,000 m in a period of 7 years 11 months 14 days.

First person to climb the "Seven Summits" The Seven Summits—the highest peaks on all seven continents—are categorized in two alternative ways. The Messner list has the highest point in Oceania as Puncak Jaya in Indonesia. The Bass list recognizes Mount Kosciuszko in New South Wales, Australia, instead. Patrick Morrow (Canada) was the first person to complete the Messner list, summiting Puncak Jaya on August 5, 1986.

Oldest female to climb the Seven Summits Caroline (Kay) LeClaire (U.S.A., b. March 8, 1949) completed her last Seven Summits climb with her ascent of Mount Everest on May 23, 2009, at the age of 60 years 77 days.

First person to climb Annapurna I solo On October 28, 2007, Tomaž Humar (Slovenia) completed his solo climb of Annapurna I. He chose a new route along the right side of the south face in pure "alpine" style—

he carried his equipment and food with him. In "expedition" style, the climber benefits from porters and fixed lines.

Fastest time to climb El Capitan The fastest ascent of the "Nose" of El Capitan in California, U.S.A., was made by Hans Florine (U.S.A.) and Yuji Hirayama (Japan) in 2 hr. 48 min. 50 sec. in September 2002.

The **fastest solo ascent of the "Nose" of El Capitan** was achieved by Hans Florine in 11 hr. 41 min. on July 30, 2005.

First ascent of K2 by a woman Wanda Rutkiewicz (Poland) reached the summit of K2—the world's second highest mountain, at 28,251 ft. (8,611 m)—on June 23, 1986.

APA'S 21 ASCENTS

Date	Expedition name
May 10, 1990	International
May 8, 1991	Sherpa Support
May 12, 1992	New Zealand
Oct. 7, 1992	International
May 10, 1993	U.S.A.
Oct. 10, 1994	International
May 15, 1995	American on Sagarmatha
Apr. 26, 1997	Indonesian
May 20, 1998	Extreme Everest
May 26, 1999	Asian-Trekking
May 24, 2000	Everest Environmental
May 16, 2002	Swiss 50th anniversary
May 26, 2003	Commemorative U.S. expedition
May 17, 2004	Dream Everest
May 31, 2005	Climbing for a Cure
May 19, 2006	Team No Limit
May 16, 2007	SuperSherpas
May 22, 2008	Eco Everest
May 21, 2009	Eco Everest
May 21, 2010	Eco Everest
May 11, 2011	Eco Everest

First ascent of K2 (west face) Russia's Andrew Mariev and Vadim Popovich completed the first successful ascent of the notoriously vicious west face of K2. The expedition—led by Viktor Kozlov (Russia)—reached the 28,251-ft.-high (8,500-m) peak on August 21, 2007, after a grueling 10-week climb. Incredibly, none of the team used oxygen for the climb.

Fastest time to climb Mount Everest and K2 Karl Unterkircher (Italy) summited the Himalayan peaks of Mount Everest (29,029 ft.; 8,848 m) on May 24, 2004, and K2 on July 26, 2004. In both cases, he achieved this without extra oxygen. There was a 63-day gap between his ascents.

First solo summit of Mount Everest Reinhold Messner (Italy) topped Mount Everest, solo, on August 20, 1980. It took Reinhold three days to make the ascent from his base camp at 21,325 ft. (6,500 m).

His climb was made all the more difficult by the fact that he did not use bottled oxygen.

Oldest person to climb Mount Everest (male) According to the Senior Citizen Mount Everest Expedition, Min Bahadur Sherchan (Nepal, b. June 20, 1931) reached the highest point on the Earth on May 25, 2008, at the age of 76 years 340 days.

Tamae Watanabe (Japan, b. November 21, 1938) became the **oldest woman to summit Everest** when she reached the peak at 9:55 a.m. on May 16, 2002, at the age of 63 years 177 days.

First ascent of Mount Everest (female) Junko Tabei (Japan, b. September 22, 1939) reached the summit of Mount Everest on May 16, 1975.

Most ascents of Mount Everest by a woman Lakpa Sherpa (Nepal) topped Mount Everest for the fifth time on June 2, 2005. She made the climb with her husband, George Dijmarescu (U.S.A.), who was himself completing his seventh ascent of Everest.

OLDEST MAN TO CLIMB MOUNT KILIMANJARO Richard Byerley (U.S.A., b. March 26, 1927) reached the summit of Mount Kilimanjaro, Tanzania, at the age of 84 years 193 days, on October 6, 2011. The farmer from Washington, U.S.A., began scaling the mountain on October 2, 2011, at noon, through the Machame route, accompanied by his grandchildren, 29-year-old Annie (left) and 24-year-old Bren (right).

First married couple to reach the summit of Mount Everest Phil and Susan Ershler (U.S.A.) were the first married couple to successfully climb Everest. They made it to the summit on May 16, 2002, the same day that a record 54 people also reached the top.

A CENTURY OF ADVENTURE (1912–2012)

 Circumnavigation

 Mountaineering

 Sea

 Polar

 Land & Air

  May 29, 1953: Edmund Hillary (New Zealand) and Sherpa Tenzing Norgay (Nepal) succeed in the **first ascent of Mount Everest**, the world's **highest peak**.

July 31, 1954: The **first ascent of K2** (the second highest mountain) is made by Achille Compagnoni and Lino Lacedelli (both Italy).

 November 1956: A U.S. Navy crew begin building the Amundsen-Scott South Pole Scientific Station, which goes on to become the **longest-serving polar research station**, continuously occupied to the present day.

January 23, 1960: Jacques Piccard (Switzerland) and Don Walsh (U.S.A.) achieve the **deepest manned submarine dive** when they descend 35,810 ft. (10,911 m) down the Mariana Trench in the Pacific Ocean.

September 3, 1966: John Ridgway and Chay Blyth (both UK) row from Cape Cod, U.S.A., to the Aran Isles, Ireland, in *English Rose III*, the first ocean row of the 20th century. The row takes place 70 years after the **first ocean row** by Norwegians George Harbo and Gabriel Samuelsen in June–August 1896.

 April 22, 1969: Robin Knox-Johnston (UK) arrives at Falmouth as the only competitor left in the *Sunday Times* Golden Globe Race, making him the **first person to sail around the world solo and nonstop**.

July 19, 1969: John Fairfax (UK) returns home triumphant after the **first solo row across any ocean**, crossing the Atlantic east to west in *Britannia*.

July 21, 1969: Neil Armstrong and Edwin "Buzz" Aldrin (both U.S.A.) become the **first humans to walk on the Moon**.

July 30–August 1, 1971: Alfred M. Worden (U.S.A.) of *Apollo 15* becomes the **most isolated human** in history. While his fellow astronauts explore the lunar surface, Worden is alone in the command module 2,234 miles (2,596.4 km) from the nearest person.

August 6, 1971: Chay Blyth (UK) becomes the **first person to sail nonstop westward** around the world on *British Steel*.

EPIC JOURNEYS

FARTHEST FLIGHT BY . . .

Airship The longest nonstop flight by an airship, both in terms of distance and duration, was one of 3,967 miles (6,384.5 km) by Hugo Eckener (Germany), piloting the *Graf Zeppelin* in November 1928. The 71-hour flight took place between Lakehurst, New Jersey, U.S.A., and Friedrichshafen, Germany.

FASTEST TIME TO CYCLE FROM CAIRO TO CAPE TOWN Robert Knol (Netherlands) cycled from Cairo, Egypt, to Cape Town, South Africa, in 70 days 3 hr. 50 min. from January 24 to April 4, 2011. The trip was unsupported and unaided. Robert's bicycle had to be repaired only once, in Zambia. In Sudan, with temperatures approaching 113°F (45°C), he drank around 3.08 gal. (15 liters) of water every day.

LONGEST JOURNEY ON CRUTCHES Guy Amalfitano (France) traveled 2,488.04 miles (4,004.12 km) through France, on crutches, ending in Orthez on July 27, 2011.

Adventure

Autogyro Wing Commander Kenneth H. Wallis (UK) holds the straight-line distance record of 543.27 miles (874.32 km) in a WA-116/F gyrocopter. His nonstop flight from Lydd, Kent, UK, to Wick, Highland, UK, took place on September 28, 1975.

Commercial aircraft From November 9 to 10, 2005, a Boeing 777-200LR Worldliner was flown 11,664 nautical miles (13,422.7 miles; 21,601.7 km) nonstop and without refueling from Hong Kong to London, UK. At 22 hr. 42 min., it was the longest flight ever by an unmodified commercial aircraft. The 777-200LR is powered by two General Electric GE90-115Bs, the world's **most powerful jet engines**. The first aircraft were delivered to customer airlines early in 2006.

Paraglider (male) The farthest straight distance achieved by a male paraglider is 312.5 miles (502.9 km) by Nevil Hulett (South Africa) at Copperton, South Africa, on December 14, 2008.

Kamira Pereira (Brazil) carried out the **farthest paraglider flight by a woman**, traveling 201.63 miles (324.5 km) in a straight line west from Quixada, Brazil, on November 14, 2009. In doing so, she beat her own record of 200 miles (323 km), which she had set six days earlier.

FASTEST TIME TO . . .

Cycle across Canada Arvid Loewen (Canada) cycled across Canada in 13 days 6 hr. 13 min. between July 1 and July 14, 2011.

Cycle across Europe (North Cape to Tarifa) From June 20 to July 29, 2011, Glen Burmeister (UK) cycled solo across Europe, north to south, in 39 days 11 hr. 24 min. 24.71 sec.

HIGHEST ALTITUDE ON A TANDEM PARAGLIDER Lifting off from the summit of Everest on May 21, 2011, Babu Sunuwar and Lakpa Sherpa (both Nepal) reached a height of approximately 29,127 ft. (8,878 m), the greatest altitude achieved on a tandem paraglider. The two men then traveled 19.3 miles (31 km) around Mount Nuptse before landing safely at the airport in Namche Bazaar, Nepal.

FACT: Human beings cannot survive extended periods at altitudes beyond around 20,000 ft. (6,000 m).

LONGEST JOURNEY ON A 50CC SCOOTER The greatest distance covered on a 50cc scooter was 7,730.66 miles (12,441.29 km) by Claudio Torresan (Italy). He traveled from Shumen, Bulgaria, to Almaty, Kazakhstan, between May 25 and November 25, 2010.

MOST TRAVELED TOY MASCOT Toy bear Raymondo, owned by ISPY (UK), flew 395,605 miles (636,714.8 km) from September 27, 2009, to September 3, 2010, via 35 countries.

Cycle across the Sahara Desert Reza Pakravan (Iran) crossed the Sahara Desert by bicycle in 13 days 5 hr. 50 min. 14 sec. He set out on March 4, at 30°00'5"N, 2°57'2"E in Algeria and completed his journey at 17°59'2"N, 30°59'4"E, in Sudan, on March 17, 2011.

Fly across the Atlantic Ocean The transatlantic flight record stands at 1 hr. 54 min. 56.4 sec. U.S.A.F Major James V. Sullivan and Major Noel F. Widdifield (both U.S.A.) flew a Lockheed SR-71A Blackbird eastward on September 1, 1974. The average speed for the New York–London stage of 3,461.53 miles (5,570.80 km) was 1,806.96 mph (2,908.02 km/h). The pilots slowed their speed only once, to allow for refueling from a specially modified tanker aircraft.

Run from John o'Groats to Land's End The fastest run between John o'Groats and Land's End, UK, lasted 9 days 2 hr. 26 min. and was achieved by Andrew Rivett (UK) from May 4 to 13, 2002.

The **fastest confirmed journey from Land's End to John o'Groats by a woman** is 12 days 15 hr. 46 min. 35 sec., by Marina Anderson (UK), from July 16 to 28, 2008.

LONGEST JOURNEY . . .

By car Emil and Liliana Schmid (Switzerland) have covered 413,653 miles (665,712 km) in their Toyota Land Cruiser since October 16, 1984. In the course of their travels, they have crossed 172 countries and territories. Although the Schmids have returned to Switzerland for short periods several times during their adventure, they have no permanent home there.

> **FACT:** Dixie and Sam exploited wind power during their trek, kite skiing for part of the way.

LONGEST UNASSISTED SNOW-KITING TREK IN ANTARCTICA On February 3, 2012, Dixie Dansercoer and Sam Deltour (both Belgium) completed their Antarctic ICE Expedition across unexplored regions of eastern Antarctica. They carried out their 3,114.93-mile (5,013-km) trip without any external assistance or the use of motorized vehicles.

By helicopter Robert Ferry (U.S.A.) piloted his Hughes YOH-6A helicopter from Culver City, California, U.S.A., to Ormond Beach, Florida, U.S.A., without refueling, a distance of 2,213.1 miles (3,561.6 km). The flight ended on April 6, 1966.

By motorcycle Emilio Scotto of Buenos Aires, Argentina, completed the longest ever journey by a motorcycle, covering more than 457,000 miles (735,000 km) and 214 countries and territories, from January 17, 1985, to April 2, 1995.

The **longest continuous journey by motorcycle within one country** is 11,371.69 miles (18,301 km) by Mohsin Haq (India), who toured all 28 states of India between October 2 and November 26, 2011.

By mouth-controlled motorized wheelchair The longest continuous journey by mouth-controlled motorized wheelchair is 17,398 miles (28,000 km) and was achieved by Chang-Hyun Choi (South Korea) between May 10, 2006, and December 6, 2007. Choi, who is affected by cerebral palsy and paralyzed from the neck down, traveled at a maximum speed of 8 mph (13 km/h) across 35 countries in Europe and the Middle East.

SNOWKITING EXPEDITION BY NUMBERS

- 74 days on the ice
- 42 miles (68 km) per day travel, on average
- 24 days on which they covered more than 62 miles (100 km)
- 11 days of enforced rest owing to inclement weather
- 10,324 ft. (3,147 m) average altitude
- −22.72°F (−30.4°C) average temperature
- 6.69 mph (10.77 km/h) average speed (on active days)

Walking backward The greatest ever exponent of reverse pedestrianism was Plennie L. Wingo (U.S.A.), who completed an 8,000-mile (12,875-km) transcontinental walk from Santa Monica, California, U.S.A., to Istanbul, Turkey, from April 15, 1931, to October 24, 1932.

A CENTURY OF ADVENTURE (1912–2012)

 Circumnavigation Mountaineering Sea

 Polar Land & Air

April 22, 1972: Sylvia Cook (UK) becomes the **first woman to row across any ocean**, as she and John Fairfax (UK) row the Pacific east to west—in absolute terms, the **first row across the Pacific**.

December 7–19, 1972: The *Apollo 17* crew take part in the **longest lunar mission**, remaining on the Moon's surface for 74 hr. 59 min. 40 sec. Commander Eugene Cernan (U.S.A.) becomes the **last man on the Moon**.

May 16, 1975: Junko Tabei (Japan) is the **first woman to reach the summit of Mount Everest**.

May 8, 1978: Reinhold Messner (Italy, right) and Peter Habeler (Austria) are the **first people to summit Mount Everest without oxygen**.

August 29, 1982: Sir Ranulph Fiennes and Charles Burton (both UK) return from the **first circumnavigation via both poles**, a 35,000-mile (56,000-km) round trip from Greenwich, London, UK.

June 14, 1983: Peter Bird (UK) becomes the **first person to row the Pacific solo**, traveling east to west in *Hele-on-Britannia*.

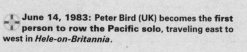

August 5, 1986: Patrick Morrow (Canada) adds Puncak Jaya in Indonesia to his mountaineering tally, making him the **first person to climb the Seven Summits** (highest peaks on each continent).

June 5, 1988: Kay Cottee (Australia) spends 189 days at sea to become the **first woman to sail nonstop around the world solo**.

May 14, 1989: Robert Swan (UK) completes the Icewalk Expedition to the North Pole, becoming the **first person to walk to both poles**. Swan had trekked to the South Pole on January 11, 1986.

May 4, 1990: Børge Ousland (pictured) and Erling Kagge (both Norway) become the **first to reach the North Pole unsupported**; a third team member—Geir Randby—is airlifted after a fall and does not complete the trip.

SEA JOURNEYS

Most solo ocean crossings In 2000, Emmanuel Coindre (France) became the first person to cross the Atlantic Ocean east to west in a pedal-powered boat. He then rowed the Atlantic east to west in 2001, west to east in 2002, and east to west in 2004 before setting a speed record, also in 2004, by rowing the Atlantic again, west to east, in 62 days 19 hr. 48 min. To cap it off, he rowed the Pacific west to east from Chōshi in Japan, to Coos Bay in Oregon, U.S.A., in 2005, taking 129 days 17 hr. 22 min.

Most ocean rows Simon Chalk (UK) has rowed oceans six times, including one solo crossing of the Indian Ocean in 2003. The remaining crossings were completed as a member of various teams of different sizes. As one half of a duo, he rowed the Atlantic east to west in 1997; as part of a five-strong team, he rowed the Atlantic east to west again in 2007–08; in an octet, he rowed the Indian Ocean east to west in 2009; in a team of 14, he rowed the Atlantic east to west in 2011; and finally, in another octet, he rowed the Atlantic east to west in 2012.

FIRST CANOEIST TO PADDLE ACROSS AN OCEAN Gábor Rakonczay (Hungary) crossed the Atlantic Ocean east to west in his 24-ft. 7-in.-long (7.5-m) canoe after 76 days at sea. He set off from Lagos in Portugal on December 21, 2011. After stopping off at Las Palmas in the Canary Islands to rest and for supplies, he continued on January 25, 2012, arriving at the Caribbean island of Antigua in the Leeward Islands, West Indies, on March 25, 2012.

First row across an ocean solo (male) John Fairfax (UK, 1937–2012) rowed the Atlantic Ocean east to west in *Britannia* between January 20 and July 19, 1969.

In addition, his crossing of the Pacific with Sylvia Cook (UK, see p. 226) made John the **first person to row two oceans**.

Youngest person to row an ocean solo On March 14, 2010, Katie Spotz (U.S.A., b. April 18, 1987) completed a 70-day row across the Atlantic Ocean east to west from Dakar in Senegal to Georgetown in Guyana. She set off on January 3, 2010, at the age of just 22 years 260 days.

FASTEST ENGLISH CHANNEL CROSSING BY CANOE (KAYAK) Paul Wycherley (UK) took just 2 hr. 28 min. to row a kayak across the English Channel between Dover Harbour, UK, and Cap Gris Nez, France, on October 2, 2011. There are busy shipping lanes in the Channel, and Paul found himself rowing around ferries and tankers en route. But he didn't mind—in fact, he found that the waves that the ships created broke up the monotony of rowing constantly!

FIRST ROW ACROSS THE PACIFIC OCEAN The first people to row across the Pacific Ocean were John Fairfax and Sylvia Cook (both UK) in *Britannia II* between April 26, 1971, and April 22, 1972.

The **youngest male to row across an ocean solo** is Tommy Tippetts (UK, b. March 26, 1989), who was 22 years 301 days old at the start of his row across the Atlantic east to west from San Sebastián in La Gomera, Canary Islands, to Barbados, West Indies, from January 21 to April 12, 2012, in *Ked Endeavour*. In all, Tippetts spent 82 days 8 hr. 40 min. at sea, raising money for Mind, a mental health charity.

Oldest person to row an ocean solo Tony Short (UK, b. March 28, 1944) was 67 years 252 days old when he began rowing the Atlantic east to west from La Gomera to Barbados in *Spirit of Corinth*. The row lasted from December 5, 2011, to January 22, 2012, a total of 48 days 8 hr. 3 min.

Longest solo row across an ocean From July 10, 2007, to May 17, 2008, Erden Eruç (Turkey) rowed the Pacific Ocean solo, east to west, from California, U.S.A., to Papua New Guinea onboard *Around-n-Over* in a time of 312 days 2 hr.

Fastest solo row across the Atlantic The fastest solo Atlantic crossing east to west in a classic ocean-rowing boat was by Fyodor Konyukhov (Russia), who made the 2,907-mile (4,678-km) journey between San Sebastián in La Gomera, Canary Islands, and Port St. Charles in Barbados in 46 days 4 hr. from October 16 to December 1, 2002.

Andrew Brown (UK) achieved a faster solo row along the same route, in a one-of-a-kind ocean-rowing boat with a modified hull—the **fastest crossing of the Atlantic east to west in an open-class ocean-rowing boat**. Andrew set off from San Sebastián on December 5, 2011, and arrived in Port St. Charles on January 14, 2012, having spent 40 days 9 hr. 41 min. at sea.

The **fastest solo row across the Atlantic east to west on the "Trade Winds II" route** was by Charles Hedrich (France), who rowed 2,507 miles (4,035 km) between Dakar in Senegal, and Guara Point in Brazil, in 36 days 6 hr. 37 min. from December 18, 2006, to January 23, 2007.

First person to sail and row the Indian Ocean James Kayll (UK) sailed from Thailand to Djibouti, onboard *Ocean Song*, from January 8 to February 13, 2005; he then rowed from Geraldton, Western Australia, to Mauritius, onboard *Indian Runner 4* from April 21 to July 6, 2011.

The trimaran *Groupama 3*, skippered by Franck Cammas (France), sailed the Indian Ocean in 8 days 17 hr. 40 min. from February 15 to 23, 2010, the **fastest sailed crossing of the Indian Ocean**.

The **first** and **youngest person to row the Indian Ocean solo** is Sarah Outen (UK, b. May 26, 1985), between April 1 and August 3, 2009, starting off at the age of 23 years 310 days.

Fastest time to swim the Persian Gulf Open-water swimming takes place in open oceans, seas, rivers, canals, and so on. The first and therefore fastest swim along the length of the Persian Gulf is by 34-year-old Mohammad Kobadi (Iran). In 84 days, between December 19, 2011, and March 12, 2012, Kobadi swam 653 miles (1,051 km), in stages, from the Strait of Hormuz to Arvandkenar, along the coast of southeastern Iran, averaging 7.2 miles (11.7 km) per day. The achievement was ratified by Open Water Source.

FIRST FEMALE TO ROW THREE DIFFERENT OCEANS British rower Roz Savage conquered the Atlantic Ocean east to west from the Canary Islands, Spain, to Antigua in the West Indies in 2005–06, the Pacific Ocean east to west from San Francisco, U.S.A., to Madang, Papua New Guinea (via Hawaii, U.S.A., and Tarawa, Kiribati) in 2008–10, and the Indian Ocean east to west from Perth, Australia, to Mauritius in 2011.

FACT: By the end of her third crossing, Roz had spent 510 days at sea, the **most days at sea by a female ocean rower**.

FASTEST CIRCUMNAVIGATION OF AUSTRALIA BY CATAMARAN Bruce Arms (New Zealand) sailed his 45-ft. 11-in. (14-m) catamaran around Australia in 38 days 21 hr. 40 min. 42 sec., setting the record for the swiftest circumnavigation of Australia. He completed his round trip at Mooloolaba, Queensland, on August 18, 2011, at 9:41:06 a.m. AEST.

Fastest time to swim around Manhattan On September 28, 2011, Oliver Wilkinson (Australia) swam around the island of Manhattan in New York, U.S.A., in a time of 5 hr. 44 min. 2 sec., beating the record of 5 hr. 44 min. 47 sec. set earlier that day by Rondi Davies (U.S.A./Australia). The achievement was ratified by NYC Swim, the governing body of the Manhattan Island Marathon Swim.

A CENTURY OF ADVENTURE (1912–2012)

 Circumnavigation

 Mountaineering

 Sea

 Polar

 Land & Air

 May 1996: Freak weather conditions result in the most deaths on Everest in a day, as eight climbers succumb to blizzards and 70-mph (112-km/h) winds; 1996 becomes the deadliest year in Everest's history.

 October 15, 1997: Andy Green (UK) drives the first car to break the sound barrier, averaging a speed of 763 mph (1,236 km/h) behind the wheel of *Thrust SSC*.

 March 20, 1999: Bertrand Piccard (Switzerland) and Brian Jones (UK) complete the first nonstop circumnavigation by balloon in the *Breitling Orbiter 3*.

July 2, 2002: Steve Fossett (U.S.A.) becomes the **first person to circumnavigate the globe by balloon solo** in the 140-ft.-tall (42.6-m) *Bud Light Spirit of Freedom*.

April 30, 2005: Park Young-Seok (South Korea) reaches the North Pole on foot, becoming the **first person to complete the Explorers' Grand Slam**: climbing the Seven Summits and the 14 peaks over 26,246 ft. (8,000 m), reaching both poles on foot and climbing Everest.

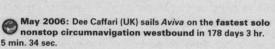

November 2005: Olivier de Kersauson (France) sets the record for the **fastest sail across the Pacific**, taking 4 days 19 hr. 13 min. 37 sec. onboard *Geronimo*.

May 2006: Dee Caffari (UK) sails *Aviva* on the **fastest solo nonstop circumnavigation westbound** in 178 days 3 hr. 5 min. 34 sec.

January 7, 2009: A Canadian team reaches the South Pole after 33 days 23 hr. 30 min.—the **fastest unsupported and unassisted journey to the South Pole**.

January 13, 2011: Christian Eide (Norway) completes the **fastest unsupported solo journey to the South Pole** after a trek lasting 24 days 1 hr.

WORLD TOUR

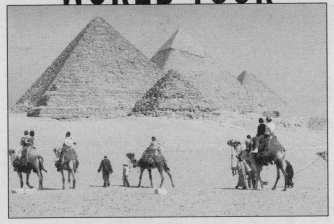

CONTENTS

GWR GOES GLOBAL Packed your suitcase? Got your passport? Then fasten your seat belt, settle back, and relax. It's time to take a trip around the world with Guinness World Records!

Over the next 18 pages, we present a tour of some of the most amazing record-breaking places on our planet. Every record you'll see is a destination you can visit as a tourist, and, taken together, they comprise a route around the globe, continent by continent. Well, we haven't sent you to Antarctica—we've limited it to places you could realistically be expected to spend a vacation. For polar adventures, meanwhile, see p. 211.

Bon voyage!

EUROPE

LARGEST TRILITHONS "Trilithon" is a Greek word that means "three stones," and describes structures comprising two upright stones with a third laid across the top. The largest trilithons are at Stonehenge, to the south of Salisbury Plain (UK), with single sarsen blocks weighing more than 49.5 tons (45 metric tonnes). The tallest upright stone stands 22 ft. (6.7 m) aboveground, with another 8 ft. (2.4 m) belowground. The earliest stage of the construction of the ditch has been dated to 2950 B.C.

MOST EXPENSIVE HOTEL ROOM The Royal Penthouse Suite at the Hotel President Wilson in Geneva, Switzerland, costs U.S. $65,000 per day. For this sum, clients have access to 18,083 sq. ft. (1,680 m²) of space plus views of Mont Blanc—through 2-in.-thick (6-cm) bulletproof windows—along with a private cocktail lounge, a jacuzzi, a fitness center, and a conference room.

LARGEST ANNUAL FOOD FIGHT On the last Wednesday in August, the town of Buñol, near Valencia, Spain, holds its annual tomato festival, La Tomatina. In 2004, 38,000 people spent one hour at this giant food fight, throwing 137.7 tons (125 metric tonnes) of tomatoes at each other. Attendants dump the red fruit from the backs of trucks on to the streets for people to throw.

MOST POPULAR CITY FOR TOURISM The city that has the greatest number of international visitors is Paris, France: 31 out of every 150 foreign tourists to the country arrive in the city. Housed in Paris's Louvre art gallery, Leonardo da Vinci's *Mona Lisa* (ca. 1503–19, left) is considered to be the **most valuable object ever stolen**. It was stolen from the Louvre on August 21, 1911 but was recovered in Italy in 1913. Vincenzo Perugia (Italy) was charged with its theft.

OLDEST AMUSEMENT PARK IN OPERATION Bakken, located in Klampenborg, north of Copenhagen, Denmark, opened in 1583 and is the world's oldest operating amusement park. It is home to five roller coasters, including the wooden "Rutschebanen," built in 1932.

LARGEST BEER FESTIVAL In terms of the quantity of beer consumed, Munich's Oktoberfest 2011 (September 17–October 3, 2011) was history's largest beer festival. Some 6.9 million visitors drank 1.98 million gal. (7.5 million liters) of beer in 35 beer tents.

LARGEST ICE STRUCTURE The Ice Hotel in Jukkasjärvi, Sweden, which is rebuilt each winter, has a total floor area of 43,000–54,000 sq. ft. (4,000–5,000 m²), and in the winter of 2004–05 featured 85 rooms. The hotel also features the Ice Globe theater—based on the design of William Shakespeare's famous playhouse—an ice bar, and an ice church. Lying 124 miles (200 km) north of the Arctic Circle, the hotel has been re-created every December since 1990.

MOST ART GALLERY SPACE You would have to walk 15 miles (24 km) to visit each of the 322 galleries of the Winter Palace within the State Hermitage Museum in St. Petersburg, Russia. The galleries are home to nearly 3 million works of art and objects of archaeological interest.

LARGEST AMPHITHEATER The Flavian amphitheater, or Colosseum, of Rome, Italy, completed in A.D. 80, covers 5 acres (2 ha) and has a capacity of 87,000. It has a maximum length of 612 ft. (187 m) and a maximum width of 515 ft. (157 m).

ASIA

MOST MUSLIM PILGRIMS The Hajj annual pilgrimage to Mecca, Saudi Arabia, attracts an average of 2 million people a year, more than any other Islamic pilgrimage. Pilgrims enter a spiritual state called *ihram*, which for men includes wearing a white seamless garment (intended to show the equality of all Muslims in the eyes of Allah).

MOST VISITED SIKH SHRINE The Golden Temple in Amritsar, India, the world's most important Sikh shrine, has up to 20,000 visitors a day. This figure rises to 200,000 on special festivals, such as Guru Purab (the birthday of one of the 10 Sikh gurus) and Baisakhi (the day Sikhism was established). The temple's second story is covered in precious stones and about 881 lb. (400 kg) of gold leaf.

LARGEST RELIGIOUS STRUCTURE Angkor Wat (City Temple) in Cambodia covers an area of 17.5 million sq. ft. (1.62 million m²) and has an external wall measuring 4,200 ft. (1,280 m). It was built for the Hindu god Vishnu by the Khmer King Suryavarman II in the period 1113–50, and housed a population of 80,000 before it was abandoned in 1432.

FACT: The Angkor settlement, which included Angkor Wat, covered more than 386 sq. miles (1,000 km²)—the world's largest preindustrial metropolis.

HIGHEST MOUNTAIN Mount Everest epitomizes humanity's sense of adventure. Located in the Himalayas, at 29,029 ft. (8,848 m) high, it was named in 1865 after Sir George Everest (1790–1866), a Surveyor-General of India. But it was only in 1953 that New Zealander Edmund Hillary and Tenzing Norgay, a Nepali from India, managed to climb it. In the snow at the top, Norgay left candies as an offering to Buddhist gods and Hillary left a small cross.

LARGEST OBSERVATION WHEEL The Singapore Flyer, in Marina Bay, Singapore, consists of a 492-ft.-wide (150-m) wheel, built over a three-story terminal building, giving a total height of 541 ft. (165 m). It was opened to the public on March 1, 2008.

STEEPEST ROLLER COASTER The Takabisha ride at the Fuji-Q Highland park in Fujiyoshida City, Japan, has a 121-degree "beyond vertical" drop for 11 ft. 2 in. (3.4 m). The carriages descend from a 141-ft.-1-in. (43-m) tower, enter the steepest stretch at 95 ft. 1 in. (29 m), and, for a stomach-churning 0.38 seconds, the riders are traveling down and inward at the same time.

FACT: Buddha was a spiritual teacher who lived about 500 years before Christ. He was born in Nepal or India and his teachings are the basis of Buddhism.

LARGEST PALACE The Imperial Palace in the center of Beijing, China, covers a rectangle measuring 3,150 × 2,460 ft. (960 × 750 m) over an area of 178 acres (72 ha). The outline survives from the construction of the third Ming Emperor, Yongle (1402–24), but most of the buildings are from the 18th century.

TALLEST STONE BUDDHA The Leshan Giant Buddha in the Sichuan Province of China was carved out of a hillside in the 8th century. It measures 233 ft. (71 m) in height, making it the tallest statue of Buddha to be carved entirely out of stone. The statue and surrounding area have been designated a UNESCO World Heritage Site.

LONGEST WALL The main part of the Great Wall of China is 2,150 miles (3,460 km) long—nearly three times the length of Britain. It also has 2,195 miles (3,530 km) of branches and spurs. Built to protect the northern border of the Chinese empire, it runs from Shanhaiguan on the Gulf of Bohai to Yumenguan and Yangguan.

FACT: Before the Ming dynasty started in 1368, the wall was built from rammed earth, stones, and wood. During Ming rule, bricks were used, quickening the wall-building.

MOST EXPENSIVE ELEPHANT PAINTING
Tourists visiting the Maesa Elephant Camp in Chiang Mai, Thailand, can marvel at the paintings produced by the pachyderms. The most expensive—entitled *Cold Wind, Swirling Mist, Charming Lanna I*—sold for 1.5 million baht (U.S. $32,970) to Panit Warin (Thailand) on February 19, 2005.

LARGEST ORANGUTAN SANCTUARY
Since 1964, the Sepilok Orangutan Rehabilitation Centre, in the Malaysian state of Sabah, in northern Borneo, has rehabilitated more than 100 orphaned orangutans back into the wild. Baby orangutans usually stay with their mothers for six years, but they often have to be rescued during logging and forest clearances, or from poachers. At Sepilok, a buddy system is used to replace a mother's teaching.

AFRICA

LARGEST MUD BUILDING The Great Mosque in Djenné, Mali, measures 328 ft. (100 m) long and 131 ft. (40 m) wide. The present structure was built in 1905 and is made from sun-baked mud bricks, secured with a mud-based mortar, and coated with a mud plaster to create a smooth, sculpted look. It is replastered every year.

TALLEST MINARET The minaret of the Great Hassan II mosque in Casablanca, Morocco, measures 656 ft. (200 m). The mosque, built from 1986 to 1993, cost 5 billion dirhams (U.S. $574 million) and can accommodate 25,000 worshippers in its prayer hall, which has a retractable roof, and an additional 80,000 people within its environs.

FACT: The far side of the Great Hassan II mosque sits above the sea. This was inspired by a Quran verse that states: "The throne of Allah was built on water."

LARGEST WATERFALL (VERTICAL AREA)
The Victoria Falls, on the Zambezi River between Zimbabwe and Zambia, is neither the tallest nor the widest waterfall in the world, but it is the largest by vertical area. At 5,604 ft. (1,708 m) wide and 354 ft. (108 m) high, it creates a sheet of falling water with an area of around 2,017,400 sq. ft. (184,400 m^2).

LARGEST SCENTED GARDEN FOR THE BLIND.
The Kirstenbosch National Botanical Gardens on the eastern slopes of Table Mountain, Cape Town, South Africa, has a Fragrance Garden for the blind that measures 88.9 acres (36 ha). A Braille Trail in the main gardens starts and ends at the Fragrance Garden.

LONGEST RIVER
The Nile's main source is Lake Victoria in east central Africa. From its farthest stream in Burundi, it extends 4,160 miles (6,695 km) in length.

LARGEST GAME RESERVE Larger than Switzerland, the Selous Game Reserve extends over 21,236 sq. miles (55,000 km²) of woodland, grassland swamp, and forest in southern Tanzania. It was designated a UNESCO World Heritage Site in 1982. This was as a result of its diverse wildlife, which includes one of the world's largest populations of wild dogs, and its undisturbed nature—there is no permanent human habitation in the reserve, only tourist facilities.

GREATEST WATERFALL (ANNUAL FLOW) The Boyoma Falls in the Democratic Republic of the Congo (formerly Zaire) has an average annual flow of 600,000 cu. ft./sec. (17,000 m³/sec). Formerly known as Stanley Falls, it has seven cataracts and extends for 60 miles (100 km) along a curve of the Lualaba River between Ubundu and Kisangani.

OLDEST ISLAND Madagascar, in the Indian Ocean, became an island around 80–100 million years ago, when it split off from the Indian subcontinent. It is now only 248.5 miles (400 km) off the coast of Africa (at the shortest point) and is considered part of the African continent. Lemurs, such as the diademed sifaka (*Propithecus diadema*) left, are indigenous to Madagascar.

TALLEST PYRAMID Khufu's pyramid at Giza, Egypt, also known as the Great Pyramid, was 481.4 ft. (146.7 m) high when completed about 4,500 years ago, but erosion and vandalism have reduced its height to 451.4 ft. (137.5 m) today. In this photo, it is the far pyramid—because it is in the distance, it looks smaller than Khafre's pyramid in the middle.

LONGEST RIFT SYSTEM The Great Rift Valley is about 4,000 miles (6,400 km) long with an average width of 30–40 miles (50–65 km). It begins in Jordan and extends along the Red Sea into east Africa. The African section, from Ethiopia to Mozambique, is about 2,175 miles (3,500 km) long and includes the Ol Doinyo Lengai volcano in Tanzania, right. The valley has been forming for about 30 million years.

OCEANIA

OLDEST OPERATING OPEN-AIR MOVIE THEATER Sun Picture Theatre, in Broome, Western Australia, first opened on December 9, 1916. The movie theater played only silent movies until 1933, when it showed its first "talkie"—*Monte Carlo* (U.S.A., 1930), a musical starring Jeanette MacDonald and Jack Buchanan (both U.S.A.).

WIDEST BRIDGE The widest long-span bridge is the 1,650-ft.-long (503-m) Sydney Harbour Bridge, Australia, which is 160 ft. (48.8 m) wide. It carries two electric overhead railroad tracks, eight lanes of roadway, and a cycle track and footway. The bridge was officially opened on March 19, 1932.

LARGEST SANDSTONE MONOLITH Uluru, also known as Ayers Rock, rises 1,143 ft. (348 m) above the surrounding desert plain in Northern Territory, Australia. It is 1.5 miles (2.5 km) long and 1 mile (1.6 km) wide. Uluru's distinctive reddish color is caused by the oxidation of iron-bearing minerals in the rock.

FACT: Uluru was originally part of an ancient mountain range. The surrounding peaks have been eroded away over hundreds of millions of years.

CARSTENSZ PYRAMID, INDONESIA
At 16,023 ft. (4,884 m), the Carstensz Pyramid (also known as Puncak Jaya), in Papua Province, Indonesia, is Oceania's tallest peak. It features on one of the two Seven Summits lists (see above). Henrik Kristiansen (Denmark) set the fastest time to climb the highest peak on each continent (Carstensz list), in 136 days from January 21, 2008, to June 5, 2008.

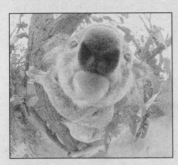

OLDEST KOALA SANCTUARY
Established in 1927 by Claude Reid (Australia), the Lone Pine Koala Sanctuary in Brisbane, Queensland, Australia, is the world's oldest koala sanctuary. The sanctuary currently houses more than 130 animals—the greatest number of koalas in captivity.

LONGEST REEF The Great Barrier Reef off Queensland, northeastern Australia, is 1,260 miles (2,027 km) in length. It is not actually a single structure, but consists of thousands of separate reefs. On three occasions (between 1962 and 1971, 1979 and 1991, and 1995 and the present), corals on large areas of the central section of the reef were eaten away by the crown-of-thorns starfish (*Acanthaster planci*).

LARGEST SAND ISLAND Fraser Island, located off the south coast of Queensland, Australia, covers approximately 402,750 acres (163,000 ha). It is home to a sand dune 75 miles (120 km) long and more than 100 freshwater lakes. In 1992, the island was recognized by the United Nations Educational, Scientific, and Cultural Organization (UNESCO) as a World Heritage Site.

MOST SOUTHERLY CAPITAL CITY Wellington, North Island, New Zealand, which had a population of around 393,000 as of June 2011, is the southernmost capital city of an independent country (41°17'S). The world's southernmost capital of a dependent territory is Port Stanley, Falkland Islands (51°43'S).

NORTH AMERICA

LARGEST JAZZ FESTIVAL The Festival International de Jazz de Montréal in Québec, Canada, is the world's largest jazz festival. The event attracted 1,913,868 people in July 2004, its 25th anniversary year.

MOST VISITED WATERFALL Located on the border between Canada and the U.S.A., Niagara Falls receives 22.5 million visitors a year. It is also the fifth most popular tourist attraction in the world, beating the Disney theme parks; the Notre Dame Cathedral in Paris, France; and the Great Wall of China.

FIRST DARK SKY PARK The International Dark Sky Association has named Utah's Natural Bridges National Monument as the first dark sky park. This is an area where the night sky can be seen clearly, without any light pollution.

OLDEST NATIONAL PARK Yellowstone National Park, U.S.A., was the first area in the world to be designated a national park. It was given its status in 1872 by U.S. president Ulysses S. Grant, who declared that it would always be "dedicated and set apart as a public park or pleasuring ground for the benefit and enjoyment of the people." The park covers 3,470 sq. miles (8,980 km²), mainly in the state of Wyoming.

HIGHEST CONCENTRATION OF THEME HOTELS There are 14 theme hotels on the Strip in Las Vegas, Nevada, U.S.A., all of which boast extravagant designs. The Luxor has a sphinx, a black pyramid, and an obelisk; New York New York recreates a scaled-down version of the New York skyline; and Paris features a half-scale Eiffel Tower.

MOST VISITED THEME PARK As of 2010, the Magic Kingdom at Walt Disney World in Florida, U.S.A., had been visited by more than 16.9 million visitors, according to a report compiled by Themed Entertainment Association (TEA) and Economics Research Associates (ERA). It was followed by Disneyland in Anaheim, California, U.S.A., which had 15.9 million guests, and Tokyo Disneyland in Japan, which had 14.4 million visitors.

HEAVIEST STATUE Unveiled on October 28, 1886, the Statue of Liberty weighs 27,156 tons (24,635 metric tonnes), of which 31 tons (28 metric tonnes) is copper, 125 tons (113 metric tonnes) is steel, and 27,000 tons (24,494 metric tonnes) makes up the concrete foundation. It was presented to the U.S.A. as a gift from France to mark the friendship between the two countries.

FACT: The Grand Canyon stretches over an area of more than 1 million acres (404,685 ha). Each year it attracts at least 5 million visitors.

LARGEST MONUMENT The volume of the Quetzalcóatl Pyramid at Cholula de Rivadavia in Central Mexico has been estimated at 151 million cu. ft (3.3 million m^3). The pyramid stands 177 ft. (54 m) tall and its base covers an area of nearly 45 acres (18.2 ha). The structure is now mostly overgrown (and a Spanish church was built on top in the 1590s) but recent excavations and renovations have revealed some of the original structure (left).

LARGEST LAND GORGE The Grand Canyon was created over the course of millions of years by the Colorado River in north-central Arizona, U.S.A. It runs from Marble Gorge to the Grand Wash Cliffs, covering a distance of 277 miles (446 km). The gorge extends to a depth of 1 mile (1.6 km) and its width ranges from 0.3–18 miles (0.5—29 km).

SOUTH AMERICA

LARGEST GEOGLYPHS
The so-called "Nazca lines" are a group of huge figures engraved on the desert ground of Nazca (Peru) representing plants, animals, insects, and various geometric shapes. Most can be appreciated only from the air. The designs occupy a 193-sq.-mile (500-km^2) area and average 600 ft. (180 m) in length.

GREATEST RIVER FLOW On average, the Amazon discharges water at 7,100,000 cu. ft./sec. (200,000 m³/sec.) into the Atlantic Ocean, increasing to more than 12,000,000 cu. ft./sec. (340,000 m³/sec) in full flood. The lower 900 miles (1,450 km) of the river average 55 ft. (17 m) in depth, but the river has a maximum depth of 407 ft. (124 m).

TALLEST MOAI "Moai" are monolithic human figures that were carved from rock on Easter Island (Rapa Nui) between 1250 and 1500. In all, 887 of these statues have been discovered so far. The tallest standing moai, which has been named "Paro," measures 32 ft. 1 in. (9.8 m) in height and is located at Ahu Te Pito Kura, Easter Island. It weighs 82 tons (74.39 tonnes).

HIGHEST NAVIGABLE LAKE The highest commercially navigable lake is Lake Titicaca, which lies in the Altiplano at a height of 12,500 ft. (3,810 m) above sea level on the Andean border between Peru and Bolivia. Its surface area covers approximately 3,200 sq. miles (8,300 km²) and it has an average depth of 460–590 ft. (140–180 m), so it is deep enough for the safe passage of commercial vessels.

LARGEST CARNIVAL Rio de Janeiro's annual carnival is usually held for four days in February or March and attracts about 2 million people each day. In 2004, the carnival drew in a record 400,000 foreign visitors, of which 2,600 were thought to have been from the *Queen Mary II* ocean liner. Samba schools spend many months creating the fabulous, colorful costumes that they wear when they dance through the city's streets.

LARGEST SWIMMING POOL The San Alfonso del Mar seawater pool in Algarrobo, Chile, is 3,324 ft. (1,013 m) long and has an area of 19.77 acres (8 ha). It was completed in December 2006, after 10 years' work. The pool employs advanced technology to draw seawater into one end of the pool from the Pacific Ocean, filter and treat it, and then pump it out at the other end.

TALLEST WATER SLIDE The world's loftiest water slide is Kilimanjaro at Águas Quentes Country Club in Barra do Piraí, Rio de Janeiro, Brazil. Constructed in 2002, it reaches a vertiginous 163 ft. 9 in. (49.9 m)—that's taller than the Statue of Liberty— and descends at an angle of 60 degrees. If you're brave enough to tackle this skyscraping slide, you'll find yourself racing downward at speeds approaching 60 mph (96 km/h)!

LARGEST SWAMP Located principally in southwestern Brazil, but with small areas within neighboring Bolivia and Paraguay, too, the Pantanal (which is Spanish for "marshland") covers a surface area of 57,915 sq. miles (150,000 km²)—greater than the total surface area of England!

HIGHEST WATERFALL The Salto Angel in Venezuela, on a branch of the Carrao River, an upper tributary of the Caroni River, has a total drop of 3,212 ft. (979 m), with the longest single drop being 2,648 ft. (807 m). The "Angel Falls" were named after the American pilot James "Jimmie" Angel, who recorded them in his log book on November 16, 1933.

LARGEST INCA DISCOVERY The two Yale University Peruvian Expeditions of 1911–12 and 1914–15, both led by historian Hiram Bingham (U.S.A.), uncovered the lost Inca cities of Machu Picchu (left)—which is the largest Inca site yet discovered—and Vitcos. These sites are regarded as two of the most important archaeological finds in the Americas. It is believed that the Spanish conquistadors, who conquered the Incas, failed to find Machu Picchu.

SOCIETY

CONTENTS

39,437

LARGEST SCHOOL The largest school in terms of pupils is the City Montessori School in Lucknow, India, which had a record enrollment of 39,437 children on August 9, 2010, for the 2010–11 academic year. The school admits boys and girls between ages two and five, who can then continue their education to degree level. In 2002, it won the UNESCO Prize for Peace Education. The City Montessori has come a long way since Jagdish Gandhi and his wife Bharti first opened it in 1959 with a loan of just 300 rupees (U.S. $63)! Then it had a grand total of five pupils!

HOW RICH CAN YOU GET?

ENDLESS PURSUIT OF WEALTH

There was a time when real wealth was largely inherited. It was tied up in land and the right to farm that land. Over time, the ability to exploit the oil, gas, minerals, and precious metals that lay beneath the surface of the land changed the face of wealth. It also served to feed the demands of emerging industries, such as steel and shipping—and the powerful men who went on to make fortunes from them.

Fortunes are still made and maintained in the old industries, but a new source of wealth has emerged based on technologies that barely existed 50 years ago. Telecoms and computing—convergent technologies that seem to change almost daily—are the new engines of wealth creation, but will today's technology billionaires ever reach, or exceed, the heady heights of the Rockefellers and the Vanderbilts? Is there a limit to just how much money one person can actually accrue?

All figures are given in U.S. dollars.

The World Bank puts the GDP of the world at $63.04 trillion. Yet John D. Rockefeller, the richest person in history, managed to acquire just a fraction of that—and at the peak of his wealth he owned 85% of the crude oil known to exist at the time and 95% of the world's oil refineries! So what might have stopped him going any further and grabbing the lot?

Economic systems require stability if they are to function properly. Any imbalance will inevitably require that the system be rebalanced. This means that while an individual might, in theory, be able to acquire all the money in the world, the tipping point for a chaotic imbalance in the system will have been reached long before they do so, causing the kind of economic crash that would result in their money not being worth the paper it was printed on.

TOP TEN RICHEST LIVING PEOPLE, 2012

The world's wealthiest according to Forbes (and how their wealth compares to the GDP of various countries—yes, these people are personally richer than some countries!)

Name	Business	Worth
1. Carlos Slim Helú (Mexico) *Richer than: Puerto Rico*	Telmex and América Móvil (telecoms)	$69 billion
2. Bill Gates (U.S.A.) *Richer than: Slovenia*	Microsoft (computing)	$61 billion
3. Warren Buffett (U.S.A.) *Richer than: Luxembourg*	Berkshire Hathaway (holdings: retail, rail, media, utilities)	$44 billion
4. Bernard Arnault (France) *Richer than: North Korea*	LVMH (apparels/accessories)	$41 billion
5. Amancio Ortega Gaona (Spain) *Richer than: Jordan*	Inditex/Zara (fashion)	$37.5 billion
6. Larry Ellison (U.S.A.) *Richer than: Honduras*	Oracle (computing)	$36 billion
7. Eike Batista (Brazil) *Richer than: Afghanistan*	EBX Group (mining, oil)	$30 billion
8. Stefan Persson (Sweden) *Richer than: Senegal*	H&M (fashion)	$26 billion
9. Li Ka-shing (China) *Richer than: Senegal*	Hutchison Whampoa & Cheung Kong Holdings (diverse)	$25.5 billion
9=. Karl Albrecht (Germany) *Richer than: Senegal*	Aldi (discount supermarkets)	$25.5 billion

FACT: Even if you spent $1,000 a day, it would take you around 2,739 years to spend $1 billion!

RICHEST PEOPLE IN HISTORY This filthy-rich lineup of billionaires represents our best estimation of the wealthiest people of all time. It includes rulers, business magnates, and entrepreneurs from across history, with their estimated wealth adjusted for inflation to allow for comparison. How do these people—all men—compare? And how do they compare with today's moneymakers?

TOP TEN RICHEST PEOPLE OF ALL TIME

WHO Cornelius Vanderbilt (U.S.A.)
WEALTH $170 billion
WHY New York and Harlem Railroad
DETAILS: At the time of his death at 82 in 1877, the engineering entrepreneur was worth $105 million—roughly 1/87th of the GDP of the entire U.S.A.!

WHO Basil II (Byzantine Empire)
WEALTH $172 billion
WHY Byzantine Emperor (976–1025)
DETAILS: Basil, aka the "Bulgarslayer," ruthlessly expanded his empire, taxing the nobility as he went; died at 67, leaving behind a full treasury.

WHO Marcus Licinius Crassus (Italy)
WEALTH $172.5 billion
WHY Consul of the Roman Republic (115–53 B.C.)
DETAILS: Historian Pliny estimated Crassus' wealth at 200 million sestertii from slavery, mining, and real estate.

GOLD! Gold was first mined by the ancient Egyptians, but 66% of the total gold now in circulation was mined after 1950. There is an estimated 153,000 tons (157,000 metric tonnes) of gold in the world—enough, if melted, to fill 3.27 Olympic-size swimming pools.

WHO Henry Ford (U.S.A.)
WEALTH $191 billion
WHY Founder of the Ford Motor Company
DETAILS: Didn't invent the automobile, but the Model-T entrepreneur was practically responsible for the assembly line.

WHO Andrew W. Mellon (U.S.A.)
WEALTH $192 billion
WHY Oil, steel, and shipping magnate
DETAILS: Banker, politician, statesman, philanthropist, art collector; wealth peaked at $400 million in 1930.

WHO Osman Ali Khan, Asaf Jah VII (Hyderabad)
WEALTH $213 billion
WHY Ruler of Hyderabad (now India)
DETAILS: His Exalted Highness The Nizam of Hyderabad (ruled 1911–48) enjoyed the royalties from Hyderabad's diamond mining—until the country was forcibly annexed by India.

WHO William Henry Vanderbilt (U.S.A.)
WEALTH $235 billion
WHY Son of Cornelius (see no. 10, page 257)
DETAILS: Inherited ca. $100 million from daddy but managed to nearly double it in just nine years by expanding the family railroad business. Famously unhappy with his wealth.

WHO Nicholas II (Russia)
WEALTH $257 billion
WHY Last (and worst?) Emperor of Russia
DETAILS: Wealthiest monarch in history, reported to be worth $881 million at the age of 48 in 1916; abdicated the following year, then murdered in 1918 by the Bolsheviks.

FACT: Are you worth your weight in gold? The average 145-lb. (66-kg) man, if made of gold, would be worth $3,607,560!

WHO Andrew Carnegie (UK/U.S.A.)
WEALTH $302 billion
WHY Steel magnate
DETAILS: Born in Dunfermline, Scotland, Carnegie emigrated to the U.S.A. in 1848, where he founded a steel company that he would eventually sell in 1901 for $480 million; gave most of it away in philanthropic ventures.

WHO John D. Rockefeller (U.S.A.)
WEALTH $322 billion
WHY Standard Oil (Esso)
DETAILS: Founded his oil company in 1870 and became America's first billionaire as the demand for petroleum and gasoline exploded; like Carnegie, he gave much of it away—he spent 40 years of his retirement as a philanthropist.

THE COAT OF ARMS

RICHEST FAMILY? The House of Rothschild—a German/Jewish dynasty that founded banks and financial institutions in 18th-century Europe—could be considered the richest family in history. Renowned for their secrecy, as well as their philanthropy, the many generations of Rothschilds are believed to have a wealth valued in excess of $1 trillion in today's money. Their businesses continue to thrive, still driven by family members. The price of gold, for example, is fixed daily at the Rothschild & Sons offices in London.

FACT: The Rothschild family coat of arms' Latin motto translates as "harmony, integrity, industry."

PETS

Farthest distance tracked by a lost dog In 1979, Jimpa, a labrador/boxer cross, arrived at his old home in Pimpinio, Victoria, Australia, after walking 2,000 miles (3,220 km) across Australia. His owner, Warren Dumesney (Australia), had taken Jimpa with him 14 months earlier when he went to work on a farm at Nyabing, Western Australia. During his trek, the dog negotiated the almost waterless Nullarbor Plain.

Largest pet gathering A group of 4,616 pets went for a walk with their owners at La Feria de las Flores ("Flower Fair") in Medellín, Colombia, on August 7, 2007.

OLDEST LIVING RABBIT Do is a Jersey Wooley owned by Jenna Antol of New Jersey, U.S.A. He was born on January 1, 1996, and was 16 years 1 month 14 days old on February 15, 2012.

TALLEST DOMESTIC CAT Savannah Islands Trouble is 1 ft. 7 in. (48.3 cm) tall. He is owned by Debby Maraspini (U.S.A.) and was measured at the Silver Cats Cat Show at the Grand Sierra Resort in Reno, Nevada, U.S.A., on October 30, 2011.

The **longest domestic cat** is Mymains Stewart Gilligan at 48.5 in. (123 cm) long. He is owned by Robin Hendrickson and Erik Brandsness (both U.S.A.) and was measured on August 28, 2010.

FACT: Savannah Islands Trouble is 0.93 in. (2.4 cm) taller than the previous record holder.

Society

PET PHOTOGRAPHED WITH THE MOST CELEBRITIES A white Maltese dog called Lucky Diamond has been photographed with 359 different celebrities, including Kim Kardashian, Richard Branson, Snoop Dogg, and Kristen Stewart (all above, left to right). Lucky's owner is Wendy Diamond (U.S.A.).

Longest cat whiskers At 7.5 in. (19 cm), the longest whiskers on a cat belong to Missi, a Maine coon who lives with her owner, Kaija Kyllönen. The whiskers were measured in Iisvesi, Finland, on December 22, 2005.

Longest dog tail As of April 12, 2012, the longest dog tail measured 26 in. (66.04 cm) and belonged to Bentley, a great dane from Colorado, U.S.A. He is owned by Patrick Malcom and his family.

Most expensive pet wedding In September 1996, two rare "diamond-eyed" cats, Phet and Ploy, were married at a lavish ceremony at Phoebus House, Thailand's biggest discotheque. The wedding cost Phet's owner, Wichan Jaratarcha, U.S. $16,241 on top of an additional dowry of U.S. $23,202.

Most prolific cat During her life, a tabby from Texas, U.S.A., named Dusty, produced 420 kittens. She gave birth to her last litter (a single kitten) on June 12, 1952.

Shortest living domestic cat The shortest cat alive is Fizz Girl, a two-year-old female munchkin cat, who measured 6 in. (15.24 cm) from the floor to the shoulders on July 23, 2010. The pint-size pet is owned by Tiffani Kjeldergaard of San Diego, U.S.A.

Wealthiest cat When Ben Rea (UK) died in May 1988, he bequeathed his £7-million (U.S. $12.5-million) fortune to Blackie, the last surviving of the 15 cats with whom he shared his mansion. The millionaire antiques dealer and recluse refused to recognize his family in his will.

Similarly, the **wealthiest dog** was a standard poodle named Toby, who was left U.S. $15 million in the will of Ella Wendel of New York, U.S.A., in 1931.

TALLEST DOG A great dane named Zeus measured 3 ft. 8 in. (111.8 cm) tall on October 4, 2011—making him both the **tallest living dog** and the **tallest dog ever.** The Olympian canine is owned by Denise Doorlag (pictured) and her family of Otsego in Michigan, U.S.A.

OLDEST . . .

Bearded dragon: Guinness, a lizard owned by Nik Vernon (UK), was born on July 26, 1997, and was 14 years 7 months 17 days old as of April 20, 2012.

Budgerigar: Charlie, born in April 1948 and owned by J. Dinsey (UK), died on June 20, 1977, when 29 years 2 months old.

Cat: A cat named Creme Puff, born on August 3, 1967, lived until August 6, 2005—an amazing 38 years 3 days! She lived with her owner, Jake Perry, in Austin, Texas, U.S.A.

The **oldest living cat** is Pinky, who was born on October 31, 1989, and lives with her owner, Linda Anno, in Hoyt, Kansas, U.S.A.

Chinchilla: A chinchilla named Bouncer, born on July 1, 1977, and owned by Jenny Ann Bowen of Great Barr in Birmingham, UK, died on October 3, 2005, at the incredible age of 28 years 94 days.

SMALLEST SERVICE DOG The smallest service dog is Cupcake (left)—a five-year-old female long-haired teacup chihuahua owned by Angela Bain of Moorestown, New Jersey, U.S.A. Cupcake is only 6.25 in. (15.87 cm) tall!

Dog: The greatest reliable age recorded for a dog is 29 years 5 months for an Australian cattle dog named Bluey (d. 1939), who was obtained as a puppy in 1910 by Les Hall of Rochester, Victoria, Australia.

Goldfish: A goldfish named Tish, owned by Hilda and Gordon Hand (UK), lived for 43 years after Hilda's son Peter won the fish at a fairground stall in 1956.

Guinea pig: Snowball the guinea pig, who lived in Nottinghamshire, UK, died on February 14, 1979, at the age of 14 years 10 months 2 weeks. Guinea pigs have an average lifespan of 4–8 years.

Mouse: A house mouse called Fritzy (b. September 11, 1977), who belonged to Bridget Beard of Edgbaston, West Midlands, UK, died at the age of 7 years 7 months on April 24, 1985. Mice usually live for 1.5–2 years.

Rat: A common rat called Rodney (b. January 1983), belonging to Rodney Mitchell of Tulsa in Oklahoma, U.S.A., died aged 7 years and 4 months on May 25, 1990.

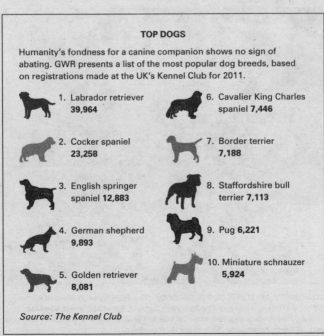

TOP DOGS

Humanity's fondness for a canine companion shows no sign of abating. GWR presents a list of the most popular dog breeds, based on registrations made at the UK's Kennel Club for 2011.

1. Labrador retriever **39,964**

2. Cocker spaniel **23,258**

3. English springer spaniel **12,883**

4. German shepherd **9,893**

5. Golden retriever **8,081**

6. Cavalier King Charles spaniel **7,446**

7. Border terrier **7,188**

8. Staffordshire bull terrier **7,113**

9. Pug **6,221**

10. Miniature schnauzer **5,924**

Source: The Kennel Club

SCHOOLS

First country to impose compulsory education Prussia made education compulsory in 1819.

Lowest pupil-to-teacher ratio San Marino has six pupils to every teacher in elementary schools. At high school level, Monaco has the lowest ratio, with 5.8 pupils per teacher.

Country with most higher education students The U.S.A. has 14,261,800 students in higher education (attending universities, colleges, and comparable institutions).

Most elementary schools India had 664,000 elementary schools, as of September 2011. China, the previous record holder, now has 456,900 elementary schools (down from 849,123 in 1997) as a result of its one-child-per-family policy.

LONGEST WAIT FOR A CLASS REUNION The 1929 class of Miss Blanche Miller's Kindergarten and Continuation School, Bluefield, West Virginia, U.S.A., had its first reunion after 70 years. Ten members of the class had died but, of those remaining, 55% were in attendance.

Most schools attended Wilma Williams, now Mrs. R. J. Horton, attended 265 schools, from 1933 to 1943, when her parents were in show-business in the U.S.A.

Most multiple birth sets in one year at one school Maine South High School in Park Ridge, Illinois, U.S.A., has 19 birth sets—16 sets of twins and 3 sets of triplets. All 41 students are due to graduate in 2014.

Most twins in one year at one school A total of 16 pairs of twins are enrolled in the 9th grade at Valley Southwoods Freshman High School in West Des Moines, U.S.A., for the academic year 2011–12.

Most triplets in one school In the school year 1998–99, Kirkby Centre School, Ashfield, Nottinghamshire, UK, had five sets of triplets enrolled as students.

COMPLETE CLASS

Here are the largest classes in some of your favorite subjects . . .

Lesson/date	Students	Location
Business November 18, 2011	1,864	DAV Centenary College in Faridabad, Haryana, India
Chemistry September 22, 2011 (B)	4,207	Multiple venues across Israel
History November 8, 2011	14,257	Third-grade children from Orange County, California, U.S.A., at Angel Stadium, California
Hockey February 11, 2009 (A)	459	Streatham & Clapham High School in London, UK
Math December 3, 2010	4,076	Multiple venues—30 schools across the UK
Meteorology May 7, 2009	16,110	"School Day at the K" at Kauffman Stadium, Kansas City, Kansas, U.S.A.
Painting September 16, 2011	879	Warren Road Primary School in Orpington, Kent, UK
Physics May 7, 2009 (C)	5,401	Coors Field in Denver, Colorado, U.S.A.

A.   B.   C.

OLDEST PERSON TO BEGIN ELEMENTARY SCHOOL Kimani Ng'ang'a Maruge (Kenya) was 84 when he enrolled at Kapkenduiyo "Primary" School, Eldoret, Kenya, in 2004. Two of his 30 grandchildren were in the school above him! He wore the school uniform and, after straight "A"s in his first end-of-term exams, he was made a senior "head boy." Mr. Maruge passed away on August 15, 2009, at the age of 90.

HIGHEST PUPIL-TO-TEACHER RATIO In the Central African Republic, there are 95 pupils for every elementary school teacher and 92 pupils for every high school teacher.

Longest lesson Kathiravan M. Pethi and 36 students (all India) took part in a lesson entitled "Gandhi's Vision and Mission in Life" that lasted 78 hr. 3 min. The lesson took place at the Association of Physicians of India, Bangalore, India, from October 31 to November 3 in 2008.

Largest class with perfect attendance In the year 1984–85, Ms. Melanie Murray's class of 23 at David Barkley Elementary School, San Antonio, Texas, U.S.A., had a perfect attendance with no absences.

Longest-running annual class reunion The class of 1929 at the Cherokee County Community High School held its 77th class reunion in Columbus, Kansas, U.S.A., on June 27, 2006.

Longest-serving "head teacher" John Aitkenhead (UK) founded the Kilquhanity House School in Dumfries and Galloway, Scotland, in 1940, and worked there for 57 years until it closed in 1997. Although he was head teacher, or principal, the school was libertarian and governed by its pupils and staff.

LONGEST CAREER AS A TEACHER Medarda de Jesus Leon de Uzcategui (b. June 8. 1899), alias La Maestra Chucha, started teaching at the Modelo de Aplicacion, Caracas, Venezuela, in 1911. In 1942, she started her own school, the Escuela Uzcategui, from her home in Caracas, where she was still teaching in 1998, so her career spanned 87 years. She is reported to have died in 2002.

Longest-serving music teacher Charles Wright (U.S.A.) taught piano for 76 years from 1931 until he died on July 19, 2007, at the age of 95.

Largest school reunion A total of 3,299 former pupils of Stadium High School, Tacoma, Washington, U.S.A., attended a reunion on September 16, 2006.

A survey of school kids by the Organization for Economic Cooperation and Development (OECD) found out some fun facts about school life around the world . . .

Mexican kids have the coolest teachers . . .
71% say their teachers really listen to them.

Australian kids are the most popular . . .
93% say they are liked by fellow students.

Latvian kids respect school the most . . .
81% believe that it is preparing them well for later life.

Uruguayan kids are the worst timekeepers . . .
57% say they are late for classes at least once every two weeks.

Indonesian kids are most likely to be math nerds . . .
70% say they enjoy the subject.

AUCTIONS

MOST EXPENSIVE . . .
The following selection of records reflects the highest prices paid for items at auction, presented in ascending order of sale price.

Calendar A wall calendar featuring sketches of costume designs for characters from *Alice in Wonderland* was sold to an anonymous bidder for £36,000 (U.S. $57,848). The sale took place as part of a fundraising auction in aid of the Muir Maxwell Trust and the Fettes Foundation (both UK). It was held at The Mad Hatter's Tea Party on The Queen's Lawn at Fettes College, Edinburgh, UK, on July 3, 2011.

Signed baseball At an auction in Dallas, Texas, U.S.A., on May 5, 2006, a baseball signed in 1961 by legendary baseball player Joe DiMaggio and movie star Marilyn Monroe (both U.S.A.)—DiMaggio's former wife—was sold for U.S. $191,200 by Heritage Auction Galleries.

MOST EXPENSIVE POPSTAR COSTUME Elvis Presley's (U.S.A.) white peacock jumpsuit—designed by Bill Belew (U.S.A.)—sold for $300,000 in an online auction on August 7, 2008.

Doll A rare French doll dating from ca. 1914, by sculptor Albert Marque, realized U.S. $263,000 at a Theriault's auction in Atlanta, U.S.A., on July 12, 2009. The doll, dressed in its period clothing to honor the Ballets Russes of Paris and first introduced to international acclaim in 1909, was won by a prominent collector from Boston, U.S.A.

Batman memorabilia A Batmobile used in director Joel Schumacher's (U.S.A.) movie *Batman Forever* (U.S.A., 1995) sold at the Kruse International collector car auction in Las Vegas, Nevada, U.S.A., in September 2006 for a record U.S. $335,000 to John O'Quinn (U.S.A.).

Soccer memorabilia The most valuable piece of soccer history is an original FA Cup—one of four produced for the first competition held in 1871 and given to the winning team between 1896 and 1910. An anonymous telephone bidder bought the cup for £420,000 (U.S. $773,136) from Christie's, UK, on May 19, 2005.

James Bond memorabilia On January 20, 2006, a Swiss businessman paid U.S. $1.9 million for a silver 1965 Aston Martin DB5 coupé used to promote the 007 movies *Goldfinger* (UK, 1964) and *Thunderball* (UK, 1965).

Guitar A Fender Stratocaster guitar signed by a host of music legends, including Mick Jagger, Eric Clapton, Paul McCartney, Jimmy Page, and Brian May (all UK) fetched U.S. $2.7 million at a charity auction for Reach Out to Asia at the Ritz-Carlton Hotel, Doha, Qatar, on November 17, 2005. The Reach Out to Asia campaign seeks to support worthy causes around the world, with particular emphasis on the Asian continent.

MOST EXPENSIVE PHOTOGRAPH *Rhein II*, a photograph of the Rhine River under gray skies taken by Andreas Gursky (Germany, b. 1955), fetched U.S. $4,338,500, including buyer's premium, at a Christie's auction in New York, U.S.A., on November 8, 2011. The glass-mounted 143 x 73-in. (363.5 x 185.4-cm) image, created in 1999, is one of an edition of six works. The buyer is unknown.

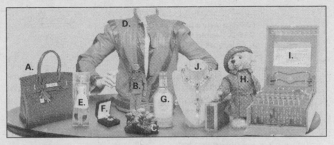

A. HANDBAG
Price: $203,150
Date: December 9, 2011
AUCTION: Heritage Auctions, Dallas, Texas, U.S.A.
Details: Hermès Diamond Birkin handbag, featuring diamond-and-white-gold hardware

B. TOY SOLDIER
Price: U.S. $200,000
Date: August 7, 2003
AUCTION: Heritage Comics Auctions, Dallas, Texas, U.S.A.
Details: First hand-crafted 1963 GI Joe prototype

C. TRUFFLE
Price: U.S. $330,000
Date: December 1, 2007
PLACE: The Grand Lisboa Hotel, Macau, China
Details: White truffle (*Tuber magnatum pico*) unearthed in Pisa, Italy, on November 23, 2007

D. JACKET
Price: U.S. $1.8 million
Date: June 26, 2011
AUCTION: Julien's Auction, Beverly Hills, U.S.A.
Details: Black-and-red calf-leather jacket with winged shoulders worn by singer Michael Jackson (U.S.A.) in his 1983 *Thriller* video

E. BARBIE DOLL
Price: U.S. $27,450
Date: May 2006
AUCTION: Held by Sandi Holder's Doll Attic (U.S.A.)
Details: Original 1959 Barbie in mint condition

F. FALSE TEETH
Price: £15,200 (U.S. $23,700)
Date: July 29, 2010
AUCTION: Keys auctioneers, Aylsham, Norfolk, UK
Details: Set of dentures that once belonged to wartime British prime minister Winston Churchill

G. WHISKEY
Price: £46,850 (U.S. $72,975)
Date: December 14, 2011
AUCTION: Bonhams, Edinburgh, UK
Details: Bottle of rare 55-year-old Glenfiddich single-malt whisky. Proceeds of the sale were donated to the charity WaterAid

H. TEDDY BEAR
Price: €213,720 (U.S. $182,400)
Date: October 14, 2000
AUCTION: Christie's, Monaco
Details: Steiff "Louis Vuitton" teddy bear made in 2000 and measuring 17 in. (45 cm) tall

I. RADIO EQUIPMENT
Price: £24,172.50 (U.S. $38,047.50)
Date: April 1993
AUCTION: Phillips, London, UK
Details: German Enigma coding (ciphering/enciphering) machine

J. PEARL NECKLACE
Price: U.S. $11,842,500
Date: December 14, 2011
AUCTION: Christie's, New York City, U.S.A.
Details: 50.6-carat necklace known as "La Peregrina," dating from the 16th century. It was a present to actress Elizabeth Taylor from her then husband Richard Burton, who bought it in an auction in 1969 for U.S. $37,000

Clock The world record for a clock sold at auction is £1,926,500 (U.S. $3,001,294) for a Louis XVI Ormulu-Mounted Ebony Grande Sonnerie Astronomical Perpetual Calendar Regulateur de Parquet. The auction took place at Christie's, London, UK, on July 8, 1999.

Letter (signed) A letter written in 1787 by George Washington to his nephew Bushrod—in which he urges adoption of the country's new constitution—sold for U.S. $3,200,000 on December 5, 2009, at Christie's, New York City, U.S.A.

Musical instrument A violin known as the "Hammer," made in 1707 by Antonio Stradivari in Cremona, Italy, sold for U.S. $3.5 million to an anonymous buyer at Christie's, New York City, U.S.A., on May 15, 2006. It is one of 620 instruments made by Stradivari thought to exist.

Dress The ivory rayon-acetate dress that was worn by Marilyn Monroe in *The Seven Year Itch* (U.S.A., 1955) raised U.S. $4.6 million in an auction at The Paley Center for Media in Los Angeles, U.S.A., on June 18, 2011.

Coin The most expensive coin is a 1933 Double Eagle—a U.S. $20 gold coin that was minted but never officially circulated (most of the coins were melted down shortly after being produced). The rare coin was auctioned at Sotheby's in New York City, U.S.A., on July 30, 2002, where it fetched U.S. $7,590,020 with premium.

Diamond A "D" color internally flawless, pear-shape diamond that weighs 100.10 carats sold for CHF 19,858,500 (U.S. $16,561,171) at Sotheby's in Geneva, Switzerland, on May 17, 1995. It also holds the record for the **most expensive jewel sold at auction**.

Chair An armchair made ca. 1917–19 by Irish-born designer Eileen Gray, which had belonged to designer Yves Saint Laurent (France), sold at auction for €21.9 million (U.S. $28 million). The buyer, Cheska Vallois (France), was the same dealer who originally sold the chair to the French designer in the 1970s. The auction took place at Christie's in Paris, France, on February 24–26, 2009.

THE ECONOMY

Largest stock-market flotation (IPO) The stock-market launch—or "Initial Public Offering" (IPO)—of the Agricultural Bank of China (aka AgBank) raised a record U.S. $22.1 billion on August 13, 2010. Shares were listed on both the Shanghai and the Hong Kong Stock Exchanges. The bank has over 30 million customers and over 440,000 employees.

Largest trading volume in a day The largest volume of shares traded at one stock exchange in one day was 5,799,792,281. This incredible figure was achieved on the New York Stock Exchange on August 16, 2007.

YOUNGEST BILLIONAIRE Facebook cofounder Dustin Moskovitz (U.S.A.) left the social networking website in 2008 to form his own company. Now at the age of 27, he is worth U.S. $3.5 billion according to Forbes.

Highest share value On March 27, 2000, the share price for one share of Yahoo! Japan stood at 120.4 million yen (U.S. $1.12 million). Yahoo! Japan is the nation's dominant information portal, and the scarcity of the stock contributed to the dramatic rise in price. As of 2004, Japanese company Softbank owned 41.93% of the company, with U.S.-based Yahoo! owning 33.49%. Yahoo! Japan's share price has increased 4,700% since December 1998.

Highest closing price on the FTSE 100 The FTSE 100 index lists the share prices of the 100 UK companies with the highest market value. It reached an overall closing high of 6,930.2 on December 30, 1999.

The **lowest closing price on the FTSE 100** was on July 12, 1984, when it fell to 978.7.

Greatest annual net loss by a company AOL Time Warner (U.S.A.) reported an annual net loss of U.S. $98.7 billion on January 30, 2003.

Largest takeover German conglomerate Mannesmann merged with Vodafone AirTouch (UK) in February 2002. Under the terms of the £112-billion (U.S. $159-billion) deal, Mannesmann shareholders received 49.5% of the merged company, with Vodafone providing 58.96 of its shares for each Mannesmann share.

LARGEST BANK COLLAPSE According to the International Monetary Fund (IMF), the worst banking crisis suffered by any country, relative to its economy, occurred in 2008–11 with the collapse of the three largest banks in Iceland.

MOST BILLIONAIRES (CITY) According to *Forbes*, the Russian capital Moscow currently boasts an unprecedented 79 billionaires. Between them, the Moscow billionaires share a total of U.S. $375.3 billion. The richest Muscovite—and Russia's richest man—is the steel magnate Vladimir Lisin. The photograph at left shows a millionaire's shopping fair in Moscow.

The U.S.A. is the country with the most billionaires: 412 out of a global total of 1,210, as of 2011.

FACT: Iceland's banks had made loans equivalent to nine times its gross domestic product (GDP).

YOUNGEST INVESTMENT BANKER John Wang Clow (U.S.A., b. May 23, 1994) passed the Investment Banking Examination (Series 79), administered by the Financial Industry Regulatory Authority (FINRA), on August 5, 2011. He became a licensed investment banker on August 8, 2011, at the age of 17 years 77 days.

Largest public company According to *Forbes*, the banking firm J.P. Morgan Chase (U.S.A.) was the world's largest public company as of 2010/11—a record for the second year running. *Forbes'* calculations are based on four categories: sales, profits, assets, and overall market value. For 2010/11, J.P. Morgan Chase registered figures of U.S. $115.5 billion in sales, U.S. $17.4 billion in profits, U.S. $2,117.6 billion in assets, and U.S. $182.2 billion in market value.

Largest company • By assets: Mortgage association Fannie Mae (U.S.A.) had assets totaling U.S. $3,222 billion, according to *Forbes'* Global 2000 list for 2010/11. **• By market value**: According to the Forbes Global 2000 list for 2010/11, the oil and gas giant Exxon Mobil had a market value of U.S. $407.2 billion as of April 2011. **• By profits**: Swiss food company Nestlé made U.S. $36.7 billion profit in 2010/11. With revenues totaling U.S. $112 billion for the 12 months up to March 11, 2011, Nestlé is also the **largest food company** in terms of annual sales. The company owns business units, including Food and Beverage, Nestlé Waters, and Nestlé Nutrition. **• By sales**: *Forbes* places Wal-Mart Stores, Inc., as the company with the highest sales, with world-beating figures of U.S. $421.8 billion.

LARGEST FINANCIAL RESCUE PLAN Between 2008 and 2012, the central banks of the U.S.A., UK, Japan, and the 17 European countries that use the euro issued loans to the value of U.S. $8.8 trillion to ease the effects of the Global Financial Crisis (GFC). This figure includes U.S. $2.95 trillion from the U.S. Federal Reserve and U.S. $3.58 trillion from the European Central Bank.

Largest corporate bankruptcy U.S. investment bank Lehman Brothers Holdings Inc. filed for bankruptcy to the tune of U.S. $613 billion on September 15, 2008. The bank succumbed to the subprime mortgage crisis, which started the worldwide recession in 2008.

Largest advertising agency (revenues) Omnicom Group Inc., whose headquarters are on Madison Avenue in New York, U.S.A., had revenues of U.S. $12.5 billion for the fiscal year ending December 31, 2010.

Richest investor Warren Edward Buffett (U.S.A.), chairman of Berkshire Hathaway, is the world's richest investor, estimated to be worth U.S. $45 billion as of September 2011.

Richest media tycoon Michael Bloomberg's (U.S.A.) media empire Bloomberg L.P., which includes the Bloomberg financial news firm, was worth an estimated U.S. $22.5 billion as of March 2011.

MOST PROFITABLE RESTAURANT CHAIN When it comes to restaurants, McDonald's (U.S.A.) is first in line. For the 2010/11 financial year, the ubiquitous burger chain served up profits of U.S. $4.9 billion, while the company itself was valued at a mouthwatering U.S. $80.1 billion. The first McDonald's fast-food restaurant opened in 1948 in San Bernardino, California, U.S.A.

Why not invest your time in auctions, on p. ■■■?

WORLD WEALTH

The World Bank calculated the yearly average Gross Domestic Product of 190 countries from 1990 to 2010. It was determined that the ten richest nations listed below own 65.5% of the world's wealth.

10. CANADA $1,577,040 million	**5. FRANCE** $2,560,002 million*
9. INDIA $1,721,111 million	**4. GERMANY** $3,280,530 million
8. ITALY $2,051,412 million	**3. JAPAN** $5,458,837 million
7. BRAZIL $2,087,890 million	**2. CHINA** $5,926,612 million[†]
6. UK $2,248,831 million	**1. U.S.A.** $14,586,736 million

*includes overseas departments
[†]excludes Chinese Taipei, Hong Kong, and Macau

CITIES

First city Dating back to around 3200 B.C., the world's first city was Uruk, located in southern Mesopotamia (modern Iraq). Home to some 50,000 inhabitants, it was the largest settlement of its time, covering 1,112 acres (450 ha) and encircled by a 5.9-mile (9.5-km) city wall. Thriving as a result of trade and agriculture, Uruk also became a great artistic center, featuring many elaborate mosaics and monuments.

First use of codes for sending mail In 1857, Sir Rowland Hill (UK) divided London into postal districts based on compass points: "N" for North, "S" for South, etc. The UK's present form of the postcode—a mixture of letters and numbers decoded by machine to allow for faster sorting—was first used in Norwich, Norfolk, UK, in October 1959. The similar ZIP (Zone Improvement Plan) code came into use in the U.S.A. in July 1963.

CITY WITH MOST SKYSCRAPERS According to the Council on Tall Buildings and Urban Habitat, in 2010 there were 2,354 buildings in Hong Kong that were at least 328 ft. (100 m) tall. They have an estimated combined height of about 205 miles (330 km), which is only 15.5 miles (25 km) shy of the altitude at which the Chinese *Tiangong 1* space station orbits Earth.

Largest arcology project An "arcology" is a city designed to provide an alternative to modern urban sprawl. First proposed by Italian-American architect Paolo Soleri in the 1960s, an arcology's aim is to be self-sufficient and prevent wasteful consumption of land, energy, and time. The largest arcology underway is Masdar City in Abu Dhabi, UAE. Initiated in 2006, it occupies 2.3 sq. miles (6 km^2) and is planned to host around 50,000 people and 1,500 businesses.

Largest city with no major road connection Iquitos, founded in the Peruvian rain forest in the 1750s, has a population of around 430,000 and is a major port on the Amazon River. The only road from Iquitos stops at the small town of Nauta, about 62 miles (100 km) to the south. This makes the city accessible only by air and river.

MOST EXPENSIVE CITY TO PARK IN According to a 2011 report by Colliers International, the most expensive urban zones in which to park an automobile are in London, UK. Median monthly parking rates are £657 (U.S. $1,083) in the City of London—the financial district—and £615 (U.S. $1,014) in London's West End—the entertainment district.

For more high-rise records, turn to p. 543.

Largest slum Neza-Chalco-Itza is one of Mexico City's *barrios* (slums). Most of its approximately four million inhabitants live there illegally. Mexico City's slums have been growing for more than 100 years, after the railroads allowed for new industry to begin in the city.

Largest shopping mall The Dubai Mall, located in Downtown Dubai, UAE, consists of four levels with a floor area of 5.9 million sq. ft. (548,127 m²). It has 1,200 retail outlets and over 160 food and beverage outlets. Construction began in 2004, with the mall opening its doors on November 4, 2008.

Busiest subway network The Moscow Metro in Russia carries 8–9 million passengers each day. By comparison, the New York City Subway, U.S.A., carries 4.5 million people each day and the London Underground, UK, carries just over 3 million.

Oldest subway system The London Underground, UK, opened its first section—from Paddington station to Farringdon—in 1863.

Subway with most stations New York City Subway has 468 stations (277 of which are underground) in a network covering 230 miles (370 km).

Longest driverless subway network The Dubai Metro (UAE) consists of two driverless lines (Red and Green) that totaled 46.41 miles (74.69 km) when the Green line was officially opened on September 9, 2011.

CITY WITH THE DENSEST POPULATION
Manila, capital of the Philippines, had 1,660,714 inhabitants, according to its 2007 census. Crammed into just 14.88 sq. miles (38.55 km²), its population density is 111,574 people per square mile.

CITY WITH MOST BRIDGES Hamburg, Germany, is located on the Elbe River at the point where it meets the Bille and Alster rivers. The canals, rivers, and streams within the city are crossed by a total of 2,302 bridges—more than the cities of Venice and Amsterdam combined.

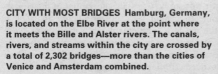

OLDEST SKYSCRAPER CITY
The population of Shibam in Yemen—amounting to about 7,000 people—live in densely clustered mud-brick, high-rise buildings, some of which are above 98 ft. 5 in. (30 m) tall and have up to 12 stories. The high-rise construction began after Shibam was flooded in 1532–33, with most of the approximately 500 towers built in the 16th century.

Longest subway escalator The St. Petersburg subway in Russia has an escalator with a vertical rise of 195 ft. (50.5 m).

Most escalators in a subway system The subway in Washington, D.C., U.S.A., has 557 escalators, which are maintained by approximately 90 technicians.

Busiest station Shinjuku Station in Tokyo, Japan, has an average of 3.64 million passengers pass through it each day. It has more than 200 exits.

Longest continuous subway The Moscow Kaluzhskaya underground rapid transit line from Medvedkovo to Bittsevsky Park, completed in early 1990, is 23.8 miles (37.9 km) long.

First parking meters Carl C. Magee (U.S.A.) invented the parking meter, the first examples of which were installed in Oklahoma City, Oklahoma, U.S.A., in July 1935, reaching New York in 1951, and London in 1958.

Largest parking lot The world's largest parking lot for automobiles can hold 20,000 vehicles and is situated at the West Edmonton Mall in Edmonton, Alberta, Canada. There are overflow facilities on an adjoining parking lot for another 10,000 vehicles.

Largest urban tram network From 1897 to the 1960s, Buenos Aires in Argentina boasted a huge tram network. At its maximum, it had an estimated 532.5 miles (857 km) of lines, including those underground. The trams were replaced by modern buses.

Oldest bus rapid-transit network Curitiba, the capital of the Brazilian state of Paraná, is home to around 1.75 million people. In 1974, it became the first city in the world to implement a bus rapid-transit network. Superior to normal bus routes, it uses dedicated lanes for buses, articulated long buses, and more frequent vehicles, allowing its 2.3 million daily users to commute at speeds similar to light rail networks.

MYSTERIOUS WORLD

First scientific treatise on spontaneous human combustion
Spontaneous human combustion (SHC) is defined as the burning of a living human body without any clear external source of ignition. Approximately 200 cases have been reported worldwide during the past three centuries alone. Author Charles Dickens even incorporated an SHC event into the plot of his novel *Bleak House* (1852). The first scientific, non-sensationalized investigation into spontaneous human combustion appeared in 1673. Entitled *De Incendiis Corporis Humani Spontaneis*, it was written by Jonas Dupont (France) and comprised SHC-related cases and studies.

LARGEST COLLECTION OF "HAUNTED" DOLLS Located south of Mexico City within a network of canals, Mexico's tiny La Isla de las Muñecas ("Island of the Dolls") houses thousands of broken, mutilated, and decaying dolls. Locals claim that at night the dolls come to life, animated by the spirits of the dead. The grotesque collection began in the 1950s, when a hermit named Don Julian Santana Barrera settled there. Claiming that he was being haunted by the ghost of a young girl who had drowned in one of the canals in the 1920s, he began placing dolls around the island as a sort of shrine to appease her restless spirit.

First "haunted" battle scene The famous Battle of Marathon between the citizens of Athens and Persian armies took place on the Plain of Marathon in 490 B.C., and was won by the Greeks. However, shortly afterward, observers claimed to have seen a ghostly "action replay" of this battle, and comparable spectral reenactments have reputedly been witnessed at the site on several occasions since then, up to modern times.

Oldest ghost Ghost Ranch, in Rio Arriba County, New Mexico, has earned its name from the many sightings of a huge ghostly reptile that have been made there over the years. Measuring 19 ft. 6 in.–29 ft. 6 in. (6–9 m) long, it has been dubbed "Vivaron, the snake-demon" by local inhabitants.

In 1947, paleontologist Edwin H. Colbert (U.S.A.) unearthed a huge cache of fossil skeletons in this same area, derived from various prehistoric reptiles. These not only included more than a thousand dinosaur specimens but also a 29.5-ft.-long (9-m) crocodile-like creature known as a phytosaur. Its discovery led to speculation that the paranormal "snake-demon" that had

been reported by the locals was the ghost of this phytosaur. If this were true—and keeping in mind that its fossil skeleton is 220 million years old, dating from the Triassic period—the phytosaur's specter would be the world's oldest ghost!

LONGEST-RUNNING PARANORMAL MAGAZINE U.S. Magazine *Fate* began in 1948 and for many years was published monthly. Since July 2009, it has appeared only bimonthly online.

TALLEST BIGFOOT According to researchers who investigate reports of the bigfoot (sasquatch), visibly different types of this hairy bipedal mystery primate occur in North America. The tallest is the so-called true giant, which, witnesses say, is 9 ft. 10 in.–19 ft. 6 in. (3–6 m) tall. The most common sightings are in the high mountains of the West and in the northern spruce forests. Pictured is GWR consultant Karl Shuker with a cast of the "Grays Harbor Footprint," taken from tracks discovered in 1982 in Washington State, U.S.A.

Longest continuous house construction

Winchester House in San Jose, California, U.S.A., was under construction for 38 years. Once an eight-room farmhouse on a 161-acre (65-ha) estate, its transformation into a mansion was begun in 1886 by the widowed Sarah Winchester, heiress to the Winchester rifle fortune. It is known as the "Winchester Mystery House" because of its many oddities, such as closets opening into blank walls, a window in the floor, and staircases leading nowhere. Some believe that after the death of her husband (son of the inventor of the famous rifle) the widow was told by a medium that endless remodeling would confuse and calm the ghosts of all the people killed by the "gun that won the West." The house has 13 bathrooms, 52 skylights, 47 fireplaces, 10,000 windows, 40 staircases, 2,000 doorways and trapdoors, and three elevators.

Most participants in a scientific study of a haunted house

Between May 26 and June 4, 2000, psychologist Richard Wiseman from the University of Hertfordshire, UK, led an experiment in which 1,027 volunteers walked around parts of Hampton Court Palace, reputedly one of the most haunted locations in the UK. The volunteers documented any unusual experiences or sensations and the results were collected for psychological analysis.

FIRST STIGMATIC The term "stigmatic" refers to a person who seems to have wounds mirroring those suffered by Jesus Christ during his crucifixion. Depicted here is Francis of Assisi (1181/2–1226, canonized 1228), who was reportedly visited by an angel in 1224 while praying. Francis later found that he bore a series of wounds corresponding to those of Jesus. Stigmatics continue to make claims to the present day (left photo).

LONGEST LOCH NESS MONSTER VIGIL Steve Feltham (UK, right) arrived
at Loch Ness, Scotland, in 1991 in search of the legendary monster,
and remains there full time. Feltham lives on the shore in a converted
bookmobile and spends every day scanning the loch (the Scottish term for
"lake") in search of the monster.

The **most prolific Nessie eyewitness** is Alex Campbell, a water bailiff
who worked at the loch for more than 40 years—he claimed to have made
17 observations of Nessie, starting in May 1934.

Largest flock of birds to invade a house On the evening of May 4,
1998, the Fire Department in Pasadena, California, U.S.A., was called to
investigate a strange happening in an empty house. Firefighters discovered
that more than 1,000 swifts (family Apidae) had flown down the chimney,
spreading soot everywhere. Some of the swifts were dead, having apparently flown headlong into the walls in panic. It took at least two hours for
the firefighters, led by Fire Dept. Battalion Chief Joe Nestor (U.S.A.), to
shoo the rest of the huge flock out of the house, through windows and
doors. It is unclear why the swifts flew down the chimney en masse.

Deadliest lake The lake responsible for the most deaths not brought
about by drowning is Lake Nyos in Cameroon, West Africa, where toxic
gases have claimed nearly 2,000 lives in recent decades. On one night in
August 1986, about 1,700 people and countless animals were killed by a
large natural release of carbon dioxide gas.

Largest area of glowing sea In 1995, scientists at the U.S. Naval Research Laboratory discovered an area of luminous sea in the Indian Ocean
off the coast of Somalia using satellite images. The patch of water measured more than 155 miles (250 km) long and had an area of around 5,400
sq. miles (14,000 km^2). Bioluminescent bacteria are believed to have been
responsible for the water's striking appearance.

Largest pink lake Retba Lake, better known as Lac Rose ("Pink Lake"), is the world's largest pink body of water, measuring around 0.9 x 3 miles (1.5 x 5 km) at low water. A shallow lagoon, located 18 miles (30 km) north of Dakar, Senegal (famous as the last leg in the Paris–Dakar Rally), the lake's intense color is the result of microorganisms and a strong concentration of minerals.

STRANGEST FALLS

ELECTRIC RAIN November 1, 1844—Paris, France
Witnessed by Dr. Morel-Deville, rain sparked and crackled as it hit the ground and buildings, and it gave off a phosphorus smell.

BIRDS' BLOOD May 15, 1890—Messignadi, Calabria, Italy
Rain of blood formally identified as birds' blood fell, but no bird carcasses were found.

GREEN RAIN June 2002—India
Fell for two days; shown to be pollen-containing droppings of a huge swarm of honeybees.

NAILS October 12, 1888—Texas, U.S.A.
Cascade of nails rained from the sky onto the wife of Point Isabel's lighthouse keeper.

BLUE RAIN April 8, 1954—U.S.A.
Blue rain fell over several U.S. towns; when examined, found to be radioactive.

HAILSTONE-ENCASED TORTOISE May 11, 1894—Vicksburg, Mississippi, U.S.A.
During a hailstorm, a gopher tortoise entirely encased in a giant hailstone and measuring 6 x 8 in. (15.2 x 20.3 cm) fell from the sky.

FROGS August 28, 1977—Canet-Plage, France
Thousands of tiny frogs the size of peas were seen falling to the ground from the sky just before a heavy rain shower began.

PWDRE SER (STAR ROT) January 21, 1803—Silesia, Germany
The day after a meteor fell to the Earth, an unexplained jellylike mass (*pwdre ser*) was found on the ground.

SILVER COINS September 30, 1956—Meshehera, Russia
A shower of silver coins fell all over the district during a storm.

ANGEL HAIR September 20, 1892—Florida, U.S.A.
Great white sheets of spiderweb-like gossamer (known as angel hair) floated down with rain, some measuring 150 ft. (45 m) or more in length; it was seen and collected by Gainesville's postmaster.

LARGEST CROP GLYPH Members of the XL D-Sign team (all Netherlands) created a 1,739 x 1,476-ft. (530 x 450-m) crop-field image of a "mothman" in Zeeland, Netherlands, over the course of one night in August 2009. It covered around 59 acres (24 ha) and was dubbed "Project Atlas." XL D-Sign has been producing huge, elaborate crop-field-sited images for more than 10 years.

NATIONS

HIGHEST BUDGET FOR HEALTHCARE The U.S.A. spent 16.2% of its Gross Domestic Product (GDP) on healthcare in 2009.

FEWEST SMOKERS According to the latest available figures from Nationmaster.com, only 17% of Canadians smoke at least one cigarette daily.

LOWEST POPULATION DENSITY Greenland has a population density of around 0.06 people per sq. mile (0.02 people per km²).

Just how long can we live for? Find out on p. ■■■.

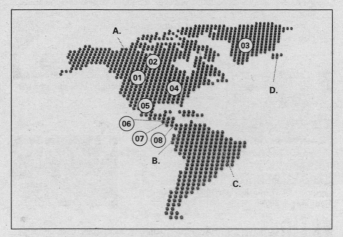

A. MOST COMPUTERS PER CAPITA Canadians had 108.6 computers per 100 citizens as of 2009.

B. LOWEST MARRIAGE RATE Colombia has an average of just 1.7 marriages per 1,000 population, according to *The Economist*.

C. LARGEST PRODUCER OF COFFEE Brazil produced more than 2.6 million tons (2.36 million tonnes) of coffee in 2009–10.

D. MOST INTERNET USERS PER CAPITA Iceland had 93.5 Internet users per 100 population as of 2009, according to *The Economist*.

FASTEST-GROWING BODY MASS INDEX The average U.S. citizen grew 2 lb. 3 oz. (1 kg) heavier per decade from 1980 to 2008.

LARGEST EMIGRANT POPULATION According to the latest World Bank report, 11.9 million Mexican citizens were living abroad as of 2010.

FACT: The U.S.A. spent U.S. $7,421 per person on healthcare in 2009—a total bill of U.S. $2.2 trillion.

LEAVING A BIG FOOTPRINT

With a population of some 500,000 people, Luxembourg is one of the tiniest nations. As of 2009, however, it had the **largest ecological footprint** of any nation. The equivalent of 25.2 acres (20.2 ha) of land would be needed to meet each Luxembourger's needs and absorb their carbon emissions.

FEWEST DIVORCES Guatemala registers just one divorce per 10,000 people, according to *The Economist*.

HIGHEST MURDER RATE The United Nations recorded 60.87 murders per 100,000 citizens in Honduras in 2008.

HAPPIEST COUNTRY As of 2009, Costa Rica ranked first on the Happy Planet Index, with a 76.1% rating.

AT A GLANCE...

GWR's one-stop guide to the world's populations:

• **Global population:** reached 7 billion on October 31, 2011

• **Population growth rate:** the annual birth rate is currently 1.915%—meaning 252 babies are born every minute; but the mortality rate is 0.812%, which means 107 deaths every minute and, therefore, a net growth of 1.092% (based on estimates for 2011)

• **Countries:** 195

• **Land boundaries:** 322

• **Total labor force:** 3.228 billion (2010 estimate)

• **Registered refugees:** at least 8.8 million (2010 estimate)

Source: CIA Factbook

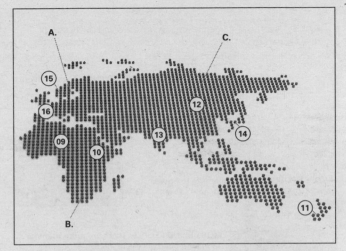

A. **HIGHEST RATIO OF FOREIGN AID** Sweden gives 1.03% of its GDP to official development aid.

B. **MOST OFFICIAL LANGUAGES** The Republic of South Africa has 11 official languages. They are: English, Afrikaans, isiZulu, isiXhosa, Sesotho, Setswana, Sepedi, Xitsonga, siSwati, isiNdebele, and Tshivenda.

C. **GREATEST GENDER DIFFERENCE IN LIFE EXPECTANCY** Russian males have a life expectancy of 59.33 years, compared with 73.14 years for females—a difference of 13.81 years.

HIGHEST BIRTH RATE Based on figures for 2005–10, there are 49.5 births per 1,000 population in Niger.

NEWEST INDEPENDENT COUNTRY On July 9, 2011, South Sudan peacefully seceded from Sudan. One day earlier, Sudan had become the first country to recognize South Sudan as a country in its own right.

FACT: A total of 46 nations and other territories are completely landlocked.

FACT: As of 2011, there are around two cows and seven sheep to every person in New Zealand.

LEAST CORRUPT COUNTRY New Zealand scores 95% on the Corruptions Perception Index.

HIGHEST POPULATION According to figures from 2010, China's population now exceeds 1.33 billion.

MOST BLIND PEOPLE There are more than 15 million blind people in India.

HIGHEST COST OF LIVING The Japanese have the highest cost of living. On an index where the U.S.A. = 100, Japan comes in at 158, based on the average cost of consumer purchases.

MOST DEMOCRATIC COUNTRY The 2011 Economist Intelligence Unit report rates Norway as the most democratic country, with a score of 9.8 out of 10.

MOST POPULAR TOURISM DESTINATION According to the United Nations, France attracted 76.8 million tourists in 2010.

Society

LIFE EXPECTANCY

The average life expectancy in the world is 66.57 years: 64.52 for males and 68.76 for females.

Average in years

†Monaco 89.73
**Japan 82.25
••Australia 81.81
†Italy 81.77
‡Canada 81.38
†France 81.19
†Spain 81.17
†Sweden 81.07
**Israel 80.96
••New Zealand 80.59
†Norway 80.20
†Ireland 80.19
†Germany 80.07
†UK 80.05
†Greece 79.92
†Netherlands 79.68
†Finland 79.27
**South Korea 79.05
†Denmark 78.63
†Portugal 78.54
‡U.S.A. 78.37
•Chile 77.70
†Czech Rep 77.19
•Argentina 76.95
**UAE 76.51
‡Mexico 76.47
•Paraguay 75.77
†Poland 76.28
†Slovakia 75.40

†Croatia 75.35
†Hungary 74.70
**Lebanon 73.66
**China 73.47
†Estonia 72.82
•Colombia 72.81
*Egypt 72.12
•Brazil 71.99
†Turkey 71.69
**Philippines 71.09
•Peru 70.74
**Indonesia 70.69
**Iraq 69.94
**India 69.89
†Ukraine 68.25
‡Belize 68.20
**Mongolia 67.65
•Bolivia 66.89
WORLD 66.57
†Russia 66.03
‡The Bahamas 65.78
**Pakistan 64.49
**N. Korea 63.81
**Yemen 63.27
••Kiribati 63.22
*Botswana 61.85
‡Haiti 60.78
**Bangladesh 60.25
*Ghana 59.85

*Senegal 59.00
*Kenya 57.86
*Côte d'Ivoire 55.45
*D.R. Congo 54.36
*Cameroon 53.69
*Gabon 53.11
*Uganda 52.72
*Tanzania 52.01
*Sudan 51.42
*Rwanda 50.52
*Mali 50.35
*Somalia 49.63
*South Africa 48.98
*Guinea-Bissau 47.90
*Chad 47.70
*Nigeria 46.94
*Zimbabwe 45.77
**Afghanistan 45.02
*Central African
  Republic 44.47
*Malawi 43.82
*Djibouti 43.37
*Liberia 41.84
*Sierra Leone 41.24
*Mozambique 41.18
*Lesotho 40.38
*Zambia 38.63
*Angola 38.20
*Swaziland 31.88

Key
*Africa
**Asia

†Europe
‡N. America

•S. America
••Oceania

Source: CIA Factbook

WORLD LEADERS

Simultaneous head of state of most countries Her Majesty, Queen Elizabeth II (UK) is head of state of 16 countries, as of March 2012. The Queen's role is nominal (she has no political powers), yet more than 128 million people in 15 Commonwealth states (plus the UK and its 14 Overseas Territories) recognize her as their monarch.

She is also the oldest British monarch ever. Her coronation was on June 2, 1953, and, in 2012, she remains on the throne at the age of 85.

First female president Maria Estela Martínez de Perón (known as Isabel, or Isabelita), the widow of General Juan Perón (both Argentina), was the first female president. She was sworn in as interim leader of Argentina on June 29, 1974, as delegated by her husband, the president, who died on July 1. She was deposed in a military coup on March 24, 1976.

LARGEST PARLIAMENT (LEGISLATIVE BODY) China's National People's Congress, or NPC, has 2,987 members and meets annually in Beijing's Great Hall of the People. Its formal leader is Wu Bangguo, who holds the title of Chairman and Party Secretary of the Standing Committee of the National People's Congress.

FACT: The NPC is China's sole legislative body. Its members are elected for five years.

Richest monarch According to *Forbes*, as of July 2011 the wealthiest monarch is Thailand's King Bhumibol Adulyadej, King Rama IX of the Chakri dynasty. Although his wealth declined by some U.S. $5 billion in the year following the global financial crisis of 2008, he is still managing to get by, with an estimated fortune exceeding U.S. $30 billion, much of which stems from investment in Thai businesses.

Oldest president Joaquín Balaguer (1907–2002) was president of the Dominican Republic in 1960–62, 1966–78, and 1986–96. He left office at the age of 89, having held the presidency for over 23 years.

The **oldest currently reigning monarch** is Abdullah bin Abdulaziz Al Saud, the King of Saudi Arabia. He achieved the record on May 11, 2007, at the age of 82 years 253 days. King Abdullah took to the throne on August 1, 2005.

Morarji Ranchhodji Desai (India, 1896–1995) was 81 when he began leading India in March 1977, the **oldest age at which a prime minister has first been appointed**.

YOUNGEST CURRENT HEAD OF STATE Kim Jong-un of North Korea ascended to the leadership position on December 17, 2011, following the death of his father, Kim Jong-il. Kim Jong-un's exact age has never been confirmed: it has been speculated that he was 27 upon succeeding his father, but his date of birth has also been listed as January 8, 1982, or the same date in 1983 or 1984. The younger Kim also holds the title of Supreme Commander of the Korean People's Army and carries the rank of Daejang, the equivalent of a general.

OLDEST CURRENT HEAD OF STATE Sir Cuthbert Montraville Sebastian (b. October 22, 1921), at 90 years old, is Governor-General of St. Kitts and Nevis, West Indies, an independent British Commonwealth realm.

FACT: Sir Cuthbert represents Queen Elizabeth II (UK, above), the realm's formal head of state.

LONGEST IMPRISONMENT FOR A DEPOSED LEADER Former Panamanian general and "Maximum Leader" Manuel Noriega (effective ruler of Panama from 1983 to 1989) was captured by U.S. military forces on January 4, 1990 and was imprisoned first in the U.S.A., then France, and finally Panama. As of March 4, 2012, he had been detained for 22 years 2 months.

FIRST FEMALE PRIME MINISTER Sirimavo Ratwatte Dias Bandaranaike (Sri Lanka, 1916–2000) was the first and longest-serving female prime minister in modern times. She held the post three times: July 21, 1960–March 27, 1965; May 29, 1970–July 23, 1977 (Ceylon renamed itself as Sri Lanka in 1972); and November 14, 1994–August 10, 2000.

Youngest monarch King Oyo—aka Rukirabasaija Oyo Nyimba Kabamba Iguru Rukidi IV—is the 20-year-old ruler of Toro, a kingdom in Uganda, East Africa. Born on April 16, 1992, he came to power at the age of three and now rules over 3% of Uganda's 33-million-strong population.

The **youngest monarchs ever** were a king of France and a king of Spain, who were sovereigns from the moment of their birth. Jean (John) I of France was the posthumous son of Louis X and succeeded at birth on November 14, 1316, but died five days later. Alfonso XIII of Spain was the posthumous son of Alfonso XII and succeeded at birth on May 17, 1886.

Tallest world leader Canadian prime minister Stephen Harper is the tallest current world leader, at 6 ft. 2 in. (188 cm). Harper edges out U.S. president Barack Obama, whose height is 6 ft. 1 in. (185 cm), and British prime minister David Cameron, who stands at 6 ft. 0.5 in. (184 cm).

The world's **shortest national leader** was Benito Juarez (1806–72), five-term president of Mexico, who served from 1858 until 1872. He stood a mere 4 ft. 6 in. (137 cm) tall. Juarez led Mexico during the period known as La Reforma. He fought the French occupation of Mexico and made early efforts to liberalize and modernize the country.

Shortest presidency The shortest presidency was that of Pedro Lascuráin, who governed Mexico for one hour on February 18, 1913. Lascuráin was the legal successor to President Madero, who was murdered on February 13, 1913. The vice president of Mexico was disqualified because he was under arrest at the time and thus Lascuráin was sworn in, immediately appointed General Victoriano Huerta as his successor, and then resigned.

First fascist dictator Benito Mussolini became Italy's youngest prime minister on October 31, 1922, having led the country's right-wing, fascist political movement since 1919. He made it clear that he would govern authoritatively and soon obtained full dictatorial powers, securing his position in a fraudulent election in 1924. He became the first of the fascist dictators, siding with Adolf Hitler's Germany in World War II. He was caught by Italian partisans and killed on April 28, 1945, while trying to flee to Switzerland.

LONGEST-SERVING HEAD OF STATE (NONROYAL) Fidel Castro (Cuba) held the top political position in his country, first as prime minister (1959–76) and then president (1976–2008), for a span of 49 years 10 months 3 days.

LONGEST IMPRISONMENT OF A FUTURE HEAD OF STATE Nelson Mandela, who was president of South Africa from 1994 to 1999, was a political prisoner interned in three different prisons (most notably Robben Island) from August 5, 1962, to February 11, 1990—a total of 27 years 6 months 6 days.

MOST FAILED ASSASSINATIONS

In 2006, an ex-bodyguard claimed that there had been 638 plots to take Castro's life. The plots included:

- Cigars packed with explosive, and others laced with poison

- Poisoned pills

- A fountain pen containing a syringe full of poison

- Infecting Castro's diving suit with a lethal fungus

- Rigging seashells, in one of Castro's favorite diving areas, with explosives

Longest time for an embalmed leader to be on public display
The body of Vladimir Ilyich Lenin (1870–1924), the first leader of the
Soviet Union, has been on public display in the Mavzoléy Lénina (Lenin's
Tomb), in Red Square, Moscow, Russia, since six days after his death on
January 21, 1924. Lenin's features are moisturized every day and preser-
vatives injected beneath his clothes. The body was removed for safety
during World War II.

LONGEST-SERVING CURRENT HEADS OF STATE

Some heads of state hold onto their position rather longer than others.
GWR presents a selection of world leaders who, as of May 4, 2012, are
still occupying the top spot. This list excludes disputed countries.

65 years
King Bhumibol Adulyadej: Thailand

60 years
Queen Elizabeth II: UK and Commonwealth

44 years
Sultan Hassanal Bolkiah: Brunei

41 years
Sultan Qaboos bin Said al Said: Oman

40 years
Queen Margrethe II: Denmark

38 years
King Carl XVI Gustaf: Sweden

36 years
King Juan Carlos: Spain

33 years
President Teodoro Obiang Nguema Mbasogo: Equatorial
New Guinea

32 years
President José Eduardo dos Santos: Angola

32 years
Queen Beatrix: Netherlands

Sources: *Daily Telegraph; CIA World Factbook*

PEOPLE AT WAR

Country least at peace According to the Global Peace Index 2011, the country least at peace is Somalia. The index, published by the Institute for Economics and Peace, ranks 153 nations and takes into account issues such as domestic and international conflict, safety and security in society, and militarization. The **country most at peace** in the index is Iceland.

Deadliest conflict since World War II The conflict that began in Zaire (now the Democratic Republic of the Congo) in August 1998, and officially ended in July 2003, is known as the Second Congo War or the Great African War. It involved Zaire, Rwanda, Uganda, Angola, Zimbabwe, Chad, Namibia, and Sudan. About 5.4 million people died—most due to disease and starvation—and many millions were displaced.

World War II remains the **deadliest conflict ever**, with around 56 million fatalities.

Country with most hostage taking The Center for Strategic and International Studies reports that Pakistan had 5,333 incidents of hostage taking in the period 2007–10.

Leading host country for refugees According to the UNHCR's Global Trends 2010 report, Pakistan has 1.9 million refugees. Developing countries host around 80% of the world's refugee population—more than half of whom are children. The report puts the global total at 43.7 million, consisting of refugees, people displaced within their country by conflict and natural disasters, and asylum seekers.

FIRST WOMAN TO COMMAND A FIGHTING WARSHIP Commander Sarah West (UK), above left, of the British Royal Navy, became the first woman to take charge of a major warship when she assumed command of the British frigate HMS *Portland*, main picture, in May 2012. On June 10, 1998, Commander Maureen A. Farren (U.S.A.) became the first woman to command a combatant ship, when she took charge of USS *Mount Vernon*, a dock landing ship.

FACT: At the end of World War II, the U.S. Navy had 6,798 active ships; in 2011, the figure was just 285.

LEADING COUNTRY OF ORIGIN FOR REFUGEES
According to the Global Trends 2010 Report from the United Nations' Refugee Agency, more than three million Afghan refugees are distributed throughout 75 countries; 96% of them are in Pakistan and Iran.

LARGEST ARMED FORCE (RELATIVE TO POPULATION) The Democratic People's Republic of Korea (DPRK, aka North Korea) boasts 1.19 million active personnel in its regular armed forces. This is the largest active armed force relative to population—almost 49 military personnel for every 1,000 head of population. It is also the world's fourth largest army (see "Armed forces" feature, p. 298). When combined with the reserve and paramilitary services, and the Peasant Red Guard, the number of military personnel rises to 7.68 million.

Youngest state leader to control nuclear weapons The leader of the Democratic People's Republic of Korea (North Korea), Kim Jong-un, who succeeded his father Kim Jong-il as leader of the country on December 24, 2011, is, according to official reports, only 29 years old (although other sources put his age at 26 or 27).

Most highly decorated servicewoman of World War II Born in New Zealand and raised in Australia, Nancy Grace Augusta Wake worked with the French Resistance during World War II as a British agent with the Special Operations Executive (SOE). The German Gestapo called her the "White Mouse" due to her ability to evade capture. Her awards include: the British George Medal; the French Croix de Guerre (with two palms); Médaille de la Resistance and Chevalier de la Légion d'Honneur; and the U.S. Medal of Freedom. She died on August 7, 2011, at 98 years old.

Most military personnel rescued at sea On May 8, 1942, 2,735 people from the U.S. aircraft carrier USS *Lexington* (CV-2) were rescued after it had been sunk by the Japanese between Australia and New Caledonia in the Battle of the Coral Sea.

MOST WANTED MAN According to the U.S. Federal Bureau of Investigation, the world's most wanted man is al-Qaeda leader Ayman al-Zawahiri (Egypt). A sum of U.S. $25 million has been offered by the Rewards for Justice Program for his capture or conviction. Although the FBI does not provide a ranking of its most wanted, no one else has a larger bounty attached to their name.

LARGEST NATO OPERATION NATO, the North Atlantic Treaty Organization, is an intergovernmental mutual-defense alliance based on the North Atlantic Treaty signed on April 4, 1949. As of June 6, 2011, NATO's International Security Assistance Force (ISAF) in Afghanistan totaled 132,457 personnel from 49 countries. ISAF was set up by the UN in 2001 and came under NATO control in 2003—its aims are to defeat the Taliban insurgency, provide economic aid, and train the police and army.

Shortest war On August 27, 1896, Britain and Zanzibar (now part of Tanzania) officially went to war at 9 a.m. The conflict ended at 9:45 a.m., with Zanzibar suffering about 500 casualties and its leader, Sultan Khalid, seeking refuge in the German consulate.

LARGEST . . .

Tank battle On July 12, 1943, during World War II, the Battle of Kursk—part of Germany's Operation Zitadelle—saw a total of 1,500 German and Russian tanks amass for close-range fighting in the Prokhorovka region of Russia. Both sides lost more than 300 tanks each in one day.

Naval battle The greatest sea battle involving only ships and submarines was the Battle of Jutland on May 31, 1916, in which 151 British Royal Navy warships squared up against 101 German warships. The Royal Navy lost 14 ships and 6,097 men, and the German fleet 11 ships and 2,545 men.

MOST SNIPER KILLS Simo Häyhä, a Finn, killed more than 500 Soviet soldiers in World War II. On March 6, 1940, Soviet soldiers finally shot the man they called "White Death" in the jaw. He survived and died in 2002.

MOST SNIPER KILLS OF 21ST CENTURY Ex-U.S. Navy SEAL Chris Kyle is the deadliest sniper so far in the 21st century. Nicknamed "the Devil of Ramadi" by Iraqis, he has 160 kills confirmed by the U.S. defense authorities.

Air and sea battle During World War II's Battle of Leyte Gulf in the Philippines, 218 Allied warships battled 64 Japanese warships from October 22 to 27, 1944. In the skies above, 1,280 U.S. and 716 Japanese aircraft were engaged in combat. In the end, 26 Japanese and six U.S. vessels were sunk and the Allies secured a base on the island of Leyte.

MILITARY MIGHT AT A GLANCE

Armed forces

The chart below identifies the top 10 largest armed forces based on the number of personnel as of 2010.

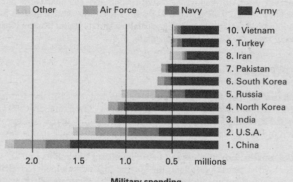

Military spending

The global expenditure on the military in 2011 was U.S. $1.73 trillion (represented by this square block). This equates to 2.6% of world Gross Domestic Product. But which countries spend the most? Here is the top 10, based on the total annual spend in U.S. $ for the year 2011.

1. U.S.A.	U.S. $711 bn
2. China	U.S. $143 bn*
3. Russia	U.S. $71.9 bn*
4. UK	U.S. $62.7 bn
5. France	U.S. $62.5 bn
6. Japan	U.S. $54.5 bn
7. Saudi Arabia	U.S. $48.2 bn
8. India	U.S. $46.8 bn
9. Germany	U.S. $46.7 bn*
10. Italy	U.S. $37 bn*

* estimates

Sources: *The Economist*, International Institute for Strategic Studies, Stockholm International Peace Research Institute.

Combined military operation On June 6, 1944, the Allied Forces launched Operation Overlord, the invasion of German-occupied mainland Europe. Three million men were assembled in the UK under General Eisenhower's command. In the first wave of landings on five beaches in Normandy, France, some 5,300 ships carried 155,000 men, supported by 1,500 tanks and 12,000 aircraft.

Evacuation of military personnel From May 26 to June 4, 1940, as France fell to Nazi Germany, 1,200 Allied naval and civil craft—including fishing boats, pleasure cruisers, and Royal National Lifeboat Institution lifeboats—evacuated 338,226 British and French troops from the beachhead at Dunkerque (Dunkirk), France.

Landlocked navy The landlocked country with the largest naval force is Bolivia. As of 2007, it had 4,800 personnel, of which marines comprised 1,700 (including 1,000 Naval Military Police). These forces patrol Lake Titicaca as well as the country's river systems, preventing smuggling and drug trafficking.

SURVIVORS

Longest time adrift at sea Captain Oguri Jukichi and one of his sailors, named Otokichi (both Japan), survived approximately 484 days after their ship was damaged in a storm off the Japanese coast in October 1813. They drifted in the Pacific before being rescued by a U.S. ship off the Californian coast on March 24, 1815.

LONGEST TIME SURVIVED WITH NO PULSE For one week, starting on August 14, 1998, surgeons used a blood pump to support Julie Mills (UK), who had severe heart failure. For three of those days, she had no pulse.

LONGEST TIME ADRIFT AT SEA ALONE Poon Lim (b. Hong Kong) lived for 133 days on a raft after his ship, the SS *Ben Lomond*, was sunk on November 23, 1942. He was picked up off the north coast of Brazil on April 5, 1943.

LONGEST FALL SURVIVED IN AN ELEVATOR Betty Lou Oliver (U.S.A.) survived a plunge of 75 stories—more than 1,000 ft. (300 m)—in an elevator in the Empire State Building in New York City, U.S.A., on July 28, 1945, after an American B-25 bomber crashed into the building in thick fog.

Greatest rescue without loss of life The U.S. ship *Susan B. Anthony* was sunk off Normandy, France, on June 7, 1944. All 2,689 passengers on board survived.

Most lightning strikes survived The only man in the world to be struck by lightning seven times was ex–park ranger Roy C. Sullivan, the "human lightning conductor" of Virginia, U.S.A. A single lightning strike is made up of several 100-million volts (with peak current in the order of 20,000 amps).

Longest time trapped in an elevator Kively Papajohn of Limassol, Cyprus, was trapped in her apartment building elevator for six days from December 28, 1987, to January 2, 1988. She was 76 years old at the time. Kively survived the cold and beat dehydration by rationing the fruit, vegetables, and bread that she had in her shopping bag.

HIGHEST SPEED SURVIVED IN A MOTORCYCLE CRASH Ron Cook (U.S.A.) crashed a 1,325 cc Kawasaki motorcycle while traveling at an estimated 200 mph (322 km/h) during the SCTA time trials at El Mirage Dry Lake, California, U.S.A., on July 12, 1998. He broke his right arm, wrist, and leg in the crash.

FIRST PERSON TO SURVIVE TWO NUCLEAR ATTACKS
Tsutomu Yamaguchi (Japan, Japan, 1916–2010) was in Hiroshima on August 6, 1945, when the U.S. Army Air Forces dropped the "Little Boy" atomic bomb on the city. Suffering burns to his upper body, Tsutomu returned to his home town of Nagasaki on August 8. The next day, U.S. forces dropped "Fat Man," a 20–22-kiloton bomb, on the city. Miraculously, Tsutomu again survived with only minor injuries—although his left eardrum was irreparably damaged and in later life he was to suffer from illness related to his exposure to radiation. In both cities, he was within 1.8 miles (3 km) of ground zero.

Farthest vertical ski fall survived In April 1997, while she was competing in the 1997 World Extreme Skiing Championships in Valdez, Alaska, Bridget Mead (New Zealand) fell a vertical distance of nearly 1,312 ft. (400 m). Remarkably, she suffered no broken bones, just bruises and severe concussion. Doctors credit her survival to her excellent physical condition and to the fact that she was wearing a helmet.

Farthest auto accident flight survived Paramedic Matt McKnight (U.S.A.) was helping at an accident scene on October 26, 2001, when he was struck by an automobile traveling at 70 mph (112 km/h). He was thrown a distance of 118 ft. (35.9 m) along Route 376, Monroeville, Pennsylvania, U.S.A. Matt dislocated both his shoulders (fracturing one), suffered a collapsed lung, had a thigh ripped open to the bone, and fractured his pelvis and legs. He made a full recovery and returned to work a year later.

Farthest distance survived in a tornado Matt Suter (U.S.A.) was caught in a tornado and carried 1,307 ft. (398 m) in Missouri, U.S.A., on March 12, 2006.

Youngest person to survive a vehicle crash On February 25, 1999, Virginia Rivero from Misiones, Argentina, went into labor at her home and walked to a nearby road in order to hitchhike to the hospital. Offered a lift by two men, she gave birth to a baby girl in the back seat of their automobile. When she told them she was about to have a second baby, the driver overtook an auto in front, only to collide with a third vehicle. Virginia and her newborn daughter were ejected through the back door of the vehicle, suffering minor injuries; but Virginia flagged down another automobile, which took them to the hospital. Once there, she gave birth to a baby boy.

FACT: Luis Urzua (below), seen here with Chilean president Sebastián Piñera, was the last man rescued.

LONGEST TIME TO SURVIVE TRAPPED UNDERGROUND "The 33 of San José" (32 Chileans and one Bolivian) were trapped 2,257 ft. (688 m) underground for 69 days after the collapse of the San José copper-gold mine, near Copiapó, Chile, on August 5, 2010. All the miners made it back to the surface in a rescue capsule. The last man was lifted to safety from the capsule at 21:55 CLDT on October 13, 2010.

Highest percentage of burns to the body survived Two people have survived burns to 90% of their bodies. David Chapman (UK) was burned after a gas canister exploded and drenched him with burning fuel on July 2, 1996. Following the accident, surgeons spent 36 hours removing his dead skin.

Tony Yarijanian (U.S.A.) underwent 25 surgeries, including multiple skin grafts, after having similar injuries from an explosion at his wife's beauty spa in California, U.S.A., on February 15, 2004.

FACT: It took around 15 minutes to winch each of the miners up to the surface in the rescue capsule.

Longest time to survive without food Doctors have estimated that a well-nourished individual can survive without medical consequences on a diet of sugar and water for 30 days or more. The longest period for which anyone has lasted without solid food is 382 days in the case of Angus Barbieri (UK) of Tayport, Fife, who lived on tea, coffee, water, club soda, and vitamins in Maryfield Hospital, Dundee, UK, from June 1965 to July 1966. During that period, his weight declined from 472 lb. (214 kg) to 178 lb. (80.74 kg).

MEDICAL MARVELS

GWR pays tribute to those individuals who have undergone major surgery and survived . . .

LONGEST SURVIVING ARTIFICIAL HEART TRANSPLANT PATIENT
Peter Houghton (UK, 1938–2007)
Date of operation: June 20, 2000
Survived: 7 years 5 months 5 days

LONGEST SURVIVING SINGLE LUNG TRANSPLANT PATIENT
Wolfgang Muller (Canada, 1934–2008)
Date of operation: September 15, 1987
Survived: 20 years 11 months 21 days

LONGEST SURVIVING HEART TRANSPLANT PATIENT
Tony Huesman (U.S.A., 1957–2009)
Date of operation: August 30, 1978
Survived: 30 years 11 months 10 days

LONGEST SURVIVAL WITH HEART OUTSIDE BODY
Christopher Wall (U.S.A., b. August 19, 1975)
Survived: 36 years 5 months 29 days, as of February 17, 2012

LONGEST SURVIVING DOUBLE-KIDNEY TRANSPLANT PATIENT
Brian K. Bourgraf (U.S.A.)
Date of operation: March 23, 1968
Survived: 43 years 331 days, as of February 17, 2012

LONGEST SURVIVING KIDNEY TRANSPLANT PATIENT
Johanna Leanora Rempel (née Nightingale, Canada, b. March 24, 1948)
Date of operation: December 28, 1960
Survived: 51 years 1 month 20 days, as of February 17, 2012

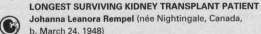

SOCIAL MEDIA

Biggest social games company Despite having only existed since July 2007, U.S. firm Zynga is the most popular social games developer. It attracted 252,274,991 monthly active users on Facebook as of May 18, 2012. Its most popular game, *CityVille*, in which players create their own city, claimed a staggering 26 million players within 12 days of its launch in 2010, making it the **fastest-growing social network game**. As of May 18, 2012, *CityVille* had 36,900,000 active monthly users.

Largest online music playlist The social entertainment site Myspace. com (launched January 2004) has a published playlist of more than 200 million tracks, with 500 new artists being added each week.

Largest video sharing website YouTube dominates video on the Internet. As of April 2012, it had more than 4 billion views a day, and more than 60 hours of video were being added every minute—the equivalent of more than 250,000 full-length movies per week. In 2010, more than 13 million hours of video were uploaded and, in 2011, it attracted 490 million unique users a month.

MOST TWEETS PER SECOND During a television screening of Hayao Miyazaki's Castle in the Sky (Japan, 2009) in Japan on December 9, 2011, Twitter went crazy, reaching 25,088 tweets per second. In the anime film, a spell of destruction is cast with the word "balse" to bring down the city of Laputa. The moment this happened, the film's fans hopped on Twitter to tweet the word "balse," too.

MOST VIEWED VIDEO ONLINE Justin Bieber's (Canada) video for "Baby," directed by Ray Kay (Norway), is not only the top music video on YouTube but the most viewed video online of any kind. As of May 18, 2012, it had 738,166,041 views on the video-sharing website. However, it is also the most "disliked" video online—as of May 18, 2012, it had 2,563,872 "dislikes." "Friday," a 2011 single by U.S. pop star Rebecca Black, was previously the most disliked video, but it was removed temporarily from YouTube for copyright reasons.

FACT: Bieber had 21,927,059 Twitter followers as of May 18, 2012—not far off Lady Gaga's record (see p. 307).

Arabic was the fastest-growing language on Twitter in 2011.

FASTEST TO 1 MILLION FOLLOWERS ON TWITTER
Actor Charlie Sheen (U.S.A.) racked up 1 million followers on Twitter in just 25 hours 17 minutes on March 1 and 2, 2011. Sheen was big news at the time, having had his contract terminated on his CBS hit sitcom *Two and a Half Men*.

FIRST TO 1 MILLION FOLLOWERS ON TWITTER In April 2009, actor Ashton Kutcher (U.S.A.) became the first person to amass over 1 million Twitter followers. Kutcher is now no longer king of the celebrity tweeters, being only the 17th most-followed, with 10,668,643 followers as of May 18, 2012. That's well behind first-placed Lady Gaga (see p. 307).

First satirical social network game *Cow Clicker* involves clicking on a picture of a cow every six hours and is designed to satirize other social network games, such as *FarmVille.* Its designer, Ian Bogost (U.S.A.), describes it as "a Facebook game about Facebook games." It drew an all-time monthly high of 54,245 users, and has spawned a puzzle game, an iPhone game, and an alternate reality game, making it the most successful satirical social game to date. It also sells new cow pictures to click on—the most expensive, the "Roboclicker," had an asking price of 5,000 "mooney" or U.S. $340.

Highest price paid for a social network developer The games developer Playdom, which initially made its reputation creating games for Myspace, was sold to the Walt Disney Company for a record U.S. $563 million in July 2010.

TWEETS ON TWITTER . . .

all in 140 characters or less:

• Twitter has donated access to all its tweets to the Library of Congress for research.

• The name Twitter was used as its definitions—"chirps from birds" and "a short burst of inconsequential information"—fitted perfectly.

• Traffic usually peaks at 1:00 p.m. Pacific Standard Time (4:00 p.m. Eastern Standard Time and 9:00 p.m. Greenwich Mean Time).

MOST PICTURES DOWNLOADED FROM A WEBSITE IN 24 HOURS Erik Kessels (Netherlands) downloaded 950,000 pictures from the Flickr website for his *What's Next?* exhibition held in Amsterdam, Netherlands, in 2011. He printed 350,000 of the images to create "a sea of images you can drown in" and left them piled on the floor. Kessels said he wanted to show "how public private photos have become" and to unnerve visitors by making them "walk over personal memories.

MOST "LIKED" VIDEO ONLINE With 908,668 thumbs-up on YouTube as of May 18, 2012, "Charlie bit my finger—again!" is the favorite online video. It shows Harry Davies-Carr having his finger bitten by his baby brother Charlie (both UK)—with a little more force than he was expecting.

First arcade game to integrate Twitter Sega's *Virtua Fighter 5: Final Showdown* is the first arcade game to let players link together their Virtua Fighter and Twitter accounts. This means players can follow each other's fortunes while they punch and kick their way through bouts. Cool combat moves are posted automatically on Twitter.

Most content uploaded to an online video service An average of 70.49 hours per minute is uploaded to Ustream.tv, a website that broadcasts live events. This figure, based on the 37.05 million hours of content uploaded to the site from June 2010 to May 2011, beats YouTube's 60 hours of content per minute.

MOST FOLLOWERS ON TWITTER Lady Gaga (U.S.A., b. Stefani Germanotta) had more than 24,285,376 Twitter followers of her @ladygaga Twitter feed as of May 18, 2012. She was also the **first tweep to attain 10 million followers**, on May 15, 2011.

LARGEST ONLINE SOCIAL NETWORK As of March 2012, Facebook boasted over 901 million monthly active users, with more than 125 billion friend connections. Each day, 3.2 billion "likes" and comments are generated by its users, who upload over 300 million photos to the service. Facebook's largest shareholder is Mark Zuckerburg (right), who was recently overtaken by fellow Facebook founder Dustin Moskovitz (both U.S.A.) as the world's **youngest billionaire** (see p.151)

MOST SOCIAL NETWORKING

• **Most comments on a Facebook item in 24 hours:** 80,030, achieved by Greenpeace on April 14, 2011. Greenpeace were trying to get Facebook itself to use green energy instead of electricity from burning coal.

• **Most comments on a single Facebook item in total:** 1,001,552, in response to a post made on October 30, 2011, by Tracey Hodgson (UK) on the Facebook page FFG Pioneers. Tracey's post was on the Zynga game Frontierville, now called The Pioneer Trail.

• **Most "likes" on a Facebook page:** 88,051,895, on Facebook for Every Phone, as of May 18, 2012.

• **Most "likes" on a Facebook item in 24 hours:** 588,243, in response to a post on February 15, 2011, by rapper Lil Wayne (U.S.A., b. Dwayne Carter, Jr.). He was competing with cookie company Oreo for the record.

Most talked-about topics on Facebook Since 2009, Facebook has been tracking the phrases most used in status updates. In 2009, "Facebook applications" was the favorite topic. In 2010, it was "HMU" (hit me up), with "World Cup" (soccer) coming in second. In 2011, it was "Death of Osama bin Laden."

IN JUST ONE DAY . . .

375 Mb of data are consumed per average household

294 billion e-mails are sent

22 billion text messages are sent

8 years of footage is added to YouTube: the equivalent of 60 hours of video every minute!

3 billion YouTube clips are viewed; in 2010, 700 billion playbacks were logged

400 million people log on to Facebook

300 million photos are added to Facebook

50 million people log on to Twitter

230 million tweets are sent—equal to 2,662 messages tweeted every second!

460,000 new Twitter accounts are opened

4.3 million new images are uploaded to Flickr, enough to fill 540,000 pages of a photo album

---

ENGINEERING

CONTENTS

LARGEST TRUCK BODY The WESTECH Flow Control Body, designed and manufactured in Wyoming, U.S.A., is the largest mining truck body by volume. Specially made for the Liebherr T 282 C truck, it was measured on June 14, 2011, at North Antelope Rochelle Mine in Wyoming carrying 16,612 cu. ft. (470.4 m³) of coal. That's about the same capacity as 5,875 bathtubs, or 600 pickup truckloads. To move such a great weight, the T 282 C has a 20-cylinder engine and a 1,171-gal. (5,350-liter) fuel tank. It costs about $5 million.

The driver needs to climb 21 steps to get to his cab . . . and sits 19 ft. 8 in. (6 m) off the ground.

The total height of the truck is 30 ft. 6 in. (9.3 m) . . . and the wheels are 11 ft. 10 in. (3.6 m) high.

The engine weighs 23,104 lb. (10,480 kg) . . . and generates a top speed of 39.7 mph (64 km/h).

HOW TALL CAN WE BUILD?

HOW HIGH CAN WE GO?

In the Old Testament tale of the Tower of Babel (below left), mankind tries to reach God by building a supertall structure to heaven. But is there any upper limit to our towering ambitions today?

The 20th century saw skyscrapers dominate city skylines. By 1980, more  than 80% of the world's buildings over 500 ft. (150 m) were in North America. Today, however, Asia and the Middle East are the preeminent builders of supertall structures. Every building now sits in the shadow of the 2,717-ft-tall (828-m) Burj Khalifa, the glittering glass-and-steel trophy that opened in Dubai, UAE, in 2010. But for how long?

CONCRETE: A superhigh-pressure pump was used to raise the concrete upward during construction of the Burj Khalifa.

LOGISTICS: The higher you build, the greater the mechanical infrastructure needed to support the building.

ECONOMICS: Supertall buildings are often begun at the end of a boom era, when money is available and confidence is high. But the long construction times involved may dissuade financiers.

HEIGHT: The Burj Khalifa was an impressive 60% taller than the previous highest building, Taipei 101. But the Kingdom Tower would be another 20% taller than the Burj Khalifa!

MAINTENANCE: The size of supertall buildings makes them highly vulnerable to the elements. The building's façade will deteriorate over time and will require repaneling. Adequate surface drainage is also vital. To avoid corrosion in a building's metal structures and components, an electrical current is sometimes passed through them, a treatment known as "cathodic protection."

FOUNDATIONS: The deepest foundations are those of the Petronas Towers, Kuala Lumpur, Malaysia, which extend 394 ft. (120 m) into the bedrock.

WIND: The top of a skyscraper can sway 3 ft. (1 m) in high winds. Typically, a tall building is designed to sway by no more than 1/500th of its height. Large objects called "mass dampers" help to shift a building's weight to balance the pressure of the wind. Pictured above is the 728-ton (660-tonne) mass damper, housed—in full public view—near the top of the 1,667-ft.-tall (508-m) skyscraper Taipei 101 in Chinese Taipei.

SKY-HIGH RENTS AND SKYSCRAPERS

OFFICE RENTAL: The cost of office space is inexorably on the rise, with rates in the **most expensive office location**—Hong Kong, China—at an eye-watering U.S. $213.70 per sq. ft. (U.S. $2,299.41 per m²) per annum as of June 2011. One way to combat these hefty costs is to build upward, instead of taking up more space on the ground.

THE RISING CHALLENGE OF WASTE DISPOSAL

SEWAGE: Tall buildings must be located where there is sufficient municipal sewage systems—otherwise there is the risk of congestion. Until recently, Dubai had an insufficient sewage system, so a constant stream of trucks had to ferry the contents of septic tanks between its tall buildings and the city's only sewage-treatment plant.

FIRE SAFETY FIRST

EVACUATION: Fire and smoke can be lethal in a tall building, as was the case in the aftermath of the terrorist attacks on the World Trade Center towers on September 11, 2001 (right).

ELEVATORS: Moving large numbers of people to a great height—and promptly—is a challenge. The higher you build, the more elevators you need, but more elevators reduce the available floor space to rent. Express elevators also have a speed limit beyond which passengers begin to feel queasy—the upper limit is around 40 mph (64 km/h).

TOP 100 TALLEST BUILDINGS

Born in the U.S.A., the skyscraper has latterly been taken to spectacular new heights in the Middle East and Asia. Our time line (right) shows the history of the 100 tallest buildings constructed—and their distribution across the world—since 1930.

Source: skyscrapercenter.com

LINE KEY

- ▬▬ Hotel
- ▬▬ Hotel/Office
- ▬▬ Hotel/Residential
- ///// Hotel/Office/Retail
- • • Office
- ▪▪ Residential
- ▏▏▏ Residential/Office
- ▦▦ Residential/Office/Hotel

Year	Region	0 (ft)	325	655	985	1,310	1,640
1930	The Americas	•	•	•	•	•	
1930	The Americas	•	•	•	•	•	
1931	The Americas	•	•	•	•	•	•
1932	The Americas	•	•	•	•		
1969	The Americas	▏▏▏▏▏▏▏▏▏▏▏▏					
1973	The Americas	•	•	•	•	•	
1974	The Americas	•	•	•	•	•	•
1975	The Americas	•	•	•	•		
1977	The Americas	•	•	•	•	•	
1982	The Americas	•	•	•	•		
1982	The Americas	•	•	•	•		
1983	The Americas	•	•	•	•	•	
1984	The Americas	•	•	•	•		
1985	The Americas	•	•	•	•		
1986	Asia	•	•	•	•		
1987	The Americas	•	•	•	•		
1989	The Americas	•	•	•	•		
1989	The Americas	•	•	•	•	•	
1990	Asia	•	•	•	•	•	
1990	The Americas	•	•	•	•	•	
1990	The Americas	•	•	•	•	•	
1990	The Americas	•	•	•	•	•	
1991	The Americas	•	•	•	•		
1992	Asia	•	•	•	•	•	•
1992	Asia	•	•	•	•	•	
1993	Asia	▬▬▬▬▬▬▬▬▬					
1993	The Americas	•	•	•	•	•	
1996	Asia	•	•	•	•	•	
1996	Asia	•	•	•	•	•	
1996	Asia	•	•	•	•		
1997	Asia	▬▬▬▬					
1997	Asia	▬▬▬▬▬▬▬					
1998	Asia	•	•	•	•	•	•
1998	Asia	•	•	•	•	•	
1998	Asia	•	•	•	•	•	
1998	Asia	•	•	•	•	•	
1999	Middle East	▬▬▬▬▬▬▬					
1999	Asia	▦▦▦▦▦▦▦▦					
1999	Asia	•	•	•	•		
2000	Middle East	▬▬▬▬▬▬					
2000	Asia	▬▬▬▬▬▬▬					
2000	Middle East	•	•	•	•	•	
2001	Asia	•	•	•	•	•	
2001	Asia	•	•	•	•	•	
2002	Middle East	▦▦▦▦▦▦▦					
2003	Asia	•	•	•	•	•	
2003	Asia	▦▦▦▦▦					
2004	Asia	///////////					
2004	Asia	•	•	•	•	•	•
2005	Asia	•	•	•	•		

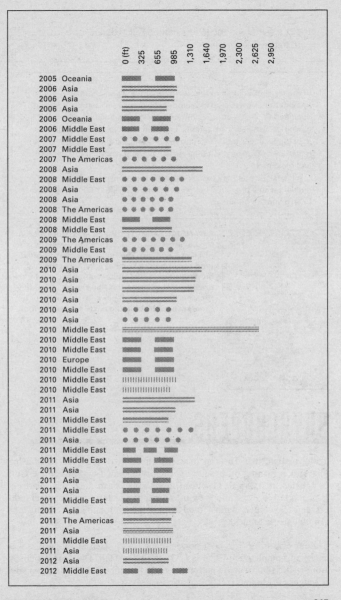

	0 (ft)	325	655	985	1,310	1,640	1,970	2,300	2,625	2,950
2005 Oceania										
2006 Asia										
2006 Asia										
2006 Asia										
2006 Oceania										
2006 Middle East										
2007 Middle East										
2007 Middle East										
2007 The Americas										
2008 Asia										
2008 Middle East										
2008 Asia										
2008 Asia										
2008 The Americas										
2008 Middle East										
2008 Middle East										
2009 The Americas										
2009 Middle East										
2009 The Americas										
2010 Asia										
2010 Asia										
2010 Asia										
2010 Asia										
2010 Asia										
2010 Asia										
2010 Middle East										
2010 Middle East										
2010 Middle East										
2010 Europe										
2010 Middle East										
2010 Middle East										
2010 Middle East										
2011 Asia										
2011 Asia										
2011 Middle East										
2011 Middle East										
2011 Asia										
2011 Middle East										
2011 Middle East										
2011 Asia										
2011 Asia										
2011 Asia										
2011 Middle East										
2011 Asia										
2011 The Americas										
2011 Asia										
2011 Middle East										
2011 Asia										
2012 Asia										
2012 Middle East										

In theory, a building's height is limited only by an architect's imagination. However, a skyscraper is a complex creation, involving engineering, architecture, economics, and even politics, with each having its own set of limitations. Location matters, too: tall buildings may topple in earthquake-prone regions and existing building materials can only withstand a certain amount of structural pressure and movement.

All these factors may explain why the Kingdom Tower is the only building with a projected height of around 3,280 ft. (1,000 m) to have been given the go-ahead.

FINANCIAL CLIMATE: When recessions kick in, the construction of showcase tall buildings is often put on hold. The Burj Dubai was finished (and renamed the Khalifa) only when the bankrupt emirate of Dubai was bailed out by the president of neighboring Abu Dhabi. Ultimately, the revenue generated per square foot must be greater than the building costs per square foot.

SKYSCRAPERS

Tallest structure The top of the drilling rig of the Ursa tension leg platform, a floating oil production facility operated by Shell in the Gulf of Mexico, is 4,285 ft. (1,306 m) above the ocean floor. The platform is connected to the seafloor by oil pipelines and four massive steel tethers at each corner, with a total weight of approximately 17,640 tons (16,000 metric tonnes).

Tallest chimney The coal power plant No. 2 stack at Ekibastuz, Kazakhstan, completed in 1987, is 1,378 ft. (420 m) tall. The diameter tapers from 144 ft. (44 m) at the bottom up to 46 ft. 7 in. (14.2 m) at the top, and it weighs 66,138 tons (60,000 metric tonnes).

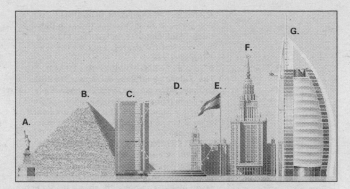

A. STATUE OF LIBERTY You can compare the height of all the buildings on these pages against the Statue of Liberty, which, from the bottom of the pedestal to the tip of the torch, is 305 ft. 1 in. (92.99 m) tall.

B. TALLEST PYRAMID The Great Pyramid of Giza, Egypt (also known as the pyramid of Khufu), was 481 ft. (146 m) high when completed around 4,500 years ago, but erosion and vandalism have reduced it to 451.4 ft. (137.5 m) today.

C. TALLEST HOSPITAL The Li Shu Pui block of the Hong Kong Sanatorium and Hospital in Wan Chai, Hong Kong, is 487 ft. (148.5 m) tall. The 38-floor hospital was designed by Wong & Ouyang (HK) Ltd. and completed in 2008.

D. TALLEST OBSERVATION WHEEL The Singapore Flyer comprises a 492-ft. (150-m) diameter wheel built over a three-story terminal building, giving it a total height of 541 ft. (165 m). It is located in Marina Bay, Singapore, and was opened to the public on March 1, 2008.

E. TALLEST UNSUPPORTED FLAGPOLE The Dushanbe Flagpole, unveiled on May 24, 2011, in the Tajikistan capital of Dushanbe, measures 541 ft. 4 in. (165 m). It flies a 196-ft. 10-in. x 98-ft. 5-in. (60-m x 30-m) Tajikistan flag.

F. TALLEST UNIVERSITY The MV Lomonosov Moscow State University on the Lenin Hills, south of Moscow, Russia, stands 787.5 ft. (240 m) tall and has 32 stories and 40,000 rooms. It was constructed between 1949 and 1953.

G. TALLEST ATRIUM The atrium of the Burj Al Arab hotel in Dubai, UAE, is 590 ft. (180 m) high. It forms a vast central cavity, around which the hotel is built.

Tallest monument The stainless steel Gateway Arch in St. Louis, Missouri, U.S.A., was completed on October 28, 1965, to commemorate the westward expansion after the Louisiana Purchase of 1803. It is a sweeping arch rising to 630 ft. (192 m).

Tallest obelisk An obelisk is a tapered four-sided column, usually with a pointed top. The Washington Monument in Washington, D.C., U.S.A., is an obelisk that stands 555 ft. (169 m) tall. Completed in 1884, it was built—without any steel enforcement—to honor George Washington, the first president of the U.S.A., making it the world's tallest unreinforced masonry structure.

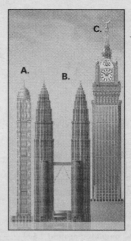

A. TALLEST RESIDENTIAL BUILDING
Completed in 2012, Princess Tower in Dubai, United Arab Emirates, is 1,356 ft. (413.4 m) high and has 101 stories, dedicated to residential use.

B. TALLEST TWIN TOWERS The 1,482-ft. 7-in.-tall (451.9-m) Petronas Towers in Kuala Lumpur, Malaysia, are the tallest matching pair of buildings. The 88-story office buildings opened in March 1996. The towers are joined at level 41 and level 42 by a double-decker "Skybridge."

C. TALLEST HOTEL The 120-story Makkah Royal Clock Tower Hotel—aka the Abraj Al-Bait Hotel Tower—in Mecca, Saudi Arabia, stands 1,972 ft. (601 m) high. The hotel is part of a seven-building complex that has a record floor space of 16.15 million sq. ft. (1,500,000 m²). The tallest all-hotel building (as opposed to a mixed-use building) is the 1,093-ft. (333-m) Rose Rayhaan by Rotana in Dubai.

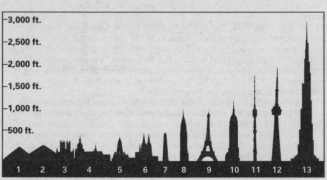

TALLEST SELF-SUPPORTING STRUCTURES Here are the world's tallest buildings since the 341-ft.-high (104-m) Red Pyramid was built for the pharaoh Sneferu in ca. 2600 B.C. The Great Pyramid, built for the pharaoh Khufu to a height of 481 ft. (146 m) in ca. 2560 B.C., soon superseded it. However, it took another 3,771 years for the record to be broken again, when Lincoln Cathedral with its central spire (now collapsed) reached 525 ft. (160 m). Today's tallest building—the Burj Khalifa at 2,716 ft. 6 in. (828 m) high—is almost eight times as high as the Red Pyramid.

1. Red Pyramid, Egypt
2. Great Pyramid, Egypt
3. Lincoln Cathedral, UK
4. St. Mary's Church, Germany
5. St. Nikolai, Germany
6. Cologne Cathedral, Germany
7. Washington Monument, U.S.A.
8. Chrysler Building, U.S.A.
9. Eiffel Tower, France
10. Empire State Building, U.S.A.
11. Ostankino Tower, Russia
12. CN Tower, Canada
13. Burj Khalifa, UAE

TALL BUILDINGS

Guinness World Records uses the definition of tall and supertall buildings as specified by the Council on Tall Buildings and Urban Habitat (CTBUH).

Tall vs. Supertall

The CTBUH defines "supertall" as taller than 984 ft. (300 m). By the end of 2011, there were only 59 completed structures worldwide.

984 ft.

Tall   Supertall

How do you measure a tall building?

GWR only recognizes buildings measured to their "architectural top," which is defined by the CTBUH as the height "including spires, but not including antennae, signage, flag poles, or other functional-technical equipment."

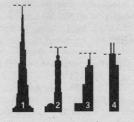

1. Burj Khalifa, UAE: 2,716 ft.
2. Taipei 101, Chinese Taipei: 1,666 ft.
3. Zifeng Tower, China: 1,476 ft.*
4. Willis Tower, U.S.A.: 1,450 ft.†

1,250 ft. to roof but spire considered part of structure

†1,729 ft. to top of antennae (not considered part of the structural height of the building)*

Buildings vs. Towers

GWR defines a "tower" as a building in which usable floor space occupies less than 50% of its height (usable floor space shown in gray).

1. Oriental Pearl Tower, China
2. Jin Mao Tower, China

FACT: Close to 26,000 glass panels, each cut by hand, were used in the exterior paneling of the Burj Khalifa.

A. TALLEST TOWER The Tokyo Sky Tree in Sumida, Tokyo, Japan, rises 2,080 ft. (634 m) to the top of its mast, making it the world's tallest tower. The Sky Tree serves as a broadcasting tower.

B. TALLEST BUILDING At 2,716 ft. 6 in. (828 m) tall, the Burj Khalifa (Khalifa Tower) in Dubai, UAE, became the tallest building in the world when it was officially opened on January 4, 2010. Part of a 490-acre (2-km²) development called Downtown Dubai, the Burj has residential, office, and hotel use.

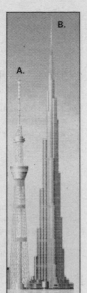

AIRPORTS

Largest airport King Fahd International Airport (DMM), near Dammam in eastern Saudi Arabia, is the largest airport by area. It occupies 301 sq. miles (780 km²), bigger than the entire country of Bahrain (which has three airports of its own).

Largest airport park A park at Amsterdam Schiphol Airport (AMS) in the Netherlands, opened on May 11, 2011, by the Dutch Princess Irene, is the world's largest (and currently only) park within an airport. The park has indoor and outdoor sections, measures 21,528 sq. ft. (2,000 m²), and features projected butterflies and the sounds of bicycle bells and children. People can recharge their cell phones in the park by pedaling static bicycles.

Largest airport library Schiphol is also home to the largest airport library in terms of area, covering 967 sq. ft. (90 m²). It opened in July 2010.

Largest airport golf course Don Mueang International Airport (DMK) in Bangkok, Thailand, is home to an 18-hole golf course. It fills much of the gap between the two runways, which are 12,139 ft. (3,700 m) and 11,482 ft. (3,500 m) long.

LONGEST ICE RUNWAY The two ice runways at Antarctica's McMurdo Station are the longest of their type in the world, each measuring 10,000 ft. (3,048 m) long and 220 ft. (67 m) wide. The runways are carved out of sea ice each year, before the ice breaks in December. They can take large aircraft, such as the Lockheed C-5 Galaxy (left).

Busiest beach airport Despite being submerged daily by the incoming tide, the Barra beach airport (BRR) in the Scottish Western Isles handles more than 1,000 flights per year. It is the only beach airport to handle scheduled airline services.

LARGEST MODEL AIRPORT Knuffingen Airport, located at Miniatur Wunderland in Hamburg, Germany, is a 494-sq.-ft. (45.9-m²) model of Hamburg's Fuhlsbüttel Airport. Built to a scale of 1:87, it took seven years to make at a cost of U.S. $4.8 million. A computer can move the planes and automobiles and, because of wires, the planes can even fly.

TOP 10 MOST EXTREME AIRPORTS

In 2010, the History Channel ranked the most challenging airports for pilots. Tenzing-Hillary tops the list—the Yeti Airlines crash there (right) in 2008 left 18 people dead.

Airport	Dangers
1. Tenzing-Hillary (LUA), Lukla, Nepal	Mountainous location with high winds and changing visibility
2. Toncontín (TGU), Tegucigalpa, Honduras	Difficult approach through hills, short runway
3. Gustaf III (SBH), St. Barthélemy, Caribbean	Steep approach and short airstrip; planes often end up on beach
4. Princess Juliana (SXM), St. Maarten, Caribbean	Short runway—planes fly in just yards above beach (pictured on next page)
5. Gibraltar (GIB)	Road runs across runway, high winds, restricted air corridors
6. Kai Tak, Hong Kong (HGK, now closed)	Nearby multistory buildings means tricky low-altitude approach
7. Courchevel (CVF), France	Mountaintop runway is short, sloping, and ends with a cliff drop
8. Eagle County (EGE), Gypsum, Colorado, U.S.A.	Difficult mountainous approach and changeable weather
9. Madeira (FNC), Funchal, Madeira, Portugal	High winds, mountainous terrain, runway built over ocean
10. San Diego (SAN), California, U.S.A.	Busy airspace, multistory parking lot close to end of runway

The three-letter airport codes are identifiers assigned by the International Air Transport Association.

FACT: Planes at Princess Juliana Airport fly just yards above the beach. A two-lane road separates beach and runway.

Highest airport At 14,219 ft. (4,334 m) above sea level, Qamdo Bangda Airport (BPX) in Tibet is the highest airport operating a scheduled service. Because planes have extended stopping distances at high altitude (due to reduced atmospheric resistance), the airport requires an extralong runway at 13,794 ft. (4,204 m).

Most northerly airport Svalbard Airport (LYR), which serves a cluster of Norwegian islands in the Arctic Ocean, is the most northerly public airport, located at 78.2° latitude and 15.4° longitude. Completed in 1975, the 7,608-ft. (2,319-m) runway is built on a layer of permafrost.

AVIATION AT A GLANCE

• Global air passenger traffic rose by 6.6% in 2010, topping the 5 billion passengers mark for the first time.

• According to the U.S. National Air Traffic Controllers Association (NATCA), there are about 5,000 (nonmilitary) planes in the sky above the U.S.A. at any one time.

• It's impossible to give an accurate figure for the actual number of people flying at any one time globally, but estimates range from 100,000 to 2 million passengers.

• NATCA claim that your chances of dying on a flight out of the U.S.A. to be 1 in 14 million; boffins at the Massachusetts Institute of Technology have deemed flying to be 22 times safer than driving.

BUSIEST CARGO AIRPORT Hong Kong International Airport (HKG), also known as Chek Lap Kok Airport, is the world's busiest airport in terms of cargo handling. According to the Airports Council International, the airport overtook Memphis International Airport (MEM) in 2010, when it handled 4,102,984 tons (4,168,852 tonnes) of cargo. With a floor area of 3.2 million sq. ft. (280,500 m²), the airport's SuperTerminal 1 is the world's largest cargo terminal under one roof.

LARGEST AIR TERMINAL Measuring 12.76 million sq. ft. (1,185,000 m²), Dubai International Airport's (DXB) Terminal 3 is the world's largest airport building in terms of floor space.

Closest airports The distance between the airports of Papa Westray (PPW) and Westray (WRY), neighboring destinations in the Scottish Orkney Islands, is a mere 1.76 miles (2.83 km). Flights between the two airports take an average of just 96 seconds (two minutes including taxiing time).

Steepest runway at an international airport Courchevel Airport (CVF) in the French Alps possesses the world's steepest runway. At just 1,722 ft. (525 m) long and angled at 18.5 degrees, it is not for the faint-hearted.

Longest airstrip on a purpose-built island Kansai International Airport (KIX), constructed on an artificial island 3 miles (4.8 km) offshore in Osaka Bay, Japan, is home to a 13,123-ft.-long (4,000-m) airstrip. The island is connected to the mainland by a road and rail bridge.

Airport with the longest bridge-supported runway extension Extended into the sea to accommodate large aircraft, such as Boeing 747s, the runway at Madeira Airport (FNC), Portugal, is 9,124 ft. (2,781 m) long, with the bridge-supported section measuring 3,346 ft. (1,020 m) long and 591 ft. (180 m) wide.

Shortest commercially serviceable runway Juancho E. Yrausquin Airport (SAB), on the Caribbean island of Saba, Netherlands Antilles, has the shortest commercially serviceable runway. At just 1,300 ft. (396 m) in length, it is only slightly longer than the runways on most aircraft carriers. At each end of the runway, cliffs drop into the sea.

BUSIEST AIRPORTS

The Airports International Council produces annual figures on the world's busiest airports based on three criteria:

ATL (89.33 million) 👤👤👤👤👤👤👤👤👤
PEK (73.94 million) 👤👤👤👤👤👤👤
ORD (66.77 million) 👤👤👤👤👤👤👤
LHR (65.88 million) 👤👤👤👤👤👤
HND (64.21 million) 👤👤👤👤👤👤

👤 = *10 million passengers arriving, departing, or transferring*

HKG (4.58 million tons) 💼💼💼💼💼
MEM (4.31 million tons) 💼💼💼💼
PVG (3.55 million tons) 💼💼💼💼
ICN (2.95 million tons) 💼💼💼
ANC (2.83 million tons) 💼💼💼

💼 = *1 million tons/tonnes of cargo loaded and unloaded*

ATL (950,119) ✈✈✈✈✈✈✈✈✈
ORD (882,617) ✈✈✈✈✈✈✈✈
LAX (666,938) ✈✈✈✈✈✈
DFW (652,261) ✈✈✈✈✈✈
DEN (630,063) ✈✈✈✈✈✈

✈ = *100,000 takeoffs and landings*

KEY TO AIRPORT CODES

ANC	Ted Stephens Anchorage (U.S.A.)	**LAX**	Los Angeles (U.S.A.)
ATL	Hartsfield Jackson Atlanta (U.S.A.)	**LHR**	London Heathrow (UK)
		ICN	Incheon (South Korea)
DEN	Denver (U.S.A.)	**MEM**	Memphis (U.S.A.)
DFW	Dallas/Fort Worth (U.S.A.)	**ORD**	Chicago O'Hare (U.S.A.)
HND	Tokyo (Japan)	**PEK**	Beijing Capital (China)
		PVG	Shanghai Pudong (China)

TRAINS & RAILWAYS

Fastest train speed • **Average speed:** A French SNCF TGV train recorded an average speed of 190.37 mph (306.37 km/h) between Calais and Marseille on May 26, 2001. The train, which was unmodified and identical to Eurostar trains, covered the 663 miles (1,067 km) between the cities in 3 hr. 29 min., reaching a top speed of 227 mph (366 km/h).

• **Maglev:** The highest speed by a manned superconducting magnetically levitated (maglev) train is 361 mph (581 km/h) by the MLX01, operated by the Central Japan Railway Company and Railway Technical Research Institute, on the Yamanashi Maglev Test Line, Yamanashi Prefecture, Japan, on December 2, 2003.

• **Jet-powered:** The M-497 Black Beetle was a prototype experimental train powered by two General Electric J47-19 jet engines. It was developed and tested in 1966 in the U.S.A. and reached speeds of up to 183 mph (296 km/h).

• **Diesel:** The former British Rail inaugurated its high-speed train (HST) daily service between London, Bristol, and South Wales, UK, on October 4, 1976, using InterCity 125 trains. One of these reached a speed of 148 mph (238 km/h) on a test run between Darlington and York, UK, on November 1, 1987.

LONGEST CONTINUALLY OPERATING TRAMWAY The St. Charles Avenue Line in New Orleans, Louisiana, U.S.A., began operation in September 1835 and still runs today. It was one of the U.S.A.'s first passenger railroads. Initially, carriages were moved by a number of different means, including mules and steam engines, until overhead electric cables were adopted in 1895.

FASTEST TRAIN—MAXIMUM SPEED On the 70.84-mile-long (114-km) Beijing–Tianjin Intercity Rail line in China, trains run at a maximum operating speed (MOS) of 217.48 mph (350 km/h). Tests have demonstrated that the trains have an unmodified capability of 244.82 mph (394 km/h), but their speed has been limited for safety reasons.

FACT: The line has cut journey times between Beijing and Tianjin from 70 minutes to 30 minutes.

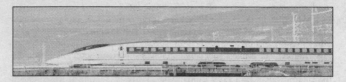

FASTEST TRAIN JOURNEY (AVERAGE SPEED) The West Japan Railway Company operates its 500-Series *Nozomi* bullet trains ("Shinkansen") at an average speed of 162.7 mph (261.8 km/h) on the 119-mile (192-km) line between Hiroshima and Kokura on the island of Honshu.

Japan has the busiest railroad network, with around 23 billion passengers recorded for the year 2010, across all rail companies. Japan Railway, the country's main rail company, recorded approximately 8.9 billion passengers alone in that year.

Japanese trains get very crowded—particularly at rush hour—so white-gloved "pushers" are used to encourage passengers to fill all available space (left).

• **Steam:** The fastest steam locomotive is the London North Eastern Railway "Class A4" No. 4468 *Mallard*. It achieved a speed of 126 mph (202.8 km/h), hauling seven coaches weighing 535,722 lb. (243 metric tonnes), down Stoke Bank, near Essendine, between Grantham and Peterborough, UK, on July 3, 1938.

Fastest scheduled speed between two rail stops Between Lorraine and Champagne-Ardenne in France, trains reach an average speed of 173.6 mph (279.4 km/h), according to the *Railway Gazette International* World Speed Survey study.

Fastest train on a national rail system The highest speed recorded by a train on a national rail network (rather than a dedicated test track) is 357.2 mph (574.8 km/h), by a French SNCF modified version of the TGV on April 3, 2007. The peak speed was achieved between the Meuse

OLDEST MODEL TRAIN SET
Made at an unknown location before 1868, the oldest model train set can be found in the Bowes Museum in Barnard Castle, County Durham, UK.

FIRST PRESERVED RAILROAD The 7.25-mile (11.6-km) Talyllyn Railway in Gwynedd, UK, dates from 1865 and was built to carry slate from local quarries. Over the years, the railroad was allowed to become run-down, but it was eventually taken over by enthusiasts and volunteers, who formed the Talyllyn Railway Preservation Society and reopened the line as a tourist attraction. The first trips on the revived railroad took place on May 14, 1951.

SMALLEST COMMERCIALLY AVAILABLE WORKING MODEL RAILROAD "T" Gauge, developed by K. K. Eishindo of Japan, has a track with a gauge of just 0.1 in (3 mm). The models are 450 times smaller than the real thing.

HIGHEST RAILROAD LINE The Qinghai-Tibet railroad in China is a 1,215-mile-long (1,956-km) line, most of which lies 13,120 ft. (4,000 m) above sea level. Its highest point reaches an altitude of 16,640 ft. (5,072 m). Carriages are pressurized, like aircraft cabins, and oxygen masks are available.

At an altitude of 16,627 ft. (5,068 m) above sea level, the Tanggula railroad station in Tibet is the **highest railroad station** in the world. The unstaffed station opened on July 1, 2006 and is located at the highest point on the Qinghai-Tibet railroad.

and Champagne-Ardenne stations on the LGV Est high-speed rail line in eastern France.

Largest railroad system The country with the most extensive railroad network is the U.S.A., with 139,679 miles (224,792 km) of railroad lines.

The country with the **shortest railroad track** is Vatican City, with a 2,828-ft. (862-m) spur entering the Holy See from Italy. It is used only for goods and supplies.

Oldest railroad station Liverpool Road station in Manchester, UK, was first used on September 15, 1830, and was finally closed on September 30, 1975. Today, part of the station serves as a museum.

The **oldest independent railroad company** is the Ffestiniog Railway (UK), which was founded by an act of Parliament on May 23, 1832. It is still operating today, running tourist trains along the 23.5-in. (597-cm) narrow-gauge tracks between Porthmadog and Blaenau Ffestiniog in Gwynedd, Wales—a distance of 13.5 miles (21.6 km).

The **oldest locomotive roundhouse** is the Derby Roundhouse, which was built in 1839 by the North Midland Railway (UK). The restored structure now forms part of the Derby College campus.

First public electric railroad The earliest public electric railroad was opened on May 12, 1881 at Lichterfelde near Berlin, Germany. It was 1.5 miles (2.5 km) long, ran on 100 V current, and carried 26 passengers at a speed of 30 mph (48 km/h).

Longest train journey without changing trains The longest run without a change of train stretches 6,346 miles (10,214 km), from Moscow in Russia to Pyongyang in North Korea. One train a week makes the journey, which incorporates sections of the famous Trans-Siberian line. The journey is scheduled to take 7 days 20 hr. 25 min. in total.

TOP 10 LONGEST RAILROAD NETWORKS

U.S.A.: 139,679 miles	**Germany:** 26,085 miles
Russia: 54,156 miles	**Australia:** 23,888 miles
China: 53,437 miles	**Argentina:** 22,969 miles
India: 39,751 miles	**France:** 18,417 miles
Canada: 28,926 miles	**Brazil:** 17,732 miles

Population per 1 mile of track

The top 10 countries ordered by the number of citizens for every 1 mile of railroad track:

1. Canada: 748	**6. Finland:** 1,457
2. Australia: 915	**7. Vatican City:** 1,550
3. Sweden: 1,171	**8. Latvia:** 1,564
4. Romania: 1,366	**9. St. Kitts and Nevis:** 1,664
5. Namibia: 1,403	**10. New Zealand:** 1,712

Canada has the **longest rail network per capita**, with each person claiming 7 ft. of track; Australians are second with 5.7 ft.

The U.S.A. has the **longest rail network** (meaning the total of all gauges of track: broad, standard, narrow, and dual). There are 2,224 people per 1 mile of track.

Source: CIA World Factbook; International Union of Railways

Longest train A 4.57-mile-long (7.35-km) train consisting of 682 ore cars pushed by eight diesel-electric locomotives was assembled by BHP Iron Ore (Australia). The train traveled 171 miles (275 km) from the company's Newman and Yandi mines to Port Hedland in Western Australia on June 21, 2001.

Longest passenger train Comprising 70 coaches and one electric locomotive, a train created by the National Belgian Railway Company—in aid of a cancer charity—measured 5,685 ft. 4 in. (1,732.9 m) on April 27, 1991. It traveled 38.9 miles (62.5 km) from Ghent to Ostend (both Belgium).

Longest runaway train On March 26, 1884, a wind of great force set eight coal cars on the move at Akron in Colorado, U.S.A. The chance event resulted in the longest journey by a runaway train: a distance of 100 miles (160 km) down the Chicago, Burlington, and Quincy Railroad east of Denver, Colorado.

Longest railroad platform The platform at Kharagpur station in West Bengal, India, is 3,517 ft. (1,072 m) long.

India is also home to the **longest 2-ft.-gauge passenger railroad line**, which runs for 124.14 miles (199.8 km) between Gwalior and Sheopur Kalan.

Longest pleasure-pier railroad The pleasure-pier railroad at Southend-on-Sea, Essex, UK, measures 6,200 ft. 1 in. (1,889.8 m) in length.

Most northerly tramway terminus The northernmost tramway terminus is St. Olav's Gate station in Trondheim on the Gråkallbanen, or Trondheim Tramway line, in Norway. The city is located at 63° 36'N latitude, 10° 23'E longitude.

Longest continuous publication of a model railroad magazine An issue of *Model Railroader* has been produced every month since issue No. 1 appeared in January 1934. As of April 2012, the magazine, which is published by Kalmbach Publishing (U.S.A.), had produced 940 monthly issues specifically related to model railroading in a variety of scales and gauges.

MANUFACTURING

First factory to use standardized parts Originally built around 1104, but extended in about 1320, the Venetian Arsenal was a group of shipyards in Venice, Italy. It was the first manufacturing factory in the modern world to use standardized and interchangeable parts to build products. At its height, it employed around 16,000 people and could make almost

one ship each day. The new techniques allowed lighter, faster, and more cost-effective ships to be built.

First production automobile factory René Panhard and Émile Levassor started as woodworkers, moved into coach building, and, in 1889, built the first factory to make gasoline-powered vehicles. Their first automobile—using a Daimler engine—rolled out of their workshop in 1890. Panhard-Levassor produced autos in the 1890s with pedal-operated clutches, chain transmission, and, crucially, a front-mounted engine driving rear wheels. A standard in the motor industry, this became known as "System Panhard."

Strongest commercially available manufacturing robot Kuka Robotics' KR 1000 Titan robot—designed for heavy lifting and placement tasks in the automotive, building, and foundry industries—has a load capacity of 2,200 lb. (1,000 kg). It can move in six independent directions at once and uses nine motors to attain better than +/- 0.1-millimeter precision handling. The robot weighs 10,912 lb. (4,950 kg) and has a reach of 10 ft. 6 in. (3.2 m).

Best-selling auto The Toyota Corolla is the world's best-selling automobile, with more than 35 million sold (to February 2011) over 10 generations since 1966. It was also the first automobile in the world to eclipse 30 million sales. However, the Volkswagen Beetle is the best-selling auto

LARGEST AUTOMATED FACTORY
The brewers Grupo Modelo have built a canning factory at Piedras Negras in Coahuila state, northern Mexico, that has 37 robots that give a total canning capacity of up to 220 million gal. (10 million hectoliters) a year. Alongside the canning robots, there are laser-guided automated transport carts. The plant cost U.S. $520 million and reached full production capacity in 2011.

FACT: The Grupo Modelo plant can produce 6,000 cans and 144,000 bottles per hour.

of a single design (the core structure and shape of the Beetle remained largely unchanged from 1938 to 2003). The Beetle's tally when production ended was 21,529,464.

Highest production of aircraft (company) The Cessna Aircraft Company of Wichita, Kansas, U.S.A., has been the most productive airspace company, with a total production of 192,991 aircraft through to the end of 2009. Company founder Clyde Cessna built and flew his first airplane in 1911.

Highest production of military jet aircraft It is estimated that over 11,000 Russian MIG-21 "Fishbed" jet fighters have been produced since the first prototype flew in 1955, making it the most common jet-powered military aircraft ever, and the military aircraft produced in the greatest numbers in the post–World War II era. The aircraft has been produced in over 30 different variants and has seen service with around 50 air forces around the world.

LARGEST . . .

Bell foundry Since 1839, John Taylor & Co. has been casting bells in Loughborough, Leicestershire, UK. It has the largest bell foundry by area, occupying half of a 107,600-sq.-ft. (10,000-m²) site, the rest of which is

LARGEST TIRE MANUFACTURER In 2010, Lego made 381 million tires, easily beating all other tire manufacturers. Lego tires may not fit an everyday automobile, but they are remarkably lifelike. Even the rubber compound used for the Lego products would be suitable for a domestic vehicle.

FACT: Lego's minifigures were all yellow until 2003, when the firm introduced realistic skin tones.

Scotland's Robert William Thomson invented the pneumatic tire in 1846.

devoted to the Taylor Museum of bell casting and tuning. John Taylor & Co. is responsible for casting many famous bells, including "Great Paul" in St. Paul's Cathedral, London, UK, the largest bell in the UK, weighing 37,483 lb. (17,002 kg). The business has been in the hands of the Taylor family since 1784.

Manufacturer of artificial limbs The Artificial Limbs Manufacturing Corporation of India (ALIMCO), based in Kanpur, Uttar Pradesh, is a nonprofit organization that makes 355 different types of artificial limbs and prosthetic aids. In the 2008–09 financial reporting period, the firm made 1,644,232 limbs.

Manufacturer of ball bearings Svenska Kullagerfabriken (SKF), a Swedish company founded in 1907 with headquarters in Gothenburg, is the biggest ball-bearing firm by turnover. In 2011, SKF, which employs around 40,000 people, had a turnover of 49,285 million Swedish krona (U.S. $33,055 million).

Manufacturer of musical instruments The Yamaha Corporation, renowned for its motorcycles and engines, is also the world's largest manufacturer of musical instruments by revenue. In 2011, their income from musical instruments was 271.1 billion yen (U.S. $3.48 billion), which accounted for 72.5% of the Yamaha group turnover. The company was

HIGHEST NATIONAL MANUFACTURING OUTPUT In 2010, China was estimated to have produced 19.8% of the world's manufactured goods, fractionally ahead of the U.S.A. at 19.4%. This broke the U.S.A.'s 110-year history as the world's leading manufacturer. China has about 100 million manufacturing workers—significantly more than any other country.

LARGEST FACTORY (VOLUME) The Boeing Everett factory in Washington, U.S.A., has a total volume of 472,370,319 cu. ft. (13,385,378 m³) and covers a floor area of 4.3 million sq. ft. (399,483 m²). The facility is used to build the Boeing 747, 767, 777, and the new 787 Dreamliner aircraft.

founded in 1887 by Torakusu Yamaha as the Japan Musical Instrument Manufacturing Corporation.

Manufacturer of snowboards With an average annual turnover of about U.S. $230 million from 2006 to 2010, Burton Snowboards is the largest money earner of all snowboard manufacturers. The firm, whose flagship store is located in Burlington, Vermont, U.S.A., was started in 1977 by Jake Burton Carpenter. He built the world's first snowboard factory in Burlington, although since March 2010 the boards have been produced in Austria.

Manufacturer of toilets Toto Ltd., a Japanese company founded in 1917, sells a range of toilets called Washlets. With an annual sales revenue in excess of U.S. $4.2 billion in 2006, the firm is the largest manufacturer of toilets.

Abandoned factory The old Packard car factory in Detroit, U.S.A., at 3.5 million sq. ft. (325,160 m²), is the largest abandoned factory by size. The factory, which once produced 75% of the world's cars, was closed in 1956 and has stood empty ever since.

UNITS PRODUCED IN ONE YEAR . . .

Lego bricks
36,000,000,000

Cell phones
1,600,000,000

Tires
1,400,000,000

Computers
364,000,000

Bicycles
105,000,000

Automobiles
51,971,000

Washing machines
50,100,000

iPads
19,500,000

Book titles published
1,004,725

WEAPONS

FIRST . . .

Boomerang The boomerang is usually associated with the Australian Aborigines, but they were also used in ancient Egypt and Europe. The oldest boomerang discovered is about 23,000 years old. It was made from a mammoth tusk and found in a cave in the Oblazowa Rock in south Poland.

Gun It is believed that the earliest guns were constructed both in China and in Northern Africa ca. 1250. The invention of the gun certainly dates from before 1326. Gunpowder may have been invented in China, India, Arabia, or Europe in the 13th century; the earliest known example of a gun was found in the ruins of the castle of Monte Varino in Italy, which was destroyed in 1341.

True flintlock mechanism Marin le Bourgeoys (France), a gun maker at the court of Louis XIII of France, invented the first true flintlock in the early 17th century. The flintlock is the firing mechanism used on muskets

MOST ADVANCED SNIPER RIFLE The L115A3, made by Accuracy International (UK) and used by the British Army since 2008, is the most advanced sniper (or long-range) rifle. Weighing 15 lb. (6.8 kg), this 8.59-mm caliber weapon is fitted with a telescopic day sight, which offers up to 25 times magnification, as well as a night sight and a laser-range finder. It can achieve a first-round hit at 1,969 ft. (600 m) and harassing fire out to more than 3,609 ft. (1,100 m).

and rifles, which includes a striking device that operates a firing pin to hit and ignite the primer in the gun cartridge. Le Bourgeoys combined and adapted earlier firing mechanisms so that the cock and trigger acted vertically instead of horizontally. His guns also incorporated a half-cocked position, which allowed it to be loaded without firing—providing greater safety for the user.

Machine gun In 1862, Richard Gatling (U.S.A.) produced the first workable, hand-cranked, multiple-barrel machine gun. Loose cartridges were fed using gravity into the open breach from a top-mounted hopper. It was this feature, rather than the multiple rotating barrels, that permitted unskilled operators to achieve high rates of fire. It was first used in warfare during the American Civil War of 1861–65. Although ca-

FINAL B53 WEAPON TO BE DISMANTLED Brought into service in 1962 and decommissioned in 1997, the U.S. B53 nuclear bomb had 9,000 kilotons of explosive power. It was a major weapon in the Cold War, often deployed on the B-52 Stratofortress aircraft. On October 25, 2011, it was announced that the last B53 had been dismantled. High-explosive material weighing 300 lb. (136 kg) was removed from the enriched uranium heart of the bomb.

MOST ADVANCED PILOT HELMET BAE Systems' (UK) newest fighter-pilot helmet projects the image of enemy aircraft onto the visor; it also tracks the pilot's eye movements, letting the weapons systems quickly lock onto the target the pilot is looking at.

pable of continuous fire, it was not a true automatic weapon because it required human power to turn it.

Automatic weapon Sir Hiram Maxim built his first self-powered, single-barrel machine gun in 1883 in the UK and demonstrated it in 1884. It used the recoil force of the fired round to extract the fired case and place another in the chamber, cocking the action in the process. By holding the trigger down, the gun fired continuously or until it overheated or jammed. Various designs of the Maxim gun were used in World War I and it also continued in service in various guises throughout World War II.

Large-scale use of poison gas in war While the earliest documented use of a biological agent in war was in the 6th century B.C., the first large-scale use of poison gas was during World War I. The German Army used a form of tear gas unsuccessfully against the Russians at the Battle of Bolimov in Poland on January 31, 1915. They then used chlorine gas during the Second Battle of Ypres in France between April 22 and May 25, 1915, when 188 tons (171 metric tonnes) of the poisonous gas were released over a 4-mile (6.4-km) front. The British first used poison gas at the Battle of Loos in France on September 25, 1915.

Battlefield ray-gun deployment A battlefield ray gun, or direct-energy weapon, was deployed for the first time in Iraq by the Americans in 2008. "Zeus"—named after the Greek god of thunder—is designed to allow operators to neutralize targets, such as roadside bombs and other

NEWEST SEA-LAUNCHED BALLISTIC MISSILE Following successful testing in December 2011, the Bulava Intercontinental Ballistic Missile (ICBM) is set to be used by the Russian Navy. The missile can carry several individually targeted warheads and has a range of 5,000 miles (8,000 km). It will be deployed on board the newest class of Russian sub, the Burei.

unexploded ordnance, at a safe distance of 984 ft. (300 m). The conventional way to neutralize bombs is by using explosives, for example, with a rocket-propelled grenade. However, compared with direct-energy weapons, this method can be inaccurate and often more expensive.

FIRST COMBAT USE OF A STEALTH AIRCRAFT Stealth aircraft cannot be detected by enemy radar. The first one used on military operations was the U.S. F-117 Nighthawk, made by Lockheed Martin. It first flew in 1981 and remained classified until November 1988; in all, 64 Nighthawks were built. The first combat use of the aircraft was in the U.S. invasion of Panama in December 1989, when it bombed the Rio Hato airfield, near Panama's south coast.

FACT: In the 1991 Gulf War, the F-117 flew for a total of 6,905 hours in nearly 1,300 combat sorties.

MOST ADVANCED . . .

Weapon for drones In 2011, the U.S. defense company Raytheon successfully tested the Small Tactical Munition bomb specifically designed to be fired from a drone, or unmanned aerial vehicle (UAV). Using a laser seeker together with GPS, the 2-ft.-long (60-cm) weapon is capable of hitting stationary and moving targets regardless of weather conditions.

Warhead casing material A new material that replaces steel in warhead casings was demonstrated at the U.S. Naval Surface Warfare Center (NSWC) in Dahlgren, Virginia, U.S.A., on December 2, 2011. Called High-Density Reactive Material (HDRM), it consists of metals and polymers that combine and explode only on impact with the target. The kinetic force of impact and the disintegration of the casing inside the target—with an additional release of chemical energy—creates an explosion up to five times greater than conventional casings. It can be used for new warheads or incorporated into current ones.

MOST ADAPTABLE ELECTRONIC CAMOUFLAGE BAE Systems' (UK) electronic camouflage system, Adaptiv, consists of an exterior cover of hexagonal tiles that can be used on tanks, aircraft, or ships. It can disguise one type of vehicle as another type, as shown above, where a tank appears to be an ordinary automobile, and it can also "merge" a vehicle with its background so it becomes invisible to thermal-imaging sensors. It works by altering the temperature of the tiles, effectively turning the vehicle's exterior into a large thermal infrared "television screen," with each tile representing a pixel.

FACT: The Adaptiv system can also send signals that enable it to be identified by friendly forces.

FIGHTING VEHICLES

Deadliest unmanned aerial vehicle The Predator C Avenger Unmanned Aerial Vehicle is capable of 460 mph (740 km/h) at 60,000 ft. (18,288 m) for up to 20 hours. The ability to carry 3,000 lb. (1,360 kg) of weapons and its stealthy design—there are no sharp angles, reducing its radar signature—make it the world's deadliest drone to date. Its first flight was on April 4, 2009.

Most Spitfires flown Alex Henshaw (UK) flew and tested more than 3,000 Spitfires between April 1932 and October 1995, when he flew his last one in a Battle of Britain memorial flight at Coningsby, Lincolnshire, UK.

FIRST TANK The British No. 1 Lincoln, modified to become "Little Willie," first ran on September 6, 1915, and first saw action on September 15, 1916, in World War I.

HEAVIEST ROUTE-CLEARANCE VEHICLE The U.S. Army's Buffalo weighs 53,500 lb. (24,267 kg) empty and has a load capacity of 22,500 lb. (10,205 kg), giving a total weight of nearly 38 tons (34.47 metric tonnes). Part of the Mine Resistant Ambush Protected (MRAP) family of vehicles, it was developed to counter the threat from land mines, improvised explosive devices (IEDs), and ambushes in Iraq and Afghanistan. Made by Force Protection Inc., the Buffalo has a V-shape hull to deflect explosions. It can carry up to 13 personnel in addition to a driver and codriver.

> **FACT:** For bomb and mine disposal, the Buffalo has a 30-ft. (9-m) robotic arm with an iron claw and a camera.

Highest rate of tank production Designed to be easily produced and maintained, the M-4 Sherman Main Battle Tank was first made in the U.S.A. in 1942 during World War II. More than 48,000 of them were turned out over three years.

Longest development of a Main Battle Tank Work on the development of the Arjun Main Battle Tank for the Indian Army started in 1972. In 1996, the Indian government decided to mass-produce the tank but tests by the Indian Army highlighted its poor performance and reliability, so the first deliveries were not made until 2004—32 years after its conception. By 2011, 124 Arjuns were in service with the Indian Army.

Most expensive single weapon system The USS *Ronald Reagan*, the CVN 76 class, nuclear-powered aircraft carrier launched in 2001, cost U.S. \$4.5 billion, including crew, armament, 85 aircraft, and defense and communication systems.

HEAVIEST ARMORED VEHICLE The Titan, a British bridge-laying vehicle that enables ground troops to cross rivers, weighs 137,789 lb. (62,500 kg) and can carry an 85-ft.-long (26-m) bridge or two 39-ft.-long (12-m) bridges. It is the **fastest bridge-laying system in the world**, able to lay the 85-ft. bridge within two minutes. Equipped with the chassis of the *Challenger 2* Main Battle Tank, the Titan has remote-controlled CCTVs to help position the bridges and a bulldozer blade to clear obstacles. The British Army has 33 Titans, the final one being delivered in 2008.

FIRST . . .

Armored auto squadron On December 3, 1914, three armored vehicles were delivered to the British Royal Naval Air Service. Each comprised a Rolls-Royce Silver Ghost chassis with a Vickers machine gun mounted on a single turret. They were used in World War I for reconnaissance and to rescue downed pilots. In the 1920s, the Royal Air Force used Rolls-Royce armored cars to protect oil supplies in Mesopotamia (modern-day Iraq).

Combat wing for an unmanned aerial vehicle On May 1, 2007, the U.S. Air Force (U.S.A.F.) created the first combat wing of unmanned aerial vehicle—the 432nd Wing of Air Force Special Operations Command. The combat wing fly Predator and Reaper drones from Creech Air Force Base in Nevada, U.S.A. They can be armed with missiles and are capable of flying remotely anywhere in the world.

Laser gunship On December 4, 2007, at Kirkland Air Force Base, New Mexico, U.S.A., Boeing completed the installation of a high-energy chemical laser on a Hercules C-130H aircraft. It was part of the development of the U.S. military's Advanced Tactical Laser, which will be able to destroy ground targets more accurately and with less collateral damage than conventional guns or missiles.

Aerial battle involving an unmanned aerial vehicle In December 2002, a U.S. Air Force RQ-1 Predator drone conducting surveillance in Iraqi airspace was engaged by an Iraqi MiG-25 fighter jet. The two planes fired air-to-air missiles at each other, with the MiG eventually downing the Predator.

FASTEST . . .

Armored four-wheel-drive carrier The Kombat T-98, an armored VIP car built by Kombat Armouring in St. Petersburg, Russia, since 2003, can reach 111 mph (180 km/h). It has an 8.1-liter V8 engine and can be equipped with gun ports and a machine gun.

LARGEST FAMILY OF PERSONNEL CARRIERS The U.S.-made BAE M113 is the most used tracked armored personnel carrier still in service worldwide. There are more than 80,000 M113s currently deployed, in over 40 variants, and they are used in more than 50 countries. The vehicle is due to retire from service from the U.S. military in 2018.

Combat jet The Russian Mikoyan MiG-25 fighter (NATO code name "Foxbat") entered service in 1970 and had a reconnaissance version, "Foxbat-B," which was tracked by radar at about Mach 3.2 (2,110 mph; 3,395 km/h).

Flying boat The Martin XP6M-1 Sea-Master, the U.S. Navy four-jet-engine minelayer flown in 1955–59, had a top speed of 646 mph (1,040 km/h).

MOST PRODUCED MAIN BATTLE TANK First produced in 1945, the Soviet T54/55 Main Battle Tanks entered production in 1947 and eventually became the most produced tank in the world. They were supplied not only to the Soviet Union but also to its allies in eastern Europe and elsewhere. Production numbers are estimated at over 80,000 and they have been deployed in nearly 80 countries.

FACT: T55 tanks were used by both sides in the Libyan Civil War that ended Gadhafi's rule in 2011.

GLOBAL FIREPOWER

Tank numbers

The Chinese People's Republic has the army with the greatest number of Main Battle Tanks. The most recent estimates give it 7,050 tanks, while the U.S. Army possesses 5,795 (excluding the 447 in the U.S. Marine Corps) and the Russian Army 2,800 (rises to 3,319 when Naval Infantry [Marines], Coastal Defense Forces, and Interior Troops are included), if the 18,000 in store are disregarded.

CHINA 7,050
U.S.A. 5,795
RUSSIA 2,800

Aircraft-carrier numbers
Source: Haze Gray & Underway World Aircraft Carrier List

U.S.A. - 11	UK - 1
Spain - 2	France - 1
Italy - 2	Russia - 1
Brazil - 1	Thailand - 1
India - 1	

Combat aircraft
Source: Haze Gray & Underway

Country	Fighters	Bombers	Attack
Egypt	644	25	—
India	1,130	118	370
Israel	233	10	264
N. Korea	899	60	211
Pakistan	325	30	250
PLAAF	901	91	110
Russia	1,264	166	1,267
S. Korea	648	60	352
UK	345	50	209
U.S.A.	3,043	171	1,185

Military submarine The Russian Alpha-class nuclear-powered submarines, produced from 1974 to 1981, had a reported maximum speed of more than 40 knots (46 mph; 74 km/h). In all, seven Alpha-class submarines were made.

Fighting Vehicles   343

Tank A production-standard S 2000 Scorpion Peacekeeper tank, developed by Repaircraft PLC (UK), attained a speed of 51.1 mph (82.23 km/h) at the QinetiQ test track in Chertsey, UK, on March 26, 2002.

Warship The U.S. Navy test surface-effect ship the SES-100B reached 91.9 knots (105 mph; 170 km/h) on January 25, 1980, at Chesapeake Bay, Maryland, U.S.A. Similar to hovercraft, surface-effect ships travel on a cushion of air, but also have two sharp, rigid hulls that remain in the water. Large fans under the ship create air pressure that is trapped between the hulls and raises the ship.

HELICOPTERS

FIRST . . .

"Helicopter" design Leonardo da Vinci (Italy, 1452–1519) proposed the idea of a helicopter-type craft for a human passenger in 1493. The so-called "air screw" consisted of a platform with a helical screw designed to allow it to take off and land vertically. Da Vinci's sketch was discovered in the 19th century.

Helicopter flight On November 13, 1907, Paul Cornu (France) flew an experimental helicopter in untethered flight for the first time in Lisieux, Calvados, France. This event is widely credited as the first free flight of a rotary-wing aircraft, but in reality it was probably no more than a hop or series of airborne hops. Another two machines were built, but the control system proved to be ineffective and no further progress was made.

FIRST TRUE HYBRID MANNED/ UNMANNED HELICOPTER On September 20, 2006, the A/MH-6X, a light-turbine helicopter constructed at the Boeing Rotorcraft Facility in Mesa, Arizona, U.S.A., flew for the first time. It combines features from Boeing's A/MH-6M Mission Enhanced Little Bird (MELB) and the Unmanned Little Bird (ULB) Demonstrator, a modified MD 530F civil helicopter. The A/MH-6X has been designed for both military and civil use.

FACT: The A/MH-6X can be piloted or programmed to fly autonomously.

**LARGEST HELICOPTER
EVER The Russian Mil Mi-
12 was 121 ft. 4.7 in. (37 m)
long, with a maximum
takeoff weight of 227,737 lb.
(103.3 metric tonnes).
Powered by four 6,500-
hp (4,847-kW) turboshaft
engines, it had a rotor
diameter of 219 ft. 10 in.
(67 m). The Mil Mi-12
first flew in 1968, but never
went into production.**

Design for a production helicopter
Igor Sikorsky (Russia, now Ukraine) designed the world's first true production helicopter. Sikorsky's U.S. Patent 1,994,488,
filed on June 27, 1931, marked the crucial
breakthrough in helicopter technology and led to the Sikorsky R-4. It
proved itself in active service for U.S. forces during World War II and
became the world's first mass-produced helicopter.

Turbine-powered helicopter The Kaman K-225 helicopter was built
in 1949, principally for use as a crop duster. In 1951, the reciprocating
engine was replaced with a Boeing 502-2 gas turbine (jet) engine to demonstrate the reduced weight, higher power-to-weight ratio—thus allowing
greater payloads—and the greater reliability and easier maintenance offered by such engines. On December 11, 1951, the modified K-225 became the first helicopter to fly with turbine-powered transmission.

Following development of his K-225, aeronautical engineer Charles Kaman (U.S.A.) introduced the world's **first twin-turbine- (jet-) powered
helicopter** in March 1954.

Remotely piloted helicopter On July 30 1957, a modified Kaman
helicopter, the HTK-1K, became the first rotorcraft to fly while being
remotely controlled. It was developed as part of a U.S. Army/Navy programme and designed for use in difficult and dangerous situations. Earlier
that year, on May 23, it had been flown from the USS *Mitscher*, while
being operated from the ship, with a safety pilot on board.

The fastest model helicopter reached a speed of 148.9 mph (239.68 km/h).

FIRST MANNED ELECTRIC MULTICOPTER On October 21, 2011, the first manned flight of the "e-volo"—an electric multicopter—took place in southwest Germany. It lasted 1 min. 30 sec. and the pilot was Thomas Senkel (Germany). Powered by 16 lithium ion batteries running electric motors, each driving its own propeller to provide lift, the multicopter is capable of flying for 20 minutes. It weighs 176 lb. 6 oz. (80 kg).

Helicopter at the South Pole The first helicopters to land at the South Pole were three Bell UH-1B turbo-powered Iroquois from Mount Weaver, Antarctica. They arrived on February 4, 1963, after a 2-hr. 24-min. flight, the aim being to fly back to McMurdo Station via the Pole. Despite arriving successfully, the helicopters were eventually dismantled and flown back to McMurdo in Lockheed Martin LC-130s.

Fully autonomous flight by unmanned helicopter In June 2010, the Piasecki Aircraft Corporation, together with the Carnegie Mellon University (both U.S.A.), demonstrated a navigation and sensor system that enables a full-size helicopter to fly, unmanned, at low altitude. It can also avoid obstacles and evaluate and select suitable landing sites in unmapped terrain.

SMALLEST HELICOPTER In terms of rotor length, the smallest helicopter is the GEN H-4 made by Gen Corporation (Japan), with a rotor length of only 13 ft. (4 m), a weight of 154 lb. 5 oz. (70 kg), and consisting of one seat, one landing gear, and one power unit. It has two sets of coaxial contrarotating rotors, removing the need for a traditional tail rotor to act as a balance.

FACT: The GEN H-4 can reach an altitude of 3,280 ft. (1,000 m) and a top speed of 56 mph (90 km/h).

The sensors—which are mounted in an unmanned Little Bird helicopter testbed—build three-dimensional maps of the ground and identify obstacles in the path of the helicopter. In time, the system will be used to let unmanned helicopters evacuate wounded soldiers from the battlefield and other dangerous situations.

Unmanned cargo resupply helicopter On December 17, 2011, the U.S. 2nd Marine Air Wing used a Kaman K-Max to make the first unmanned helicopter cargo delivery to troops on a battlefield. Having successfully demonstrated a remotely controlled, unmanned resupply helicopter to the U.S. Marine Corps in January 2010, some 3,500 lb. (1,590 kg) of freight was moved from Camp Dwyer to Combat Outpost Payne in the Helmand Province, Afghanistan, in around 1.5 hours.

Electric helicopter On August 4, 2011, the first authenticated, manned flight of a helicopter powered by an electric motor took place at Venelles, France. The aircraft was flown by Pascal Chretien (France) and hovered about 19 in. (50 cm) above the ground for 2 min. 10 sec. The first flight was tethered, but the machine later made its first free flight on August 12, 2011. In July and August 2011, the aircraft flew for a total of 99.5 minutes in 29 flights, some of which extended for 6 minutes.

LARGEST HELICOPTER CARRIER Few classes of ship cater to helicopters in force. The largest ships in this role currently in service, by tonnage and helicopter capacity, are those of the U.S. Wasp Class, such as the USS *Boxer* (left), of which eight are in use. If not carrying fixed-wing aircraft, they can carry 42 CH-46 Sea Knight helicopters or 22 MV-22 Osprey aircraft.

SPEC:

Length: 830 ft.
Beam: 104.3 ft.

Draft: 26.6 ft.
Displacement: 45,360 tons

In search of an airport? Land on p. 320.

Swarming mini choppers A team from General Robotics, Automation, Sensing and Perception (GRASP) Laboratory at the University of Pennsylvania, U.S.A., has developed a fleet of mini four-bladed helicopters, named "quadrotors." About the size of a human hand, they are designed to carry out autonomous, synchronous flying. Working together as a swarm, they are capable of carrying items through small openings, and it is envisaged that they will operate in environments dangerous to humans, such as on oil rigs or in war or disaster zones. At the beginning of 2012, the helicopters were demonstrated operating in "swarms" (multiple formations) of up to 20 aircraft.

HOW WE LEARNED TO HOVER

In the 4th century B.C., children in China tied feathers to small sticks, spun them, and watched them rise into the air. But it took nearly 2,000 years before the first plans for a practical 'copter were drawn up. GWR presents highlights from the history of the helicopter:

1493
Leonardo da Vinci (Italy) sketches his idea for a human-powered "air screw."

1784
Launoy and Bienvenu (both France) demonstrate a small model helicopter, propelled by a tightly wound cord, for the French Academy of Sciences.

1907
Gyroplane No. 1—created by Louis and Jacques Breguet, under the direction of Charles Richet (all France)—becomes the first rotary-wing craft to be manned; is unsteerable and reaches up just 2 ft. (60 cm).

1907
Bicycle manufacturer Paul Cornu (France) makes the first true "free" manned helicopter flight.

1931
Igor Sikorsky (Russia) secures a patent for the first production helicopter, the Sikorsky R-4.

1959
Bell UH-1 Iroquois "Huey" military helicopters enter production.

WACKY VEHICLES

First flying automobile The ultimate off-roader, the Terrafugia Transition is the first "roadable" aircraft—or flying automobile. Previous efforts have needed extra equipment or wings to be added, but this two-seater plane can, at the touch of a button, fold its wings and turn into an automobile. The Transition took flight for the first time in March 2009 at Plattsburgh International Airport in New York State, U.S.A. It can reach a top speed of 100 knots (115 mph; 185 km/h) in the air—but Terrafugia have not said how fast it can go on land. The company is now developing a production version, which they are marketing with the line: "Simply land at the airport, fold your wings up, and drive home."

First submarine automobile The Swiss company Rinspeed created the world's first true submersible automobile, called the "sQuba." First shown at the Geneva Motor Show in March 2008, it is powered electrically by three rechargeable lithium-ion batteries. It can drive straight into the sea and then float until a hatch opens to let water flood the body and gradually sink the vehicle. Underwater, it effectively flies at a depth of 33 ft. (10 m).

Longest bicycle The longest true bicycle (with only two wheels) measures 117 ft. 5 in. (35.79 m). It was built by the Mijl van Mares Werkploeg (gang of workers) in Maarheeze, Netherlands, and ridden on August 5, 2011. Two people ride the bike: one steers at the front and one pedals at the back.

Tallest unicycle ride Sem Abrahams (U.S.A.) rode a 114-ft. 9-in.-tall (35-m) unicycle for a distance of 28 ft. (8.5 m) at the Silverdome in Pontiac, Michigan, on January 29, 2004.

Largest tricycle Made by Kanyaboyina Sudhakar (India) and ridden in Hyderabad, India, on July 1, 2005, the largest pedal tricycle is 37 ft. 4 in. (11.37 m) long with a height of 41 ft. 7 in. (12.67 m).

SMALLEST VAN The smallest roadworthy van is *Wind Up*, which measures 41 in. (104.14 cm) high, 26 in. (66.04 cm) wide, and 52 in. (132.08 cm) long. Perry Watkins (UK) made the van from a Postman Pat coin-in-the-slot children's ride in seven months up to May 2011. The vehicle has all the usual features, including lights and windshield wipers, and it is insured and taxed.

FASTEST SCOOTER Colin Furze (UK) has supercharged a mobility scooter so that it can reach a top speed of 71.59 mph (115.21 km/h). It took Colin three months to convert the scooter, which features five gears, a 125-cc motorbike engine, and twin exhausts.

Most transformations of a vehicle An Ellert—a three-wheel automobile—was successfully transformed in Denmark into a hot rod, a rocket-powered hydrofoil, and, finally, on September 8, 2006, an aircraft. Each of these transformations took two weeks to complete.

FASTEST . . .

Automobile powered by compressed air Toyota's three-wheel KU:RIN automobile reached a speed of 80.3 mph (129.2 km/h) at the Japan Automobile Research Institute's Ibaraki test track on September 9, 2011. The vehicle has a compressed-air "fuel tank"—as air is released, it generates thrust.

Vehicle powered by powertool Jon Bentley (UK) reached 72.74 mph (117 km/h) on a dragster powered by a chainsaw for the 200th episode of *The Gadget Show* at Santa Pod Raceway, Northamptonshire, UK, on August 22, 2011.

Bicycle powered by electric-ducted fans Ortis Deley (UK) recorded a top speed of 72 mph (115.87 km/h) on a bicycle fitted with electric-ducted fans—propellers used for model aircraft. The fans, along with about 22 lb. (10 kg) of batteries, were attached to the back rack of the bike. Ortis completed his feat for the 200th episode of *The Gadget Show* at Santa Pod Raceway in Northamptonshire, UK, on August 24, 2011.

Powered street luge Lying down on his jet-powered street luge, Jason Bradbury (UK) attained a speed of 115.83 mph (186.41 km/h) for *The Gadget Show*'s 200th episode in Bentwaters Parks, Suffolk, UK, on August 9, 2011. Jason's luge, essentially a liquid-fuel-powered skateboard, did not have any brakes—so Jason superglued pieces of tire to his boots to help him stop.

In March 2010, Jason also attained the **fastest speed in a water-jet-powered automobile**. He reached a record speed of 16.65 mph (26.8 km/h) on *The Gadget Show* at Wattisham Airfield, Ipswich, UK.

The hairiest automobile features 220 lb. (100 kg) of human hair!

> **FACT:** Built by Louis Borsi (UK), the **lightest automobile** weighed 21 lb. (9.5 kg), with a 2.5-cc engine.

LOWEST AUTOMOBILE The *Mirai* ("future" in Japanese) measures 1 ft. 5.79 in. (45.2 cm) from the ground to the highest part of the vehicle. It was created on November 15, 2010, by Hideki Mori (pictured) and his students on the automobile engineering course at Okayama Sanyo High School in Asakuchi, Japan. Previous projects on the course have included building an amphibious automobile and a huge glider plane.

FASTEST BATHROOM The *Bog Standard*, created by Edd China (UK), consists of a motorcycle and sidecar hidden under a bathroom suite—including a bathtub, basin, and laundry basket. Using controls hidden under the basin, Edd has driven the vehicle at a top speed of 42.25 mph (68 km/h).

> **FACT:** Edd China also holds the record for **fastest garden shed**, **fastest bed**, and **fastest office**.

HEAVIEST RIDEABLE PEDAL BIKE

Built by Wouter van den Bosch (Netherlands), the *Monsterbike* weighs 1,650 lb. (750 kg) and was ridden for the first time in Arnhem, Netherlands, in May 2010. It is made from steel tubes, bicycle parts, four small tires at the back, and one mammoth Michelin tractor tire, measuring 6 ft. 4.7 in. (1.95 m) high, at the front. Wouter made the bike for his fine art degree—but he is not sure whether or not it is art.

SNAPSHOT

• The photographer Ranald Mackechnie almost ended up in one of Arnhem's canals trying to get far enough back to capture the whole bike in the shot!

• During the shoot, a police van stopped and all the policemen inside had their photos taken with the bike.

• When taking his bike for a spin, Wouter finds that most people stare and smile—but a few fellow cyclists get annoyed because the bike tends to block cycle lanes.

TITANIC TIRES

Looking for a tire for your giant mining truck? You need a Titan 63, the new **largest production tire**:

12,500 lb. (5,670 kg)
14 ft. (4.26 m) tall

But that's nothing. The **tallest tire** of all—the 78-ft. 9-in. (24-m) Uniroyal Giant in Michigan, U.S.A.—is nearly six times as big!

78 ft. 9 in. (24 m) tall

ROADS

Longest continuous road Australia's Highway One circumnavigates the whole country via a network of fully interconnected roads. Its total length is 9,024 miles (14,523 km), making it more than 2,200 miles (3,500 km) longer than its nearest rival, the Trans-Siberian Highway.

Longest straight road Built originally as a private road for Saudi Arabia's King Fahd, the road that connects the Harad area with Badha in Saudi Arabia is 149.13 miles (240 km) long. It cuts straight through the desert with no bends to the left or right, and no significant rise or fall.

SHORTEST STREET
The length of Ebenezer Place in Wick, Caithness, Scotland, UK, was found to be only 6 ft. 9 in. (2.05 m) when measured on October 28, 2006. The stunted street has a mail address (No. 1), a doorway, and even a street sign above the door.

STEEPEST ROAD Located in Dunedin, New Zealand, Baldwin Street is the world's steepest paved road over a continuous distance of more than 33 ft. (10 m). At just over 1,150 ft. (350 m) in length, with 34 houses located along it, the road rises a total of 227 ft. (69.2 m) at a rate of 3 ft. 4 in. (1 m) vertically for every 9 ft. 4 in. (2.86 m) horizontally traveled. The road is surfaced with specially grooved concrete so automobiles can grip the surface.

FACT: The "Baldwin Street Gutbuster" is an annual race up and down the steepest street.

MOST COMPLEX JUNCTION The Judge Harry Pregerson Interchange in Los Angeles, U.S.A., is a multiple-stack highway interchange that connects Interstate Highway 105 and Interstate Highway 110 with the Harbor Gateway North area of Los Angeles. A four-level interchange, it offers the possibility of driving from any direction on to any other direction of travel on the intersecting roads, as well as possessing restricted access lanes for high-occupancy vehicles. The uppermost lane stands at a height of 120 ft. (36.5 m).

Longest one-way road The M2 Southern Expressway in Adelaide, South Australia, is 13 miles (21 km) long and allows only one direction of traffic flow at a time. The road runs toward Adelaide in the morning, swapping to a southbound flow in the afternoon.

Longest circular road The M25 London Orbital Motorway is 121.8 miles (195.5 km) long. Work on the road, which circles London, began in 1972 and was completed in 1986 at an estimated cost of U.S. $1.33 billion.

Most lanes on a road The Toll Plaza of the San Francisco–Oakland Bay Bridge has 23 lanes running eastbound through the tolls.

Oldest road surface still in use Stretches of the Via Appia (the Appian Way) in Italy date from its original construction in 312 B.C. The route formed the main connection between Rome and Brindisi, southeast Italy. On the best-preserved parts, close to Rome itself, people may walk or cycle on the old stone-paved road. In the area of Velletri, it is still possible to drive on the original Roman-paved surface.

First highway In 1924, the world's first dual-carriage highway built for higher-speed traffic was opened between the Italian towns of Milan and Varese, with a single lane in each direction separated by a crash barrier. Today, it is part of the A8 and A9 highway network.

MOST CROOKED ROAD Comprising eight tight hairpin turns as it meanders down a hill in San Francisco, U.S.A., Lombard Street is the world's most crooked road. Many roads twist and turn, but only a 0.25-mile-long (400-m) section of Lombard Street, which descends a 27-percent incline, has so many hairpin turns in such a short distance—a total of 1,440 degrees twisted and turned.

First solar-powered road The A18 Catania–Siracuse highway in Sicily incorporates three tunnels covered with more than 80,000 individual solar panels, which provide power for lighting, tunnel fans, emergency phones, and signs. The road is estimated to produce 12 million kWh of power per year across the 1.7-mile (2.8-km) length covered by the tunnels.

Coldest road The Kolyma Highway (M56) in Russia passes through some of the coldest inhabited places on Earth. The road is 1,262 miles (2,031 km) long and goes from Nizhny Bestyakh in the west to Magadan in the east. Temperatures as low as −89.86°F (−67.7°C) have been recorded along this route.

Most southerly road The McMurdo–South Pole Highway is a 900-mile (1,450-km) road constructed in Antarctica from the McMurdo Station to Amundsen-Scott base at the South Pole. The road is made from flattened and graded ice and snow.

15,420-ft. (4,700-m) drop

MOST DANGEROUS ROAD The road considered by many to be the most lethal in the world is the North Yungas Road that runs for 43 miles (69 km) from La Paz to Coroico in Bolivia, and sees up to 300 deaths annually—6.9 per mile (4.3 per km). For most of the stretch, the single-lane mud road (with two-way traffic) has an unbarricaded vertical drop, measuring 15,420 ft. (4,700 m) at its highest point. It's most deadly in the rainy season.

FACT: The North Yungas Road is known in Spanish as El Camino de la Muerte—"Road of Death."

TOP 10 LONGEST ROAD NETWORKS

238,600 miles: Distance from Earth to the Moon.

10. Spain 423,339 miles

9. Australia 508,503 miles

8. France 591,048 miles

7. Russia 610,186 miles

6. Canada 647,655 miles

5. Japan 1,747,992 miles

863,700 miles: Diameter of the Sun.

4. Brazil 1,088,560 miles

ca. 1,864,000 miles: Distance traveled by light in 10 seconds.

3. India 2,063,207 miles

2. China 2,400,000 miles

*2,900,000 miles: Distance driven as of December 2010 by a 1966 P-1800S Volvo owned by Irvin Gordon (U.S.A.), the **highest vehicle mileage** for a single automobile.*

*3,001,276 miles: Distance driven by professional truck driver William Coe, Jr. (U.S.A.) between 1986 and 2009, the **greatest distance driven without accident in a commercial vehicle**.*

*3,458,300 miles: Total distance driven annually by drivers for every 0.6 miles of road in Hong Kong, the nation with the **most used road network** in the world. The **most crowded roads**, however, are in Kuwait, where there are nearly 271 vehicles per 0.6 mile of road!*

1. U.S.A. 4,042,768 miles

Source: The Economist

FACT: Peruvians drive more than any other nationality—the average Peruvian drives 23,956 miles each year!

There is a five-star hotel on the roundabout!

LARGEST ROUNDABOUT
One roundabout in Putrajaya, Malaysia, has a 2.1-mile (3.4-km) circumference. Circled by the Persiaran Sultan Salahuddin Abdul Aziz Shah road, it has 15 entry/exit points.

Oldest functional traffic signal The oldest working traffic signal was first installed on a junction in Ashville, Ohio, U.S.A., in 1932 and operated until 1982. The signal has four faces, and a rotating red/green lamp inside alternately illuminates each face. Designed by Ashville resident Teddy Boor, it still works today and was only retired from service because color-blind individuals found it more difficult to read than modern lights.

First road-traffic death On August 31, 1869, Mary Ward (Ireland) fell out of her cousin's experimental steam car and was run over, breaking her neck. The speed of the vehicle was estimated to be 3.5–4 mph (5.6–6.4 km/h).

Most complex roundabout The "Magic Roundabout" in Swindon, UK, comprises five smaller roundabouts (a type of circular road junction) around the circumference of a larger roundabout. A car can travel in both directions around the larger roundabout to exit via the chosen road. Each of the smaller roundabouts has three entry and three exit lanes.

Deepest road tunnel The Eiksund road tunnel in Norway connects the Norwegian mainland with Hareidlandet island and lies 942 ft. (287 m) below sea level. It is 25,476 ft. (7,765 m) long and was opened in 2008.

EPIC ENGINEERING

ON LAND

Longest bridge The Danyang-Kunshan Grand Bridge on the Jiangsu high-speed railroad (from Beijing to Shanghai) is 102 miles (164 km) long. This line, opened in June 2011, also crosses the 70.8-mile (114-km) Langfang–Qingxian viaduct, the second longest bridge in the world.

LARGEST CONCRETE DAM The Three Gorges Dam on the Yangtze River in China was begun on December 14, 1994, and was operational from 2005. It has a concrete volume of 525 million cu. ft. (14.86 million m³) and is 7,661 ft. (2,335 m) long, with the top 607 ft. (185 m) above sea level. The dam is still in progress, but it is reported to be the most expensive single construction project on Earth, with unofficial estimates over U.S. $75 billion.

Longest bridge over continuous water The Second Lake Pontchartrain Causeway, completed in 1969, joins Mandeville and Metairie, Louisiana, U.S.A. and is 23.87 miles (38.42 km) long.

Longest footbridge The 1.28-mile (2.06-km) Poughkeepsie Bridge (also known as the "Walkway Over the Hudson State Historic Park") in New York, U.S.A., was reopened to the public on October 3, 2009, as the world's longest pedestrian bridge.

Longest road bridge The six-lane elevated Bang Na Expressway (also known as the Burapha Withi Expressway) runs 33.5 miles (54 km) through Bangkok, Thailand. Made with 63.5 million cu. ft. (1.8 million m³) of concrete, it was opened on February 7, 2000, at a total cost of U.S. $1 billion.

LONGEST SUSPENSION BRIDGES

1. Akashi-Kaikyō Bridge Length: 6,532 ft. (1,990.8 m) Links: mainland Japan (Honshu) to Shikoku Island Built: 1998

2. Xihoumen Bridge Length: 5,414 ft. (1,650 m) Links: mainland China to Zhoushan Archipelago Built: 2009

3. Great Belt Bridge Length: 5,328 ft. (1,624 m) Links: Danish islands of Zealand and Funen Built: 1998

Longest canal The Belomorsko-Baltiysky Kanal, or the White Sea–Baltic Canal, from Belomorsk to Povenets in Russia, is 141 miles (227 km) long and has 19 locks. It was built using forced labor between 1930 and 1933.

Longest big-ship canal The Suez Canal in Egypt, linking the Red Sea and Mediterranean Sea, is 100.8 miles (162.2 km) long from Port Said lighthouse to the town of Suez. Opened on November 17, 1869, it took 10 years to build, with a workforce of 1.5 million, of whom 120,000 died during the construction. It has a maximum width of 1,198 ft. (365 m).

Highest dam The Nurek Dam, on the Vakhsh River in Tajikistan is 984 ft. (300 m) high and was completed in 1980.

Longest dam Completed in 1964, the Kiev Reservoir across the Dnieper River in Ukraine has a crest length of 25.6 miles (41.2 km).

Longest rubber dam The Xiaobudong Rubber Dam, on the Yihe river in Shandong Province, China, measures 3,723 ft. (1,135 m) long and consists of 16 sections, each 229 ft. (70 m) long. It was completed on July 1, 1997.

HIGHEST CABLE-STAYED BRIDGE A cable-stayed bridge has cables supporting the bridge deck from one or more columns (often called towers or pylons). The deck of the 3,688-ft.-long (1,124-m) cable-stayed Baluarte Bicentennial Bridge in Mexico is, at its highest point, 1,321 ft. (402.57 m) above the average water level of the Baluarte River. The bridge is supported by 12 concrete towers, the tallest of which measures 502 ft. (153 m) from its underground foundations to the road level.

FACT: The bridge has a maximum drop of 1,279 ft (390 m)—enough space to fit the Eiffel Tower underneath!

HIGHEST SUSPENSION BRIDGE The deck of the Si Du River Bridge in Badong County, Hubei, China, is 1,549 ft. (472 m) above the bottom of the valley—more than high enough to accommodate the Empire State Building beneath it.

Strongest dam The Sayano-Shushenskaya Dam on the Yenisey River in Russia, is designed to bear a record load of 19,841,600 tons (18 million metric tonnes) from a filled reservoir of 1,100,000 million cu. ft. (31,300 million m³) capacity. The dam, completed in 1987, is 803 ft. (245 m) high.

AT SEA

Longest bridge spanning open sea The 22.4-mile-long (36-km) Hangzhou Bay Bridge, linking the cities of Cixi and Zhapu in the Zhejiang Province of China, is the bridge spanning the greatest width of open ocean. Construction on the U.S. $1.4 billion bridge began in June 2003 and ended in 2007. It was officially opened in 2008.

LARGEST LAND VEHICLE The largest machine capable of moving under its own power is the 15.648-ton (14,196-tonne) RB293 bucket wheel excavator, manufactured by MAN TAKRAF of Leipzig, Germany. Used to move earth in an open-cast coal mine in the German state of North Rhine-Westphalia, it is 722 ft. (220 m) long, 310 ft. (94.5 m) tall, and capable of shifting 8.475 million cu. ft. (240,000 m³) of earth per day.

Ship with greatest lifting capacity The MV *Fairplayer* and MV *Javelin*, operated by Jumbo Shipping of Rotterdam, Netherlands, are J-class megaships with two Huisman mast cranes each capable of carrying a load of 992 tons (900 metric tonnes), giving a lifting capacity of 1,984 tons (1,800 metric tonnes). Each cargo ship has a transport capacity (deadweight tonnage or DWT) of 13,969 tons (12,673 metric tonnes). Especially heavy loads are welded to the deck.

Heaviest object lifted at sea The crane vessel *Saipem 7000*, the second largest in the world, broke the offshore weight-lifting record when it transported a 13,393-ton (12,150-metric tonne) single integrated deck (SID) from a heavy-transport carrier to the Sabratha platform in Libya's Bahr Essalam gas field in October 2004. The lift took four hours. The lifting capacity, from two 459-ft.-long (140-m) 15,600-hp (11,630-kW) fully revolving Amhoist cranes, is 15,432 tons (14,000 metric tonnes).

Largest cruise ship At 1,187 ft. (362 m) long, 216 ft. (66 m) wide, and weighing 225,282 gross tonnage, MS *Allure of the Seas* (U.S.A.) is the largest passenger ship. It has 16 passenger decks and can take 6,318 passengers.

LARGEST TUNNEL BORING MACHINE The Mixshield tunnel boring machine built by Herrenknecht AG (Germany) measures 50 ft. (15.43 m) in diameter and weighs 2,500 tons (2,300 metric tonnes). Two Mixshields were used to create two tunnels under the Yangtze River in China from Shanghai to Changxing Island. The tunnels, built from 2006 to 2008, are 4.64 miles (7.47 km) long and 213 ft. (65 m) deep.

FACT: The Mixshield can tunnel distances of up to 85 ft. (26 m) per day.

BRIDGE TYPES

Drawbridge (bascule)
Has two "leaves" that can be raised to enable ships to pass underneath; the **longest drawbridge** is the Charles Berry Bridge across the Black River in Lorain, Ohio, U.S.A., at 333 ft. (101.5 m).

Span suspension bridge
Deck is suspended by cables attached to vertical supports; the **longest suspension bridge for both road and rail traffic**— with a main span of 4,517 ft. (1,377 m), a width of 131.2 ft. (40 m), and a length of 1.3 miles (2.2 km)—is the Tsing Ma Bridge in Hong Kong (China).

Steel arch bridge
Deck passes beneath a steel arch and through (often) concrete supports; the **longest steel arch bridge** is the Chongqing-Chaotianmen Bridge over the Yangtze River in China with a main span of 1,811 ft. (552 m).

Swing bridge
Movable bridge that pivots horizontally (as opposed to upward like a drawbridge). The El Ferdan Railway Bridge across the Suez Canal near Ismailia, Egypt, has a central span of 1,115 ft. (340 m) that rotates 90° in order to let ships pass and is the world's **longest swing bridge**.

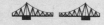

Tibetan bridge
A narrow walkway between two banks and supported loosely by cables or ropes; the world's **longest Tibetan bridge** has a span of 1,227 ft. (374 m) over the Po River in Turin, Italy.

Largest container ship With a length of 1,300 ft. (397 m), a beam of 183 ft. (56 m), and a depth from deck to keel of 98 ft. (30 m), the MV *Emma Maersk* (Denmark) is the largest container vessel. It could fill a freight train over 43.5 miles (70 km) long.

SCIENCE

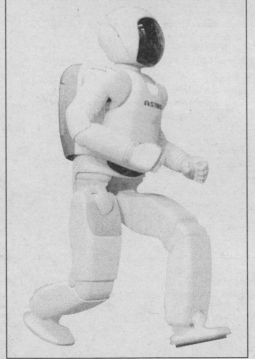

CONTENTS

LARGEST PARTICLE ACCELERATOR The Large Hadron Collider—a 17-mile-long (27-km) circular underground tunnel on the Franco-Swiss border near Geneva, Switzerland—is history's largest, most complex machine. Its purpose is to smash together two opposing beams of protons at high energies to study the results. In use, the collider's 9,300 magnets are frozen at -456.3°F (-271.3°C), colder than deep space, making the collider the world's largest refrigerator!

WHAT'S THE SPEED LIMIT?

CAN ANYTHING TRAVEL FASTER THAN LIGHT?

The biggest news in physics in 2011 was the revelation that the **fastest speed possible** may have been broken. One of the backbones of science is that nothing can travel faster than the speed of light in a vacuum. This speed limit affects everything—heat, gravity, radio waves. However, an experiment that fired tiny particles called neutrinos through Earth toward a detector seemed to show these subatomic particles traveled slightly faster than the speed of light. Was our understanding of the universe wrong?

Neutrinos, unlike protons and electrons, have no electric charge. They can easily pass through matter. Every second, the Sun produces over two hundred trillion trillion trillion of them, and every second, billions of them pass through your body.

The sensational results of 2011 came from a beam of artificial neutrinos fired from CERN in Switzerland, home to the Large Hadron Collider. The beam was aimed through Earth to the OPERA detector at Gran Sasso in Italy, 454 miles (732 km) away. The mystery was that the CERN neutrinos appeared to arrive 60.7 billionths of a second earlier than they should have if traveling at the speed of light.

Inside the particle accelerator
1. PIONS AND KAONS To create the neutrinos, a beam of protons is first generated by the Super Proton Synchrotron (SPS) at CERN. The beam of protons hits a graphite target that creates subatomic particles known as pions and kaons.

2. NEUTRINOS The subatomic particles produced by the SPS enter a 0.62-mile-long (1-km) tunnel, where they decay into muons and muon neutrinos. They are then focused into a beam and fired in the direction of the detector at Gran Sasso. When these particles encounter solid rock, only the muon neutrinos pass through.

3. THROUGH EARTH The neutrinos travel straight through Earth—7 miles (11.4 km) from the surface at the deepest point—and make the 454-mile (732-km) journey to Italy. GPS is used to monitor even the most subtle shifting of Earth.

Gran Sasso National Laboratory
4. GRAN SASSO At Gran Sasso, the neutrinos arrive and are detected by OPERA after traveling 454 miles through Earth's crust in just 0.0024 seconds. They appeared to be arriving 0.000000067 seconds earlier than they should have if they were obeying the speed of light.

5. OPERA DETECTOR The OPERA detector consists of 150,000 "bricks" of photographic film separated by lead sheets. It is located underground at Gran Sasso, insulating it from other particles and radiation that cannot pass through matter as easily as neutrinos. When a neutrino interacts with the matter making up the bricks, the photographic film records the event, which can then be analyzed by developing the film in each brick separately.

The OPERA team measured the speed of the CERN neutrinos 16,000 times, and each result showed the particles arriving faster than they should have. The race was on to independently measure neutrino velocities. If a different lab could confirm the results, then the speed of light barrier could indeed have been broken.

The ICARUS experiment, also at Gran Sasso, used liquid argon to detect neutrinos arriving in the beam from CERN and found no sign of the faster-than-light anomaly. In the meantime, the team at OPERA discovered a faulty connection between a fiber-optic cable and a GPS receiver used to synchronize timing measurements between CERN and Gran Sasso. It seems that scientists, including Albert Einstein and James Clerk Maxwell, were right all along and that the speed of light *is* the **fastest possible speed in the universe**, even for neutrinos!

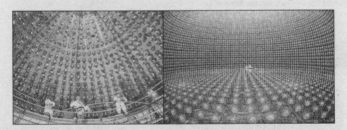

BOREXINO The Borexino Experiment is designed to detect low-energy neutrinos emanating from the Sun. Situated underground at Gran Sasso, Italy, it is shielded from cosmic rays but not from neutrinos, which pass through the rock around it. Photomultiplier tubes detect individual photons produced whenever a neutrino from the Sun interacts with an atom in the detector's internal fluid (right, showing liquid filling the detector).

FACT: Pictured here are some of the 2,200 photomultiplier detector tubes in the Borexino (BORon EXperiment) detector.

SPEED OF LIGHT Albert Einstein's Theory of Special Relativity proposes that the speed of light is the maximum speed at which all energy and matter can travel. The idea that light has a "speed" was first demonstrated by Denmark's Ole Christensen Rømer (1644–1710), whose studies of the moons of Jupiter led to a better understanding of how light travels. Today, the speed is ratified as a constant by the Conférence Générale des Poids et Mesures—the body that manages the International System of Units.
Sun to Earth: 8 min. 19 sec.
Moon to Earth: 1.3 sec.

MEASURING THE SPEED OF LIGHT

The figures below track the increasing accuracy with which scientists throughout history have determined the speed of light.

Date:	Scientist:	Speed of light (km/s):
1675	Ole Rømer (Denmark) and Christiaan Huygens (Netherlands)	136,700
1729	James Bradley (UK)	187,000
1849	Hippolyte Fizeau (France)	195,700
1862	Léon Foucault (France)	185,168±500
1907	Edward Rosa and Noah Dorsey (both U.S.A.)	186,231±30
1926	Albert Michelson (U.S.A.)	186,284±4
1950	Louis Essen and A. C. Gordon-Smith (both UK)	186,282.4 ±30
1958	Keith Davy Froome (UK)	186,282.4 ±0.10
1972	K. M. Evenson (U.S.A.) et. al	186,282.395 ±0.0011
1983	17th Conférence Générale des Poids et Mesures	186,282.39705 (exact)

SCIENCE FRONTIERS

Deepest multicellular life In June 2011, scientists announced the discovery of a new species of nematode worm that lives at depths of 0.8–2.2 miles (1.3–3.6 km) below the Earth's surface. The nematodes (*Halicepha-*

MOST DETAILED MAP OF ANTARCTIC BEDROCK BEDMAP2, by the British Antarctic Survey (BAS), is a view of Antarctica beneath its ice. It is a digital map created from some 27 million data points collected by radar, which can "see" through the ice. The data has been compiled from measurements taken from aircraft, satellites, and dog-sled teams. BEDMAP2 was first shown in December 2011 and updated the first BEDMAP, made in 2000.

lobus mephisto) survive in rock fractures filled with fluid, where they eat bacteria. Find out more on p. 204.

First living laser In June 2011, Malte Gather and Seok Hyun Yun at the Wellman Center for Photomedicine at Massachusetts General Hospital, U.S.A., said they had used a cell derived from the human kidney to create laser light. The scientists injected the kidney cell with DNA from glowing jellyfish, which made the kidney cell glow green when bombarded with blue light. By using mirrors, they eventually made the cell emit green laser light. The cell survived the process, even after several minutes of emitting laser light.

Highest frequency microelectronic device In January 2012, researchers at Technische Universität Darmstadt, Germany, announced they had created an experimental resonance tunnel diode less than 0.04 sq. in. (1 mm^2), which can transmit at 1.111 THz, or 1,111 billion cycles per second. The tiny transmitter, which works at room temperature, could lead to new methods in medical diagnostics.

MOST ACCURATE CLOCK The cesium-fountain atomic clock, CsF2, at the UK's National Physical Laboratory, Teddington, London, is part of a global network of highly accurate atomic clocks providing consistent time measurements for the world. As of August 26, 2011, the CsF2 clock was accurate to one part in 4,300 trillion, meaning it would take 138 million years for it to lose or gain less than one second.

LARGEST CHERENKOV TELESCOPE The Major Atmospheric Gamma Ray Imaging Cherenkov (MAGIC) Telescope consists of a pair of almost identical telescopes on La Palma in the Canary Islands, Spain. Each telescope has a diameter of 55 ft. 9 in. (17 m) and a surface area of 2,540 sq. ft. (236 m²). They detect faint blue Cherenkov radiation produced in the Earth's atmosphere by high-energy gamma rays from distant cosmic events. The two telescopes began operation in 2004 and 2009.

Longest trapped antimatter On June 5, 2011, scientists working on the ALPHA experiment at CERN, Geneva, Switzerland, reported they had successfully trapped 112 antihydrogen atoms for 16 minutes. The ALPHA experiment mixed antiprotons with positrons in a vacuum chamber, where they combined to form antihydrogen. This was then trapped within a magnetic bottle. The antihydrogen atoms were detected by turning off the magnetic field within the magnetic bottle and observing flashes of light as each antihydrogen atom met normal matter. Both the normal and antimatter atoms were annihilated.

Fastest camera In December 2011, the Massachusetts Institute of Technology, U.S.A., revealed a camera that acquires visual data from repetitive events at a rate of half a trillion frames per second. The camera, which builds up the data from many repetitions of the event, therefore, has an effective shutter speed of two-trillionths of a second. It can show a pulse of light moving through a bottle.

First image of charge distribution in a single molecule On February 27, 2012, scientists at IBM Research in Zurich, Switzerland, announced that they had used "Kelvin probe force microscopy" to image and measure the positive and negative charge distribution in a molecule of naphthalocyanine. This breakthrough should make it possible to investigate charges at a molecular level when chemical bonds are formed.

HIGHEST LASER ENERGY (ON A SINGLE TARGET) The laser at the National Ignition Facility at Lawrence Livermore National Laboratory, San Francisco, U.S.A., consists of 192 laser beams. In October 2010, it fired a one-megajoule shot on a peppercorn-size pellet of nuclear fuel. The energy crushed the pellet instantly, releasing about 10 trillion neutrons and signaling the successful fusion of some tritium and deuterium atoms. Ultimately, the objective is to create a fusion reaction that offers unlimited, pollution-free energy.

FASTEST-RUNNING HUMANOID ROBOT ASIMO (short for Advanced Step in Innovative Mobility) is the latest in a series of prototype humanoid robots developed by Honda (Japan) since 2000. On November 8, 2011, Honda revealed the latest ASIMO, which can run at 5.6 mph (9 km/h) with both feet momentarily leaving the ground. For more robots, just turn the page.

Darkest man-made substance A low density carbon-nanotube array created by researchers from Rensselaer Polytechnic Institute and Rice University (both U.S.A.) demonstrated reflectance of 0.045% when tested at Rensselaer Polytechnic Institute on August 24, 2007.

EVOLUTION OF THE SUPERCOMPUTER

The human brain can perform no more than about five calculations per second, while the fastest computers (see right) can now perform more than 10 quadrillion calculations in the same time. Here, we look at the number of calculations (operations) per second by computers over time:

OPS *Operations per second*	1943	5,000 OPS
	1944	100,000 OPS
	1955	400,000 OPS
MFLOPS *Millions of floating point operations per second (FLOPS)*	1960	1.2 MFLOPS
	1964	3 MFLOPS
	1969	36 MFLOPS
	1974	100 MFLOPS
	1976	250 MFLOPS
	1981	400 MFLOPS
	1983	941 MFLOPS
GFLOPS *Gigaflops: 10^9—1,000,000,000 (one billion)—FLOPS*	1984	2.4 GFLOPS
	1985	3.9 GFLOPS
	1989	10 GFLOPS
	1990	23.2 GFLOPS
	1993	43 GFLOPS
	1994	170 GFLOPS
	1996	368 GFLOPS
TFLOPS *Teraflops: 10^{12}—1,000,000,000,000 (one trillion)—FLOPS*	1997	1.34 TFLOPS
	1999	2.38 TFLOPS
	2000	7.23 TFLOPS
	2002	35.8 TFLOPS
	2004	70.7 TFLOPS
	2005	280 TFLOPS
	2007	478 TFLOPS
PFLOPS *Petaflops: 10^{15}—1,000,000,000, 000,000 (one quadrillion)—FLOPS*	2008	1.1 PFLOPS
	2009	1.76 PFLOPS
	2010	2.5 PFLOPS
	2011	10.51 PFLOPS

Sources: Peer1 Hosting; TOP500

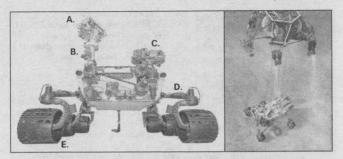

LARGEST PLANETARY ROVER On November 26, 2011, NASA launched its Mars Science Laboratory mission toward the planet Mars. Onboard was the *Curiosity* rover, which is 9 ft. 10 in. (3 m) long and weighs 1,984 lb. (900 kg), including 176 lb. (80 kg) of scientific instruments. It is designed to travel at up to 0.056 mph (0.09 km/h) while it explores the geology of Gale crater on Mars.

A. Laser and camera to analyze rocks and soil
B. Meteorological sensor
C. Spectrometer and camera on robotic arm for close-up rock studies
D. Suspension built for driving over Mars rocks
E. Wheels double up as landing gear

Smallest magnetic memory bit In January 2012, IBM and the German Center for Free-Electron Laser Science announced they had managed to store one bit of data on a storage device consisting of just 12 atoms of iron, measuring 4 x 16 nanometers. By comparison, a modern PC requires around one million atoms to do the same. The device was created atom by atom using a scanning tunneling microscope at IBM's Almaden Research Center in San Jose, California, U.S.A.

Fastest computer The K computer at the RIKEN Advanced Institute for Computational Science in Kobe, Japan, is the world's fastest supercomputer, achieving 10.51 quadrillion calculations per second using LIN-PACK benchmarking. Built in conjunction with Fujitsu, it took its second consecutive top place in the TOP500 list—which ranks the most powerful supercomputers—in 2011.

AI & ROBOTICS

Most advanced synthetic human brain Researchers at the Blue Brain Project, part of the Swiss Federal Institute of Technology in Lausanne, are building an artificial human brain by simulating the operation of individual brain cells, or "neurons," inside a supercomputer. In 2008, scientists on the project perfected the software needed to describe the behav-

FIRST STEALTH GAME WITH COLLECTIVE AI *Metal Gear Solid 2* (2001) featured guards working as a team, able to communicate with other guards offscreen. Such levels of AI are now integral to stealth games.

FIRST AI ROBOT TOY The Furby—built by Tiger Electronics (Japan)—was the first truly robotic cyberpet with artificial intelligence (AI). It went on sale in 1998 and took the form of a cuddly toy, resembling Gizmo from the *Gremlins* movies, which had to be fed (by placing objects in its mouth to activate a button), could "learn" to speak English, and would take naps (snoring as it did so). It sold in excess of 40 million units in three years.

ior of a human "neocortical column"—a subunit in the brain consisting of some 10,000 neurons. In 2011, 100 of these virtual neocortical columns were joined together to form a network of a million artificial neurons. This marks the most sophisticated software emulation of a human brain to date.

Deadliest antipersonnel robot In 2010, South Korea recruited some serious robotic firepower in the form of the Super aEgis 2—a robot sentry gun packing a heavy-duty 12-mm machine gun, 40-mm grenade launcher, and even surface-to-air missiles. The weapon uses infrared sensors and a camera to lock on to human targets up to 1.8 miles (3 km) away in daylight and

MOST LIFELIKE ANDROID In March 2011, a team of scientists from Osaka University and robotics company Kokoro (both Japan) unveiled an android—a robot with features modeled closely on those of a human—that is the most lifelike yet. Named Geminoid DK, the android has been made in the likeness of technology professor Henrik Scharfe, of Aalborg University in Denmark. It cost U.S. $200,000 to develop.

FACT: Geminoid DK has rubber "skin." Pneumatic devices enable it to show expressions and move.

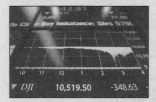

BIGGEST STOCK-MARKET CRASH CAUSED BY AUTOMATED TRADING On May 6, 2010, the Dow Jones, an index of value on the U.S. stock market, plunged more than 600 points (about 6%). It recovered 20 minutes later. Dubbed the "flash crash," it was thought to have been caused by "algorithmic trading"— a term that describes AI computers trading automatically in accordance with preprogrammed rules.

1.3 miles (2.2 km) at night. Targets are recognized and tracked in the images using sophisticated artificial intelligence algorithms. A laser range finder enables the computer to adjust its aim, while a gyroscope helps it correct for recoil.

First computer movie critic British company Epagogix has developed an artificial intelligence computer program that can accurately predict the box-office returns of movies. First, human readers score a prospective script, assigning numerical values to hundreds of variables describing its content. The software then compares these numbers to those of previously released movies—together with their box-office receipts—which yields a forecast of what a full production of the new script is likely to make. The company claims its software can estimate a movie's box-office takings to within +/- U.S. $10 million.

HIGHEST SCORE ON A QUIZ SHOW BY A COMPUTER In 2011, IBM fielded a computer named "Watson" in the U.S. TV game show *Jeopardy!* against two highly successful contestants; it comprehensively defeated them both, winning U.S. $77,147. On many questions, its opponents simply couldn't press their buzzers fast enough to beat the machine. Prior to the game, engineers fed Watson with a huge volume of data. This not only taught it how humans communicate, but also turned it into a general-knowledge genius.

First human killed by a robot: Robert Williams (U.S.A.) in 1979.

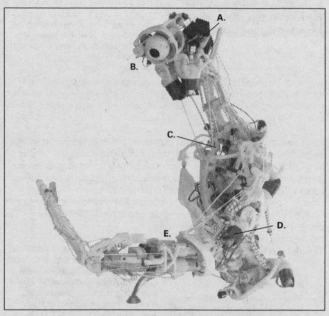

MOST ADVANCED HUMANOID ROBOT In June 2011, scientists at the University of Zurich, Switzerland, unveiled a remarkable humanoid robot called Ecci. The robot has the electromechanical equivalent of muscles, tendons, and nerves to move the bones in its skeleton. These are controlled by a highly advanced synthetic brain—a computer that learns from its experiences. This enables Ecci to develop coordination skills and ensure that it doesn't repeat its mistakes. Ecci's development involved 25 scientists, working for a period of three years.

A. Brain that learns from errors
B. Single eye powerful enough to match human stereoscopic vision
C. Tendons, muscles, and bones made from a special plastic
D. Electric motors move joints
E. Rotatable forearms

RISE OF THE ROBOTS

The idea of a machine capable of independent movement dates back to ancient times. Mechanisms for entertainment, such as toy figures, clockwork toys, and music boxes, have existed for centuries. However, genuinely functional robots, or machines capable of processing calculations, are a far more recent development. . . .

MECHANICAL CALCULATOR

Definition: any automated counting device
First example: Antikythera Mechanism, considered the **oldest analog computer** (early 1st century B.C.)

INDUSTRIAL ROBOT

Definition: nonhuman-like machine used to perform tasks in industrial manufacturing
First example: Unimate robot, introduced by General Motors (1961)

HUMANOID

Definition: more autonomous robot; anthropomorphic structure: head, arms, trunk, sometimes legs
First example: WABOT-1 (1973)

ANDROID (female equivalent: "gynoid")

Definition: robot with features that convincingly mimic those of humans, and which can process information and respond to it
First examples: early 2000s, including the Actroid and EveR-1 (both 2003)

CYBORG

Definition: partly mechanical, partly organic being, fitted with integral, advanced technology*
First example: British scientist Kevin Warwick, who implanted an electronic chip into his nervous system (2002)

not including humans with artificial aids, such as hearing aids, prosthetic limbs, or false eyes

First computer to beat a world chess champion (regular time controls) On May 11, 1997, world chess champion Garry Kasparov (Russia) was beaten by the IBM chess computer Deep Blue—a superpowerful parallel processor capable of evaluating 200 million board positions every second, and holding in its memory details of 700,000 past games played by grandmasters.

Turn to p. 392, where science meets sci-fi.

First poker bot to beat human professionals in a live tournament
In 2008, a program called "Polaris," written by computer scientists from
the University of Alberta, Canada, beat a six-strong team of human professionals in a tournament held in Las Vegas, U.S.A. Against each of the
pros, it played a 500-hand game of Limit Texas Hold'em ("limit" means
the bet sizes are fixed). Whoever finished each game with the most chips
was the winner. Polaris won three games, lost two, and tied one.

Fastest time to solve a Rubik's Cube by a robot A robot can
now solve a Rubik's Cube faster than a human. On November 11, 2011,
CubeStormer II finished a scrambled 3 x 3 cube in 5.27 seconds at *Wired*
magazine's offices in London, UK. It was commissioned by ARM Holdings and built by Mike Dobson and David Gilday (all UK) from four
LEGO Mindstorms NXT kits and a Samsung Galaxy S2 cell phone. The
human record, held by Feliks Zemdegs (Australia), stood at 5.66 seconds
as of February 18, 2012.

First AI scientist In 2009, researchers at the Creative Machines Lab,
part of Cornell University in New York, U.S.A., unveiled a software program called Eureqa. Feed the program data on pretty much anything and
it will try to come up with a mathematical law explaining how the data is
related. As a proof of concept, the team fed the program data on the motion of a pendulum—to which it responded by "discovering" Newton's
second law of motion and the conservation of energy.

NUMBERS

Most precise value of pi Pi (π) is a number that is frequently used in ge-
ometry, where it denotes the ratio of a circle's circumference to its diameter.
It has the value 3.141592, but that is only the value to six decimal places—
because it is an "irrational" number, it is impossible to write down its full
value. The most digits of pi ever calculated were worked out in 2011 by
Shigeru Kondo (Japan) and student Alexander J Yee (U.S.A.). Kondo used
computer software written by Yee to calculate pi to 10,000,000,000,000
(10 trillion) decimal places—a computation that took 371 days!

Oldest irrational number The first irrational number discovered was
the square root of 2, by Hippasus of Metapontum (then part of Magna
Graecia in southern Italy), in around 500 B.C.

Largest named number The largest lexicographically accepted named
number in the system of successive powers of 10 is the "centillion," first

recorded in 1852. It is the hundredth power of a million, or 1 followed by 600 zeroes (although only in the UK and Germany).

The words googol (10^{100}) and googolplex (10^{googol}) have entered the language to describe large numbers but are mostly used informally.

Largest prime number A "prime" number is any positive number divisible only by 1 and itself. The largest prime number found to date was discovered by the Great Internet Mersenne Prime Search project on August 23, 2008. It is a Mersenne prime, which means it can be written as 2^n-1, where "n" is a prime; $2^{43112609}-1$ contains around 12,978,189 digits. The **lowest prime number** is 2.

Lowest composite number A "composite" number is a number higher than 1 that can be divided exactly by numbers other than 1 or itself. Examples are 22 (2 x 11) and 20 (2 x 10, 4 x 5).The lowest of the composite numbers is 4.

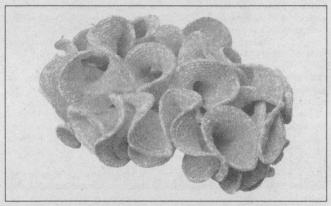

LARGEST HYPERBOLIC CROCHET The ancient Greek philosopher Euclid argued that parallel lines remain parallel forever. Later, however, mathematicians realized that his laws apply only in flat space. On the earth's curved surface, for example, lines of longitude are parallel at the equator but cross at the poles. Mathematicians have also envisaged theoretical curved spaces in which lines start as parallel but then diverge; such "hyperbolic" spaces have a kind of saddle shape. Daina Taimina, a Latvian mathematician, has crocheted models of hyperbolic shapes. The largest one measures 27.5 x 27.5 x 19.6 in. (70 x 70 x 50 cm) and weighs 13 lb. 14 oz. (6.3 kg). It is woven from 4.8 miles (7.8 km) of yarn.

FACT: Coral grows "hyperbolically," expanding its surface area to take in more nutrients.

	5	3			7				
	6			1	9	5			
		9	8					6	
	8				6				3
	4			8		3			1
	7				2				6
		6					2	8	
				4	1	9			5
					8			7	9

FASTEST TIME TO COMPLETE AN EASY SUDOKU PUZZLE Thomas Snyder (U.S.A.) completed an Easy Sudoku puzzle in 2 min. 8.53 sec. at BookExpo America, Washington, DC, U.S.A., on May 20, 2006. Sudoku is one of the world's most popular number puzzles—pictured above are some of the 1,714 students from Fairfield Methodist Primary School in Singapore who set the record for **most people playing Sudoku simultaneously,** on August 1, 2008.

Lowest perfect number A number is said to be "perfect" if it is equal to the sum of all its divisors (i.e., all the other numbers that go into that number exactly) other than itself. For example, 28 is perfect: $1 + 2 + 4 + 7 + 14 = 28$. The next two perfect numbers are 496 and 8,128. The lowest perfect number is, therefore, 6, as $1 + 2 + 3 = 6$.

Oldest unsolved number problem All the perfect numbers discovered so far are even—but could a perfect number ever be odd? This puzzle perplexed the ancient Greeks, back to the time of Nicomachus of Gerasa in the 1st century and maybe even back as far as Euclid, who lived 500 years earlier. In the centuries since, other mathematicians, including Pierre de Fermat and René Descartes, have attempted a solution, but none have so far succeeded.

Newest number Most numbers are not invented or discovered; they just "are." But one number had to be invented: zero. It was introduced by the Babylonians in the 4th century B.C. to indicate nothing—the absence of any other number. Originally, the Babylonians used a space (and later a placeholder symbol) between numerals to indicate the lack of a digit or value; the symbol "0" did not arise until the 8th century in India.

CULTURE WITH THE FEWEST NUMBERS The Pirahã tribe, who live in the Amazon region of Brazil, South America, have a special vocabulary: it has no numbers. As a result, the Pirahã are unable to count (although they do have expressions for "more than" and "less than"). Other linguistically innumerate societies (such as Australia's Aborigines) borrow number systems from other languages, but the Pirahã seem to show no interest in learning to count.

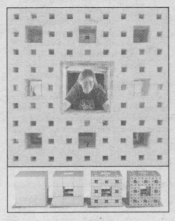

LARGEST MENGER SPONGE

A Menger sponge (named after its originator, Austrian mathematician Karl Menger) is a kind of fractal made by taking a cube, dividing each face into nine squares (like a Rubik's Cube) and from each face removing the middle square and all the material beneath it. The process is then repeated on every remaining square on the cube. The largest model of a Menger sponge measures 4 ft. 6 in. (1.4 m) along each side and weighs 154 lb. 5 oz. (70 kg). It was built from 66,048 business cards by computer scientist Dr. Jeannine Mosely (U.S.A.). She spent 10 years on the task, finishing in 2005.

FASTEST TIME TO TYPE FROM 1 TO 1,000,000 Les Stewart (Australia, above left), has typed from 1 to 1,000,000, in words, on 19,990 sheets of quarto-size paper. Starting in 1982, he became a "millionaire" on December 7, 1998.

In a related record attempt in 2007, Jeremy Harper (U.S.A., above right) verbally counted up to one million in a series of live Internet broadcasts. Starting on June 18, 2007, he reached 1,000,000 on September 14, 2007, after 89 days, averaging just over 11,200 numbers per day—the **highest sequence of numbers counted out loud.**

MOST IRRATIONAL NUMBER Numbers are considered "irrational" if they cannot be written down precisely as a fraction or in decimal form—you would need an infinite number of digits. The geometric constant pi is one example (see p. 378).

The most irrational number is 1 plus the square root of 5 all divided by 2—a figure roughly equal to 1.618. This number is known as the "Golden Ratio." Shapes with side lengths in this proportion tend to be especially pleasing to the eye—a fact that was known to artists and architects dating back to the 5th century B.C. The painting above, which uses the "Golden Ratio," is *Bathers at Asnières* (1884) by Georges Pierre Seurat.

Most popular number Of the numbers 1–9, the most commonly occurring is the number 1. You might expect all numbers to occur with equal likelihood, but studies of data in many forms, from train times to fundamental constants of nature, show that 1 crops up with a probability of 30%, and that higher numbers occur with steadily diminishing frequency.

Longest proof Originally proposed in 1971 by Daniel Gorenstein, the "Enormous Theorem" relates to the symmetry of geometric shapes. It took 100 mathematicians and some 15,000 pages of workings to prove it, a task that was finally completed in 2004.

PUT YOUR BRAIN TO THE TEST—AND BREAK A RECORD

Jayasimha Ravirala (India) committed to memory a binary number sequence consisting of a record 264 numbers, in just one minute, at the Holy Mary Institute of Technology in Hyderabad, India, on March 8, 2011. (It took him 9 minutes to accurately recall every number!) Can you beat his record? Below is a string of 265 numbers, and if you can memorize them all in just one minute, you'll be a record-breaker. Give it a go!

111101100101100111111011100110111110010010100100000111001
001000001010010011001001111000110010000110100001000110111 1
100010110001100000101110101101111001001000000011011111010
001100111010010000011101110110010011010010000010000001010 1
010111000010100100011100100101000

Longest binary number memorized in five minutes The everyday numbers we use are termed "base-10," meaning there are 10 basic numbers (0, 1, 2, 3, 4, 5, 6, 7, 8, 9) from which all others are constructed. For example, 625 stands for six hundreds, two tens, and five units. The term "binary" is another name for base-2 numbering. In binary, there are just two basic numbers: 0 and 1. The number 6 would be written 110—one 4, one 2, and zero units. In 2008, Ben Pridmore (UK) set the world record for memorizing the most binary digits in five minutes—accurately reciting every digit from a randomly generated sequence 930 digits long. Ben set his impressive record at the 2008 UK Memory Championships in London, UK, and he was also the overall winner of the event. *See p. 382 for a binary record attempt that you can try yourself.*

LIGHT FANTASTIC

Longest underwater fiber-optic cable Fiber-optic cables transmit light and form the basis of modern communication. There are many thousands of miles of fiber-optic cables at the bottom of the oceans. The longest of these "light pipes" is the Sea-Me-We-3 (Southeast Asia–Middle East–Western Europe), which is 24,000 miles (39,000 km) long. Operated by India's Tata Communications and fully commissioned in late 2000, the cable provides a high-speed connection from Germany to Australia and Japan. From Germany, the cable runs around Europe via the North Sea, Atlantic, and Mediterranean, then into the Red Sea and Indian Ocean. It splits in two just below Thailand; one branch goes north to Japan and one goes south to Australia.

Fastest single-core fiber-optic cable In April 2011, NEC Laboratories, in Princeton, New Jersey, U.S.A., demonstrated a data-sending rate of 101.7 terabits a second through 103 miles (165 km) of fiber-optic cable. This is the equivalent of sending 250 Blu-ray discs a second and was achieved by sending light from 370 separate lasers of different wavelength outputs into the fiber. Each laser emitted its own waveband of infrared light, containing several polarities, phases, and amplitudes to code information.

Oldest light The oldest light in the universe is the Cosmic Microwave Background (CMB), created in the Big

LONGEST BURNING LIGHTBULB The Livermore Centennial Light Bulb, at Firestation 6 in Livermore, California, U.S.A., has been burning since it was installed in 1901. The hand-blown bulb has operated at about 4 watts, and has been left on 24 hours a day to provide illumination of the fire engines. In 2011, the city of Livermore threw a street party to celebrate the lightbulb's 110th birthday.

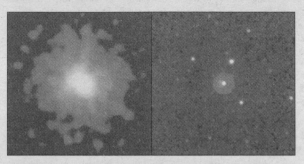

BRIGHTEST LIGHT EVER OBSERVED In March 2008, the SWIFT satellite saw a galaxy explode and produce a light a few hundred million, billion times brighter than our Sun.

Bang. The radiation has been cooled and stretched out by the expansion. It is present everywhere and almost uniformly distributed. It was discovered in 1964 by astronomers Arno Penzias and Robert Wilson (both U.S.A.), who noticed a faint glow in space not related to any star, galaxy, or other object. The current estimated age of the CMB light, and hence the universe itself, is 13.75 ± 0.13 billion years (4.336×10^{17} seconds in SI units, or 13.75 gigayears).

First calculation using an optical computer In 2009, scientists at the University of Bristol, UK, used four photons of light to interact with silicon chips to implement an algorithm to calculate the factors of 15 (3 and 5). The calculation was a simple process, but the work should pave the way for superfast optical computers that will ultimately calculate at the speed of light.

GREATEST COLOR VISION Stomatopod crustaceans, which include the mantis shrimp, contain eight different types of color photoreceptor. This compares to four in most birds and reptiles, three in humans and other primates, and two in most other mammals. The stomatopods can distinguish numerous shades within the electromagnetic spectrum's ultraviolet waveband—which is entirely invisible to humans. The eyesight may be used to identify prey (which are often semitransparent), or avoid predators.

First hologram In 1962, Emmett Leigh and Juris Upatnieks of the University of Michigan, U.S.A., made the first hologram—a three-dimensional image captured on a two-dimensional surface. It showed a toy train and a bird and was captured on photographic silver halide film emulsion on glass. The image is viewed by shining a laser from behind the image. Later in 1962, Soviet physicist Yuri Denisyuk (1927–2006) invented what became known as a reflection hologram that could be viewed using a simple lightbulb in front of the image. Capturing a three-dimensional image on a photographic plate was first conceived by Hungarian-British physicist Dennis Gabor (1900–79) in 1947. However, holography became possible in the early 1960s only with the development of the laser, which creates coherent light that generates an interference pattern.

First infrared photograph Infrared light is electro-magnetic radiation with a wavelength longer than that of visible light—it sits beyond the "red" end of the spectrum. The first photographic emulsions capable of capturing infrared light were developed by Professor Robert Williams Wood (U.S.A., 1868–1955). He published the first infrared photographs in the October 1910 journal printed by the Royal Photographic Society (RPS). Today, infrared photography has many practical as well as artistic uses. Infrared cameras are used to detect changing blood flow, overheating in electrical apparatus, and heat loss in buildings. Military night-vision devices also use infrared illumination—as do many household appliances, including heaters, TV remote controls, and the solid state lasers that play CDs.

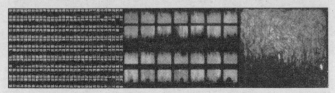

FIRST LIVING "NEON" SIGN Scientists at the University of California, San Diego, U.S.A., have created bioluminescent bacteria that have been biologically programmed to synchronize their blue flashes like a neon sign. The scientists are hoping to use the bacteria as low-cost biosensors—in the presence of pollutants or disease-causing organisms, for instance, they would change the rate at which they flash.

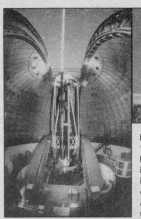

FIRST ARTIFICIAL GUIDE STAR On June 1, 1992, scientists at Lick Observatory and Lawrence Livermore National Labs (both in California, U.S.A.) shot a laser beam into the sky to create an artificial "star" of glowing atmospheric sodium ions. Astronomers used this star to observe how much "distortion" the Earth's atmosphere introduced into a telescope's image. They could then compensate for this distortion when viewing other objects in space, creating much more accurate images. The laser technology was developed from the U.S.A.'s "Star Wars" missile defense system of the 1980s and 1990s.

LARGEST LIGHTBULB Appropriately, the world's largest lightbulb is at the top of the Thomas Alva Edison Memorial Tower, a monument dedicated to the inventor of the electric lightbulb. The bulb is 13 ft. (3.96 m) tall, weighs 8 tons (7,257 kg), and is illuminated at night. The 131-ft. (40-m) tower was built in 1937, on the site of Edison's laboratory in Menlo Park, New Jersey, U.S.A.

Longest optical tape measure Optical tape measures use lasers instead of a physical piece of tape and are used in the construction industry. The longest optical tape measure, however, works all the way to the Moon. Light from lasers based in the U.S.A., France, and Russia can be bounced off reflectors left on the Moon's surface from 1969 to 1971 by the astronauts of the U.S.A.'s *Apollo 11, 14,* and *15* missions. From these lasers, it is possible to measure the distance of the Moon from Earth. The distance averages 238,855 miles (384,400 km) now—but because the

Moon moves away from Earth by 1.5 in. (38 mm) each year, this record will continually be broken. The light takes a 2.5-second round trip.

MAD SCIENCE

Fastest cell On December 3, 2011, the American Society for Cell Biology announced the results of their first World Cell Race: some 50 laboratories across the world chose different types of cells to compete in a race along a 0.01-in. (0.4-mm) racetrack. The winner was a line of fetal mesenchymal bone marrow cells from Singapore, which were clocked at 5.2 microns per minute, or 0.000000194 mph (0.000000312 km/h).

Highest prize offered for a scientific proof of paranormal ability The James Randi Educational Foundation Million Dollar Paranormal Challenge was first offered in 1968 by American magician and skeptic James Randi, initially as a prize of U.S. $100. The money has increased to U.S. $1 million, which will be awarded to the first group to scientifically prove the existence of paranormal or supernatural abilities. Between 1997 and 2005, some 360 applications were made. No one has yet been awarded the prize.

Lowest Bacon number In 1994, a trivia game emerged based on the "small world phenomenon," linking people in the movie industry to U.S.

MOST EXPENSIVE CONVERSION ERROR On September 23, 1999, NASA's *Mars Climate Orbiter* probe passed behind the planet Mars—and disintegrated in the Martian atmosphere. The cause? Human error. The onboard software had been written using metric units of thrust, but U.S. standard units had been used to enter course correction commands from the ground. The mission had cost U.S. $327.6 million.

FIRST ESP EXPERIMENT IN SPACE On the *Apollo 14* mission from January 31 to February 9, 1971, Lunar Module Pilot Edgar Mitchell tried a private, prearranged extrasensory perception (ESP) experiment. He looked at, and thought about, five shapes on Zener cards, in random order, hoping that his thoughts would be received by four friends on Earth. Out of 200 attempts, his friends got 51 right.

FIRST REMOTE-CONTROLLED BULL In 1963, Spanish physiology professor José Manuel Rodriguez Delgado implanted a device he had created, called a "stimoceiver," into the brains of bulls at a breeding ranch in Córdoba, Spain. He was later able to use a handheld transmitter to halt a charging bull by using the stimoceiver to stimulate the animal's caudate nucleus.

actor Kevin Bacon (below left). A person's Bacon number marks the fewest steps from them to Bacon, based on movie appearances. For example, UK actor Sir Patrick Stewart was in *Star Trek Generations* (U.S.A., 1994) with Glenn Morshower (U.S.A.), who was in *X-Men: First Class* (U.S.A., 2011) with Bacon. This gives Stewart a Bacon number of 2. Kevin Bacon has the lowest Bacon number: zero.

LOWEST ERDÖS–BACON NUMBER An Erdös–Bacon number is the sum of an "Erdös" number (the fewest steps to link academics to the prolific Hungarian mathematician Paul Erdös) and a "Bacon" number. Two people share the record for the lowest Erdös–Bacon number. Professor Daniel Kleitman (U.S.A., bottom left) has coauthored multiple research papers with Erdös, giving him an Erdös number of 1. Kleitman was also a consultant and extra in the movie *Good Will Hunting* (U.S.A., 1997)—starring Minnie Driver (UK), who starred with Bacon in *Sleepers* (U.S.A., 1997). This gives him a Bacon number of 2 and a resulting Erdös–Bacon number of 3.

Bruce Reznick (U.S.A.) was an extra in *Pretty Maids All in a Row* (U.S.A., 1972) with Roddy McDowall (UK)—who starred with Bacon in *The Big Picture* (U.S.A., 1989)—giving him a Bacon number of 2. Reznick also has an Erdös number of 1. This gives him an Erdös–Bacon number of 3.

FACT: Daniel Kleitman (above) teaches applied mathematics at Massachusetts Institute of Technology.

> **FACT:** A "Rube Goldberg" is an overcomplex machine created to perform a very basic task.

LARGEST RUBE GOLDBERG In 2012, the Purdue Society of Professional Engineers (PSPE) Rube Goldberg Team (all U.S.A.) made a machine with 300 "steps." Its goal? To blow up and pop a balloon.

First complete robotic digestive system Ecobot III was created in 2010 by scientists at the Bristol Robotics Laboratory (University of the West of England and University of Bristol), UK. It is a robot powered by organic matter, which, along with water, can collect itself from its environment. The organic matter, which can include human waste, is digested by an array of 48 onboard microbial fuel cells in order to generate electricity. The organic waste products from this process are then excreted by the robot.

First graphene distillery Discovered by scientists at the University of Manchester, UK, and the Institute for Microelectronics Technology, Russia, in 2004, graphene is the **thinnest material** known to science. It forms a sheet made from a single layer of carbon atoms and its discoverers earned the Nobel Prize in Physics in 2010. In January 2012, researchers at the University of Manchester announced they had used a membrane of graphene oxide to seal a bottle of vodka "just for a laugh," and discovered that the liquor became stronger over time as water molecules escaped through the membrane.

FIRST ELECTRONIC DIALOGUE BETWEEN NERVOUS SYSTEMS In March 2002, UK scientist Kevin Warwick had a tiny 100-electrode array (seen below left, on a UK 5 pence coin) set into the median nerve fibers of his left arm. A second implant was surgically added to Kevin's wife, Irena. The implants communicated over the Internet, allowing Kevin to feel signals from Irena's implant. Via a radio transmitter/receiver connected to the implant, Kevin also interacted with objects without touching them. His arm movements are making his wife's necklace glow in the photograph at left.

FACT: The concept of "tin-foil hats" first emerged in the book *The Tissue-Culture King* (1927) by Julian Huxley.

FIRST SCIENTIFIC PROBE INTO "TIN-FOIL HATS" Many conspiracy theorists believe that a hat made from metal foil can protect the brain from telepathic interference. In 2005, a group of graduate students at the Massachusetts Institute of Technology (MIT), U.S.A., concluded that aluminum foil hats can actually amplify radio signals at some frequencies that are controlled by the U.S. government.

IG NOBEL PRIZE

A satirical version of the Nobel Prizes, the Ig Nobels have been awarded annually by the Annals of Improbable Research since 1991. Each year, 10 awards are given for research that "first makes people laugh and then makes them think." Recent awards include:

BIOLOGY, 2011
For discovering that a certain kind of beetle is attracted to a certain kind of Australian beer bottle.

PEACE, 2011
Awarded to the Mayor of Vilnius, Lithuania, for demonstrating that the problem of illegally parked luxury automobiles can be solved by running them over with an armored tank.

MEDICINE, 2011
For demonstrating that people make better decisions about some kinds of things—but worse decisions about other kinds of things—when they have a strong urge to urinate.

ENGINEERING, 2011
For perfecting a method to collect whale snot using a remote-controlled helicopter.

PHYSICS, 2010
For demonstrating that, on icy walkways in wintertime, people slip and fall less often if they wear socks on the outside of their shoes.

MANAGEMENT, 2010
For demonstrating mathematically that organizations would become more efficient if they promoted people at random.

First sensory deprivation tank In 1954, U.S. scientist John Lilly built a soundproofed and darkened tank filled with warm salty water, at body temperature, designed to isolate the human brain from external stimuli. Lilly—who, with a colleague, was the first person to try the tank—reported that he entered dreamlike, euphoric states within its environment. Sensory deprivation tanks are now commonly used for meditation and in alternative therapies.

Longest man-made lightning Nikola Tesla (Croatia) created the longest manmade bolt of lightning—130 ft. (40 m)—in 1899, at his laboratory in Colorado, U.S.A. The accompanying thunderclap was reported to have been heard 22 miles (35 km) away.

First identical snow crystals A commonly believed statement about snow is that two snowflakes are never alike. In 1988, however, Nancy Knight (U.S.A.), a scientist at the National Center for Atmosphere Research in Boulder, Colorado, U.S.A., found two identical examples while studying snow crystals from a storm in Wisconsin, U.S.A., using a microscope.

First heat-ray gun The Active Denial System projects an invisible heat-energy microwave beam within a range of 1,640 ft. (500 m). Typically, the gun is mounted on a Humvee vehicle, and while a human target would feel a burning sensation, the weapon is nonlethal. It was first publicly demonstrated at Moody Air Force Base in Georgia, U.S.A., on January 24, 2007.

Most radiation-resistant lifeform The red-colored bacterium *Deinococcus radiodurans* can resist 1.5 million rads of gamma radiation, about 3,000 times the amount it would take to kill a human.

SCI-FI SCIENCE

First Earthlike extrasolar planet **Sci-fi:** The forested planet of Pandora in *Avatar* is located in the Alpha Centauri system.

Science: To date, more than 700 planets have been found that orbit other stars, but the first potentially Earthlike example is Kepler-22b—so its discovery, announced on December 5, 2011, caused excitement among astronomers. The planet is about 2.4 times the size of Earth and orbits its sunlike star in around 290 days. The luminosity of its star, coupled with the orbital distance, means Kepler-22b is believed to reside within its star's habitable zone. If the planet has an Earthlike greenhouse effect, then its surface temperature could be a comfortable 71.6°F (22°C).

First planet found to orbit two stars **Sci-fi:** Luke Skywalker's home planet of Tatooine from *Star Wars* is in a binary (two-sun) system.

Science: Kepler-16b was discovered by NASA's Kepler mission and unveiled on September 15, 2011. The planet is similar in mass to Saturn and it orbits the binary star Kepler-16 every 229 days in a stable, roughly circular orbit.

Largest tractor-beam study **Sci-fi:** A technology familiar to fans of *Star Trek* and *Star Wars*, tractor beams can pull large objects from a distance.

Science: In October 2011, NASA awarded a U.S. $100,000 grant to scientists at its Goddard Space Flight Center in Greenbelt, Maryland, U.S.A., to study three potential methods for manipulating and transporting particles using laser light. NASA hopes to use future tractor-beam technology for tasks including extraterrestrial sampling and the cleaning up of space debris.

FIRST PREHISTORIC EXTINCT CLONING PROJECT **Sci-fi:** In *Jurassic Park*, extinct dinosaurs are brought back to life using DNA manipulation.

Science: Some intact specimens of woolly mammoths have been found in Siberian permafrost. In January 2011, Japanese researchers announced plans to insert woolly mammoth DNA into African elephant cells to create an elephant-mammoth hybrid. It will take around two years before an embryo is ready to be implanted into an elephant.

FIRST INTER-SPECIES WEB CHAT **Sci-fi:** *Rise of the Planet of the Apes* features great apes with artificially boosted intelligence.

Science: Koko the gorilla has been taught more than 1,000 American Sign Language signs and more than 1,000 spoken words. On April 28, 1998, she took part in a Web chat in which around 8,000 AOL subscribers asked her questions. Her teacher, Dr. Penny Patterson, put the questions to Koko, interpreted her signs, and replied to the questioners via AOL.

FACT: R Bot 001's first test patrol ended in failure—rain caused the nonwaterproof robot to short-circuit!

FIRST ROBOT POLICEMAN Sci-fi: The *Robocop* TV shows and movies feature a robot-human hybrid law-enforcement agent.

  Science: In 2007, the Russian city of Perm gained a fully robotic real-life version. R Bot 001 is a 5-ft. 6-in.-tall (1.7-m) robot crime fighter that moves on four wheels and scans its environment with five cameras to look for crimes being committed. It can issue simple orders and serve as a point of contact for its human counterparts.

FACT VS. FICTION

The *International Space Station (ISS)* is the **largest space station** ever built, while the Space Shuttle is, to date, the **largest reusable space craft**. But how do these real-world examples compare with their sci-fi counterparts? Below are some classic fictional craft—how many can you identify? *(Answers on p. 600.)*

Shuttle: 122 ft. (37.2 m) long

ISS: 347 ft. (105.8 m) wide

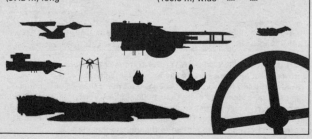

GREATEST TIME DILATION Sci-fi: In the *Back to the Future* movies, Marty McFly travels through time in a modified Delorean DMC-12 sports car.

Science: The greatest "time travel" experienced by an individual is around 1/48th of a second, for cosmonaut Sergei Krikalev (USSR)—a consequence of the 803 days 9 hr. 39 min. he has spent in orbit, traveling at around 17,000 mph (27,000 km/h). Relative to everyone else, he has essentially "time traveled" a fraction of a second into the future.

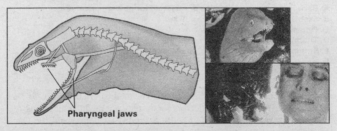

Pharyngeal jaws

FIRST DOCUMENTED USE OF PHARYNGEAL JAWS TO CATCH PREY Sci-fi: The Xenomorphs in the *Alien* movies have a second—and very vicious—set of protruding jaws.

Science: Known as pharyngeal jaws, these exist within the throats of around 30,000 species of fish. While most species with these extra jaws use them to help swallow food, moray eels project theirs forward into their mouths to help capture prey.

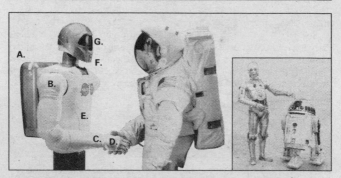

FIRST DEXTROUS ROBOTIC ASTRONAUT IN SPACE Sci-fi: Science fiction is populated with intelligent robot droids, such as *Star Wars'* C-3PO and R2-D2.

Science: In February 2011, the space shuttle *Discovery* set off for the *International Space Station*. Part of its cargo was Robonaut 2, a humanoid robot designed to test how robots can assist astronauts in space. On February 15, 2012, in its latest test, it performed a firm handshake with *ISS* commander Daniel Burbank.

A. Backpack contains batteries or a system for power conversion
B. Each arm can hold 19 lb. 13 oz. (9 kg)
C. Fingers controlled by tendons
D. Thumb has four joints
E. Stomach houses 38 PowerPC processors
F. Infrared camera for depth perception
G. Four cameras behind visor

Largest tricorder competition Sci-fi: The medical tricorder in *Star Trek* is a handheld device used by doctors for on-the-spot medical diagnosis.

Science: On January 10, 2012, the X-Prize Foundation and the Qualcomm Foundation announced a U.S. $10-million incentive for the first working version of a medical tricorder. The prize will be awarded to the research group that develops a mobile platform able to best diagnose a set of 15 diseases in 30 people in three days.

Oldest automated nuclear weapons control system Sci-fi: In the *Terminator* movies, Skynet is a computer-controlled "Global Digital Defense Network" that maliciously launches the U.S. nuclear arsenal toward Russia, resulting in a global nuclear war that kills half of humanity.

Science: When U.S. President Ronald Reagan announced his Strategic Defense Initiative in 1983, the Soviet Union saw it as a sign that the U.S.A. may be preparing for a nuclear "first strike" against them. In response, they developed "Perimeter," a doomsday weapon that would automatically retaliate. Perimeter became active in 1985 and was designed to seismically detect nuclear strikes in the USSR.

Most powerful radio signal deliberately beamed into space Sci-fi: In *Close Encounters of the Third Kind* and countless other sci-fi fables, humans make contact with an alien race.

Science: In 1974, scientists at the Arecibo Radio Telescope in Puerto Rico transmitted basic data on humanity, in the form of a 2,380-MHz binary radio signal, to the M13 globular cluster in the constellation of Hercules. The 169-second message will arrive in around 25,000 years—although it will take another 25,000 years for us to receive any answer. . . .

SOUND

Deepest note in the universe The lowest note in the universe is caused by acoustic waves generated by a supermassive black hole in the center of the Perseus cluster of galaxies, 250 million light-years away. The sound, which propagates through the extremely thin gas surrounding the black hole, is that of a B-flat note, 57 octaves below middle C. The sound waves are estimated to have been consistently produced by the black hole for around 2.5 billion years.

Loudest sound The island-volcano Krakatoa, in the Sunda Strait between Sumatra and Java, Indonesia, exploded in an eruption on August 27, 1883. The sound was heard 3,100 miles (5,000 km) away. The noise is estimated to have been heard across 8% of the Earth's surface and to have had 26 times the power of the largest ever H-bomb test.

Loudest unexplained underwater sound In the 1960s, the U.S. Navy began installing arrays of underwater microphones in the South Pacific and North Atlantic regions to track the movements of Soviet submarines. In the summer of 1997, a sound was heard that rose in frequency for one minute and was powerful enough to be detected by multiple sensors

LOUDEST BURP Paul Hunn (UK, left, with GWR's Craig Glenday), blasted out a burp at 109.9 decibels (dB). Decibels measure sound intensity, with silence equal to 0 dB, a normal conversation registering at 60 dB and a large orchestra at 98 dB. Hunn claimed his record for the loudest male burp at Butlins in Bognor Regis, UK, on August 23, 2009.

LOUDEST POSSIBLE SUSTAINED SOUND IN AIR Sound takes the form of a wave, and the loudness of any sound relates to how high and low the peaks and troughs of the wave are. The peaks and troughs of a sound wave oscillate at an average of 1 atmospheric pressure. The lowest possible troughs of a wave are at 0 atmospheres, or a pressure of zero. The highest troughs of such a wave would be at 2 atmospheres. A sound wave with an amplitude range of 2 atmospheres corresponds to 194 dB. Any event louder than 194 dB is considered a shock wave.

in the Equatorial Pacific Ocean autonomous hydrophone array. Analysis of the signal suggested it originated far off the west coast of southern South America, giving a range of around 3,100 miles (5,000 km). Nicknamed "The Bloop," this sound was picked up several times that summer and has never been detected since. Its origin remains unknown, although some scientists have speculated it was caused by ice calving in Antarctica or even an unknown giant marine species.

Strongest measured sonic boom created by an aircraft In 1967, the U.S. Government performed a series of tests to discover whether or not an aircraft's sonic boom could be used as a weapon. An F-4 Phantom was used to perform extremely low and fast flybys over Nevada, one of which resulted in a sonic boom measuring 144 lb.-force per sq. ft (703 kg-force/m^2). No injury was reported by the researchers who were present, despite them being exposed to a sonic boom produced by a jet fighter traveling at Mach 1.26 and at an altitude of just 95 ft. (29 m) above ground level.

LOUDEST SIREN The Chrysler air raid sirens are the loudest sirens ever constructed, capable of producing 138 dB at a distance of 100 ft. (30 m). The sirens are so loud that a normal person would be deafened within 200 ft. (60 m) of one during operation.

LARGEST ACOUSTIC MIRROR Acoustic mirrors were developed by the British as an experimental early warning system to detect enemy aircraft. The two largest examples were built in the 1920s and early 1930s near Dungeness, UK (above), and Maghtab in Malta. Both had the same design: a curved concrete wall 200 ft. (61 m) long by 27 ft. (8.2 m) high, which focused sound into a "listening trench" in which microphones were installed. The invention of radar made them obsolete.

Loudest animal sound Blue whales (*Balaenoptera musculus*) and fin whales (*B. physalus*) emit a low-frequency pulse when communicating. These calls reach an amazing 188 dB on the decibel scale, the loudest sounds by any living source.

First voice recording The oldest recorded human voice is a 10-second fragment of the French folk song "Au Clair de la Lune." It was recorded on April 9, 1860, by inventor Édouard-Léon Scott de Martinville (France,

LOUDEST LAND ANIMAL Male howler monkeys (*Alouatta*) of Central and South America have an enlarged bony structure at the top of the windpipe, allowing sound to reverberate. In full voice, they are audible 3 miles (4.8 km) away.

FIRST MAN-MADE OBJECT TO BREAK THE SOUND BARRIER Bullwhips have been used by humanity for millennia. The sharp "crack" that a whip makes when it is cast occurs because the tip of the whip has broken the speed of sound.

FACT: In the photo above, Adam Winrich (U.S.A.) is casting the **longest whip ever cracked**: 216 ft. (65.83 m).

1817–79). Discovered in 2008 by researchers in Paris, the clip was created on paper using a phonautograph, a device for recording sounds visually, without being able to play them back. The paper recording was analyzed by scientists at Lawrence Berkeley National Laboratory (U.S.A.), who used optical imaging as a "virtual stylus," allowing the clip to be played back for the very first time.

Rarest speech sounds The least common speech sound is "ř" in Czech—technically speaking, a "rolled post-alveolar fricative." It occurs in very few languages and is the last sound mastered by Czech children.

In the southern Bushman language "!xo," there is a click articulated with both lips, which is written "Â." This character is usually referred to as a "bull's-eye" and the sound—essentially a kiss—is termed a "velaric ingressive bilabial stop."

LARGEST ANECHOIC TEST CHAMBER The Benefield Anechoic Facility at Edwards Air Force Base in California, U.S.A., is a vast echo-free chamber with a volume of 4.62 million cu. ft. (130,823 m³). The chamber is insulated from outside noise and its interior surfaces do not reflect sound or electromagnetic waves. Built in 1988–89, it is used to test aerospace and defense projects, including tanks, aircraft, and air-defense systems.

FACT: The term "dBA" covers sound levels audible to the human ear, so it excludes extreme highs and lows.

FACT: The speed of sound is 1,123 ft. per sec. (342.3 m/sec) in dry air at 68°F (20°C).

If you prefer the sound of music, see p. 422.

SOUND SPECTRUM

GWR explores the extremes of sound, from the faintest rustling of leaves to the eardrum-popping noises of guns and fireworks.

Decibel scale

Painful and dangerous

Avoid or use hearing protection	140	Fireworks
		Gunshots
		Custom auto stereos at full volume
	130	Jackhammers
		Ambulances

Uncomfortable

Dangerous over 30 seconds	120	Jet planes during takeoff

Very loud

Dangerous over 30 minutes	110	Concerts
		Auto horns
		Sporting events
	100	Snowmobiles
		MP3 players at full volume
	90	Lawn mowers
		Power tools
		Blenders
		Hair-dryers

Over 85 dB for extended periods can cause permanent hearing loss

Loud	80	Alarm clocks
	70	Traffic
		Vacuum cleaners
Moderate	60	Normal conversation
		Dishwashers
	50	Moderate rainfall
Soft	40	Quiet library
	30	Whisper
Faint	20	Leaves rustling

Source: American Academy of Audiology; South Carolina Department of Health and Environmental Control

Most common language sound No language lacks the vowel "a" (as in the English word "father").

First acoustic hyperlens In October 2009, scientists at the U.S. Department of Energy's Lawrence Berkeley National Laboratory announced that they had created an acoustic hyperlens—a device to magnify details obtained by sound imaging, including submarine sonar and ultrasound fetal scans. Their hyperlens consists of 36 brass fins arranged in a fan shape. This arrangement allows physical manipulation of imaging sound waves in order to resolve details one-sixth the size of the sound waves themselves.

Quietest spot on Earth The world's quietest place is the Anechoic Test Chamber at Orfield Laboratories in Minneapolis, Minnesota, U.S.A. Ultrasensitive tests in this specially constructed room on January 21, 2004, gave a background noise level of just -9.4 dBA (decibels, A-weighted).

Loudest pipe organ The Vox Maris organ produced a reading of 138.4 dBA when tested in Urspringen, Germany, on October 21, 2011.

Least appealing sound A year-long survey by Trevor Cox, Professor of Acoustic Engineering at Salford University, UK, found the most repellent sound to the human ear is someone vomiting. It beat such sounds as a baby wailing and a dentist's drill.

Loudest insect The African cicada (*Brevisana brevis*) makes a calling song with an average sound pressure level of 106.7 dB at a distance of 50 cm (1 ft 7.5 in). Its songs play a vital role in communication and reproduction.

ENTERTAINMENT

CONTENTS

HIGHEST REVENUE GENERATED BY AN ENTERTAINMENT PRODUCT IN 24 HOURS Within 24 hours of its launch on November 8, 2011, military shooter *Call of Duty: Modern Warfare 3* had sold more than 6.5 million copies in the U.S.A. and UK. The record sales generated around U.S. $400 million according to the game's publisher, Activision Blizzard.

HOW FAMOUS CAN YOU GET?

WHO IS THE MOST FAMOUS PERSON ON EARTH?

Fame, renown, repute, glory—there are many words for the state of being known or talked about by a lot of people. However, what is fame, how can we quantify it, and what, if any, are the limits on fame?

We live in an age where the line between fame and celebrity is blurred. Where once someone became famous for their extraordinary deeds, many people are now celebrated merely for being famous.

The great Julius Caesar (100–44 B.C.) was known throughout the Roman Empire and beyond, having extended Rome's power to the west across the

MOST FAMOUS CELEBRITY According to our rinse of celebrity statistics, Lady Gaga is currently the most famous celeb on the planet. The First World bias of the list reflects the ubiquity of the Internet in the West. How will a shift in this balance change the face of celebrity in the future?

TOP 10 MOST INFLUENTIAL PEOPLE IN HISTORY

1	Mohammed	Prophet of God, founder of Islam
2	Isaac Newton	English scientist, devised laws of motion
3	Jesus Christ	Son of God, central figure of Christianity
4	Buddha	Indian teacher, philosopher, founder of Buddhism
5	Confucius	Chinese teacher, philosopher, founder of Confucianism
6	St. Paul	Christian apostle, missionary, Bible contributor
7	Cài Lún	Chinese inventor of papermaking process
8	Johannes Gutenberg	German inventor of printing press and movable type
9	Christopher Columbus	Italian navigator, explorer, led to European colonization of the New World
10	Albert Einstein	German physicist, devised theory of relativity

Source: The 100: A Ranking of the Most Influential Persons in History, *Michael H. Hart*

English Channel and to the north into the Rhinelands. Even then, his fame (or infamy) cannot compare with that of Justin Bieber, who has conquered the Internet with three entries in the top ten most popular YouTube videos of all time (see p. 425), reaching well over a billion people in the process. Admittedly, Bieber also attracted a record number of "dislikes," but he fared somewhat better than Caesar, who received multiple stab wounds from *his* "dislikers"!

In essence, there would appear to be two ages of fame: pre- and post-Internet. *The 100*, a book that ranks those people who have played a pivotal role in the course of human history, features not a single person in its top ten who was born after the beginning of the 20th century. ·

Who's had the most Facebook "likes" this year? Find out on p. 307.

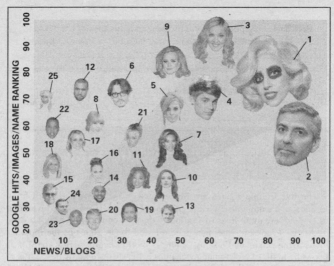

CELEBRITY SNAPSHOT 2011–12 Plotted here are the top 25 celebrities currently making the news (to the year ending March 14, 2012), in terms of hits on Google, news sites, and picture sites, as well as Forbes' power rating, imdb star rating, and first-name rank (chance of a Google hit from only the first name).

The ratings given—and the corresponding celebrities' head sizes—have been calculated by assigning a score out of 100 to each of the criteria mentioned above. The larger the head, the more "famous" the face . . .

Interestingly, if you take the average age, occupation, and nationality from a list of the top 50 celebs, we end up with a 34-year-old male musician from the U.S.A. The top 25 celebrity who fits this profile most closely is rapper/songwriter/producer Kanye West (who actually appears at No. 12 on the list)!

1 LADY GAGA	10 ANGELINA JOLIE	19 BRAD PITT
2 GEORGE CLOONEY	11 OPRAH WINFREY	20 DONALD TRUMP
3 MADONNA	12 KANYE WEST	21 RIHANNA
4 JUSTIN BIEBER	13 ROGER FEDERER	22 JAY-Z
5 KATY PERRY	14 LEBRON JAMES	23 KOBE BRYANT
6 JOHNNY DEPP	15 ELTON JOHN	24 LEONARDO
7 BEYONCÉ KNOWLES	16 JENNIFER LOPEZ	DICAPRIO
8 TAYLOR SWIFT	17 BRITNEY SPEARS	25 NICKI MINAJ
9 ADELE	18 JENNIFER ANISTON	

The five leading figures are Mohammed, Isaac Newton, Jesus Christ,
Buddha, and Confucius—clearly significant figures. However, who among
us could quote more lines of Confucius than we could the lyrics of a song
by Michael Jackson—the man once referred to (in 2006) as the most famous living person on Earth by Guinness World Records? How many of us
know the limits of Newtonian mechanics better than we know the chorus of
"Poker Face" by Lady Gaga, the most famous of the faces in our 2011–12
snapshot of celebrity fame (see page 407)?

**Facebook currently has 845 million active users, and between them
the faithful helped to generate revenues in excess of U.S. $3.7 billion in
2011.** This networking site drives much of the traffic on the Internet, with
users tipping off each other about new uploads from musicians, actors, or
simply ordinary people. For a fleeting moment, these celebrities manage to
attract the kind of fame that eluded Julius Caesar—just by walking into a
door, falling off a skateboard, or getting bitten by a baby.

As access to the net grows, which it inevitably will, so too will the limits of fame—in June 2011, the United Nations declared that free access to
the Internet was a fundamental human right, on a par with access to clean
water. Only when everyone is online will these limits be reached, and, by
then, perhaps we will *all* be afforded our allotted 15 minutes—or at least 15
megabytes—of fame.

COMICS

First comic Most experts agree that Swiss cartoonist Rodolphe Töpffer's
Histoire de M. Vieux Bois ("The Adventures of Mister Wooden Head"),
created in 1827 and first published a decade later, was the earliest comic.
The story, published in North America in 1842 as *The Adventures of Oba-
diah Oldbuck*, consisted of around 30 pages of comic strip. Each page was
cut into six panels, with a narrative caption below each drawing.

MOST TRANSLATED COMIC *The Adventures of Asterix*, created by René Goscinny and Albert Uderzo (both France) in 1959, has been translated into 111 languages and dialects, including Welsh, Latin, Swiss German, and Esperanto. It sold 320 million copies worldwide and has been adapted nine times as a cartoon for TV and three times for the cinema.

MOST EXPENSIVE COMIC A copy of *Action Comics* #1, first published in 1938, was bought by an anonymous bidder via the U.S. auction website ComicConnect.com for U.S. $2.161 million on November 30, 2011. The comic, which features the first appearance of Superman, was graded at Very Fine/Near Mint: 9.0 by the Certified Guaranty Company (CGC).

First sequential newspaper strip *Hogan's Alley*, by Richard Felton Outcault (U.S.A.), is credited as the first regular newspaper strip. It featured Mickey Dugan, better known as the "Yellow Kid" because of his distinctive long, yellow nightshirt. The sequential strip version of *Hogan's Alley* appeared in Randolph Hearst's *New York Journal* from October 25, 1896, and continued for three series.

MOST EXPENSIVE PAGE OF COMIC ART An unknown collector paid €312,500 (U.S. $461,503) for one hand-drawn page from the 1963 Tintin book *The Castafiore Emerald* on May 10, 2009. The selling price was three times that of its catalog estimate.

LARGEST COMIC FESTIVAL Japan's Comiket, a three-day comics festival held in Tokyo in the summer and winter each year, attracted 560,000 visitors during summer 2009. The last day—Sunday, August 16—was the busiest, with around 200,000 visitors attending. This record was equaled at the summer 2010 Comiket. The event is especially known for its *dojinshi*—self-published manga comics.

First graphic novel Graphic novels are book-length comics. The term "graphic novel" first appeared in 1976 on the dust jacket of *Bloodstar* by illustrator Richard Corben and author Robert E. Howard (both U.S.A.). In the same year, George Metzger's (U.S.A.) comic book *Beyond Time and Again* was subtitled "A Graphic Novel," and *Red Tide* by Jim Steranko (U.S.A.) was labeled both a "visual novel" and a "graphic novel."

Best-selling comic (single edition) Created by Chris Claremont (UK) and Jim Lee (U.S.A.), *X-Men 1*, published by Marvel Comics, sold a total of 8.1 million copies. Lee also drew four variant covers for the issue, all of them published simultaneously and which integrated to form one image, bearing the cover date October 1991.

Most expensive Silver Age comic The years 1956 to 1970 mark the "silver age" of comics. A copy of *Amazing Fantasy* #15, first published in 1962, was purchased by an anonymous buyer via the U.S. auction website ComicConnect.com for U.S. $1.1 million, in March 2011. The comic marked the debut of Spider-Man.

FIRST SUPERHERO Contrary to popular belief, Superman was not the first comic-strip superhero. That honor falls instead to The Phantom, created in 1936 by the American cartoonist Lee Falk, two years before Superman. The *Phantom* newspaper strip featured the adventures of Kit Walker, who sported a mask and a figure-hugging purple outfit as "the ghost who walks."

Longest-running weekly comic British humor comic *The Beano* was launched on July 30, 1938, and has been published weekly ever since—except for a period during World War II, when its frequency was reduced due to paper shortages. As of February 11, 2012, *The Beano* has been published for 3,622 issues, making it the longest-running weekly comic to have retained its name and numbering system throughout its history. It is published by DC Thompson & Co. (UK).

Most editions of any comic The Mexican comic *Pepín* printed its first edition on March 4, 1936, as a weekly comics anthology. It eventually became a daily, running until October 23, 1956. In all, 7,561 issues were published.

Largest publisher of comics Marvel Comics is the biggest publisher of comics, boasting the greatest market share of any comic publisher, claiming an amazing 45.63% of the total market at the end of 2009. The second largest is DC Comics with 35.22%.

Most professional contributors to a graphic novel In one working day in September 1991, a group of 133 cartoonists gathered at the Guinness World of Records museum at the Trocadero in London, UK, to create a 250-ft.-long (76-m) comic strip entitled *The Worm*. The strip's story—concerning a cartoonist who journeys through time—was conceived by legendary writer Alan Moore (UK). The finished comic was published in 1999 by Slab-O-Concrete Press to help raise money for the Cartoon Art Trust.

Fastest time to produce a comic book Kapow! Comic Con produced a comic book in 11 hr. 19 min. 38 sec. in London, UK, on April 9, 2011.

MOST MOVIE ADAPTATIONS OF A COMIC CHARACTER Batman has starred in eight full-length live-action movies, from *Batman* (U.S.A., 1966) to *The Dark Knight Rises* (U.S.A., 2012).

Prefer batsmen to Batman? Then fly to p. 479.

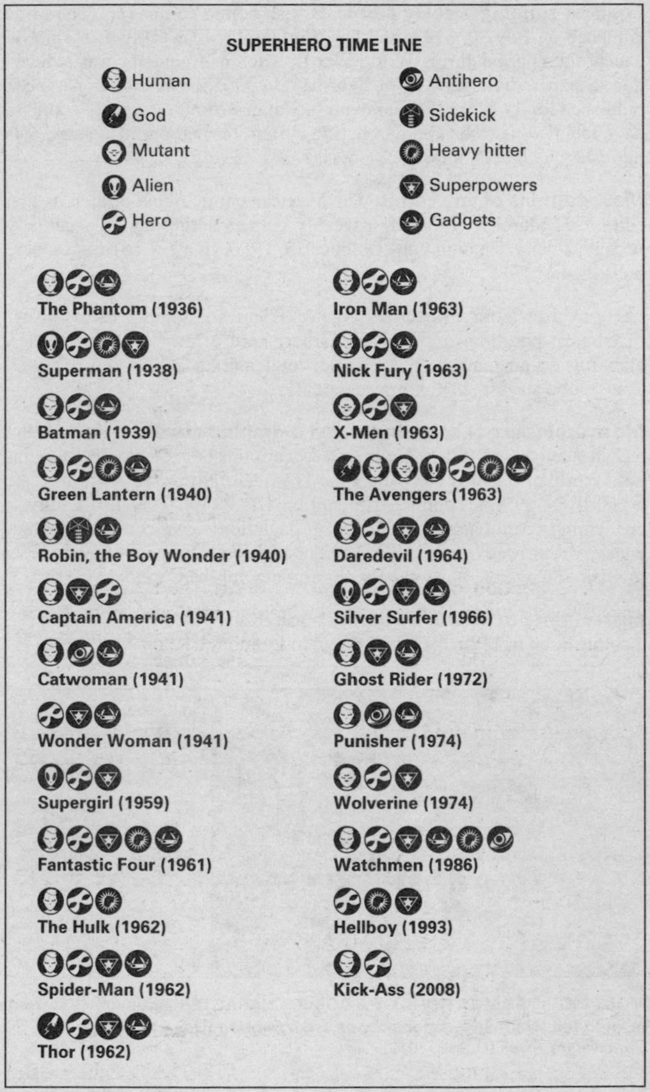

SUPERHERO TIME LINE

- 🦸 Human
- 🦸 God
- 🦸 Mutant
- 🦸 Alien
- 🦸 Hero

- 🦸 Antihero
- 🦸 Sidekick
- 🦸 Heavy hitter
- 🦸 Superpowers
- 🦸 Gadgets

🦸🦸🦸
The Phantom (1936)

🦸🦸🦸🦸
Superman (1938)

🦸🦸🦸
Batman (1939)

🦸🦸🦸🦸
Green Lantern (1940)

🦸🦸🦸
Robin, the Boy Wonder (1940)

🦸🦸🦸🦸
Captain America (1941)

🦸🦸🦸
Catwoman (1941)

🦸🦸🦸
Wonder Woman (1941)

🦸🦸🦸🦸
Supergirl (1959)

🦸🦸🦸🦸🦸
Fantastic Four (1961)

🦸🦸🦸
The Hulk (1962)

🦸🦸🦸🦸
Spider-Man (1962)

🦸🦸🦸🦸
Thor (1962)

🦸🦸🦸
Iron Man (1963)

🦸🦸🦸
Nick Fury (1963)

🦸🦸🦸
X-Men (1963)

🦸🦸🦸🦸🦸🦸🦸🦸
The Avengers (1963)

🦸🦸🦸🦸
Daredevil (1964)

🦸🦸🦸🦸
Silver Surfer (1966)

🦸🦸🦸
Ghost Rider (1972)

🦸🦸🦸
Punisher (1974)

🦸🦸🦸
Wolverine (1974)

🦸🦸🦸🦸🦸🦸
Watchmen (1986)

🦸🦸🦸
Hellboy (1993)

🦸🦸
Kick-Ass (2008)

Category	Winner	Details	
Best writer	Alan Moore (UK)	Nine-times winner, 1988–2006	
Best artist/penciller	P. Craig Russell and Steve Rude (both U.S.A.)	Four wins each	
Best painter/multimedia artist (interior art)	Alex Ross and Jill Thompson (both U.S.A.)	Five wins each	
Best letterer	Todd Klein (U.S.A.)	Has won 16 times since category opened in 1993	
Best cover artist	James Jean (U.S.A.)	Won six times consecutively between 2004 and 2009	

SMALLEST COMIC *Agent 327*, drawn and written by Martin Lodewijk (Netherlands), was published by Comicshop "Sjors" in June 1999. It measured just 1 x 1.4 in. (2.58 x 3.7 cm). Printed in full color with 100 lines per 0.4 in. (1 cm), 2,000 copies of the 16-page comic were made, each sold with a free magnifying glass.

Largest collection of comics in a museum The Serial and Government Publications Division of the Library of Congress in Washington, D.C., U.S.A., houses more than 5,000 titles and over 100,000 individual issues. The oldest comic book in the collection is *Popular Comics*, first published in February 1936.

Most movies from the work of a comic-book creator As of March 2012, the comic-book creations of Stan Lee (U.S.A.) have been adapted into Hollywood movies 15 times.

Largest auction of comic books On May 5 and 6, 2011, an auction of comic books, art, and comic-related memorabilia took place in New York City, U.S.A. Conducted by Heritage Auction Galleries, the auction raised U.S. $6,077,355.

AT THE MOVIES

Highest-grossing movie series As of July 19, 2011, the eight movies of the Harry Potter series had grossed U.S. $6,853,594,569 at the international box office. The first movie, *Harry Potter and the Sorcerer's Stone* (U.S.A./UK), came out in 2001.

HIGHEST-GROSSING MIDNIGHT SCREENING Directed by David Slade (UK), *The Twilight Saga: Eclipse* (U.S.A., 2010), the third movie in the *Twilight* series, opened with midnight screenings (including one in Los Angeles, U.S.A., right) on June 30, 2010, in over 4,000 U.S. movie theaters, grossing an estimated U.S. $30 million.

Oldest actor to receive an Oscar At the 84th Academy Awards on February 26, 2012, Christopher Plummer (Canada) won the Best Supporting Actor category for his role in *Beginners* (U.S.A., 2010). At the age of 82 years 65 days, this makes him the oldest ever winner of an acting Oscar.

MOST SUCCESSFUL FEATURE-FILM SPIN-OFF The Hasbro Transformers toy line first appeared on screen as a cartoon series in the 1980s. It has had three live-action feature-film spin-offs, the most successful being *Transformers: Dark of the Moon* (U.S.A., 2011), which had accumulated over U.S. $1 billion by the start of 2012. The movie also holds the record for the **most vehicles destroyed in the making of a movie**—532 automobiles were "totaled," easily surpassing the record of 150 held by *The Junkman* (U.S.A., 1982). According to director Michael Bay (U.S.A.), they were flood-damaged vehicles donated by the movie's insurance company: "By law, the cars have to be crushed. So I am a perfect guy to do that."

FACT: Technically, "dark of the Moon" is the last few days of the lunar cycle, when the night sky is devoid of moonlight.

HIGHEST-GROSSING OPENING WEEKEND
During the weekend of its domestic release on May 4–6, 2012, *The Avengers* (U.S.A., 2012) grossed U.S. $207,438,708, beating the record set by *Harry Potter and the Deathly Hallows: Part II* in 2011. The Marvel-inspired movie hit the U.S. $150-million mark within 48 hours of its release, grossing U.S. $150,371,975 by the end of Saturday May 5.

Longest red carpet at a première At the world première of *Harry Potter and the Deathly Hallows—Part 2* (U.S.A./UK, 2011) in London, UK, on July 7, 2011, Warner Bros. created a red carpet that stretched 1,492 ft. 9 in. (455 m) from Trafalgar Square to Leicester Square.

MOST . . .

Money lost by a movie Costing about U.S. $98 million (£63 million) to produce, and with a U.S. domestic gross of just U.S. $10,017,322 (£6,411,086), *Cutthroat Island* (U.S.A., 1995) made a net loss of U.S. $104,982,678 (£67,188,914).

"Original Screenplay" Oscar wins At the 84th Oscars ceremony in February 2012, Woody Allen (U.S.A.) won the best "Original Screenplay" award for *Midnight in Paris* (Spain/U.S.A., 2011), his third award in the category, following previous wins for his movies *Hannah and Her Sisters* (U.S.A., 1986) and *Annie Hall* (U.S.A., 1977). He also holds the record for the **most "Original Screenplay" nominations**, with 15.

"Razzie" nominations in a year Adam Sandler (U.S.A.) holds the dubious honor of having earned 11 separate nominations for the 2012 "Razzie" Awards (also known as the Golden Raspberries), reflecting his work as actor, producer, or screenwriter for such critically reviled 2011 movies as *Bucky Larson*, *Just Go with It*, and his cross-dressing comedy *Jack and Jill* (all U.S.A.).

MOST OSCAR NOMINATIONS FOR AN ACTRESS
Meryl Streep (U.S.A.) has been Oscar nominated 17 times. She's won three of them, including the 2012 Best Actress for playing former UK prime minister, Margaret Thatcher, in *The Iron Lady* (UK/France, 2011).

FACT: Jean Dujardin became the first French winner of the Best Actor Oscar for *The Artist* (France/Belgium, 2011).

HIGHEST-GROSSING LIMITED OPENING In its 425-movie theater U.S. opening weekend on December 16–18, 2011, *Mission: Impossible—Ghost Protocol* (U.S.A./UAE) grossed U.S. $13 million, the highest amount for an opening in fewer than 600 movie theaters. The record was previously held by *Bridget Jones: The Edge of Reason* (UK/France/Germany/Ireland/U.S.A., 2004).

Portrayed character in movies The Devil has been featured in 544 different movies as of March 2012. The second most common character is Santa Claus, with 303 portrayals; third is the Grim Reaper, with 290; fourth is Jesus Christ, with 239; and fifth is God, with 231. Count Dracula is the **most portrayed literary character on screen**, with 155 portrayals, followed by Sherlock Holmes, with 147.

Successful box-office month The release of *Harry Potter and the Deathly Hallows—Part 2* (U.S.A./UK), *Captain America*, *Transformers: Dark of the Moon*, and *Cars 2* (all U.S.A., 2011) helped to make July 2011 the highest-earning month at the worldwide box office, with ticket sales totaling U.S. $1,395,075,783.

Sequels released in one year During 2011, Hollywood broke its record for most sequels released in a calendar year. According to Box Office Mojo, 27 movies released in 2011 were sequels, beating the 24 released in 2003. That averages about one every other week and roughly one-fifth of total releases.

Product placements in a movie *POM Wonderful Presents: The Greatest Movie Ever Sold*, directed by Morgan Spurlock (U.S.A.) and released on April 22, 2011, had 3,463 product placements. The movie is a documentary about advertising and product placement, and, ironically, its finance came from advertising and product placement. The **greatest product placement return for a movie** is held by the James Bond movie *Die Another Day* (UK/U.S.A., 2002); it earned MGM £45 million (U.S. $71 million). In all, 20 companies had their product featured in the movie, including Ford, British Airways, Sony, and Finlandia Vodka.

Most wins by a film: 11

Ben-Hur (1959), *Titanic* (1997), *The Lord of the Rings: The Return of the King* (2003)

Films that have won the "Big Five" (Best Picture/Director/Actor/Actress/Screenplay): 3

• *It Happened One Night* (1934) Frank Capra/Clark Gable/Claudette Colbert/Robert Riskin

• *One Flew Over the Cuckoo's Nest* (1975) Miloš Forman/Jack Nicholson/Louise Fletcher/Lawrence Hauben and Bo Goldman

• *The Silence of the Lambs* (1991) Jonathan Demme/Anthony Hopkins/Jodie Foster/Ted Tally

Most Best Director: 4

John Ford for *The Informer* (1935), *The Grapes of Wrath* (1940), *How Green Was My Valley* (1941), *The Quiet Man* (1952)

Most Best Leading Actor: 2

Spencer Tracy, Fredric March, Gary Cooper, Marlon Brando, Dustin Hoffman, Tom Hanks, Jack Nicholson, Daniel Day-Lewis, Sean Penn

Most Best Leading Actress: 4

Katharine Hepburn for *Morning Glory* (1934), *Guess Who's Coming to Dinner* (1967), *The Lion in Winter* (1968), *On Golden Pond* (1981)

Most Best Cinematography: 4

• Leon Shamroy for *The Black Swan* (1942), *Wilson* (1944), *Leave Her to Heaven* (1945), *Cleopatra* (1963) • Joseph Ruttenberg for *The Great Waltz* (1938), *Mrs. Miniver* (1942), *Somebody Up There Likes Me* (1956), *Gigi* (1958)

Winner of both Best Actor/Actress and Best Screenplay: 1

Emma Thompson for *Howards End* (1992) and *Sense and Sensibility* (1995)

THE ACTING A-LIST

According to research published in 2011 by the U.S. media company Forbes, the highest-earning Hollywood actors and actresses are . . .

	Actor/actress	Yearly earnings (U.S. $)
01	Leonardo DiCaprio	$77 million
02	Johnny Depp	$50 million
03	Adam Sandler	$40 million
04	Will Smith	$36 million
05	Tom Hanks	$35 million
06	Ben Stiller	$34 million
07	Robert Downey, Jr.	$31 million
08 =	Angelina Jolie	$30 million
08 =	Sarah Jessica Parker	$30 million
10 =	Jennifer Aniston	$28 million
10 =	Mark Wahlberg	$28 million
10 =	Reese Witherspoon	$28 million

SFX characters portrayed As of May 6, 2011, Bill Blair (U.S.A.) had played 202 special-effects (SFX) characters in U.S. feature movies and TV shows. These include a caveman in *Dinosaur Valley Girls* (1996), a captured human pet in *Masked and Anonymous* (2003), a mummy in *Monster Night* (2006), zombies in *Voodoo Moon* (2006) and *Resident Evil: Afterlife* (2010), and assorted Klingons, Bajorans, Asoths, Cardassians, Vulcans, and Borgs in the TV series *Star Trek: Deep Space Nine* (1993–99).

BOX-OFFICE HITS

ANIME *Spirited Away* (Japan, 2001) U.S. $275 million

ANIMATION SERIES *Shrek* (U.S.A., 2001–07) U.S. $2.2 billion *total gross*

FANTASY *The Lord of the Rings: The Return of the King* (U.S.A./New Zealand, 2003) U.S. $1.1 billion

DISASTER *2012* (U.S.A., 2009) U.S. $770 million

BOND *Casino Royale* (UK/Czech Republic/U.S.A./Germany/The Bahamas, 2006) U.S. $587.6 million

CRIME *Ocean's Eleven* (U.S.A., 2001) U.S. $451 million

VIDEO GAME SPIN-OFF *Prince of Persia: The Sands of Time* (U.S.A., 2010) U.S. $326.8 million

GANGSTER *The Departed* (U.S.A./Hong Kong, 2006) U.S. $290 million

ZOMBIE *Resident Evil: Afterlife* (Germany/France/U.S.A., 2010) U.S. $296 million

HORROR *The Twilight Saga: New Moon* (U.S.A., 2009) U.S. $710 million

THE ULTIMATE BLOCKBUSTER

The movies on these pages grossed more than any other movie in their genre. But what elements should the ideal blockbuster include? GWR has created a composite movie that *should* be box-office gold. The calculations are based on the *average* box-office grosses for the most successful movies and moviemakers since 1995.*

 GENRE: Superhero **Gross:** U.S. $131.7 million

 DIRECTOR: Steven Spielberg (U.S.A.) **Gross:** U.S. $150.9 million

 PRODUCER: David Heyman (UK) **Gross:** U.S. $192.7 million

 LEAD ACTOR: Daniel Radcliffe (UK) **Gross:** U.S. $244.4 million

 LEAD ACTRESS: Emma Watson (UK) **Gross:** U.S. $245.6 million

 SCREENPLAY: George Lucas (U.S.A.) **Gross:** U.S. $224.9 million

 COMPOSER: John Williams (U.S.A.) **Gross:** U.S. $139 million

 PRODUCTION METHOD: Animation/live action **Gross:** U.S. $138.4 million

 DISTRIBUTED BY: DreamWorks SKG **Gross:** U.S. $77.7 million

 RATED: PG-13 **Gross:** U.S. $42.3 million

 SOURCE: Comic/graphic novel **Gross:** U.S. $86.5 million

 RELEASE TIME: summer

* *Sources: the-numbers.com; boxofficemojo.com. The box-office figure for each category is based on a minimum of 10 movies.*

ANIMATION *Toy Story 3* (U.S.A., 2010) U.S. $1.063 billion

SCI-FI (AND HIGHEST-GROSSING MOVIE OF ALL TIME) *Avatar* (U.S.A./UK, 2009) U.S. $2.71 billion

SILENT *The Artist* (France/Belgium, 2011) U.S. $105.5 million

POST-APOCALYPTIC *I Am Legend* (U.S.A., 2007) U.S. $585 million

MUSICAL *Mamma Mia!* (U.S.A./UK/Germany, 2008) U.S. $610 million

HIGH-SCHOOL COMEDY *Superbad* (U.S.A., 2007) U.S. $170 million

SUPERHERO *The Dark Knight* (U.S.A./UK, 2008) U.S. $1.002 billion

MARTIAL ARTS *The Karate Kid* (U.S.A./China, 2010) U.S. $359 million

SPY *The Bourne Ultimatum* (U.S.A./Germany, 2007) U.S. $443 million

SWASHBUCKLER *Pirates of the Caribbean: Dead Man's Chest* (U.S.A., 2006) U.S. $1.066 billion

COMEDY *The Hangover: Part II* (U.S.A., 2011) U.S. $581 million

FOREIGN LANGUAGE *The Passion of the Christ* (U.S.A., 2004) U.S. $604.3 million

PICK OF THE POPS

First solo artist to have three No. 1 U.S. albums before the age of 18 Justin Bieber (Canada, b. March 1, 1994) claimed three chart-topping U.S. albums before reaching his 18th birthday: the singer's *My World 2.0* made its debut at No. 1 on April 10, 2010, with first-week sales of 283,000, *Never Say Never: The Remixes* made its chart-topping entrance on March 5, 2011, with sales of 165,000, and *Under the Mistletoe* was the first Christmas album by a male artist to debut at No. 1 on the U.S. albums chart. *Under the Mistletoe* topped the countdown on November 19, 2011 after first-week sales of 210,000.

First artist to win two Mercury Music Prizes *Let England Shake*, the eighth studio album by UK alternative rock singer PJ Harvey, claimed the prestigious Mercury Music Prize on September 6, 2011, making her the only artist to win the award twice in its 20-year history. In 2001, Harvey became the first female to take home the prize with her fifth studio effort, *Stories from the City, Stories from the Sea*.

Most simultaneous hits on UK singles chart (solo female) On February 25, 2012, Whitney Houston (U.S.A.) had 12 new entries in the top 75, including three tracks in the top 40: "I Will Always Love You" (No. 14), "I Wanna Dance with Somebody (Who Loves Me)" (No. 20), and "One Moment in Time" (No. 40). The record-breaking artist was found dead at the Beverly Hilton Hotel in Beverly Hills, California, U.S.A., on February 11, 2012.

YOUNGEST CHART ENTRANT (U.S.A.) The "breathing, cries, and coos" of Blue Ivy Carter, the daughter of Beyoncé and Jay-Z (both U.S.A.), appeared on Jay-Z's track "Glory." It charted just days after her birth on January 7, 2012.

FIRST FEMALE WITH FIVE NO. 1 U.S. SINGLES FROM ONE ALBUM When "Last Friday Night (T.G.I.F.)" followed "California Gurls," "Teenage Dream," "Firework," and "E.T." to the singles chart summit in August 2011, it gave singer Katy Perry (U.S.A., b. Katheryn Hudson) a fifth U.S. chart-topper from her No. 1 album *Teenage Dream*. The only other artist to achieve five U.S. No. 1 singles from one album is Michael Jackson (U.S.A.), who notched up five No. 1s from his 1987 album *Bad*.

First UK group to debut at No. 1 in U.S.A. with debut album

UK boy band One Direction (Niall Horan, Zayn Malik, Liam Payne, Harry Styles, and Louis Tomlinson) became the first UK group to make a chart-topping bow on the *Billboard* 200 albums chart, with *Up All Night*'s first-week sales of 176,000 on March 31, 2012. The band finished third in the 2010 series of talent show *The X Factor* (UK, 2004–present).

Most simultaneous tracks on U.S. singles chart by a solo artist

Grammy-winning American rapper Lil Wayne (b. Dwayne Carter, Jr., aka Weezy) placed an unprecedented 12 tracks on the *Billboard* Hot 100 on September 17, 2011. Weezy scored eight new entries to add to his four existing Hot 100 entries in the same week his *Tha Carter IV* album debuted at No. 1 on the *Billboard* 200.

Fastest-selling U.S. digital album

Lady Gaga's (U.S.A., b. Stefani Germanotta) *Born this Way* is the fastest-selling digital album in Nielsen SoundScan history (that is, since March 1991, when accurate sales figures were introduced in the U.S.A.), generating 662,000 first-week sales to debut at No. 1 on June 11, 2011. *Born this Way*—the **first album to debut in a social network game** (*GagaVille*)—sold 1.1 million copies in its first week (retailing on Amazon for just 99 cents).

LONGEST GAP BETWEEN TOP 10 ALBUMS (UK) When Leonard Cohen (Canada) debuted at No. 2 on February 11, 2012 with his 12th studio album, *Old Ideas*, it was his first showing in the top 10 since *Songs of Love and Hate* in 1971.

ADELE-UGE OF RECORDS

Adele has been sweeping up records since *21* was released in January 2011. Here are some of them:

Biggest-selling UK album by a solo female By April 7, 2012, *21* had sold 4,181,000 in the UK.

Biggest-selling UK album artist in one year In 2011, *21* sold 3,772,346 units and *19* sold 1,207,600 units—4,979,946 units in total.

Biggest-selling U.S. digital track in one year "Rolling in the Deep," the lead single from *21*, was downloaded 5.81 million times in 2011.

Fastest album to reach U.S. digital sales of one million *21* registered 1 million U.S. digital sales on July 16, 2011, just 19 weeks after its No. 1 debut on March 12, 2011.

BIGGEST-SELLING DIGITAL ALBUM IN U.S.A. AND UK Adele (UK, b. Adele Adkins) raised the bar for digital album sales in both the U.S.A. and the UK in 2011. Within five months of its February 2011 release, *21* had eclipsed Eminem's *Recovery* as the biggest-selling digital album in U.S. chart history, with sales of 1.1 million units. By the end of the year, sales were 1.8 million. In the UK, *21*'s digital sales rose to more than 700,000 in 2011, replacing Lady Gaga's *The Fame* as the biggest-selling UK digital album.

YOUNGEST MALE TO ENTER U.S. ALBUMS CHART AT NO. 1 Scotty McCreery (U.S.A.), winner of the 10th season of *American Idol*, was 18 years 13 days old when he made his albums chart bow with *Clear as Day* on October 22, 2011. McCreery, the sixth *American Idol* contestant to crown the *Billboard* 200, was also the first country artist to enter at No. 1 with a debut studio album.

FACT: *Clear as Day* sold 197,000 copies in week one to debut at the top of the albums chart.

YOUTUBE SENSATIONS

Here are the top 10 most viewed music videos on YouTube. The total number of views (y axis) are charted over time (x axis) to show how rapidly the songs reached their total viewing figures. Also listed are the numbers of "likes" and "dislikes" for each. Data sourced on March 24, 2012.

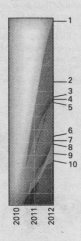

4 Lady Gaga "Bad Romance" (2009) 454,870,832 views 584,025 likes 128,366 dislikes

5 Eminem feat. Rihanna "Love the Way You Lie" (2010) 444,146,358 views 992,029 likes 30,984 dislikes

6 Eminem "Not Afraid" (2010) 326,439,734 views 1,061,097 likes 27,102 dislikes

7 Don Omar feat. Lucenzo—"Danza Kuduro" (2010/11) 325,290,637 views 405,014 likes 29,529 dislikes

8 Justin Bieber feat. Jaden Smith "Never Say Never" (2010/11) 307,746,944 views 549,818 likes 241,697 dislikes

9 Justin Bieber "One Time" (2009/10) 288,637,158 views 400,707 likes 391,432 dislikes

10 Miley Cyrus "Party in the U.S.A." (2009) 277,926,168 views 443,677 likes 99,653 dislikes

1 Justin Bieber feat. Ludacris "Baby" (2010) 720,028,324 views 1,139,137 likes 2,383,464 dislikes

2 Jennifer Lopez feat. Pitbull "On the Floor" (2011) 512,466,800 views 929,039 likes 71,191 dislikes

3 Shakira feat. Freshlyground "Waka Waka (This Time for Africa)" (2010) 456,150,127 views 471,495 likes 25,877 dislikes

FACT: Madonna's Super Bowl performance attracted more viewers than the game itself!

BIGGEST TV AUDIENCE FOR A SUPER BOWL ACT A record 114 million people watched Madonna's (U.S.A., b. Madonna Ciccone) half-time show at Super Bowl XLVI, at Lucas Oil Stadium, Indianapolis, Indiana, U.S.A., on February 5, 2012. The performance also featured UK rapper M.I.A. (b. Mathangi Arulpragasam) and U.S. hip-hop star Nicki Minaj (b. Onika Minaj) on Madonna's new single, "Give Me All Your Luvin'."

BIGGEST-SELLING U.S. DIGITAL ARTIST By the end of 2011, Rihanna (Barbados, b. Robyn Rihanna Fenty) had sold an incredible 47.57 million digital tracks in the U.S.A., according to sales tracked by Nielsen SoundScan. The 24-year-old singer, who made her debut in 2005, held off The Black Eyed Peas (42.4 million career digital sales), Eminem (42.29 million), Lady Gaga (42.08 million), and Taylor Swift (41.82 million).

Fastest-selling rock concerts in UK history On October 21, 2011, The Stone Roses (UK) sold 220,000 tickets in 68 minutes for their three comeback gigs at Heaton Park in Manchester, UK, on June 29–July 1, 2012. A total of 150,000 tickets for the first two concerts were bought in just 14 minutes from 9:30 a.m.; 70,000 tickets for the third date were made available at 10 a.m. and sold out in 38 minutes. The event grossed over £12 million (U.S. $19.04 million) in ticket sales.

HIGHEST-GROSSING TOUR U2's (Ireland) mammoth 360° world tour grossed U.S. $736,137,344 from 110 shows between June 30, 2009, and July 30, 2011, as 7,268,430 fans enjoyed the spectacle.

ROCK OF AGES

Most consecutive U.S. No. 1 singles Whitney Houston (U.S.A., 1963–2012) achieved seven consecutive No. 1 singles on the *Billboard* Hot 100 between 1985 and 1988: "Saving All My Love for You" (1985), "How Will I Know" (1986), "Greatest Love of All" (1986), "I Wanna Dance with Somebody (Who Loves Me)" (1987), "Didn't We Almost Have it All" (1987), "So Emotional" (1987), and "Where Do Broken Hearts Go" (1988).

The Grammy-winning soundtrack to the blockbuster movie *The Bodyguard* (1992), in which Houston starred, remains the **best-selling soundtrack**, with more than 44 million copies sold worldwide. The album, which has been certified for shipments of 17 million copies in the U.S.A. alone, spent 20 nonconsecutive weeks at No. 1 between December 12, 1992, and May 29, 1993.

First video on MTV The first music video aired on the Music Television network (based in New York City, U.S.A., and launched on August 1, 1981) was the appropriately titled "Video Killed the Radio Star," a UK No. 1 single for The Buggles (UK) in 1979.

The first video seen on MTV Europe, launched on August 1, 1987, was "Money for Nothing" by Dire Straits (UK), which topped the *Billboard* Hot 100 in 1985. The track starts and ends with the lyric: "I want my MTV."

BEST-SELLING SINGLE Bing Crosby's (U.S.A.) "White Christmas" has sold an estimated 50 million copies worldwide. Written by Irving Berlin (U.S.A.) in 1940, it reached No. 1 in the U.S.A. in October 1942, where it remained for 11 consecutive weeks.

The record for the **most cumulative weeks on the U.S. chart (one album)** is held by Pink Floyd's (UK) 1973 album *The Dark Side of the Moon*. On April 28, 2012, it recorded its 802nd week—more than 15 years—on the *Billboard* 200.

FACT: Claims on the internet that *Dark Side* was written as a soundtrack for *The Wizard of Oz* are denied by the band!

A. The **first album to debut at No. 1 in the U.S.A.** was *Captain Fantastic and the Brown Dirt Cowboy* by Elton John (UK, b. Reginald Dwight), which hit the top spot on June 7, 1975. The second album to go straight to No. 1 was Elton's next album, *Rock of the Westies*.

B. ABBA (Sweden), along with Led Zeppelin (UK), see next page, hold the record for the **most successive UK No. 1 albums**, with eight. ABBA first ascended to No. 1 with their *Greatest Hits* collection, above, in May 1976 and scored their eighth consecutive chart-topper with *The Singles—The First Ten Years* in November 1982.

C. The Beatles (UK) hold the record for the **most consecutive weeks at No. 1 on the UK albums chart (group, one album)**, with their chart debut *Please Please Me* (1963). It topped the chart for 30 weeks from May 11 to November 30, 1963.

D. Released in November 1982, *Thriller* by Michael Jackson (U.S.A., 1958–2009) is the world's **biggest-selling album**. Sales figures vary, but *Thriller* has definitely exceeded the 65-million mark.

Largest rock concert TV audience On July 13, 1985, an estimated global audience of 1.9 billion people in 150 countries watched the dual-venue Live Aid charity concerts to raise money for famine-hit Ethiopia. Organized by musicians Bob Geldof (Ireland) and Midge Ure (UK), the event was broadcast simultaneously from Wem-

FIRST SINGLE TO SELL ONE MILLION COPIES In 1955, "Rock Around the Clock" by Bill Haley and the Comets (U.S.A.) became the UK's first million-selling single. It is also the only single to return to the top 20 on five separate occasions.

A. Fleetwood Mac's *Rumours* has spent the **most weeks on the UK albums chart**. Between February 26, 1977, and April 28, 2012, the album racked up 490 weeks in the top 75 (the chart was a top 100 from 1981 to 1989).

B. Oasis (UK) claimed the record for the **fastest-selling album in UK chart history** when their third studio album, *Be Here Now*, sold 663,389 copies in just three days on August 21–23, 1997, including 350,000 copies on the first day. The album sold its millionth copy 17 days after its release.

C. Led Zeppelin (UK) share with ABBA (Sweden), see previous page, the record for the **most successive UK No. 1 albums**, with eight. Led Zeppelin's chart-topping run began with *Led Zeppelin II*, above, in February 1970 and concluded with *In Through the Out Door*—recorded at ABBA's Polar Studios in Stockholm, Sweden—in September 1979.

D. Released on March 21, 2000, *No Strings Attached* by *NSync (U.S.A.), the group that introduced Justin Timberlake to the world, is the **fastest-selling album in the U.S.A.** It shifted a staggering 2.42 million copies in its first week, more than doubling the 1.13 million copies sold by Backstreet Boys' *Millennium* in 1999.

bley Stadium in London, UK, and John F. Kennedy Stadium in Philadelphia, Pennsylvania, U.S.A., and featured many of the biggest names in rock including The Beach Boys, David Bowie, Bob Dylan, Elton John, Led Zeppelin, Paul McCartney, Queen, and U2. The concerts raised about £40 million (then U.S. $50 million).

> **FACT:** As a youngster, future *NSync member Justin Timberlake performed at beauty pageants.

Most UK No. 1 versions of the same song Four different versions of "Unchained Melody" have topped the UK chart. Jimmy Young (UK, 1955), The Righteous Brothers (U.S.A., 1990), Robson Green and Jerome Flynn (UK, 1995), and Gareth Gates (UK, 2002) have all scored No. 1s with this 1955 ballad written by Alex North and Hy Zaret (both U.S.A.).

Most simultaneous hits on UK singles chart (group) Two months after The Jam (UK) announced their split in December 1982, the New Wave trio's entire singles back catalog was reissued. Thirteen tracks reached the top 75 on February 5, 1983, most notably the double A-side "Going Underground"/"Dreams of Children" at No. 21.

Most charts topped with one album Released on November 14, 2005, *Confessions on a Dance Floor* by Madonna (U.S.A.), topped charts in 40 countries around the world. The lead single, "Hung Up," reached No. 1 in the singles charts of 41 countries.

Most No. 1 singles In little more than six years, between 1964 and 1970, The Beatles (UK) crowned the *Billboard* Hot 100 a record 20 times, including six times in 1964 and four in 1965. Their first No. 1 was "I Want to Hold Your Hand" in January 1964 and their last "The Long and Winding Road" in June 1970.

First group inducted into the Songwriters Hall of Fame Queen (Freddie Mercury [b. Zanzibar], Brian May, Roger Taylor, and John Deacon, all UK) were the first complete group inducted into the Songwriters Hall of Fame, in 2003. The first induction ceremony was staged in 1969, and 389 individuals have been inducted since then.

THEATER

First permanent theater The Theater of Dionysius was the world's oldest theater, built in ancient Athens in approximately 500 B.C. With an estimated capacity of up to 17,000 people, the outdoor theater was "in the round," with stone rows built up a slope overlooking the stage.

Both tragedies and comedies were performed there and it was used for "competitions," in which the audience served as judges to vote for a prize for best play.

Oldest indoor theater The Teatro Olimpico in Vicenza, Italy, was designed in the Roman style by Andrea di Pietro, alias Palladio (1508–80). Work on the theater began three months before his death and was finished by his pupil Vicenzo Scamozzi in 1583. It is preserved today in its original form.

Largest theater The Great Auditorium is part of the Great Hall of the People (Renmin Dahuitang) in Tiananmen Square, Beijing, China, which was completed in 1959. The Auditorium is 249 ft. (76 m) long, 196 ft. (60 m) wide, and 108 ft. (33 m) high. When used as a theater, it seats 10,000.

The **smallest regularly operated professional theater** is the Kremlhof theater in Villach, Austria, which has a maximum capacity of eight seats. It is jointly run by the organizations VADA and kärnöl (both Austria) and has hosted regular performances since January 12, 2010.

LONGEST THEATRICAL RUN As of April 23, 2012, there have been 24,757 continuous performances of *The Mousetrap* by Dame Agatha Christie (UK). The show opened at the Ambassadors Theatre in London's West End on November 25, 1952, transferring to St. Martin's Theatre in 1974. The legendary whodunit will mark its diamond anniversary (60 years) on November 25, 2012.

MOST EXPENSIVE THEATER PRODUCTION By the time *Spider-Man: Turn Off the Dark*, the musical based on the legendary comic superhero, opened on June 14, 2011 at the Foxwoods Theatre on Broadway, its cost had climbed to U.S. $75 million. It is the largest investment for a theatrical production anywhere in the world. With 182 previews (performances before an official opening) from November 28, 2010, until its official opening on June 14, 2011, it has also registered the **most previews for a Broadway show.**

Largest theater stage The Hilton Theater at the Reno Hilton in Reno, Nevada, U.S.A., measures 175 × 241 ft. (53.3 × 73.4 m). The stage has three main lifts, each of which can raise 1,200 performers (up to a total weight of 143,961 lb./65.3 metric tonnes), as well as two turntables, each with a circumference of 62 ft. 6 in. (19.1 m).

Largest theater cast A total of 2,100 children appeared in the finale of the *Rolf Harris Schools Variety Spectacular* held at Sydney Entertainment Centre, Sydney, Australia, in November 1985.

Oldest national theater Founded in 1680 by Louis XIV of France, the Comédie Française is the oldest national theater in the world. During the French Revolution of 1789, the theater's company split: the conservatives went to the Théatre de la Nation, while the more revolutionary actors be-

came the Théatre de la République at the Palais Royal. In 1803, the Comédie Française was reformed and has remained in existence ever since.

AGILE AYCKBOURN Sir Alan's writing output has also encompassed 2 short, one-act plays, 11 revues, 7 plays for children, 5 adaptations (also full length plays), 1 screenplay, and 1 book, *The Crafty Art of Playmaking*.

HIGHEST WEEKLY GROSS FOR A ONE-MAN SHOW ON BROADWAY
Hugh Jackman (Australia) grossed U.S. $2,057,354 during the holiday week December 27, 2011–January 1, 2012, performing *Hugh Jackman, Back on Broadway* at the Broadhurst Theater in New York City, U.S.A.

Jackman also took the record for the **most money raised for a charity by a Broadway show**: U.S. $1,789,580 for Broadway Cares/Equity Fights AIDS.

Best-selling playwright English playwright William Shakespeare (1564–1616) is the world's best-selling playwright, with sales of his plays and poetry thought to have exceeded 4 billion copies since his death. He is also the third most translated author in history, behind Agatha Christie (UK) and Jules Verne (France).

The **most valuable edition of a Shakespeare work** is one of only five copies of the First Folio, dated 1623, which was sold at Christie's in New York City, U.S.A., on October 8, 2001, for U.S. $6,166,000. It is also the highest price ever paid for a 17th-century book.

Longest solo theatrical performance Adrian Hilton (UK) recited the complete works of Shakespeare in 110 hr. 46 min. in a "Bardathon" at the Shakespeare Festival in London and Gold Hill Baptist Church in Chalfont St. Peter (both UK) on July 16–21, 1987.

YOUR TICKET TO BROADWAY

• New York's world-renowned Broadway Theater District includes Times Square and stretches from West 41st Street to West 54th Street, between 6th Avenue (Avenue of the Americas) and 8th Avenue. It includes 39 professional theaters.

• Its nickname, the "Great White Way," alludes to the district's adoption of electric advertising signs and lighting in the late 19th century.

• "Off Broadway" theaters usually have between 100 and 499 seats. Even smaller professional productions can be seen in "Off Off Broadway" venues seating under 100. The smallest Broadway theater has 650 seats.

AND THE WINNER IS . . .

The UK's Laurence Olivier Awards and the U.S.A.'s Tony Awards are benchmarks of theatrical excellence. GWR raises the curtain on the most lauded performers and productions.

Most Tony Awards for a play *The Coast of Utopia*, by Tom Stoppard (UK)—7

Performer with the most Tony Award nominations Julie Harris (U.S.A.)—10

Most Tony Awards for an actor Boyd Gaines (U.S.A.)—4

Most Tony Awards for an actor/actress in performance Julie Harris (U.S.A.) and Angela Lansbury (U.S.A., b. UK)—5 (Julie Harris also has a Lifetime Achievement Tony)

Most Tony Awards (individual) Harold Prince (U.S.A.)—21

Most Tony Awards for a composer Stephen Sondheim (U.S.A.)—8

Most Olivier Awards for a show *Matilda the Musical*, from the book by Roald Dahl (UK)—7

Most Olivier Awards for an actor Sir Ian McKellen (UK)—6

Most Olivier Awards for an actress Dame Judi Dench (UK)—7 (including the Special Award for Outstanding Contributions to the British Theatre)

Most Olivier Awards (individual) Dame Judi Dench and designer William Dudley (both UK)—7

Usually, GWR considers only world records. London's West End and New York's Broadway are such cornerstones of the theater, however, that we have also included records specific to those districts.

Longest continually operating theatrical management organization The Theatrical Management Association (TMA) was founded in London, UK, 108 years ago, on January 24, 1894, although initially under a variant of this name. The great English actor-managers Sir Henry Irving and Sir Herbert Beerbohm Tree were among its creators, with Irving becoming the organization's first president.

Oldest opera The Chinese form of opera, *Kunqu*, appeared in the 14th century during the Yuan Dynasty (1271–1368). It combined opera with ballet, drama, and the recitation of poetry and music, drawing on earlier Chinese theatrical forms, such as mime and acrobatics. "Kun" refers to Kunshan (the district where the opera originated, near Suzhou, in modern Jiangsu Province, China) and "qu" means music.

Most prolific contemporary playwright Sir Alan Ayckbourn (UK) has written 76 full-length plays since 1959. His first full work, *The Square Cat*, debuted at the Library Theatre in Scarborough, North Yorkshire, UK, when Ayckbourn was just 20. His latest play, *Surprises*, is due to debut in 2012. He has had a new full-length play produced nearly every year for more than 53 years. Only six of those years have not seen the premiere of a new Ayckbourn play.

Most performances in one Broadway show George Lee Andrews (U.S.A.) gave 9,382 performances in the Broadway staging of *The Phantom of the Opera*. The show opened on January 26, 1988, at the Majestic Theater with Andrews in the cast, and he played several roles in the show until September 3, 2011.

Longest-running show on Broadway The Andrew Lloyd Webber (UK) musical *The Phan-*

tom of the Opera is the longest-running show in the history of Broadway—musical or play—having reached the milestone 10,000 performances at the Majestic Theater in New York, U.S.A., on February 11, 2012.

The **longest-running musical in London's West End** is *Les Misérables* by Claude-Michel Schönberg (France), which opened on December 4, 1985, and is currently in its 27th year. It celebrated its 10,000th performance on January 5, 2010.

TV

Most widely viewed factual program Airing in 212 different territories worldwide, the UK's *Top Gear* (BBC) is the most widely viewed factual program on television. The motoring show began in 1977 and relaunched in 2002. It is currently hosted by Jeremy Clarkson, Richard Hammond, and James May (all UK).

First regular TV broadcasts At 3 p.m. on November 2, 1936, in London, UK, the BBC launched the world's first regular public television broadcasts. However, experimental services had operated across the world from the 1920s.

First TV broadcaster to show a live sporting event in 3D BSkyB was the first TV broadcaster to relay a sporting event live in 3D. On January 31, 2010, it screened a soccer match between Arsenal and Manchester United in 3D via its Sky Sports platform to a public audience in selected pubs in the UK.

First TV sitcom Character actor James Hayter (UK) starred as J. Pinwright, owner of the smallest multiple store in the world, in the first television sitcom *Pinwright's Progress* (BBC, 1946–47).

HIGHEST-RATED TV SERIES (CURRENT) The Metacritic website assembles ratings for movies, TV shows, music, and games releases from several sources and provides an average value for each. As of March 9, 2012, the fourth season of *Southland* (TNT)—starring Michael Cudlitz and Lucy Liu, pictured left—registered the highest ratings for a current show, with a score of 90/100. The **highest-rated TV series of all time** was season four of Baltimore-based crime show *The Wire* (HBO), which scored 98/100.

Longest-running sitcom (episode count) The current (and, in fact, all-time) longest-running sitcom on U.S. television is *The Simpsons* (Fox), which completed its 23rd series in spring 2012. The show debuted on December 17, 1989, and its 500th episode was broadcast on February 19, 2012. Doh!

MOST WATCHED MAN ON TV Actor David Hasselhoff (U.S.A.) is the most watched man in television history. Having debuted as the eponymous hero of the popular U.S. series *Knight Rider* (NBC), he went on to star as LA County lifeguard Mitch Buchannon in the series *Baywatch* (NBC), which, at its peak in 1996, had an estimated weekly audience of 1.1 billion viewers.

HIGHEST-PAID COMEDY ACTOR As of 2011, Ashton Kutcher (U.S.A., center left) earned U.S. $700,000 per episode for sitcom *Two and a Half Men* (CBS), making him TV's highest-paid comedy actor. He replaced previous record holder Charlie Sheen (U.S.A.).

FACT: Sheen had earned as much as U.S. $1.2 million per episode on the same show.

Longest-running TV variety show *Sábado Gigante* (Univision Television Network) is a Spanish-language U.S. TV variety show that has been broadcast every Saturday evening since August 8, 1962. It was created—and has been continually hosted—by Mario Kreutzberger (Chile), more popularly known as "Don Francisco." Each three-hour episode is filmed in front of a live audience.

Longest marathon TV talk show Lasting 52 hours, the longest marathon TV talk show took place on Channel 5 (Ukraine) from August 23 to August 25, 2011. The hosts were Pavlo Kuzheyev and Tetiana Danylenko (both Ukraine) at the Channel 5 Studio in Kiev, Ukraine.

Most durable TV presenter Sir Patrick Moore (UK) has hosted the monthly UK series *The Sky at Night* (BBC) since the first edition aired in 1957. The series is also the **longest-running TV show presented by the same host**.

Longest TV career by an entertainer (male) Sir Bruce Forsyth (UK) made his TV debut in 1939 as an 11-year-old on the BBC (UK) show *Come and Be Televised* and hosted his first show, *Sunday Night at the London Palladium* (ATV/ITV, UK), in 1958. His most recent TV appearance was on December 25, 2011, when he co-hosted the BBC's *Strictly Come Dancing Christmas Special*, giving him a TV career of 72 years.

Most expensive TV commercial A four-minute feature film made by director Baz Luhrmann (Australia) advertising Chanel No. 5 perfume is the world's most expensive TV advertisement, costing U.S. $33 mil-

MOST EXPENSIVE TV SERIES Screened in late 2011, Steven Spielberg's 13-part series *Terra Nova* (Fox, 2011) carried a U.S. $70-million price tag—that's around U.S. $200,000 for each minute of action. Not far behind were the HBO giants *Game of Thrones*—U.S. $60 million for its first series—and *Boardwalk Empire*—U.S. $50 million per series.

FACT: The pilot episode of *Boardwalk Empire* cost U.S. $18 million alone!

---

lion to produce. It premiered on U.S. TV on November 11, 2004, and starred Nicole Kidman (Australia) as a Marilyn Monroe–style actress who is hounded by paparazzi. Kidman, who wore couture outfits by designer Karl Lagerfeld in the ad, was paid U.S. $3.7 million for her appearance (the **highest fee for a TV commercial**).

Highest advertising rates for a TV show Excluding specials and one-off sporting events, the costliest television series for advertising slots is currently *American Idol* (Fox), during which a 30-second advertisement will cost U.S. $623,000, earning the show a healthy U.S. $7 million every 30 minutes. However, the hour-long final episode of *Friends* (NBC) holds the all-time record for a TV series, costing advertisers U.S. $2 million per 30 seconds on May 6, 2004.

HIGHEST-PAID TV ACTRESS Eva Longoria (above left) of *Desperate Housewives* (ABC), which finished in 2012, and Tina Fey (above) of *30 Rock* (NBC) each earned a record U.S. $13 million a season. Fey's salary also includes her writing fees.

TV'S TOP GENRES

In 2009, we all broke records by watching more TV than ever before, a global average of 3 hr. 12 min. per day! But what were we watching?

Fiction (42%)	Entertainment (38%)	Factual (20%)
Series (63%)	*Event (30%)*	*News (52%)*
Movies (12%)	*Reality show (28%)*	*Magazine (27%)*
Soap operas (12%)	*Variety show (18%)*	*Politics (10%)*
Telenovelas (9%)	*Game show (12%)*	*Documentary (9%)*
Cartoons (2%)	*Talk show (7%)*	*Religious (1%)*
TV movies (2%)	*Comedy (5%)*	
Sitcoms (1%)		

Source: International Television Expert Group (2009 figures)

MOST EXPENSIVE GAME SHOW The most expensive TV game show ever was the UK's *Red or Black* (ITV), devised by Simon Cowell (UK, *see below*) and hosted by Ant & Dec (aka Anthony McPartlin and Declan Donnelly, both UK, pictured). The program was stripped—that is, shown on consecutive nights—across seven nights in September 2011, and four contestants each walked away with £1 million (U.S. $1.5 million). The budget for the show was £15 million (U.S. $23 million).

Highest annual earnings for a TV talent show judge His appearances as a judge on the television shows *Pop Idol* (UK), *American Idol* (U.S.A.), and *The X Factor* (UK) have made Simon Cowell (UK) the highest-paid TV talent show judge. He earned £56.7 million (U.S. $90 million) in 2010–11 according to *Forbes*.

Highest-paid TV cast The cast of *The Sopranos* (HBO), a New Jersey–based Mob drama, earned a combined salary of U.S. $52 million for their work on the show's seventh series. According to *Forbes'* Celebrity 100 list, James Gandolfini (U.S.A.), who played the Mob boss Tony Soprano, secured himself a fee of U.S. $1 million for each of the last eight episodes.

Highest annual earnings ever for a television actor *Seinfeld* star Jerry Seinfeld (U.S.A.) made an estimated U.S. $267 million in 1998 according to the 1999 *Forbes* Celebrity 100 list.

STAR WARS

Highest average box-office gross for a director The six feature movies directed by George Lucas, from *THX 1138* (U.S.A., 1971) to *Star Wars: Episode III—Revenge of the Sith* (U.S.A., 2005), have grossed a total of U.S. $1.74 billion at the box office, at an average of U.S. $290.6 million per movie.

(Of those movie directors who have made 10 movies or more, U.S. director Steven Spielberg has the highest average box-office gross; see p. 420.)

LARGEST FORTUNE MADE FROM A MOVIE FRANCHISE Instead of taking a director's fee for *Star Wars* (U.S.A., 1977), George Lucas (U.S.A.) acquired the rights to all sequels and future merchandise. In 2011, Forbes assigned him a net worth of U.S. $3.2 billion.

The 15 movies *written* by George Lucas have grossed U.S. $3.33 billion in global box-office receipts, the **highest box-office gross for a screenwriter**.

Highest-grossing space-opera movie *Star Wars: Episode I—The Phantom Menace* (U.S.A., 1999) had grossed U.S. $924 million worldwide by February 3, 2000.

Largest simultaneous premiere—territories *Star Wars: Episode III—Revenge of the Sith* (U.S.A., 2005) was released simultaneously in 115 territories by 20th Century Fox on May 19, 2005. It went on to secure an international gross of U.S. $303 million.

Most Oscars won for visual effects Dennis Muren (U.S.A.) won the Academy Award for Visual Effects a total of six times between 1983 and 1994. He has also received two Special Achievement Awards, in 1981

LARGEST ENTERTAINMENT VOICE-OVER PROJECT More than 200,000 lines of dialogue were recorded by several hundred voice actors for the LucasArts video game *Star Wars: The Old Republic* (Electronic Arts, BioWare, and LucasArts, 2011). The MMORPG (massively multiplayer online role-playing game) was first released on December 20, 2011. Pictured above are some of the game's creative team.

FACT: "*Star Wars* Theme/Cantina Band" was a U.S. No. 1 hit in 1977.

FIRST *STAR WARS* VIDEO GAME The inaugural *Star Wars* video game, *The Empire Strikes Back* (Parker Brothers, 1982) was based on the second movie in the series and made for the Atari 2600 and Intellivision.

for *Star Wars: Episode V—The Empire Strikes Back* (U.S.A., 1980) and in 1984 for *Star Wars: Episode VI—Return of the Jedi* (U.S.A., 1983). He also won the Technical Achievement Award in 1982 "For the development of a Motion Picture Figure Mover for animation photography."

In addition, Muren holds the record for the **most Oscar nominations for visual effects**. He has been nominated on 13 occasions, the first being in 1982 for *Dragonslayer* (U.S.A., 1981) and the most recent being in 2006 for *War of the Worlds* (U.S.A., 2005).

Best-selling single of instrumental music A 1977 disco arrangement of John Williams's (U.S.A.) music to *Star Wars*—entitled "*Star Wars* Theme/Cantina Band"—by record producer Meco, aka Domenico Monardo (U.S.A.), remains the only instrumental single to have reached platinum status, according to the Recording Industry Association of America (RIAA), having sold more than 2 million units. The track featured on the album *Star Wars and Other Galactic Funk* (1977), which outsold the original movie soundtrack and was also certified platinum.

Most successful book series based on a movie series Lucas Licensing has recorded more than 100 million sales of *Star Wars*–related books, with over 850 novelizations, original novels, reference books, chil-

---

THE EMPIRE STRIKES GOLD

Taking into account the original movies, rereleases, and special editions, the six *Star Wars* movies represent the **highest-grossing sci-fi series ever**. Take a look at the worldwide box-office figures . . .

$475.1 M
*Star Wars: Episode VI—
Return of the Jedi*

$538.4 M
*Star Wars: Episode V—
The Empire Strikes Back*

$649.4 M
*Star Wars: Episode II—
Attack of the Clones*

$775.4 M
*Star Wars: Episode IV—
A New Hope*

$848 M
*Star Wars: Episode III—
Revenge of the Sith*

$1.026 B
*Star Wars: Episode I—
The Phantom Menace*

Sources for box-office figures: boxofficemojo.com; imdb.com

MOST SPOOFED FILM SERIES There have been direct references to the *Star Wars* series in more than 170 feature movies, and in countless TV shows, comics, advertisements, and online videos. One episode of the cartoon comedy *Family Guy*, "Blue Harvest" (Fox, 2007, above left), was an hour-long parody of the movie.

A number of full-length *Star Wars* spoofs have been made, of which the best known is *Spaceballs* (U.S.A., 1987, above right). Individual *Star Wars* spoof scenes have been a staple of comedy movies for more than 30 years, from *Airplane II: The Sequel* (U.S.A., 1982) and *Get Crazy* (U.S.A., 1983) to *Austin Powers: The Spy Who Shagged Me* (U.S.A., 1999) and *The Simpsons Movie* (U.S.A., 2007).

dren's books, and role-playing supplements, including 80 *New York Times* bestsellers. The first original novel based on *Star Wars* characters was *Splinter of the Mind's Eye* (1978), written by Alan Dean Foster (U.S.A.).

Largest movie merchandising campaign In May 1996, PepsiCo (owners of Pepsi, Pizza Hut, KFC, Taco Bell, and Frito Lay) signed a deal with Lucasfilm for the right to link their products with *Star Wars* during the Special Edition rereleases of the original trilogy, leading up to the 1999

FACT: George Lucas made U.S. $500 million in 1977–80 from *Star Wars* merchandise alone.

MOST SUCCESSFUL MERCHANDISING FRANCHISE IN MOVIES As of 2012, the value of the *Star Wars* franchise is estimated at U.S. $30.57 billion, of which the box-office returns for the six movies in the series account for only U.S. $4.27 billion. Lucas Licensing on behalf of Lucasfilm has noted more than U.S. $20 billion in sales of tie-in merchandise globally, along with more than U.S. $3 billion profit from *Star Wars* video games and U.S. $2.5 billion in DVD sales.

release of *Episode I—The Phantom Menace*. At a reported U.S. $2 billion, it is the most extensive single cross-promotion deal in history.

Most prolific video-game series based on a licensed property As of April 2012, a total of 279 *Star Wars* video games had been released across 41 different platforms.

Most successful action-figure range As of 2007, the *Star Wars* toy lines from Kenner/Hasbro had generated more than U.S. $9 billion in sales. In 1978 alone, Kenner's first range of *Star Wars* figures sold more than 40 million units, earning in excess of U.S. $100 million.

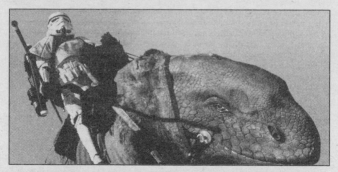

BIGGEST OPENING WEEKEND EVER FOR A RERELEASED MOVIE Shown in movie theaters in 1997 as the first of Lucasfilm's 20th anniversary Special Editions of the original *Star Wars* trilogy, *Episode IV—A New Hope* (U.S.A.) grossed U.S. $35,906,661 in U.S. movie theaters on the weekend of January 31–February 2, 1997. *A New Hope* took U.S. $579,646,015 worldwide to June 1997, making this the **highest theatrical gross for a movie rerelease**.

VIDEO GAMERS

Best-selling computer game console The PlayStation 2 (PS2), made by Sony and released in 2000, had sold over 153.6 million units as of November 21, 2011. The second best-selling console is the Nintendo DS, released in 2004. The DS overtook the PS2 in January 2011, when it registered 147 million sales, but has since lost ground.

Best-selling music game As of May 2011, more than 7.32 million copies of Ubisoft's Wii game *Just Dance 2* (2010) had been sold around the globe, making it more successful than the single-platform versions of all other music games. The second best-selling title in the genre is the original *Just Dance* (Ubisoft, 2009), with sales of 5.78 million.

Biggest MMO hack In April 2011, Sony revealed that, due to a huge online hack, user details from 24.6 million accounts in its enormous multiplayer online (MMO) gaming arm, Sony Online Entertainment (SOE), may have been stolen. The games affected were *EverQuest I & II*, *Free Realms*, *Vanguard*, *Clone Wars Adventures*, and *DC Universe Online*. About 12,700 credit or debit card numbers and expiration dates, plus 10,700 direct-debit records, could have been compromised as part of the hack, leading to SOE taking all of its MMOs offline for 12 days.

First fitness game In 1979, a full 25 years before Nintendo popularized fitness gaming, Mattel's Intellivision blazed a trail for health-conscious software with Jack LaLanne's *Physical Conditioning*. The game featured

MOST PROLIFIC DANCING GAME HIGH SCORER Elizabeth "Kitty McScratch" Bolinger (U.S.A.) holds more Twin Galaxies high-score records for *Dance Central*, *Just Dance*, and *Just Dance 2* than any other player. She is first on the leaderboard for more than 85 different songs. Her highest score is for *Dance Central* track "C'mon Ride It (The Train)" by Quad City DJs, for which she scored 432,793 points on December 5, 2010.

FACT: The International Video Game Hall of Fame is based in Kitty's hometown, Ottumwa, Iowa, U.S.A.

FACT: To use this controller like a standard handheld pad, you would need to be 167 ft. (51 m) tall.

LARGEST VIDEO GAME CONTROLLER Officially verified in August 2011 as the largest console game controller, this fully functional Nintendo Entertainment System (NES) pad measures an enormous 12 ft. x 5 ft. 3 in. x 1 ft. 8 in. (366 cm x 159 cm x 51 cm). Its main creator is engineering student Ben Allen (bottom right), who was helped by Stephen van't Hof and Michel Verhulst, all of whom study at the Delft University of Technology in the Netherlands. The fantastic facsimile is 30 times the size of a standard NES controller, and requires two gamers to navigate its enormous buttons.

the recorded voice of veteran U.S. fitness fanatic LaLanne (then 65 years old), encouraging gamers to try various exercises, while basic animations showed the movements on screen.

Largest collection of video games Richard Lecce (U.S.A.) had a total of 8,068 different video games when counted in Delray Beach, Florida, U.S.A., on December 22, 2011.

Largest fee paid for an appearance in a video-game advertisement Helen Mirren (UK) was paid a reported £500,000 (U.S. $800,000) to appear in a series of television ads for *Wii Fit* (Nintendo, 2007) from October 2010.

Largest game of *Angry Birds* The March 3, 2011, edition of *Conan*, the American talk show hosted by Conan O'Brien, featured a man-size, real-life version of *Angry Birds* (Rovio, 2009) in the studio set. The game was re-created by the show's production staff and featured obstacles made from furniture, while inflatable balls were used to represent the game's birds and pigs.

Largest cell phone gaming party On April 13, 2011, a total of 316 participants joined a cell phone gaming party organized by Kick Energy (UK) at the *Gadget Show Live*, in the NEC, Birmingham, UK.

For even more gaming world records, check out **GWR Gamer's Edition 2013!**

FASTEST COMPLETION OF *MARIO KART* CIRCUIT 1 Speedy Sami Çetin (UK) has been a fixture of the competitive *Mario Kart* scene for over 10 years, but 2010 was his golden season. He took the checkered flag for the fastest completion of the iconic Circuit 1 on the very first game in the series, *Super Mario Kart* (Nintendo, 1992). He holds the record on both the PAL and NTSC versions of the game, with times of 58.34 seconds and 56.45 seconds respectively, as of August 2011.

First video game theme to win a Grammy award On February 13, 2011, *Civilization IV* became the first game to feature a Grammy-winning theme song. Composer Christopher Tin (U.S.A.) won in the Best Instrumental Arrangement Accompanying Vocalist(s) category with "Baba Yetu."

Most expensive PlayStation 3 game sold at auction On August 2, 2011, Damian Fraimorice (Israel) sold a factory-sealed copy of *NBA Elite 11* (EA, 2011) to a buyer in the U.S.A. for U.S. $1,500. Damian also holds the record for the **most expensive Xbox 360 game sold at auction**. On February 2, 2011, he sold a copy of *Dead Space Ultra Limited Edition* to a buyer in New York, U.S.A., for U.S. $2,999.

Most gamers voting in a gaming award In a poll conducted by the entertainment news service IGN at the 2011 Gamescom exhibition in Cologne, Germany, a total of 258,367 people voted for their favorite game. The winner, *DOTA 2* (2012) from Valve Software, collected 68,041 votes.

Most guns in a video game *Borderlands* (Gearbox Software, 2009) has a tagline boasting "87 bazillion" guns in the game. In reality, the figure is

MOST INTERNATIONAL *STREET FIGHTER* WINS Ryan Hart (UK) won more than 450 *Street Fighter* events in 13 different countries from 1998 to 2011. He also holds the record for the **longest winning streak on *Street Fighter IV*** (Capcom/Dimps, 2009). Ryan remained unbeaten for 169 matches at the GAME event in the Prospect Centre, Hull, UK, on March 27, 2010.

FACT: Ryan dressed as the character Ryu for a special Guinness World Records shoot in London's Chinatown.

17,750,000—still by far the most guns in any video game. Weapons are generated randomly, with different ammo, components, and elemental effects.

Most prolific video games magazine Enterbrain, Inc. (Japan) had published 1,120 issues of *Famitsu* as of December 1, 2011. The first issue appeared on June 20, 1986.

Most valuable Xbox sold at auction Excluding one-off competition prizes and consoles not on general sale, the rarest Xbox is the white Panzer Dragoon–theme original, released to promote *Panzer Dragoon Orta* (Sega, 2002). Only 999 were produced. On June 10, 2011, one was sold on eBay for U.S. $1,250.

SPORTS

CONTENTS

MOST PRIZE MONEY IN AN ATP SEASON Novak Djokovic (Serbia) served up a stunningly successful 2011 season on the Association of Tennis Professionals (ATP) circuit, which saw him net a hefty U.S. $12.6 million in prize money. By winning 10 titles in all—including the Australian Open, Wimbledon, and the U.S. Open—the world No. 1 took his career earnings to U.S. $32.9 million, making him the fourth highest-earning tennis player of all time.

HOW FAST CAN WE RUN?

HOW QUICKLY CAN A HUMAN RUN 100 METERS?

When Usain Bolt (Jamaica) ran the 100 meters in 9.58 seconds, he smashed not only the world record but also the mathematical theories about athletic ability. Scientists did not expect anyone to go that fast until 2060. Can he go faster? If so, what's the fastest speed that it is physically possible to reach?

Sports scientist John Brenkus has written about this very subject in his book *The Perfection Point*. The perfect athlete would benefit from the ultimate in genetics, nutrition, and training. But how much faster than Usain Bolt could this perfect athlete travel at if he were to make a flawless run in ideal conditions?

1. REACTING TO THE GUN: Starting pistols are a thing of the past. Why? The sound takes 0.025 seconds to travel the 36 ft. (11 m) from lane 1 to lane 9, giving the first athlete an advantage. Today, the race starts with a beep from a speaker placed behind each runner. The key is to react quickly, but not too quickly. The perfect start is one-tenth of a second (100 milliseconds) after the beep. Moving off the blocks sooner than this will trigger a false start. If Usain Bolt had managed to get away in one-tenth of a second for his record-breaking run in 2009, he would have finished in 9.51 seconds.

2. GETTING OUT OF THE BLOCKS: While it's good to have strong calf and thigh muscles to get that explosive start, if they're too powerful they'll be too heavy for a record-worthy sprint.

3. ACCELERATING TO YOUR TOP SPEED (SEE ASAFA POWELL, RIGHT): Air resistance increases as the square of the speed, which means that if you double your speed, the drag increases fourfold. At speeds of 25 mph (40 km/h), this is four times the resistance a marathon runner will face. Luckily, tailwinds up to 4.4 mph (2 m/sec) are allowed by the Olympic committee. (Bolt broke his record with no tailwind; imagine how much quicker he would have been *with* one!) If the track is at an altitude of 3,280 ft. (1,000 m), the air will be thinner and provide less resistance. Any higher, and records don't count.

4. SLOWING DOWN AS LITTLE AS POSSIBLE (SEE CARL LEWIS, LEFT): The final challenge is not decelerating too quickly. Air resistance continues to act on runners, but by now their muscles will start to tire, too, and they won't be able to speed up the rate at which they are taking individual steps. Instead, they should increase their stride length—so that they can cover as great a distance as possible with each pace.

USAIN BOLT

As Brenkus explains, the 100 meters is a simple concept—you run from A to B as quickly as possible—but this involves four key stages (see photos above and on page 451).

So, taking Usain Bolt's record time of 9.58 seconds and adjusting for what we've learned from the four stages, the result is a potential time of 9.01 seconds.

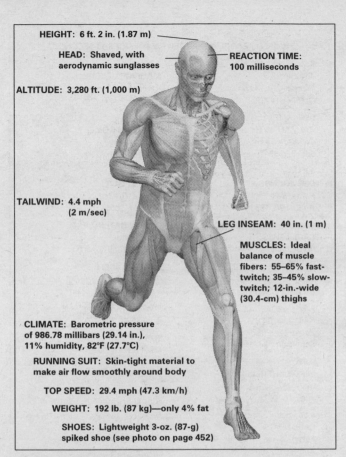

HEIGHT: 6 ft. 2 in. (1.87 m)

HEAD: Shaved, with aerodynamic sunglasses

REACTION TIME: 100 milliseconds

ALTITUDE: 3,280 ft. (1,000 m)

TAILWIND: 4.4 mph (2 m/sec)

LEG INSEAM: 40 in. (1 m)

MUSCLES: Ideal balance of muscle fibers: 55–65% fast-twitch; 35–45% slow-twitch; 12-in.-wide (30.4-cm) thighs

CLIMATE: Barometric pressure of 986.78 millibars (29.14 in.), 11% humidity, 82°F (27.7°C)

RUNNING SUIT: Skin-tight material to make air flow smoothly around body

TOP SPEED: 29.4 mph (47.3 km/h)

WEIGHT: 192 lb. (87 kg)—only 4% fat

SHOES: Lightweight 3-oz. (87-g) spiked shoe (see photo on page 452)

THE PERFECT 100-METER ATHLETE

But just think. It took humanity 190,000 years of development to run a mile in under 4 minutes. Once this barrier was breached—a barrier more psychological than physical—it took just 46 days for someone else to do it; 10 years later, 336 people had achieved it!

So if 9.01 seconds seems an absolute scientific limit, then breaking the 9-second barrier will become the new holy grail of athletics. And as humans seem to have an inbuilt desire to overcome apparently insurmountable obstacles, it is surely conceivable that the barrier will be broken. Therefore, the real limit is 8.99 seconds.

How Fast Can We Run?

WORLD RECORD 100-METER RUNS UNDER 10 SECONDS

9.95
JIM HINES
Mexico City, Mexico
October 14, 1968

9.93
CALVIN SMITH
Colorado Springs, U.S.A.
July 3,1983

9.83
BEN JOHNSON*
Rome, Italy
August 30, 1987

9.93
CARL LEWIS
Rome, Italy
August 30, 1987

Zürich, Switzerland
August 17, 1988

9.92
CARL LEWIS
Seoul, South Korea
September 24, 1988

9.90
LEROY BURRELL
New York, U.S.A.
June 14, 1991

9.86
CARL LEWIS
Tokyo, Japan
August 25, 1991

9.85
LEROY BURRELL
Lausanne, Switzerland
July 6, 1994

9.84
DONOVAN BAILEY
Atlanta, U.S.A.
July 27, 1996

9.79
MAURICE GREENE
Athens, Greece
June 16, 1999

9.78
TIM MONTGOMERY
Paris, France
September 14, 2002

9.77
ASAFA POWELL
Athens, Greece
June 14, 2005

JUSTIN GATLIN*
Doha, Qatar
May 12, 2006

ASAFA POWELL
Gateshead, England
June 11, 2006

Zürich, Switzerland
August 18, 2006

9.74
ASAFA POWELL
Rieti, Italy
September 9, 2007

9.72
USAIN BOLT
New York, U.S.A.
May 31, 2008

9.69
USAIN BOLT
Beijing, China
August 16, 2008

9.58
USAIN BOLT
Berlin, Germany
August 16, 2009

*These records were later rescinded

AMERICAN FOOTBALL

Longest NFL field goal The NFL record for longest field goal is 63 yards, by Sebastian Janikowski (Poland) of the Oakland Raiders against the Denver Broncos on September 12, 2011. He equaled the record set by Jason Elam (U.S.A.) of the Denver Broncos, against the Jacksonville Jaguars, on October 25, 1998, and Tom Dempsey (U.S.A.) of the New Orleans Saints, against the Detroit Lions, on November 8, 1970.

Most passes thrown without an interception Quarterback Tom Brady (U.S.A.) achieved an NFL regular-season record by throwing 358 consecutive passes in a row without one being intercepted while playing for the New England Patriots from October 17, 2010, to September 12, 2011. Brady, who joined the team in 2000, broke the record of 319 attempts without an interception set by Bernie Kosar (U.S.A.), playing for the Cleveland Browns in 1990 and 1991.

MOST FIRST DOWNS BY A TEAM IN A SEASON Darren Sproles (U.S.A., pictured left) helped the New Orleans Saints set a National Football League (NFL) record for most first downs in a season, with 416 in 2011.

MOST FIELD GOALS CONVERTED (50 YARDS OR MORE) Jason Hanson (U.S.A.) shares the NFL record for most successful field goals of 50 yards or greater in a regular season, with 8. He achieved this in 2008, placekicking for the Detroit Lions. Jason equaled the 1995 record set by Morten Andersen (Denmark) with the Atlanta Falcons.

FACT: Drew Brees set the NFL record for **most passing yards in a season** with 5,476 while playing for the New Orleans Saints (U.S.A.) in 2011.

Most passes completed in a Super Bowl game The NFL record for most completions in a Super Bowl game is 32, by Tom Brady for the New England Patriots in 2004's Super Bowl XXXVIII. His record was equaled by Drew Brees (U.S.A.) for the New Orleans Saints in Super Bowl XLIV in 2009. Both players' teams went on to victory. The Patriots defeated the Carolina Panthers 32–29 and the Saints beat the Indianapolis Colts 31–17.

NFL SEASONS

Most receptions by a tight end The most catches made by a tight end in a season is 102, by Tony Gonzalez (U.S.A.) while playing for the Kansas City Chiefs in 2004. He also set the record for **most catches made by an NFL tight end during a career**, with 1,149, playing for the Kansas City Chiefs and Atlanta Falcons.

Most penalty yards by a team The Oakland Raiders set an NFL record for most penalty yards in a season with 1,358 in 2011. In the same year, they also set the NFL record for **most penalties incurred by a team in a season**, with 163.

Most receiving yards by a tight end Rob Gronkowski (U.S.A.) racked up 1,327 receiving yards while playing for the New England Patriots in the 2011 season. Gronkowski also claimed the NFL record for **most touchdown catches in a season by a tight end**, making 17 for the Patriots in the same year.

MOST PASS COMPLETIONS IN A PLAYOFF Drew Brees (U.S.A.) set the NFL record for most pass completions in a playoff game with 39. He was playing for the New Orleans Saints against the Seattle Seahawks on January 8, 2011. He also holds the NFL record for **highest completion percentage by a quarterback in a season** with 71.2%, playing for the New Orleans Saints in 2011. Brees completed 468 of 657 attempts to break his own mark of 70.6% in 2009.

LONGEST TOUCHDOWN RECEPTION A 99-yard touchdown reception has been made 13 times, most recently by New York Giants teammates Victor Cruz from Eli Manning. The record was claimed when the Giants played the New York Jets (all U.S.A.) on December 24, 2011.

MOST PASSING YARDS IN A ROOKIE SEASON The NFL record for most passing yards by a quarterback playing in his first season is 3,893, set by Cam Newton (U.S.A.) playing for the Carolina Panthers in 2011.

Newton also set the NFL record for **most passing yards in an NFL debut**, with 432 against the Green Bay Packers on September 18, 2011. That same year he also set the NFL record for **most rushing touchdowns by a quarterback in a season**, with 14.

MOST FIELD GOALS IN A SEASON David Akers (U.S.A.) set the NFL record for most field goals in a season with 44, for the San Francisco 49ers in 2011. Akers secured his 44 successful goals out of a record 52 attempts—the most field goals attempted in a single season by an individual. Akers joined the 49ers in July 2011, after an 11-year career with the Philadelphia Eagles.

MOST PUNT RETURN TOUCHDOWNS IN A CAREER The NFL record for most punt return touchdowns is 12, by Devin Hester (U.S.A.). He has played for the Chicago Bears since 2006. Devin also has the record for the **most punt return touchdowns in an NFL season**, with four in 2007. Patrick Peterson (U.S.A.) equaled it for the Arizona Cardinals in 2011.

Most offensive yards by a team The New Orleans Saints achieved the most offensive yards in a season, with 7,474 in 2011. The Saints also set an NFL record for the **most yards passing by a team in a season**, with 5,347 in 2011.

The **most passing yards by both teams in a single game** is 971, set when the Green Bay Packers (469) beat the Detroit Lions (502) 45–41 on January 1, 2012.

Most seasons at the same NFL team The most seasons played with one team is 20, shared by three players:
• Offensive tackle Jackie Slater (U.S.A.), playing for the Los Angeles Rams from 1976 to 1995
• Cornerback Darrell Green (U.S.A.), playing for the Washington Redskins between 1983 and 2002
• Placekicker Jason Hanson (U.S.A.), currently active, has played for the Detroit Lions since 1992.

Most kick returns for a touchdown Devin Hester (U.S.A.) set the NFL record for the most combined kick return touchdowns, with 17. Hester had 12 punt return touchdowns and five kickoff return touchdowns. He also holds the NFL record for **most kickoff return touchdowns by an individual in a regular season game**, with two against the St. Louis Rams on December 11, 2006.

NFL CAREERS

Most points scored Morten Andersen (Denmark) scored 2,544 points in his career as a placekicker from 1982 to 2007. He played for the New Orleans Saints, Atlanta Falcons, New York Giants, Kansas City Chiefs, and Minnesota Vikings.

Andersen also holds the NFL record for **most field goals in career**, with 565.

Most fumble return touchdowns Jason Taylor (U.S.A.) achieved six fumble return touchdowns as a defensive end and a linebacker, playing for the Miami Dolphins, Washington Redskins, and New York Jets between 1997 and 2011.

Most receiving yards by a tight end Tony Gonzalez (U.S.A.) racked up 13,338 yards playing for the Kansas City Chiefs and Atlanta Falcons from 1997 through the 2011 season.

An average of 111 million viewers watched the 2012 Super Bowl.

Most punts The NFL record for most career punts is 1,713, by Jeff Feagles (U.S.A.) during his 22-year career with the New England Patriots, Philadelphia Eagles, Arizona Cardinals, Seattle Seahawks, and New York Giants from 1988 to 2009. Feagles also holds the record for **most career punting yards** with 71,211.

Highest field goal percentage Nate Kaeding's (U.S.A.) career field goal percentage is 86.5%, playing for the San Diego Chargers since 2004.

CHAMPIONSHIP WINS, TOUCHDOWNS, AND STADIUMS

Most Super Bowls won	6	Pittsburgh Steelers
	5	Dallas Cowboys San Francisco 49ers
	4	Green Bay Packers New York Giants
Most AFC Championships won	8	Pittsburgh Steelers
	7	New England Patriots
	6	Denver Broncos
Most NFC Championships won	8	Dallas Cowboys
	5	Washington Redskins New York Giants San Francisco 49ers
Most NFL touchdowns	208	Jerry Rice (San Francisco 49ers, Oakland Raiders)
	175	Emmitt Smith (Dallas Cowboys, Arizona Cardinals)
	162	LaDainian Tomlinson (San Diego Chargers, New York Jets)
Largest stadiums (by capacity)	109,901	Michigan Stadium Home of Michigan Wolverines Ann Arbor, Michigan
	107,282	Beaver Stadium Home of Penn State Nittany Lions University Park, Pennsylvania
	102,455	Neyland Stadium Home of Tennessee Volunteers Knoxville, Tennessee

Statistics correct as of March 19, 2012

BALL SPORTS

MOST PASS COMPLETIONS IN A CFL CAREER Anthony Calvillo (U.S.A.) has completed 5,444 passes in the Canadian Football League (CFL) with the Las Vegas Posse (U.S.A.), the Hamilton Tiger-Cats, and the Montreal Alouettes (both Canada). He set the record from 1994 to 2011, when he also recorded the most touchdown passes in a CFL career, with 418, and the most passing yards in a CFL career, with 713,412.

CHAMPIONS AND AWARD WINNERS

Canadian football

Most Grey Cups (first awarded in 1909)	15	Toronto Argonauts (Canada)
	13	Edmonton Eskimos (Canada)
	10	Winnipeg Blue Bombers (Canada)
Grey Cup MVP awards (first awarded in 1959)	3	Sonny Wade (U.S.A.)
		Doug Flutie (U.S.A.)
		Damon Allen (U.S.A.)

Aussie rules

Most VFL/AFL premiers (VFL first held in 1897; superseded by AFL in 1990)	16	Carlton (Australia), last in 1995
		Essendon (Australia), last in 2000
	15	Collingwood (Australia), last in 2010

Gaelic football

Most Sam Maguire Cups (awarded to All-Ireland Championship winners since 1928)	36	Kerry (Ireland)
	23	Dublin (Ireland)
	9	Galway (Ireland)
Largest stadiums (by capacity)	82,300	Croke Park, Dublin (Ireland)
	53,500	Semple Stadium, Tipperary (Ireland)
	50,000	Gaelic Grounds, Limerick (Ireland)

Statistics correct as of April 12, 2012

MOST PASS RECEPTIONS IN GREY CUP HISTORY The Grey Cup is awarded to the winners of the Canadian Football League (CFL). Ben Cahoon (U.S.A.) is the all-time leading receiver in Grey Cup history, making 46 catches in the championships. Playing with the Montreal Alouettes (Canada) from 1998 to 2010, he also set the CFL record for **most pass receptions in a career**, with 1,017. The **single season CFL record for most pass receptions** was set by Derrell Mitchell (U.S.A.), with 130 for the Toronto Argonauts (Canada) in 1998.

MOST JOCK MCHALE MEDALS WON CONSECUTIVELY Jock McHale Medals are given to the coach of the winning Premiership team and two coaches have won three years in a row. Norm Smith won for Melbourne between 1955 and 1957, and Leigh Matthews (left) for Brisbane from 2001 to 2003.

MOST AFL GRAND FINALS PLAYED Michael Tuck (Australia) has competed in 11 Grand Finals—more than any other individual player. He joined Hawthorn in 1972 and made his record-breaking appearances between 1975 and his retirement as a player in 1991. He was made captain of the team in 1986.

GAELIC FOOTBALL

Most All-Ireland Ladies Championship wins Kerry won the All-Ireland Ladies Gaelic Football Championship a record 11 times between 1976 and 1993. The first Championships were held in 1974, the year in which the Ladies Gaelic Football Association itself was formed.

Most players in an exhibition match Whitehall Colmcille GAA Club (Ireland) organized a Gaelic football exhibition match with 399 players in

YOUNGEST FEMALE SOCCER REFEREE
When Daisy Goldsmith (UK) celebrated her 14th birthday, she also received her level-nine qualification from the Football Association (a soccer organization), on March 10, 2010, in Puriton, Somerset, UK. She became the youngest of 25,502 qualified referees in the nation at the time of her appointment. Only 407 of her colleagues are also female.

Dublin, Ireland, on May 22, 2011. The participants ranged in age from the club's under-8 members to its senior players.

Largest attendance A crowd of 90,556 people saw Down beat Offaly at the All-Ireland final at Croke Park, Dublin, Ireland, in 1961.

Largest lesson The largest Gaelic football lesson involved 528 participants at an event organized by St. Joseph's Gaelic Athletic Club in Glenavy, Northern Ireland, UK, on May 9, 2010.

Most doubles Kerry won the All-Ireland Football Championship and the National Football League double on 11 occasions between 1929 and 2009.

Instituted in 1925, the Irish National Football League is a competition organized, like the more prestigious All-Ireland Championships, at an intercounty level.

Kerry won the League 19 times between 1928 and 2009, the **most National Irish Football League wins recorded by a single team**. Their most recent triumph was achieved in 2009 over Derry.

AUSSIE RULES

Most consecutive Grand Final wins The Brisbane Lions won the Australian Football League (AFL) Grand Final three times in a row in

MOST CHAMPIONS LEAGUE WINS (FEMALE) FFC Frankfurt (Germany) has won the premier competition in women's European club soccer three times, in 2002, 2006, and 2008. Formerly known as the UEFA Women's Cup, the competition was renamed the UEFA Women's Champions League in 2009–10 and has been running since 2001.

2001–03. The team lost to Port Adelaide at its fourth consecutive Grand Final appearance in 2004.

Most consecutive matches kicking goals Peter McKenna kicked at least one goal in each one of 120 consecutive matches playing for Collingwood from 1968 to 1974. He played for the team between 1965 and 1975.

Most goals kicked in a single Grand Final Two players have managed to kick a record nine goals in an AFL Grand Final. Gordon Coventry set the record playing for Collingwood against Richmond in 1928, and Gary Ablett repeated the feat 61 years later, playing for Geelong against Hawthorn in 1989.

SOCCER FREESTYLERS John Farnworth (UK, left) has the record for the **most soccer ball touches with the toes in one minute**, with 109. He showed off his fleet feet on the BBC's *Match of the Day Kickabout* in London, UK, on September 16, 2011.

Ash Randall (UK, right) completed the record for the **most soccer ball touches with the shin in one minute**, with 138, outside the Wales Millennium Centre in Cardiff, UK, on February 16, 2012. Ash is part of a collective of urban sports freestylers called SBX Entertainment. For both these records, the ball could not hit the ground.

Most Michael Tuck Medals won Nick Stevens has won a record two Michael Tuck Medals, first while playing for Port Adelaide in 2002 and then with Carlton in 2007. The Michael Tuck Medal is awarded to the player judged to be the best and fairest in the final of the AFL preseason cup.

Most Leigh Matthews Trophies Gary Ablett, Jr. was awarded a record three Leigh Matthews Trophies in consecutive years while playing for Geelong from 2007 to 2009. The trophy is presented each year by the AFL Players Association to the league's most valuable player.

Most preseason cups won Hawthorn won four preseason AFL cups, in 1988, 1991–92, and 1999—a record matched by Essendon with wins in 1990, 1993–94, and 2000.

The AFL preseason cup began in 1988. The 18 AFL clubs play four matches and the two teams with the best record play in the final.

CANADIAN FOOTBALL

Most yards rushing Mike Pringle (U.S.A.) rushed for a career record of 16,425 yards with the Edmonton Eskimos (Canada), Sacramento Gold Miners (U.S.A.), Baltimore Stallions (U.S.A.), and Montreal Alouettes (Canada) in 1992–2005.

Most kicks blocked Barron Miles (U.S.A.) blocked 13 kicks in 1998–2009, playing in the CFL with the Montreal Alouettes and then the BC Lions (both Canada).

Most points scored Lui Passaglia (Canada) scored 3,991 points, a CFL career record. He played 408 games with BC Lions from 1976 to 2000, the **most games played in a regular CFL season**.

BALL FEATS

Longest duration spinning a basketball on a toothbrush Thomas Connors (UK) kept a basketball spinning for a duration of 13.5 seconds while it was balanced on a toothbrush held in his mouth. Connors set the record in Cardiff Bay, Cardiff, UK, on February 16, 2012.

Most basketball circles around the waist in 30 seconds Thaneswar Guragai (Nepal) passed a basketball around his own waist 56 times in 30 seconds, in Kathmandu, Nepal, on April 4, 2012. He overtook the previous record holder by three circles.

Most baseballs held in a baseball glove Ashrita Furman (U.S.A.) managed to hold 24 baseballs in one standard-size baseball glove. Furman grasped the record on December 28, 2011, in New York City, New York, U.S.A.

SOCCER

MOST APPEARANCES BY A FOREIGN PLAYER IN THE PREMIER LEAGUE The most appearances in the English Premier League by a foreign player is 468, by goalkeeper Mark Schwarzer (Australia) playing for Middlesbrough and Fulham between 1998 and the end of the 2011–12 season.

First English Premier League goal The very first goal scored in the English Premier League was by striker Brian Deane (England) for Sheffield United, which beat Manchester United 2–1 on August 15, 1992.

Most consecutive hattricks Masashi Nakayama (Japan) scored hattricks in four consecutive games playing for Júbilo Iwata in the Japanese J League. He netted five goals against Cerezo Osaka at Nagai Stadium on April 15, 1998; four against Sanfrecce Hiroshima at Júbilo Iwata Stadium on April 18, 1998; another four against Avispa Fukuoka at Kumamoto City Stadium on April 25, 1998; and a hattrick against Consadole Sapporo at Júbilo Iwata Stadium on April 29, 1998.

MOST EXPENSIVE FOOTBALL PLAYER A transfer fee of £80 million (U.S. $131.86 million) was quoted for Cristiano Ronaldo's (Portugal) move to Real Madrid (Spain) from Manchester United (England) on July 1, 2009. Ronaldo also garnered the highest combined transfer fees for an individual soccer player: £92.2 million (U.S. $152.1 million) for his moves from Sporting Lisbon (Portugal) to Manchester United and then Real Madrid.

FACT: Schwarzer has played 94 times for Australia—more times than any of his countrymen.

MOST PREMIER LEAGUE APPEARANCES Ryan Giggs (Wales) played 598 times for Manchester United in the English Premier League between 1992 and the end of the 2011–12 season. The remarkably enduring Giggs is the **only player to have appeared in every Premier League season**—20 seasons in all—and the **only player to have scored in every Premier League season.** He has also won the **most Premier League winner's medals, with 12.**

SOCCER'S TOP TOURNAMENTS

Most FIFA World Cups (first held 1930)	5	Brazil (1958, 1962, 1970, 1994, 2002)
	4	Italy (1934, 1938, 1982, 2006)
	3	Germany (1954, 1974, 1990)
Most European Championships (first held 1960)	3	Germany (1972, 1980, 1996)
	2	Spain (1964, 2008)
		France (1984, 2000)
Most European Cups (first held 1956; renamed in 1992 as the Champions League)	9	Real Madrid, Spain (1956, 1957, 1958, 1959, 1960, 1966, 1998, 2000, 2002)
	7	AC Milan, Italy (1963, 1969, 1989, 1990, 1994, 2003, 2007)
	5	Liverpool, England (1977, 1978, 1981, 1984, 2005)
Most Copa Américas (first held 1916)	15	Uruguay (1916, 1917, 1920, 1923, 1924, 1926, 1935, 1942, 1956, 1959, 1967, 1983, 1987, 1995, 2011)
	14	Argentina (1921, 1925, 1927, 1929, 1937, 1941, 1945, 1946, 1947, 1955, 1957, 1959, 1991, 1993)
	8	Brazil (1919, 1922, 1949, 1989, 1997, 1999, 2004, 2007)

Statistics correct as of April 10, 2012

Most own goals in a domestic league soccer match On October 31, 2002, in a league fixture in Madagascar, Stade Olympique l'Emyrne (SOE) lost 149–0 to AS Adema—with every goal an own goal! This unusual tactic was in protest against a refereeing decision that went against SOE in a previous play-off match.

Most UEFA Champions League goals The most prolific goal scorer in the UEFA Champions League is Raúl González Blanco (Spain), who scored 71 times in 144 matches playing for Real Madrid (Spain) and Schalke 04 (Germany) from 1992 to the end of the 2011 season.

Largest tournament (by players) Copa Telmex 2011 was contested by 181,909 players and a total of 10,799 teams. The competition was held in Mexico from January 2 to December 11, 2011.

MOST WINS OF THE BALLON D'OR On three occasions, diminutive South American dynamo Lionel Messi (Argentina) has been awarded the trophy for the most outstanding soccer player of the year. Johan Cruyff, Marco van Basten (both Netherlands) and Michel Platini (France) have matched this feat. Messi's wins have come in consecutive years, from 2009 to 2011. (The trophy was renamed the FIFA Ballon d'Or in 2010.)

Messi also scored the **most goals in a UEFA Champions League match,** when he notched up five goals in FC Barcelona's 7–1 demolition of Bayer Leverkusen (Germany) on March 7, 2012.

FACT: In March 2012, Messi's goal tally for FC Barcelona (Spain) hit 234, making him its all-time top scorer.

Most goals in the FIFA World Cup (team) Brazil has scored 210 goals at the FIFA World Cup finals.

Brazil is the only team to have qualified for all 19 World Cup tournaments since 1930, the **most appearances at the FIFA World Cup Finals**.

Most goals in a single FIFA World Cup (player) Just Fontaine (France, b. Morocco) scored 13 goals in the 1958 World Cup in Sweden in just six matches.

Most goals in a single FIFA World Cup (team) Runners-up Hungary netted 27 goals at the 1954 tournament in Switzerland.

Most clean sheets at the FIFA World Cup Two goalkeepers have each kept 10 clean sheets (matches in which they have conceded no goals) in their World Cup finals career. Peter Shilton (England) achieved the feat playing for England between 1982 and 1990. Fabien Barthez equaled the record between 1998 and 2006 playing for France, with whom he won the 1998 World Cup.

Largest attendance at a World Cup match A crowd of 174,000 watched the game between Uruguay and Brazil at the Maracanã Stadium in Rio de Janeiro, Brazil, on July 16, 1950. Uruguay won 2–1.

Most wins of the FIFA women's World Cup Germany won the women's World Cup in 2003 and again in 2007. This equals the record achieved by the U.S.A., who won the inaugural tournament in 1991 and triumphed for a second time in 1999.

Most goals scored in the FIFA women's World Cup Birgit Prinz (Germany) has scored 14 goals in FIFA women's World Cup matches. Her last goal was scored in the final at the Hongkou Stadium in Shanghai, China, on September 30, 2007.

The **most goals scored by an individual player in a women's World Cup tournament** is 10, by Michelle Akers (U.S.A.) in 1991.

Most times sent off in the FIFA World Cup Two players have been sent off twice in World Cup matches. The record is shared by Rigobert Song (Cameroon), who was sent off in a game against Brazil in 1994 and then against Chile in 1998, and Zinedine Zidane (France), who first received his marching orders against Saudi Arabia in 1998, and then again in the final against Italy in 2006.

Most own goals in a FIFA World Cup match There were two own goals in a World Cup match between the U.S.A. and Portugal in Suwon, South Korea, on June 5, 2002. The first was scored by Jorge Costa (Portugal), and the second by Jeff Agoos (U.S.A.). The U.S.A. won the match 3–2.

Most Olympic soccer titles The greatest number of Olympic soccer titles won is three, by Great Britain in 1900 (unofficial competition), 1908, and 1912, and Hungary in 1952, 1964, and 1968.

Women's soccer was introduced to the Olympic Games in 1996. The **most women's Olympic soccer titles** is three, by the U.S.A. in 1996, 2004, and 2008.

Most goals in an Olympic match The greatest number of goals scored in an Olympic soccer match by both teams is 18, in the game between France and Denmark in London, UK, on October 22, 1908. Denmark won the match 17–1.

The **most goals scored by an individual male player in an Olympic soccer tournament** is 12, by Ferenc Bene (Hungary) in 1964 in Tokyo, Japan. Hungary went on to win the title that year, beating Czechoslovakia 2–1.

The **most goals scored by an individual female player in an Olympic soccer tournament** is five, by Cristiane (Brazil) and Birgit Prinz (Germany) at the 2004 finals in Athens, Greece.

Most valuable team in sports Manchester United (England) are worth U.S. $2.24 billion according to Forbes, making them the most valuable sports team of any kind. The figure is based on enterprise value (equity plus debt) and revenue for 2010–11. Second is soccer team Real Madrid (Spain), worth U.S. $1.88 billion, and joint third are baseball's New York Yankees and the NFL's Dallas Cowboys (both U.S.A.), at $1.85 billion.

RUGBY

UNION

Biggest win in the World Cup On October 25, 2003, Australia beat Namibia 142–0 in Adelaide, Australia. The Wallabies scored a World Cup record 22 tries, with fullback Chris Latham scoring five and wing Lote Tuqiri and fly-half Matt Giteau each scoring three. Mat Rogers kicked 16 conversions.

Longest drop goal Gerald Hamilton "Gerry" Brand kicked a drop goal 255 ft. (77.7 m) for South Africa vs. England at Twickenham, UK, on January 2, 1932.

YOUNGEST WORLD CUP FINAL REFEREE Craig Joubert (South Africa, b. November 8, 1977) was 33 years 349 days old when he refereed the Rugby Union World Cup Final between New Zealand and France in Auckland, New Zealand, on October 23, 2011.

YOUNGEST WORLD CUP TRY SCORER George North (UK) was just 19 years 166 days old when he scored for Wales in a Rugby Union World Cup match against Namibia (left, North pictured second left) at New Plymouth in New Zealand on September 26 2011. North is the third youngest player to play for Wales, making his international debut against South Africa on 13 November 2010 at the Millennium Stadium in Cardiff, Wales, aged 18 years 214 days.

Largest paying attendance for an international A crowd of 109,874 witnessed New Zealand's 39–35 victory over Australia at Stadium Australia in Sydney, Australia, on July 15, 2000. Winger Jonah Lomu sealed the win with a try.

Largest paying attendance at a club match A crowd of 83,761 saw Harlequins beat Saracens 24–19 in the English Aviva Premiership, at Wembley Stadium, London, UK, on March 31, 2012.

Highest score In Denmark, Comet beat Lindo by 194–0 on November 17, 1973. The highest British score is 177–3 by Norwich against Eccles and Attleborough in a Norfolk Cup match in 1996.

MOST HEINEKEN CUP WINS The Heineken Cup is the premier European club competition, and Toulouse (France) has won it four times (1996, 2003, 2005, and 2010). On the last occasion, they beat Biarritz Olympique, France, 21–19 at the Stade de France in Paris.

Most appearances in a Super Rugby career Since his debut in 1999, Nathan Sharpe (Australia) has played 157 times for the Queensland Reds and Western Force, as of May 9, 2012.

Most British and Irish Lions tours as captain Only one player has captained the British and Irish Lions rugby team on two separate tours: Martin Johnson (UK) in 1997 and 2001. In 1997, the Lions won 2–1 in South Africa, while in 2001 they lost to Australia 2–1. Johnson also toured with the Lions in 1993.

Most points in a Heineken Cup final The most points scored by a player in a Heineken Cup final is 30, by Diego Domínguez (Italy), playing for Stade Français against Leicester in Paris, France, on May 19 2001.

LEAGUE

Fastest hattrick On May 19, 2002, Chris Thorman (UK) scored a hattrick of tries just 6 min. 54 sec. after the start of a match. He was playing for Huddersfield Giants against Doncaster Dragons in the semifinal of the Buddies National League Cup at Doncaster, South Yorkshire, UK.

Highest score in an international match France defeated Serbia and Montenegro 120–0 during the Mediterranean Cup at Beirut, Lebanon, on October 22, 2003.

Largest attendance A crowd of 107,558 attended the National Rugby League Grand Final at Stadium Australia in Sydney, New South Wales, Australia, on September 26, 1999, to see Melbourne beat St. George Illawarra 20–18.

Rugby Union

Caps	139	George Gregan (Aus, 1994–2007)
	123	Brian O'Driscoll (Ire/Lions, 1999–)
	123	Ronan O'Gara (Ire/Lions, 2000–)
Points	1,250	Dan Carter (NZ, 2003–)
	1,246	Jonny Wilkinson (Eng/Lions, 1998–2011)
	1,090	Neil Jenkins (Wal/Lions, 1991–2002)
Tries	69	Daisuke Ohata (Jap, 1996–2006)
	64	David Campese (Aus, 1982–96)
	60	Shane Williams (Wal/Lions, 2000–11)

Rugby League

Caps	59	Darren Lockyer (Aus, 1998–2011)
	55	Ruben Wiki (NZ, 1994–2006)
	46	Mick Sullivan (GB, 1954–63)
		Garry Schofield (GB, 1984–94)
		Mal Meninga (Aus, 1982–94)
Points	278	Mal Meninga (Aus, 1982–94)
	228	Neil Fox (GB, 1959–69)
	204	Darren Lockyer (Aus, 1998–2011)
Tries	41	Mick Sullivan (GB, 1954–63)
	35	Darren Lockyer (Aus, 1998–2011)
	33	Ken Irvine (Aus, 1959–67)

Statistics correct as of March 19, 2012

Largest attendance for a World Cup final On October 24, 1992, a total of 73,631 people attended the World Cup final between Australia and Great Britain at Wembley Stadium in London, UK.

Longest drop goal On March 25, 1989, Joe Lydon (UK) scored from 183 ft. 8 in. (56 m) for Wigan against Warrington in a Challenge Cup semifinal at Maine Road in Manchester, UK.   .

Most appearances for the same club The most appearances for one club is 774, by Jim Sullivan (UK) for Wigan, UK, from 1921 to 1946. He played a record 928 first-class games in all.

MOST FOUR NATIONS TITLES The most wins of the Four Nations competition is two, by Australia in 2009 and 2011. The competition is contested between Australia, England, New Zealand, and one qualifier. It superseded the Tri-Nations (1999–2006), contested by Australia, Great Britain, and New Zealand. Australia also holds the record for the **most Tri-Nations wins**, with three. New Zealand has won it once, in 2005.

Most Australian premierships South Sydney have won 20 premierships since 1908. The competition was known as the New South Wales Rugby League between 1908 and 1994, the Australian Rugby League between 1995 and 1997, and the National Rugby League (NRL) from 1998. The Brisbane Broncos have won the **most NRL titles**, with three (1998, 2000, 2006), in addition to premiership wins in 1992, 1993, and 1997.

Most Australian top-flight appearances Darren Lockyer (Australia) made 355 league appearances for the Brisbane Broncos from 1995 to 2011 in the Australian Rugby League, Super League, and National Rugby League.

Most consecutive Super League titles Leeds Rhinos achieved three Super League titles between 2007 and 2009. On each occasion, the Rhinos defeated St. Helens in the final.

Most points in an international (individual) Hazem El Masri of Lebanon scored 48 points (16 goals, 4 tries) against Morocco in a World Cup qualifying match at Avignon, France, on November 17, 1999.

Most siblings to play in an international Four Keinhorst brothers—James, Kristian, Markus, and Nick—represented Germany against the Czech Republic in the European Rugby League Shield in Prague, Czech Republic, on August 4, 2007.

Most teams in a World Cup tournament In all, 16 teams took part in the 2000 World Cup held at venues across the UK and France.

Oldest player in the Challenge Cup At the age of 52, Sid Miller (UK) appeared for Littleborough against Redhill in a first-round tie in December 1993.

FACT: Pictured above is Australia vs. New Zealand during the first round of the 2011 Four Nations.

BASEBALL

Highest paid player On December 13, 2007, Alex Rodriguez (U.S.A.) signed a contract with the New York Yankees worth U.S. $275 million over 10 years, the largest in baseball history. According to money mavens Forbes in March 2012, Rodriguez's on- and off-field earnings in 2012 are expected to reach U.S. $32 million, $5 million more than the next highest MLB earner, Joe Mauer (U.S.A.).

Oldest player to hit a home run At 48 years 254 days, Julio Franco (Dominican Republic) became the oldest MLB player to hit a home run when he connected off Randy Johnson (U.S.A.) for a two-run home run to help lead the New York Mets to a 5–3 win over the Arizona Diamondbacks at Chase Field in Phoenix, Arizona, U.S.A., on May 4, 2007.

Largest attendance On March 29, 2008, a crowd of 115,300 turned out for an exhibition game between the Los Angeles Dodgers and the Boston Red Sox at the Los Angeles Memorial Coliseum in California, U.S.A. The game was in celebration of the Dodgers' 50th anniversary in Los Angeles—previously the team had been based in Brooklyn, New York.

Largest television audience for a World Series The highest average viewing figures per game for a World Series is 44,278,950 viewers for the 1978 event between the New York Yankees and LA Dodgers on October 10–17, 1978. Broadcasted on NBC, the games averaged a 56% share of the TV audience and reached almost 24.5 million homes. The Yankees won the series 4–2.

Oldest diamond Labatt Park in London, Ontario, Canada, was established in 1877 and is the oldest continually used diamond.

CAREER BATTING RECORDS

• Barry Bonds (U.S.A.) has the **most home runs** in the MLB, with 762 for the Pittsburgh Pirates and San Francisco Giants from 1986 to 2007. Henry Aaron is next on the list with 755 home runs, and "Babe" Ruth is third with 714.

• Ty Cobb (U.S.A.) has the **highest batting average**— .367 for the Detroit Tigers and Philadelphia Athletics from 1905 to 1928. Rogers Hornsby is next with an average of .358 and Ed Delahanty is third with an average of .350.

FACT: Pujols (see page 475) has hit 30 or more home runs in every season since the start of his career in 2001.

Highest batting average by a catcher Joe Mauer's (U.S.A.) .365 batting average playing for the Minnesota Twins during the 2009 season was an MLB record for a catcher. It was Mauer's third batting title in four seasons.

MOST . . .

At bats without recording a hit Eugenio Vélez (Dominican Republic) of the Los Angeles Dodgers set a post-1900 MLB record for a nonpitcher by going hitless in 46 consecutive at bats in 2010 and 2011. Vélez broke the record of 45 straight at bats by Bill Bergen (U.S.A.) of the Brooklyn Superbas in 1909, Dave Campbell (U.S.A.) of the San Diego Padres and St. Louis Cardinals in 1973, and Craig Counsell (U.S.A.) of the Milwaukee Brewers in 2011.

MOST HITS IN A WORLD SERIES GAME Two batters have recorded five hits in a World Series game: Paul Molitor (U.S.A.) for the Milwaukee Brewers in Game 1 of the 1982 World Series against the St. Louis Cardinals on October 12, 1982, and Albert Pujols (Dominican Republic, left) for the St. Louis Cardinals in Game 3 of the 2011 World Series against the Texas Rangers on October 22, 2011. In his game, Pujols also set the record for most **total bases in a World Series game**, with 14. He hit three home runs (12 total bases) and two singles (2 total bases).

MOST GRAND-SLAM HOME RUNS IN A GAME The New York Yankees hit three grand-slam home runs in their 22–9 victory over the Oakland Athletics on August 25, 2011. The grand-slam home runs were hit by Robinson Canó (Dominican Republic), Russell Martin (Canada), and Curtis Granderson (U.S.A., right). A grand-slam home run occurs when the bases are "loaded," so the team scores four runs.

MOST CONSECUTIVE LOSING SEASONS The Pittsburgh Pirates endured 19 MLB losing seasons from 1993 to 2011. Left, Ronnie Cedeno of the Pirates argues an umpire's call in another defeat: 9–1 to the St. Louis Cardinals in 2010.

MOST CAREER RUNS BATTED IN BY A DESIGNATED HITTER David Ortiz (Dominican Republic) has batted in 1,097 runs as a designated hitter playing for the Minnesota Twins and Boston Red Sox since 1997.

Consecutive winless games by a starting pitcher Three MLB starting pitchers have recorded 28 consecutive winless games: Jo-Jo Reyes (U.S.A.) for the Atlanta Braves and the Toronto Blue Jays from 2008 to 2011; Matt Keough (U.S.A.) for the Oakland Athletics in 1978–79; and Cliff Curtis (U.S.A.) for the Boston Braves in 1910–11.

Home runs hit in a postseason series Nelson Cruz (Dominican Republic) hit six home runs while playing for the Texas Rangers against the Detroit Tigers in the 2011 American League Championship Series.

In this series, Cruz also set an MLB record for **most runs batted in (RBIs) in a postseason series**, with 13.

Hits by a shortstop Derek Jeter (U.S.A.) has recorded 3,053 hits for the New York Yankees since 1995. He is the Yankees' all-time leader in hits.

Games played at shortstop Omar Vizquel (Venezuela) has played 2,699 MLB games as a shortstop for the Seattle Mariners, Cleveland Indians, San Francisco Giants, Texas Rangers, and Chicago White Sox since 1989. Vizquel also has the record for **most seasons played at shortstop**, with 23.

Games played at catcher Iván Rodríguez (Puerto Rico) has played 2,427 MLB games as a catcher while playing for the Texas Rangers, Florida Marlins, Detroit Tigers, New York Yankees, Houston Astros, and Washington Nationals since he made his MLB debut at the age of 19 on June 20, 1991.

Runs batted in (RBIs) in a single postseason David Freese (U.S.A.) batted in 21 runs in the 2011 postseason for the St. Louis Cardinals.

MAJOR LEAGUE BASEBALL [MLB] RECORDS

Team

Most World Series titles (first awarded in 1903)	27	New York Yankees
	11	St. Louis Cardinals
	9	Philadelphia/Kansas City/Oakland Athletics
Largest current stadiums (by seating capacity)	56,000	Dodger Stadium (Los Angeles, California, U.S.A.), home of the Los Angeles Dodgers
	50,490	Coors Field (Denver, Colorado, U.S.A.), home of the Colorado Rockies
	50,291	Yankee Stadium (Bronx, New York, U.S.A.), home of the New York Yankees
Oldest clubs (year founded)	1870	Chicago Cubs
	1871	Boston/Milwaukee/Atlanta Braves
	1882	St. Louis Cardinals
		Cincinnati Reds
		Pittsburgh Pirates
Individual		
Most MVP of the Year awards (first awarded in 1911)	7	Barry Bonds
	3	Jimmie Foxx, Joe DiMaggio, Stan Musial, Roy Campanella, Yogi Berra, Mickey Mantle, Mike Schmidt, Albert Pujols, Alex Rodriguez

Statistics correct as of the end of the 2011 season

RBIs in an inning Fernando Tatís (Dominican Republic) batted in eight runs playing for the St. Louis Cardinals on April 23, 1999. Tatís hit a record two grand-slam home runs in the innings, both against Los Angeles Dodgers pitcher Chan Ho Park (South Korea).

Consecutive games Cal Ripken, Jr. played 2,632 MLB games for the Baltimore Orioles from May 30, 1982, to September 19, 1998.

MOST SAVES FOR A ROOKIE PITCHER Craig Kimbrel (U.S.A.) saved 46 games for the Atlanta Braves in 2011, his first full season in the MLB. He made such an impression that he was selected by San Francisco Giants manager Bruce Bochy for the 2011 All-Star Game.

Consecutive World Series victories The New York Yankees won the World Series five times from 1949 to 1953.

Games won by a pitcher Denton True "Cy" Young (U.S.A.) won 511 MLB games from 1890 to 1911 for the Cleveland Spiders, St. Louis Cardinals, Boston Red Sox, Cleveland Indians, and Boston Braves.

Cy Young Awards Since 1956, the Cy Young Award has been given annually to the outstanding pitcher in the major leagues. Roger Clemens (U.S.A.) has won seven Cy Young Awards, playing for the Boston Red Sox in 1986, 1987, 1991; Toronto Blue Jays in 1997–98; New York Yankees in 2001; and Houston Astros in 2004.

Wild pitches thrown in an inning Several pitchers have thrown four wild pitches in an innings: R. A. Dickey (U.S.A.) is the most recent, playing for the Seattle Mariners on August 17, 2008.

MOST GAMES PITCHED WITH ONE TEAM Mariano Rivera (Panama) pitched 1,042 games for the New York Yankees from 1995 to the end of the 2011 season. Rivera also holds the record for most career saves, with 603. A save is credited when a relief pitcher holds onto a winning lead of three runs or fewer.

FACT: Rivera also holds the record for **most games finished in a career**, with 883.

CRICKET

Highest partnership in a Test match Mahela Jayawardene and Kumar Sangakkara scored 624 together for Sri Lanka against South Africa in Colombo, Sri Lanka, on July 27–29, 2006. Jayawardene hit 374—the fourth highest Test innings by an individual—and Sangakkara 287 as Sri Lanka scored 756 for 5 declared. Sri Lanka won the match by an inning and 153 runs.

Highest Test batting average Sir Don Bradman (Australia) averaged 99.94 playing for Australia in 52 Tests between 1928 and 1948. He needed just four in his last innings against England at The Oval to attain a career average of 100, but he was out for a duck!

Highest score in a Test inning (team) Sri Lanka scored 952 for 6 against India at Colombo in August 1997. This beat England's score of 903 for 7 against Australia at The Oval, London, UK, in August 1938.

HIGHEST INDIVIDUAL SCORE IN AN ODI India captain and opener Virender Sehwag struck 219 runs from 149 balls against the West Indies at Holkar Cricket Stadium in Indore, India, on December 8, 2011. Sehwag's extraordinary innings, which lasted 208 minutes and included 25 fours and seven sixes, beat Sachin Tendulkar's (India) record ODI score of 200 not out. India scored 418 for five, their highest ODI score, and won the match by a whopping 158 runs.

MOST TEST SERIES WHITEWASHES The country with the most Test series "whitewashes" is 19, by Australia between 1920 and the 4–0 thrashing of India in 2011–12 (left). This record includes series with a minimum of three matches.

FACT: Gayle (see page 480) hit 6, 6 (off a no-ball), 4, 4, 6, 6, 4—so with one run for the no-ball, 37 runs came off the over.

RUNS, WICKETS, AND WORLD CUP WINS

Test cricket

Most runs	15,470	Sachin Tendulkar (Ind, 1989–)
	13,288	Rahul Dravid (Ind, 1996–2012)
	13,200	Ricky Ponting (Aus, 1995–)
Most wickets	800	Muttiah Muralitharan (SL, 1992–2010)
	708	Shane Warne (Aus, 1992–2007)
	690	Anil Kumble (Ind, 1990–2008)

One-Day Internationals

Most runs	18,342	Sachin Tendulkar (Ind, 1989–)
	13,704	Ricky Ponting (Aus, 1995–2012)
	13,430	Sanath Jayasuriya (SL,1989–2011)
Most wickets	534	Muttiah Muralitharan (SL, 1993–2011)
	502	Wasim Akram (Pak, 1984–2003)
	416	Waqar Younis (Pak, 1989–2003)
Most World Cup wins	4	Australia (1987, 1999, 2003, 2007)
	2	India (1983, 2011)
		West Indies (1975, 1979)
	1	Pakistan (1992)
		Sri Lanka (1996)

Statistics correct as of April 1, 2012

MOST RUNS OFF AN OVER IN THE IPL Chris Gayle (Jamaica) of the Royal Challengers hit 37 off an over by Prasanth Parameswaran (India) of the Kochi Tuskers in Bangalore, India, on May 8, 2011.

FASTEST PLAYERS TO 1,000 ODI RUNS Three players have reached 1,000 ODI runs in only 21 innings: Viv Richards (West Indies) on January 22, 1980; Kevin Pietersen (England) on March 31, 2006; and Jonathan Trott (England, above), on August 27, 2009. Ironically, Trott scored a duck in his first ODI against Ireland in Belfast on August 21, 2009.

MOST CENTURIES IN INTERNATIONALS When he scored 114 against Bangladesh in an ODI on March 16, 2012, the "Little Master" Sachin Tendulkar (India) became the first player to score 100 international centuries.

Longest Test match Before World War II, Test matches were often "timeless"—that is, played until one side won. The longest timeless Test was between England and South Africa at Durban, South Africa, on March 3–14, 1939. The total playing time was 43 hr. 16 min. and a record Test match aggregate of 1,981 runs were scored. Ironically, the match still did not have a positive result—it was abandoned after 10 days, with the eighth day rained off, because the ship taking the England team home was due to leave. The **shortest Test** was the rain-hit England-Australia match at Trent Bridge on June 12, 1926, which saw only 50 minutes of play.

Most consecutive wins in Test cricket Australia recorded a run of 16 successive Test victories when they beat India by 10 wickets at Mumbai, India, in March 2001. Australia was all set to make it 17 against India at Eden Gardens, Kolkata, India, later that month—however, although they gained a first-innings lead of 274 runs and enforced the follow-on, India eventually won the match by 171 runs. This is the **greatest margin of victory after following-on**. Australia repeated its feat of 16 wins in a row from December 26, 2005 to January 2, 2008.

FACT: Tendulkar has the **most runs overall (ODI, Test and Twenty20)**—33,906 as of April 25, 2012.

MOST DUCKS IN TWENTY20 INTERNATIONALS The most scores of 0 recorded by an individual batsman in Twenty20 international matches is six, by Jean-Paul Duminy (South Africa, left), between 2007 and 2011. The record for the **most ducks in IPL Twenty20 cricket** is seven, held by Shane Warne (Australia) playing for Rajasthan Royals between 2008 and 2011.

Lowest team score in a Test match innings The lowest innings total in Test cricket is 26, by New Zealand versus England at Auckland on March 28, 1955.

Most runs scored in a Test match Graham Gooch (England) scored 456 in total (333 in the first innings and 123 in the second) against India at Lords, London, England, between July 26 and 31, 1990. The **most runs scored by a female player in a Test match** was by Pakistan opener Kiran Baluch, who scored 264 in total (242 in the first innings and 22 in the second) in the Test against West Indies at Karachi, Pakistan, on March 15–18, 2004.

Most dismissals in a Test match career Mark Boucher (South Africa) has 555 Test dismissals in Tests (532 catches and 23 stumpings). Boucher also has the **most dismissals in international cricket**, with 998 (952 catches and 46 stumpings). All figures as of April 24, 2012.

Most sixes by a player in a first-class inning Three batsmen have hit 16 sixes in a first-class inning: Andrew Symonds (Australia) for Gloucestershire against Glamorgan at Abergavenny, Wales, UK, on August 24–25, 1995; Graham Napier (UK) for Essex against Surrey, at Whit-

---

SACHIN'S 100 HUNDREDS

• Sachin's first international century was scored on August 14, 1990, at Old Trafford, Manchester, against England.

• Of his 100 hundreds, Sachin scored 51 in Test cricket and 49 in ODI cricket (the most in both forms of cricket).

• Australia is his favorite victim—he scored 20 of his 100 centuries against them.

• He hit his 99th century against South Africa on March 12, 2010, but had to wait 1 year 4 days for his 100th against Bangladesh. That was the second longest period between any of his centuries—the longest came after his first century.

---

gift in Surrey, UK, on May 19, 2011; and Jesse Ryder (New Zealand) for New Zealand against Australia A at Brisbane, Australia, on November 27, 2011.

Highest partnership in an ODI Rahul Dravid and Sachin Tendulkar hit 331 in a One-Day International (ODI) for India against New Zealand in Hyderabad, Andhra Pradesh, India, on November 8, 1999. Dravid made 153 and Tendulkar 186 not out in India's total of 376, and India won by 174 runs.

Most ODI appearances (female) Charlotte Edwards has played 155 matches for England in ODIs since 1997. She has scored 4,755 ODI runs with a top score of 173 not out.

Most sixes by a player in a Twenty20 international In only his second Twenty20 international, Richard Levi hit 13 sixes for South Africa as he destroyed the New Zealand attack in Hamilton, New Zealand, on February 19, 2012. He scored 117 not out, equaling the **highest Twenty20 international individual score**, in South Africa's winning total of 174 for 2.

Most expensive IPL player Gautam Gambhir (India) was bought for U.S. $2.4 million by the Kolkata Knight Riders in the Indian Premier League (IPL) Season 4 on January 8, 2011.

ICE HOCKEY

Most overtime game winners Joe Sakic (Canada) set the NHL record for the most overtime game-winning play-off goals, with eight, all scored for the Colorado Avalanche (U.S.A.) from 1996 to 2008.

Most Stanley Cup finals refereed Bill McCreary (Canada) has skated as the referee in 44 career Stanley Cup finals games in the NHL. His 44th outing was Game 5 of the 2010 finals on June 6, but it was with his 43rd, Game 3 of the 2010 finals on June 3, that he surpassed the previous record of 42, held by Bill Chadwick (U.S.A.). McCreary has refereed more than 1,600 games since, making his debut in the 1984–85 season; his first Stanley Cup final series appearance was in 1994.

FACT: In 2011, Thomas made the **most saves in a single postseason**, with 798 in the Stanley Cup playoffs, and the **most saves in a single Stanley Cup final**, with 238 playing against the Vancouver Canucks.

• Marcus Vinnerborg (Sweden) became the **first European-trained referee in an NHL game**, overseeing a 2–1 win for the Dallas Stars over the visiting Anaheim Ducks (both U.S.A.) on November 16, 2010.

• Evgeni Nabokov (Russia) became the **first goalie to score a powerplay goal**, for the San Jose Sharks (U.S.A.) with a man advantage over the Vancouver Canucks (Canada), on March 10, 2002.

• It wouldn't be a list of firsts without an appearance from Martin Brodeur (Canada), the **first NHL goalie to win 600 career games**, hitting the mark when the New Jersey Devils defeated the Atlanta Thrashers (both U.S.A.), 3–0, on April 6, 2010.

MOST GOALS SCORED IN AN NHL CAREER BY A U.S. PLAYER Mike Modano (U.S.A.) racked up an amazing 561 goals in his career for the Minnesota North Stars, Dallas Stars, and Detroit Red Wings (all U.S.A.) from the 1989–90 season through to the end of the 2010–11 season. Only three other U.S.-born players have scored 500 or more goals: Jeremy Roenick, Joe Mullen, and Keith Tkachuk. Wayne Gretzky (Canada) has the **most goals in NHL history**, with 894.

Fastest ice hockey shot The hardest known ice hockey shot was a 110.3-mph (177.5-km/h) slap shot by Denis Kulyash (Russia) of Avangard Omsk, made in the Kontinental Hockey League's All-Star skills competition, held in St. Petersburg, Russia, on February 5, 2011. Kulyash's shot has earned him the nickname "Tsar Cannon," after a 1586 cannon outside the Kremlin.

Kulyash's effort beat Zdeno Chára (Slovakia) of the Boston Bruins (U.S.A.), who hit a 105.9-mph (170.4-km/h) slap shot in the NHL All-Star SuperSkills competition in Raleigh, North Carolina, U.S.A., on January 29, 2011.

Longest ice hockey marathon Brent Saik (Canada) and friends really had to get their skates on when they played hockey for 242 hours at Saiker's Acres in Sherwood Park, Alberta, Canada, from February

> **FACT:** Modano is the highest-scoring U.S.-born player in NHL history, with 1,374 career points—561 goals and 813 assists.

11 to 21, 2011. The group of 40 was split into two teams called Blue and White. The Whites were the winners, with the final score standing at 2,067–2,005. It was the fourth attempt on the record by Saik and his associates, who were using the match to raise funds for cancer treatment.

Most consecutive professional wins The Cardiff Devils (UK) had a winning streak of 21 in the Elite Ice Hockey League (UK) from October 31, 2010, to January 15, 2011. The Devils outscored opponents by a combined score of 111–38 during their perfect run.

Fewest wins in an NHL season The fewest wins recorded by a team in a single NHL season—playing at least 70 games—is eight, by the Washington Capitals (U.S.A.) in 1974–75. The "Caps" also had the **most consecutive losses in NHL history** that season, with 17.

Most consecutive seasons scoring over 100 points The Detroit Red Wings (U.S.A.) topped 100 points in a record nine straight seasons from 1999–2000 to 2008–09.

GOAL-TENDERS

Oldest winner of the Conn Smythe Trophy Tim Thomas (b. April 15, 1974) of the Boston Bruins was, at 37 years 62 days, the oldest player in National Hockey League history to win the Conn Smythe Trophy, awarded to the Most Valuable Player of the Stanley Cup playoffs. He received the award on June 15, 2011.

Most regular season games played in an NHL career By the end of the regular season on April 7, 2012, Martin Brodeur, goalie for the New Jersey Devils, had played the most career regular season games, with 1,191 since 1993–94.

HIGHEST GOALIE SAVE PERCENTAGE Tim Thomas (U.S.A.) saved 1,699 goals while playing for the Boston Bruins (U.S.A.) in the 2010–11 regular season and set a record NHL save percentage of .938. Fan favorite Thomas also set the record for the highest save percentage by a goaltender in the NHL Stanley Cup finals, with .967.

FIRST NHL TEAM TO WIN THREE SEVEN-GAME SERIES IN A POSTSEASON During the 2011 NHL playoffs, the Boston Bruins became the first team in the league's history to win a Game 7 three times in the same postseason. The Bruins won a clinching Game 7 victory over the Montreal Canadiens (Canada) in the first round, the Tampa Bay Lightning (U.S.A.) in the Eastern Conference finals and Vancouver Canucks in the Stanley Cup finals.

Brodeur had racked up the **most NHL career regular season minutes**, with 70,029. In the 2006–07 season, he had 48 wins, the **most matches won by a goaltender in a regular season**. Overall, he has 371 losses, the **most regular season NHL career losses**, yet has managed the **most regular season NHL career shutouts by a goalie**, with 119.

Most NHL shutouts in playoffs Patrick Roy (Canada) recorded 23 shutouts in a career with the Montreal Canadiens (Canada) and Colorado Avalanche (U.S.A.) from 1985–86 to 2002–03. His shutouts have been equaled by Martin Brodeur in his career with the New Jersey Devils.

Most regular season goals allowed in a career During the 1999–2000 season, Grant Fuhr (Canada) let in his 2,756th goal and—possibly not the most coveted title in the NHL—tied the record for most regular season goals conceded by a goaltender in a career. Fuhr played for the Edmonton Oilers, Toronto Maple Leafs (both Canada), Buffalo Sabres, Los

NATIONAL HOCKEY LEAGUE

Most Stanley Cup titles (first held 1893–94)	24	Montreal Canadiens (Canada)
	13	Toronto Maple Leafs (Canada)
Most regular season games	1,767	Gordon "Gordie" Howe (Canada)
	1,756	Mark Messier (Canada)
Most regular season goals	894	Wayne Gretzky (Canada)
	801	Gordon "Gordie" Howe (Canada)
Largest capacity arena	21,273	Bell Centre, Montreal (Montreal Canadiens)
	20,066	Joe Louis Arena, Detroit (Detroit Red Wings)

Statistics correct as of April 5, 2012

MOST SAVES BY A GOALTENDER IN A CAREER The dazzling Martin Brodeur just can't help breaking goaltending records. By April 2012, he had set another in the NHL for the most regular season career saves by a goaltender, with 27,312. Brodeur, who has played with the New Jersey Devils (U.S.A.) for his entire career, reached the total playing from the 1993–94 season. He also holds the record for **most NHL regular season career wins by a goaltender, with 656.**

Angeles Kings, St. Louis Blues (all U.S.A.), and Calgary Flames (Canada) from 1981–82 to 1999–2000. The total was first reached by Gilles Meloche (Canada), who played between 1970–71 and 1987–88.

Youngest to record a shutout At 18 years 65 days, Harry Lumley (Canada, 1926–98) became the youngest NHL netminder to record a shutout. Lumley was playing for the Detroit Red Wings when he blanked the Toronto Maple Leafs (Canada) 3–0 on January 14, 1945. It was his only shutout of the 1944–45 season.

Lumley also holds the record for **youngest goalie to play in an NHL game**. He was 17 years 42 days old when he first took to the ice as a New York Rangers (U.S.A.) rookie in the 1943–44 season.

Most matches won in overtime in a career Roberto Luongo (Canada) of the Vancouver Canucks set the NHL record for most overtime wins by a goaltender over the course of a career, with 49.

TEAMS ROUND-UP

NETBALL

Oldest club The Poly Netball Club was founded in London, UK, in 1907 by a team from the Regent Street Polytechnic and has been in continuous existence ever since. The club's first recorded match was a 40–4 victory over the Northampton Institute in January 1909.

NETBALL, WATER POLO, AND HOCKEY VICTORIES

Netball

Most World Championships (first awarded in 1963, held every four years) *three-way tie	10	Australia (1963, 1971, 1975, 1979*, 1983, 1991, 1995, 1999, 2007, 2011)
	4	New Zealand (1967, 1979*, 1987, 2003)
	1	Trinidad and Tobago (1979*)

Water polo

Most men's Olympic golds (first awarded in 1900)	9	Hungary (1932, 1936, 1952, 1956, 1964, 1976, 2000, 2004, 2008)
	4	Great Britain (1900, 1908, 1912, 1920)
	3	Italy (1948, 1960, 1992)
Most women's Olympic golds (first awarded in 2000)	1	Australia (2000)
		Italy (2004)
		Netherlands (2008)

Hockey

Most men's World Cups (first awarded in 1971)	4	Pakistan (1971, 1978, 1982, 1994)
	3	Netherlands (1973, 1990, 1998)
	2	Germany (2002, 2006)
		Australia (1986, 2010)
Most women's World Cups (first awarded in 1974)	6	Netherlands (1974, 1978, 1983, 1986, 1990, 2006)
	2	Argentina (2002, 2010)
		Germany (1976, 1981)
		Australia (1994, 1998)
Most men's Olympic golds (first awarded in 1908)	8	India (1928, 1932, 1936, 1948, 1952, 1956, 1964, 1980)
	3	Germany (1972, 1992, 2008)
		Great Britain (1908, 1920, 1988)
Most women's Olympic golds (first awarded in 1980)	3	Australia (1988, 1996, 2000)
	2	Netherlands (1984, 2008)

Statistics correct as of April 3, 2012

Most points scored at a World Championships Irene van Dyk (New Zealand, b. South Africa) scored 543 points in the 1995 World Championships, the most for a single tournament. She also holds the record for the **most international appearances**, with 202 as of April 20, 2012. These comprise 72 caps for South Africa and 130 caps for New Zealand (van Dyk moved to New Zealand in 2000 and became a citizen in 2005).

Longest game Netball Alberta organized a match between Team Rockers and Team Rollers that lasted 61 hours at the South Fish Creek recreation complex in Calgary, Alberta, Canada, on September 16–19, 2011. Team Rockers won 2,759–1,405.

Most World Series wins New Zealand has won the World Series twice, in 2009 and 2010.

MOST CHAMPIONS LEAGUE HANDBALL WINS The European Handball Federation (EHF) Champions League, started in 1956, is Europe's premier club handball competition. FC Barcelona's (Spain) handball team have won the Champions League eight times, in 1991, 1996–2000, 2005, and 2011. In 2011, Barca beat BM Ciudad Real (Spain) 27–24 in Cologne, Germany, on May 29, under the captaincy of László Nagy (kissing the trophy, above). VfL Gummersbach (Germany) is the second most successful team, with five wins.

MOST NETBALL SUPERLEAGUE WINS The Netball Superleague, held since 1996, is the premier netball club competition in Britain. Team Bath (left), which originates from the University of Bath, UK, have won the competition a record four times, in 2006–07 and 2009–10. The Hertfordshire Mavericks have won two titles, in 2008 and 2011.

MOST VOLLEYBALL WORLD GRAND CHAMPIONS CUP WINS Volleyball's World Grand Champions Cup, inaugurated in 1993, is held every four years between six teams: the host nation, four continental champions, and one wild card. Brazil has won three times in the men's event, in 1997, 2005, and in 2009, the year they were the first team to defend the Cup.

In the women's event, also held since 1993, Cuba, Russia, China, Brazil, and Italy all have one win.

BEACH VOLLEYBALL

Highest earnings for a player (female) Misty May-Treanor (U.S.A.) has earned U.S. $2,078,083 in professional beach volleyball earnings up to April 2012. She took U.S. $1,062,945 from international beach volleyball matches and U.S. $1,015,138 from domestic matches. She also holds the record for the **most career tournament victories**, with 110–69 domestic and 41 international wins.

Oldest person to win a title At the age of 44 years 284 days, Karch Kiraly (U.S.A.) won the Huntington Beach Open in California, U.S.A., on August 13, 2005.

Youngest person to win a title At 17 years 99 days, Xue Chen (China) won the China Shanghai Jinshan Open in Shanghai, China, on May 28, 2006.

MOST MEN'S HANDBALL SUPER GLOBE WINS The International Handball Federation Super Globe is a handball competition contested between the champion clubs from continental confederations. BM Ciudad Real (Spain) have the most Super Globes, with two, in 2007 and 2010. Left, BM Ciudad Real player Luc Abalo tries to score against Qatar's Al-Sadd in the 2010 tournament in Doha, Qatar.

LACROSSE

Most men's World Championships U.S.A. has won 9 of the 11 World Championships, in 1967, 1974, 1982, 1986, 1990, 1994, 1998, 2010, and 2011. Canada won the two other titles, in 1978 and 2006.

Most women's World Cups U.S.A. has won six World Cups, in 1982, 1989, 1993, 1997, 2001, and 2009. Canada is the only other winner, in 1978 and 2006.

Fastest lacrosse shot Paul Rabil (U.S.A.) recorded a lacrosse shot of 111 mph (178 km/h) at the Major League Lacrosse All-Star Game's Fastest Shot competition in Boston, Massachusetts, U.S.A., on July 8, 2010, matching a shot he made in 2009. In the competition, each participant shoots 10 yards (9 m) away from the goal and only shots that enter the goal count.

MOST WATER POLO WORLD LEAGUE WINS Serbia has won the men's FINA Water Polo League six times, in 2005–08 and 2010–11. In the 2011 competition, they beat Italy 8–7 in a dramatic final in Florence, Italy, on June 26, shown above.

The most wins of the FINA Water Polo World League by a women's national team is also six, by the U.S.A. in 2004, 2006–07, and 2009–11. The men's World League has been contested every year since 2002 and the women's event since 2004.

FACT: Serbia's Filip Filipović (above) and Italy's Stefano Luongo compete in the 2011 World League final.

KORFBALL

Most Europa Cup wins Korfball, a mixed-gender sport with teams of four men and four women, is similar to netball and basketball, and the Europa Cup has been held since 1967. The most wins of the Europa Cup is six, by PKC (Netherlands) in 1985, 1990, 1999–2000, 2002, and 2006.

Highest score in a Europa Cup final The highest score recorded by a club team in a Europa Cup final is 33, by Koog Zaandijk (Netherlands) in Budapest, Hungary, on January 22, 2011. Koog Zaandijk beat Royal Scaldis SC (Belgium) 33–23—this match's 56 points also represents the **highest total points in a Europa Cup final**.

HOCKEY

Highest score in international hockey (women) England defeated France 23–0 in Merton, London, UK, on February 3, 1923.

Most men's EuroHockey Nations Championship wins The Euro-Hockey Nations Championship, held since 1970, is the premier international hockey competition in Europe. Germany (formerly West Germany) won the Championship seven times between 1970 and 2011.

FLOORBALL

Most World Championships Floorball is a type of indoor hockey, and Sweden has won the men's World Championships six times, from 1996 to 2006. Finland is the only other winner (in 2008 and 2010). Sweden also holds the record for the **most women's World Championships**, with five from 1997 to 2011. Finland, in 1999 and 2001, and Switzerland, in 2005, are the only other winners.

HURLING

Most All-Ireland Championships wins Hurling is a 15-a-side sport of Gaelic origin, in which players attempt to score points by hitting a ball with a stick, known as a hurley, into or over their opponent's goal. Kilkenny won 33 All-Ireland Championships between 1904 and 2011. Kilkenny's four Championships in 2006–2009 is a record for the **most successive All-Ireland Championships**, equaling the achievement of Cork in 1941–44.

Most All-Ireland Camogie Championships wins as captain Camogie is the women's version of hurling. The most wins of the Camogie Championship by a team captain is six, by Sophie Brack (Ireland, d. 1996) for Dublin between 1948 and 1955.

Dublin has won the **most All-Ireland Senior Camogie Championships** with 26 victories between 1932 and 1984.

BASKETBALL

NBA

Highest percentage shooting three-point field goals in a career
Playing for six different teams from 1988–89 to 2002–03, Steve Kerr (U.S.A., b. Lebanon) recorded a three-point field-goal percentage of .454. Kerr made 726 of 1,599 attempts.

Most championship titles won by a coach Phil Jackson (U.S.A.) won 11 NBA championships. He picked up six titles as coach of the Chicago Bulls, in 1991–93 and 1996–98, and five as coach of the Los Angeles Lakers, in 2000–02 and 2009–10.

Jackson holds the record for **most NBA career playoff games by a coach**. His total of 333 was achieved with the Chicago Bulls from 1989 to 1998 and the Los Angeles Lakers from 1999 to 2011. During the same period, he set a new record for the **most NBA playoff wins by a coach**. His 229 victories of 333 playoffs yielded a winning percentage of .688, the **highest winning percentage by a coach in NBA playoffs**.

MOST THREE-POINT FIELD GOALS CONVERTED BY AN NBA TEAM IN A PLAYOFF The Seattle SuperSonics converted 20 three-point field goals against the Houston Rockets on May 6, 1996, a feat matched by the Dallas Mavericks against the Los Angeles Lakers on May 8, 2011. The Mavericks' Peja Stojaković (Serbia) is shown (left) with the Lakers' Derek Fisher (U.S.A.).

MOST FREE THROW CONVERSIONS WITHOUT A MISS IN AN NBA PLAYOFF Dirk Nowitzki (Germany) of the Dallas Mavericks set an NBA playoff record by converting 24 straight free throws during a 121–112 defeat of the Oklahoma City Thunder in the first game of the Western Conference playoffs on May 17, 2011.

FACT: In 2006–07 Dirk was the first European to win the NBA's Most Valuable Player (MVP) award.

MOST SEASONS WITH THE LEADING FIELD-GOAL PERCENTAGE Shaquille O'Neal (U.S.A.) held the leading NBA field-goal percentage for a record 10 seasons. He achieved the feat while playing for the Orlando Magic in 1993–94, the Los Angeles Lakers from 1997–98 to 2003–04, the Miami Heat from 2004–05 to 2005–06 and the Phoenix Suns in 2008–09. He also achieved the NBA highest career field-goal percentage, with .582 between 1992 and 2011. O'Neal converted 11,330 of 19,457 attempts.

Largest attendance A crowd of 108,713 watched the NBA All-Star Game at Cowboys Stadium in Dallas, Texas, U.S.A., on February 14, 2010.

Most three-point field goals in a career Ray Allen (U.S.A.) scored a three-point field goal for the 2,561st time in his career during the first quarter of a game playing for the Boston Celtics against the Los Angeles Lakers on February 10, 2011, surpassing the previous mark of 2,560 held by Reggie Miller (U.S.A.) of the Indiana Pacers. Allen, who has also played for the Milwaukee Bucks and Seattle SuperSonics since 1996, had scored a total of 2,718 three-point field goals as of April 23, 2012.

Allen holds the record for the **most career three-point field goals attempted by an individual**, with 6,788 as of April 23, 2012. He also scored eight three-point field goals for the Boston Celtics against the Los Angeles Lakers at the Staples Center in Los Angeles, California, U.S.A., on June 6, 2010, a record for the **most three-point field goals scored by an individual in an NBA Finals game**.

Finally, Allen has scored the **most three-point field goals by an individual in an NBA Finals series**, with 22 against the Los Angeles Lakers in 2008.

Most wins in a season The Chicago Bulls racked up 72 wins and just 10 losses in the 1995–96 season.

HIGHEST THREE-POINT FIELD-GOAL PERCENTAGE IN AN NBA SEASON Kyle Korver (U.S.A.) achieved a .536 three-point field-goal percentage while playing for the Utah Jazz during the 2009–10 season. Korver converted 59 of 110 attempts.

FACT: Sharp-shooting must be in Korver's genes. His mother once netted 74 points in a high-school match.

Most losses in a season The Philadelphia 76ers had the least successful regular season of all time, with 73 losses and only nine wins in 1972–73. The **most consecutive losses by a team** stands at 26, made by the Cleveland Cavaliers between December 20, 2010 and February 11, 2011.

Youngest player On November 2, 2005, Andrew Bynum (U.S.A., b. October 27, 1987) was 18 years 6 days old when he played for the Los Angeles Lakers against the Denver Nuggets.

The **youngest winner of the NBA Most Valuable Player award** is Derrick Rose (U.S.A.) of the Chicago Bulls. Rose was aged just 22 when he received this accolade for his efforts in the 2010–11 season.

WNBA *

Most games played in a career Tangela Smith (U.S.A.) has played in 448 games during her Women's National Basketball Association (WNBA) career with the Sacramento Monarchs, Charlotte Sting, Phoenix Mercury, and Indiana Fever since 1998.

Most field goals scored in a career Tina Thompson (U.S.A.) scored an NBA record of 2,385 field goals playing for the Houston Comets and Los Angeles Sparks from 1997 to the end of the 2011 season.

The prolific Thompson has played 14,561 minutes, the **most minutes played in a WNBA career**, and also shares the record for the **most minutes played per game in an WNBA career**—33.6—with Katie Smith (U.S.A.).

Smith has scored the **most three-point field goals in a WNBA career**. Her 834 three-point field goals have come during her stints with the Minnesota Lynx, Detroit Shock, Washington Mystics, and Seattle Storm from 1999 to the end of the 2011 season.

Most assists in a career Since 1998, Ticha Penicheiro (Portugal) has made 2,560 assists in 435 games for the Sacramento Monarchs and Los Angeles Sparks. She also has **most assists per game**: 5.9.

HIGHEST REBOUNDS PER GAME AVERAGE (WNBA) Tina Charles (U.S.A., left) has recorded an average of 11.4 rebounds per WNBA game playing for the Connecticut Sun since 2010. Charles also recorded a single-season record 398 rebounds in 34 games by the end of the 2011 season.

All WNBA records until end of 2011 season.

FIBA (International Basketball Federation)

Most FIBA World Championships (first held in 1950)	5	Yugoslavia/Serbia
	4	U.S.A.
	3	Soviet Union
Most FIBA Women's World Championships (first held in 1953)	8	U.S.A.
	6	Soviet Union
	1	Australia

NBA (National Basketball Association)

Most NBA titles (first held in 1946–47)	17	Boston Celtics
	16	Minneapolis/Los Angeles Lakers
	6	Chicago Bulls
Most NBA career appearances	1,611	Robert Parish (U.S.A.)
	1,560	Kareem Abdul-Jabbar (U.S.A.)
	1,504	John Stockton (U.S.A.)
Most NBA career points	38,387	Kareem Abdul-Jabbar (U.S.A.)
	36,928	Karl Malone (U.S.A.)
	32,292	Michael Jordan (U.S.A.)

WNBA (Women's National Basketball Association)

Most WNBA titles (first held in 1997)	4	Houston Comets
	3	Detroit Shock
	2	Los Angeles Sparks
		Phoenix Mercury
		Seattle Storm
Most WNBA career appearances	448	Tangela Smith (U.S.A.)
	435	Ticha Penicheiro (Portugal)
	433	Tina Thompson (U.S.A.)
Most WNBA career points	6,751	Tina Thompson (U.S.A.)
	6,263	Lisa Leslie (U.S.A.)
	6,015	Katie Smith (U.S.A.)

Statistics correct as of April 2, 2012

Most steals in a career Tamika Catchings (U.S.A.)—who in 2011 was named as one of the top 15 players in WNBA history—has recorded 775 steals for the Indiana Fever in 313 games since 2002.

Most double-doubles in a season The greatest number of double-doubles (recording double-figures in points scored and rebounds in the same game) is 23, by Tina Charles (U.S.A.) playing for the Connecticut Sun in 2011.

Fewest points scored in a quarter by a team The record for fewest points scored in a quarter is one, by the Chicago Sky in the fourth quarter of a 59–49 defeat to the New York Liberty on August 4, 2011.

Most consecutive losses by a team The Tulsa Shock started the 2011 season by winning just one of their first 10 games. The coach and his interim successor were both replaced but the team ended the season with a record 20 straight losses.

TRACK & FIELD—MEN

OLYMPICS

First to feature athletes from all continents The first modern Olympics was held in Athens, Greece, in 1896 but it was not until the fifth Games in Stockholm, Sweden, in 1912, that the Games could finally boast athletes from every continent (excluding Antarctica). In making its debut in the Olympics, Japan became the first Asian nation to compete in the Games and was represented by marathon runner Shizo Kanakuri and sprinter Yahiko Mishima.

Oldest track & field medalist Tebbs Lloyd Johnson (UK, 1900–84) was aged 48 years 115 days when he came in third in the 50,000 m walk at the 1948 Olympics in London, UK.

LONGEST TRIPLE JUMP Jonathan Edwards (UK) hopped, skipped, and jumped 60 ft. 0.78 in. (18.29 m) at the 1995 World Championships in Gothenburg, Sweden, on August 7. He had already set the world record with an earlier jump of 59 ft. 6.96 in. (18.16 m). Edwards also jointly holds the record for the most men's European Athlete of the Year trophies, with two (1995 and 1998). Javelin thrower Jan Železný (Czech Republic, p. 500) and triple jumper Christian Olsson (Sweden) have also won the trophy twice.

FASTEST 4 × 100 M The Jamaican team of (from left, above) Nesta Carter, Michael Frater, Yohan Blake, and Usain Bolt ran the 4 × 100 m relay in 37.04 seconds at the 2011 World Championships at Daegu, South Korea, on September 4. They broke the record of 37.10 seconds set by Jamaica's 2008 Olympic team, which included Asafa Powell instead of Blake.

The oldest track & field gold medalist is Irish-born Patrick "Babe" McDonald (U.S.A., 1878–1954), who was 42 years 26 days when he won the 56-lb. (25.4-kg) weight throw at Antwerp, Belgium, on August 21, 1920.

Most Olympic gold medals by an athlete Paavo Nurmi (Finland) won nine golds at the 1,500 m, 3,000 m, 5,000 m, 10,000 m, and cross-country events from 1920 to 1928. Carl Lewis (U.S.A.) repeated the feat with nine golds at the 100 m, 200 m, 4 × 100 m relay, and long jump from 1984 to 1996.

Most gold medals, 1,500 m Sebastian Coe (UK) won two medals in the men's 1,500 m event in 1980 and 1984. As Lord Coe, he later headed London's bid for the 2012 Olympics, taking on the role of chairman of the London Organizing Committee for the Olympic Games (LOCOG).

FACT: Jan (see page 500) has the five top javelin performances of all time, with his best at 323 ft. 1.16 in. (98.48 m).

MOST OLYMPIC JAVELIN GOLD MEDALS
Jan Železný (Czech Republic) won three golds at successive Olympics in 1992, 1996, and 2000. Železný also holds the record for **most wins of the men's javelin at the World Championships,** with three, in 1993, 1995, and 2001. He is also the only man to have thrown the new javelin, introduced in 1986, over 308 ft. (94 m).

WORLD CHAMPIONSHIPS

Most appearances Jesús Ángel García (Spain) appeared in walking events at 10 World Championships between 1991 and 2009.

Most gold medals Carl Lewis and Michael Johnson (both U.S.A.) each won eight World Championship golds: Lewis in 1983–91 in the 100 m, 4 × 100 m, and long jump; Johnson in 1991–99 in the 200 m, 400 m, and 4 × 400 m.

Most 100 m wins Carl Lewis and Maurice Greene (both U.S.A.) have each won the World Championship 100 m three times: Lewis in 1983, 1987, and 1991; Greene in 1997, 1999, and 2001.

Most 1,500 m wins Hicham El Guerrouj (Morocco)—winner of the **most IAAF World Athlete of the Year trophies** (three in 2001–03)—has won the World Championship 1,500 m four times, in 1997, 1999, 2001, and 2003.

Most marathon wins Three athletes have won the World Championship marathon twice: Abel Antón (Spain) in 1997 and 1999, Jaouad Gharib (Morocco) in 2003 and 2005, and Abel Kirui (Kenya) in 2009 and 2011.

FASTEST 30,000 M On June 3, 2011, Moses Cheruiyot Mosop (Kenya) ran the 30,000 m in 1 hr. 26 min. 47.4 sec. in Eugene, Oregon, U.S.A. En route to the 30,000 m finish, he also ran the fastest 25,000 m, taking 1 hr. 12 min. 25.4 sec. Japan's Toshihiko Seko had previously held both records after his run in Christchurch, New Zealand, on March 22, 1981, yielding times of 1 hr. 13 min. 55.8 sec. for the 25,000 m and 1 hr. 29 min. 18.8 sec. for the 30,000 m. Mosop was the first man in 30 years to break the records.

MOST WORLD CHAMPIONSHIP LONG JUMP WINS Two athletes have won the men's long jump at the World Championships four times: Iván Pedroso (Cuba) and Dwight Phillips (U.S.A., above). Pedroso won his titles consecutively in 1995, 1997, 1999, and 2001; he also won three consecutive Pan American Games golds in 1995, 1999, and 2003.

Phillips won his World Championship golds in 2003, 2005, 2009, and 2011. In 2011, he was randomly assigned the bib number "1111." After winning, Phillips proudly pointed to the number which reflected his position in the four championships. He commented: "From the moment I saw the bib, I said this championship is mine."

MOST EUROPEAN CROSS COUNTRY CHAMPIONSHIP WINS Serhiy Lebid (Ukraine) won the European Cross Country Championships nine times from 1998 in Ferrara, Italy, to 2010 in Albufeira, Portugal.

FACT: Serhiy has competed in a record 18 European Cross Country Championships.

OUTDOOR TRACK EVENTS

Event	Time	Name & Nationality	Location	Date
100 m	9.58	Usain Bolt (Jamaica)	Berlin, Germany	Aug 16, 2009
200 m	19.19	Usain Bolt (Jamaica)	Berlin, Germany	Aug 20, 2009
400 m	43.18	Michael Johnson (U.S.A.)	Seville, Spain	Aug 26, 1999
800 m	1:41.01	David Lekuta Rudisha (Kenya)	Rieti, Italy	Aug 29, 2010
1,000 m	2:11.96	Noah Ngeny (Kenya)	Rieti, Italy	Sep 5, 1999
1,500 m	3:26.00	Hicham El Guerrouj (Morocco)	Rome, Italy	Jul 14, 1998
1 mile	3:43.13	Hicham El Guerrouj (Morocco)	Rome, Italy	Jul 7, 1999
2,000 m	4:44.79	Hicham El Guerrouj (Morocco)	Berlin, Germany	Sep 7, 1999
3,000 m	7:20.67	Daniel Komen (Kenya)	Rieti, Italy	Sep 1, 1996
5,000 m	12:37.35	Kenenisa Bekele (Ethiopia)	Hengelo, Netherlands	May 31, 2004
10,000 m	26:17.53	Kenenisa Bekele (Ethiopia)	Brussels, Belgium	Aug 26, 2005
20,000 m	56:26.00	Haile Gebrselassie (Ethiopia)	Ostrava, Czech Republic	Jun 26, 2007
25,000 m	1:12:25.4	Moses Cheruiyot Mosop (Kenya)	Eugene, Oregon, U.S.A.	Jun 3, 2011
30,000 m	1:26:47.4	Moses Cheruiyot Mosop (Kenya)	Eugene, Oregon, U.S.A.	Jun 3, 2011
3,000 m steeplechase	7:53.63	Saif Saaeed Shaheen (Qatar)	Brussels, Belgium	Sep 3, 2004
110 m hurdles	12.87	Dayron Robles (Cuba)	Ostrava, Czech Republic	Jun 12, 2008
400 m hurdles	46.78	Kevin Young (U.S.A.)	Barcelona, Spain	Aug 6, 1992
4 × 100 m relay	37.04	Jamaica (Yohan Blake, Nesta Carter, Michael Frater, Usain Bolt)	Daegu, South Korea	Sep 4, 2011
4 × 200 m relay	1:18.68	Santa Monica Track Club, U.S.A. (Michael Marsh, Leroy Burrell, Floyd Heard, Carl Lewis)	Walnut, U.S.A.	Apr 17, 1994

4 × 400 m relay	2:54.29	U.S.A. (Andrew Valmon, Quincy Watts, Harry Reynolds, Michael Johnson)	Stuttgart, Germany	Aug 22, 1993
4 × 800 m relay	7:02.43	Kenya (Joseph Mutua, William Yiampoy, Ismael Kombich, Wilfred Bungei)	Brussels, Belgium	Aug 25, 2006
4 × 1,500 m relay	14:36.23	Kenya (Geoffrey Rono, Augustine Choge, William Tanui, Gideon Gathimba)	Brussels, Belgium	Sep 4, 2009

OUTDOOR FIELD EVENTS

Event	Record	Name & Nationality	Location	Date
High jump	2.45 m (8 ft. 0.45 in.)	Javier Sotomayor (Cuba)	Salamanca, Spain	Jul 27, 1993
Pole vault	6.14 m (20 ft. 1.73 in.)	Sergei Bubka (Ukraine)	Sestriere, Italy	Jul 31, 1994
Long jump	8.95 m (29 ft. 4.36 in.)	Mike Powell (U.S.A.)	Tokyo, Japan	Aug 30, 1991
Triple jump	18.29 m (60 ft. 0.78 in.)	Jonathan Edwards (UK)	Gothenburg, Sweden	Aug 7, 1995
Shot	23.12 m (75 ft. 10.23 in.)	Randy Barnes (U.S.A.)	Los Angeles, U.S.A.	May 20, 1990
Discus	74.08 m (243 ft. 0.53 in.)	Jürgen Schult (Germany)	Neubrandenburg, Germany	Jun 6, 1986
Hammer	86.74 m (284 ft. 7 in.)	Yuriy Sedykh (Russia)	Stuttgart, Germany	Aug 30, 1986
Javelin	98.48 m (323 ft. 1.16 in.)	Jan Železný (Czech Republic)	Jena, Germany	May 25, 1996
Decathlon	9,026 points	Roman Šebrle (Czech Republic)	Götzis, Austria	May 27, 2001

Statistics correct as of March 30, 2012

TRACK & FIELD——WOMEN

Most European Cross-Country Championships Paula Radcliffe (UK) in 1998 and 2003, and Hayley Yelling (UK) in 2004 and 2009 have both won the European Cross Country Championships twice.

Fastest 20 km road walk Vera Sokolova (Russia) completed the 20 km walk in 1 hr. 25 min. 8 sec. at the Russian Winter Walking Championships in Sochi, Russia, on February 26, 2011. The 23-year-old former world junior champion smashed the previous mark of 1 hr. 25 min. 41 sec., set by her compatriot Olimpiada Ivanova at the 2005 World Championships in Helsinki, Finland.

Oldest female world record holder in athletics Marina Stepanova (USSR) was 36 years 139 days old when she set a world record of 52.94 seconds for the 400 m hurdles at Tashkent, USSR, on September 17, 1986.

OLYMPICS

Youngest track & field gold medalist At just 15 years 123 days old, Barbara Pearl Jones (U.S.A.) was a member of the winning 4 × 100 m relay team at the Olympics in Helsinki, Finland, on July 27, 1952. She also won gold in the 4 × 100 m at the 1960 Rome Games.

Most track & field medals Merlene Ottey (Jamaica) won nine Olympic medals from 1980 to 2000—three silver and six bronze—in the 100 m, 200 m, and 4 × 100 m relay. Merlene has also won the **most medals at the World Championships**, with 14. She won three gold, four silver, and seven bronze from 1983 to 1997.

MOST WORLD CHAMPIONSHIP APPEARANCES Susana Feitor (Portugal) competed in walking events in 11 World Championships between 1991 and 2011. In 2005, she won bronze in the 20 km walk.

FACT: Gulnara (see page 505) first broke the 3,000 m steeplechase record in 2003 with a time of 9 min. 8.33 sec.

FASTEST HALF MARATHON Mary Keitany (Kenya) smashed the half marathon world record at Ras Al-Khaimah in the UAE on February 18, 2011, with a time of 1 hr. 5 min. 50 sec. This took an incredible 35 seconds off Lornah Kiplagat's (Netherlands) 2007 record, set when winning the World Half Marathon Championships at Udine, Italy. During her half marathon, Keitany also ran the **fastest 20,000 m,** in 1 hr. 2 min. 36 sec.

FASTEST 3,000 M STEEPLECHASE In winning the Olympic 3,000 m steeplechase gold medal at the 2008 Beijing Olympics, Gulnara Samitova-Galkina (Russia) set a new world record of 8 min. 58.81 sec. Silver medalist Eunice Jepkorir (Kenya) came in a massive 8.6 seconds behind.

Youngest world record holder When Wang Yan (China), at the age of 14 years 334 days, completed a 5,000 m walk in 21 min. 33.8 sec. in Jinan, China, on March 9, 1986, she became the world's youngest individual female track & field record holder.

WORLD CHAMPIONSHIPS

Most gold medals From 2005 to 2011, Allyson Felix (U.S.A.) won eight World Championship golds, in the 200 m at Helsinki, Finland, in 2005; the 200 m, 4 × 100 m, and 4 × 400 m at Osaka, Japan, in 2007; the 200 m and 4 × 400 m in Berlin, Germany, in 2009; and the 4 × 100 m and 4 × 400 m in Daegu, South Korea, in 2011.

Most 1,500 m wins Two athletes have won the World Championship 1,500 m twice: Tatyana Tomashova (Russia) in 2003 and 2005, and Maryam Yusuf Jamal (Bahrain, born in Ethiopia) in 2007 and 2009.

Most javelin wins Trine Hattestad (Norway) in 1993 and 1997, and Mirela Manjani (Greece) in 1999 and 2003, have both won the World Championship javelin twice.

Most high jump wins Stefka Kostadinova (Bulgaria) in 1987 and 1995, Hestrie Cloete (South Africa) in 2001 and 2003, and Blanka Vlašić (Croatia) in 2007 and 2009, have all won the World Championship high jump event twice.

To see how fast humans can run, hotfoot it to p. 451.

OUTDOOR TRACK EVENTS

Event	Time	Name & Nationality	Location	Date
100 m	10.49	Florence Griffith-Joyner (U.S.A.)	Indianapolis, U.S.A.	Jul 16, 1988
200 m	21.34	Florence Griffith-Joyner (U.S.A.)	Seoul, South Korea	Sep 29, 1988
400 m	47.60	Marita Koch (GDR)	Canberra, Australia	Oct 6, 1985
800 m	1:53.28	Jarmila Kratochvílová (Czech Republic)	Munich, Germany	Jul 26, 1983
1,000 m	2:28.98	Svetlana Masterkova (Russia)	Brussels, Belgium	Aug 23, 1996
1,500 m	3:50.46	Qu Yunxia (China)	Beijing, China	Sep 11, 1993
1 mile	4:12.56	Svetlana Masterkova (Russia)	Zurich, Switzerland	Aug 14, 1996
2,000 m	5:25.36	Sonia O'Sullivan (Ireland)	Edinburgh, UK	Jul 8, 1994
3,000 m	8:06.11	Wang Junxia (China)	Beijing, China	Sep 13, 1993
5,000 m	14:11.15	Tirunesh Dibaba (Ethiopia)	Oslo, Norway	Jun 6, 2008
10,000 m	29:31.78	Wang Junxia (China)	Beijing, China	Sep 8, 1993
20,000 m	1:02.36	Mary Keitany (Kenya)	Ras Al-Khaimah, UAE	Feb 18, 2011
25,000 m	1:27:05.90	Tegla Loroupe (Kenya)	Mengerskirchen, Germany	Sep 21, 2002
30,000 m	1:45:50.00	Tegla Loroupe (Kenya)	Warstein, Germany	Jun 6, 2003
3,000 m steeplechase	8:58.81	Gulnara Samitova-Galkina (Russia)	Beijing, China	Aug 17, 2008
100 m hurdles	12.21	Yordanka Donkova (Bulgaria)	Stara Zagora, Bulgaria	Aug 20, 1988
400 m hurdles	52.34	Yuliya Pechonkina (Russia)	Tula, Russia	Aug 8, 2003
4 × 100 m relay	41.37	GDR (Silke Gladisch, Sabine Rieger, Ingrid Auerswald, Marlies Göhr)	Canberra, Australia	Oct 6, 1985
4 × 200 m relay	1:27.46	United States "Blue" (LaTasha Jenkins, LaTasha Colander-Richardson, Nanceen Perry, Marion Jones)	Philadelphia, U.S.A.	Apr 29, 2000

| 4 × 400 m relay | 3:15.17 | USSR (Tatyana Ledovskaya, Olga Nazarova, Maria Pinigina, Olga Bryzgina) | Seoul, South Korea | Oct 1, 1988 |
| 4 × 800 m relay | 7:50.17 | USSR (Nadezhda Olizarenko, Lyubov Gurina, Lyudmila Borisova, Irina Podyalovskaya) | Moscow, Russia | Aug 5, 1984 |

OUTDOOR FIELD EVENTS

Event	Record	Name & Nationality	Location	Date
High jump	2.09 m (6 ft 10.28 in)	Stefka Kostadinova (Bulgaria)	Rome, Italy	Aug 30, 1987
Pole vault	5.06 m (16 ft 7.21 in)	Yelena Isinbayeva (Russia)	Zurich, Switzerland	Aug 28, 2009
Long jump	7.52 m (24 ft 8.06 in)	Galina Chistyakova (USSR)	St. Petersburg, Russia	Jun 11, 1988
Triple jump	15.50 m (50 ft 10.23 in)	Inessa Kravets (Ukraine)	Gothenburg, Sweden	Aug 10, 1995
Shot	22.63 m (74 ft 2.94 in)	Natalya Lisovskaya (USSR)	Moscow, Russia	Jun 7, 1987
Discus	76.80 m (252 ft)	Gabriele Reinsch (GDR)	Neubrandenburg, Germany	Jul 9, 1988
Hammer	79.42 m (260 ft 6.76 in)	Betty Heidler (Germany)	Halle, Germany	May 25, 2011
Javelin	72.28 m (253 ft 6 in)	Barbora Špotáková (Czech Republic)	Stuttgart, Germany	Sep 13, 2008
Heptathlon	7,291 points	Jackie Joyner-Kersee (U.S.A.)	Seoul, South Korea	Sep 24, 1988
Decathlon	8,358 points	Austra Skujyte (Lithuania)	Columbia, U.S.A.	Apr 15, 2005

Statistics correct as of March 30, 2012

WORLD CUP

Most points scored Marita Koch (East Germany) was representing Europe when she scored 46 points in the 200 m and 400 m between 1979 and 1985. In each World Cup, at least eight teams took part—five continental and three national (occasionally the host nation would also compete, making it nine entrants). The event was renamed the Continental Cup in 2010 and limited to four teams: Africa, the Americas, Asia/Pacific, and Europe.

The **most points scored in a single event** is 33, by Maria Mutola (Mozambique) in the 800 m between 1992 and 2002. The only person to have scored more is Javier Sotomayor (Cuba), with 35 points in the men's high jump between 1985 and 1998.

Most wins by a team The most World Cup wins by a female team stands at four, by the East Germans in consecutive World Cups held in 1979, 1981, 1985, and 1989.

Greatest span of appearances The longest time between first and final appearances in World Cup competitions is 15 years, by Tessa Sanderson (UK), representing Europe in the javelin between 1977 and 1992. Sanderson has the greatest span for any athlete, beating the men's record of 14 years held by pole vaulter Okkert Brits (South Africa).

MOST WORLD CHAMPIONSHIP LONG JUMP WINS
Three athletes have won the World Championships twice: Jackie Joyner-Kersee (U.S.A.) in 1987 and 1991; Fiona May (Italy) in 1995 and 2001; and Brittney Reese (U.S.A.), left, in 2009 and 2011. Reese also has two World Indoor Championship golds, won in Doha, Qatar, in 2010 and Istanbul, Turkey, in 2012.

FARTHEST HAMMER THROW Betty Heidler (Germany) threw the hammer 260 ft. 6.76 in. (79.42 m) in Halle, Germany, on May 25, 2011. Heidler, who won the World Championships in 2007, eclipsed the previous mark of 256 ft. 10.67 in. (78.30 m) set by the 2009 world champion Anita Wlodarczyk of Poland in Bydgoszcz, Poland.

FACT: The first woman to throw a hammer over 70 m (229 ft. 7.9 in.) was Olga Kuzenkova (Russia) in 1997.

MARATHONS

FASTEST MARATHON (MALE) On September 25, 2011, Patrick Makau (Kenya) ran the 38th Berlin Marathon, Germany, in 2 hr. 3 min. 38 sec. Previous record holder Haile Gebrselassie (Ethiopia) was also in the race, but Makau left him behind shortly after the halfway point before shattering his record by 21 seconds. In doing so, he also ran the **fastest 30 km (road)** in 1 hr. 27 min. 38 sec.

FASTEST MARATHON (FEMALE) Paula Radcliffe (UK) won the London Marathon, UK, on April 13, 2003, in a record time of 2 hr. 15 min. 25 sec. She also holds the two other fastest times, one set when she won the 2002 Chicago Marathon and one in the 2005 London Marathon. Paula also ran the **fastest 10 km (road)**, in 30 min. 21 sec. at the 2003 World's Best 10K, in San Juan, Puerto Rico.

Oldest marathon The Boston Marathon (U.S.A.) is the oldest continuously run annual marathon. It was first held on April 19, 1897, over 24 miles 1,232 yards (39 km), instead of today's official distance of 26 miles 385 yards (42.195 km). Although he had run on a shortened course, the 1897 winner, John J. McDermott (U.S.A.), recorded a time of 2 hr. 55 min. 10 sec., over 50 minutes short of today's world record (see above)!

Most marathons in a calendar year (male) R. Laurence Macon (U.S.A.) completed 113 marathons from January 1 to December 31, 2011, while Yolanda Holder (U.S.A.) has the record for the **most marathons run in a calendar year (female)**, with 106 between January 1 and December 31, 2010. Holder, nicknamed "Walking Diva," estimated her attempt cost U.S. $25,000 in travel, accommodation, and entry fees.

Most marathons run on consecutive days (male) Akinori Kusuda (Japan) ran 52 marathons on 52 days in Besshonuma Park, Saitama, Japan, from January 30 to March 22, 2009. And when Cristina Borra (Italy) completed 13 marathons between February 16 and 28, 2010, all run in

---

FACT: Makau (above) celebrates his 2011 Berlin Marathon win, his second in a row, in front of the Brandenburg Gate.

HOTTEST MARATHON The Badwater Ultramarathon, held every July on a 135-mile (217-km) course from Death Valley to Mt. Whitney in California, U.S.A., registers temperatures of up to 131°F (55°C). The finish is 8,000 ft (2,530 m) above sea level.

GREATEST DISTANCE RUN BAREFOOT IN 24 HR. Abhijeet Baruah (India), a 22-year-old police constable, ran 97 miles (156.2 km) barefoot in Jorhat, Assam, in northeast India, on January 30–31, 2012.

Ruffini Park, Turin, Italy, she achieved the record for the **most marathons run on consecutive days (female)**.

Most finishers in a marathon A total of 47,323 runners out of 47,763 starters finished the New York Marathon, New York, U.S.A., on November 6, 2011.

Most money raised by a marathon runner At the London Marathon on April 17, 2011, Steve Chalke (UK) raised £2,330,159.38 (U.S. $3,795,581.14) for Oasis UK, a charity that helps vulnerable young people.

Most runners linked to complete a marathon Organized by Robin Gohsman (U.S.A.), 62 runners, linked by ropes, finished the Milwaukee Lakefront Marathon in Milwaukee, Wisconsin, U.S.A., on October 2, 2011.

Most northerly marathon The North Pole Marathon has been held annually since 2003, on a course certified by the Association of International Marathons and Distance Races. Thomas Maguire (Ireland) recorded the fastest time of 3 hr. 36 min. 10 sec. in 2007. Cathrine Due (Denmark) is the fastest woman, with a time of 5 hr. 37 min. 14 sec. in 2008.

FACT: Grete (see page 511) strides to victory at the 1983 London Marathon, which she finished in a then world record 2 hr. 25 min. 29 sec.

MOST WINS OF WORLD MARATHON MAJOR RACES (FEMALE) The Majors consist of the annual marathons in London (UK), New York, Boston, Chicago (all U.S.A.), and Berlin (Germany) plus the Olympic and the World Championship marathons. Grete Waitz (Norway) won 12 Majors between 1978 and 1987, comprising nine in New York, two in London, and one World Championship marathon. Bill Rodgers has the most wins (male), with eight from 1975 to 1980, comprising four in Boston and four in New York.

Lowest marathon The finish of the Dead Sea Marathon, held every April, is located 1,312 ft. (400 m) below sea level at Amman, Jordan.

Most consecutive days running an ultramarathon Enzo Caporaso (Italy) ran seven ultramarathons in seven consecutive days from June 13 through 19, 2010. All the races started in Turin, Italy, and covered 100 km (62.14 miles). Caporaso ran the first in 11 hr. 28 min. 43 sec., but slowed to 19 hr. 23 min. 11 sec. by his last.

Youngest runner to complete 100 marathons (female) Melanie Johnstone (UK, b. December 7, 1974) was 34 years 279 days old when she completed her 100th marathon, the 2009 Moray Marathon, in Elgin, Scotland, UK, on September 13, 2009. Melanie's first marathon was the 2003 London Marathon.

> **FACT:** A total of 170,150 applied to enter the 2012 London Marathon—50,200 were accepted.

2012 VIRGIN LONDON MARATHON: NEW WORLD RECORDS While marathon running is a serious business for elite athletes, such as those featured on page 509, for others it is a great excuse to have some fun on the run—and where better to have it than at the world's premier marathon event: the London Marathon?

A. TALLEST COSTUME David Lawrenson's Blackpool Tower measured 26 ft. 2 in. (7.976 m) 7 hr. 19 sec.

B. FASTEST ON STILTS George and Charley Phillips (brother and sister) 6 hr. 50 min. 2 sec.

C. FASTEST RUN BY A PARENT AND CHILD Jeff and Russell Whittington 5 hr. 42 min. 1 sec.

D. FASTEST DRIBBLING A SOCCER BALL Tony Barrance 5 hr. 36 min. 24 sec.

E. FASTEST HULA HOOPING Sasha Kenney 5 hr. 5 min. 57 sec.

F. FASTEST IN A TWO-PERSON PANTOMIME COSTUME Billy and Tom Casserley (brothers) 4 hr. 49 min. 18 sec.

G. FASTEST DRESSED AS A STAR Ian Gear 4 hr. 33 min. 10 sec.

H. FASTEST DRESSED AS A MASCOT (FEMALE) Wendy Shaw running as Alfie (of Guide Dogs for the Blind, UK) 4 hr. 6 min. 6 sec.

I. FASTEST DRESSED AS A VEGETABLE (FEMALE) Helen Juckes as a carrot 3 hr. 47 min. 15 sec.

J. FASTEST DRESSED AS A MONK Gavin Long 3 hr. 45 min. 14 sec.

K. FASTEST IN A WEDDING DRESS Naomi Garrick 3 hr. 41 min. 40 sec.

L. FASTEST DRESSED AS A BOOK CHARACTER (FEMALE) Julie Donald dressed as Waldo's friend Wenda 3 hr. 39 min. 49 sec.

M. FASTEST DRESSED AS A DAIRY PRODUCT (MALE) Chris Atkins as a tub of ice cream 3 hr. 37 min. 22 sec.

N. FASTEST DRESSED IN SCHOOL UNIFORM (MALE) Tony Audenshaw 3 hr. 36 min. 51 sec.

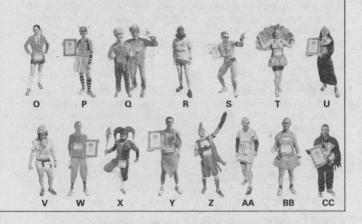

O. **FASTEST DRESSED IN SCHOOL UNIFORM (FEMALE)** Amy Tanner
   3 hr. 33 min. 52 sec.
P. **FASTEST DRESSED AS AN INSECT (FEMALE)** Magdalene Bennett as a bee
   3 hr. 32 min. 30 sec.
Q. **FASTEST DRESSED AS A VIDEO GAME CHARACTER** Joint holders:
   Dan McCormack as Luigi and Nash Pradhan as Mario 3 hr. 29 min. 41 sec.
R. **FASTEST WEARING A GAS MASK** Andy McMahon 3 hr. 28 min. 38 sec.
S. **FASTEST DRESSED AS A LIFEGUARD** Hamish Khayat 3 hr. 26 min. 35 sec.
T. **FASTEST IN AN ANIMAL COSTUME (FEMALE)** Susannah Gill as a peacock
   3 hr. 18 min. 9 sec.
U. **FASTEST DRESSED AS A NUN** Kevin Day 3 hr. 17 min. 58 sec.
V. **FASTEST DRESSED AS A BABY** Michael Brigham 3 hr. 11 min. 53 sec.
W. **FASTEST DRESSED AS A GOLFER (MALE)** Simon Le Mare
   3 hr. 10 min. 4 sec.
X. **FASTEST DRESSED AS A JESTER** Alexander Scherz 3 hr. 1 min. 56 sec.
Y. **FASTEST DRESSED AS A VEGETABLE (MALE)** Edward Lumley as a carrot
   2 hr. 59 min. 33 sec.
Z. **FASTEST DRESSED AS A ROMAN SOLDIER** David Tomlin 2 hr. 57 min.
AA. **FASTEST DRESSED IN A NURSE'S UNIFORM (MALE)** Kevin Harvey
   2 hr. 51 min. 37 sec.
BB. **FASTEST DRESSED AS A FAIRY** Martin Hulbert 2 hr. 49 min. 44 sec.
CC. **FASTEST DRESSED AS A BOOK CHARACTER (MALE)** David Mark Stone
   as Dracula 2 hr. 42 min. 17 sec.

CYCLING

Most participants in a Furnace Creek 508 The Furnace Creek 508 race in California, U.S.A., attracted 217 participants on October 8–10, 2011. Billing itself as "The toughest 48 hours in sport," the race is 508 miles (817.5 km) long, from Santa Clarita (just north of Los Angeles) to Twentynine Palms via the Mojave Desert, Death Valley, and 10 mountain passes.

Most Vélo d'Or awards Awarded annually since 1992 by *Vélo Magazine* (France) to the best rider of the year, the Vélo d'Or (Golden Bicycle) is widely regarded as the most prestigious accolade in cycle racing. Lance Armstrong (U.S.A.) won five Vélo d'Or awards in 1999–2001 and 2003–04.

Fastest women's team 3 km, standing start On April 5, 2012, Laura Trott, Danielle King, and Joanna Rowsell cycled the 3 km team pursuit in 3 min. 15.720 sec. to take gold for GB at the World Championships in Melbourne, Australia.

Fastest men's team 750 m, unpaced standing start René Enders, Maximillian Levy, and Stefan Nimke (all Germany) cycled the three-lap 750 m track in 42.914 seconds at Cali in Colombia, on December 1, 2011.

Fastest time to cycle 10,000 km Guus Moonen (Netherlands) cycled 10,000 km (6,213 miles) in 22 days 15 hr. 34 min. 9 sec. around three circuits of the village of Oisterwijk, Netherlands, from June 5 through 28, 2010.

FASTEST 3 KM, UNPACED STANDING START (FEMALE) Sarah Hammer (U.S.A.) cycled the 3 km unpaced from a standing start in 3 min. 22.269 sec. at the Pan American Championships in Aguascalientes, Mexico, on May 11, 2010.

FACT: In 2011, Sarah became the first American to win three medals at the World Championships.

FASTEST MEN'S TEAM 4 KM PURSUIT On April 4, 2012 at the Hisense Arena in Melbourne, Australia, GB's Ed Clancy, Peter Kennaugh, Steven Burke, and Geraint Thomas struck gold at the World Championships in 3 min. 53.295 sec. They broke the record of 3 min. 53.31 sec. that the GB team (Ed Clancy, Bradley Wiggins, Paul Manning, and Geraint Thomas) had set winning gold at the 2008 Beijing Olympics in China.

In the men's team pursuit, two teams ride against each other, starting on opposite sides of the velodrome. The object is to catch the other team or record the fastest time, determined by the time of the third rider.

Fastest 500 m, unpaced flying start (female) Olga Streltsova (Russia) cycled the 500 m unpaced in 29.481 seconds in Moscow, Russia, on May 29, 2011.

Greatest distance cycled in 48 hours on a mountain bike Dave Buchanan (UK) cycled 354.8 miles (571 km) on an off-road trail between Cardiff and Caernarfon, in Wales, UK, from May 13 to 15, 2011.

Greatest distance cycled in a year Thomas Godwin (UK) cycled 75,065 miles (120,805 km) in 1939, an average of 205.65 miles (330.97 km) per day. He then went on to clock up a total of 100,000 miles (160,934 km) in the 500 days to May 14, 1940. His feat was completed on a four-gear steel bike weighing in excess of 30 lb. (13.5 kg).

Longest static cycling marathon Patrizio Sciroli (Italy) cycled for an epic 224 hr. 24 min. 24 sec. from May 6 to 15, 2011, on a static bike in Teramo, Italy. To achieve the record, he had to maintain a speed of at least 12 mph (20 km/h).

FASTEST 200 M UNPACED FLYING START (FEMALE) On April 5, 2012, Anna Meares (Australia) cycled the flying 200 m in 10.782 seconds in the first round of qualifying at the World Championships at the Hisense Arena in Melbourne, Australia.

MOST CYCLO-CROSS WORLD CUPS Sven Nys (Belgium) won six cyclo-cross World Cups between 1999 and 2009. Cyclo-cross consists of many laps of a short course—typically 1.5–2 miles (2.5–3.5 km)—featuring short, steep hills, sharp corners, and obstacles that require the rider to carry the bike. The terrain varies throughout and can include tarred roads, hardpack dirt, grass, mud, and sand. Daphny van den Brand (Netherlands, above right) has won the **most women's cyclo-cross World Cups**, with three victories between 2005 and 2012.

TOUR DE FRANCE

Fastest average speed Lance Armstrong (U.S.A.) finished first in the 2005 Tour, with an average speed of 25.882 mph (41.654 km/h). He finished the 2,241-mile-long (3,607-km) Tour in 86 hr. 15 min. 2 sec. Armstrong announced his retirement after this race, but he returned to cycling in 2009 and finished third in the Tour that year.

Longest solo escape Breaking away from the *peloton* (field) is risky, as it leaves no chance of slipstreaming (or "drafting") other riders. The longest solo escape was 157.2 miles (253 km) by Albert Bourlon (France) in 1947 to win the 14th stage between Carcassonne and Luchon.

Largest victory margin Fausto Coppi (Italy) finished 28 min. 27 sec. in front of Stan Ockers (Belgium) in 1952.

Youngest winner Henri Cornet (France) was aged 19 years 350 days when he won the second ever Tour, in 1904. Cornet actually finished in fifth position, but was awarded the victory after the first four riders—Maurice Garin, Lucien Pothier, César Garin, and Hippolyte Aucouturier (all France)—were disqualified. In this controversial tour, riders were attacked to stop them, and nails were thrown over the road to cause punctures. Riders were also alleged to have used vehicles for lifts.

Oldest winner Firmin Lambot (Belgium) won the Tour de France at the age of 36 years 4 months in 1922.

Longest Tour de France Today, the Tour de France covers around 2,000 miles (3,200 km), but in 1926 the race totaled 3,569.77 miles (5,745 km)—farther than the distance between Paris and Moscow and back again. The race was won by Lucien Buysse (Belgium).

Most Tours completed Hendrik "Joop" Zoetemelk (Netherlands) finished 16 Tours in 1970–73 and 1975–86. Over the 16 races, Joop recorded one Tour win, in 1980, and six second-place finishes. In 1985, at the age of 38, he won the World Road Championship.

FASTEST WOMEN'S TEAM SPRINT (500 M) On April 4, 2012, at the Hisense Arena in Melbourne, Australia, Germany's Miriam Welte and Kristina Vogel clocked a time of 32.549 seconds to beat Australians Anna Meares and Kaarle McCulloch in the final of the World Championships women's team sprint. Welte and Vogel had already set a world record earlier in the day of 32.630 seconds in qualifying against Lithuania.

In the women's team sprint, the two riders race for two laps—one rider leads off while the other follows, centimetres behind, in her slipstream. On the second lap, the second rider sprints to the finish by herself.

TOUR DE FRANCE WINS

Most Tour de France wins (Tour first held in 1903; yellow jersey, for overall winner, first formally awarded in 1919)	7	Lance Armstrong (U.S.A.)
	5	Jacques Anquetil (France)
		Bernard Hinault (France)
		Miguel Indurain (Spain)
		Eddy Merckx (Belgium)
	3	Louison Bobet (France)
		Greg LeMond (U.S.A.)
		Philippe Thys (Belgium)
Most Tour de France green jerseys (best sprinter, first awarded in 1953)	6	Erik Zabel (Germany)
	4	Sean Kelly (Ireland)
	3	Jan Janssen (Netherlands)
		Eddy Merckx (Belgium)
		Freddy Maertens (Belgium)
		Djamolidine Abdoujaparov (Uzbekistan)
		Robbie McEwen (Australia)
Most Tour de France red polka-dot jerseys (King of the Mountains, first awarded in 1933)	7	Richard Virenque (France)
	6	Federico Bahamontes (Spain)
		Lucien Van Impe (Belgium)
	3	Julio Jiménez (Spain)

GIRO D'ITALIA WINS

Most Giro d'Italias (first held in 1909)	5	Alfredo Binda (Italy)
		Fausto Coppi (Italy)
		Eddy Merckx (Belgium)
	3	Giovanni Brunero (Italy)
		Gino Bartali (Italy)
		Fiorenzo Magni (Italy)
		Felice Gimondi (Italy)
		Bernard Hinault (France)
	2	11 cyclists

Statistics correct as of April 2, 2012

RACING SPORTS

SKIING

Fastest speed Simone Origone (Italy) skied at a speed of 156.83 mph (252.40 km/h) at Les Arcs, France, on April 20, 2006.

The **fastest speed by a female skier** is 150.73 mph (242.59 km/h), by Sanna Tidstrand (Sweden), also at Les Arcs, on April 20, 2006.

Youngest Alpine skier to win Olympic gold On February 16, 1992, Kjetil André Aamodt (Norway) won the first of his four golds in Albertville, France, aged 20 years 167 days.

Ktejil is also **the oldest Alpine skier to win Olympic gold**. He won his fourth gold at the super-giant slalom in Turin, Italy, on February 18, 2006, aged 34 years 169 days.

FASTEST ROW, SINGLE SCULLS, LIGHTWEIGHT On July 24, 2011, Jeremie Azou (France) finished the single sculls (that is, using two oars) in 6 min. 46.93 sec. at the World Rowing Under-23 Championships in Amsterdam, Netherlands.

LARGEST TRIATHLON RACE The most participants in a single triathlon race of international distance was 4,546 at the Nation's Triathlon in Washington, D.C., U.S.A., on September 12, 2010. International, or Olympic, distance triathlons consist of a 0.93-mile (1.5-km) swim, 24.85-mile (40-km) bicycle ride, and 6.21-mile (10-km) run. The event raised more than U.S. $3 million for the Leukemia and Lymphoma Society.

RICHEST HORSE RACE The largest prize fund for a single horse race is U.S. $10 million for the Dubai World Cup, held at Meydan Racecourse in Dubai, United Arab Emirates. The 2012 race, held on March 31, was won by 20/1 outsider Monterosso, ridden by the 20-year-old Mickael Barzalona (France).

FACT: Barzalona celebrated his 2012 win by standing up in his stirrups and waving his whip before the finish.

Longest race The Vasaloppet Nordic ski race is 56 miles (90 km) long and is held annually every March in northwest Dalarna, Sweden. The fastest finish time is 3 hr. 38 min. 41 sec. by Jörgen Brink (Sweden) in 2012. In contrast, the first winner in 1922, Ernst Alm (Sweden), took 7 hr. 32 min. 49 sec.!

Longest downhill race The annual "Schlag das ASSingerh," organized by the municipality of Nassfeld Hermagor (Austria), is 15.91 miles (25.6 km) long. The race starts at Gartenkofel and finishes at Tröpolach.

Longest marathon ski The longest time spent skiing nonstop is 202 hr. 1 min. by Nick Willey (Australia) at Thredbo, a ski resort in New South Wales, Australia, on September 2–10, 2005.

BOBSLED

Most Olympic golds Three competitors have won three Olympic bobsled golds. Meinhard Nehmer and Bernhard Germeshausen (both GDR, now Germany) won theirs in the 1976 two-man and the 1976 and 1980 four-man races, while André Lange, also of Germany, won gold in the 2006 two-man and the 2002 and 2006 four-man races.

Oldest Olympic champion Jay O'Brien (U.S.A.) was 47 years 357 days old when he won the gold medal with the four-man bobsled team during the 1932 Winter Olympics held at Lake Placid in New York, U.S.A.

LUGE

Most doubles World Cup wins The luge World Cup has been held annually since 1977 and Hansjörg Raffl and Norbert Huber (both Italy) have won the doubles at the event eight times, from 1983 to 1993. In the luge, competitors ride feetfirst and face up on the sled.

Most women's World Cup wins The most overall wins of the women's luge World Cup is five, by Silke Kraushaar-Pielach (Germany) between 1998 and 2007.

MOST WINS IN MEN'S LUGE WORLD CUP Two men have secured 10 overall wins of the men's luge World Cup: Markus Prock (Austria) between 1987 and 2002, and Armin Zöggeler (Italy, left) between 1999 and 2011.

FACT: Zöggeler won gold in the single luge at the 2002 and 2006 Winter Olympics.

MOST CLASSIC LUGE WORLD CUP WINS Road luge involves riding a wheeled board down an inclined paved road or course. The riders negotiate bends by leaning, and brake by using their feet on the road. Between 2007 and 2011, Michael Serek (Austria) won five International Gravity Sports Association (IGSA) Classic Luge World Cups.

SKELETON

Fastest speed In the skeleton, the racer rides headfirst, facedown on the sled. Alexander Tretyakov (Russia) and Sandro Stielicke (Germany) both hit speeds of 90.96 mph (146.4 km/h) at the Winter Olympics in Whistler in British Columbia, Canada, on February 19, 2010. On the same day, the **fastest speed for an individual female on a bobsled skeleton** was recorded by Marion Trott (Germany), who reached 89.78 mph (144.5 km/h).

Oldest competitor at the Winter Olympics James Coates (GB) cõmpeted in the skeleton at the 1948 Olympics in St. Moritz, Switzerland, at the age of 53 years 328 days. Coates finished seventh in the final, 5.4 seconds behind the winner.

SPEED SKATING

Fastest short-track 5,000-m relay (men) Jon Eley, Richard Shoebridge, Paul Stanley, and Jack Whelbourne (GB) completed the 5,000-m relay in 6 min. 37.877 sec. at the ISU Short Track Speed Skating World Cup in Dresden, Germany, on February 20, 2011. The short-track event is 111 m, compared with the 400 m long track.

Most Olympic golds (men) Two men have won five gold medals at speed skating: Clas Thunberg (Finland) in 1924 and 1928; and Eric Arthur Heiden (U.S.A.), at one Games at Lake Placid in New York, U.S.A., in 1980.

STAIR CLIMBING

Most Empire State Run-Up wins (men) The Empire State Building Run-Up is a foot race up 1,576 steps from ground level to the 86th-floor observation deck. It has been held annually since 1978 and the most wins is seven, by Thomas Dold (Germany), consecutively from 2006 to 2012. Cyclist Paul Crake (Australia) has the **fastest time for the Run-Up**—9 min. 33 sec. in 2003. Crake is the only man to do it in under 10 minutes. The last four of his five wins from 1999 to 2003 were all under 10 minutes.

Most Empire State Run-Up wins (female) Cindy Moll-Harris (U.S.A.) has won the women's Run-Up four times, in 1998, 2000–01, and 2003. In 2006, Andrea Mayr (Austria) set the **fastest female time for the Run-Up**—finishing in 11 min. 23 sec.

ROWING

Most World Coach of the Year Awards Richard Tonks (New Zealand), in 2005 and 2010, and Gianni Postiglione (Greece) in 2006 and 2011, have both won the World Rowing Coach of the Year Award twice.

Most World Rowing Cup wins The World Rowing Cup has been held annually since 1997 and is won by the country that picks up the most points from three regattas. Germany has won the Cup 10 times, between 1998 and 2011. Great Britain has won it four times, consecutively from 2007 to 2010. Switzerland won the inaugural competition.

Most Olympic golds One man and two women have five rowing golds. Steven Redgrave (GB) won golds at consecutive Olympics from 1984 to 2000. Elisabeta Lipă (Romania) won golds in 1984, 1992, 1996, 2000, and 2004; and Georgeta Damian (Romania) won two in 2000, two in 2004, and one in 2008.

Fastest 24,901-mile (Equator) indoor row David Holby (UK) rowed 24,901 miles (40,075 km)—the equivalent of the length of the Equator—in 2 years 6 months 20 days at The Malls shopping mall in Basingstoke, Hampshire, UK. Holby, who became known as "Dave the Rower" to the shoppers, rowed on average 186.62 miles (300.34 km) a week from May 2008 to December 2010.

Longest open-sea race The Indian Rowing Race covers 3,140 nautical miles (3,615 miles) from Geraldton, Western Australia, to Port Louis, Mauritius. It has been held twice, in 2009 and 2011.

SWIMMING

Fastest 200 m short-course backstroke (female) Melissa "Missy" Franklin (U.S.A.)—the 2011 FINA female Swimmer of the Year—swam

FASTEST 1,500 M LONG-COURSE FREESTYLE SWIM At the FINA World Championships on July 31, 2011, Sun Yang (China) won gold in the 1,500 m freestyle in 14 min. 34.14 sec. at the Oriental Sports Center in Shanghai, China. In doing so, Yang beat the longest-standing men's swimming world record of 14 min. 34.56 sec. set by Grant Hackett (Australia) at the 2001 World Championships in Fukuoka, Japan. (Long-course records take place in 50-m-long pools.)

the short-course 200 m backstroke at the 2011 World Cup in Berlin, Germany, on October 22 in a time of 2 min. 0.03 sec. Six weeks later, on December 16, the 16-year-old and her Team U.S.A. colleagues swam the **fastest 4 × 100 m short-course medley relay** at the Duel in the Pool in Atlanta, Georgia, U.S.A., with a time of 3 min. 45.56 sec.

Fastest 200 m long-course medley (male) Ryan Lochte (U.S.A.) swam the 200 m long-course medley in 1 min. 54 sec. in Shanghai, China, on July 28, 2011.

FABULOUS PHELPS

• Michael Phelps (U.S.A.) is the most successful swimmer of all time. He took up the sport at the age of 7 and qualified for the 2000 Sydney Olympics at 15, where he finished fifth in the final of the 200 m butterfly.

• At the 2004 Athens Olympics, while still a teenager, he won eight medals— six gold and two bronze—equaling the record for **most medals won at a single Olympics.**

• Michael won eight medals again at the 2008 Olympics— this time, however, they were all gold, so he broke the record for the **most golds at a single Olympics**. His tally comprised five individual records and three as part of relay teams.

• He has won the **most World Championships swimming golds**—one in 2001, four in 2003, five in 2005, seven in 2007, five in 2009, and four in 2011—a total of 26.

• He also holds the record for the **most World Swimmer of the Year Awards**, with six, won in 2003–04 and 2006–09.

FACT: At the 2011 World Championships, Sun Yang also won gold in the 800 m freestyle.

POWER SPORTS

HEAVIEST OVER-105 KG SNATCH (MALE)
Behdad Salimikordasiabi (Iran) lifted 214 kg in the men's over-105 kg snatch category at the 2011 World Weightlifting Championships in Paris, France, on November 13. He broke the previous record of 213 kg, lifted by Salimikordasiabi's fellow Iranian and two-time Olympic champion Hossein Rezazadeh in 2003.

HEAVIEST 63 KG SNATCH (FEMALE)
Svetlana Tsarukaeva (Russia) lifted 117 kg in the 63 kg weight category of the snatch competition at the 2011 World Weightlifting Championships in Paris, France, on November 8, 2011. Here, Svetlana is shown at the 2011 World Championships in the clean and jerk, where the bar is first lifted to the collar bone. In the snatch, the bar is lifted in one smooth, continuous movement.

MOST JUDO WORLD CHAMPIONSHIP TITLES
Teddy Riner (France) won six judo World Championship golds from 2007 to 2011—four at heavyweight (over-100 kg), one at openweight, and one in men's teams. Riner also has a silver in openweight, so he shares the record for **most medals won at the World Championships** with seven, along with Naoya Ogawa (Japan), with four gold and three bronze from 1987 to 1995, and Robert Van de Walle (Belgium), with two silver and five bronze from 1979 to 1989.

FACT: Riner was the **youngest to win a World Championship**. He was 18 years 192 days old when he took the heavyweight gold in 2007.

FACT: Behdad won an Asian Games gold in 2010 despite being affected by swine flu and collapsing during one lift.

LONGEST WOMEN'S WRESTLING WINNING STREAK Saori Yoshida (Japan) won 119 consecutive matches between 2002 and 2008. Yoshida eventually lost her unbeaten record in a match against Marcie Van Dusen (U.S.A.) in a Team World Cup event in Beijing, China, on January 20, 2008. Left, Yoshida is shown competing against Tonya Verbeek (Canada) on her way to gold in the 55 kg weight class at the 2008 Beijing Olympics.

MOST CONSECUTIVE UFC FIGHT WINS Anderson "The Spider" Silva (Brazil) won 15 UFC fights between 2006 and 2011. His 15th victory was against Yushin Okami (Japan) on August 27, 2011—after flooring Okami with a short right hook, Silva finished him off with a brutal ground-and-pound.

BOXING

Longest reigning world champion Joe Louis (U.S.A.) was undefeated heavyweight champion for 11 years 252 days, from June 22, 1937, when he beat Jim Braddock (U.S.A.), through to his retirement on March 1, 1949. Floyd Mayweather, Jr. (U.S.A.) first became world champion on October 3, 1998, and, up to his win against Miguel Cotto (Puerto Rico) on May 5, 2012, was undefeated for 13 years 214 days. However, Floyd retired for a period during that time.

FACT: Saori won nine World Championships in the 55 kg category from 2002 to 2011.

MOST BOXING WORLD TITLES IN DIFFERENT WEIGHT DIVISIONS Manny Pacquiao (Philippines) won his eighth world title at different weights when he defeated Antonio Margarito (U.S.A.) to win the WBC super welterweight title on November 13, 2010. He has also held sanctioned belts in the WBC flyweight, super featherweight (which he won against Mexico's Juan Manuel Márquez, left), and lightweight divisions, plus The Ring featherweight, IBF super bantamweight, IBO and The Ring light welterweight, and WBO welterweight.

Most professional bouts (female) Stephanie M. Dobbs (U.S.A.) fought 62 professional bouts from her first fight on March 2, 2002, to June 5, 2010.

Oldest active boxer Steve Ward (UK) was aged 55 years 219 days at the time of his most recent bout on March 19, 2011, in Chesterfield, Derbyshire, UK. Ward boxed as an amateur from the age of 11 to 21 before embarking on a 10-year professional career. He retired for 23 years from 1987 to 2010, before returning to fight three times in 2010 and 2011, with all fights sanctioned by the European Boxing Federation.

Oldest winner of a major world championship At 46 years 126 days, Bernard "The Executioner" Hopkins (U.S.A.) defeated Jean Pascal (Canada, b. Haiti) in Montreal, Canada, on May 21, 2011, to capture the WBC, IBO, and The Ring light heavyweight belts.

Heaviest heavyweight world champion Nikolay Valuev (Russia) weighed in at a massive 328 lb. (148.7 kg) for his WBA heavyweight title fight with Monte Barrett (U.S.A.) at Allstate Arena, Rosemont, Illinois,

---

A MAN OF MANNY TALENTS

• In May 2010, Manny was elected congressman for Sarangani on the Philippine island of Mindanao. He is the first professional boxer to hold national public office while active in the ring.

• Manny has starred in movies, including the boxing superhero movie *Wapakman* (2009), an entry in the Metro Manila Film Festival.

• Manny is also a keen singer. His albums include *Pac-Man Punch* (2007) for MCA Records, and his 2011 duet with singer-songwriter Dan Hill, "Sometimes When We Touch," reached No. 19 on the U.S. *Billboard* Adult Contemporary chart.

U.S.A., on October 7, 2007. Valuev won the bout via a technical knockout in round 11.

Most Fighter of the Year Awards Muhammad Ali (U.S.A.) won five Fighter of the Year Awards, given by *The Ring* magazine, in 1963, 1972, 1974–75, and 1978.

Most Trainer of the Year Awards Freddie Roach (U.S.A.) has won five Trainer of the Year Awards, in 2003, 2006, and 2008–10.

WRESTLING

Most men's Freestyle Wrestling World Championships Two competitors have won the men's Freestyle Wrestling World Championships seven times: Aleksandr Medved (Belarus) in the 97 kg, over-97 kg, and over-100 kg classes between 1962 and 1971; and Valentin Jordanov (Bulgaria) in the 52 kg class between 1983 and 1995.

Most Olympic golds Five wrestlers have won three Olympic titles: Carl Westergren (Sweden) in 1920, 1924, and 1932; Ivar Johansson (Sweden) in 1932 (two) and 1936; Aleksandr Medved (Belarus) in 1964, 1968, and 1972; Aleksandr Karelin (Russia) in 1988, 1992, and 1996; and Buvaysar Saytiev (Russia) in 1996, 2004, and 2008.

SUMO

Most bouts won in a calendar year In 2009, *Yokozuna* Hakuhō Shō (Mongolia, birth name Mönkhbatyn Davaajargal) won 86 out of the 90 regulation bouts that a top *rikishi* (sumo wrestler) fights annually.

Heaviest wrestler Samoan-American Saleva'a Fuauli Atisano'e (aka Konishiki), weighed in at 589 lb. (267 kg) at Tokyo's Ryōgoku Kokugikan on January 3, 1994. He put his massive weight down to eating a high-protein stew called *chankonabe*.

Most top-division wins The most *makuuchi*, or top division, wins in sumo wrestling by a *rikishi* is 815, by Kaiō Hiroyuki (Japan, birth name Hiroyuki Koga) from 1993 to 2010. There are 42 wrestlers in the *makuuchi*, ordered into five ranks.

TAEKWONDO

Most World Championship finweight titles won Yeon-Ho Choi (South Korea) has won four finweight World Championship gold medals, in 2001, 2003, 2007, and 2009.

JUDO

Most women's World Championships medals Ingrid Berghmans (Belgium) won 11 medals—comprising 6 gold, 4 silver, and 1 bronze—at the World Championships between 1980 and 1989.

Youngest female judo world champion Ryoko Tani (née Tamura, Japan) was 18 years 27 days when she won the under-48 kg title at the World Championships in Hamilton, Canada, in 1993.

GOLF

Farthest golf shot Flight Engineer Mikhail Tyurin (Russia), assisted by caddy Commander Michael Lopez-Alegria (U.S.A.), teed-off during a spacewalk outside the *International Space Station* on February 23, 2006. NASA estimated the ball would orbit for three days and travel 1.26 million miles (2.02 million km) before burning up in the atmosphere.

The **longest golf shot at an altitude below 3,280 ft. (1,000 m)** is 408 yd. (373.07 m), by Karl Woodward (UK) at Golf del Sur, Tenerife, Spain, on June 30, 1999.

LOWEST TOTAL SCORE IN THE U.S. OPEN Rory McIlroy (UK) won the U.S. Open at Congressional Country Club in Bethesda, Maryland, U.S.A., on June 16–19, 2011, with a score of only 268 (65-66-68-69). This score, 16 under par, was also the **lowest score to par in a U.S. Open**. The win was Rory's first Major and, at age 22 years 46 days, he became the youngest U.S. Open champion since Bobby Jones (U.S.A.) in 1923 and the youngest Major winner since Tiger Woods (U.S.A.) won at the U.S. Masters in 1997.

FACT: Rory was 16 years 42 days when he won the 2005 Irish Amateur Close Championship.

MOST EUROPEAN TOUR EVENT WINS
The most event wins on golf's European Tour is 50, including five Majors, by Severiano "Seve" Ballesteros (Spain, 1957–2011) between 1976 and 1995. He also holds the record for most consecutive years with at least one event win on the European Tour—seven years from 1976 to 1992.

OLDEST WINNER ON EUROPEAN TOUR Des Smyth (Ireland) was at the age of 48 years 34 days when he won the Madeira Island Open at Santo da Serra, Portugal, on March 17, 2001. He hit a round of 270, 18 under par, to win by two strokes.

Highest-altitude golf course The Yak golf course, part of an Indian Army base, is 13,025 ft. (3,970 m) above sea level in Kupup, East Sikkim, India. Natural ponds and mountain streams provide hazards.

Largest golf range The SKY72 Golf Club Dream Golf Range in Jung-gu, Incheon, South Korea, has 300 individual bays.

Largest golf facility Mission Hills Golf Club in Shenzhen, China, has 12 fully operational 18-hole courses.

Largest bunker The Hell's Half Acre bunker on the 585-yd. (535-m) seventh hole of the Pine Valley course, Clementon, New Jersey, U.S.A., starts 280 yd. (265 m) from the tee and extends another 150 yd. (137 m) up the fairway.

Longest hole The seventh hole (par 7) of the Satsuki golf course in Sano, Japan, measures 964 yd. (881 m).

Longest holed putt in a top-flight tournament Jack Nicklaus (U.S.A.) in the 1964 Tournament of Champions, and Nick Price (Zimbabwe) in the 1992 United States PGA, both sank putts of 110 ft. (33.5 m). Bob Cook (U.S.A.) holed a putt measured at 140 ft. 2.75 in. (42.74 m) on the 18th at St. Andrews, Scotland, in the International Fourball Pro Am Tournament on October 1, 1976.

Lowest score to par after 72 holes in a top-flight tournament Chapchai Nirat (Thailand) hit 32 under par at the 2009 SAIL Open (on the Asian Tour) at the Classic Golf Resort, Gurgaon, India, on March 21, 2009.

Most consecutive birdies in a PGA Tour event Mark Calcavecchia (U.S.A.) hit nine birdies in the third round of the Canadian Open at Oakville in Ontario, Canada, on July 25, 2009. All nine of Calcavecchia's putts were within 15 ft. (4.72 m) of the hole. Despite his amazing start, he ended the third round with a score of 71 (one under par).

Longest individual unbeaten streak in the Ryder Cup Lee Westwood (UK) from 2002 to 2008, and Arnold Palmer (U.S.A.) from 1965 to 1971, both went 12 matches unbeaten in the Ryder Cup. Westwood lost two matches at the end of the 2008 Ryder Cup, but stormed back in the 2010 event, winning three matches and halving one, to help Europe regain the trophy.

Most consecutive Major wins Tiger Woods (U.S.A.) claimed four consecutive Major titles in 2000–01, winning the U.S. Open, the British Open, and the PGA Championship in 2000 and the U.S. Masters in 2001. This achievement has been dubbed the "Tiger Slam"; a true Grand Slam involves winning all the Majors in one calendar year.

MOST WINS, HIGHEST EARNINGS, LOWEST ROUNDS

Most Majors won *British Open, U.S. Masters, U.S. Open, and U.S. PGA Championship*	18	Jack Nicklaus (U.S.A.), 1962–86
	14	Tiger Woods (U.S.A.), 1997–2008
	11	Walter Hagen (U.S.A.), 1914–29
Highest career earnings—U.S. Tour	$95,516,542	Tiger Woods (U.S.A.)
	$65,944,204	Vijay Singh (Fiji)
	$65,286,308	Phil Mickelson (U.S.A.)
Highest career earnings—European Tour	€26,985,651	Lee Westwood (UK)
	€26,472,392	Ernie Els (South Africa)
	€24,387,862	Colin Montgomerie (UK)
Lowest rounds—only major tours	58 (−12)	Ryo Ishikawa (Japan) The Crowns tournament, 2010, Japan Golf Tour
	59 (−13)	Al Geiberger (U.S.A.) Danny Thomas Memphis Classic, 1977, U.S. PGA Tour
	59 (−13)	Chip Beck (U.S.A.) Las Vegas Invitational, 1991, U.S. PGA Tour

Statistics correct as of March 19, 2012

YOUNGEST WINNER ON THE EUROPEAN TOUR At the age of 17 years 188 days, Matteo Manassero (Italy) won his first European Tour event—the Castello Masters at Club de Campo del Mediterraneo in Costa del Azahar, Spain, on October 24, 2010. He soon proved this victory was not a fluke. On April 17, 2011, he won his second European Tour event—the Malaysian Open at the Kuala Lumpur Golf & Country Club—at the age of 17 years 363 days to become the only golfer to win two European Tour events before turning 18.

HIGHEST CAREER EARNINGS ON THE ASIAN TOUR Thongchai Jaidee (Thailand) earned U.S. $4,472,290 on golf's Asian Tour from 1999 to March 19, 2012. Jaidee also holds the most event wins on the Asian Tour with 13, the first being the Kolon Korea Open in 2000.

Highest prize money for a golf tournament The Players Championship, contested at Sawgrass, Florida, U.S.A., has a total prize pool of U.S. $9,500,000, with U.S. $1,710,000 going to the winner. K. J. Choi (South Korea) won the event in 2011.

Highest season's earnings on the Ladies' European Tour Laura Davies (England) earned €471,727 (U.S. $698,084) on the 2006 European Tour.

Highest season's earnings on the Ladies U.S. Tour On the 2007 U.S. Ladies PGA Tour, Lorena Ochoa (Mexico) earned U.S. $4,364,994.

Most consecutive U.S. Opens started Jack Nicklaus (U.S.A.) started all 44 U.S. Opens from 1957 to 2000.

Most holes of golf played in one year Richard Lewis (U.S.A.) played 11,000 holes, all at the Four Seasons Resort and Club in Irving, Texas, U.S.A., from January 1 to December 31, 2010. Lewis played 611 full rounds of golf, plus an additional two holes, averaging at more than 30 holes played per day!

Most British Opens hosted The Royal and Ancient Golf Club of St. Andrews—established in Fife, Scotland, UK, in 1754 and patronized by King William IV in 1834—hosted the Open golf championships on a record 28 occasions between 1873 and 2010.

Most wins of the women's British Open Karrie Webb (Australia) and Sherri Steinhauer (U.S.A.) have both won the British Open three times: Webb in 1995, 1997, and 2002; Steinhauer in 1998, 1999, and 2006.

Youngest female to play in the Curtis Cup Michelle Wie (U.S.A.) appeared in the Curtis Cup aged 14 years 244 days, at Formby Golf Club, in Merseyside, UK, on June 11–12, 2004. The Cup is the best-known team trophy for women amateur golfers, played between the U.S.A. and Great Britain & Ireland since 1932.

RACKET SPORTS

MOST MEN'S WHEELCHAIR WORLD CHAMPIONSHIPS
Between 1995 and 2004, David Hall (Australia)
won six International Tennis Federation men's
wheelchair singles World Championships, awarded on
performances throughout the year. David had both legs
amputated after being hit by an automobile at the age
of 16 on October 11, 1986. In 1987, he started playing
wheelchair tennis and, by 1992, he was representing
Australia at the Paralympics.

**MOST MEN'S DOUBLES WINS AT THE BADMINTON
WORLD CHAMPIONSHIPS** The most wins of the men's
doubles event by the same pair is four, by Cai Yun and
Fu Haifeng (China) in 2006 and 2009–11. Their victory
in the 2011 final came in straight sets against Ko Sung-
Hyun and Yoo Yeon-Seong (both South Korea).

**LONGEST MEN'S TENNIS GRAND
SLAM FINAL** Rafael Nadal (Spain, left)
and Novak Djokovic (Serbia, see page
534) played for 5 hr. 53 min. in the
Australian Open final at Melbourne,
Australia, on January 29, 2012, a
record for the Open era. Djokovic won
the match, widely regarded as one
of the greatest finals of all time, 5–7, 6–4, 6–2, 6–7, 7–5. Nadal had lost to
Djokovic in the previous two Grand Slam finals (Wimbledon and the U.S.
Open) and so set an unwanted record of three for the **most consecutive
tennis Grand Slam final losses in the Open era.** (The Open era began
in 1968, when professional players were first allowed to enter Grand Slam
tournaments—with the first being the French that year.)

TENNIS

Most consecutive weeks at No. 1 (male) Roger Federer (Switzerland) spent 231 weeks at the top of the singles rankings, from February 2,
2004, to July 7, 2008. He lost the top spot to Rafael Nadal (Spain) after
falling to the Spaniard in a five-set Wimbledon final. The previous best

---

FACT: In 2010, Nadal became the seventh player in history to
win all four Grand Slams.

was 160 weeks by Jimmy Connors (U.S.A.), from July 29, 1974, to August 22, 1977.

First tennis player to achieve the "golden" Grand Slam In 1988, Steffi Graf (Germany) won the four Grand Slams—the Australian Open, the French Open, Wimbledon, and the U.S. Open—as well as the Olympic gold medal to complete the "golden" Grand Slam. She is the only person to have achieved this feat in singles in a calendar year. Two other players—Andre Agassi (U.S.A.) and Rafael Nadal (Spain)—have completed a "golden" Grand Slam over their careers.

Fastest serve Ivo Karlović (Croatia), who stands 6 ft. 10 in. (2.08 m) tall, served a ball at 156 mph (251 km/h) in a doubles match against Germany in the Davis Cup on March 5, 2011.

The **fastest serve by a woman** is 130 mph (209 km/h), by Brenda Schultz-McCarthy (Netherlands) in the first round of the Western & Southern Financial Group Women's Open on July 15, 2006. This was matched by Venus Williams (U.S.A.) at the final of the Zurich Open in 2008.

Highest attendance A crowd of 35,681 saw Kim Clijsters (Belgium) defeat Serena Williams (U.S.A.) 6–3, 6–2 in Brussels, Belgium, on July 8, 2010, in an exhibition match. The figure beat the "Battle of the Sexes" match between Billie Jean King and Bobby Riggs (both U.S.A.), which drew 30,472 people to the Astrodome in Houston, Texas, U.S.A., on September 20, 1973.

Largest Grand Slam fine Serena Williams (U.S.A.) was fined U.S. $82,500 for verbal abuse during the 2009 U.S. Open semifinal at Flushing Meadows, New York, U.S.A., on September 12, 2009. Williams's out-

MOST GRAND SLAM TITLES WON BY A MOTHER Kim Clijsters (Belgium, left), from 2009 to 2011, and Margaret Court (Australia) in 1973, have both won three Grand Slam singles titles after giving birth.

burst occurred on match point against her, after she was called for a foot fault. She was given a one-point penalty, which meant her opponent, Kim Clijsters, was awarded the match.

Longest professional match The 2010 first-round match at Wimbledon between John Isner (U.S.A.) and Nicolas Mahut (France) lasted 11 hr. 5 min. and stretched over three days. After playing 183 games, Isner finally defeated Mahut 70–68 in the final set. Ironically, the pair were drawn against each other at the 2011 Wimbledon—this time, Isner won in straight sets in only 34 games.

Longest rally Identical twins Ettore and Angelo A. Rossetti (U.S.A.) played a 25,944-stroke rally at North Haven Health & Racquet in North Haven, Connecticut, U.S.A., on August 9, 2008. The attempt lasted 15 hours.

BADMINTON

Fastest hit When testing Yonex rackets, Tan Boon Heong (Malaysia) hit a shuttlecock at 261.6 mph (421 km/h) at the Tokyo Metropolitan Gymnasium in Tokyo, Japan, on September 26, 2009. The **fastest hit recorded in competition** is 206 mph (332 km/h), by Fu Haifeng (China) in the 2005 Sudirman Cup.

Longest match The men's singles final at the 1997 World Championships at Glasgow, UK, on June 1 lasted 124 minutes, with Peter Rasmussen (Denmark) overcoming Sun Jun (China) 16–17, 18–13, 15–10.

Most World Championship wins (men's singles) Lin Dan (China) has won four World Championships—in 2006, 2007, 2009, and 2011.

MOST CONSECUTIVE WOMEN'S SQUASH WORLD OPENS Nicol David (Malaysia, left) won four women's World Opens in a row from 2008 to 2011. She claimed the 2011 title by beating Jenny Duncalf (England, b. Netherlands) in the final in straight sets. David also holds the most women's World Opens in total, with six, having also won in 2005 and 2006. She also has the most Women's International Squash Players Association Player of the Year awards, with six from 2005 to 2010.

Most World Championship wins (mixed doubles) Two mixed pairs have won the World Championships twice: Park Joo-Bong and Chung Myung-Hee (South Korea) in 1989 and 1991, and Nova Widianto and Lilyana Natsir (Indonesia) in 2005 and 2007.

Most World Championship wins (women's doubles) Gao Ling and Huang Sui (China) have won the World Championships three times—in 2001, 2003, and 2006.

TABLE TENNIS

Longest rally Brian and Steve Seibel (U.S.A.) played a rally lasting 8 hr. 15 min. 1 sec. at the Christown YMCA in Phoenix, Arizona, U.S.A., on August 14, 2004.

The **longest rally in a competition** was in a 1936 Swaythling Cup match in Prague between Alojzy "Alex" Ehrlich (Poland) and Paneth Farkas (Romania). The 2-hr. 12-min. rally was the first of the match.

SQUASH

Most World Championship wins (team, women) The women's title has been won nine times by Australia, in 1981, 1983, 1992, 1994, 1996, 1998, 2002, 2004, and 2010.

Longest recorded competitive match Jahangir Khan (Pakistan) took 2 hr. 45 min. to beat Gamal Awad (Egypt) 9–10, 9–5, 9–7, 9–2 in the final of the Patrick International Festival at Chichester, West Sussex, UK, on March 30, 1983. The first game alone lasted a record 1 hr. 11 min.

TENNIS, SQUASH, AND TABLE TENNIS

Tennis		
Most Grand Slam singles—men	16	Roger Federer (Switzerland)
	14	Pete Sampras (U.S.A.)
	12	Roy Emerson (Australia)
Most Grand Slam singles—women	24	Margaret Court (Australia)
	22	Steffi Graf (Germany)
	19	Helen Wills Moody (U.S.A.)
Largest stadium capacity—ATP Tour and Grand Slams	23,200	Arthur Ashe Stadium, New York, U.S.A. (used for U.S. Open)
	17,500	O2 Arena, London, UK (used for ATP World Tour Finals)
	16,100	Indian Wells Tennis Garden, California, U.S.A. (used for Indian Wells Masters)

Squash		
Most British Opens—men (first held in 1930)	10	Jahangir Khan (Pakistan)
	8	Geoff Hunt (Australia)
	7	Hashim Khan (Pakistan)
Most British Opens—women (first held in 1922)	16	Heather McKay (Australia)
	10	Janet Morgan (England)
	8	Susan Devoy (New Zealand)
Most World Opens—men (first held in 1976)	8	Jansher Khan (Pakistan)
	6	Jahangir Khan (Pakistan)
	4	Geoff Hunt (Australia)
Most World Opens—women (first held 1979)	6	Nicol David (Malaysia)
	5	Sarah Fitz-Gerald (Australia)
	4	Susan Devoy (New Zealand)

Table Tennis		
Most World Championship singles—men (first held 1926)	6	Viktor Barna (Hungary)
	4	Richard Bergmann (England, b. Austria)
	3	Zhuang Zedong (China)
		Wang Liqin (China)
Most World Championship singles—women (first held 1926)	6	Angelica Rozeanu (Romania)
	5	Mária Mednyánszky (Hungary)
	3	Gizella Farkas (Hungary)
		Deng Yaping (China)
		Wang Nan (China)

Correct as of March 27, 2012

TARGET SPORTS

ARCHERY

Highest FITA 24-hour score by a team of two Sergeants Martin Phair and Jamie Fowler (both UK) scored 37,359 points shooting FITA (International Archery Federation) 59-ft. (18-m) rounds at the Royal Air Force Benson gymnasium in Benson, Oxfordshire, UK, on June 17–18, 2009. Phair even managed to shoot a rare "Robin Hood"—firing one arrow directly into the back of another.

Largest archery tournament On August 4, 2010, 1,024 participants took part in an archery contest organized by the People's Government of Xiwuzhumuqin County, in Balaga'ergaole, Inner Mongolia Autonomous Region, China. The tournament was carried out under standard Mongolian archery rules.

Farthest accurate distance (men's) Under regulated FITA conditions, Peter Terry (Australia) shot an arrow 656 ft. 2 in. (200 m) at the Kalamunda Governor Stirling Archers club in Perth, Western Australia, on December 15, 2005. Terry's feathered feat was accomplished using a compound bow, and he hit two out of six on a FITA 48-in. (122-cm) target.

Highest score, indoor (59-ft./18-m) On March 6, 2011, compound archer Christopher Perkins (Canada) broke the junior and senior indoor 59-ft. (18-m) archery records with a score of 599 at the Canadian Indoor Championships.

DARTS

Most 180s in a Premier League Darts match Gary Anderson (UK) hit a total of 11 maximum scores of 180 while playing Simon Whitlock (Australia) on April 21, 2011. Anderson's sharp-shooting dartsmanship took place during a Premier League Darts match at the National Indoor Arena in Birmingham, UK.

Longest singles marathon Ryne Du Shane and Dylan Smith (both U.S.A.) played a marathon darts game lasting 41 hours at the Itty Bitty Bar in Holland, Michigan, U.S.A., from May 16 to 18, 2011. The duo played a variant of darts called "Cricket," with Du Shane winning 105 to 66.

> **FACT:** Johnny Archer has been WPA World Nine-Ball Champion twice, in 1992 and 1997.

MOST MOSCONI CUP APPEARANCES Johnny Archer (U.S.A.) has appeared in the nine-ball Mosconi Cup pool tournament—the "Ryder Cup of Pool"—15 times, playing for the U.S.A. between 1997 and 2011. He shares the record with Ralf "The Kaiser" Souquet (Germany), who has also notched up 15 appearances, for the European team.

MOST WEBER CUP APPEARANCES The Weber Cup is a tenpin bowling contest played between Europe and the U.S.A. since 2000. Tim Mack has represented the U.S.A. in 10 Weber Cups between 2000 and 2010—the largest number of appearances.

Mack won the Cup six times between 2000 and 2008, the **most wins of the Weber Cup by an individual**. The **most team wins of the Weber Cup** is seven, by the U.S.A., in 2000–02, 2006–08, and 2011.

FARTHEST THROWN BULL'S-EYE Cricket star Andrew "Freddie" Flintoff (UK) scored a darts bull's-eye from 16 ft. 6.8 in. (5.05 m) as part of his BT Sport Relief Challenge, Flintoff's Record Breakers, in London, UK, on March 19, 2012.

MOST ARCHERY WINS IN MEN'S RECURVE Brady Ellison (U.S.A.) has won two men's titles, using a recurve bow, in the FITA World Cup in 2010 and 2011. The other category in the World Cup, which began in 2006, features the compound bow, and the record for **most wins in the men's compound World Cup** is also two, by Sergio Pagni (Italy) in 2009 and 2010.

FACT: Among other records for Sport Relief 2012 set by Freddie on the day was the **fastest time to drink a cup of hot chocolate**: 5.45 seconds.

Fewest darts to score 1,000,001 On August 21–23, 2010, a team of eight men—Mickey Mansell, Mickey Taggart, Felix McBrearty, Daryl Gurney, Campbell Jackson, Ronan McMahon, Eamonn McGovern, and Thomas Stoga (all UK)—threw 35,698 darts in more than 46 hours to reach a score of 1,000,001 at The Weigh Inn bar in Omagh, County Tyrone, UK.

Highest darts score in an hour (men's team) Martin Cotter, Damian O'Driscoll, Steven Coveney, John O'Shea, Craig Sproat, Jason Kavanagh, Kevin McDonnell, and James Corcoran (all Ireland) of the Cork Darts Organisation scored 35,087 in an hour at St. Vincent's GAA Club in County Cork, Ireland, on March 20, 2010.

POOL

Most wins of the World Cup of Pool The World Cup of Pool—a nine-ball competition for doubles—has been won twice by two countries. The Philippines, represented by Efren Reyes and Francisco Bustamante, took the honors in 2006 and 2009. China—Li Hewen and Fu Jianbo—triumphed in 2007 and 2010.

Largest tournament The eight-ball division of the 2010 American Poolplayers Association National Team Championships recorded the largest ever pool contest when 5,361 participants played in Las Vegas, Nevada, U.S.A., from August 19 to 28, 2010.

Longest singles marathon Colin Pilcher and Marc Murray (both UK) cued up for 72 hr. 2 min.—a charity marathon record achieved at the Stateside sports bar in Consett, County Durham, UK, from July 31 to August 3, 2011.

MOST PREMIER LEAGUE DARTS APPEARANCES Premier League Darts is played weekly from February to May across the UK. Darts sensation Phil Taylor (UK) is the only player to take part in all eight editions of the competition since its inception in 2005. As of April 23, 2012, he has won the title five times, the **most Premier League Darts titles held.** He also has the **most wins of the darts World Grand Prix**, with 10 from 1998 to 2011. The World Grand Prix is held in Dublin, Ireland, every October.

MOST SNOOKER PREMIER LEAGUE TITLES Ronnie O'Sullivan (UK) won the Snooker Premier League title on a record 10 occasions between 1997 and 2011. The round-robin competition was originally known as the Matchroom League from its debut in 1987 to 1998. Stephen Hendry (UK) is O'Sullivan's nearest rival with six wins (1987–2004).

O'Sullivan has also recorded the **most competitive 147 breaks in snooker**, with 11 in total. Hendry equaled his record, with a 147 against Stuart Bingham (UK) in the first round of the 2012 World Championship.

Youngest pool world champion Wu Chia-Ching (Chinese Taipei, b. February 9, 1989) won the pool world championships at the age of 16 years 121 days old. The championship was staged at Kaohsiung, Chinese Taipei, on June 10, 2005.

SNOOKER

Youngest professional to score a break of 147 Thanawat Thirapongpaiboon (Thailand) was 16 years 312 days old when he sunk a maximum break at the Euro Players Tour Championship in Rüsselsheim, Germany, on October 22, 2010.

The record for the **youngest player to score a maximum 147 in a televised snooker match** was set by Ding Junhui (China), at the age of 19 years 288 days while playing at the Masters tournament at Wembley, UK, on January 14, 2007.

Longest singles marathon Gerry Cunningham and Gary McDonald (both UK) set the record for the longest singles snooker marathon when

Snooker		
Most WPBSA World Snooker Championships (first held in 1969)	7	Stephen Hendry (UK)
	6	Ray Reardon (UK)
		Steve Davis (UK)
Most UK Snooker Championships (first held in 1977)	6	Steve Davis (UK)
	5	Stephen Hendry (UK)
	4	Ronnie O'Sullivan (UK)
Darts		
Most Men's World Darts Championships (British Darts Organisation and Professional Darts Corporation)	15	Phil Taylor (UK)
	5	Eric Bristow (UK)
		Raymond van Barneveld (Netherlands)
Most Women's World Darts Championships (British Darts Organisation, first held in 2001)	9	Trina Gulliver (UK)
	2	Anastasia Dobromyslova (Russia)
	1	Francis Hoenselaar (Netherlands)

Statistics correct as of April 1, 2012

they played for 50 hours at the Chatham Pool & Snooker Club in Chatham, Kent, UK, between February 27 and March 1, 2009. McDonald had only stepped in after Cunningham's original partner became ill.

TENPIN BOWLING

Most strikes in a minute Colin Champion (U.S.A.) made eight tenpin bowling strikes in a minute at the Kegel Training Center in Lake Wales, Florida, U.S.A., on January 24, 2011. Champion, a member of the Webber International University bowling team, required 10 rolls to complete his record attempt.

Longest marathon Charity fundraiser Stephen Shanabrook (U.S.A.) bowled for 134 hr. 57 min. (more than five days!) at Plano Super Bowl in Plano, Texas, U.S.A., from June 14 to 19, 2010. In the course of his record tenpin session, Shanabrook completed 643 full games.

Youngest bowling world champion Paeng Nepomuceno (Philippines, b. January 30, 1957) won the 1976 Bowling World Cup in Tehran, Iran, at the age of 19 years 292 days. Nepomuceno—named the "International Bowling Athlete of the Millennium"—also holds the record for winning the **most tenpin bowling World Cups (four times, in 1976, 1980, 1992, and 1996)** and the most bowling titles in a career (124).

HIGH FLYERS

FASTEST SPEED ON A 70-M CANOPY-PILOTING COURSE (FEMALE) Canopy piloting, also known as swooping, involves a skydiver deploying the parachute (canopy) at 5,000 ft. (1,525 m), then entering a steep rotating dive before leveling out and completing a course. On July 31, 2011, Jessica Edgeington (U.S.A., left) flew the 70-m (230 ft.) course in 2.301 seconds in Longmont, Colorado, U.S.A. This equates to an average speed of 68.07 mph (109.55 km/h).

The fastest time to complete a 70-m course by a male canopy pilot is 2.093 seconds, by Greg Windmiller (U.S.A.) in Johannesburg, South Africa, on December 5, 2009. This equates to an average speed of 74.8 mph (120.38 km/h).

BASE BASICS

• BASE jumpers perform daredevil leaps from stationary structures (instead of aircraft), gliding to the ground with a parachute.

• "BASE" stands for "Buildings, Aerials, Spans, and Earth." "Spans" denotes bridges; "Earth" denotes cliffs or rock faces. BASE jumpers leap from all of them, often illegally.

• Unlike parachutists, BASE jumpers do not carry a second 'chute—mainly because their jumps are relatively low and there's no time to deploy it.

• In freefall, a BASE jumper reaches a speed of around 120 mph (190 km/h).

• It's dangerous! A 2008 study concluded that 1 in 60 BASE jumps ends in death.

• The most common cause of death is "offheading"—flying in an unintended direction and hitting a solid object.

FACT: The first canopy-piloting competitions were organized in the U.S.A. in 1996.

You'll find more acts of epic endeavor on p. 222.

FIRST WORLD AIR GAMES The inaugural World Air Games took place on September 15–21, 1997, at six different sites in Turkey. Events included parachuting, air racing, aerobatics, aeromodeling, microlight, hang gliding, paragliding, and ballooning. The Games are staged every four years and were held in 2001 in Spain and 2009 in Italy; the 2005 Games were canceled because of organizational difficulties.

AEROBATICS

Most consecutive rolls by an aircraft Zoltán Veres (Hungary) performed a head-spinning 408 consecutive rolls in an airplane during the Al Ain Aerobatic Show in Al Ain, UAE, on January 29, 2007.

Longest inverted flight The longest flight sustained with an aircraft upside down lasted 4 hr. 38 min. 10 sec. and was performed by Joann Osterud (Canada), flying from Vancouver to Vanderhoof, Canada, on July 24, 1991.

GLIDING

Farthest distances • Free distance (one straight-line leg): 1,362.6 miles (2,192.9 km), by Terence Delore (New Zealand) at El Calafate, Argentina, on December 4, 2004.

• **Out-and-return distance** (two straight-line legs, one turn point): 1,396.5 miles (2,247.6 km) by Klaus Ohlmann (Germany) from Chapelco, Argentina, on December 2, 2003.

• **Overall distance** (at least one, but not more than three, turn points): 1,869.7 miles (3,009 km) by Klaus Ohlmann from Chapelco, Argentina, on January 21, 2003.

Highest speed The highest speed in a glider to set an official Fédération Aéronautique Internationale (FAI) record is 190.6 mph (306.8 km/h), over an out-and-return course of 310 miles (500 km), by Klaus Ohl-

FACT: Skydivers generally carry out between 200 and 500 jumps before they try flying in a wingsuit.

MOST PARAGLIDING WORLD CUPS Competitors in the Paragliding World Cup must negotiate a number of different courses at various sites worldwide. Each course has set turning points and a finishing line; the winner is the paraglider who is fastest to the line. Christian Maurer (Switzerland, left) has won three Paragliding World Cups, in 2005–07.

MOST WORLD BASE RACE VICTORIES The annual World BASE Race has been held at Innfjorden in Rauma, Norway, since August 2008. Dressed in wingsuits, competitors leap from a mountainside and glide 2,500 ft. (760 m) downward. The winner is the BASE racer who reaches the ground most quickly— and, of course, without fatal injury. Frode Johannessen (Norway, left) has won the World BASE Race twice, in 2009 and 2011.

mann (Germany) on December 22, 2006, at Zapala, Argentina. He flew a Schempp-Hirth Nimbus-4DM.

The **highest average speed achieved in a glider by a woman** when setting an official FAI world record is 141.54 mph (227.8 km/h), by Ghislaine Facon (France) at Chos Malal, Argentina, on November 22, 2005.

Fastest speed (out-and-return course) On December 26, 2009, pilots Jean-Marie Clement (France) and Bruce Cooper (UK) set a new gliding world record for speed on an out-and-return course when they flew their Schempp-Hirth Nimbus-4DM at an average speed of 129.36 mph (208.19 km/h) over a distance of 620 miles (1,000 km). The duo began and finished their flight at Bariloche, Argentina.

HANG GLIDING

Most consecutive loops Chad Elchin (U.S.A.) performed 95 loops consecutively at the Highland Aerosports flight park at Ridgely in Maryland, U.S.A., on July 16, 2001. Elchin was towed to 15,900 ft. (4,846 m) and looped his Aeros Stealth Combat nonstop down to 700 ft. (213 m) at speeds of 18–80 mph (28–128 km/h).

FASTEST SPEED IN A WINGSUIT On May 28, 2011, in the skies above Yolo County, California, U.S.A., Shinichi Ito (Japan) reached a speed of 225.6 mph (363 km/h). He also traveled 14.35 miles (23.1 km), the **greatest horizontal distance in a wingsuit**.

Most World Championships The men's World Hang Gliding Championships were first held in 1976. The most individual wins is three, by Tomas Suchanek (Czech Republic) in 1991, 1993, and 1995, and Manfred Ruhmer (Austria) in 1999, 2001, and 2003.

The **most individual wins of the women's World Hang Gliding Championships** is four, by Corinna Schwiegershausen (Germany) in 1998, 2004, 2006, and 2008. The competition was inaugurated in 1987.

MICROLIGHT

Fastest speed Pavel Skarytka (Czech Republic) achieved an average speed of 120.67 mph (194.2 km/h) in a B-612 microlight aircraft over a 9.3-mile (15-km) course near Bubovice, Czech Republic, on October 11, 2003.

Highest altitude The highest altitude achieved in a microlight is 31,890 ft. (9,720 m), by Serge Zin (France) over Saint-Auban, France, on September 18, 1994.

Most microlights airborne at once A group of 30 microlights completed two circuits (counterclockwise) within a 2.2-mile (3.7-km) radius above the Wrekin hill in Shropshire, UK. The event was organized on May 6, 2000, by Shropshire Microlight Flying School and Telford Business Club (both UK) to raise money for charity.

PARACHUTING

Fastest freefall style In the freefall style discipline, skydivers must compete a predetermined set of maneuvers in the quickest time. The fastest time for the men's parachuting freefall style is 5.18 seconds, by Marco Pflueger (Germany) over Eisenach, Germany, on September 15, 2007.

The **fastest women's parachuting freefall style** is 6.10 seconds, by Tatiana Osipova (Russia) over Békéscsaba, Hungary, on September 19, 1996.

Farthest nonstop flight by a powered parachute The official FAI record for the longest distance flown in one hop by powered parachute is 686 miles (1,105 km), by Juan Ramón Morillas Salmerón (Spain) from Jerez in Cadiz, to Lanzarote in the Canary Islands, Spain, on April 23, 2007.

Largest canopy formation The largest canopy formation consisted of 100 parachutes and was formed by an international team over Lake Wales in Florida, U.S.A., on November 21, 2007.

Most tandem jumps in 24 hours On July 10, 2011, a total of 130 tandem parachute jumps took place in an event organized by Khalsa Aid and Skydive Hibaldstow (both UK) at Hibaldstow Airfield in Lincolnshire, UK.

The record for the **most tandem parachute jumps by an individual in 24 hours** is 105 and is shared by Luther Kurtz and Angela Bishop (both U.S.A.) at Harbor Springs Airport in Harbor Springs, Michigan, U.S.A., on June 29–30, 2010. Kurtz served as the instructor on all jumps, with Bishop (his sister) as his tandem traveler.

PARAGLIDING

Farthest out-and-return distance The greatest out-and-return distance achieved by a paraglider is 161.3 miles (259.7 km), by Aljaz Valic (Slovenia) at Soriska Planina, Slovenia, on July 20, 2006.

On August 19, 2009, Nicole Fedele (Italy) covered 102.2 miles (164.6 km) from Sorica, Slovenia, to Piombada, Italy, in a paraglider, the **farthest out-and-return distance by a female paraglider**.

Farthest flight in a tandem paraglider Richard Westgate and Phillip Bibby (both UK) flew 221.3 miles (356.2 km) without landing from Vosburg to Krompoort Farm, South Africa, on December 7, 2006.

Greatest altitude The greatest height gain in a paraglider is 14,849 ft. (4,526 m), by Robbie Whittall (UK) at Brandvlei, South Africa, on January 6, 1993. In comparison, Boeing 747s normally cruise at 35,000 ft. (10,000 m).

The **greatest altitude gained in a paraglider by a female** is 14,189 ft. (4,325 m), by Kat Thurston (UK) over Kuruman, South Africa, on January 1, 1996.

Most loops Raúl Rodríguez (Spain) carried out 108 continuous loops in his paraglider above Passy Plaine-Joux, France, on June 15, 2006.

SKYDIVING

Fastest speed Switzerland's Christian Labhart reached a speed of 327.41 mph (526.93 km/h) in Utti, Finland, at the International Speed Skydiving Association (ISSA) World Cup on June 4–6, 2010.

The **highest speed achieved by a woman in a speed skydiving competition** is 275.09 mph (442.73 km/h), by Clare Murphy (UK) in Utti, Finland, at the ISSA World Cup on June 15–17, 2007.

Largest wingsuit formation On November 16, 2009, 68 wingsuited skydivers jumped from four aircraft over Lake Elsinore, California, U.S.A. They formed a complex diamond pattern for 2 miles (3.2 km) at

---

FACT: Wingsuit flyers typically descend at a speed of 50–60 mph (80–100 km/h).

---

an average speed of 100 mph (160 km/h). This is the largest formation recognized by the United States Parachute Association (USPA).

Longest banzai skydive On September 2, 2000, over Davis, California, U.S.A., Yasuhiro Kubo (Japan) jumped from a plane at an altitude of 9,842 ft. (3,000 m) without a parachute. In 50 seconds, he hooked onto a parachute that had been thrown out prior to his jump!

BOARD SKILLS

SKATEBOARD

Most Summer X Games medals The greatest number of ESPN Summer X Games skateboard medals won to date is 19 by Andy Macdonald (U.S.A.). He won his first medal in 1999.

Highest hippy jump A "hippy jump" is a trick in which the rider jumps off the skateboard and over an obstacle while the skateboard rides on underneath it. The highest skateboard hippy jump is 40.5 in. (102.87 cm), and it was achieved by Patrick Neal Rushing (U.S.A.) at Fish Creek Park in Arlington, Texas, U.S.A., on November 12, 2011.

Most consecutive kickflips The greatest number of consecutive kickflips performed on a skateboard is 1,546, by Zach Kral (U.S.A.) at 4 Seasons Skate Park in Milwaukee, Wisconsin, U.S.A., on November 30, 2008.

Longest board slide Rob Dyrdek (U.S.A.) produced a 100-ft. 5.75-in. (30.62-m) board slide on MTV's *Rob & Big* show in Los Angeles, California, U.S.A., on September 17, 2007.

Fastest time to slalom 50 cones On August 28, 2011, Janis Kuzmins (Latvia) slalomed through 50 cones in just 10.02 seconds at the Nike Riga Run in Mežaparks, Riga, Latvia.

Most consecutive ollies Eric Carlin (U.S.A.) carried out 242 consecutive skateboard ollies at Mount Laurel in New Jersey, U.S.A., on July 16, 2011. Carlin had three failed attempts (of 55, 122, and 20 consecutive ollies) before breaking the record on his fourth attempt of the day.

FACT: The ollie was originally known as a "no-hands aerial" . . . .

HIGHEST SKATEBOARDING OLLIE An "ollie" involves raising all four wheels of the board off flat ground simultaneously. The highest ollie measured 45 in. (114.3 cm) and was achieved by Aldrin Garcia (U.S.A.) at the Maloof High Ollie Challenge in Las Vegas, Nevada, U.S.A., on February 15, 2011. Garcia was required to ollie over a rigid high bar without it making contact with any part of his body or board.

The ollie has a special place in the skate hall of fame: It was the **first skateboard trick** ever performed—by Alan Gelfand (U.S.A.) in 1976.

Most shove-its in 30 seconds In a "shove-it," the skateboarder keeps the lead foot on the board while propelling his or her board with the other foot. The greatest number of skateboard shove-its executed in 30 seconds is 26, by Nicholas Hunter Heath (U.S.A.) in Ocoee, Florida, U.S.A., on September 4, 2011.

Most tricks invented Widely regarded as the most influential skater of all time, freestyler Rodney "The Mutt" Mullen (U.S.A.) invented at least 30 skateboard tricks between 1997 and 2008.

SNOWBOARD

Most Winter X Games gold medals As of January 2012, Shaun White (U.S.A.) had won a record 12 Winter X Games golds. White won his 12th gold at Winter X Games 16 in 2012, when he scored the **first perfect 100 in the snowboard superpipe**. All of his gold medals came in snowboard superpipe and snowboard slopestyle. White has won 17 medals in all, the **most X Games medals won by an individual**.

MOST WOMEN'S TTR WORLD SNOWBOARD TOUR TITLES To date, Jamie Anderson (U.S.A.) has picked up two Ticket To Ride (TTR) World Snowboard Tour titles, in 2007–08 and 2010–11.

Shaun, a two-time Olympic gold medalist, also holds the snowboard record for the **highest air on a superpipe**, reaching 23 ft. (7 m) at Winter X Games 14 in Aspen, Colorado, U.S.A., in 2010.

Most men's TTR World Snowboard Tour titles Peetu Piiroinen (Finland) won three consecutive TTR World Snowboard Tour titles, from 2008/09 to 2010/11.

Most World Snowboarding Championships The greatest number of World Snowboarding Championship titles won (including Olympic titles) is seven, by Karine Ruby (France, 1978–2009). She won giant slalom in 1996, snowboard cross in 1997, Olympic gold in 1998, giant slalom, parallel slalom, and snowboard cross in 2001, and snowboard cross in 2003.

Ruby also won the **most Fédération Internationale de Ski (FIS) Snowboard World Cups**, with 20 victories in the following categories: overall (1996–98, 2001–03); slalom/parallel slalom (1996–98, 2002); giant slalom (1995–98, 2001); snowboard cross (1997, 2001, 2003–04); and big air (2004).

MOST WAKEBOARDING WORLD SERIES WINS Phillip Soven (U.S.A.) won the Wakeboarding World Series (WWS) four times, consecutively, between 2007 and 2010. In 2011, he just missed out and finished second.

FACT: The WWS began in 2006 and ranks competitors based on their performance at a set of events worldwide.

MOST X GAMES SKATEBOARD VERT WINS (MEN) Pierre-Luc Gagnon (Canada) won the skateboarding vert competition (riding on a vertical ramp) at the Summer X Games five times from 2002 to 2010.

The **most men's FIS Snowboard World Cups won** is six, by Mathieu Bozzetto (France),with victories in the overall (1999–2000) and slalom/parallel slalom (1999–2002) categories.

Fastest speed The greatest speed by a snowboarder is 125.459 mph (201.907 km/h), by Darren Powell (Australia) at Les Arcs in Savoie, France, on May 2, 1999.

Longest rail grind Calum Paton (UK) performed a rail grind measuring 258 ft. 2.4 in. (78.7 m) at the Milton Keynes Xscape in Buckinghamshire, UK, on December 2, 2011. The record was broken at an event organized by *Whitelines* snowboarding magazine, which saw professional and amateur riders attempt to break the record. No one matched the previous record until the very end of the event, when it was bettered by more than 32 ft. 9.7 in. (10 m).

SURFING

Most wins of the ASP Longboard World Championship Nat Young (Australia) has won the Association of Surfing Professionals (ASP) men's Longboard World Championship four times, in 1986 and 1988–90.

FACT: To date, Gagnon has won 16 X Games medals—seven of which are gold.

The **most wins of the ASP women's Longboard World Championship** is two, by Jennifer Smith (U.S.A.) in 2007 and 2009.

Largest wave surfed (unlimited) On November 1, 2011, Garrett McNamara (U.S.A.) surfed a wave measuring 78 ft. (23.77 m), trough to crest, off Praia do Norte, Nazaré, Portugal. The term "unlimited" denotes that the surfer is towed to the wave, enabling him or her to catch waves that would be too strong to be caught by paddling in.

Gary Saavedra (Panama) surfed a wave for 43.1 miles (66.47 km) on the Panama Canal on March 19, 2011—the **longest wave surfed**. Saavedra followed a wave-creating boat for 3 hr. 55 min. 2 sec. during the event, also breaking the record for the **longest time to surf a wave**.

Longest marathon Kurtis Loftus (U.S.A.) surfed 29 hr. 1 min. at Jacksonville Beach, Florida, U.S.A., on October 26–27, 2011. The 50-year-old Loftus surfed 313 waves during his time in the ocean, using the same board throughout.

Oldest big-wave competition The inaugural Eddie Aikau Memorial took place in Hawaii, U.S.A., in 1984. The first event was staged at Sunset Beach on Oahu's North Shore before moving the following year to its current location in Waimea Bay. The event has been held only eight times because of the precondition that the ocean swell must reach 66 ft. (20 m).

MOST ASP WORLD TITLES (MEN)
Kelly Slater (U.S.A.) has won the men's ASP world title 11 times, in 1992, 1994–98, 2005–06, 2008, and 2010–11.

He has also recorded the **most consecutive wins of the men's ASP world title, with five wins in 1994–98.**

The **most ASP world titles won by a woman is seven, by Layne Beachley (Australia), in 1998–2003 and 2006.**

Prefer web surfing? Try social media, p. 304.

WAKEBOARD

Most world titles Wakeboarding involves riding a board over water, usually pulled by a boat, and employs water-skiing, snowboarding, and surfing techniques. The World Wakeboard Association (WWA) World Championships were first held in 1994 and Darin Shapiro (U.S.A.) has won the men's title the most: three times in 1999, 2001, and 2002. Two boarders share the record for the **most women's world championships**. Tara Hamilton (U.S.A.) won the title in 1998 and 2002; Maeghan Major (U.S.A.) won in 1999 and 2000.

Most inverts in a minute On August 30, 1999, Julz Heaney (UK) achieved 15 inverts (somersaults) in a minute on a wakeboard at the John Battleday Water Ski center in Chertsey, Surrey, UK.

Longest rail slide The longest wakeboard rail slide measured 153 ft. 9.2 in. (46.87 m) and was achieved by Borij Levski (Slovenia) in Ptuj, Slovenia, on July 2, 2011. Borij used a cable lift (similar to a ski lift) to tow him.

Longest ramp jump Jérôme Macquart (France) performed a 49-ft. 2-in. (15-m) ramp jump on a wakeboard on the set of *L'Été De Tous Les Records* in Argelés-Gazost, France, on July 14, 2004.

The **longest ramp jump on a wakeboard by a woman** is 42 ft. 2 in. (13 m), by Sandrine Beslot (France) on the same TV show and at the same location but on July 7, 2005.

WATER SPORTS

AQUABIKING

Most Pro Offshore World Championship wins (men) Cyrille Lemoine (France) has won the Union Internationale Motonautique (UIM) men's Pro Offshore World Championship three times, in 2006, 2008, and 2010.

MOST WINS OF THE WOMEN'S AQUABIKE WORLD CHAMPIONSHIP Julie Bulteau (France) has won the Union Internationale Motonautique (UIM) women's Pro Ski World Championship three times, consecutively, in 2009–11.

MOST WINS OF THE DIVING WORLD SERIES 3-M SPRINGBOARD (MEN) Qin Kai (China) has won the Fédération Internationale de Natation (FINA/Midea) Diving World Series men's 3-m springboard event four times, in 2007, and consecutively in 2009–11.

LONGEST-DISTANCE UNDERWATER SWIM WITH ONE BREATH Carlos Coste (Venezuela) swam 492 ft. (150 m) in the Dos Ojos cave system in Quintana Roo, Mexico, on November 3, 2010. Coste's swim, which lasted 2 min. 32 sec., is the longest with one breath in open water.

DIVING

Most wins of the Diving World Series 3-m springboard (women) The most wins of the FINA Diving World Series women's 3-m springboard event is three, by He Zi (China) in 2009–11.

Most World Series 10-m Platform wins (men) Qui Bo (China) notched up three consecutive wins in the FINA Diving World Series men's 10-m platform event, in 2009–11.

First "perfect 10" in the World Championships The first award of a score of 10 to a diver in the World Aquatic Championships was achieved by Greg Louganis (U.S.A.) at Guayaquil, Ecuador, on August 5, 1982. Louganis won gold medals in both the 3-m springboard and 10-m platform competitions.

Most World Championships Guo Jingjing (China) won 10 FINA diving world titles in the women's 3-m springboard, individual, and synchronized events five times: 2001, 2003, 2005, 2007, and 2009.

Youngest world champion Fu Mingxia (China, b. August 16, 1978) won the women's world title for 10-m platform diving at Perth, Western Australia, on January 4, 1991, at the age of 12 years 141 days. The following year, aged 13, she won the same event at the Barcelona Olympics.

KITE SURFING

Youngest world champion (female) Gisela Pulido (Spain, b. January 14, 1994) won her first Kiteboard Pro World Tour (KPWT) world championship on November 4, 2004, at 10 years 294 days old. She went on to win her first Professional Kiteboard Riders Association (PKRA) championship on August 26, 2007, at 13 years 224 days old.

Fastest speed kite surfing (male) Rob Douglas (U.S.A.) reached 55.65 knots (64 mph; 103 km/h) at the 2010 Lüderitz Speed Challenge in Lüderitz, Namibia, on October 28, 2010.

The **fastest speed kite surfing by a woman** was 50.43 knots (58 mph; 93 km/h), by Charlotte Consorti (France) at the 2010 Lüderitz Speed Challenge in the same location on the same day.

Longest distance covered in 24 hours Rimas Kinka (Lithuania) kite surfed for 313.6 miles (504.8 km) off the coast of Islamorada, Florida, U.S.A., on November 13, 2011.

WATERSKIING

Longest jump The farthest waterski jump by a male is 246 ft. 8 in. (75.2 m), by Freddy Krueger (U.S.A.) at Seffner in Florida, U.S.A., on November 2, 2008.

The **longest waterski jump by a woman** measured 187 ft. 4 in. (57.1 m), by June Fladborg (Denmark) in Lincoln, UK, on August 24, 2010.

Most flips (30 seconds) Nicolas Le Forestier (France) completed 16 full 360-degree flips on one waterski in 30 seconds on the set of *L'Été De Tous Les Records* in Lac de Biscarrosse, France, on August 5, 2003.

The **most waterski flips by a woman (30 seconds)** is eight, by Duan Zhenkun and Han Qiu (both China) in Xichang City, Sichuan Province, China, on November 17, 2011.

Barefoot slalom Skiing on his bare feet, Keith St. Onge (U.S.A.) performed 20.6 crossings of the wake in 30 seconds at the Gauteng North Barefoot Waterski Championships in Bronkhorstspruit, South Africa, on January 6, 2006.

The **most barefoot crossings of the wake by a female waterskier in 30 seconds** is 17, by Nadine De Villiers (South Africa) on January 5, 2001, in Wolwekrans, South Africa.

WHEEL SKILLS

BMX

Highest vertical air Mat Hoffman (U.S.A.) carried out a 26-ft. 6-in. (8.07-m) air on a BMX bicycle from a 24-ft.-tall (7.31-m) quarterpipe ramp on March 20, 2001, in Oklahoma City, Oklahoma, U.S.A. He was towed by a motorcycle in the run up to the jump.

The **highest air on a halfpipe** is 19 ft. (5.8 m), by Dave Mirra (U.S.A.) off an 18-ft.-tall (5.4-m) ramp in San Diego, California, U.S.A., in January 2001.

> **FACT:** Bad Habit weighs 10,200 lb. (4,626.6 kg). Each tire is 66 in. (167.6 cm) wide.

LONGEST RAMP JUMP IN A MONSTER TRUCK Joe Sylvester (U.S.A.) carried out a 208-ft. (63.58-m) ramp jump in his professional monster truck *Bad Habit* at the 10th Annual Cornfield 500 in Columbus, Pennsylvania, U.S.A., on September 5, 2010. He made three attempts overall. During the first attempt, the truck landed on its nose, shattering the front suspension.

LONGEST NOSE WHEELIE ON A MOTOCROSS BIKE Riding a Kawasaki KX250T8F, Gary Harding (U.S.A.) maintained a nose wheelie for 282 ft. (86.2 m) at Mason Dixon Dragway in Boonsboro, Maryland, U.S.A., on August 22, 2010. Immediately after the attempt, Harding proposed to his girlfriend on the very same track. She quickly accepted!

Most backflips (single leap) On May 28, 2011, Jed Mildon (New Zealand) performed three backflips on a bicycle in a single leap at the Unit T3 Mindtricks BMX Jam at Spa Park in Taupo, New Zealand. Mildon first rode his BMX bike down a 45-degree ramp from a height of 65 ft. 7 in. (20 m) before taking off from the up ramp.

Most gyrator spins in one minute Takahiro Ikeda (Japan) carried out 59 gyrator spins in a minute on the set of *100 Handsome Men and Beautiful Women*, at the Kojimachi NTV studio in Tokyo, Japan, on November 13, 2011.

MOTORCYCLE

Longest front flip On November 17, 2008, Jim DeChamp (U.S.A.) performed a 47-ft. 8-in.-long (14.52-m) motorcycle front flip at Godfrey Trucking/Rocky Mountain Raceway in Salt Lake City, Utah, U.S.A., for the MTV show *Nitro Circus*. This was the first time anyone has successfully front flipped a motorcycle.

First double backflip Travis Pastrana (U.S.A.) made the first successful double backflip on a motorcycle at ESPN X Games 12 in Los Angeles, California, U.S.A., on August 4, 2006.

Highest tightrope crossing On October 16, 2010, in Benidorm, Spain, the aptly named Mustafa Danger (Morocco) motorcycled across a 2,185-ft.-long (666.1-m) tightrope set at a height of 426 ft. (130 m).

Highest trials motorcycle wall climb On January 21, 2009, Jordi Pascuet and Marcel Justribó (both Spain) each climbed a vertical wall onto a platform at a height of 10 ft. 6.38 in. (3.22 m) on the set of *Guinness World Records*, in Madrid, Spain.

Longest reverse ride Hou Xiaobin (China) rode a motorcycle backward for 93.21 miles (150 km) in Binzhou City, China, on October 4, 2006.

WHEELCHAIR

First landed backflip Aaron Fotheringham (U.S.A.) landed the first wheelchair backflip at Doc Romeo skate park in Las Vegas, Nevada, U.S.A., on October 25, 2008.

Longest stationary manual A "stationary manual" is a position in which the wheelchair is held balanced on its rear wheels alone. Hermann van Heerden (South Africa) held this position for 10 hr. 1 sec. in Bloemfontein, South Africa, on October 11, 2011.

Longest wheelie Eliza McIntosh (U.S.A.) sustained a continuous rear-wheel wheelie for 12.39 miles (19.93 km) at the East High School athletics track in Salt Lake City, Utah, U.S.A., on October 8, 2011.

She completed 48 laps of the athletics track without the front wheels of the wheelchair touching the ground.

MOST WORLD ROLLER FIGURE SKATING CHAMPIONSHIPS Tanja Romano (Italy) won nine World Roller Figure Skating Championships at the women's combined event from 2002 to 2010.

The most **World Roller Figure Skating Championships at the men's combined is five**, by Karl-Heinz Losch (Germany), from 1958 to 1966, and Sandro Guerra (Italy), from 1987 to 1992.

FACT: Born in Trieste, Italy, Tanja Romano began skating when she was just five years old.

Most manual spins On February 23, 2011, Gulshan Kumar (India) carried out a dizzying 63 manual wheelchair spins in one minute on the set of *Guinness World Records—Ab India Todega* in Mumbai, India.

AUTOSPORTS

AUTOS

Most points scored by an F1 driver Michael Schumacher (Germany) scored 1,517 points between August 25, 1991, and the end of the 2011 season.

Most consecutive F1 grand prix victories by a constructor McLaren (UK) won 11 grands prix in a row in the 1988 season. Ayrton Senna (Brazil, 1960–94) won seven of the races and his fellow McLaren driver and archrival Alain Prost (France) won four. Senna went on to win the World Drivers' Championship, pipping Prost by three points.

Fastest lap of Le Mans Loïc Duval (France) was driving a Peugeot 908 HDi FAP in the Le Mans 24-hour race when he recorded a lap of 3 min. 19.07 sec., on June 12, 2010.

Closest finish in NASCAR racing There are two instances of a NASCAR race being won by just 0.002 seconds. Ricky Craven beat Kurt Busch (both U.S.A.) by 0.002 seconds at Darlington Raceway in Darlington, South Carolina, U.S.A., on March 16, 2003. Jimmie Johnson beat Clint Bowyer (both U.S.A.) by the same margin to win the 2011 Aaron's 499 race at Talladega Superspeedway, in Talladega, Alabama, U.S.A., on April 17.

Most NASCAR titles by auto make Chevrolet (U.S.A.) provided the vehicle for the NASCAR champion 35 times between 1957 and 2011, including every year since 2003.

MOST F1 POLE POSITIONS IN A SEASON Sebastian Vettel (Germany), driving for Red Bull-Renault (UK/Austria), secured 15 Formula One pole positions from the 19 races in the 2011 season. Vettel won 11 grand prix races in the season (nine from pole position) and won the Drivers' Championship with 392 points, the **most points won in an F1 season.**

MOST CHAMPIONSHIP WINS

Formula One

Most World Drivers' Championships (first awarded in 1950)	7	Michael Schumacher (Germany, 1994–95, 2000–04)
	5	Juan Manuel Fangio (Argentina, 1951, 1954–57)
	4	Alain Prost (France, 1985–86, 1989, 1993)
Most World Constructors' Championships (first awarded in 1958)	16	Ferrari (Italy, 1961, 1964, 1975–76, 1977, 1979, 1982–83, 1999–2004, 2007–08)
	9	Williams (UK, 1980–81, 1986–87, 1992–94, 1996–97)
	8	McLaren (UK, 1974, 1984–85, 1988–91, 1998)

NASCAR (National Association for Stock Car Auto Racing)

Most Sprint Cup Series Drivers' Championships (first awarded in 1949)	7	Richard Petty (U.S.A., 1964, 1967, 1971–72, 1974–75, 1979)
		Dale Earnhardt (U.S.A., 1980, 1986–87, 1990–91, 1993–94)
	5	Jimmie Johnson (U.S.A., 2006–10)
	4	Jeff Gordon (U.S.A., 1995, 1997–98, 2001)

Rallying

Most World Rally Championships (first awarded in 1977)	8	Sébastien Loeb (France, 2004–11)
	4	Juha Kankkunen (Finland, 1986–87, 1991, 1993)
		Tommi Mäkinen (Finland, 1996–99)
	2	Walter Röhrl (Germany, 1980, 1982)
		Miki Biasion (Italy, 1988–89)
		Carlos Sainz (Spain, 1990, 1992)
		Marcus Grönholm (Finland, 2000, 2002)

Statistics correct as of April 3, 2012

Fastest speed in NHRA drag racing, top fuel Top-fuel autos are the fastest drag racers—they have the engine at the back and a sleek "rail" design. The highest terminal velocity at the end of a 440-yd. (402-m) run by a top-fuel car is 337.58 mph (543.16 km/h) by Tony Schumacher (U.S.A.) in Brainerd, Minnesota, U.S.A., on August 13, 2005, in his U.S. Army dragster.

Fastest speed in NHRA drag racing, funny car "Funny cars" have the engine in the front and bodywork similar to a production automobile. Mike Ashley (U.S.A.) reached a terminal velocity of 334.32 mph (538.04 km/h) from a standing start over 440 yd. (402 m) in a Dodge Charger in Las Vegas, Nevada, U.S.A., on April 13, 2007.

First female IndyCar winner Danica Patrick (U.S.A.) won the Indy Japan 300 in Motegi, Japan, on April 20, 2008. Danica began her career in kart racing and Formula Ford.

BIKES

Most AMA Superbike Championships (manufacturer) Suzuki (Japan) won 13 AMA (American Motorcyclist Association) Superbike titles between 1979 and 2009.

Most Superbike World Championships (manufacturer) Ducati has won 17 Superbike World Championships, in 1991–96, 1998–2004, 2006, 2008–09, and 2011.

Fastest speed in NHRA drag racing, pro-stock Pro-stock bikes cannot use artificial induction, such as turbocharging, supercharging, or nitrous oxide. The highest terminal velocity for a pro-stock motorcycle is 197.65 mph (318.08 km/h), by Michael Phillips (U.S.A.) in Baton Rouge, Louisiana, U.S.A., on July 18, 2010.

Most Motocross des Nations wins Motocross takes place on off-road circuits and the Motocross des Nations, also known as the "Olympics of Motocross," has been contested annually between national teams since 1947. The U.S.A. has won the competition 22 times. Great Britain is second with 16, and Belgium is third with 14.

MOST MOTOGP MANUFACTURERS' CHAMPIONSHIPS
Yamaha (Japan) have won five Moto Grand Prix Manufacturers' Championships, in 2004–05 and 2008–10. Honda has won four championships (2003–04, 2006, and 2011) and Ducati one (2007).

MOST SUPERSPORT WORLD CHAMPIONSHIPS Sébastien Charpentier (France) has won two Supersport World Championships (SWC), in 2005–06. In the SWC, the riders use models of motorcycles available to the public.

Longest motorcycle race circuit The 37.73-mile (60.72-km) "Mountain" circuit on the Isle of Man, over which the principal TT (Tourist Trophy) races have been run since 1911 (with minor amendments in 1920), has 264 curves and corners.

Most wins at the Isle of Man TT festival Ian Hutchinson (UK) won all five solo races at the Isle of Man TT festival in 2010.

Fastest lap at the Isle of Man TT John McGuinness (UK), riding a Honda in 2009, completed the "Mountain Circuit" in 17 min. 12.30 sec. His average speed on the lap was 131.578 mph (211.754 km/h).

First female in the British Superbike Championship In 2011, Jenny Tinmouth (UK) competed in the British Superbike Championship for the Splitlath Motorsport team.

MOST WINS IN THE MODERN ERA OF NASCAR The NASCAR Sprint Cup Series has been awarded since 1949, but the modern NASCAR era is usually dated from 1972, when the season was shortened from 48 races (including two on dirt tracks) to 31. Jeff Gordon (U.S.A.) has the most NASCAR wins in the modern era with 85. He won his 85th race (left) at the AdvoCare 500 Race at Atlanta Motor Speedway, in Hampton, Georgia, U.S.A., on September 6, 2011.

YOUNGEST AND OLDEST

• The **youngest F1 grand prix winner** was Sebastian Vettel (Germany), who won the Italian Grand Prix at Monza on September 14, 2008, at the age of 21 years 73 days. In this race, Vettel was also the **youngest F1 grand prix driver to attain pole position.**

• The **oldest F1 grand prix winner** is Tazio Nuvolari (Italy), who won the Albi Grand Prix at Albi, France, on July 14, 1946, at the age of 53 years 240 days.

• Troy Ruttman (U.S.A.) is the **youngest winner of the Indianapolis 500**—he won the race at the age of 22 years 80 days on May 30, 1952.

• At 19 years 93 days old, Graham Rahal (U.S.A.) became the **youngest winner in major open-wheel racing history** when he won the IndyCar Honda Grand Prix of St. Petersburg in Florida, U.S.A., on April 6, 2008.

Open-wheel racing cars have wheels outside the car's main body (and often just one seat), so they include Formula One vehicles.

MOST F1 WINS, MANUFACTURER The most Formula One grand prix wins by a manufacturer is 216, achieved by Italian constructor Ferrari between 1961 and 2011. Ferrari also has the **most starts in F1: 830** from 1950 to 2011.

MOST CONSECUTIVE WORLD RALLY CHAMPIONSHIPS The most consecutive World Rally Championship (WRC) titles is eight, won by Sébastien Loeb (France) between 2004 and 2011. The next highest is four, by Tommi Mäkinen (Finland) between 1996 and 1999. Loeb won all eight titles in a Citroën, which is a record for **most consecutive World Rally Championship titles won by a manufacturer.**

FACT: Loeb, above, leaps forward in the WRC rally in Portugal on March 25, 2011

ACKNOWLEDGMENTS

Guinness World Records would like to thank the following for their help in compiling this year's edition:

Actors' Equity Association; Ruth Adams and Smokey; Dr. John Andrews, OBE; Ascent Media; Eric Atkins; Back-to-back worldwide competition; Nigel Baker (Boxing Monthly); Josh Balber; Patrick Barrie (English Tiddlywinks Association); BBC Sport Relief; Sarah Bebbington; Dr. George Beccaloni (Natural History Museum; Bender Helper Impact; Morty Berger (NYC Swim); Justin Bieber; Dr. Janet Birkett; Bleeding Cool; Chelsea Bloxsome; Bolina; Boneau/Bryan-Brown; Bonhams; Michael Borowski; Catherine Bowell; The British Library; Broadway League; Lindsey Brown; Matt Burrows; Karumi Bustos (Zone Diet); Ronald "Ron" Byrd Akana; Cameron Mackintosh Limited; Hayley Campbell; The Cartoon Museum (London); Jennifer Cartwright; CCTV China (Guo Tong, Liu Ming, Wang Wei, Lin Feng, Liu Peng); Alan Cassidy, OBE (British Aerobatic Association); Clara and Camille Chambers; Georgina Charles; David Checkley (British Cave Research Association); Leland Chee; Mark Chisnell; Simone Ciancotti; City Montessori School; CITVC China (Wang Qiao); Joyce Cohen; Collaboration (Mr. Suzuki, Miho, Masumi); Adam Cloke; Comic Connect; Connection Cars (Rob and Tracey Dunkerley); Don Coulson; Council on Tall Buildings and Urban Habitat; Kenneth and Tatiana Crutchlow; Andrew Currie; Dr. Patrick Darling; Anastassia Davidzenka; Walter Day (Twin Galaxies); DC Thomson; Denmaur Independent Papers Limited; Mrs. M. E. Dimery; The Dock Museum, Barrow-in-Furness; Joshua Dowling; Helen Doyle; Europroduzione/Veralia (Marco, Stefano, Gabriel, Renato, Carlo); Toby and Amelia Ewen; Eyeworks Germany (Kaethe, Andi, Michael, Oliver, Martin); Eyeworks Australia and New Zealand (Julie, Alison); F J T Logistics Limited (Ray Harper, Gavin Hennessy); Benjamin Fall; Rebecca Fall; Joanna Fells; Rebecca Fells; Simon Fells; Hannah Finch (Virgin London Marathon); Noah Fleisher; Patrik Folco; Esteve Font Canadell; Formulation Inc. (Marcus, Ayako, Kei); Justin Garvanovic (Editor-in-Chief, European Coaster Club); Gerontology Research Group; Gerosa Group; Stewart Gillies; Sean Glover; Paul Gravett; Jackie Green; Martin Green; Victoria Grimsell; Alyson Hagert; Megan Halsband; Kristin Mie Hamada; Hampshire Sports and Prestige Cars (Richard Johnston); Carmen Alfonzo de Hannah; Stuart Hendry; Heritage Auctions; High Noon Entertainment (Pam, Jim, Andrew, Fred, Peter, Rachel); Highest Bridges.com; Graham Hill (Aerobatics); Deb Hoffmann; Hal Holbrook; Marsh K. Hoover; Alan Howard (Archives Director, International Jugglers Association); Dora Howard; Matilda Howard; Katherine Howells; Colin Hughes; Paul Ibell; ICM (Michael and Greg); INP Media (Bryn Downing); Integrated Colour Editions Europe (Roger Hawkins, Susie Hawkins, Clare Merryfield); International Planetarium Society; Amy Isobel; Itonic (Lisa Bamford and Keren Turner); Nicolas Janberg (Structurae); Melanie Johnson; Roger Johnson (The Sherlock Holmes Journal); Rich Johnston; Barbara Jones (Lloyds Register Reference Library); Eberhard Jurgalski (8000ers.com); Mark Karges; Yuriko Katsumata; Alex Keeler; Iryna Kennedy (Irish Long Distance Swimming Association); Siobhan Kenney (Protected Areas Programme, UNEP-WCMC); Anne B. Kerr; Erik Kessels; Keys; Rishi Khanna; Christopher Knee (International Association of Department Stores); Dr. Jennifer Krup; Siddharth Lama; Orla Langton; Thea Langton; The Library of Congress; Martin Lindsay; Ashley Fleur Linklater; Lion Television; Nickie Lister (Shiver Productions); Ashley Lodge; David Lotz; Peter Lowell; Dave McAleer; Sean Macaulay; Ewen Macdonald (Sea Vision UK); Eshani Malde; Albert, Stan and Sami Mangold; Steve Marchant; Duane Marden (Roller Coaster Database); Clodomiro Marecos; Mike Margeson; Missy Matilda; Clare "Babes" McLean (Flawless Files); Alex Meloy; Metropolis Collectibles, Inc. & ComicConnect.com; Miditech (Niret, Nivedith, Tarun, Alphi, Nikita); Jerry Mika (Asian Trekking); Mark Millar; Tamsin Mitchell; Harriet Molloy; Sophie and Joshua Molloy; Anikó Németh Móra (International Weightlifting Federation); Mark Muir (GRG); Steven Munatones (Open Water Source); Simon Murgatroyd; Kevin Murphy (Channel Swimming and Piloting Federation); National Maritime Museum (Claire Hyde, Sheryl Twigg, Rosie Linton); Captain Dexter Nelson (Oklahoma City Police Department); Forrest Nelson (Catalina Channel Swimming); Gemma Nelson; New Jersey Performing Arts Center; Jessica Nichols; Greg O'Connor (The Boston Light Swim Association); Nicola Oakey (Virgin London Marathon); Ralph Oates (boxing); Shaun Opperman (Battersea Dog Refuge); Michael Oram; Rubén Darío Orué Melgarejo; Tiffany Osborne (Virgin London Marathon); Peace One Day; Andrew and Charlotte Peacock; Daniel Phillips; Dr. Clara Piccirillo; Elena Polubochko; Sarah Prior; Dr. Robert Pullar; Shawn Purdy; Miriam Randall; Lauren Randolph; Dr. Donald Rau; Simon Raw; Robert Reardon; Amnon Rechter; Dr. Ofra Rechter; Re:fine Group; John Reed (WSSR Council); Rachel Reiner; Brian Reinert; Tom Richards; Fran Ridler (Virgin London Marathon); Jenny Robb (Curator and Assistant Professor at Billy Ireland Cartoon Library & Museum, Ohio State University); Gus and Dan Robertson; Jennifer Robson; Royal Shakespeare Company; Rosy Runciman; Richard Salisbury (The Himalayan Database); Tore Sand; Santa Barbara Channel Swimming Association (Scott Zornig and Evan Morrison); Schleich; Shaun Scarfe (Four One Four Ltd (BMX)); The Shakespeare Guild; Sean Shannon; Bill Sharp (Billabong XXL Global Big Wave Awards); Ang Tshering Sherpa; Appa Sherpa; Dawa Sherpa; Elisa Shevitz; Samantha Shutts (Columbus Zoo and Aquarium); Richard Sisson; Tom Sjogren (ExplorersWeb); Lottie, Jemima and Emma Skala; SLATE PR; Ben Smith; Society of London Theatres (SOLT); Maria Somma; Lyle Spatz; Spectratek Technologies, Inc. (Mike Foster, Mike Wanless); Square Four; Peter Stanbury; Jennifer Stewart (The Broadway League); Stora Enso Veitsiluoto; Storyvault Films (Olivia Lichtenstein, Kieran Carruthers, Georgia Cheales);

Strongman Champions League (Ilkka Kinnune and Marcel Mostert); Tej Sundher; Amy Taday; Emily Taday; Daina Taimina; Charlie, Daisy and Holly Taylor; John Taylor (Skyhawk Aerobatics); Theatrical Management Association (TMA), London; Themed Entertainment Association; Spencer Thrower; TNR; Julian Townsend; truTV (Marissa, Adam, Angel, Marc, Stephen, Michael); UIM (Union Internationale Motonautique); V&A Theatre & Performance Enquiry Service; Alex Valerio; Pedro Vázquez; Lorenzo Veltri; Gabriela Ventura; Viacom18 (Sandhya, Romil); Anneka Wahlhaus; Charley Wainwright; Adam West; Beverley Williams; Adam Wilson; Stewart Wolpin; Lydia Wood; Dan Woods; World Planetarium database—APLF (France); Tobias Hugh Wylie-Deacon; X-Leisure and West India Quay; Nada Zakula; Cherry Zhu; Zippy Production (Mitsue); Zodiak Rights; Eric Zuerndorfer; Vincent Zurzolo. Plus the children and staff at St. Thomas' Hospital, and all of our incredible record holders

PICTURE CREDITS

xi: Sam Christmas/GWR **xiii:** Str/Reuters; Sipa Press/Rex Features; Sipa Press/Rex Features; Pascal Parrot/Sygma/Corbis; Georges Gobet/AP/PA **xiv:** Mark Greenberg/Virgin Oceanic; Keystone USA-ZUMA/Rex Features **xv:** James Crisp; James Crisp; Rahav Segev/Photopass.com **xvi:** White House/Chuck Kennedy; Mark Wilson/Getty Images **xvii:** Anthoula Lelekidis; NBAE **xviii:** Lou Rocco/ABC, inc. **xx:** Kena Betancur/Reuters **xxii:** Maxwell photography/GWR; Tokyo-Skytree **xxiii:** Paul Michael Hughes/GWR; Michael Hughes/GWR; Tesco; Alexander Pihuliak/GWR; Alexander Pihuliak/GWR **xxv:** Gerard Farrell/GWR; Matt May/GWR; Adrian Holerga; Matt May/GWR **xxvi:** Sam Christmas/GWR; Sam Christmas/GWR; Sam Christmas/GWR **xxvii:** Sam Christmas/GWR; Sam Christmas/GWR; Sam Christmas/GWR; Sam Christmas/GWR **xxx:** Simone Joyner/Getty Images **xxxi:** Peace One Day Ltd.; AFP/Getty Images; Stuart Wilson/Getty Images **xxxii:** Samir Hussein/Getty Images **xxiii:** Peace One Day Ltd; Stuart Wilson/Getty Images; Amnesty International **xxxiv:** AFP/Getty Images; Jorge Lopez/Reuters; Getty Images; Eric Vandeville/GAMMA/Getty Images **3:** Getty Images; Getty Images; Roger Ressmeyer/Corbis **4:** NASA; Getty Images; NASA; Antonio Rosario/ Getty Images **5:** NASA; NASA; NASA; Jaxa/ISAS/ Ciel et Espace Photos; Perspectx; NASA **6:** NASA; Pline; Getty Images; ESO; NASA **7:** Getty Images; ESA; NASA **8:** Detlev van Ravenswaay/Science Photo Library; Don P. Mitchell **9:** Getty Images **10:** NASA **11:** Getty Images; Max Planck Institute **12:** ESA **13:** NASA; NASA **14:** NASA **15:** NASA **16:** NASA **17:** NASA **18:** Getty Images **19:** Science Photo Library **20:** NASA; Rex Features; Getty Images; Getty Images; NASA **22:** Boeing; Michael Stonecyphe/USAF **24:** Getty Images **25:** Getty images **26:** David A. Aguilar (cfa) **27:** NASA **28:** Science Photo Library; NASA **29:** Science Photo Library; Science Photo Library **31:** Paul Harris/Getty Images **33:** Carsten Peter/Getty Images **34:** Mann et al. **35:** Steven

Kazlowski/Getty Images; Alex Tingle; Fleetham Dave/Getty Images; William West/Getty Images **36:** Robert Nickelsberg/Getty Images; NOAA/Getty Images **37:** Mike Sega/Reuters; Munish Sharma/Reuters; Tomas Benedikovic/isifa/Getty Images **38:** James P. Blair/Getty Images; NASA **39:** Kevin Lee/Getty Images **41:** David Prutchi; Reuters; Reuters **42:** Ho New/Reuters; Boris Horvat/Getty Images **43:** Getty Images; Images; Zoltan Balogh/Getty Images **46:** Alamy; Tony Wu/Getty Images **47:** Peter Walton/Getty Images; Paul Harris/Getty Images **48:** Woods Hole Oceanographic Institution; Swedish Museum of Natural History **49:** Richard Bonson/Getty Images; Charles Fisher **51:** Rodrigo Baleia; Alamy **52:** Karl Brodowsky; Alamy **53** National Geographic; Thomas Hamler **54:** Forestry Tasmania **55:** Andy Murch/Oceanwide **57:** Kevin Scott Ramos **61:** Gary Bell/Oceanwide Images **62:** Andy Murch/Oceanwide Images; Jennifer Crites; Rand McMeins/Getty Images **63:** Steve Bloom/Alamy **65:** Katherine Feng/FLPA **67:** NHPA; Andrea Florence/Ardea; Mark Jones/Getty Images; Gary Ombler/Getty Images **70:** Michael Kern/Corbis **71:** Joel Sartore/Getty Images; J & C Sohns/Getty Images; Laurie Campbell/Getty Images **72:** Jurgen & Christine Sohns/FLPA; George Grall/Getty Images **74:** SuperStock; John Binns **75:** Oceanlab/Uni of Aberdeen **76:** Caters; Caters; Richard Bradbury/GWR **77:** FLPA; Nature PL **79:** E.R. Degginger/Alamy; Juniors Bildarchiv/Alamy; Paul Nicklen/Getty Images **80:** Tom Walker/Getty Images; Mark Bowler/Photoshot **81:** FLPA **83:** Vano Shlamov **84:** Paul Sawyer/FLPA **85:** Andy Rouse/Nature PL; Elliott Neep/Getty Images; Anup Shah/Getty Images **86:** Splash News; AP/Pa **87:** Slobodan Djajic/Getty Images **88:** Kevin Scott Ramos/GWR **90:** Paul Michael Hughes/GWR; James Ellerker/GWR **94:** Ryan Schude/GWR; Paul Michael Hughes/GWR; James Ellerker **97:** Kevin Scott Ramos/GWR **99:** Navesh Chitrakar/Reuters **100:** Reuters; Francois Mori/AP/PA **101:** Frank Schwere/Getty Images; Frank Schwere/Getty Images; Frank Schwere/Getty Images; Getty Images; Science Photo Library **103:** iStock; Getty Images; iStock; Casula/Getty Images; Getty Images **106:** Lowell Mason **108:** Anne Kerr; Don Coulson; Paul Michael Hughes/GWR **110:** Rex Features; Craig Connor/North News **111:** Getty Images; James Ambler/Getty Images **114:** AP/PA **117:** Rick Wilking/Reuters; Reuters **119:** Kevin Scott Ramos/GWR **120:** James Ellerker/GWR; Shinsuke Kamioka/GWR **124:** Daniel Bazan/GWR **125:** Kevin Scott Ramos/GWR; Paul Michael Hughes/GWR **127:** Ranald Mackechnie/GWR **128:** Splash News; Tomas Bravo/GWR **129:** PA; Imagno/Getty; Nir Elias/Reuters **130:** Richard Bradbury/GWR; Prakash Mathema/GWR; Prakash Mathema/GWR **131:** Punit Paranjpe/Getty Images; Ashesh Shah/GWR **132:** Maria Elisa Duque/GWR; John Wright/GWR; Owee Salva/GWR; Prakash Mathema/GWR; Jonathan Lewis/GWR; Gary Parker; John Wright/GWR **133:** Getty Images; Liu Hong Shing/AP/PA **134:** Owee Salva/GWR; Owee Salva/GWR **137:** Richard Bradbury/GWR **139:** Paul Michael Hughes/GWR; Doug Pensinger/Getty Images; Action Plus Sports Images/Alamy **140:** MedicalRF.com/Getty Images **141:** Dorling Kindersley/Getty Images **142:** Dorling Kindersley/Getty Images **143:** Bertrand Guay/Getty Images; Ahmad Yusni/Getty Images **145:** Sebastien Pirlet/Reuters; Sebastien Pirlet/Reuters **150:** Niall Carson/PA **151:** Bikas Das/AP/

PA; Piyal Adhikary/EPA **154:** Ryan Schude/GWR **157:** Richard Bradbury/ GWR; Kevin Scott Ramos/GWR **158:** Kevin Scott Ramos/GWR **160:** Cindy Ord/Getty Images **161:** Adam Harnett/Caters **163:** Xavier La Canna/ PA **164:** Kevin Scott Ramos/GWR **165:** Christopher Furlong/Getty Images **168:** Paul Michael Hughes/GWR **169:** Paul Michael Hughes/GWR **170:** David Jones/PA **171:** James Ellerker/GWR **172:** Cheryl Ravelo/Reuters; Cheryl Ravelo/Reuters; Cheryl Ravelo/Reuters **173:** Ranald Mackechnie/ GWR; WENN **175:** Shinsuke Kamioka/GWR **176:** Ryan Schude/GWR; Ranald Mackechnie/GWR **180:** James Ellerker/GWR **181:** Ryan Schude/ GWR; Ranald Mackechnie/GWR **185:** Francois Lenoir/Reuters; Otto Greule Jr./AP/PA **186:** Rex Features **187:** Paul Michael Hughes/GWR **188:** Kevin Scott Ramos/GWR; David Grubbs/AP/PA **189:** Steve Marcus/ Reuters; Steve Marcus/Reuters **190:** Paul Michael Huges/GWR **193:** Dave Thompson/PA; Dave Thompson/PA **194:** Bonnie Salzman; Madalyn Ruggiero/Eyevine **195:** Jens Meyer/AP/PA **198:** Alexander Pihuliak/GWR **201:** APPI **203:** Sacha Kenyon **204:** Stephen Alvarez/Getty Images; Gaten Borgonie/University Ghent **205:** NOAA; Jamstec **206:** Mark Thiessen/AP/ PA **208:** Alamy; Stephane Mahe/Reuters **209:** Gerardo Garcia/Reuters; Mercedes Benz **210:** Getty Images; Getty Images; Getty Images; Getty Images **211:** Getty Images; Getty Images; Getty Images **212:** Robert Hollingworth; Leon Neal/Getty Images **213:** Reuters; Reuters **216:** Getty Images; Getty Images; Rex Features; AP/PA **217:** Getty Images; Ho New/Reuters **218:** Photoshot **220:** Robin Paschall **221:** Alamy; Getty Images; Michael Burnett/Rex Features **222:** NASA **223:** APPI **225:** Polar Circles-Dixie Dansercoer **226:** AP/PA; Chien-min Chung/Getty Images; Alamy **227:** Rex Features; Alamy; David Cheskin/PA; AP/PA **228:** Angel Medina G./epa/ Corbis; Huntswood **229:** Mirrorpix **230:** Roz Savage **231:** Paul Scambler; Getty Images **232:** Getty Images; ABACA/PA; Getty Images **233:** Tarek Mostafa/Reuters **235:** iStock; Hans Elbers/Getty Images; Jochem D Wijnands/Getty Images; Lucy Nicholson/Reuters **237:** Niels Poulsen/Alamy; Thomas Lohnes/Getty Images; Getty Images; Walter Bibikow/Getty Images **238:** Getty Images; Bazuki Muhammad/Reuters; Narinder Nanu/Getty Images; Adrees Latif/Reuters **239:** Ang Tshring Sherpa/Reuters; Shilpa Harolikar/Getty Images; Yoshikazu Tsuno/Getty Images **240:** iStock; Getty· Images; Steve Allen/Getty Images **241:** James Balog/Getty Images; Yves Herman/Reuters; Pascal Rossignol/Reuters **242:** Larry Dale Gordon/Getty Images; Nigel Dennis/Getty Images; Peter Adams/Getty Images **243:** Bertrand Rieger/Getty Images; Alamy; Ariadne Van Zandbergen/Getty Images; Tarek Mostafa/Reuters **244:** Ulrich Doering/Alamy; Roger Smith; Alamy; Getty Images **245:** Robert Cameron; Lone Pine Koala Sanctuary; Jeff Hunter/Getty Images **246:** James D. Morgan/Rex Features; Getty Images; Getty Images **247:** Enrique R. Aguirre Aves/Getty Images; Mark Ralston/Getty Images; George Rose/Getty Images **248:** Mark Ashman/ Getty Images; A & L Sinibaldi/Getty Images **249:** Gordon Sinclair/Photoshot; John Mitchell/ Alamy; David Muench/Getty Images; Jacob Halaska/ Getty Images **250:** Ingo Arndt/Getty Images; Getty Images; Danita Delimont/Getty Images **251:** Vanderlei Almeida/ Getty Images; Jon Arnold/ Alamy; Martin Bernetti/Getty Images **252:** Theo Allofs/Getty Images; Fabio Filzi/Getty Images; Jan Cobb/Getty Images **253:** Getty Images **255:** Rishi Khanna/Montessori School **256:** Peter Foley/Getty Images; Scott Olson/Getty Images; Scott Olson/Getty Images; Eric Piermont/Getty Images; Xurxo Lobato/Getty Images; Stephen Lam/Getty Images; Chris Goodney/ Getty Images; Nick Harvey/Getty Images; Ed Jones/Getty Images **257:** Getty Images; Getty Images; Alamy **258:** Getty Images; Getty Images; AP/ PA; Corbis; Getty Images **259:** AP/PA; AP/PA; **260:** James Ellerker/GWR **262:** Kevin Scott Ramos/GWR; Philip Robertson/GWR **265:** Gili Yaari **266:** Africa 24 Media/Peter Greste; David Lewis/Reuters **268:** Alamy; Ted Thai/Getty Images **269:** Sandi Holder's Doll Attic, Inc; Rex Features; Justin Sullivan/Getty Images; Peter Brooker/Rex Features; Tony Gentile/ Reuters; Rex Features; The Teddy Bear Musuem, Korea; Christie's Images **271:** Araya Diaz/Getty Images **272:** Getty Images; Denis Sinyakov/Getty Images **273:** James Ellerker/GWR **274:** Hannelore Foerster/Bloomberg via Getty Images; Jason Alden/Bloomberg via Getty Images **276:** Getty Images; Ken Mackay/Rex Features **277:** iStock; Ingolf Pompe/Getty Images **278:** Aldo Pavan/4 Corners **280:** Anne Lewis/Alamy; Alamy **281:** C. McIntyre/Getty Images; PA; Getty Images **282:** Getty Images; Rex Features **284:** Joop van Houdt/XL D-sign **284:** Warren Diggles/Getty Images; Alamy; Peter Adams/Alamy **285:** iStockphoto; Peter Dazeley/Getty Images; Mark Ralston/Getty Images **286:** Danita Delimont/Alamy; Danny Ramirez/Reuters; Mayela Lopez/Getty Images **287:** iStockphoto; Alan Boswell/Getty Images; Roberto Schmidt/Getty Images **288:** John Nicholson/Getty Images; Gareth Jones/Getty Images; Subir Halder/Getty Images;Gleb Garanich/Reuters; Nils-Johan Norenlind/Getty Images; Shaun Egan/Getty Images **290:** Nelson Ching/Getty Images **291:** AFP/Getty Images; Fiona Hanson/ AFP **292:** Bob Sullivan/Getty Images; Robert Nickelsberg/Getty Images; Keystone/Getty Images **293:** Adalberto Roque/AFP/ Getty Images; Walter Dhladhla/AFP/Getty Images **295:** Royal Navy; Alamy **296:** Paula Bronstein/Getty Images; Getty Images; Getty Images **297:** Romeo Gacad/Getty Images **300:** Ben Hider/Getty Images; Ernie Sisto/Eyevine **301:** Jemal Countess/Getty Images **302:** Ho New/Reuters; Ho New/Reuters; Ho New/Reuters **304:** Studio Ghibli; You Tube **305:** Brian To/FilmMagic/Getty Images; Henry S. Dziekan III/Getty Images **306:** 24 Hrs Photos Installatie Erik Kessels Gijs van den Berg/Caters News; You Tube **307:** Andrew H. Walker/Getty Images; Justin Sullivan/Getty Images; Kim White/Greenpeace **309:** Jeddah Economic Company/Adrian Smith + Gordon Gill Architecture **311:** James Ellerker/GWR; Imagno/Austrian Archives/Getty Images **312:** Jeddah Economic Company/Adrian Smith + Gordon Gill Architecture; Reuters; AFP/Getty Images **313:** AFP/ Getty Images; AFP Getty Images; David Handschuh/ NY Daily News Archive/Getty Images; Kuni Takahashi/Getty Images **316:** AFP/Getty Images **317:** Cliff Tan Anlong; Cliff Tan Anlong; Cliff Tan Anlong; Cliff Tan Anlong; Cliff Tan Anlong; Cliff Tan Anlong; Cliff Tan Anlong **318:** Cliff Tan Anlong; Cliff Tan Anlong; Cliff Tan Anlong **320:** Cliff Tan Anlong; Cliff Tan Anlong; USAF/Getty Images **321:** Stuart Franklin/Getty Images; Suraj Kunwar/AP/PA **322:** Angelo Cavalli/Photoshot **323:** Vincent Yu/AP/PA; Alamy **325:** Veolia Transportation, In Service to the Regional Transit Authority of New Orleans; Mu Xiang Bin/Redlink/Corbis **326:** AFP/Getty Images; Superstock; Syd Neville **327:** Donald Nausbaum/ Corbis; Yuriko Nakao/Reuters; China Photos/Getty Images **330:** Aaron M. Sprecher/Getty images **331:** Chealion **332:** Aly Song/Reuters **333:** Stephen Brashear/Getty Images **335:** Chris Ison/PA; Rex Features; Ho New/Reuters **336:** BAE Systems; BAE Systems; Paul Bratcher **337:** Lockheed Martin Aeronautics **338:** BAE Systems; BAE Systems **339:** Andrew Skudder; Defense Imagery; Defense Imagery **340:** Crown Copyright; Crown Copyright **341:** USAF **342:** Lockheed Martin; Sasa Kralj/AP/PA **344:** Pavel/Planespotters.net **345:** Sergey Riabsev/JetPhotos.net **346:** Beate Kern; Shinsuke Kamioka/GWR **347:** Oscar Espinoza/US Navy **349:** Ben Stansall/Getty Images **350:** Paul Michael Hughes/GWR **351:** Shinsuke Kamioka/GWR; Paul Michael Hughes/ GWR **352:** Ranald Mackechnie/GWR **353:** Robert MacDonald; Stefan Wermuth/Reuters; Natacha Pisarenko/AP/PA **354:** SuperStock; PA **355:** Alamy; Spencer Platt/Getty Images **358:** STR/Reuters **359:** Handout/ Reuters **360:** Richard Bradbury/GWR **361:** Herrenknecht AG **363:** Yoshikazu Tsuno/Getty Images **366:** Cern; KAMIOKA; NASA; Paolo Lombardi/INFN-MI **367:** AFP/Getty Images; AFP/Getty Images **368:** NASA **369:** Dr. Hamish Pritchard; Dr. Hamish Pritchard **370:** Robert Wagner/Max-Planck-Institut/Munich **371:** Yoshikazu Tsuno/Getty Images; Tomohiro Ohsumi/Getty Images **373:** NASA; NASA **374:** Tim Boyle/Getty Images; Nichlas Hansen **375:** Lucas Jackson/Reuters; Seth Wenig/AP/PA **379:** Georges Seurat; Diana Taimina **380:** Dan Everett **381:** Rick Friedman/ Corbis; Solkoll; YouTube **382:** Francois Nascimbeni/Getty Images **383:** Dick Jones **384:** NASA; NASA; NHPA **385:** NHPA; Jeff Hasty Lab/UC San Diego; Jeff Hasty Lab/UC San Diego **386:** Laurie Hatch; Laurie Hatch; AP/PA; James Nesterwitz/Alamy **388:** NASA; Getty Images; Andy Crawford/Getty Images **390:** Rex Features; Ethan Miller/Getty Images; Murray Close/Getty Images; Ronald Cohn/The Gorilla Foundation; 20th Century Fox **394:** Skyvision Entertainment **395:** Shamil Zhumatov/Reuters; Science Photo Library; 20th Century Fox/Moviestore **396:** NASA; Lucasfilm/Moviestore **397:** Ranald Mackechnie/GWR **398:** Dr Gary Settles/Science Photo Library; Chrysler Group LLC. **399:** Andrew Grantham; Andrew Grantham; Thomas Marent/Ardea **400:** Thomas Powell/ASAF **403:** La Petite Reine **407:** Danny Martindale/Getty Images; Frazer Harrison/Getty Images; Steve Granitz/Getty Images; Frederick M. Brown/Getty Images; AFP/Getty Images; Nick Harvey/Getty Images; Noel Vasquez/ Getty Images; Jason LaVeris/Getty Images; Steve Granitz/Getty Images; Mike Ehrmann/Getty Images; Cindy Ord/Getty Images; Dominique Charriau/Getty Images; Dave M. Benett/Getty Images; Bruce Glikas/Getty Images; Jeffrey Mayer/Getty Images; Mike Marsland/Getty Images; Pascal Le Segretain/ Getty Images; Rob Kim/Getty Images; Dan MacMeda/Getty Images; Matthew Stockman/Getty Images; X Factor/Getty Images; Steve Granitz/Getty Images; Lester Cohen/Getty Images; Paul Morigi/Getty Images **409:** Rex Features; Getty Images; Hachette **410:** Stormstill; King Features; Rex Features; Rex Features; Dominic Winter/Rex Features **413:** Kazam Media/Rex Features **414:** Summit Entertainment; John Sciulli/Rex Features; Paramount Pictures **415:** Marvel/Paramount Pictures; Jeff Kravitz/Getty Images

416: Paramount Pictures **418:** Frazer Harrison/Getty Images; Francois Durand; Getty Images; Dreamworks; Studio Ghibli **419:** New Line Cinema; Columbia; MGM; Warner Bros; Walt Disney Pictures; Warner Bros; Summit Entertainment; Sony Pictures **420:** WireImage/Getty Images; WireImage/Getty Images; Pixar **421:** 20th Century Fox; La Petite Reine; Warner Bros; Columbia; Universal; Warner Bros; Columbia; Universal; Walt Disney Pictures **422:** Warner Bros; Icon Productions; Ed Burke/AP/PA **423:** Eamonn J. McCabe; David Wolff/Getty Images **424:** Kevork Djansezian/Getty Images **425:** Getty Images; Getty Images; Getty Images; Getty Images; Getty Images; Getty Images; Getty Images **426:** Jeff Kavitz/Getty Images; Universal Music; Ernesto Ruscio/Getty Images **427:** MCA Records; Harvest/Capital **428:** MCA Records; Epic Records; Parlophone/EMI; Epic Records; Decca **429:** Warner Bros Records; Creation; Atlantic Records; Jive Records **431:** Ranald Mackechnie/GWR; Paul Brown/Rex Features **432:** Redux/Eyevine; Redux/Eyevine; Rex Features **433:** Redux/Eyevine **435:** WireImage/Getty Images; Michael Stravato/The New York Times/ Eyevine **436:** Doug Hyun/Turner Network Television **437:** Paul Michael Hughes/GWR; Matt Hoyle/Getty Images **438:** Vince Valitutti/Fox; Fox **439:** Frederick M. Brown/Getty Images; Bobby Bank/Getty Images **440:** ITV/Rex Features **441:** Lucasfilm/ 20th Century Fox/ Kobal Collection; Electronic Arts/Bioware/Lucasfilms **443:** Lucasfilm/ 20th Century Fox/ Kobal Collection; 20th Century Fox/ Everett/Rex Features; Brooks Films/ Ronald Grant **444:** Hasbro/Getty Images; David Crausby/Alamy; Lucasfilm/ 20th Century Fox/ Kobal Collection **445:** Ryan Schude/GWR **446:** Ranald Mackechnie/GWR **447:** Richard Bradbury/GWR **449:** David Sherman/NBAE/Getty Images **451:** Stan Honda/Getty Images; Clive Brunskill/ Getty Images; Getty Images **452:** Gunnar Berning/Getty Images; Tiziana Fabi/Getty Images; Getty Images; Getty Images **453:** iStockphoto **455:** Kevin C. Cox/Getty Images; Al Messerschmidt/ Getty Images **456:** Otto Greule Jr./Getty Images **457:** Jim McIsaac/Getty Images; Ronald Martinez/ Getty Images; Michael Zagaris/Getty Images; Brian Kersey/Getty Images **460:** Nathan Denette/AP/PA **461:** Fred Greenslade/Reuters; Darren England/Getty Images; Tony Feder/Getty Images **463:** Bongarts/Getty Images **465:** Michael Steele/Getty Images; Jasper Juinen **466:** Mike Hewitt/Getty Images **467:** Jeff Gross/Getty Images; David Ramos/Getty Images **470:** Gabriel Bouys/Getty Images; Stu Forster/Getty Images **471:** Lionel Bonaventure/Getty Images **473:** Dave Howarth/PA **475:** Rob Carr/Getty Images; Chris Trotman/Getty Images; Dilip Vishwanat/Getty images **476:** Elsa/ Getty Images **477:** Daniel Shirey/Getty Images **478:** Jim McIsaac/Getty Images **479:** Getty Images; Hamish Blair/Getty Images **480:** Getty Images **481:** Getty Images; Getty Images **482:** Getty Images **484:** Claus Andersen/ Getty Images **485:** Barry Chin/ Getty Images **486:** John Tlumacki/ Getty Images **487:** Andy Marlin/NHLI/Getty Images **489:** Martin Meissner/AP/ PA; Clare Green/Team Bath **490:** AFP/Getty Images; Mohammed Dabbous/Reuters **491:** Fabrizio Giovannozz/AP **493:** Andrew D Bernstein/ NBAE/Getty Images; MCT/Getty Images **494:** David Sherman/NBAE/ Getty Images **495:** Melissa Majchrzak/NBAE/Getty Images **496:** Scott Cunningham/NBAE/Getty Images **498:** Eric Feferberg/AFP/Getty Images

499: AP/PA; Angelos Zimaras/Demotix/PA 500: Simon Bruty/Getty Images; Don Ryan/AP/PA 501: Bob Martin/Getty Images; Ermindo Armino/AP/PA 504: Alexander Hassenstein/Bongarts/Getty Images 505: www.photorun.NET; Gary Hershon/Reuters 508: Peter Parks/AFP/Getty images; Andreas Rentz/Bongarts/Getty Images 509: AFP/Getty Images; Michael Steele/Getty images 510: AFP/Getty Images 511: Allsport/Getty Images 512: GWR; GWR; GWR; GWR; GWR; GWR; GWR; GWR; GWR; GWR; GWR; GWR; GWR; GWR 513: GWR; GWR; GWR; GWR; GWR; GWR; GWR; GWR; GWR; GWR; GWR; GWR; GWR; GWR 514: Attila Kisbenedek/AFP 515: Joe Castro/AAP/PA 516: Rick Rycroft/AP/PA; Offside; Offside 517: Quinn Rooney/Getty Images 519: Olaf Kraak/Getty Images; AFP Getty Images 520: Stefano Rellandini/Reuters 521: IGSA 523: AFP/Getty Images; Dilip Vishwanat/Getty Images 524: AFP/Getty Images; AFP/Getty Images; Stephane Reix/Corbis 525: Jeff Gross/Getty Images; Jim Kemper/ Zuffa LLC./Getty Images 526: Robert Beck/ Sports Illustrated/Getty Images 528: Jim Watson/Getty Images; David Cannon/Getty Images 529: Stephen Munday/Getty Images; Reuters 531: Domenech Castello/Corbis; Ian Walton/Getty Images 533: Robert Cianflone/Getty Images; Julian Finney/Getty Images; Mark Blinch/Reuters; 534: AFP/Getty Images 535: AFP/Getty Images 536: AFP/Getty Images 539: AFP/Getty Images; MATCHROOM SPORTS; Comic Relief; Paul Gilham/Getty Images; 541: MATCHROOM SPORTS; AFP/Getty Images 543: Ori Kuper 544: Reuters 545: Martin Scheel; Ivar Brennhovd 549: AFP/Getty Images 550: Carols Hauck 551: Bo Bridges/Getty Images 552: Pierre Tostee/ASP/Getty Images 553: Vittorio Ubertone/Aquabike Promotion Ltd. 554: Ezra Shaw/Getty Images 557: RISPORT 558: Mark Thompson/Getty Images 560: Koichi Kamoshida/Getty Images 561: AFP/Getty Images; Jeff Burke/Getty Images 562: AFP Getty Images; Massimo Bettiol/Getty Images 602: Geoff Caddick/PA 603: Mario Tama/Getty Images 604: Matt Lingo/Red Bull Contest Pool 605: Sam Christmas

IN MEMORIAM

Vasiliy Alekseyev (**most weightlifting records broken**); Leila Denmark (**oldest ever practicing doctor**); Whitney Houston (**best-selling soundtrack album, first album by a solo female to debut at U.S. No.1**); Steve Jobs (**lowest paid CEO, largest options grant**); Evelyn Bryan Johnson (**most flying hours logged**); Ken LeBel (**most barrels jumped over by a man on ice skates**); Patrick Musimu (**deepest variable-weight freedive**); William Lawlis Pace (**longest time with a bullet in the head**); István Rózsavölgyi (**fastest 1,500-m**); Maria Gomes Valentim (**oldest woman**); Park Young-Seok (**first person to complete the explorers' grand slam**)

INDEX

This year's index is organized into two parts: by subject and by superlative. **Bold entries** in the subject index indicate a main entry on a topic, and **BOLD CAPITALS** indicate an entire chapter. Neither index lists personal names.

SUBJECT INDEX

A

BMX, 555–56
Board Skills, 548–53
boats/ships: circumnavigations, xv, 208, 209; container, 362; military, 295, 297, 298, 342, 343, 344; nuclear-powered, 44, 340
bobsleds, 520
bodybuilders, 106, 108
body burn, 199
body mass index (BMI), 130
body modification, 122–26
Body Parts, 118–22, 140, 183, 303, 373, 390
bog snorkeling, 195
Bolivia, 289, 299, 355
bookmarks, 178
books: authors, 188; collections, 173, 178; illustrations, 186; movie-based, 442–43; publishing, 334
boomerangs, 334
Borexino Experiment, 367
Bosnia and Herzogovina, 191, 340
Botswana, 289
bottles: beer, 178; champagne, 173, 198; manufacturing, 330; Moutai, 174; plastic, 185; whiskey, xx
bowling, 539, 542
boxing, 525–27
Box-Office Hits: movies, 418–22, 440–44; theater, 433, 435
Boyoma Falls (DR Congo), 243
brain, 373–74, 391
Brazil: biodiversity, 252; cities, 279; coffee production, 285; gun ownership, 337; life expectancy, 289; military, 343; railroads, 328; roads, 356; wealth, 275
breath: holding underwater, 200
bridges, 244, 277, 357–60, 362
British Open: golf, 531; squash, 537
Broadway, 432–36
broccoli, 165
Brunei, 294
Brussels sprouts, 165
bubblegum, 169
Buddhism, 240
budgerigars, 262
budgets: healthcare, 284; military, 298
Buenos Aires, Argentina, 279
buffalo, 72, 80, 91
building height, xiii, xiv, xxii, 312, 318, 319; *see also* skyscrapers
bulls, 67, 81, 90, 389
Burj Khalifa (Dubai, UAE), xiv, 311, 312, 313, 318, 319, 416
burns, survived, 302
burps, 397
Burundi, 340
buses, 278
But Is It Art?, 182–87
butterflies, 175
buttons, 178

C

cabbage, 165
Caesarean sections, 113, 114
calculators, 375
calendars, 267
Cambodia, 130, 340
cameras, 370, 385
Cameroon, 289
camouflage, 338
Canada: collectors, 178; computer use, 285; life expectancy, 289; railroads, 328; roads, 356; smokers, 284; wealth, 275
canals, 42, 359
cancer screening, xviii
candles, 171
candy, 167–70
cannibalism, 75
canoeing, 228
canopy piloting, 543
cantaloupe, 165
capital cities, 246
carbon dioxide (CO_2), 35, 36–37, 160, 282
carnivals, 251
carnivores, 59, 60, 71
carrots, 165
cars *see* automobiles
Carstensz Pyramid (Indonesia), 245
cartoons, 184
catamarans, 231
cats, 68, 77–78, 79, 87, 175, 260–62; *see also* big cats
cattle, 75, 81, 88, 90
cauliflower, 165
caves, 33, 204
celebrities: in cat photos, 261; costumes, 268; newsmaking, 407–08
celery, 165
cell phones, 334, 446
centipedes, 77
Central African Republic, 289
CERN (European Organization for Nuclear Research), 44, 365, 366, 370
Ceylon *see* Sri Lanka
CFL (Canadian Football League), 460, 461, 464
Chad, 191, 289, 295
chains: bracelets, xv; kissing, xxiv
chainsaws, 199, 350
chairs, 271
charity events, 152
Charlie's Angels memorabilia, 172
checkers, 192
cheese, 163
cheetahs, 83, 84, 85, 87, 96
chefs, 606
chelonians *see* turtles/tortoises/terrapins
Chernobyl (Ukraine), 43
cherries, 165

food: auctioned, 270; calories, 602; desserts, 167–70; eaten, xv, 157–62; grown, 163, 165; irradiation, 43, 44; prepared, 163–67; production, 91, 92; in space, 18, 20; survival without, 303

food fights, 236

football: American, 190, 455–59; Australian rules, 462–64; Canadian, 460, 461, 464; Gaelic, 460, 461–462; *see also* soccer

foreign aid, 287

forests, 47–50, 54; *see also* rainforests

Formula One racing, 190, 558, 559, 562

fossil fuels, 39

fractals, 381

France: gun ownership, 337; head of state, 292; life expectancy, 289; military, 298, 343; nuclear power, 41, 42; railroads, 328; roads, 356; storm destruction, 53; tourism, 288; wealth, 275; in World War II, 299

Fraser Island, 246

Fresh Kills Landfill (Staten Island, NY, U.S.A.), 37

frogs, 78, 95, 283

fruits, 165

fudge, 169

funny cars, 560

Fun with Food, 157–62

fuzzy dice, xviii

G

Gabon, 289

galaxies, 26–29, 384

game consoles, 445, 446

game reserves, 243

games: checkers, 192; chess, 189, 377; conkers, 192, 194; horseshoes, 192, 194; movie spin-offs, 419; online, 304, 305, 306, 423, 445; poker, 189, 378; stealth, 374; tiddlywinks, 193; trivia, 388; video, 151, 306, 441, 442–48

game shows, 440

garden gnomes, 151, 177, 179

gardens, 237, 242

garlic, 165

Gateway Arch (St. Louis, MO, U.S.A.), 317

geese, 69

geoglyphs, 249

gerbils, 68

Germany: collectors, 178; gun ownership, 337; life expectancy, 289; military, 298, 299; railroads, 328; wealth, 275

gestation: amphibian, 66; big cat, 85; human triplets, 112; mammal, 66; sharks, 63, 66

Ghana, 289

ghosts, 280

giraffes, 58, 83

Giro d'Italia (cycling), 518

glaciers, 34

gliding, 544–46

Global Financial Crisis (GFC), 274

Global Positioning System (GPS), 23, 25, 342

gloves, 180

goats, 68, 73, 76, 88, 89, 90, 91

gold: mining, 40, 204, 257, 258, 302; value, 259

Golden Ratio, 382

goldfish, 263

Golf, 528–32

golf courses, 320, 529

gorges, 249

gorillas, 59

graffiti, 184

Grammy Awards (music), 107, 423, 447

Grand Canyon (Arizona, U.S.A.), 249

Grand Finals (Australian football), 461, 462, 463

Grand Slam (tennis), 533, 534, 535, 537

grand slams (baseball), 475

grapefruit, 165

graphene, 390

graphic novels, 410

gravy wrestling, 193

Great African War, 295

Great Barrier Reef, 49, 245

Great Britain, 297; *see also* United Kingdom

Great Lakes, 39, 54

Great Pyramid (Egypt), xiii, 243, 317, 318

Great Rift Valley, 244

Great Wall (China), 240

Greece, 289, 498

GREEN EARTH, 31–54

greenhouse gases, 36

Greenland, 35, 46

Grey Cup (Canadian football), 461

gross domestic product (GDP): by country, 275; defined, 259; for foreign aid, 287; in recession, 274; U.S.A., 284; world, 256

Guatemala, 286

guide stars, 386

Guinea-Bissau, 289, 340

guinea pigs, 68, 92, 94, 95, 263

guitars, 268

guns, 21, 24, 332, 334–35, 337, 392, 398, 447

gurning, 192

GWR Day, xxii–xxv

gymnasts, 108

gyrocopters, 223

H

hacking, 445

hailstones, 283

hair: body, 121; facial, 121, 197; head, 120, 121, 143

hairstyles: afro, xx; Mohican, 120, 122

Haiti, 289

movie-watching, xxix; pool, 540; skiing, 520; snooker, 541; surfing, 552

Marathons (running), xiv, 107, 128, 500, **509–13**; half, 203, 505

Marianas Trench, xiv, 206, 221

marine life, 46, 48, 50

Mariner spacecraft, 9, 12

Mario Kart, 447

marriage: age, 117; rates, 118, 285; *see also* weddings

married couples, 133, 218, 221

Mars, 5, 7, 373

marsupials, 67, 70, 79

Masdar City, UAE, 276

matchbook covers, 178

matchbox labels, 178

mazes, 604

McMurdo Station, Antarctica, 320, 346, 355

meatballs, 166

meat production, 91

media tycoons, 274

medical tricorder, 396

memorabilia, xxi, 171–77

memory devices, 373

Menger sponge, 381

Mercury, 8

Mercury Music Prize, 422

Mexico, 267, 285, 289, 292, 293, 337

Mexico City, Mexico, 277, 279

mice, 68, 263

Michael Tuck Medals (Australian football), 464

Mickey Mouse memorabilia, 177

microelectronic devices, 369

microlights, 546

Middle East, 311, 314–15

military: forces, 295–99; rockets, 24, 25; in space, 22, 23; vehicles, 339–44, 345, 347, 348

milk, 91

Milky Way, 29, 30, 38

millionaires, 187

millipedes, 77

minarets, 241

mining, 40, 204, 302

models: airport, 321; automobile, xxiv, 172, 178; human organs, 183; trains, 326, 327

molecular charge, 370

mollusks, 70, 71

Monaco, 264, 289

Mona Lisa, 236

monarchs, 129, 290, 291, 292, 294

Mongolia, 36, 289

monkeys, 399

monoliths, 244, 250

monster trucks, 556

monuments, 48, 247, 317

Moon, 6, 13, 20, 414

moose, 59, 80

moray eels, 395

mosaics, xx

Mosconi Cup (pool), 539

Moscow, Russia, 272, 277, 317

Motocross des Nations, 560

motorcycles, 148, 225, 300, 556–57, 560–61

mountain climbing, 210, 211, 216, 601

Mountaineers, 217–22, 226, 227

movies: awards, 190, 414, 415, 417, 441–42; blockbusters, 64; box office, 413–16, 418–22, 440–44; cameras, 174; characters, 416, 418; comics-based, 411, 413; critics, 375; directors, 106, 188, 417, 420, 440, 441; merchandising, 443, 444; premieres, 415, 441; producers, 189, 420; projectors, 174; sequels, 416; spoofs, 443; stars, 187, 420; theaters, 244; watching, xxix

Mozambique, 289

MTV, 427

mudflats, 49

mules, 91

multicopter, 346

multiplayer online (MMO) gaming, 445

multiple births, 104, 106, 110, 112, 114, 265

Mumbai, India, 279

murders, 286

murres, 71

muscles; 452, 453

music: awards, 106–07, 422, 447; broadcasts, 17–18; composers, 189; festivals, 246; games, 445; instrumental, 149, 442; online, 304; performances, 204; popular, xix, 422–31; singing, 148

musical instruments, 268, 270, 332–33

musicals, 436

musicians, 408

MVP awards: baseball, 477; basketball, 493; football, 460; ice hockey, 485

Myspace, 304, 305

Mysterious World, 279–84

N

Namibia, 295, 328

NASA (National Aeronautics and Space Administration), 18, 21, 22

NASCAR, 558, 559, 561

NATO (North Atlantic Treaty Organization), 297

Natural Bridges National Monument (Utah, U.S.A.), 247

Nauru, 130

Nazca lines (Peru), 249

NBA (National Basketball Association), xvii, 493–96, 497

necks (human), 122, 153, 197

nematodes, 204, 368–69

nerve implants, 390

nests: bird, 77; dinosaur, 68

netball, 487–89

S

Sahara desert, 224
sailing, 208, 221, 229–32
Saint Kitts and Nevis, 291, 328
Saint Mary's Church (Germany), 318
Saint Nikolai (Germany), 318
salami, 163
salsa, 67
Salto Angel (Venezuela), 252
San Francisco, CA, 354
San Marino, 264
São Paulo, Brazil, 279
sasquatch, 281
satellites, 11, 22–25
Saudi Arabia, 291, 298, 353
saunas, 193
scarification, 122
Schools, 264–67
SCIENCE, 363–402
Science Frontiers, 368–73
Sci-Fi Science, 392–97
scooters, 224
scouting, 191
scratchcards, 178
screenplays, 415, 417
screwdrivers, 182
scuba diving, 203
sculpture, 184, 185, 186, 604
sea: level, 34, 35; rescues, 299, 300
Sea Journeys, 227–32
seaplanes, 211
Second Congo War, 295
Senegal, 289
serval, 87
Seven Summits, 218, 245
Shanghai, China, 279
Sharks, 61–65; attacks on humans, 64–65;
    gestation, 63, 66; speed, 62, 96
shaving, 19, 151
She Collects . . . , 175–78
sheep, 81, 89, 90, 91, 94
Shibam, Yemen, 278
ships *see* boats/ships
shipwrecks, 205, 296, 299
shoes, xix, 176, 177, 182, 606
shopping malls, 277
shot put, 503, 507
siblings: age, 104–05; birthdays, 110; height,
    131; rugby players, 473
Sierra Leone, 289
Singapore, 191, 239
singing, 148
sirens, 398
sitcoms, 436, 437
skateboarding, xv, 181, 548–49, 551, 604
skeleton, 521
skiing, 212, 215, 225, 301, 519–20
skin, 122

skydiving, 544, 547, 548
Skyscrapers, 276, 278, 311–15, **316–20**
sleep, 20
Slovakia, 191, 289
slums, 277
smog, 39
smoking, 284
snails, 167, 260
snakes, 57, 73, 76, 96
snipers, 297
snooker, 541–42
snowboarding, 333, 549–51
snowflakes, 392
snow leopards, 83, 84
soap bubbles, 151
Soccer, xxi, 189, 268, 461–64, **465–69**
Social Media, 304–08
SOCIETY, 253–308
soda fountains, 160, 161
solar phenomena, 13–16
solar power, xv, 209, 355
Solar System, 4, 5, 8, 9, 11, 13, 15, 16
Somalia, 191, 289, 295
Songwriters Hall of Fame, 431
sonic booms, 398
Sound, 397–402
soundtracks, 427
South Africa, 287, 289, 293
South America, 249–52, 314–15
Southern Ocean, 204
South Korea, 191, 289, 298, 343
South Pole, xv, 210–15, 221, 232, 346
South Sudan, 287
Soviet Union, 342, 396–97; *see also* Russia
SPACE, 1–30, 41
spacecraft, 7, 18–22, 394
spaceflight: interplanetary, 9; lunar, 226;
    manned, 7, 17, 18, 24, 222
space sickness, 19
space stations, 6, 17–20, 23, 25, 394
spades/shovels, 179
Spain, 178, 289, 292, 294, 343, 356
spectrum: light, 385, 387; sound, 401
speech, 400
speed: light, xii, 27, 365–68, 384; running,
    451–54; sound, 400
speed skating, 521
Spice Girls memorabilia, 177
spiders, 75, 76, 77, 185
sponges, 71
spontaneous human combustion (SHC),
    279
SPORTS, 449–562; air sports, 543–48;
    autosports, 558–62; ball sports, 460–64;
    board sports, 548–53; broadcasting, xix;
    memorabilia, xxi; power sports, 524–28;
    racing sports, 519–23; racket sports,
    533–37; target sports, 538–42; team
    sports, 487–92; on TV, 436; water sports,

FACT vs. FICTION

How did you get on with our sci-fi ships quiz on p. ■■■? Here are the answers:

USS *Enterprise*
(*Star Trek*)

Millennium Falcon
(*Star Wars*)

Serenity
(*Firefly/Serenity*)

Bird of Prey
(*Star Trek*)

Vigilant
(*Farscape*)

Battlestar *Galactica*
(*Battlestar Galactica*)

Tripod
(*War of the Worlds*)

Nostromo
(*Alien*)

Station V
(*2001: A Space Odyssey*)

STOP PRESS

Highest altitude driven by automobile Gonzalo Bravo and Eduardo Canales (both Chile) drove a 1986 modified Suzuki Samurai to an altitude of 21,942 ft. (6,688 m) on the slopes of Chile's Ojos Del Salado volcano on April 21, 2007.

First woman to climb all 8,000-m peaks without oxygen Gerlinde Kaltenbrunner (Austria) summited K2 on August 23, 2011—her 14th "8,000-er" (a peak situated beyond 8,000 m, or 26,247 ft., above sea level) climbed without supplemental oxygen.

Heaviest mantle of bees On May 6, 2012, Ruan Liangming (China) covered himself in a 136-lb. 14.51-oz. (62.1-kg) mantle of bees in Jiangxi Province, China.

Longest duration wing-suit flight Jhonathan Florez (Colombia) was airborne in a wing suit for 9 min. 6 sec. above La Guajira, Colombia, on April 20, 2012.

The following day, he flew the **greatest horizontal distance in a wing suit**—16.315 miles (26.257 km), again above La Guajira. He flew 17.52 miles (28.91 km) that day—the **greatest absolute distance flown in a wing suit**.

MOST JAFFA CAKES EATEN IN A MINUTE Peter Czerwinski (Canada, left) scoffed 13 Jaffa Cakes in just one minute in London, UK, on May 1, 2012. Stijn Vermaut (Belgium) matched Peter's feat in Vichte, Belgium, on May 6, 2012.

FACT: Competitive eater Peter holds two other GWR records. What are they? See pp. 158–162.

Longest literary work in Pilish "Pilish" is a style of English writing in which the lengths of successive words correspond to the digits of π (pi, or 3.14159 . . .). The longest text written in Standard Pilish is *Not a Wake* by Michael Keith (U.S.A.), following the first 10,000 digits of the mathematical constant. The opening lines run: "Now I fall, a tired suburbian in liquid under the trees/Drifting alongside forests simmering red in the twilight over Europe," representing the digits 3.14159265358979323846 . . .

Most calorific burger commercially available The Heart Attack Grill in Las Vegas, Nevada, U.S.A., offers the 3-lb. 2.9-oz. (1.4-kg) Quadruple Bypass burger, packing 9,982 calories, or 195.95 calories per oz. (6.91 calories per g). In April 2012, the burger sold for U.S. $16.63—bacon included, sales tax excluded.

Oldest company to supply Olympic medals The UK Royal Mint produced the 2012 Summer Olympics medals. It was instituted in A.D. 886, which makes it more than 1,100 years old.

Oldest Eurovision Song Contest entrant (male) Engelbert Humperdinck (UK, b. Arnold Dorsey, India, May 2, 1936) represented the UK at the 2012 Eurovision Song Contest aged 76 years 24 days. Humperdinck performed the track "Love Will Set You Free" at the 57th annual contest, which took place in Baku, Azerbaijan, on May 26, 2012.

LONGEST TAXI RIDE Leigh Purnell, Paul Archer, and Johno Ellison (all UK) left Covent Garden in London, UK, by taxi on February 17, 2011 and traveled 43,319.5 miles (69,716.12 km) around the globe, arriving back at their starting point on May 11, 2012. The journey, in *Hannah* the taxi—a 1992 LTI Fairway FX4 London black taxicab—clocked up £79,006.80 (U.S. $127,530) on the meter.

FACT: In China, the trio reached 17,143 ft. (5,225.4 m)—the **highest altitude in a taxi**.

HIGHEST PRICE FOR AN ARTWORK *The Scream*, an 1895 pastel by Edvard Munch (Norway), was sold to an anonymous buyer for U.S. $119.9 million at Sotheby's, in New York City, U.S.A., on May 2, 2012. The price included the buyer's premium.

OLDEST FEMALE TANDEM PARAGLIDER Margaret "Peggy" Mackenzie McAlpine (UK) was 104 years 5 months 16 days old when she completed a tandem paraglide in northern Cyprus on April 14, 2012. The feat saw her regain the title, which she had held at the age of 100.

Oldest pig Born on December 20, 1990, Peeper (also known as "Pete") lived with his owners Ed and Denise Stottmann (U.S.A.) in Louisville, Kentucky, U.S.A., until the age of 21 years 30 days.

Oldest woman to climb Mount Everest Tamae Watanabe (Japan, b. November 21, 1938) summited the 29,029-ft.-high (8,848-m) peak of Everest for the second time on May 19, 2012—aged 73 years 180 days.

FASTEST . . .

Completion of *Teamwork Temple, Wii Party* (Wii) Francisco Franco Pêgo and Sofia Franco Ruivo (both Portugal) completed *Teamwork Temple, Wii Party* (Wii) in 60 seconds in Coimbra, Portugal, on May 4, 2012.

Mile hula hooped (male) On March 24, 2012, Ashrita Furman (U.S.A.) covered a mile (1.6 km) while hula hooping in 11 min. 21.06 sec. in New York City, U.S.A.

LARGEST . . .

Chess piece The Chess Club and Scholastic Center of Saint Louis and the World Chess Hall of Fame (both U.S.A.) created a "king" chess piece measuring 14 ft. 7 in. (4.46 m) tall and 6 ft. (1.83 m) in diameter at its base. It was measured in Saint Louis, Missouri, U.S.A., on April 24, 2012.

FIRST PERSON TO SKATE A 1080 Tom Schaar (U.S.A.) performed a "1080" (three full rotations while airborne) on a skateboard using a "mega ramp" at Woodward West in Tehachapi, California, U.S.A., on March 26, 2012. Above, Tom receives his certificate from GWR's Kevin Lynch.

Chocolate sculpture François Mellet (France/U.S.A.) created a chocolate sculpture weighing 18,239 lb. 8 oz. (8,273.3 kg) and measuring 6 ft. (1.8 m) tall and 10 ×10 ft. (3.5 × 3.5 m) at its base. It was presented in Irvine, California, U.S.A., on April 20, 2012.

Crocodile in captivity On November 9, 2011, Lolong, a saltwater crocodile (*Crocodylus porosus*), was measured at 20 ft. 2.8 in. (6.17 m) at Agusan del Sur province, Mindanao, in the Philippines. He weighed some 2,370 lb. (1,075 kg).

Diaper sculpture Huggies (Kimberly-Clark Argentina) created a diaper sculpture 16 ft. 10 in. (5.14 m) tall and measuring 43 ft. 4 in.(13.2 m) in diameter at the Golden Center, Buenos Aires, Argentina, on April 14, 2012.

Glow-in-the-dark painting SZITIC Commercial Property (China) created a 1,121.38-sq.-ft. (104.18-m²) glow-in-the-dark painting in Shenzhen, China, on March 29, 2012.

Indoor Ferris Wheel The government of Turkmenistan created an indoor Ferris Wheel with a diameter of 156 ft. 2 in. (47.6 m). It was measured in Ashgabat, Turkmenistan, on April 30, 2012.

Temporary straw bale maze The MEGA MAZE, which measured 96,847 sq. ft. (8,997.38 m²), was constructed by Garden Cents (U.S.A.) in Rupert, Idaho, U.S.A., and was verified on October 1, 2011.

MOST BALLS JUGGLED Juggler extraordinaire Alex Barron (UK) kept 11 balls in the air and achieved 23 consecutive catches in what is known as a "qualifying" juggling run. This feat was achieved at Roehampton Squash Club, London, UK, on April 3, 2012. He was 18 years old at the time.

MOST . . .

Likes on a Facebook item As of May 21, 2012, the most likes on a Facebook item is 1,045,272, in response to the announcement of Facebook founder Mark Zuckerberg's marriage to Priscilla Chan on May 19, 2012.

People dressed as chefs A group of 2,111 people dressed up as chefs on May 2, 2012, in an event organized by the World Association of Chefs Societies (WACS) and Daejeon Metropolitan City Government in Daejeon, South Korea.

People dressed as leprechauns A total of 1,263 leprechauns—each boasting the prerequisite green top hat and waistcoat, red beard, and black buckled shoes—filled the streets of Bandon in County Cork, Ireland, on March 17, 2012.

People in one pair of underpants A total of 169 participants squeezed themselves into a single pair of oversized underpants at an event organized by Dr Pepper (UK) at Thorpe Park in Chertsey, Surrey, UK, on March 24, 2012.

LARGEST SNEAKER COLLECTION It all began back in 1999, when Jordy Geller (U.S.A.) started selling footwear on eBay. Jordy now has 2,388 pairs of sneakers in his "ShoeZeum" in San Diego, California, U.S.A. All but six of those pairs are made by Nike.